THE GLOBAL BUSINESS ENVIRONMENT

Challenges and Responsibilities

Please note that this book is also available for purchase as an interactive ebook through VitalSource, https://www.vitalsource.com

Also by Janet Morrison and published by Palgrave:

The International Business Environment
International Business
Business Ethics

THE GLOBAL BUSINESS ENVIRONMENT

4th edition

4th edition

Janet Morrison

Challenges and Responsibilities

 macmillan education palgrave

First edition published 2002
Second edition published 2006
Third edition published 2011
Fourth edition published 2017 by
PALGRAVE

Palgrave in the UK is an imprint of Macmillan Publishers Limited,
registered in England, company number 785998, of 4 Crinan Street,
London, N1 9XW.

Palgrave® and Macmillan® are registered trademarks in the United States,
the United Kingdom, Europe and other countries.

ISBN 978–1–137–48374–4 paperback

This book is printed on paper suitable for recycling and made from fully
managed and sustained forest sources. Logging, pulping and manufacturing
processes are expected to conform to the environmental regulations of the
country of origin.

A catalogue record for this book is available from the British Library.

A catalog record for this book is available from the Library of Congress.

CONTENTS IN BRIEF

CONTENTS

Contents

LIST OF FIGURES

LIST OF TABLES

CASE STUDY GRID

Chapter short title	Short title of case study	Geographic focus	Main topics	Page
1 The business in focus	Google	US; global	High-tech entrepreneurs; corporate control; ethics	4
	Global business in action: From a start-up in Australia to markets worldwide	Australia; Sri Lanka; global	Entrepreneurial SME; global markets; regulation and CSR	13
	South Korean business groups	South Korea	Manufacturing; industrialization; family-dominated business groups	20
	Tesco	UK	Retailing; competitive strategies; financial accountability	34
2 Globalization	Zara	Spain; global	Fast fashion retailing; globalization; CSR	37
	Mozambique's resource riches	Mozambique	Natural resources; governance; sustainable development	57
	Global business in action: Reaching global consumers	UK; global	Global consumer markets; branding in diverse markets; CSR	64
	India as a manufacturing location	India	Industrialization and the role of government; FDI; societal goals	71
3 Cultural environment	McDonald's	US; global	Fast-food sector; changing consumer preferences; CSR	76
	Cultural change in Iran	Iran	Social and cultural change; the role of religion; women in society; individual freedoms	87
	Domestic workers	Global	Social and cultural norms; employment law; human rights	112
4 Economic environment	Alibaba	China	Ecommerce; corporate control and governance; business in China	115
	Ethiopia's economic development	Ethiopia	Sustainable development; governance; democracy; human well-being	130
	Sweden's economic model	Sweden	Social market capitalism; family-dominated corporate control	153
5 Political environment	Russia's gas resources	Russia	National resource wealth; authoritarian governance	156
	Risks to democracy in Turkey	Turkey	Cultural diversity; rule of law; risks to constitutional protections of democratic institutions	177
	Hong Kong's political future	Hong Kong	Constitutionalism; democracy; integration with mainland China	194

Chapter short title	Short title of case study	Geographic focus	Main topics	Page
6 Legal environment	Uber	US; global	Disruptive innovation in taxi services; regulation; globalization	197
	Global business in action: Opening access to research and data	UK; Romania; global	Intellectual property law; widening access to data; management of research outputs	208
	Manufacturing in the Philippines	The Philippines	Low-cost manufacturing; regulation of health and safety	212
	Brazil's Petrobras	Brazil	Corporate control and governance; corrupt business-political links	229
7 Trade	BHP Billiton	Australia; South Africa; Brazil	Mining; globalization; stakeholders and CSR	234
	The fuel additive, MMT	US; Canada; South Africa	Investor-state dispute settlement (ISDS); public health; CSR	253
	Glencore	Switzerland; global	Global commodities markets; mining; ethics	268
8 Finance	HSBC	Switzerland; UK	Banking; financial regulation; ethics; executive accountability	271
	Argentina's sovereign debt	Argentina	Sovereign default; hedge funds; governance; ethics	289
	Global business in action: Acquisition strategies at Cargotec	Finland; global	Business development through mergers and acquisitions (M&A); innovation and sustainability in cargo handling	300
	AB InBev and the 'megabrew' takeover	Brazil; US; South Africa; China	Global brewing industry; takeover strategy; competition law and regulation	305
9 Technology	ARM: Cambridge start-up behind the smartphone	UK; global	Technological innovation; SME clusters; co-operative R&D	308
	Czech automotive industry	Czech Republic	Car manufacturing; FDI; globalization of supply chains and impacts on workers	325
	GSK	China	Pharmaceutical industry; corporate culture; ethics in marketing; CSR	334
10 Ecology	Solar power in Morocco	Morocco	Solar power plants; energy policies; climate change challenges in developing countries	340
	Wild fires in Indonesia	Indonesia	Impacts of deforestation; responsibilities for environmental protection; sustainable development	356
	Global business in action: Recycling and sustainability	UK; Tunisia; global	Innovation in recycling agricultural waste; consumer awareness of green issues; ethics	367
	Uruguay's social and environmental profile	Uruguay	Wind farms and other clean energy policies; social well-being; labelling of cigarettes and ISDS litigation	373

Chapter short title	Short title of case study	Geographic focus	Main topics	Page
11 Ethics and CSR	Apple	US; China; global	Outsourced manufacturing; ethics; corporate reputation	376
	Rise of the United Arab Emirates (UAE)	UAE	Human rights; ethics; social and cultural aspects of development	392
	Global business in action: Sustainable chocolate	UK; Ghana; US	Fair trade; sustainable livelihoods; social enterprise; empowerment of women; stakeholders and corporate governance	398
	Volkswagen emissions scandal	Germany; global	Ethics; management responsibilities; corporate culture	410
12 Towards a new perspective	Coca-Cola in Mexico	Mexico	Public health; rise in corporate power; ethics	413
	Economic growth in Bangladesh	Bangladesh	Sustainable development; climate change; textile industry; CSR	421
	Wal-Mart	US	Inequality; low-paid work and the living wage; CSR	438

AUTHOR'S ACKNOWLEDGEMENTS

Writing a book of this size and scope is a daunting task, especially for a sole author. While the research and writing fell to me alone, I am greatly indebted to the staff of my publishers, Palgrave. They include my editor, Ursula Gavin, and my development editor, Nikini Jayatunga. For the book's imaginative cover design, I owe thanks to Alex Connock. And I am grateful to the copy-editor, Ann Edmondson, who helped to sharpen the clarity and precision of expression that is vital in a student textbook.

I am indebted to the numerous anonymous reviewers who have contributed to the final shape and content of this book. They include those who gave advice on how the third edition could be improved, much of it based on their experience of using the book and the feedback from their students. I also appreciate the feedback I received from the reviewers who read this new edition at the manuscript stage and offered many valuable suggestions. I am grateful for their patience in reading a manuscript that still had many rough edges, and for all their remarks and suggestions. I have incorporated as many as possible in the final book.

On a personal note, I owe thanks to my husband, Ian Morrison, for his continuing moral support and words of encouragement, now extending to four editions. Throughout these years, I have seen this book as contributing to the academic study of business – a goal that overlaps with its aim of serving the needs of students and lecturers. When I was a student myself, I once went to a public lecture given by the distinguished scholar, Isaiah Berlin, whose words, which I tried to scribble down, left an enduring impression that still resonates in these uncertain times (see Note). In the course of writing this book, I have drawn on the insights and observations of many scholars, including Berlin. To all those scholars, whose works are cited in these pages, I owe utmost gratitude.

Note: Isaiah Berlin's lecture series was later published as *The Roots of Romanticism* (1999), ed. by Henry Hardy (London: Chatto & Windus).

ABOUT THE AUTHOR

Janet Morrison, now retired, was a senior lecturer in strategic and international management at Sunderland University Business School in the UK, where she enjoyed a long career in teaching, research, curriculum development and course administration. She taught international business modules at undergraduate and postgraduate levels, including International Business Environment, Management in a Global Environment, Japanese Business and the Social and Cultural Environment of International Business. She was programme leader for undergraduate international business degrees and the MBA in International Management.

Janet's academic background goes back to her first degree (in political science and history) at Mary Washington College of the University of Virginia in the US (now the University of Mary Washington), followed by a master's degree from the University of Toronto in Canada and, later, a law degree from the University of Newcastle-upon-Tyne in the UK. She also studied in Chicago, Oxford and Nagoya in Japan.

Her published research includes articles in a range of areas, including corporate governance, Japanese business and corporate social responsibility. She is the author of *International Business* (2009) and *Business Ethics* (2015), both published by Palgrave.

PREFACE TO THE FOURTH EDITION

The challenges and responsibilities of businesses, highlighted in this book's subtitle, are mirrored in those that confronted me as the author. In a fast-moving business environment, capturing the changes taking place in both businesses and societies is essential for a textbook addressed to business students. At the same time, foundation concepts and background information, presented in a balanced and orderly format, are essential in order for readers to make sense of what is happening around them – and what might happen in the future. Writing this fourth edition, I have found that I am more aware than ever of the responsibilities to the reader, not to simply 'update' in a superficial sense, but to impart some sense-making overview of current trends in the business environment. Much of the strength of earlier editions lay in their lucid explanations of foundation material, which remain the best basis on which to understand the environmental shifts taking place, along with their impacts on organizations. Hence, foundation concepts are still core to the book. These are interpreted in new contexts and explored in new case studies and thought-provoking themes under the broad headings of social responsibility, governance and sustainability. In this new edition, the expanding scope of international business is reflected in the wider variety of business contexts that feature in these chapters, along with a wider perspective on social responsibility, taking in environmental and ethical concerns across geographic boundaries.

A technological development that has proceeded rapidly since the last edition has been digitalization. Today's students are less likely to be disadvantaged by a lack of information on business than saturated by an overload of information and images, much of it from social media sources of varying degrees of reliability and accuracy. Why would the student still need to buy a conventional textbook? After all, the textbook cannot possibly keep up to date with events. Writing for a broad public nowadays is increasingly associated with material for instant consumption offered by blogs and social media, rather than with traditional printed books. Moreover, digitalization now makes it possible to produce and deliver an ebook such as a novel to readers globally in a very short timeframe. By contrast, the completion and production of a book of broad scope and complexity is a large project – one requiring a long timeframe, considerable expense, and the expertise of numerous people along the way. This book falls into that category: a carefully constructed textbook in the traditional sense. Despite the tide of digitalization, I fervently believe that a quality textbook provides an invaluable asset for students that the confusing mass of internet sources cannot match. At the same time, this book offers the student the benefits of digital content and accessibility, through the accompanying digital resources and ebook version.

This text remains focused on meaningful engagement with the needs of a student readership, wherever in the world the book is accessed. As with the approach of previous editions, I have borne in mind the needs of students at both undergraduate and postgraduate levels, including those with little background in business studies and those for whom English is a second language. This book's clear expression and easy-to-read writing style have been highly valued by students since the book's first publication. The book's relevance to students from a variety of educational backgrounds who are studying on a variety of business courses has been among its enduring strengths, which I have kept at the forefront of my approach to this new edition.

I am pleased that students and lecturers in a wide range of countries have found this book helpful, and that international students have found the text easy to read. This new edition has been written with this wide readership in mind. I hope that it will again prove stimulating, relevant and enjoyable for readers. For readers familiar with previous editions, I hope the finished book will measure up to your expectations, and for those new to this book, I hope especially that student readers will find it enjoyable as well as illuminating.

Janet Morrison

INTRODUCTION

The image on this book's cover features a compass, an instrument that transformed ocean navigation, opening new vistas in world trade – probably the most quintessentially international of all business activities. This book was originally conceived as offering international perspectives that ventured far beyond those of existing business environment textbooks, grounded as they were in UK or US managerial outlooks. The first edition, back in 2002, aimed to broaden that focus, geographically and culturally, adopting an approach that set it apart from competitors. This fourth edition continues in that spirit, offering content and analysis that act as navigational guides for the reader in a rapidly-changing global environment.

What makes this book stand out?

An international approach is now expected by readers of any business environment textbook. All are now intended to be international in scope. Why does this one remain different? This text aims to illuminate the interactions and tensions between players in the business environment, probing behind the scenes to uncover realities hidden from immediate view. The reader thus gains an insight that neither texts on formal systems nor media reports alone could provide. Here are three examples of how this approach unfolds:

- Who are the key players? This new edition spans business on all continents, at differing stages of development and in diverse cultural contexts – not simply as market opportunities for western businesses, but as players on the global scene in their own right. Governments increasingly come into this picture, active in global investment and seeking to attract foreign investors. Case studies reflect these trends. They feature decision-making dilemmas of executives in companies such as Alibaba, the Chinese e-retailer, on the one hand, and, on the other, government leaders in African countries, such as Ethiopia, seeking to promote development through global integration. Like private-sector companies, governments, as we will see, now seek the services of marketing organizations to manage media communications globally.
- Why are law and politics important? Surely, law is just for specialists? Despite their importance in shaping strategies, the legal and political environments have received only cursory attention in other textbooks, sketching out formal systems, but giving little inkling of the actions and policies of business leaders in practice. This book offers substantive analysis of how legal and political considerations impact on basic decision-making in diverse environments. This in-depth approach to legal issues has proved to be another of the ways in which this text has been more forward-looking than its rivals in highlighting future challenges for businesses in the twenty-first century.

- Many companies, large and small, feature in these pages. Who owns and controls the company in question? Why does it matter? From the first edition onwards, corporate ownership and control have featured in both the text and case studies. While other textbooks have settled for bland statements about companies taking decisions, this book has looked behind the corporate façade to ask, 'who in the company is taking the decisions, and in whose interests?' Insightful answers to these questions have never been as vital, or as revealing, as they are now. Corporate governance and stakeholder issues are more prominent in this edition, reflecting the rise in critical awareness of issues of corporate accountability around the world.

Successive editions have continued to stress an underlying international approach, aiming to acquaint readers with the issues and trends now shaping the global environment, and also those that are likely to feature prominently in the future. Key to this aim is attention to the academic background underpinning discussion of current issues in each chapter, and, it is hoped, helping readers to form their own critical perspectives. As globalization has enveloped an increasing number of countries and every type of business – from agriculture to taxis – international interactions have multiplied beyond what most people would have thought possible. New players come onto the international scene virtually every day, including companies, business groupings, international organizations and individual people – each of whom is capable of making a difference in the way business is conceived and carried on. New complexities can be exciting, but can also be daunting to take on board without the appropriate background in the business environment.

How does a start-up become a multi-billion-dollar global business in just a few years? This – and many other – intriguing aspects of the current international environment are explained and explored in this new edition. This edition, like earlier ones, presents a critical focus, reflected in the book's subtitle: *Challenges and responsibilities*. Identifying the challenges is the easier task. Establishing where responsibilities lie is much harder, but nonetheless essential. Too often, when things go wrong, we hear that responsibilities were 'shared', or that the 'system' was responsible. And, in the end, no one gets the blame. This book aims to delve behind these vague explanations. While the spotlight falls naturally on international businesses and their managers, the spotlight also extends to political and regulatory authorities, with whom businesses constantly interact. This conceptual framework is presented in the next section.

The global environment: challenges and responsibilities

The book focuses on themes of challenges and responsibilities. Throughout the chapters that follow, we identify the challenges presented to the many diverse players in the global environment. In addition, we assess where responsibilities fall, and explore where they *should* fall. The book's international approach combines with this critical focus to distinguish it from others on the international environment.

The book sets out seven sets of challenges and responsibilities. These are grouped under three broad headings, as shown in the figure. These are not just issues, but ways of going about business activities in contexts where legal and moral

Interlocking challenges and responsibilities

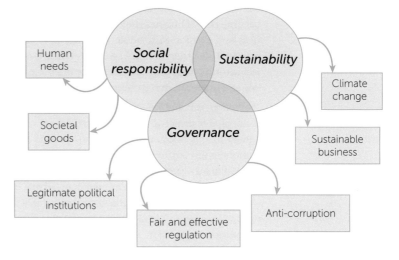

Challenges and
responsibilities

responsibilities arise, and where societies and values matter. They are listed below, with an explanation of each:

- **Sustainability**

  Building sustainable businesses – Business enterprises everywhere are faced with the challenges of sustainable use of resources, along with enduring impacts in societies and the environment. Sustainability is now viewed by businesses as part of their mission. Facing the challenges calls for significant changes in behaviour. At the same time, demands on firms for increased profitability raise potential conflicts between traditional short-term strategies and long-term sustainability imperatives.

  Adopting measures to address climate change and resource stress – Climate change affects everyone, including communities, governments and businesses. While governments and international bodies can guide and legislate, firms have responsibilities for sustainability even in the absence of legal obligations. Accepting these responsibilities, however, involves rethinking the ultimate goals of the firm, and also rethinking the ways in which it goes about its business activities. Firms can no longer simply wait for legislation to prompt them to make changes in their environmental management.

- **Governance**

  Establishing legitimate political institutions – In today's world, businesses play an active role in governance at the national and international levels, working with governments and non-governmental bodies, and influencing policies. Much of that interaction is positive, helping to adapt business aims to societal needs. However, many businesses view these interactions as self-serving, for example, in efforts to persuade governments and lawmakers to bend laws and policies towards their interests. Such an approach might satisfy shareholders in the short term, but an alignment of business aims with societal goals will support the legitimacy of both governments and business players in the long term.

  Combating corruption – Close ties between governments and businesses, while positive in many respects, can breed practices where self-interested gain, either for companies or individuals, becomes the norm, and public goals are squeezed out. While most countries have laws prohibiting corrupt practices, corruption has become part of business behaviour in many contexts. Elites in the spheres of business and politics gain, while societies lose out. Obedience to the law is a more nuanced idea than it might seem, and businesses are now subjected to more critical scrutiny than ever. Businesspeople are expected to adhere to the spirit of the law as a matter of moral obligation.

Promoting fair and effective regulation – The advance of free-market values in national economies around the world is one of the features of globalization highlighted in this book. With spreading markets has come the growth of regulatory authorities aiming to maintain transparent and fair market mechanisms. But these are national – not global – regulators. National regulators face challenges in confronting global companies, some of which dwarf their own economies. The mismatch can be glaring. Global companies might well see themselves as being above national regulators, but globalized companies still operate in local environments that are subject to regulation. Are multinational companies now becoming more aware of the need to willingly accept obligations to comply with regulatory authorities?

- **Social responsibility**

Fulfilling human needs – Businesses provide jobs, incomes to employees, goods and services that people want, and much else that contributes to human well-being. Large agricultural companies and commodities traders are major determinants of food supply and prices in global markets. These private-sector giants exist to increase the wealth of their owners, but their activities have crucial impacts on whole societies. These social responsibilities can be viewed in an ethical perspective, as recognized in the concepts of human dignity and human rights. International human rights law obliges governments to preserve human rights, but, increasingly, companies are coming into this sphere of responsibility.

Promoting societal goods – Businesses play vital roles in shaping how societies function and change. Much of the discussion in this book focuses on globalization and how it is transforming not just production, but whole societies. While these changes are beneficial in, for example, providing employment and rising incomes, they can also be detrimental to human well-being and to societies. This is especially the case where production relies on migrant workers, separated by long distances from their families and community ties. Social setbacks also occur when people and whole communities are displaced to make way for industrial and mining projects. Businesses are now called on to take a broad view of stakeholder interests, which includes societal impacts.

In each chapter, an assessment of challenges and responsibilities is set out in a section just before the conclusions. The issues raised in these discussions are revisited in the book's final chapter.

Plan of the book

The book has been re-organized since the last edition. This has aimed to improve the logical progression of chapters from the more fundamental contexts to the more business-oriented contexts. It also reflects the organization of this subject that is adopted in many course syllabuses. Part 1 retains the structure of the last edition, with an introduction to the business enterprise in Chapter 1, and an overview of globalization in Chapter 2. Globalization remains a dominant feature of the business environment, and Chapter 2 has been expanded to bring its many ramifications into perspective. The main change in the book's organization is that chapters on the dimensions of the environment, including culture, politics and law, have been brought forward to form a new Part 2, 'Framing the business environment', along with chapters on the global economic environment. The reasoning behind this shift was mainly based on the logic of exploring the underlying dimensions of the environment as a foundation for understanding aspects of the global competitive environment, which now feature in Part 3. The new Part 3, 'Shaping international business environments', groups chapters on trade, finance and innovation. These chapters have a more applied feel, drawing on the contextual analysis of the environment that features in Part 2. The new Part 4 is devoted to sustainability and issues of social responsibility, with a concluding chapter on challenges and responsibilities. It is hoped that readers will find the new organization helpful. There follows an outline of the chapters, with a brief description of each.

Part 1: Business in the global environment

Chapter 1 – The business enterprise in focus

This chapter introduces basic concepts and terms that describe business organizations and processes. It takes the reader through the basics of business formation, ownership and corporate governance. Outline guides to the dimensions of the business environment and the spheres of the environment – local, national and international – are presented. Many readers will already be acquainted with the basic concepts defined here, but I would urge that it is helpful to take time to become re-acquainted with them in a bit more depth, as provided here. Companies differ. What exactly does owning a share in Google involve? Possibly not what many people might assume.

Chapter 2 – Globalization and the business environment

Theories of globalization from the perspective of the firm are the foundation of this chapter, which examines processes and impacts of globalization critically. The chapter looks at developments in global production and global markets, asking what economic benefits have flowed, and to whom. It looks at negative impacts of globalization, highlighting issues of human well-being that have cast a shadow over the economic gains that have been realized.

Part 2: Framing the business environment

Chapter 3 – Culture and societies

Culture lays the foundation in values and norms of behaviour that influences many of the other environmental dimensions. Despite globalization, differences between national cultures remain vibrant, highlighting the importance of cross-cultural understanding in business contexts. Theories of culture are examined critically, highlighting the need to look behind categories such as 'individualist' and 'collectivist', which have tended to cloud more complex cultural realities. Substantial sections on migration, urbanization and ageing societies are included, reflecting the growing challenges facing businesses and governments.

Chapter 4 – The global economic environment

Basic concepts used to describe economic systems are introduced. Economic indicators shed light on national economic systems, but, looking behind the statistics, their limitations are evident. Human development criteria are defined, giving a more revealing picture of societies, and also revealing the effects of inequality, which is

discussed in depth in this edition. National economic systems are described and critically assessed. Is China still considered the glowing economic model of emerging markets, or has the gloss worn off?

Chapter 5 – The political environment: state and business actors

Basic theories and concepts of politics and political systems are introduced, including sources of authority and legitimacy in government. Internal and external political risks are discussed at length. Democratic and authoritarian systems are described, noting that there now seem to be shortcomings in accountability and inclusiveness in the many versions of both of these basic types of governance. Political systems are classified, with analysis of the ways that the functions of government in practice shape societies. Politics at the global level is seeing shifts in the balance of power. Which countries are becoming tomorrow's global political players?

Chapter 6 – The legal environment

Legal risk, too, has become a growing consideration for businesses globally. We look at national legal systems, assessing the extent to which the rule of law is recognized within court systems. We also look at how companies have changed their approach to legal risk, from one of navigating around laws to a more robust approach of confronting legal obstacles through litigation, lobbying and using procedures such as the investor-state dispute settlement system. The growing influence of international law is now evident in the business environment, alerting companies to obligations that extend beyond national legal systems.

Part 3: Shaping international business activities

Chapter 7 – International trade and globalization

Trade theories provide the foundational concepts for this chapter. International trade should benefit not just trading companies, but consumers, workers in trading industries, governments and whole economies. However, in reality, relations between trading nations are highly unequal: richer countries benefit and poorer countries are at a disadvantage. The World Trade Organization (WTO) has long attempted to achieve multilateral trade agreements designed to the benefit of all, but national interests still take precedence. Recent developments in trade and investment agreements outside the WTO framework are discussed, focusing on the elusive issue of fair trade for all.

Chapter 8 – Global finance

Cross-border finance benefits companies and whole economies, but globalization of financial markets has also led to increasing risks, culminating in the financial crisis of 2008. This chapter looks at the finance function for businesses and for economies, including recent developments that have sought to restore global financial stability. The roles of the International Monetary Fund (IMF) and World Bank are assessed, especially in respect of handling national financial crises. Excessive borrowing has affected companies, householders and whole economies. Rethinking finance in terms of challenges and responsibilities requires a rethink of the fundamentals: should finance be devoted to serving productive activities and consumers, or does moneymaking as an end in itself have a role to play?

Chapter 9 – Technology and innovation

Innovation lies at the heart of economic development and improvements in wellbeing. Globalization offers the prospect for developing countries to benefit technologically from foreign investment, global supply chains and trade. But advances in technology are not easily diffused, and the owners of much technology, such as patented inventions, take steps to retain control over their use. Technology offers the prospect of improvements in many areas of human well-being, including medicine, agriculture and clean energy. At issue, however, is the extent to which these public goods should be in the control of private companies. A concern is that benefits, such as life-saving medicines, are available to the few, not the many.

Part 4: Confronting global challenges

Chapter 10 – Ecology and climate change

This chapter begins with outline explanations of the impacts of climate change and environmental degradation on the natural environment and societies. Rising emissions, notably from the extensive use of fossil fuels in the large emerging economies, such as China and India, have given impetus to international efforts to avert the worst impacts of climate change, especially the risks to low-lying countries from rising sea levels. These efforts led to the Paris agreement of 2015, which was unique in reaching a consensus between developed and developing countries. Businesses are vital in translating government targets into real progress in the necessary technology and infrastructure.

Chapter 11 – Ethics and social responsibility

This chapter begins with the philosophical foundation of ethical theories, taking into account cultural diversity and differing perspectives of morality. For a business, ethical dilemmas arise constantly. Many managers might think pragmatically that, if they are able to get away with unethical or illegal behaviour, then they are in the clear. Ethical obligations are one of the dimensions of corporate social responsibility (CSR), which takes in the interests of all stakeholders. CSR also focuses on legal obligations, which are increasingly framed in terms of international standards. Human rights law, which receives more coverage in this edition, is one of these developments. Human rights affect all businesses, but particularly those in which migrant labour is common, including outsourced manufacturing, mining, agriculture and domestic work. The human rights of vulnerable workers are often poorly protected in national law. Employers are now expected to conform to international human rights law, regardless of national norms.

Chapter 12 – Challenges and responsibilities: towards a new perspective

This chapter summarizes the challenges and responsibilities highlighted in each of the earlier chapters, in areas of sustainability, governance and social responsibility. A highly focused discussion of global risks is presented, with examples from the ecological, economic, political and social dimensions of the environment. What are the risks in the global environment that have become the most troubling? Among them are inequality, threats to social well-being and political instability. The chapter goes on to assess the roles of both governments and businesses in terms of social and environmental goals. The chapter concludes by pointing towards a new, more responsible, role for businesses in the global environment.

Chapter features

This book is designed to present the content in a logical and easily accessible manner. Although ideally a reader would begin with Chapter 1 and read each successive chapter in order, the book has been designed so that any chapter can be read independently. The reader is guided by references to earlier relevant material. In some cases, key words that are introduced in earlier chapters are highlighted again in later chapters, along with a brief explanation. For readers who have read all the previous chapters, please consider the repetitions just a helpful reminder.

Chapter features are outlined below, divided between those at the beginning of the chapter, those in the body of the text, and those at the end of each chapter.

At the beginning of each chapter ...

- An **Outline** of the sections in the chapter.
- The **Learning objectives** of the chapter clarify particular outcomes which the reader can expect.
- An **Opening case study** sets the scene for the chapter, raising issues which will arise in the text. This case study usually features a company's responses to the changing environment in national and international contexts. Four questions for discussion and references for further exploration are given.

In the body of the chapter ...

- **Key words** appear in bold, and are defined in the text as they appear. These include concepts, principles and major international institutions. They also feature in a Glossary at the end of the book.
- **References** are given in parentheses in the text, for example, (Tellis, 2009). There is a references section at the end of each chapter.
- **Web references** appear after the name of the relevant organization in the text. Most refer to companies or organizations that relate to the point being discussed. In addition, there are many web links provided in the sources for figures, sources for case studies, and references in the text. Every effort has been made to ensure that these addresses are accurate, but websites change constantly, and web links often become outdated. If any of these web references fails, a key-word search should supply an up-to-date link.
- **Case study on the changing business environment** – This is a case study feature in the middle of each chapter. This case study focuses on a country, an industry or a group of countries, highlighting challenges in the global environment. Questions for discussion and references are given.
- **The way I see it ...** – This new feature focuses on a quote from a person or organization, expressing a particular point of view and a distinctive perspective. The quote is followed by the name of the person who said it, and where. Typically, the quote raises a normative issue or poses a dilemma. There are two of these in each chapter. The variety of individual perspectives is immense, ranging from a CEO of a large company to a migrant farm labourer. Also featured are political leaders and leaders of international organizations. A question is posed at the end, inviting the reader to respond: How do *you* see it?
- **Pause to reflect** boxes appear throughout the chapter. They raise questions and issues which invite the reader to examine the topic critically, often exploring further implications.
- **Global business in action** videos – This is a new interview feature that appears in selected chapters. It consists of structured interviews with people who are active in a variety of business and management roles. The text feature provides background information and suggested reading. There are also follow-up questions for individual study or group discussion. These interviews can be accessed via the freely accessible companion website or the interactive ebook (described below in the section on digital resources).

At the end of the chapter ...

- **Review questions** are designed to cover all the topics in the chapter. There are 15 questions. They are an aid to learning for self-study, or they can be the basis of group discussion. They are also a helpful revision aid.
- Two **assignments** are given after the review questions. These are broader in scope than the review questions. They require some independent research and offer an opportunity to present a considered analysis in a structured way.
- **Further reading** gives an indication of other sources to read that provide both further information and differing critical perspectives on the topics in the chapter.
- **Closing case study** – This case study features a company or national environment, raising relevant issues in national and international contexts. All raise issues of sustainability, governance and social responsibility, reflecting the book's conceptual framework. Questions for discussion and references for further exploration are provided.

He should have gone for Morrison's *The Global Business Environment*, with its free companion website and interactive ebook version.

Source: iStock.com/zaemiel.

Other learning aids in the book

Other learning aids are listed below:

- **Glossary** of key words. This is at the end of the book. It contains all the key words highlighted in bold in the text.
- **Index** – There is a comprehensive index at the end of the book. The index is divided into three sections: organizations, people and subjects.
- There is a section of **maps** at the end of the book. Identifying and understanding the geographical location of countries and regions might seem incidental, but is immensely useful in understanding the substantive issues discussed in the text.

This new edition is intended to build on the strengths and distinctiveness of earlier editions, while opening new vistas on the challenges and responsibilities facing businesses in the global environment. It is hoped that, in addition to its academic value, it will be interesting and stimulating to read.

TOUR OF BOOK

Outline of chapter and learning objectives

The opening page of each chapter provides a quick guide to what is covered in the outline of chapter. The learning objectives will help you organize your study and track your progress

Outline of chapter

Introduction

What does the business enterprise exist to do?
Purpose and goals
The company in society: stakeholders and responsibilities

How does the enterprise carry out its goals?
It all starts with entrepreneurs
Companies: the engines of business activities
Functions within the enterprise
The multinational enterprise (MNE)
Corporate governance: shareholders and other stakeholders

An overview of the global environment
Multiple dimensions
The multi-layered environment

The enterprise in a dynamic environment: challenges and responsibilities

Conclusions

This chapter will enable you to

- Identify the range of purposes pursued by business enterprises in the changing environment, notably the role of diverse stakeholders
- Evaluate the differing types of ownership and decision-making structures through which enterprises pursue their goals
- Gain an overview of the dimensions and layers of the international business environment, together with an ability to see how their interactions impact on firms

---

| 76 | Framing the business environment |

OPENING CASE STUDY

The golden arches lose their shine

From its modest beginnings as a hamburger restaurant in the 1950s, McDonald's pioneered the fast food restaurant, its golden arches becoming a familiar feature of the American landscape. Offering

time when it needed to concen... core brand (Peterson, 2015). Mc... Chipotle had differing ideas ab... restaurant, McDonald's had...

Questions for discussion

- Why did McDonald's not spot the changes taking place in consumer tastes?
- Why are the 'fast casual' restaurants proving more popular than fast food?
- McDonald's has had a poor reputation in employee relations. Why?
- What changes should Mr Easterbrook introduce that would win customers back and improve employee relations?

Opening and closing case studies

Case studies at the beginning and end of each chapter feature businesses of all sizes, from every corner of the globe. Questions at the end of each case study give you a chance to reflect further

---

Case study on the changing business environment

Focusing on an industry, country or group of countries, this case study feature highlights some of the central challenges of the globalized business environment

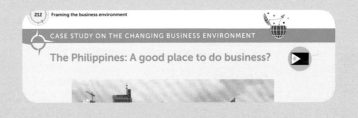

| 212 | Framing the business environment |

CASE STUDY ON THE CHANGING BUSINESS ENVIRONMENT

The Philippines: A good place to do business?

...orld trade: impacts of globalization

Trade involves the exchange of something of value, usually goods or services, for a price, usually money. **Exports** are products leaving a country, and **imports** are products entering a country. Trade in physical goods (merchandise), which amounted to over $18 trillion globally in 2013, is greater than trade in services, which totalled $5 trillion (UNCTAD, 2015: Key stats doc, p. 1). Goods traded are classified as 'primary' and 'secondary' products. Primary goods include natural resources and agricultural

Glossary

Key terms are highlighted in bold colour and defined in the text where they appear, and collated in an alphabetical glossary at the back of the book for reference

Pause to reflect

These boxes invite you to think critically about thought-provoking issues or questions

Identifying with the nation-state

Think of a nation-state which you are familiar with. Does it have a strong national culture, or is there a mixture of diverse cultural identities within its borders? If the latter, explain what they are.

The way I see it...

On business failures, 'My experience is that we learn much more from failure than we do from success. When you stop learning, you stop developing and you stop growing.'

A.G. Lafley, former CEO of Procter & Gamble (P&G), in *Harvard Business Review*, April issue, 2011.

Recall situations from your own experience when handling failure became a positive way to go forward and learn from mistakes.

The way I see it ...

Quotes from a range of business people and organizations raise different perspectives or pose dilemmas for you to consider, either on your own or in discussion with others. Rival viewpoints are sure to emerge

Global business in action videos

These video interviews appear in selected chapters, showcasing the experiences and insights of real-life business people. Follow-up questions will help you to gain a fuller picture of their businesses in global contexts

GLOBAL BUSINESS IN ACTION

From a start-up in Australia to markets worldwide

Ram Krishnamoorthy

Ram Krishnamoorthy is the founder and CEO of LongLeaf Tea Vodka (www.longleaf.com.au), which started life in Australia in 2010. The company's unique product is an artisan vodka made entirely of organic ingredients. The business originated with Ram's idea of making a premium tea-flavoured vodka, drawing on his family's expertise in tea growing, which goes back to his Sri Lankan heritage. Beginning with experiments in the kitchen, he created a product flavoured with organic black tea imported from Sri Lanka. LongLeaf was first marketed in Australia, and has now reached markets around the world. It has won prestigious international awards as the best tea vodka, helping to establish LongLeaf on the global stage. Ram has an MBA degree and had worked in investment banking prior to founding LongLeaf. As the interview with him shows, becoming an entrepreneur and getting a start-up off the ground has brought new challenges all the time.

References

Hooker, L. (2015) 'Vodafone offers global mate www.bbc.com/news

Moens, G. and Gillies, P. (1998) *International Tr* (Sydney: Cavendish Publishing).

Naidoo, K. (2013) 'Fukushima disaster: holding 11 March, at www.theguardian.com

Provost, C. and Kennard, M. (2015) 'The obscur countries', *The Guardian*, 10 June, at www.

Pratley, N. (2014) 'GSK still has questions to ans *Guardian*, 19 September, at www.theguardi

UNCTAD (2013) *World Investment Report 2013*

Vestager, M. (2015) 'Enforcing competition rule New York, 20 April, at www.ec.europa.eu/c

Zeller, T. (2011) 'Experts had long criticized pot reactor, *New York Times*, 15 March, at www

Zweigert, K. and Kötz, H. (1998) *Introduction to* Clarendon Press).

Multiple choice questions

Go to the companion website: www.palgraveh a quick multiple choice quiz on what you have

Review questions

1 What is meant by the interlocking spheres Which is the most important in the busines
2 What are the differences between civil and
3 What are the legal risks in countries where

What criticisms has it incurred?

15 In what ways is the International Criminal Co obligations on international businesses?

✓ Assignments

1 Compare the legal risks that arise for busines established with those that arise in countries
2 In what ways does international law impact o aspects and those that constrain or impose li

📖 Further reading

Adams, A. (2014) *Law for Business Students*, 8th

August, R., Mayer, D. and Bixby, M. (2012) *Interna Readings*, 6th edn (Harlow: Pearson).

Bell, S., McGillivray, D. and Pedersen, O. (2013) *E* OUP).

Harris, D. and Sivakumaran, S. (2015) *Cases and I* (London: Sweet & Maxwell).

Schaffer, R., Earle, B. and Augusti, F. (2011), *Inter Environment*, 8th edn (Cengage Learning).

Shaw, M. (2014) *International Law*, 7th edn (Cam

Wild, C. and Weinstein, S. (2013) *Smith and Keen*

🌐 Visit the companion website at www.palgravehigher for further learning and teaching resources.

Review and revise

The end of each chapter has a number of features to help you review and revise what you have studied, from review questions and multiple choice questions on the companion website, to assignments and suggestions for further reading

DIGITAL RESOURCES

Companion website

The companion website (**www.palgravehighered.com/morrison-gbe-4e**) hosts a number of additional resources to aid teaching and learning.

Teaching resources

Instructors who adopt this book on their course gain access to a selection of password protected resources to help plan and deliver their teaching:

- Chapter-by-chapter Microsoft® PowerPoint slides
- Suggested answers to case study questions, along with guidelines for group discussion
- Guideline answers to questions in the 'Pause to reflect' boxes, and 'The way I see it ...' boxes
- Outline answers to the end of chapter Review questions and assignments
- A testbank of multiple choice questions
- Updated case studies from previous editions of the book
- The Global business in action videos to play in lectures

Learning resources

Global business in action videos: These video interviews feature a range of business-people from around the globe, who share their thoughts on how they have dealt with global business challenges.

> Hear from:
> **Ramanan Krishnamoorthy**, Founder and CEO Longleaf Tea Vodka (in Chapter 1)
> **JR Little**, Global Head of Innovation, Carat (in Chapter 2)
> **Mark Hahnel**, Founder and CEO, Figshare (in Chapter 6)
> **Toni Rannikko**, Director of Strategy and M&A Cargotec (in Chapter 8)
> **Fabienne Pessayre**, Director of Zembra Ltd (in Chapter 10)
> **Sophi Tranchell**, Managing Director, Divine Chocolate (in Chapter 11)

- Multiple choice questions for each chapter, to check and reinforce your learning.
- Updated case studies from previous editions of the book
- Flashcards of useful key terms in the book

The Global Business Environment
Challenges and Responsibilities, 4th Edition
by Janet Morrison
Business Ethics
International Business

HOME

TEACHING RESOURCES

LEARNING RESOURCES

ABOUT THIS BOOK

Learn, revise and think critically about the global business environment

On this website you'll soon find detailed information about the fourth edition of this book, together with an extensive range of teaching and learning resources. These will be uploaded to the site by October 2016 and will include:

REQUEST ACCESS >

Teaching resources

Instructors who adopt this book on their course gain access to a selection of password protected resources to help plan and deliver their teaching:

- Chapter-by-chapter **lecture slides**

- **Case study teaching notes**, including suggested answers to questions and guidelines for group discussion

- **Guideline** answers to in-text questions in the 'Pause to reflect' boxes, and "The way I see it..." boxes, and for end-of-chapter Review questions and Assignments

- A **testbank** of multiple choice questions

- **Updated case studies** from previous editions of the book

- The **Global Business in Action videos** to play in lectures

Learning Resources

- **Updated case studies** from previous editions of the book

- **Flashcards** of useful key terms in the book

LIST OF ABBREVIATIONS

AGM	annual general meeting
BRIC	Brazil, Russia, India and China
CEO	chief executive officer
CSR	corporate social responsibility
EU	European Union
FDI	foreign direct investment
GATT	General Agreement on Tariffs and Trade
GDP	gross domestic product
GMO	genetically-modified organism
GNI	gross national income
ICC	International Criminal Court
ICJ	International Court of Justice
ICCPR	International Covenant on Civil and Political Rights
ICESCR	International Covenant on Economic, Social and Cultural Rights
IMF	International Monetary Fund
ISDS	investor-state dispute settlement
IT	information technology
ILO	International Labour Organization
IP	intellectual property
IPO	initial public offering
M&A	merger and acquisition (activity)
MNE	multinational enterprise
NAFTA	North American Free Trade Agreement
NGO	non-governmental organization
OECD	Organisation for Economic Co-operation and Development
PLC	public limited company
PPP	purchasing power parity
RTA	regional trade agreement
R&D	research and development
SDGs	Sustainable Development Goals
SME	small-to-medium-sized enterprise
TPP	Trans-Pacific Partnership
TRIPS	Trade-Related Aspects of Intellectual Property Rights (agreement)
TTIP	Transatlantic Trade and Investment Partnership
UK	United Kingdom
UN	United Nations
US	United States of America
WHO	World Health Organization

1 BUSINESS IN THE GLOBAL ENVIRONMENT

The two chapters in this part form a foundation for the book as a whole. In any study of business, there is a distinction between matters relating to the enterprise itself, often termed the 'internal' environment of the business, and matters relating to the external environment, such as markets where it aims to sell its products. Although this division is oversimplified, as we will find in later chapters, it helps to use these contexts for the initial formulation of concepts and identification of issues, which will become nuanced in later chapters.

Chapter 1, *The business enterprise in focus*, examines the business itself, its goals and how it goes about achieving them. The chapter begins by looking at the most basic question of all: what does the business exist for? Many issues come into play, including what the enterprise exists to do, what it is offering the public and how it should be run. To a great extent, the answers to these questions reflect the values and backgrounds of the founders. But founders also encounter the many dimensions of the business environment, such as differing cultural and legal frameworks around the world, that will shape the ways their firms carry out their objectives. Businesses are part of the societies in which they operate. Increasingly, businesses are expected to address the social impacts of their activities. These challenges multiply as the business extends its activities globally. The last two sections in Chapter 1 introduce the business in its external environment, setting out the dimensions which will form the basis of separate chapters.

In Chapter 2, *Globalization and the business environment*, we change our focus to the external environment, with rapidly changing markets and production based on global supply chains. The many processes which are grouped together under the broad heading of 'globalization' are examined critically, assessing impacts on business organizations, governments and societies. Globalization represents a range of different processes, from high-speed communications to converging consumer tastes. These processes are unfolding unevenly, some bringing about transformational change and some emerging only gradually. Globalization has led to economic benefits flowing to companies and to national economies, but negative impacts in societies are increasingly causing concern, raising questions of responsibilities for governments and businesses.

CHAPTER

1

THE BUSINESS ENTERPRISE IN FOCUS

Outline of chapter

Introduction

What does the business enterprise exist to do?
Purpose and goals
The company in society: stakeholders and responsibilities

How does the enterprise carry out its goals?
It all starts with entrepreneurs
Companies: the engines of business activities
Functions within the enterprise
The multinational enterprise (MNE)
Corporate governance: shareholders and other stakeholders

An overview of the global environment
Multiple dimensions
The multi-layered environment

The enterprise in a dynamic environment: challenges and responsibilities

Conclusions

This chapter will enable you to

- Identify the range of purposes pursued by business enterprises in the changing environment, notably the role of diverse stakeholders
- Evaluate the differing types of ownership and decision-making structures through which enterprises pursue their goals
- Gain an overview of the dimensions and layers of the international business environment, together with an ability to see how their interactions impact on firms

Google: from start-up to internet giant

'Google is not a conventional company. We do not intend to become one.' So spoke Google's founders in 2004, in a letter to prospective investors (Schmidt, 2010). Founded in 1998 by Larry Page and Sergey Brin, Google started life as a search engine company, based in Silicon Valley in California, the hub of technology companies. Brin and Page saw their company as essentially an innovation start-up, with a 'quirkiness' of spirit and a mission of 'don't do evil'. Now worth over $400 billion and employing 55,000 people, it is one of the world's largest companies in market value, making Page and Brin multibillionaires. Has Google retained its innovative spirit as a young start-up, or has it become simply a large organization that has found a successful formula for generating handsome profits?

Google's founders have branched out, investing in a wide range of new technologies, including self-driving cars, drones, robotics and even a biotech company dedicated to anti-ageing research. However, 90% of the company's revenues derive from its internet business, mainly through advertising linked to its search business, as well as the apps and services linked to its Android mobile platform. Observers might conclude that Google is more like a digital advertising company. A reorganization of the company in 2015 reflected the split in focus. A parent company called Alphabet was created, and under it there are separate divisions. The internet business became a division on its own, which takes the name Google Inc., while the many smaller businesses were separated out into other divisions. This rebranding might have looked like a paper exercise, but the company has said that these separate divisions add transparency to the organizational structure. Investors inevitably focus on the profitable business of Google and its advertising platforms. The company was launched on the stock exchange in 2004, with shares priced at $85 each. By 2015, they had risen to over $700. They are now transformed into shares in Alphabet. Transparency hardly extends to the share structure, now comprising three classes of shares.

At the outset, Google's founders were determined to retain control of the company, and set up a dual share structure. Class A shares, which carry one vote each, were offered to the public. Class B shares carry 10 votes each, and are owned mainly by Brin and Page. This gives the founders over 50% of the votes, enabling them to control corporate decision-making. An example is a big purchase of another company, such as YouTube. A third class of shares was introduced in the 2015 restructuring. C shares have no vote at all in the annual general meeting (AGM). In practice, there is little difference between A and C shares, as neither can influence voting outcomes. The principle of one-share-one-vote is usually held up as good practice, reflecting an equal voice for all shareholders according to their stakes in the company. After all, the shareholders take the risk associated with share ownership, with or without a vote. As for share price, history suggests that what goes up can come down. The financial crisis of 2007–8 was a salutary warning that markets can be unstable.

As Google's power has grown, its founders have become more engaged in the big issues of policy that face the company in the long term. One is the collection of private data of millions of users, which has aroused concern among users. Largely in response to the success of Facebook, Google has made a number of forays into social networking, which yields considerably more personal data than its core search activities. Data privacy is a matter for regulatory authorities everywhere. European Union (EU) authorities have accused Google of breaching privacy laws. While the mission of 'don't do evil' suggested a purity of motives, Google has spent large sums of money lobbying politicians in the US and EU. In common with many other companies, Google has set up a political action committee (PAC) to channel its political funding, often funding the campaigns of candidates that are pivotal in legislatures. Areas of concern include policies on granting visas for skilled immigrants, who are keenly sought by technology companies. Also relevant are policies on the collection of personal data by US national security agencies. Taxation is another sensitive issue. Google deposits some $47 billion of revenues in foreign tax havens, thus avoiding US taxation. This is common practice among large US companies. Google, in conjunction with other companies, has lobbied the US government for reforms to lighten the tax burden. In 2014, Google spent more money on political campaigns – a total of $1.43 million – than Goldman Sachs, the American bank noted for its generous political donations.

Does Google increasingly look like a conventional company, with controlling owners, intent above all on conserving their wealth, or does it retain the idealism of its early days? Page said in 2014 that Google is still imbued with altruistic principles: 'The societal goal is our primary goal ... We've always tried to say that with Google' (Waters, 2014).

Sources: Waters, R. (2014) 'A new Page', *Financial Times*, 2 November; Schmidt, E. (2010) 'How I did it: Google's CEO on the enduring lessons of a quirky IPO', *Harvard Business Review*, May 2010, at www.hbr.org; Dougherty, C. (2015) 'Google to reorganize as Alphabet to keep its lead as innovator', *New York Times*, 10 August, at www.nyt.com.

Questions for discussion

- How has Google shifted towards being a conventional company?
- What are the challenges facing Google?
- How do you view Google's political lobbying – just doing what businesses do everywhere, or engaging in money politics that is unethical?
- What criticisms can be levelled at the Google (now Alphabet) share structure?

Introduction

Business activities shape the daily lives and aspirations of people all over the world, from the farmer in rural Africa to the executive of a large American bank. Business enterprises present a kaleidoscope of different organizations and goals, catering for customers ranging from the shopper purchasing a loaf of bread to the giant oil company agreeing to carry out exploration for a government. Business enterprises and their environments have become more complex and interconnected in recent years, with expanding and deepening ties in diverse locations. Expansion has brought increased risks and greater challenges for managers. They must adapt to differing environments and rapidly changing circumstances. They also serve a more informed public than that of only a few decades ago. The international public is more aware than ever of corporate activities, largely due to the pervasiveness of the internet and social media. Challenges for managers are heightened by a growing perception that companies bear responsibilities for their actions in societies. All business organizations, whatever their size and geographical scope, are faced with key questions to which they must respond.

We begin this chapter by identifying these key questions behind the business enterprise, which are, 'What do we exist to do?' and 'How should we be carrying out our goals?' We then look at how enterprises come into existence, how decision-making takes place and, importantly, the responsibilities of decision-makers for their actions. A number of basic terms relating to companies and their governance are introduced. Business discourse often refers to 'shareholder value', but what exactly is a 'share' in a company, and why does it matter? These basic concepts are crucial in describing the organizational aspects of the company, which reflect its values and influence its behaviour. As will be seen, the company's ownership, organization and behaviour are shaped by aspects of the business environment.

The small-scale business activities of this farmer in the Ivory Coast might not seem to have much in common with a large multinational, but both play roles in global business.

Source: Photodisc.

As the global economy has expanded, there is a wider range of companies and countries engaged in global business. Moreover, states and state-related organizations are playing increasingly active roles. We highlight two cross-cutting views of the international environment. The first is the differing dimensions of the environment, including economic, cultural, political, legal, financial, ecological and technological. The second is that of spheres, from the local through to the national, regional and global. We thus provide a practical framework for understanding how enterprises interact through each dimension in multiple geographical environments. The last section of the chapter focuses on the challenges and responsibilities that have been highlighted, in particular, building a sustainable business and the regulatory environment.

What does the business enterprise exist to do?

The street trader in India and the Silicon Valley executive might not seem to have much in common: they are worlds apart in geography, culture and technology. But they have more in common than meets the eye. Both seek to offer products that will please customers, and both must respond to changing tastes and lifestyles in order to make money to keep the enterprise afloat. This is the essence of business everywhere. **Business** refers to any type of economic activity in which goods or services (or a combination of the two) are supplied in exchange for some payment, usually money. This definition describes the basic exchange transaction. The types of activity covered include trading goods, manufacturing products, extracting natural resources and farming. **International business** refers to business activities that straddle two or more countries. Businesses nowadays routinely look beyond the bounds of their home country for new opportunities. Moreover, although it used to be mainly firms in the more advanced regions of the world (such as North America, Europe and Japan) which aspired to expand into other countries, we now see businesses from a much wider range of countries 'going global'. These include Chinese, Indian, African and Latin American firms. Consequently, in most countries, there are likely to be both

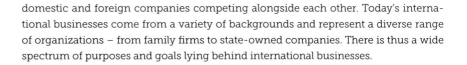

domestic and foreign companies competing alongside each other. Today's international businesses come from a variety of backgrounds and represent a diverse range of organizations – from family firms to state-owned companies. There is thus a wide spectrum of purposes and goals lying behind international businesses.

Purpose and goals

A business enterprise does not simply come into existence of its own accord. It is created by people with ideas about products or services, who may emerge in any society or geographic location, and who bring their own values and experience to bear on it. Particular national environments, with their distinctive values and social frameworks, are formative influences on founders of businesses. They might simply seek personal gain for themselves and their families, but many will envisage an overarching purpose or mission of contributing to society through employment and wealth creation. They will have some idea of what type of entity they wish to create in terms of organization. They must also focus on the specific goods or services they wish to offer, and to whom. These objectives might change frequently, while broader goals are more enduring. Both the decision-makers and the circumstances will change, but the underlying question confronting them is 'what purpose are we fulfilling or should we be fulfilling?' Most of the world's businesses aim to make money, and are sometimes referred to as **for-profit** organizations, to distinguish them from **not-for-profit** organizations, such as charities, which serve specific good causes in societies. A third category exists – the **social enterprise** – which lies somewhere between the two: it aims to make money for a social cause rather than as profit for the owners.

Although for-profit enterprises aim to make a financial gain, most founders would say that their goal is not simply to make money, but to offer products which will satisfy customers. It need not be a wholly new product, but one that is more innovative technologically, a better design or cheaper than those offered by rivals. It could be a 'greener' product than those of rivals, such as a more fuel-efficient car. In the opening case study, Larry Page of Google sounded an idealistic note in highlighting the company's goal to serve society. But Google's founders are far from altruistic, having built the company into a huge profit-generating empire in which they retain control.

Apple of the US has acquired an enviable reputation for its iconic iPhone, sold at premium prices, but the company has come under fire over the working conditions in the factories in which the phones are made, mainly in China. The strategy of having products manufactured in low-cost locations is repeated across many sectors of global business (discussed in the next chapter), and is increasingly criticized as unethical. The huge profits Apple accumulates from iPhone sales are deposited in foreign locations, in order to avoid the tax bills that would arise in the US (see the opening case study in Chapter 11). These arrangements, too, can be criticized as unethical. Apple is not alone. Many companies now routinely arrange their businesses to reduce tax burdens. They would argue that the pursuit of economic goals is, after all, what they are founded to do. This approach, however, sits uneasily with the utterances of founders, such as Larry Page, who speak of serving human needs. Moreover, consumers and investors have increasingly criticized an aggressive profit-seeking approach, pointing out that companies are part of the societies in which they operate: their economic power entails social responsibilities. The for-profit company is just that, but it is arguable that a pursuit of both economic and social goals is, in the long term, a more sustainable way in which to frame business goals (Carroll and Shabana, 2010). This point recurs throughout this book.

The company in society: stakeholders and corporate social responsibility (CSR)

As the last section highlighted, answering the question, 'what do we exist to do?' is more complex than might appear. A business seeks to enrich its owners, but it will not succeed unless it satisfies customers who purchase its products and services. Its activities involve employing people, acquiring productive assets, using resources and interacting with official authorities and other organizations in communities. These relationships all involve the business in society. These interests are referred to broadly as stakeholders. A **stakeholder** may be anyone, including individuals, groups and even society generally, who exerts influence on the company or whom the company is in a position to influence (Freeman, 1984). The influences may be direct or indirect, affecting identifiable people or a more general notion of the community as something distinct from its current members. Stakeholders who have direct relations with the company include owners, employees, customers, suppliers and business partners. These might be located in any country where the firm does business. The government can be a direct stakeholder, especially if it has an ownership stake, or it can be an indirect stakeholder, framing the legal environment in which the firm operates. Indirect stakeholders, while they affect and are affected by the company's operations, cover a range of broader societal interests, which enjoy fewer direct channels of communication with managers. They include the local community, society generally and the ecological environment affected by the company's operations. Employees in a company's supply chains are also stakeholders, but commonly do not directly interact with the lead company.

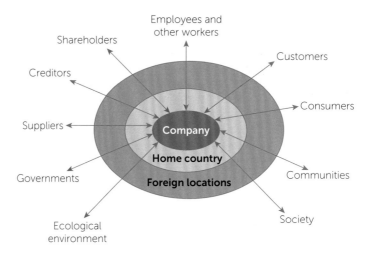

Figure 1.1 Stakeholders, home and abroad

Figure 1.1 identifies a variety of stakeholders across home and foreign environments. In a company which operates mainly in its own domestic market, managers have a fairly clear idea of their main stakeholders. Their employees and customers are readily identifiable. In a company which operates internationally, identifying stakeholders is far more difficult – and more challenging. The company's branded products could be made by workers in other locations, who are employed by a different company and have little contact with the company whose brand appears on the products. This strategy exemplifies **outsourcing**, a term used to cover any activity which a company considers can be more advantageously carried out in a location other than its home country. Outsourced manufacturing is one of the more prominent of these. It is exemplified by Nike, Gap and other familiar brands. Numerous business functions can be outsourced. Among them are IT and call centres. This is often referred to as 'business process outsourcing' (BPO). Another term closely associated with this approach is **offshoring**. Offshoring can refer to any outsourced activity, including financial arrangements designed to benefit from low-tax jurisdictions. The policy of seeking the most advantageous location for each aspect of the business is one of the major trends associated with globalization, which we discuss in the next chapter. But it also exemplifies an aggressively profit-maximizing approach to the business which arguably jeopardizes stakeholder interests.

How can I help you? The call centre, which can be continents away from the customers it serves, is an example of globalization's reach.

Source: © Royalty-Free/ Corbis.

For the company with activities and supply links in different countries, identifying and responding to stakeholder interests can be complex and involve taking decisions which have profound impacts in societies. A decision to close a factory can be made for purely internal economic reasons, but its impacts on employment and communities can be far-reaching. Stakeholders are important interests that impact on the firm's business performance, but stakeholder management also has a normative dimension, as an aspect of business ethics (Carroll and Shabana, 2010). For example, managers introduce measures to foster the health and well-being of employees not simply because people will work harder if they have healthier lives, but because it is the right thing to do. This reflects the firm's broader role in society. The approach to business activities which accords with that view rests on concepts of **corporate social responsibility (CSR)**. CSR as an approach recognizes that, in addition to economic responsibilities, the firm has legal, moral and social roles. CSR has become rather an umbrella term, covering a spectrum of approaches to business objectives, which are highlighted throughout this book and are brought together in a critical assessment in Chapter 11.

CSR takes a long-term view of the company's goals. Pure profit-seeking is a short-term approach that, in reality, can jeopardize the ability of the company to continue to generate profits. In what is often called the 'business case' for CSR, the firm places economic goals in a longer timeframe, maintaining its capacity to generate profits in the future. This longer-term approach involves the **sustainability** of the firm's business, which rests on the idea that today's business should be carried out in ways which do not cause a detriment to the ability of future generations to fulfil their needs. Sustainability takes into account the firm's impacts on communities and the natural environment. The principle of sustainability encourages a business to think of stakeholders in the future, not just the present. Most firms would probably say they uphold goals of stakeholder involvement, CSR and sustainability, but firms differ markedly in their commitment of resources to these goals. Many see these as costs which jeopardize the company's profit-making activities. Possible conflicts between social goals and economic goals underlie much of the discussion of challenges and responsibilities which occurs throughout the book.

What does the business exist to do?

Think of a company whose products you regularly purchase. Which goals does it prioritize, and do these priorities influence you to continue buying its products?

How does the enterprise carry out its goals?

Although we speak of a *firm* forming goals and carrying them out, it is actually the *people* running the firm who take key decisions. In this section, we look at the players and processes which make it function. We focus here initially on the forms, structures and processes which constitute a legal framework; this is a necessary consideration before the firm can get on with what it is 'really' about, such as manufacturing. Most businesses start in a small way, with founders who become the first owners. They bear considerable responsibility, especially in the early stages of the business. Having a great idea for a business is only the beginning. They must create a legal and organizational structure to carry it out, and decide on how it will be financed and managed. Each of these aspects of the business has an international dimension for many enterprises, adding to the possible complications, but also offering tantalizing opportunities.

This entrepreneur selling his terracotta pots in Belém, Brazil, is serving local needs and making a living, but he has little prospect, or the means, of expansion.

Source: SUPERSTOCK.

It all starts with entrepreneurs

A person who starts up a business, usually with his or her own money, is known as an **entrepreneur**. This is a broad category. Entrepreneurs exist in every society, but they differ markedly in their goals and outlooks. In developing countries, most entrepreneurs are highly localized in their activities and market. In villages throughout developing countries, the 'subsistence entrepreneur' serves the local community, managing to make a living but harbouring no intentions to expand (Schoar, 2010). The majority of entrepreneurs in developing countries are subsistence entrepreneurs. It is often observed that what is needed to propel economic development in poor countries is the more ambitious and innovative entrepreneur, who aspires to grow from a start-up to a bigger business (Schoar, 2010). The 'transformational entrepreneur' is that kind of person, reflecting the predominant image of the entrepreneur as a person with a sense of mission, a great deal of energy and a willingness to take risks. When governments speak of the need to encourage entrepreneurs, it is this type of highly-motivated businessperson they have in mind. The business environment plays an important role in encouraging – or discouraging – the entrepreneur, as shown in Figure 1.2.

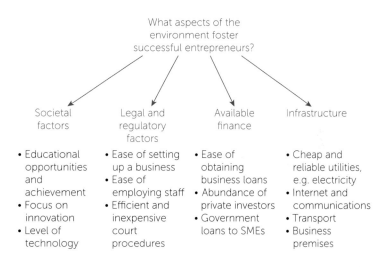

Figure 1.2 Country factors contributing to entrepreneurship

While all of the factors highlighted in Figure 1.2 are influential, some are more immediate in their impacts, and others are broad aspects of a country's environment. Availability of finance and business regulation have immediate impacts on start-up businesses. When the formalities of forming a business are reduced or access to finance is facilitated, a rise in new businesses is likely to result. The effects of improvements in education are slower in their impacts, as are improvements in infrastructure. On the other hand, the relaxation of strict labour laws can have a more immediate effect, as a change in the law encourages businesses to hire more staff. It could also be observed that where labour laws are very restrictive, for example limiting an employer's ability to dismiss an unsatisfactory employee, informal employment is common and workers are vulnerable to exploitation. India is an example of this restrictive environment (see the closing case study in Chapter 2). Facilitating entrepreneurs by encouraging them to employ people formally is likely, in practice, to lead to more secure livelihoods for workers.

The founder of a business typically begins as a **sole trader**, also referred to as a self-employed person. The business of the sole trader has no independent existence separate from its owner. In practice, this means that if the business fails, the personal wealth of its owner can be used to cover the business's debts. In the worst scenario, the owner's resources could be wiped out in order to pay business debts. This risk is known as 'unlimited liability', and is one of the major drawbacks of being self-employed. Securing finance is one of the major challenges of the start-up business. The business at this stage might have only one or two employees, or even none, although it is common for family members to help out. It is a **small-to-medium-sized enterprise (SME)**.

This category covers the vast majority of the world's business enterprises. The classification of SMEs is given below:

- Micro: 0–9 employees
- Small: 10–49 employees
- Medium: 50–249 employees
- Large: 250 or more employees

SMEs range from informal micro-enterprises to firms with up to 249 employees, making this a highly diverse category. These firms provide an important source of employment and economic activity in all countries. SMEs employ more people worldwide than large firms, in both developed and developing countries. In developing countries, where levels of poverty are high, SMEs can be significant in job creation (de Kok et al., 2013). SMEs are a vital source of innovation, from agriculture to pharmaceuticals. SMEs in the high-technology sector are actively sought by large enterprises, keen to exploit their innovative ideas. High-technology SMEs set their sights on global markets from the outset. These are often referred to as **born-global firms** (Tanev, 2012). Whereas a firm traditionally expands gradually from its local and national environment, the born-global firm's owners think from the outset in terms of international markets. Most are not the flamboyant risk-takers that are sometimes depicted in the media. The successful entrepreneur is more likely to pursue a prudent strategy based on assessing each risk and keeping it within reasonable bounds (Murman and Sardana, 2012).

Many well-known firms have grown from start-ups into global organizations. McDonald's, founded as a single hamburger outlet in the 1950s, is an example, as is Microsoft (founded in 1975) and Google (founded in 1998). Of the three, it is striking that Google, the most recent, has grown the quickest, becoming the world's dominant internet search engine in just a few years. The fact that these firms are all American is indicative that the cultural environment, as well as the legal and financial institutions, is favourable to entrepreneurs.

For individual entrepreneurs, the franchise provides an attractive route to starting a business. The **franchise** agreement allows a businessperson to trade under the name of an established brand, backed by an established organization (the 'franchisor'), while retaining ownership of the business. Under the agreement, the business owner ('franchisee') pays fees to the franchisor organization for the right to sell its products or services. The franchisee does not have the freedom over the business that an independent owner would have, but stands a greater chance of success due to the strength of the established business 'formula' of the brand. The degree of control exerted by the franchisor, in the case of McDonald's, has become an employment issue, discussed in the opening case study of Chapter 3. Besides McDonald's, Burger King and other fast-food chains, there are numerous other goods and services providers, such as car rental companies, which have grown through the use of franchising.

The way I see it ...

On business failures, 'My experience is that we learn much more from failure than we do from success. When you stop learning, you stop developing and you stop growing.'

A.G. Lafley, former CEO of Procter & Gamble (P&G), in *Harvard Business Review*, April issue, 2011.

Recall situations from your own experience when handling failure became a positive way to go forward and learn from mistakes.

GLOBAL BUSINESS IN ACTION

From a start-up in Australia to markets worldwide

Ram Krishnamoorthy

Ram Krishnamoorthy is the founder and CEO of LongLeaf Tea Vodka (www.longleaf.com.au), which started life in Australia in 2010. The company's unique product is an artisan vodka made entirely of organic ingredients. The business originated with Ram's idea of making a premium tea-flavoured vodka, drawing on his family's expertise in tea growing, which goes back to his Sri Lankan heritage. Beginning with experiments in the kitchen, he created a product flavoured with organic black tea imported from Sri Lanka. LongLeaf was first marketed in Australia, and has now reached markets around the world. It has won prestigious international awards as the best tea vodka, helping to establish LongLeaf on the global stage. Ram has an MBA degree and had worked in investment banking prior to founding LongLeaf. As the interview with him shows, becoming an entrepreneur and getting a start-up off the ground has brought new challenges all the time.

In the interview, Ram explains some of the history of LongLeaf – how it got going and how it has expanded, breaking into new markets following its success in Australia. He stresses the uniqueness of the product in the wider market for alcoholic beverages. Other flavoured vodkas contain synthetic flavourings, whereas LongLeaf is based on natural tea and organic vodka, giving it a premium status. He explains the trends taking place globally in beverages markets, which he hopes will benefit LongLeaf. As a start-up, his company has faced competition from large established companies with extensive global networks. He stresses the need to continue to innovate and to maintain the premium status of LongLeaf products.

Before watching the interview, it will be helpful to read this section on entrepreneurs again, looking particularly at Figure 1.2. Ram mentions the importance of owning the IP (intellectual property) related to the product. IP is defined later in this chapter, under the heading, 'Technological environment', which is part of the PEST analysis. It will also be useful to look at the section on R&D and innovation, under 'Functions within the enterprise'.

Visit www.palgravehighered.com/morrison-gbe-4e to watch the video, then think about the following questions:

1. What are the key factors Ram identifies as having contributed most to LongLeaf's success and growth?
2. What are the two lessons that he says a start-up must learn in order to succeed?
3. On the competitive environment, what are the global trends he highlights that are favourable to LongLeaf? What new products is he planning to introduce, and how do they fit in with the company's core product?
4. What are the challenges facing the company in the regulatory environment, notably in terms of taxation? What are the issues arising from the heavy taxation of spirits?
5. What advice does Ram offer to other entrepreneurs with a business idea?

Companies: the engines of business activity

A business can carry on indefinitely as an unincorporated association or enterprise, that is, without formal corporate status. However, when it grows beyond a size that can be managed personally by the owner, it is usual for the owner to register it as a company, to give the business a separate legal identity and separate financial footing. The **company**, also called a 'corporation', is a legal entity separate from its owners. Registration with the correct authorities in each country (or individual state in the US) constitutes its formal creation, drawing a line between the company's obligations and those of the owner(s). This means that its finances and legal obligations, such as tax, are separate from its owners. It is also possible to register as a European company within the EU, although for purposes such as taxation, the company is still considered a national entity. The company takes on a separate existence from its owners at the point when it is registered, by filing documents of its purpose and constitution with national authorities.

Companies vary widely in their formation, legal status, ownership and goals. Most of the companies featured in this book are registered companies that are commercial enterprises whose founders go through the process of registration in a particular location. The person who invests money in the company, either at its formation or later, acquires shares in it. The **share** represents ownership of the company to the extent of the amount invested. The whole of a company's shares are its share capital, also known as its **equity**. The **shareholder** is liable up to the amount invested, and therefore enjoys **limited liability**. The founders are likely to be the first and largest shareholders (also known as stockholders). The introduction of limited liability made owning shares more attractive as an investment, and paved the way for widespread share ownership by the investing public. The shareholder who buys the company's shares is providing capital to enable it to function. The larger the stake (that is, holding of shares), the more influence the shareholder will expect to exert, although, in practice, controlling interests may make this difficult. A share in a company carries certain rights, including the right to receive dividends and (normally) vote in annual general meetings (AGMs). Importantly, the shareholder is a 'member' of the company, whereas the creditor of the company is not.

Registered companies may be private or public companies. The main distinction between the two is that shares in a public company (or a portion of them) are traded on a stock exchange, whereas shares in a private company cannot be traded on exchanges. The **private limited company** tends to resemble the family business in which the owner retains control. It has few shareholders, and these are 'insiders', often related. It is not allowed to sell its shares to the public. Private companies often face problems over raising capital, but some, such as Silicon Valley start-ups, have been successful in finding financial backers known as 'venture capitalists', who are willing to invest large sums in their businesses. Uber is an example, discussed in the opening case study in Chapter 6. So long as financial backers continue to invest in a new company, owners are likely to keep the company private, thereby ensuring their continuing control of the business.

The private company faces fewer requirements for disclosure of its financial position than the public company. Although most are SMEs, many large international businesses choose to remain private companies. An example is Bosch, the German engineering company. Private companies are key economic players in Germany and many other countries. Private companies are thus significant players in the global economy.

The **public limited company (PLC)** is a registered company that offers shares to the public, and is usually referred to simply as a public company. It invites the public to subscribe for its shares in an **initial public offering (IPO)**, also known simply as a 'listing' on a stock exchange. Stock exchanges are regulated under national legal frameworks, and also governed by their own listing rules (see Chapter 8). Typically, they specify that only a portion of a company's shares need be 'floated' publicly, that is, offered to the general public, in order to be listed. This portion can be only 20%, or even lower. The remaining shares are generally owned by a few insiders, or, in some cases, government bodies. For example, Gazprom, the Russian gas giant, is listed on the London Stock Exchange, but the company is majority owned by the Russian government (see the opening case study of Chapter 5). This arrangement is not uncommon, and can seem confusing. A public limited company listed on a stock exchange is considered legally to be in the *private sector*, whereas a *public-sector* entity is owned and controlled by the state. When a government decides to 'privatize' a state-owned organization, it begins by registering the company as a PLC. Gazprom, for example, was formerly the gas ministry of the Soviet Union. Conversely, when a PLC is taken over by the state, it is said to be 'nationalized'.

The public company faces scrutiny of its accounts by national regulators in the country in which it is registered, and in countries where its shares are listed on exchanges. It should be noted, however, that global scanning for the most advantageous location affects these decisions, just as it affects the location of production facilities. The company might register in an offshore location such as a Caribbean state, where oversight is minimal, and it could well decide to list on a stock exchange where the regulatory burden is weak, and where the dominance of insiders is not an obstacle. In the US, nearly half of all public companies are registered in the tiny state of Delaware, considered the most advantageous location for business founders who wish to maintain control of their companies. Its advantages include the ease with which company registration is facilitated and the business-friendly stance of its courts. The number of registered corporate entities in Delaware actually exceeds the number of human beings in the state: there are just over 900,000 registered companies and under 900,000 people (Wayne, 2012). It is thus worthy of note at this early juncture that founders of companies which 'go public' often wish to 'have their cake and eat it': they wish to attract the public to buy shares, but they also wish to retain control of the company and take the major decisions themselves. Google, for example, has a dual share structure whereby founders' shares carry more voting rights than ordinary shares (they are weighted 10 to 1). Alibaba, the Chinese ecommerce company, is another example (discussed in the opening case study of Chapter 4).

Should we take the plunge and go public?

If an entrepreneur has a successful business as a private company, why would he/she be tempted to go public?

Functions within the enterprise

Every enterprise, whether large or small, involves a number of different types of activity, or **business functions**, which form part of the overall process of providing a product for a customer. Physical resources, including plant, machinery and offices must be organized, and functions such as finance, purchasing and marketing must be co-ordinated, to enable the entire enterprise to function smoothly as a unit. Every business carries out basic functions, such as finance, even though a small business is unlikely to hire specialists in each area. By contrast, a large organization has separate departments and, increasingly, an in-house legal department for specialist advice. The importance of particular functions depends in part on the type of business. Product design and production, along with research and development, feature mainly in manufacturing firms, whereas all firms have need of finance, human resource management (HRM) and marketing functions. The functions cover the entire life of a product, from the design stage to the delivery of a final product to the customer. They even extend beyond the sale, to include after-sales service and recycling. The main functions are set out in Figure 1.3.

Figure 1.3 Business functions in the organizational environment

In Figure 1.3, the headings in the rectangles represent the co-ordinating activities. The company's overall strategy determines what its goals are, and central managers must co-ordinate all the firm's activities to achieve those goals. We look at the part played by each of these functions in turn:

- **Finance and accounting** – This function concerns control over the revenues and outgoings of the business, aiming to balance the books and to generate sufficient profits for the future health of the firm. This function is far more complex in large public companies than in SMEs. Trends towards more innovative finance and international operations have called for considerable professional expertise. At the same time, as discussed earlier, the legal duties of financial reporting and disclosure are now increasingly under the spotlight. The company's chief financial officer (CFO) is a board member, and bears responsibilities for compliance with legal requirements.

- **Operations** – Operations covers the entire process of producing and delivering a product to the consumer. This function covers tangible goods and services, and often a combination of both. Production focuses on the operational processes by which products are manufactured. Quality, safety and efficiency are major concerns of production engineers and managers. Quality and safety have become more challenging as manufacturing has shifted to diverse locations, and in some instances, companies have brought back to the home country operations that had been carried out by low-cost workers in outsourced factories. This is likely to

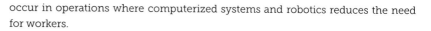

occur in operations where computerized systems and robotics reduces the need for workers.

- **Human resource management (HRM)** – Formerly known as 'personnel management', HRM focuses on all aspects of the management of people in the organization, including recruitment, training, and rewarding the workforce. In the large, hierarchical organization, these activities are formally structured, whereas in the small organization, they tend to be carried out informally, with less paperwork and less reliance on formal procedures. Organizations have become sensitive to the need to take into account the individual employee's own goals and development, as well as the needs of the company. International HR strategy is challenging. Each country has its own set of employment laws, and in each country, social and cultural factors play important roles in work values and practices. International HR managers increasingly realize the fact that motivating staff in different locations requires differing approaches and reward systems.

- **Marketing** – Marketing focuses on satisfying the needs and expectations of customers. Marketing covers a range of related activities, including product offering, branding, advertising, pricing, and distribution of goods. It might be assumed that the global company devises a global marketing strategy for all markets, but, in fact, it is common to adapt products and marketing communications to differing country markets. Language, religion and values are all aspects of culture which affect consumer preferences in different markets. As focus shifts to the large emerging markets, especially China and India, companies encounter considerable cultural diversity. These are some of the greatest challenges in international marketing, but the market potential makes these countries attractive.

- **Research and development (R&D)** – R&D is the function of seeking new knowledge and applications which can lead to new and improved products or processes. R&D activities are part of the larger focus on innovation in the company, and can take place within any of the functions listed in this section. **Innovation** covers the full range of activities carried out by all within the organization to seek improvements and new ways of doing things which can enhance competitiveness. (Innovation is discussed fully in Chapter 9.) R&D tends to focus on scientific and technical research, which is key to new product development. Pharmaceutical companies typically spend huge sums on R&D, as new medicines are their chief source of profits (see the closing case study on GSK in Chapter 9). For a media or internet company, innovation relies on creating new content (often adapted to new markets) and new ways of delivering content to the consumer.

Each of the business functions adapts and changes as a business expands internationally, as the following examples show:

- Financial reporting will involve different regulatory environments and accounting standards.
- Operations will be linked in global production networks.
- HRM will adapt to different cultures and laws.
- Marketing strategy will be designed for differing markets.
- R&D will be configured in different locations according to specialist skills in each.

For the international manager, an understanding of the differing cultural environments where the company operates, and the various functional activities which take place in each unit, is crucial to the overall achievement of the company's goals. A company's approach to these challenges depends heavily on its own background and its relations with stakeholder organizations.

The multinational enterprise (MNE)

Both private and public companies abound in the international environment. As they extend their operations outwards from their home countries, their organizations become more complex. A company can grow 'organically' by increasing its capacity and going into new markets without making major structural changes to the organization. When company executives become more ambitious internationally, they contemplate changes with deeper structural implications. A result has been a thriving global market in corporate ownership and control. As its strategy evolves, a company might buy other companies and sell those it no longer wishes to own. It might also buy stakes in other companies, often as a means of participating in a network of firms, rather than for purely ownership motives. This constant re-configuration of companies and businesses has become a prominent feature of the global business environment. In these ways, companies can grow relatively quickly internationally and adapt their businesses organizationally as changes in the competitive environment occur. The main organizational arrangement through which these changes take place is the multinational enterprise.

The **multinational enterprise (MNE)** is a broad term signifying a lead company (the parent company) which has acquired ownership (whole or partial) and other contractual ties in other organizations (including companies and unincorporated businesses) outside its home country. The parent company co-ordinates the business activities carried out by all the organizations within the MNE's broad control.

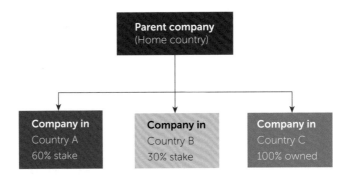

Figure 1.4 The multinational enterprise (MNE)

The MNE as an organizational form is not a strictly legal category, but it is recognized as central in international business organization and has been a key driver of globalization, discussed in the next chapter. The term covers businesses of all sizes, from SMEs to global companies with hundreds of thousands of employees. It covers private companies as well as public ones. Typically, the parent company located in the home country co-ordinates the activities of other companies in the group. If the parent company owns a majority stake in another company, that other company is a **subsidiary**. Where the ownership stake is less than half, the other company is considered an **affiliate** company. The MNE thus operates through a range of subsidiaries and affiliates. The parent company can exert strong control of a subsidiary, or it can operate on a loosely co-ordinated basis, delegating much decision-making to local managers. A simple MNE is shown in Figure 1.4. In the figure, only the company in Country C is wholly owned and controlled. It is thus a subsidiary company. The parent has a 60% equity stake in the company in Country A, making it also a subsidiary, as this gives the parent a controlling stake. The 30% stake in the company in Country B makes this company an affiliate. MNEs can have quite complex webs of affiliates, and in some countries, especially in Japan and South Korea, affiliates own shares in each other, known as 'cross-shareholding', thereby giving the parent company effective control over an affiliate even though it might own only a small stake itself (see the case study that follows).

The MNE parent company can be a **holding company**, that is, simply an umbrella company that owns the multiple companies or divisions that make up the business. An example is Alphabet, featured in the opening case study. The parent company is likely to be registered in its home country, and its subsidiaries registered in the countries where they carry out their activities. Hence, the subsidiary can be viewed as a 'local' company, even if controlled by a foreign parent. In some countries, foreign investors are not permitted by law to own 100% of a local company, but a sizeable stake can bring considerable power. In another twist, a private parent company can control subsidiaries which are publicly listed in their countries of operation (an example is the steel company, ArcelorMittal). Managing subsidiaries in different country environments is one of the major challenges for today's international managers, heightened by the expansion of competitive MNEs from developing and emerging economies.

Corporate governance: shareholders and other stakeholders

The sole trader or sole owner of a company may well take all the major decisions for the business, unfettered by the wishes of other owners and not accountable to anyone else within the business. Still, even a micro-enterprise has stakeholders, in that it exists in a community, has customers, makes an environmental impact and must comply with regulatory authorities. A company's highest decision-making processes constitute its corporate governance.

Corporate governance refers to the highest decision-making structures and processes in the company. It differs from business to business, and is influenced by national economic, social, cultural and legal environments. It reflects broad perspectives on the company's role in society, which have come under the spotlight in the wider debate on corporate governance and CSR in recent years. A company's own heritage and corporate culture influence its corporate governance, both formally and informally. National governments are in a position to set legal requirements for corporate governance, as part of their regulatory frameworks. **Regulation** refers to the rules relating to a particular type of activity or sector. The term covers both formal legal requirements and less formal guidance such as codes of practice (see closing case study on Tesco). These rules vary in their mandatory status. Many would prefer the law to lay down broad principles rather than prescriptive frameworks, on the grounds that a one-size-fits-all approach is not appropriate. The UK's Combined Code of Corporate Governance takes this more flexible approach. The **Organisation for Economic Co-operation and Development (OECD)** (www.oecd.org), which was established by representatives of the world's main developed economies in 1960, has been active in giving guidance on corporate governance. The OECD's

CASE STUDY ON THE CHANGING BUSINESS ENVIRONMENT

How sustainable are South Korea's global businesses?

South Korea had become an economic powerhouse years before China embarked on its opening up to market forces and economic growth. Back in the 1960s and 1970s, South Korea was building up expertise in innovations that would be crucial to industrial development, including microchip technology. It thus gained a valuable lead on its huge neighbour, China, in technology and innovation. When China's leaders started in earnest to introduce market reforms in 1990, they focused on large-scale manufacturing in low-technology sectors, for which abundant cheap labour was available. At that time, South Korea's technological strengths did not seem to be threatened by Chinese manufacturing, but the balance is now shifting as China is moving into manufacturing that draws on higher technology. China has also seen the growth of globally competitive companies, such as Huawei and Xiaomi, whose smartphones are competing with those of Samsung. How well are South Korea's companies able to respond, and where are the new South Korean innovators?

South Korea's economy is dominated by family-owned business groups, or 'chaebol'. The company names are familiar to consumers worldwide. Samsung Electronics, Hyundai Motors, and LG are all global brands. And so are their products, which range from cars to smartphones. Each family group consists of many separate companies that make up sprawling corporate empires, with a web of cross-shareholdings among subsidiary companies. The effect is to perpetuate the power of the family dynasties that control them. From the 1960s, the families have spearheaded South Korea's economic development, assisted by favourable government policies and by the availability of government-funded loans to aid investments. Close links with political leaders have ensured continued favoured treatment and, at the same time, ensured that companies outside the chaebol networks would not be able to thrive. The ruling families claim that their strengths derive largely from their long-term vision, rather than the focus on short-term profits that characterizes most capitalist

companies. But the ordinary shareholders in these companies, many of them foreign investors, do not always share this vision, complaining about weakening growth and poor dividends. The families would seem to prefer hoarding profits to passing on dividends to shareholders. The unaccountability of the controlling families gives these vast groups a reputation for poor corporate governance. When Hyundai paid out the equivalent of $10 billion for a piece of land on which to build a new headquarters, some investors expressed dismay, one referring to the extravagance as a 'violation of shareholder rights' (Mundy, 2014). One explanation is that the families do not take much account of non-family shareholders, even ones with large stakes: the families 'feel like the whole company is theirs' (Mundy, 2014).

South Korea's president, Park Guen-hye, elected in 2012, campaigned strongly on a pledge to rein in the chaebol in order to make the economy more dynamic and innovative. In particular, she urged the creation of a 'creative economy', in which SMEs would be encouraged (Song, 2014). However, delivering on these goals has proved difficult in a business environment which has long protected ruling business families. Even when convicted of crimes, family members have been allowed by the justice system to carry on running companies, and have even been granted pardons, impliedly reflecting their importance to the national economy. The perception that the business families are above the law gives little cause for hope that South Korea can rejuvenate its industries through letting new managerial talent emerge. It has been argued that what is needed is greater transparency and improved corporate governance, particularly in light of increased global competitive pressures (Powers, 2010).

Sources: Powers, C. (2010) 'The changing role of chaebol', *Stanford Journal of East Asian Affairs*, 10(2): 105-16; Mundy, S. (2014) 'Sparks fly over the chaebol', *Financial Times*, 3 November; Song, Jung-a (2014) 'S Korea chaebol growth model hits limits', *Financial Times*, 19 November, at www.ft.com; Evans, S. (2015) 'Can South Korea's chaebol retain their grip?' BBC News, 10 August, at www.bbc.com.

- What are the business strengths of the chaebol?
- What are the corporate governance weaknesses of the chaebol?
- How sustainable are South Korea's large businesses?
- What kinds of reform by government could dent the power of the chaebol?

overarching principles support market economies and democratic institutions. It publishes *Principles of Corporate Governance*, which are intended to guide companies generally on best practice (OECD, 2004). These appear in Table 1.1. This guidance was under review in May 2016, and a new version of the principles was forthcoming. However, the existing version serves well to highlight the basic concepts. Of note among these principles are the recognition of the role of stakeholders, the protection of the status of minority shareholders and the assertion of the need for non-executive directors to be independent.

Table 1.1 Corporate governance principles recommended by the OECD

Principle	The corporate governance framework should:
I	* Promote transparent and efficient markets * Be consistent with the rule of law * Identify responsibilities of different regulatory and supervisory authorities
II	* Protect and facilitate the exercise of shareholder rights
III	* Ensure the equitable treatment of all shareholders, including minority and foreign shareholders
IV	* Recognize the rights of stakeholders established by law or through mutual agreements * Encourage active co-operation between corporations and stakeholders in creating wealth, jobs, and the sustainability of financially sound enterprises
V	* Ensure that timely and accurate disclosure is made on all material matters regarding the corporation, including the financial situation, performance, ownership, and governance
VI	Board responsibilities: * Monitor management effectively * Align key executive and board remuneration with the longer term interests of the company and shareholders * Consider a sufficient number of non-executive board members capable of exercising independent judgment

Source: OECD (2004) *OECD Principles of Corporate Governance*, at www.oecd.org.

Although the senior executives are probably the most influential people in the company, the highest legal authority is its board of directors. **Directors** bear ultimate responsibility for the company's activities. Collectively, they constitute the **board of directors**, accountable to the company's shareholders. Structures differ from country to country. In Germany and other European countries, a two-tier board of directors is the norm. A supervisory board holds the ultimate authority for major decisions, while a management board is responsible for day-to-day management. The single board is the norm in the Anglo-American type of structure, shown in Figure 1.5. It is based on the belief that shareholders' interests are paramount. Board members have oversight over major decisions and owe duties to act in the best interests of the company as a whole, which, in practice, is equated with the interests of the shareholders. Where the state controls a company, there is a potential conflict between the government's political goals and the best interests of the company as an enterprise. For example, executives might wish to slim down the workforce, but political leaders wish to retain as many jobs as possible (as an example, see the closing case study on Brazil in Chapter 6). The supervisory board in the two-tier system includes employee representation, reflecting the principle of **co-determination**. The two-tier model is often said to represent a stakeholder approach to governance, in contrast to the focus on shareholder value that characterizes the single-tier model. However, the supervisory board in the German two-tier structure has also been criticized as being under the control of dominant shareholders (Enriques and Volpin, 2007).

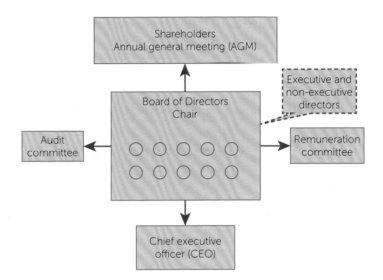

Figure 1.5 The single-tier board of directors

The directors who actively manage the company are its **executive directors**, headed by a **chief executive officer (CEO)**. The CEO occupies a pivotal role in decision-making and management of the company. The CEO is at the pinnacle of the company's **management**, which consists of all the processes of planning, organizing and controlling the firm's business. The firm's managerial staff are all responsible to the CEO. In turn, the CEO must answer to the board, maintain the confidence of shareholders, inspire the company's workforce and deal with an array of stakeholders. Whenever the company's fortunes take a turn for the worse, the CEO is in the firing line.

Non-executive directors are considered independent of the firm's management and owners, although independence is questionable in some cases: in many countries personal ties and ownership stakes are considered not to impact on independent status. The non-executive director carries out board duties on a part-time basis and, in theory, exerts more objective judgment on the company's activities than working managers do. On the other hand, knowledge about the business is now seen as necessary, following the 2008 financial crisis in which directors' failure to curb excessive risk has been highlighted. The onus is on non-executives to take their responsibilities seriously, and actively query the CEO over strategy. Non-executives are equally liable legally for corporate wrongdoing which they ought to have been aware of. There has been a tendency to appoint other CEOs and retired CEOs as non-executive directors. This approach is now changing, as uncritical boards have been implicated in a number of situations where misguided strategies and excessive executive rewards were allowed to go unchecked. An example is Enron, the energy trading company which collapsed in 2001. Enron had a corporate governance system which looked admirable on paper. However, its senior executives were able to steer the company towards their own goals, and the bodies which should have provided a check on their actions (such as the board and its committees) failed to do so. Legislation in the US, in the form of the Sarbanes-Oxley Act of 2002, focused on liability and penalties for false financial reporting, but did not address structural issues of governance.

More recently, excessive risk-taking is blamed in a series of bank failures which led to the global financial crisis of 2008, including Lehman Brothers of the US, once the country's fourth-largest investment bank, which collapsed under a mountain of $60 billion in bad debts. Other banks, deemed to be too big to fail, such as Citigroup, were rescued by US government bailouts. The UK government came to the rescue of major banks, RBS and Lloyds, which had become highly globalized and indebted (see Chapter 8). It was acknowledged that regulatory failures, as well as excessive risk-taking by managers, had been to blame. Public confidence in corporate governance had suffered, and regulatory reform was again perceived as necessary. Executives of failed banks seemed to escape unscathed following the crisis, even continuing to receive bonus payments. Public clamour for accountability has been a factor bringing about pressure to cap bankers' pay. There have also been pressures for criminal sanctions for 'reckless mismanagement' by bankers whose institutions have failed (*Financial Times*, 2014). The governor of the Bank of England has voiced criticism of UK bankers in the years following the financial crisis (Treanor, 2014). What was needed, he has said, was culture change among bankers themselves, but this has not occurred. He became persuaded that the imposition of stricter regulation seems to be the only way to bring about a more sustainable banking sector, which would regain public confidence (Treanor, 2014).

Although corporate executives routinely claim that their main objective is enhancing shareholder value, ordinary shareholders themselves have tended to have little direct influence in a number of important matters, such as executive remuneration and the appointment of directors. In separate initiatives, the US, UK and EU have taken steps to rein in excessive pay awards in the financial sector (discussed in Chapter 8). Politicians have been blamed for failing to regulate the financial sector during the pre-crisis boom years, and using taxpayers' money to fund bailouts of banks deemed to be 'too big to fail'. It did not escape notice that banks have engaged in tax avoidance schemes themselves and, indeed, profited from selling others their know-how. In terms of corporate governance, shareholders, who watched banks come to near-collapse, are now taking a more active interest in governance.

Regulation and corporate governance take place in the business environment generally, which, as we describe below, can be seen through multiple dimensions. Corporate governance focuses on the internal dimension, whereas regulation brings external influences to bear on the business and its organization. Managers must respond to the changing external environment, which, more than ever, involves engagement with stakeholders.

An overview of the global environment

The dimensions of the business environment stem largely from the characteristics which go to make up societies: every society has a cultural heritage, a social makeup, distinctive economic activities, political arrangements, one or more legal frameworks and technological capacities. A description of each of these aspects of a society gives a picture of the society as a whole. However, these dimensions do not stop at national borders. Any dimension will have a layered perspective in terms of geography. For example, the political environment is made up of local community, national government and international relations. These are shown in Figure 1.6. For enterprises, it is necessary to see the small picture, such as local politics, as well as the big picture, which might be the country's position in relation to trading partners. In fact, understanding the big picture sometimes helps in understanding local currents, and vice versa. Thus, local political leaders could well be influential in attracting a foreign investor wishing to build a factory from a country with which the national government has concluded a trade and investment agreement. We first identify the dimensions and layers.

Figure 1.6 The dimensions and layers of the international environment

Multiple dimensions

The dimensions of the environment are shown in Figure 1.6. These key dimensions can be grouped in a **PEST** analysis, which stands for political, economic, social and technological dimensions. Detailed elements of the PEST framework are shown in Table 1.2.

Table 1.2 PEST analysis in the international business environment

Political-legal
• Political stability • Form of government, e.g. democratic, authoritarian • Level of freedoms, e.g. freedom of expression and association • Incentives to foreign investors • Competition law and policy • Employment law
Economic
• Level of economic development • Trends in GDP • Rate of inflation • Wage levels and level of unemployment • Strength of currency and convertibility • Rates of taxation
Socio-cultural
• Growth rate of population and age distribution of population • Language(s) • Main religious and cultural groupings • Educational attainment levels • Level of social cohesion • Role of women
Technological
• Government spending on R&D • Legal regime for patent protection • Energy availability and costs • Transport infrastructure and costs • Innovation system, including availability of skilled workforce • Level of technology transfer

To make the PEST analysis more complete, the legal environment is considered with the political, and the cultural environment is taken with the social, making it the socio-cultural environment. This book recognizes the usefulness of the latter combination, as reflected in Chapter 3. However, we focus on the political and legal environments separately (in Chapters 5 and 6), highlighting the interconnections between the two dimensions. We add three further dimensions: the financial, technological and ecological environments, in Chapters 8, 9 and 10. All these dimensions interact to some extent. The PEST analysis, therefore, is a blunt tool for understanding societies. It also tends to take a rather static view, not capturing changes over time. In this book, we aim to do both: to look at background forces and the changes taking place. In many instances, there is tension between established norms and institutions, on the one hand, and newer forces seeking to bring about changes – often changes emanating from outside the country. Bearing these dynamics in mind, we describe each of these dimensions below:

• **Cultural and social environment** – covers values, attitudes, norms of behaviour and social relations among people who can be identified as a coherent group. Cultures are usually grouped as national cultures, which are held together by language, a historical sense of belonging and loyalty to a national homeland. As indicated above, however, national cultures are only part of a person's identity. Religions, which have adherents worldwide, may play an important part. Lifestyle, such as the modern consumer lifestyle, is also relevant to people. Lifestyle reflects many aspects of a person's life apart from national culture, including age, education, and whether he or she lives in an urban or rural setting.

- **Economic environment** – covers the kind of economic activities which make up people's livelihoods, the country's sources of wealth and the extent of the country's industrialization. These aspects of the economy provide a picture of the country's economic development, and, specifically, whether the country is promoting growth based on **sustainable development**, that is, development that looks beyond current needs to those of future generations. Globalization, and especially the role of foreign direct investment (discussed in the next chapter), have been major trends, promoting economic growth in many developing economies.

- **Political environment** – covers the country's system of government and the powerful groups and individuals who shape the way it operates in practice. All businesses, domestic and foreign, seek a stable political environment, preferably one which encourages enterprise activities. In some countries political power is concentrated and in others democratic processes are more influential in determining who wields political power. The existence of freedom of expression for individuals and media is also an indication of the type of political environment in a country.

- **Legal environment** – covers the system of laws within a country, backed up by the authority of the state. It covers how laws are made and how they are enforced in practice. In any country, businesses look for clarity and predictability in the laws which pertain to them, with fair, impartial implementation and enforcement. These characteristics indicate the existence of the rule of law in a country. Where a country is fragmented, with differing lawmaking authorities in separate regions, instability can result, making it more difficult to do business in the country, especially for foreign firms unfamiliar with the differing authorities. Cross-border legal actions, involving both national and international law, have become more significant for companies in the era of deepening international ties.

- **Technological environment** – covers the nature and extent of applied scientific knowledge, which is used for practical purposes. The depth of a country's scientific education and training, as well as the extent of government funding for R&D, are indicators of the country's technological environment. It is important for businesses that new products and inventions are protected in law. These assets are referred to as **intangible assets**, as they represent rights over products, which can be exploited. They can be contrasted with **tangible assets**, which are physical assets such as machinery and stock. Intangible assets are protected by laws relating to **intellectual property (IP)**. They include patents for the firm's inventions; copyright for written works, music, film and software; and trade marks, such as company logos. As countries climb the technological ladder, the protection and enforcement of IP rights are demanded by businesses, discussed in Chapter 9.

- **Financial environment** – covers banking and other financial services which serve other businesses as well as consumers. National financial systems differ in their openness to outsiders, their transparency and their levels of regulation. Most countries' financial systems have become more open in recent years to outside investors, such as foreign banks wishing to set up operations in the country or invest in domestic companies. Financial markets are prone to volatility, and investors look to well-capitalized banks and sound regulatory systems to maintain confidence and stability. When confidence wanes in one part of the world, it can quickly spread across financial institutions in other parts of the world, as the crisis of 2008 demonstrated.

- **Ecological environment** – covers all living things and relationships between them in their natural habitats. Environmental degradation in today's world has been caused largely by human activity, especially through industrialization, urbanization and modern large-scale agriculture. Businesses are gaining greater knowledge and awareness of the environmental impacts of their operations in differing locations, as well as their impacts on global phenomena such as climate change. Resource scarcity and climate change are increasingly becoming imperatives for corporate strategists to take into account.

The multi-layered environment

It is common to speak of *global* firms facing competition in the *global* environment, but in fact, global competition is frequently played out in local environments. Local companies, with their intimate knowledge of local markets, can be some of the toughest competitors which global companies encounter. An example is the stiff competition faced by McDonald's in China from local fast-food chains. The international environment can be conceived as layered spatial areas, visualized as concentric circles, beginning with the smallest unit, the local community. Local communities exist in the larger unit of the country, which is itself part of a geographic region, and beyond that, the world. These layers are shown in Table 1.3. The table gives examples of key phenomena as well as relevant institutions and organizations in each sphere. There is considerable interaction and interdependence among these different spheres as countries and regions become more interconnected. Growing connectedness among people and organizations is a quintessential aspect of globalization, discussed in the next chapter. It is tempting to fall for the view that all aspects of the business environment are inevitably moving towards the global, but this would be a mistake. Some aspects of the international environment have seen greater international co-operation, such as the Paris climate change agreement of 2015, but each layer of the environment has its own characteristics and players. Although they are becoming interconnected, they are not melding together into a whole, but retain distinctiveness, which business strategists ignore at their peril.

We look at each of these layers from the perspective of the business:

- **Local community** – Wherever the MNE operates or where its products are made, there will be a local community in which its impacts are immediate. A factory or other industrial process affects local people and the natural environment in the area. Production can bring jobs and wealth, but impacts on the environment can potentially be damaging. These are stakeholder issues which involve dialogue within local communities.

- **Country** – The national environment is probably the most influential for a business. National laws cover company regulation, employment conditions and the

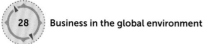

Table 1.3 Dimensions and layers of the international environment

Layers and dimensions	Local community	Country	Region	World
Cultural and social	Families; local customs; schools; urban or rural	National culture; language; sense of shared history	Cultural affinity across the region; movement of people between countries	Human rights; world religions; consumer culture
Economic	Local businesses; predominant industries	National industries; industrial structure; national income and economic growth	Degree of economic integration; regional trade relations	Global economic integration; WTO and multilateral trade agreements; global companies and industries
Political	Local government and politics	Political system; degree of civil and political freedoms	Degree of political co-operation; shared institutions (e.g. the EU)	International governmental co-operation (e.g. the UN)
Legal	Delegated lawmaking; planning; health and safety	Rule of law; independent judiciary and court system; national legislation	Legal harmonization; mutual recognition of court judgments	International law and the International Court of Justice (ICJ)
Technological	Schools and colleges; research centres	National school system; universities; government funding for R&D	Cross-border research ties; co-operation among universities	Global spread of breakthrough technology; global R&D networks
Financial	Penetration of banks and financial services	National financial system; regulatory system	Cross-border financial flows; regional regulation (e.g. the European Central Bank)	Global financial flows; international institutions (e.g. the IMF and World Bank)
Ecological	Ecosystems; pollution levels; air quality	Areas of environmental stress; environmental protection laws	Regional institutions; co-operation over regional resources (e.g. rivers)	Climate change; international co-operation on emissions reduction

environment. A country's national culture is influential in strategic decisions about potential markets and location of operations. A country's political system and leadership decide the policies which influence how stable it will be for foreign business investors.

- **Region** – Every country is located in a region and is drawn into relations with neighbouring countries. These relations can give rise to conflicts – regional wars are sadly not uncommon. But, more often, relations between neighbours are beneficial. Regional trade agreements have flourished in recent years, allowing for the free movement of goods between countries in the region. The European Union (EU) is the most highly developed regional grouping (discussed in Chapters 4 and 5). Regions can pool resources to deal with common threats such as climate change.

- **World** – There is increasing awareness of global phenomena, such as climate change, which require co-operation among all players, both businesses and governments, at all levels. To co-ordinate this co-operation, global regulatory frameworks are emerging. This is happening in respect of climate change. It is also happening in the area of human rights and financial regulation. Although national structures have been dominant in these areas, international frameworks are gaining authority. The international organizations highlighted in Table 1.3 are introduced in the next chapter. Business strategists are now looking beyond national regulation to rule-making at international level.

The way I see it ...

On the competitive environment, 'The lesson to me is differentiate yourself... Move up the value chain. Being cheaper isn't enough. Being the low-cost provider is temporal.'

Sam Palmisano, former CEO of IBM, in an interview with CRN technology news, 23 February, 2011, at www.crn.com

How does the advice of Palmisano fit in with ideas of the sustainable business?

The enterprise in a dynamic environment: challenges and responsibilities

Decisions about what the firm ought to be doing, how, and where give rise to numerous challenges, and also highlight responsibilities. The challenges become more complex as the business becomes extended globally through supply chains, diverse investors and evolving markets. An issue raised early on in this chapter was that of how the firm sees its business in the future. Apart from the subsistence entrepreneur, who has few aspirations except making a living, businesses seek more than simply to carry on in existence in the future. Most businesses have goals that reflect values and purpose of a higher order, such as innovating to produce better products or products that use fewer scarce resources. Indeed, the firm that assumes 'business as usual' will suffice in today's international markets could face a harsh awakening when rivals' innovations win over its customers.

It has become customary to say that the company exists to enhance shareholder value, as we have noted. But while this is often equated with rising share price and rising profits, these goals, too, look rather limited in today's world. Challenges and responsibilities are shown in Figure 1.7, introduced in the Introduction to this book. Stakeholders have a role in each of the three interlocking circles: sustainability, governance and social responsibility. All stakeholders, including shareholders, look for innovative products, but also products which reflect high ethical standards, including attentiveness to issues such as human rights and social goals. These are among the challenges of the sustainable business. Just looking to the next set of profit figures is short term. The sustainable business thus embraces responsibilities that reflect its participation in society.

Large firms have become adept at designing a global strategy which takes account of local differences. Indeed, local differences can be turned into a source of competitive advantage for the MNE. We see this thinking behind the decisions of large MNEs to outsource manufacturing in low-cost countries. This trend, discussed further in the next chapter, has had significant impacts in both home and host countries. Consumers in developed countries have benefited from a huge range of products at lower

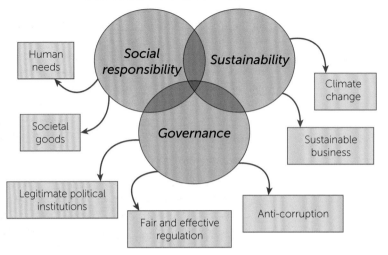

Figure 1.7 Interlocking challenges and responsibilities

prices than those manufactured in their own countries. Host economies have bene-fited from the investment of foreign companies, the employment created and the opportunities to gain valuable technological expertise.

However, when a firm fails or chooses to close down operations in a given loca-tion, the impacts can be far-reaching, extending well beyond the loss of jobs in that firm. Other businesses in the community, such as retailers and caterers, will become precarious. Unemployment inevitably rises, and so does public spending on unem-ployment and other benefits. People who had no direct connections with the com-pany could well find themselves out of work and struggling financially. It is no wonder that governments come under political pressure to tighten the regulation of foreign investors. Most regulation occurs at the national level, but global companies can – and do – choose countries on the basis of their 'light-touch' regulation, avoiding those that are more stringently regulated. We have highlighted national regulatory failures in the finance sector. Banks and other financial institutions now face greater regulation. Competition among countries to attract foreign investors has become a familiar feature of the global environment. Countries where taxes and social charges levied on companies are high tend to attract fewer foreign investors than countries without these provisions. This apparent 'race to the bottom' in any sector is unlikely to be altered without co-operation among governments to co-ordinate regulations. While this might seem unlikely in a competitive economic environment, political leaders as well as corporate decision-makers are now recognizing the need for encouraging sustainability in wealth-generating activities.

Conclusions

This chapter has highlighted internal aspects of a variety of business enterprises, including goals, organization and governance, which influence how they go about their activities and how decisions are taken. The relevant terminology, from IPOs to stakeholders, will recur throughout the book. The values and interests of the indi-vidual people behind corporate logos are key to shaping how the business behaves. The backgrounds of these actors on the business landscape have become increasingly diverse. Understanding diverse business environments has thus risen as a priority for managers. As this chapter has shown, the context provides much valuable information about firm behaviour in the past, and the ways in which changes might take place in the future. The chapter has provided an overview of the multiple dimensions of the environment which will be explored in future chapters. It has also set out the differing geographic layers of the environment, from local to international, which impact on the business enterprise. An awareness of these layers helps to understand why firms behave as they do. A local issue, such as emissions from a factory, is a matter for the inhabitants of the community most affected. It is an issue that should be addressed by their government (both local and national). But it is now also a global concern in that emissions contribute to rising temperatures globally.

The geographical scanning of MNEs has had consequences in the ways companies perceive the international environment. Developing countries which host outsourced manufacturing are no longer perceived as remote by brand owners and consumers. Workers in outsourced factories are stakeholders of the MNE, even though not employed by it. The host country's government, too, is a stakeholder, whose law and policies are influential for the MNE. In addition, growing concern at international level regarding human rights has heightened awareness of this issue among the company's most valued stakeholders – its shareholders. For the student of international business, the coming together of global and local forces is one of the aspects of the business environment which is becoming the most challenging.

References

Carroll, A.B. and Shabana, K.M. (2010) 'The business case for corporate social responsibility: a review of concepts, research and practice', *International Journal of Management Reviews*, 12(1): 85–105.

De Kok, J., Deijl, C. and Veldhuis-Van Essen, C. (2013) *Is Small Still Beautiful? Literature Review of Recent Empirical Evidence on the Contribution of SMEs to Employment Creation* (Geneva, ILO).

Enriques, L. and Volpin, P. (2007) 'Corporate governance reforms in continental Europe', *The Journal of Economic Perspectives*, 21(1): 117–140.

Financial Times (2014) 'Hold Britain's banks to higher standards', 8 October, at www.ft.com.

Freeman, R.E. (1984) *Strategic Management: A Stakeholder Approach* (Boston, MA: Pitman).

Maon, F., Lingreen, A. and Swaen, V. (2009) 'Designing and implementing corporate social responsibility: an integrative framework grounded in theory and practice', *Journal of Business Ethics*, 87(1): 71–89.

Murman, J. and Sandana, D. (2012) 'Successful entrepreneurs minimize risk', *Australian Journal of Management*, 38(1): 191–215.

OECD (2004) *OECD Principles of Corporate Governance*, at www.oecd.org

Schoar, A. (2010) 'The divide between subsistence and transformational entrepreneurship' *Innovation Policy and the Economy*, 10(1): 57–81.

Tanev, S. (2012) 'Global from the start: the characteristics of born-global firms in the technology sector', *Technology Innovation Management Review*, March, 5–8.

Treanor, J. (2014) 'Mark Carney: Dock bankers' pay for misconduct', *The Guardian*, 17 November, at www.theguardian.com
Wayne, L. (2012) 'How Delaware thrives as a corporate tax haven', *New York Times*, 30 June, at www.nytimes.com

☞ Multiple choice questions

Go to the companion website: www.palgravehighered.com/morrison-gbe-4e to take a quick multiple choice quiz on what you have read in this chapter.

⑦ Review questions

1 How does a business decide what its goals will be?
2 Define stakeholders and explain the stakeholder approach to corporate strategy.
3 What is CSR, and why is it becoming more important in the formation of corporate goals?
4 What are the advantages and disadvantages of being a sole trader?
5 What are the aspects of the limited company which distinguish it from other types of business ownership?
6 What is distinctive about the entrepreneurial enterprise?
7 What is a franchise arrangement? Give some examples.
8 How does a private company differ from a public limited company (PLC)?
9 What is distinctive about the MNE as a type of organization?
10 How does corporate governance differ from the day-to-day management of a company?
11 Why are independent (non-executive) directors considered essential in corporate governance?
12 Explain the shareholder and stakeholder perspectives on corporate governance.
13 What is the role of stakeholders in the two-tier board of directors?
14 Describe each of the main functions within the business enterprise.
15 What are the advantages and limitations of a PEST analysis?

✓ Assignments

1 Offer advice to the following CEO: Steve is the CEO of a manufacturing company in an EU country. He is worried about rising costs and competitive pressures from low-cost manufacturers in developing countries. Steve feels the pressures from shareholders to be more competitive, but he is reluctant to shift production to a low-cost country as the company has a long association with its home location.
2 The PEST analysis was designed to illuminate specific dimensions of a national environment. How can it be adapted to take into account other dimensions and broader scope, bringing in regional and global impacts?

📖 Further reading

Bartlett, C. and Ghoshal, S. (2002) *Managing Across Borders: The Transnational Solution*, 2nd edn (Boston: Harvard Business School Press).
Hickson, D. and Pugh, D.S. (2007) *Writers on Organizations* (London: Penguin).
Kay, J. (2007) *Foundations of Corporate Success* (Oxford: Oxford University Press).

Mullins, L. (2013) *Management and Organizational Behaviour*, 10th edn (London: Financial Times Publishing).

Prahalad, C.K. (2009) *The Fortune at the Bottom of the Pyramid* (Philadelphia: Wharton School Publishing).

Pugh, D.S. (ed.) (2008) *Organization Theory: Selected Readings*, 5th edn (London: Penguin Books).

Solomon, J. (2013) *Corporate Governance and Accountability*, 4th edn (London: Wiley).

Wheelen, T. and Hunger, J. (2009) *Strategic Management and Business Policy*, 12th edn (New Jersey: Addison Wesley).

Visit the companion website at www.palgravehighered.com/morrison-gbe-4e for further learning and teaching resources.

CLOSING CASE STUDY

Rescuing Tesco

Large supermarkets are increasingly facing challenges in satisfying shoppers' expectations in terms of quality and price.
Source: Getty.

When Dave Lewis took over as CEO of Tesco in 2014, he had plenty on his plate. The UK's largest retailer had been shaken by a series of shocks, and urgently needed to devise a rescue strategy. Tesco had plunged to a loss of £6.4 billion in 2014, the biggest loss ever recorded by a UK retailer. Accounting irregularities had emerged in Tesco's finances, leaving a black hole of £263 million, which was being investigated by the Serious Fraud Office. Tesco was also investigated by the grocery industry's watchdog, the Grocery Code Adjudicator, and, in 2016, was found to have delayed paying suppliers in order to bolster its finances – a practice in breach of the industry's code of practice. The company's reputation suffered from the stream of negative media stories. As the UK's biggest supermarket chain, it had seen a fall in the number of customers to its large hypermarkets, the

superstores in out-of-town locations. Consumers were shifting to smaller supermarkets including the discount chains. With his background in marketing at the consumer products company, Unilever, Mr Lewis was the first outsider to take over the helm of Tesco in its 97-year history, suggesting that the board felt radical change was needed. His marketing background would be valuable in his new role as he faced the task of rebuilding the brand, as well as refocusing the company.

In common with Walmart in the US and Carrefour in France, Tesco's growth had been built mainly on large out-of-town hypermarkets, the Tesco Extra stores – vast warehouse-like stores that sell a wide range of food and non-food products. While it also operates many smaller supermarkets, its expansion plans had focused largely on the superstores. It was assumed that shoppers in the UK were wedded to the large weekly shopping trip, not minding the fact that they might have to drive some distance to the out-of-town location. The company had not always been welcomed by local communities; in particular, small shops fear losing business. In addition, Tesco introduced 24-hour shopping in many stores, and met resistance in some locations. The company continued to purchase land for future stores, even though it had no immediate plans to build them. This apparent hoarding of land has given rise to criticism. It also added to the company's woes when property values fell. But an overriding worry for its executives has been changing shopping habits. Shoppers started to shun the large weekly shopping trip, preferring to shop more often and buy less, often at local stores rather than hypermarkets. They have also turned in greater numbers to the discount chains, Lidl and Aldi. Although the two discounters have a combined share of only 10% of the UK grocery market – compared to Tesco's 28% – Aldi's and Lidl's sales are growing annually at rates of 17% and 16% respectively, while Tesco's have been falling by about 1%. At the same time, the more upmarket offerings of Waitrose and Marks & Spencer are attracting customers. Tesco seems to be stuck in the middle.

In response, Lewis decided Tesco would need to cut prices on basic goods and also improve the offering of quality products that would excite customers. Cutting costs was a major priority. Assets had to be sold. Much of the land bank was sold off to property developers. Some 43 Tesco stores were closed, and plans to build 49 new stores were cancelled. Lewis also turned his attention to the company's international operations. Tesco had suffered from the failure of its foray into the US, having sold its US chain of loss-making stores in 2013. It had had more success in Asia and Central Europe. It was decided to sell the South Korean stores, which comprised 140 hypermarkets, as well as supermarkets and convenience stores. These were successful retail outlets, and the sale brought in £4 billion.

By 2015, Lewis felt that the rescue plan was starting to work. Inevitably, profits had fallen, largely because of price-cutting, but it seemed that the new offers and low prices were attracting more customers. Retail analysts are not so sure. One has said that Tesco, like the other big supermarkets, '... are having an identity crisis, and need to pick a side. They either have to push themselves to the premium end of retailing or push themselves to the discount end' (Shadbolt, 2015). Mr Lewis would not agree. Despite the brand losing some of its lustre, he believes in its turnaround as a refocused business. Will shareholders agree? Tesco's shares lost 18% of their value in a year, but Mr Lewis remained optimistic. A resurgent Tesco might cheer up shareholders.

Sources: Butler, S. and Walsh, F. (2015) 'Tesco profits tumble by more than half', *The Guardian*, 7 October, at www.theguardian.com; BBC (2015) 'Tesco posts record £6.4 billion annual loss', 22 April, at www.bbc.com; Shadbolt, P. (2015) 'How the discounters are beating the supermarkets', BBC News, 23 September, at www.bbc.com; Butler, S. (2016) 'Tesco failed to treat suppliers fairly, watchdog rules', *The Guardian*, 26 January.

Questions for discussion

● What are the causes of Tesco's declining financial performance?
● What aspects of the business environment that have impacted on Tesco are mentioned in the case study?
● How sound has Lewis been so far in his turnaround plans? What would you have done differently?
● Do you agree with the retail analyst who is convinced that Tesco has an identity crisis? Give your reasons.

GLOBALIZATION AND THE BUSINESS ENVIRONMENT

This chapter will enable you to

- Gain an overview of globalization
- Identify and interpret differing impacts of globalization in differing national environments, including developed and developing countries
- Distinguish the main modes of internationalization, together with their underlying rationales
- Appreciate globalization's impacts on societies

Outline of chapter

OPENING CASE STUDY

Zara, or how to succeed in global fashion

Inditex, the fashion empire based in Spain, is known worldwide as the creator of the Zara brand. Since its formation in Galicia in northern Spain in 1975, Zara's founder, Amancio Ortega, has revolutionized the business of retail fashion, from design through to production and distribution to its shops. In the process, Zara has shaped consumer expectations about fashion retailing in the world's shopping centres. Where once fashion retailers would offer a new range each autumn and spring, Zara continually renews the offering, at intervals as short as two weeks. When a line is successful, follow-up orders can also be delivered at very short notice, supplanting lines that are not popular. This constant renewal and responsiveness is at the heart of 'fast fashion', and Zara has become its most successful exponent. How has this company, with origins in an area of Spain thought of as a backwater, managed to revolutionize an industry? The keys to its success lie largely in the close ties between store managers and designers, as well as an efficient supply chain that gives Zara an edge on rivals in capturing the latest fashion trends.

Zara store managers see firsthand what lines are popular and which are not. They are given considerable scope to take decisions on orders, and they are in frequent contact with the company's headquarters in Spain, where the commercial managers and designers can respond immediately. In turn, factories are set up to fill orders rapidly. The role of the store managers is crucial. They are well paid by industry standards, and, in addition, can earn bonuses for meeting sales targets. The Inditex CEO says, 'They feel like the owner of the store' (Ruddick, 2014). From the customer's perspective, the Zara offering is constantly changing, reflecting fast-changing trends. This formula has proved popular with consumers. Zara has 6,500 shops in 88 countries, usually in high-profile main shopping districts. By contrast, the company spends very little on advertising. Inditex has expanded rapidly in China, where it has 456 stores and plans for further expansion. The company's online retailing has grown since 2012, and there are now online shops in 27 countries.

The responsiveness of the manufacturing process owes much of its efficiency to the fact that Inditex relies heavily on factories in relatively close proximity to its HQ. About 50% of its products are made in Spain, Portugal, Morocco and Turkey. Morocco and Turkey offer relatively low-cost labour. Labour in these countries is not as cheap as in Asia, but the lower transport costs and speed of fulfilling orders make these closer manufacturing locations advantageous. On the other hand, much manufacturing for the Zara brand does take place in Asia, where much of the world's garment manufacturing is now concentrated. Inditex has been involved in Bangladesh, where the collapse of the Rana Plaza factory, in which over a thousand people died, brought to the world's attention the dangerous conditions suffered by migrant workers. Inditex has signed an accord on fire and building safety, along with other western companies, including Tesco and M&S.

Low-cost labour is a crucial issue for fast fashion. Inditex brands are manufactured in 67 factories in Brazil, where accusations of 'sweatshop' practices, such as excessive hours and lack of rest days, have led to criticisms by the Brazilian authorities. The company has a corporate social responsibility director, and it is committed to raising standards in its supply chains. However, tight deadlines and low prices paid to suppliers are inevitable aspects of the business model. To meet deadlines, suppliers resort to subcontracting, sometimes without the knowledge of the brand owner. In these situations, there is a greater risk of breaches of human rights.

The Inditex approach to global fashion retailing has been highly profitable. Surging sales in emerging markets are now helping to ensure future growth. Ortega, who owns 60% of the company's shares, is one of the world's richest people, with a fortune estimated to be worth $71 billion. This would make him second only to Bill Gates, the founder of Microsoft. In earlier eras, a fashion shop in Galicia would probably have seen the Spanish market as the limit of its ambition, but Inditex has excelled in turning the business into a global empire.

Sources: Ruddick, G. (2014) 'How Zara became the world's biggest fashion retailer', *The Telegraph*, 20 October, at www.telegraph.co.uk; Butler, S. (2015) 'Zara owner Inditex faces fines in Brazil over poor working conditions claim', *The Guardian*, 12 May, at www.theguardian.com; BBC (2013) 'Zara and H&M to sign Bangladesh safety accord', 14 May, BBC News, at www.bbc.com.

Questions for discussion

- What are the aspects of the Inditex business model that have proved crucial to its success?
- The hundreds of factories that produce garments for Inditex and other fashion retailers are mainly in countries where wages are low. Does this make the business model unsustainable, in your view?
- What are the negative aspects of fast fashion from a perspective of corporate social responsibility?
- Can these negative aspects be overcome with greater attention to oversight of supply chains?

Introduction

Since about the second half of the twentieth century, the world has experienced changes in all dimensions of the environment, which have come to be grouped together under the heading 'globalization'. These changes have by now touched nearly everyone, from city dwellers in the rich economies to farmers in rural Africa. Every type of business activity and all sizes of organization have been affected. Industries such as oil stand out as global in nature, but so too are industries like textiles and clothing, which have traditionally been local and national. Multinational enterprises (MNEs) have been the main drivers of these changes, but small-to-medium-sized enterprises (SMEs), too, have benefited from opportunities to broaden their horizons in numerous sectors. Hallmarks of globalization are interconnectedness and interdependence between people, organizations and governments. These ties have been facilitated by improvements in technology, especially in telecommunications, the internet and transport. Yet, while all would agree that the global economy is a reality, the extent and depth of its reach, along with its impacts, are continually debated. Globalization is often praised for its role in economic development, but criticized for social and environmental impacts. There have been winners and losers in terms of countries, industries and employment, as this chapter will highlight. It will also join the debate on the future of globalization and its impacts in differing contexts.

The chapter begins by defining globalization, highlighting differing perspectives. The expansion of global production has contributed to economic development, but we find that for many developing countries the good news comes laced with bad, and development's benefits often do not reach the whole of society. Who is to blame? MNEs as key players are a focus of the chapter. Their internationalization strategies are discussed, highlighting the leading theories. While foreign direct investment (FDI) has been transformative, its growth has taken place alongside the broad trend towards global supply chains and outsourcing. These trends have had unequal impacts in the global economy. We identify winners and losers, but we find that the task is more fraught than it seems. A country can be a winner today, attracting significant FDI, but if investors turn away or fail to live up to expectations, FDI can look more like a detriment than a blessing. Such are the contradictions of globalization. These are highlighted in a section on the depth of globalization across the different dimensions of the global environment. We find that negative impacts on societies have multiple causes, including both corporate behaviour and government policies. The challenges and responsibilities are discussed in the final section of the chapter.

What is globalization?

We are constantly being reminded that we live in a globalized world. People in the world's richer countries have become accustomed to low-cost consumer goods, internet access from just about anywhere, and worldwide travel as a routine occurrence. At the same time, people are fearful for their livelihoods, living conditions and natural environment, both in richer and poorer countries. They are also fearful about the future of core moral values that are central to human dignity, including fulfilling careers, self-expression, political voice and other human rights.

Globalization can be defined as processes by which products, people, companies, money and information are able to move quickly around the world as decision-makers desire, with few cross-border impediments in their way. It is facilitated by an opening of markets in each of these respects. This essentially capitalist notion of the market is a crucial assumption. The **market** refers to mechanisms for exchange of something of value, usually goods or services, for a price, usually money. While in the narrow sense, the market is a place where transactions take place, in the broader sense, the market can refer to the aggregate of transactions in a sector or a geographic area, even globally. Markets thrive where there is freedom for individuals and organizations to pursue transactions as they desire: the fewer impediments, the greater the scope for free markets. While these assumptions can be queried (as discussed later in this chapter), it is helpful to be reminded of the closeness between free-market assumptions and globalization, highlighted by Thomas Friedman (2000). Where barriers to trade proliferate and governments protect their national economies, globalization cannot thrive. The era of the Great Depression leading up to the Second World War was such a period. The dismantling of trade barriers in the post-war period led to more open markets and growth in cross-border flows of goods and services, in processes we now group together as globalization.

Businesses thrive on an ability to enter foreign markets easily, and MNEs have had the organizational ability to make the most of the opportunities of global markets. The driving processes have seen changes in both production and in markets. **Globalized production** refers to MNEs' ability to co-ordinate different stages of production in the most advantageous location. Subsidiaries, affiliates and contractual partners all play roles in the different stages, forming a **value chain** from sourcing of materials through to production, distribution and delivery to the end consumers. Each stage in the chain contributes value to the final product. **Globalization of markets** refers to MNEs' ability to serve consumers across the world with their products, in contrast to an approach which views national markets as essentially separate. Globalized production has become highly developed, and MNEs are now able to co-ordinate complex supply chains. Globalized markets have developed in standardized products, but in many sectors, national differences are still marked. Globalization in these sectors has taken the form of global strategies to deliver specific products to local markets. Food is a sector in which local tastes matter. McDonald's has been famous for its ability to adapt to local tastes while focusing on the brand's core products, although this formula has come under strain with the rise of innovative competitors (see the opening case study in Chapter 3).

> **The way I see it …**
>
> Referring to Apple and Starbucks, 'I love the consistency – knowing that anywhere in the world you can depend on having the same experience in the store or being served a latte with the same taste in the same cup. That's great branding.'
>
> Angela Ahrendts, former CEO of Burberry, in Harvard Business Review, January–February issue, 2013.
>
> Do you agree with Ms Ahrendts on what makes a great brand? What else makes a great brand?

Although international trading links and colonialism in the eighteenth and nineteenth centuries connected nations around the globe, these earlier eras did not see the depth of interaction which characterizes globalization as we experience it today. The use of the term began only in the 1960s and gained common currency only in the 1980s (Waters, 2001). A divergence of views has emerged on the nature and extent of these trends. An extreme view, known as 'hyperglobalization', sees globalization in a positive light, bringing about a 'borderless' world in which local differences melt away and a global civil society emerges. This rather idealistic view gathered momentum in the late 1990s. Its proponents thought that all countries and communities would become connected through the spread of free-market capitalism, and that the autonomy of individual nation-states would gradually shrink (Ohmae, 2000). Friedman viewed technology, especially the internet, as a key force in this process, bringing about the integration of markets and empowering individuals and investors. As these processes unfolded, the division of the world into nation-states would become less significant (Friedman, 2000). The depiction of globalization by the hyperglobalizers is optimistic, stressing empowerment facilitated in the globalized environment. But this view has aroused both sceptics and critics. Sceptics point to the continuing differences between developed and developing countries, as well as the assertiveness of governments keen to preserve national interests. Critics voice fears that the rise of global capitalism has had detrimental consequences in societies, their cultures and the natural environment. Friedman can point to the fact that the citizen who is empowered by the internet can be a potent force in these respects, helping to bring decision-makers to account (Friedman, 2016). However, global companies and governments also have the tools of the internet to reinforce their power, sometimes in repressive ways.

Critics have focused particularly on the post-war economic power of the US, evidenced in the might of its multinationals, and the influence of the US in international relations. The concentration of economic power in the hands of large corporate forces, able to bend states to their will, sent alarm bells ringing in many quarters. The debate moved to the streets as anti-globalization protests become a regular occurrence at international governmental conferences, such as that of the WTO in 1999 in Seattle, Washington.

In the ensuing decade, the integration of numerous countries into the global economy provided a more finely grained picture of how globalization was actually affecting differing countries' economies and societies. Globalization, it emerged, is not a single, all-encompassing process sweeping the globe, but processes which reflect the independent actions of many different players in different places.

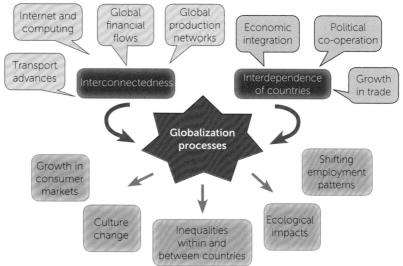

Figure 2.1 Globalization processes and their outcomes

Globalization processes are set out in Figure 2.1. The two overarching themes are interconnectedness, and interdependence. The first, **interconnectedness**, is facilitated mainly by advances in technology, computing and the internet, which allow networking to take place routinely between people in different geographical locations. Moreover, business interactions increasingly overlap with social networking sites. Advances in transport, such as container shipping, have facilitated trading ties. MNEs have become the drivers of globalized production, evolving supply chains to deliver products to consumers in an ever-increasing range of markets. Financial flows have also benefited from the internet and IT, allowing cross-border investments and transactions to be made quickly and easily.

Turning to the second theme in Figure 2.1, growing **interdependence** among countries has taken place. It might appear that countries would thereby lose their autonomy, but more subtle processes are taking place. Rather than the withering away of national autonomy, we are seeing countries asserting a sovereign right to act and willingly co-operating with other countries for common goals. In processes not unlike those transforming companies, countries are seeing themselves as linked together in their pursuit of prosperity and well-being. As economic integration deepens, so does interdependence, between countries and between business enterprises. A gradual opening up of national economic and financial systems to outside investors has occurred, accompanied by the liberalization of trade. These trends towards market liberalization have been seized on by some as indicators of the spread of global capitalism, a central tenet of the hyperglobalizers. However, market reforms have varied in both their substance and pace among countries. Countries with authoritarian systems, such as China, have used market tools to achieve national aims rather than to transform themselves into free-market systems. Governments see foreign investment as leading to economic growth, especially in the form of domestic jobs, but are wary of allowing the loss of control over these economic forces. Countries that have seen impressive economic growth from globalization, including China, South Korea and India, have not wholeheartedly embraced free markets, but retained governmental controls and policies such as subsidizing key industries (Rodrik, 2011).

Globalization processes have taken place unevenly, affecting different dimensions of the environment in different ways. Rodrik points out that globalization processes are essentially disruptive. For example, shifts in manufacturing to new locations in developing countries are disruptive in both the new environment and the one left behind. These processes have affected countries in differing ways, leading to inequality emerging both within and between countries, between those who have benefited and those who have not. Beneficiaries have included the favoured locations for low-cost production, while low-skilled jobs in advanced economies have been rapidly disappearing.

Globalization for better or worse?

Which of the schools of thought on globalization best represents your own views, and why?

Economic development: country differences

Every country has distinctive characteristics which influence the nature of the economic activities which make up its national economy. Economic activity can be divided into three broad sectors: **primary production**, which includes agriculture, mining and fishing; **secondary production**, which is industrial production; and the **tertiary sector**, which consists of services, such as tourism and financial services. All three types of activity are carried out in every economy, but there are big differences in their proportions. It is usual for countries to progress economically in stages from primary industries to manufacturing and then to services, which are considered more advanced. There are exceptions to this pattern. Some countries rich in natural resources rely mainly on these activities to generate wealth, but this can be a short-sighted policy as the day will come when the resources run out. Seeking to diversify to maintain steady growth is more advisable, although not always easy to achieve in practice. We will look at national economic systems closely in the next chapter, but here we look at how countries are broadly classified in terms of economic activities, noting especially the effects of globalization.

Globalization is closely linked with industrialization, which normally drives economic development. **Industrialization** is the process of transformation of an economy from mainly agricultural production for domestic consumption to an economy based on factory production, with potential for export. Industrialization enhances a country's capacity for wealth creation and economic growth, especially if its companies grow into successful MNEs. Industrialization is therefore linked to economic development.

Although **economic development** can refer to any change in a country's overall balance of economic activities, it usually refers to the industrialization and resultant changes in society whereby jobs are increasingly located in industrial sectors. Britain was the earliest country to industrialize, from the early nineteenth century onwards, followed by other European countries and the US. Many inventions, such as the steam engine, electric turbine and railway locomotive, originating in Britain, spread to Europe and the US. Following the Second World War, when many European countries and Japan faced the task of rebuilding infrastructure and industrial capacity, the

US was well placed to forge ahead with large-scale manufacturing, meeting growing demand for consumer goods. By the late 1960s, however, Japan's industrial development was gaining momentum, turning it into a global industrial power in sectors such as car manufacturing. By the 1980s, Japanese manufacturers threatened American industrial domination. By then, South Korea was gaining ground in some of the same sectors as Japan, such as electronics and cars. Samsung and LG have become global forces in electronics, and Hyundai has become a global carmaker (recall the case study in the last chapter). More recently, China and, to a lesser extent, India have enjoyed the rapid growth associated with economic development driven by industrialization.

It is customary to classify countries according to economic indicators. Broadly, the countries with greater income are the most developed; the poorest are the least developed. Of course, economic criteria alone do not tell the whole story: 'development' encompasses criteria other than economic indicators. The UN Development Programme (www.undp.org) uses the broader notion of 'human development' for its **Human Development Index (HDI)** (www.hdr.undp.org) which ranks countries according to three sets of criteria: economic, health (including life expectancy) and education (UNDP, 2014). The HDI provides a fuller picture of well-being in societies than economic criteria alone. Nonetheless, economic criteria are widely used indicators, and are helpful for country comparisons, but their limitations should be borne in mind.

The UN and World Bank are the chief international organizations that classify all the world's economies. The World Bank (www.worldbank.org) focuses on gross national income (GNI) per capita, that is, per head of population, in US dollars. Its categories are as follows (World Bank, 2013):

Low income: $1,035 or less
Low middle income: $1,036 to $4,085
Upper middle income: $4,086 to $12,615
High income: $12,616 or more

The World Bank designates all low- and middle-income countries as developing countries. Only those in the high-income category are developed. The UN uses three broad categories: developed, developing and transition economies. These overlap with those used by the World Bank. The world's **developed countries** are mostly industrialized economies, highly integrated in the global economy (see Table 2.1). They include North America, EU countries and Japan, which are known as the **triad countries**. Australia and New Zealand are also in this category. The new EU member states in Central and Eastern Europe have now joined this group. Thirty-four of the world's economies are members of the **Organisation for Economic Co-operation and Development (OECD)** (www.oecd.org). From its creation in 1960, the OECD has had a membership of mainly advanced, high-income countries. With increasing globalization, its membership has become more mixed, to include developing countries and also to develop relations with the large emerging countries. Its members as of 2015 were Australia, Austria, Belgium, Canada, Chile, Czech Republic, Denmark, Estonia, Finland, France, Germany, Greece, Hungary, Iceland, Ireland, Israel, Italy, Japan, South Korea, Luxembourg, Mexico, Netherlands, New Zealand, Norway, Poland, Portugal, Slovakia, Slovenia, Spain, Sweden, Switzerland, Turkey, UK and US (OECD, 2015). Of these, Mexico and Turkey are developing countries, and would fall within the loose grouping of emerging economies, discussed below.

Countries changing from agricultural to industrial production fall within the broad category of **developing countries**. These countries have often been referred to as the 'third world', but this term is now seldom used as it reflects the polarized thinking of the post-war period known as the 'cold-war' era, which was dominated by tension between the western capitalist countries, the 'first world', and the communist bloc countries, the 'second world'. These cold-war categories have been rather superseded by events, mainly the fall of the Soviet Union and the rise of market economic reforms around the world.

The vast majority of the world's countries are within the category of developing countries. There are huge variations in levels of development and extent of industrialization among these countries. Some base industrial development on abundant low-cost labour, as China has done. Some are resource-rich exporters, such as Nigeria, which is an oil producer. Many of the more globalized of these economies are referred to as 'emerging' economies, discussed below. Developing countries are mainly in South America, Africa and Asia. The UN has a separate category for the **transition economies** of Central and Eastern Europe and CIS (Commonwealth of Independent States, including Russia). Since the fall of the Soviet Union in 1991, these countries have been making the transition from planned economies to market-based economies.

Table 2.1 Economic development: UN classification of countries

Category	Countries
Developed	Australia, Austria, Belgium, Bulgaria, Canada, Croatia, Cyprus, Czech Republic, Denmark, Estonia, Finland, France, Germany, Greece, Hungary, Iceland, Ireland, Italy, Japan, Latvia, Lithuania, Luxembourg, Malta, Netherlands, New Zealand, Norway, Poland, Portugal, Romania, Slovakia, Slovenia, Spain, Sweden, Switzerland, UK, US
Transition economies	Albania, Armenia, Azerbaijan, Belarus, Bosnia and Herzegovina, Croatia, Georgia, Kazakhstan, Kyrgyzstan, Macedonia (TFYR), Moldova, Montenegro, Russian Federation, Serbia, Tajikistan, Turkmenistan, Ukraine, Uzbekistan
Developing	*(selected)* Algeria, Argentina, Bolivia, Botswana, Brazil, Chile, China, Columbia, Costa Rica, Cuba, Cyprus, Ecuador, Egypt, Guatemala, India, Indonesia, Iraq, Kenya, Kuwait, Lesotho, Malaysia, Mexico, Mongolia, Morocco, Nicaragua, Nigeria, Pakistan, Peru, Philippines, Saudi Arabia, Singapore, South Africa, Thailand, Tunisia, Turkey, United Arab Emirates, Uruguay, Venezuela, Vietnam
Least developed	*(selected)* Afghanistan, Angola, Bangladesh, Benin, Burkina Faso, Cambodia, Chad, Comoros, Equatorial Guinea, Democratic Republic of Congo, Ethiopia, Gambia, Guinea-Bissau, Haiti, Malawi, Mali, Mozambique, Myanmar (Burma), Nepal, Niger, Rwanda, Sierra Leone, Somalia, Sudan, Tanzania, Timor Leste, Togo, Uganda, Yemen, Zambia

Source: Created using data from UN (2014) *World Economic Situation and Prospects 2014* (New York: UN) (Table A, p. 145, Table B, p. 145, Table C, p. 146 and Table F, p. 149). Reprinted with the permission of the United Nations.

The UN's last category is the **least-developed countries**, which are the poorest of the developing countries. They are located mainly in sub-Saharan Africa and South Asia. These countries, which have the world's fastest-growing populations, are mainly primary agricultural producers, with little industrialization. Most have been adversely affected by globalization, suffering from volatility in global commodities markets, weak transport infrastructure and poor communications networks. These societies have fallen behind other developing countries, experiencing extreme poverty, poor health conditions and limited educational systems. Moreover, these

Fishing, shown here in Cambodia, is typical of economic activities in the world's least-developed countries.

Source: PhotoDisc/ Getty Images.

countries, which are those most at risk from the effects of climate change and extreme weather, are those with the least resources to meet the challenges.

A final category of country is the **emerging economy**, or emerging market. This is a fluid category of developing countries – mostly large in area and population – that have enjoyed rapid economic growth and have gained in importance in the global economy. The grouping of the **BRIC** countries – Brazil, Russia, India and China – was coined in 2001. They have come together in summit meetings and, in 2010, were joined by South Africa, adding the 'S' to make them the BRICS. These five countries are home to about 40% of the world's population, making them large potential markets. However, as noted, the category is a fluid one: Indonesia and Mexico both have larger populations than South Africa (South Africa's population is about 53 million, whereas Indonesia's is 250 million). At the other end of the spectrum, the resource-rich states of the Middle East, although small in area and in population, have become important global players. These countries all fall within the UN's category of developing economies. All have seen economic growth from globalization, but have also experienced slowdowns in recent years.

The emerging economies represent a diverse picture in terms of globalization. In Asia, China has led the world in manufacturing mass-produced goods, and based its development on exports. Russia and Brazil have seen growth derived from natural resources: Russia's wealth is based mainly on gas and Brazil is a large exporter of iron ore and agricultural commodities. India has benefited from a growth in manufacturing, although its progress has been slow (see the closing case study). The Middle Eastern states have been dependent on oil and gas which, like other resources, are subject to price volatility in global markets. Some of these states have diversified into financial services, but this sector, which is highly globalized, is also volatile. Emerging markets are thus exposed to the opportunities of globalization, but also the risks. Countries relying on exports, such as China, have been adversely affected by slowdowns in spending in the advanced economies, while the resource-rich countries, such as Russia and Brazil, have seen slowing demand for energy and commodities.

Developing countries have been among the major beneficiaries of globalization processes, and have seen strong economic growth as a result. The emerging countries have been among the leading performers in this respect. However, the ways in which flows of wealth are used and the need for sustainable development to maintain gains for all in society remain issues in these countries. Also of global concern is the huge gap that remains between the world's rich countries and the poorest – those classified as the least-developed. Globalization is now reaching many of these countries, such as Ethiopia and Bangladesh, raising questions over the human dimension of development (see the case study on Ethiopia in Chapter 4).

National economies and globalization

Weigh up the benefits and risks associated with globalization from the perspective of: (1) a developing country that has abundant oil reserves; and (2) a developing country with abundant low-cost labour.

MNEs and internationalization

In this section, we shift our perspective to the MNE. The company which seeks to expand internationally eyes the potential gains from production and markets outside its home country. The internationalization of its activities offers opportunities which greatly exceed those offered at home, even if its home is a large country such as the US or China. Most MNEs do not simply go on a shopping spree, acquiring ownership of foreign assets, but build strategic ties with foreign organizations, such as suppliers, which enhance their ability to create value.

Companies from a wide range of countries have now become players in global supply chains and markets, challenging the established MNEs in both mature consumer markets and newer emerging markets. SMEs, once seen as essentially local, can now become part of worldwide supply chains, raise capital from foreign investors and recruit talented people globally. In this section, we look at why and how companies internationalize.

Why do companies internationalize?

A company does not decide to branch out internationally on the basis of rather abstract observations that we now live in a global economy, but because the firm itself sees business opportunities such as efficiencies in production and new markets. For companies, as for people, the grass might seem greener on the other side, but there is much at stake. For a business, a failed foreign venture can lead not just to financial loss, but can bring down the entire company. Companies therefore need good reasons to venture abroad, and reasonable confidence that the potential benefits outweigh the risks. There are both **'pull' factors** which attract the company to a foreign location and **'push' factors** which drive the company out of its home country or other countries where it currently does business. The following motives come into play:

- New markets – A new market is a strong 'pull' factor for a company, especially if growth in its home market begins to slow. However, the new market needs to be one where the firm's products are likely to be popular and lead to growth in market share.

- More efficient production – Companies are constantly seeking ways of producing products and delivering services more efficiently. They seek to benefit from scale economies, that is, savings which come with large-scale production. The country with relevant skills and low labour costs is thus attractive, although transport costs and long delivery times must be taken into account.
- Proximity to key resources – A company that requires abundant supplies of a key raw material is likely to choose a location close to supply. For this reason, food processing plants are often located in agricultural areas.
- Access to technology and skills – A company which relies on specialist technology tends to seek out locations where these activities are flourishing, and where skilled researchers are available. For this reason, SMEs in life sciences often locate in the proximity of large pharmaceutical companies.
- Proximity to customers – A company that has traditionally exported its products might find that it can deliver a better, more customized, service if it establishes a presence near its customers. It thus learns more about the market firsthand.
- Deterioration in the home business environment – There are many possible 'push' factors which influence companies to look beyond their home country or to shift from a foreign country where they have become established. Market saturation is one. For the large retailer, market saturation could be reached if the availability of large sites becomes limited or planning regulations become stricter. Changes in taxation and regulation in a country can contribute to an exodus of companies to more advantageous locations.

Push and pull factors can combine to encourage companies to globalize. For example, a company that sees limited scope to grow in established markets in advanced economies is likely to look to emerging markets for better prospects of market growth.

Modes of internationalization

MNEs choose from a variety of methods to internationalize, known as **modes of internationalization**, shown in Figure 2.2. A firm might choose different modes in different locations and at different stages in its internationalization experience. The firm embarking on international activities for the first time tends to choose a low-risk strategy, such as **exporting** its products from its home country. If foreign demand is promising, it might establish sales offices in selected foreign markets, giving it a presence in the market and allowing it to control activities such as customer service.

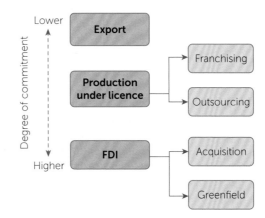

Figure 2.2 Modes of internationalization

By means of **foreign direct investment (FDI)**, the company invests in productive assets in a foreign country, acquiring them wholly or partly and using this ownership stake to exert control over operations. The investing company thereby acquires deeper involvement in the host country than the company which simply relies on exporting its products to foreign countries, without a physical presence in them. FDI is generally considered to be the main driver of globalization (Dunning, 1993), as it is characterized by this deeper level of integration in global production networks.

As Figure 2.2 shows, the MNE contemplating FDI has a number of options. As we found in Chapter 1, a parent company might set up a foreign subsidiary which it wholly owns, or it might take a lower stake, still aiming to control operations. The subsidiary gives it a legal footing in the country, from which it can grow. If the MNE is a manufacturing company, it might decide to invest in building a plant on a **greenfield** site. This type of project is typically carried out by a subsidiary set up for the purpose. The greenfield investment represents a significant commitment to the country as it involves a large capital outlay, with probably little prospect of immediate profits. This is a long-term strategy which MNEs might consider for a variety of reasons. They include the attraction of lower costs than in its home country, the availability of skilled labour in the host country and the existence of trade restrictions which deter exporters from building a presence in the host country's market

The MNE in a hurry to gain a foothold in a foreign market often chooses to purchase an existing business. **Acquisition** allows the MNE to start operations in the country almost immediately, and is common in sectors such as retailing and mining. In manufacturing, there might be a time lag while the plant is adapted to make the new owner's products, but this is shorter than would be possible on a greenfield site where the plant is built from scratch. Some acquirers purchase the whole business, including the brand, and carry on production under the new management. An acquisition in a new market can also be advantageous in that the MNE can gain local knowledge and expertise from the acquired firm. In emerging economies, many of the companies that are sold are through government privatizations of old, inefficient businesses. In this situation, the MNE takes on an ambitious project, needing to inject capital and retrain staff.

A company that is reluctant to enter a foreign market on its own, or is barred from doing so by state controls, can form a **joint venture** whereby it works with a partner firm to carry out FDI. The MNE's partner in the joint venture tends to be a local firm whose local knowledge will enhance their chances of success. The joint-venture partner can be a state-owned company. The partners form a new company, each taking an equity stake. In many emerging economies, foreign companies are required to go down the joint-venture route, as foreigners are legally barred from wholly owning a locally-registered company. This restriction is gradually being relaxed as countries open their markets.

The middle range of options presented in Figure 2.2 is **production under licence**. **Outsourced production** is a favoured choice of brand owners. Outsourcing rests on agreement by the MNE with a local company that the latter will produce the goods or deliver the service within the terms of a contract between the local company and the MNE. The local company is sometimes a foreign investor itself. Much of the manufacturing of Apple's iPhones and iPads in China, for example, is carried out by firms such as Foxconn, a Taiwanese company, which also manufactures for other brand owners, both in China and other countries. For MNEs in clothing and other consumer products, the outsourcer manufactures under licence from the MNE brand owner, being required to produce the products as needed to the specifications laid down in the licence agreement. The aim of outsourced production tends to be to reduce costs by locating production in a low-cost country, from where products are exported to consumers in other markets. This strategy has been key to MNE investment in China and other Asian economies.

In some sectors, such as fast food and hotels, companies have opted for **franchising**, which involves a licence agreed with a producer to make and deliver the product in accordance with the brand owner's instructions (see the discussion in Chapter 1). The local businessperson who owns the franchise makes a considerable capital investment, but probably feels this is money well invested, as the brand attracts customers. The brand owner, in turn, is able to expand internationally through a network of franchises, without the burden of significant capital outlay in each country. On the other hand, the franchisor must be alert to the different regulatory environment in each country, as well as differences in local tastes. McDonald's has famously adapted its offerings to cultural preferences in different countries. It takes direct ownership of outlets in some foreign markets, whereas its outlets in the US are generally franchise operations.

The MNE that desires to internationalize, but is reluctant to invest in physical assets, might choose **portfolio investment**, which consists of buying shares or other securities in a foreign company, with a view to making financial gains on the investment. These gains are often viewed as short-term. The portfolio investor usually acquires small stakes in companies, and is sometimes restricted legally or politically from big purchases through capital controls in the country. **Sovereign wealth funds**, which are entities owned by a sovereign state, are familiar portfolio investors in many sectors. Usually keeping investments below 10% in any one company, sovereign wealth fund managers maintain a focus on the public purposes for which they are responsible. Where an investor is able and willing to acquire a large stake, usually 30% or more, it gains a strong position from which it can exert considerable control in both corporate governance and management. In this case, its role would shift closer to that of the foreign direct investor, who combines ownership and control.

Companies design internationalization strategies to derive the greatest potential from each market, using different entry modes in different countries, influenced by the local conditions and government policies in each. Their choice also depends on the strengths of the firm itself and the degree of risk the company is willing to undertake. In some markets, such as the large emerging markets, companies see so much growth potential that they are often willing to take greater risks. For this reason, FDI in emerging markets has become a major trend.

Choosing a mode of internationalization

What mode of entry would you recommend for each of the following, and why?

- A US car manufacturer who wishes to sell cars in European markets
- A large food retailer from a European country who wishes to enter the Chinese market
- A Chinese manufacturer of appliances such as refrigerators and washing machines who wishes to enter the American market

FDI and the global economy

FDI has been a major contributor to globalization. As we have just seen, it is by no means the only mode of internationalization, but it is the one which represents the deepest commitment in a host country, whereby the investor and host society develop the deepest interactions. In this section, we analyse these cross-border activities and their impacts.

Theories of FDI

Why firms choose one mode of internationalization over another and one country over another are questions that theorists and researchers have long sought to explain. Theories are constantly being devised and adjusted as global interactions have deepened over time. Discerning the relationship between trade and FDI has been a theme in these theories. Trade has taken place since ancient times, while FDI is a relatively new phenomenon. Why did FDI come to be considered a better strategic option for the firm, and how has trade changed in a world of deepening FDI? We attempt to glean some historical perspective in this section by looking at how the main theories have evolved.

Foreign investment by companies flourished in the nineteenth and early twentieth centuries. Although transnational manufacturing took place in the Victorian era, the big overseas investors were in primary sectors such as mineral extraction and agricultural products. In the period before 1914, the UK was the largest holder of foreign capital assets, the majority in developing countries where British colonial rule provided an institutional umbrella (Dunning, 1993). The inter-war period saw the rise of protectionist barriers between countries, which discouraged trade and encouraged companies to focus on home markets. However, the political leaders who met to devise a framework for new co-operative agreements after the Second World War paved the way for an era of growing prosperity, which we now link to globalization.

Until about the 1960s, firms tended to carry out manufacturing activities in their home countries. But FDI was beginning to take off, leading early theorists of the phenomenon to ask why. One of these was Stephen Hymer, who sought to explain what advantages would be gained from the firm's perspective (Hymer, 1975). He spoke of **location advantages** of some countries over others. These are advantages of country or region, such as access to transport and lower costs than in the firm's home country. Such advantages are not an unqualified benefit, though, as the firm would be entering a foreign environment where it had little local knowledge. Why would a firm undertake the risk rather than simply investing in shares? The answer lay in the ability of the foreign firm to make the most of its **ownership advantages** in the host country. The foreign firm would have resources such as technology, production skills and organizational skills which local firms lacked. These ownership advantages were firm-specific, giving the foreign firm a competitive advantage.

A second relevant theory is the **product life cycle theory** of Raymond Vernon (Wells, 1972). Writing in the 1960s, when American companies were in the ascendant, Vernon envisaged all new products as originating in the US. He wrote particularly about the growing American appetite for mass-produced consumer goods such as televisions and washing machines. He traced the life cycle of the new product from its launch in the US to export to other markets and, finally, to being manufactured in cheaper locations for export to US consumers. In the early phase, demand at home leads to expansion, and demand overseas, which is limited to high-income groups, is satisfied by exports. As the market matures and overseas demand grows, foreign production begins to take off, and these products supplant US imports in overseas markets. At the same time, cost factors come into play, the product becomes more standardized and production is increased. US producers are likely to shift production overseas, first to the higher-income markets (such as Europe). These production facilities are able to export to other countries, and even back to the US, but as costs rise in Europe, companies shift production again, this time to low-cost locations such as Asian developing countries.

Vernon combined concepts of location advantages and ownership advantages. In his rather US-centric view of the world, innovation capacity was an ownership advantage enjoyed by US companies, and other countries were not as competitive. Nonetheless, the core idea that companies will locate production in the most advantageous place was to be influential in later theories. Most notable among these has been Dunning's **eclectic paradigm**, also known as the 'OLI paradigm', based on three sets of advantages: ownership (O), location (L) and internalization (I) (Dunning, 1993). The OLI paradigm was designed to explain FDI from the firm's perspective, mainly focusing on foreign production. It was called 'eclectic' because the three variables derived from diverse theories and disciplines. The ownership and location variables were to be found in trade theories, and internalization derived from transaction cost economics. The three variables are summarized below:

- *Ownership-specific advantages* – These include property rights over assets, broadly defined to include both tangible resources (such as manufacturing plants) and intangible resources (such as intellectual property rights). Ownership of capital and natural resources strengthen the firm's competitive position. The firm's technology in the form of patents reflects its innovative capacity which generates future innovations. Crucial to the exploitation of these resources are the firm's organizational and entrepreneurial skills.

- *Location-specific advantages* – These include the economic, cultural and political environments of a country as a potential location in which the firm is contemplating investment, in comparison with its home country. Low-cost labour as a location advantage was highlighted by earlier theorists, but Dunning expanded the notion in the FDI context. In addition to low-cost labour, access to raw materials, transport and infrastructure, he highlighted political policies such as government incentives to foreign investors. The size of the potential market for the firm's products in the country (and region) is another location advantage, although one which might involve a longer-term horizon in the case of developing countries. More recently, technological capacity in a country such as India is a location advantage, as R&D activities there are less costly than in developed countries. Dunning's highlighting of incentives for foreign investors has turned out to be more important than he perhaps envisaged when writing in the 1990s. Most foreign investors nowadays look to negotiate advantageous packages of terms with the host government, including benefits such as tax holidays. Without them, a greenfield FDI project is unlikely to go ahead.

- *Internalization advantages* – These look to the reduction in transaction costs through hierarchical organization as an alternative to reliance on markets. A firm might find it advantageous to gain control of the supply of raw materials or components by buying the supplier outright. The firm thus avoids the transaction costs associated with obtaining supplies on an exchange basis in markets. Taking over the supplier leads to **vertical integration**, which gives the firm greater control over supplies. This can be advantageous from several viewpoints. It allows the firm to monitor quality more closely than would be possible when dealing with an independent supplier. The firm can also keep tighter control of intellectual property, which can be a risk in countries where legal protections are weak. In this respect, there is overlap between ownership and internalization advantages. On the other hand, the advantages of vertical integration must be weighed against the costs and risks associated with outright ownership, which involves a long-term commitment (Buckley and Hashai, 2009). If the firm relies on exchange deals for supply, it is in a position to change suppliers relatively easily if a better deal presents itself, using global scanning to seek out the best deal. The flexibility offered by supply chains has thus persuaded many MNEs of their benefits over internalization, due to the liabilities arising from organizational arrangements.

The OLI paradigm aids firms contemplating FDI by highlighting the different variables and their interactions. It can thus help in weighing up the likely benefits against the risks and costs. Dunning's theory coincided with rapid growth in FDI, as firms were seeking greater efficiencies of globalized production. These MNEs were mainly from the developed countries. In today's world, MNEs originate in a wide range of countries, but the theory remains relevant. For example, Samsung manufactures its smartphones mainly in China, due to low costs of labour.

What impacts do sizeable inflows of FDI have on a host economy, and what about the countries which do not attract FDI? Perhaps the latter countries are better off in the long term as they can develop their own home-grown industries, noting that the more opportunistic foreign investors might decide to leave for more advantageous locations in a few years. Certainly, the latter possibility is implied in Dunning's theory, but what are the impacts? These are explored in the next section.

Global trends in FDI

The movements of FDI around the world can be measured in terms of types of investments, their origins and destinations. This information provides valuable insights into globalization processes. **FDI inflows** are the aggregate value of investments which flow into a country, and **FDI outflows** are the aggregate value of investments from a country's organizations to overseas destinations. These are calculated on an annual basis. The total value of foreign investments that a country has attracted is its **FDI inward stock**, and the total value of investments made by its nationals is its **FDI outward stock**. The extent of a country's firms' involvement in FDI is a good indicator of its economic integration and interdependence with other countries. Where a country's outflows and inflows are unbalanced, say, by strong outflows and weak inward investment, it might be an indication of a weak domestic business climate. Japan is an example. Where the balance is tipped towards inward investment, it might be an indication that the country enjoys location advantages, but its domestic firms are not globally competitive – as yet. China is often cited as an example, but in recent years Chinese MNEs, many of them state-owned, have become more active globally, as shown in Figure 2.3. In 2002, Chinese companies spent a total of $2.7 billion in outward investment on acquisitions and greenfield projects. This had increased to a staggering $108 billion in 2013 (Anderlini, 2014). At the same time, inward flows of FDI to China have slowed as costs of production in China have crept up in the last few years. China's economic growth has slowed from over 10% annually to rates closer to 7%.

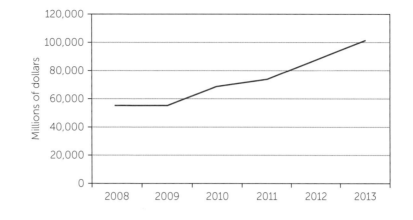

Figure 2.3 Growing FDI outflows from China

Source: Created using data from UN (2014) *World Investment Report 2014* (Geneva: UN) Annex, Table 1, p. 206. Reprinted with the permission of the United Nations.

Outward movements of capital have long been dominated by developed economies, while inflows have mainly targeted developing economies. But, as the example of China shows, this pattern is now changing. Inflows are increasingly targeting developing countries for their location advantages. The predominant trend in FDI has been the shift of production of a huge range of products from the high-cost countries to the low-cost countries. For this reason, emerging countries such as China have enjoyed rapid economic growth. China's economy overtook Japan's in size in 2009. Between 1986 and 2013, the US economy doubled, whereas the Chinese economy grew 12-fold (Euromonitor International, 2014).

FDI flows to developed countries have slowed. The transition economies of Central and Eastern European countries have attracted growing inflows, especially those that joined the EU in 2004. The flows into these countries have come mainly from other EU countries (see the case study on the Czech Republic in Chapter 9). FDI fell globally in 2008, following the financial crisis. FDI inflows into developed countries fell 32% that year, seriously affected by the drying up of debt finance to fund investment. But flows to developing countries withstood the crisis better, rising 3.6% over the previous year. Since then, FDI flows into developing countries have powered ahead, while flows to developed countries have stuttered (see Figure 2.4). In 2013, flows to developed countries were 39% of global flows, whereas flows to developing countries were 54% of the total.

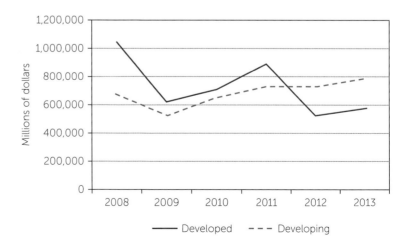

Figure 2.4 World inflows of FDI

Source: Created using data from UN (2014) *World Investment Report 2014* (Geneva: UN) Annex, Table 1, p. 205. Reprinted with the permission of the United Nations.

Outflows from developing countries have also strengthened. The outflows from developing and transition economies amounted to 39% of global outflows in 2013 – a remarkable growth from the early 2000s, when they were only 12% of the total (UN, 2014).

Emerging MNEs, often owned or controlled by a state, have gained confidence from their own fast-growing economies. These companies have enjoyed success through FDI in developing countries, benefiting from their familiarity with issues common to most developing economies, such as a weak institutional environment. As they have gained in confidence, they have also set their targets on developed countries, asserting their global competitiveness. The Indian conglomerate, Tata, is an example, featured in the box that follows.

The acquisition of American banana company, Chiquita, by Brazilian businessmen signified the ambitions of Brazil as a large emerging economy.

Source: PhotoDisc/Getty Images.

Brazilian companies are also active globally. In 2014, Chiquita, the US banana company dating back to the 1870s, was acquired by Brazilians. One of Brazil's largest orange companies, Cutrale, and its investment partner, Safra, mounted a takeover bid for Chiquita, thwarting the efforts of the Irish banana group, Fyffes, which had hoped to merge with Chiquita to form the world's biggest banana company. The merger with Fyffes had found favour with the board of Chiquita, as it would have facilitated transferring the merged companies' headquarters to Ireland, with its attractive low-tax regime for MNEs (a process referred to in the US as 'inversion'). However, Chiquita shareholders were won over by the superior offer made by the Brazilians, who were willing to pay a premium price for Chiquita as a global brand. The controlling families of Safra and Cutrale intended to take the company private. Cutrale's long history in agribusiness was a factor which also weighed with investors. Those with a sense of history, however, will have paused to consider the implications of the South American takeover of a US company long seen as a symbol of American imperialist behaviour in its banana plantations in Central and South America.

The way I see it ...

On Tata's goals to 'go global', '... not just to increase our turnover, but also to go to places ... where we would participate in the development of the country. We have endeavoured to play that role in Bangladesh, South Africa, Sri Lanka, Dubai and Singapore.'

Ratan Tata, Chairman of Tata Group, in an interview in August, 2006, 'Vision of the future', at www.tata.com

How did Tata's vision of the company's global ambitions differ from theories of internationalization? Tata is an Indian company. Does the goal of participating in development reflect a different perspective from that of MNEs from advanced economies?

FDI inflows and outflows: impacts in different countries

FDI can be highly beneficial to national economies, whether as a destination for foreign investors or a source of growth for the country's own companies. But impacts differ widely. Investments often result in a combination of both positive and negative aspects. FDI inflows can be highly beneficial to host economies, both developed and developing. They bring jobs, wealth creation and economic growth in the host country. A country's outward FDI generates wealth for its companies and revenues for the government. Its consumers also benefit, as they will pay less for the goods and services imported from MNEs that have shifted production and sourcing to low-cost countries. However, FDI's benefits are unevenly spread. Figure 2.5 contrasts the gains and losses from FDI in developed and developing countries.

Who gains and loses from FDI?

In developed economies –

- Foreign investor **gains** from location advantages, e.g. growing market.
- Host communities **gain** jobs.
- Host governments **gain** revenues.
- Workers in host country **gain** in prosperity from employment.
- Workers in uncompetitive domestic industries **lose** out.
- Companies in domestic industries can **lose** out to competition from foreign investors.
- Consumers **gain** from greater choice.

In developing economies –

- Foreign investor **gains** from location advantages, e.g. cheap labour.
- Host communities **gain** jobs.
- Workers in industries favoured by FDI **gain** in prosperity.
- Host governments **gain** revenues.
- Host economy can **gain** from technology transfer, but...
- Domestic companies can **lose** out.
- Workers in industries not favoured by FDI investors often **lose** out.
- Where FDI is in resource extraction, host government **gains** from expertise and revenues, but society can **lose** out.

Figure 2.5 Uneven benefits of FDI

As Figure 2.5 shows, gains in any country, whether developed or developing, flow mainly to those directly involved in FDI activities. These are mainly the corporate players involved, their affiliates and employees. Also benefiting are the governments within whose territories investments are located. For societies, the picture is more ambiguous. Shifts in the location of manufacturing, for example, affect people in work – and out of work – and their families. The effects differ between developed and developing countries.

Developing countries

For developing countries, the benefits of inward FDI can be transformational, promoting industrialization and formal employment with salaried work. FDI can boost economic development and bring **technology transfer**, whereby skilled workers in the host country are able to learn from the technology of the foreign investor. These **spillover effects** from FDI are also possible where the foreign investor, for example in a greenfield project, uses local suppliers and service providers. The latter companies can gain both technological and managerial skills which can be valuable in building domestic innovative capacity. However, FDI inflows do not always deliver hoped-for benefits, as Figure 2.5 shows. Much FDI, especially in poor countries, is adversely affected by weak governance and weak accountability, which can lead to gains being concentrated in government and business hands rather than societal well-being. Workers in outsourced manufacturing are stakeholders, but they are not employees of the MNE. The MNE can take the position that legally it has no responsibility for them. However, when reports of mistreatment are publicized, public opinion tends to the view that the global brand owner shoulders some of the blame.

MNEs derive value from the ownership of technology embodied in intellectual property. They often seek to limit technology transfer in host economies, for fear of nurturing local competitors (see Chapter 9). Much manufacturing FDI is of a low-skilled nature. A concern for governments is that attracting low-technology FDI can lead to the country struggling to rise up the technological ladder to higher-value manufacturing and high-tech industries.

There is also a concern over the sustainability of the low-cost manufacturing model exemplified by China. The model relies heavily on cheap labour, especially migrant workers coming from rural areas to the industrial complexes run by the manufacturers. Separated from their families, these workers are housed in the factory complex, where a highly-regimented way of life is maintained, dominated by long hours of repetitive work. These workers often endure poor living and working conditions. Migrant workers, in particular, are vulnerable to exploitation. A growth in migrant labour has been an aspect of globalization, raising issues of human rights and responsibility for the well-being of workers. Factory owners who have outsourcing agreements with MNEs are responsible as employers, but the situation becomes complicated when the factory owner contracts work out to subcontractors, as is commonly the case. MNE brand owners could be said to be morally responsible, if not directly legally responsible. Often, they are not aware that manufacturing is being carried out by subcontractors. MNEs are attracted to countries where workers' legal protections are weak. Worker discontent has led to social unrest and strikes in China, where the authorities have responded with higher wages. Improving wages, reducing hours, enforcing rest days and allowing workers to organize leads to better working conditions, but these developments are not viewed so positively by the companies involved, who tend to focus on rising costs. Where costs rise, foreign investors seek other locations where costs are lower and regulation weaker. This poses dilemmas for the government and for the foreign investor.

For resource-rich developing countries, FDI offers the possibility of wealth generation on a big scale. But exploiting resources can be fraught with difficulties, including technical challenges, infrastructure deficiencies and corruption. For this reason, many poor developing countries suffer from a 'resource curse', which has been a source of disappointment in so many, especially in Africa (UNECA, 2013). Major oil companies, such as Royal Dutch Shell and BP, are long established in developing countries and have built up expertise in oil and gas exploration and extraction. These skills are vital to unlock resource potential, especially if reserves are located in difficult environments, both geologically and politically. Resource-rich countries, including Nigeria, Russia, Iraq, Sudan and Venezuela, are some examples of countries that have suffered from poor governance and political instability. Their governments wish to realize gains from ownership and control over energy assets, but they are compelled to rely on foreign investors, who are awarded exploitation rights and production contracts. Although energy-rich countries have turned to western expertise in the past, they are now attracting the BRIC countries. An example is Mozambique, featured in the case study in this chapter.

For the developing country, the prospect of a deep-pocketed foreign investor is a mixed blessing. Host-country governments focus on the benefits of FDI to their economies as portrayed by the foreign investor. However, in reality, the investing firm is more focused on returns to its investors than on the benefits to the host country. For the MNE, location advantages are constantly shifting, and inward investors migrate as the balance of advantage shifts to new locations.

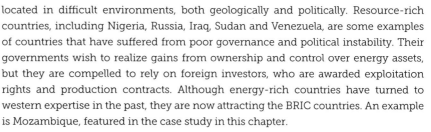

CASE STUDY ON THE CHANGING BUSINESS ENVIRONMENT

Mozambique: resource riches for whom?

The prospect of unfathomable resource riches flowing to one of the world's poorest countries would seem like a dream come true, but the history of how such resource finds are translated into reality reads more like a nightmare for many countries. The 'resource curse' has afflicted a number of African countries, such as Nigeria, where corruption, poor governance and theft from oilfields have led to continuing failure to transform the wealth into improvements in social well-being. Will Mozambique go the same way? A country like Norway has reaped the rewards of resource riches, benefiting the economy and society. But there are doubts about Mozambique's ability to follow a path closer to that of Norway.

Mozambique suffered from a long civil war that ended in 1992 with the establishment of a one-party state. Since the end of the civil war, Mozambique's government has sought to attract foreign investors, with priority given to large projects, such as the Mozal aluminium smelter, which involved a huge investment by the global mining company, BHP Billiton. Projects such as this have propelled economic growth, but have not brought the impetus for jobs and business enterprises at grassroots level. The UN's Conference on Trade and Development (UNCTAD) has found that the government operated a 'regulatory bias in favour of mega-projects', at the expense of encouraging smaller investments which would fulfill social objectives (Zhan, 2013).

The president, Filipe Nyusi, elected in 2014, has promised to ensure that the wealth is equitably distributed in society. But prospects are not very optimistic. Nyusi is the latest president to take office representing Mozambique's ruling party, Frelimo, which has been in power since the country's independence from Portugal in 1975. Frelimo has close links with business and is often accused of corruption. Lingering hostilities between Frelimo and the rebel group, Renamo, destabilized the country for many years after the end of the civil war. An accord signed between the rulers and the rebel group in 2014, on the eve of Nyusi's election, aimed to end the conflict.

Huge gas reserves have been discovered off the coast of Mozambique. When transformed into liquefied natural gas (LNG), exports could ultimately generate many billions of dollars in revenues. Mozambique has long benefited from mining resources, including coal, but, for the gas discoveries, new investment in exploration and infrastructure is needed. The government is awarding exploration and mining licences to numerous multinational companies. These include Italy's Eni and the US company, Anadarko – companies that specialize in gas discoveries. But they also include emerging multinationals, China National Petroleum Corporation (CNPC) and India's Oil and Natural Gas Corporation. Observers are concerned that these licences are not being awarded in a

Mozambique's leaders aspire to rapid development, but in rural areas such as this, development seems a distant prospect for most of the population.

Source: iStock.com/tropicalpixsingapore.

transparent way, and that the country's rulers, who have links with businesses, are benefiting personally. Some of these contracts were awarded a decade or more ago, at a time when Mozambique was considered a dangerous, high-risk location. Incentives, such as exemptions from tax for 15 years, were used to entice these investors. A fear is that the deals struck will not yield the money for the country's treasury that might have been obtainable. Further contracts for construction and logistics have been awarded, and these, too, are raising queries as to their transparency. A civil society organization that focuses on anti-corruption has said of these contracts, 'There isn't a system to find out whether the government has done good business' (Akwagyiram, 2013).

Mozambique is classified as one of the world's least-developed countries, with GNI per capita in 2013 of just $610 (in current US dollars). Coal exports have helped to lift the country to growth rates of over 7% for a number of years, but continued growth has not resulted in the societal gains that would have been expected. Its ranking in the UN's Human Development Index is 178 out of a total of 187 countries (UNDP, 2014). The percentage of the population living in severe poverty (defined as less than $1.25 per day) is 60%. Life expectancy of just 50.3 years is lower than in other low-income countries, including those of sub-Saharan Africa. Seventy per cent of its inhabitants rely on agriculture for their livelihoods. In 2012, only 35% of the rural population had access to clean water. Mozambique's new president hopes that Palma, the coastal city nearest to the new gas fields, will become a gleaming conurbation of hotels, shopping malls and golf courses (England, 2014). His vision is very remote from the reality of most Mozambicans.

Sources: England, A. (2014) 'Mozambique prepares to exploit gas bonanza', *Financial Times*, 27 October, at www.ft.com; UNDP (2014) *Human Development Report 2014* (New York: UNDP); World Bank (2014) 'World Development Indicators, World Bank Data', at www.data.worldbank.org; Akwagyiram, A. (2013) 'Will Mozambique end up like Nigeria or Norway?', BBC news, 4 April, at www.bbc.com; Zhan, J. (2015) 'Making foreign investment work: lessons from Mozambique', *The Guardian*, 30 July, 2013, at www.theguardian.com.

Questions for discussion

- What is the resource curse, and why has it been a risk in Mozambique?
- Why are energy companies in a strong position with respect to negotiating for licences in countries such as Mozambique?
- To what extent would the prospect of transparency and equitable distribution of wealth be promoted if investing companies had a strong sense of social responsibility?
- What policies could be implemented by the Mozambique government that would help to direct the resource wealth to social goods rather than prestige projects?

Developed countries

FDI inflows to developed countries are typically market oriented. The investor seeks to manufacture or assemble products in or near large markets. Manufacturing locally can also bypass tariff barriers which would apply to imports. Arguably, this situation leads to both foreign and domestic companies improving their products to grab the consumer's attention. However, it does not always work out like that. In the US, Japanese car manufacturers built greenfield factories to sidestep trade barriers in the 1970s, locating in areas outside the large centres such as Detroit, Michigan, where American car manufacturers were entrenched. From these greenfield factories, they (and many other businesses) were able to serve US customers. So competitive were the newcomers that they oversaw a gradual decline in the fortunes of the three large American car companies. Detroit's heyday was in the post-Second World War era of economic boom in the US. Known as 'motor city' or 'motown', Detroit suffered dramatic decline: the number of manufacturing jobs stood at 200,000 in 1950, and by 2012 had declined to 20,000. Vast areas became industrial wastelands, and the population decreased from 1.86 million in 1950 to 700,000 in 2012. Two of the three large American car companies, General Motors and Chrysler, collapsed financially, requiring bailouts by the US government following the financial crisis of 2008. These companies are now back on their feet, but their new incarnations are very unlike the sprawling giants of Detroit's 'motown'. Both are now more globalized in both production and markets, targeting large emerging markets especially.

De-industrialization of the advanced economies has been a major – and highly visible – aspect of the shift in manufacturing to lower-cost locations. In the US motor industry, much of the motor manufacturing shifted to locations in other parts of the country, notably the southern states, where workers were not members of the powerful trade unions that had dominated the older plants in traditional manufacturing centres like Detroit. FDI flowed into southern states, where foreign manufacturers, including the large German and Japanese car companies, became highly competitive.

Consumers in developed countries have benefited from the flow of imported goods produced in low-cost countries. Manufacturing of everything from apparel to toys has relocated to countries in the developing world, mainly China and other Asian countries. As a result, domestic toy making in developed economies has almost totally disappeared. Barbie dolls, Hot Wheels cars and other branded toys of Mattel, the large American toy company, are mainly manufactured in China, Indonesia, Malaysia, Mexico and Thailand (Mattel, 2013). Mattel manufactures some of its brands in its own factories in Asia. Others are made in outsourced factories whose owners have a licence to manufacture Mattel's branded toys. Others are even more remote: products purchased from companies with which Mattel has no ongoing relationship.

FDI is part of a bigger picture of globalized supply chains linking a range of MNEs and their affiliates through a variety of arrangements, as the example of Mattel shows. Mattel has been repeatedly cited for human rights violations in the factories producing its products, including one it owns (Crowe, 2012). Millions of its products have had to be recalled on safety grounds, such as the presence of lead in paint. With its hundreds of suppliers in developing countries, Mattel is an example of a successful global business. In 2013, its toys were enjoyed by 5 million children in over 150 countries, generating $7.1 billion in sales for the company (Mattel, 2013). Its shift to production in developing countries has helped to generate employment in the hundreds of firms that supply its toys. But on the other side of the coin are negative impacts on human well-being and the environment. Are these impacts simply the 'price' that must be paid for economic growth globally, or can globalized production be managed more responsibly to benefit society as a whole? Companies and governments play crucial roles, facing challenges and responsibilities that are discussed later in this chapter. Also influential have been an array of international organizations and agreements, which are discussed in the next section.

Globalization across key dimensions of the environment

This section takes an overview of globalization across the dimensions of the international environment, highlighted in Chapter 1. These dimensions will be discussed in detail in the chapters that follow. Here, we highlight the varied impacts of globalization in each, identifying the players involved. We place both positive and negative impacts in contexts, revealing inherent tensions in globalization processes. These tensions are shown in Figure 2.6. As the figure shows, within each dimension there are counterpoised forces at work, often revolving around conflicts between local or national pressures and global concerns. In each of the boxes, the local or national factor is listed first, followed by the wider global factors. We now look at these in more detail.

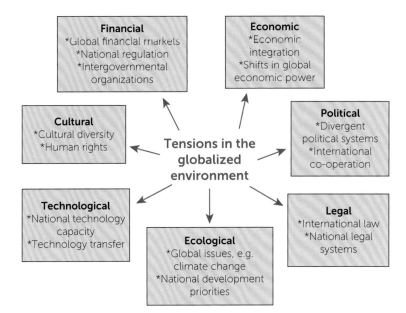

Figure 2.6 Unfolding tensions stemming from globalization

Economic environment – Countries have their own distinctive economic systems which have evolved over long periods, some more market oriented and others more state controlled. Globalization has brought greater integration among national economies. They have become interdependent, but this does not mean that they have converged. Some countries have benefited greatly from globalization: the emerging economies are examples, as their manufacturing prowess (in the case of China) and abundant natural resources (in the case of Brazil) serve global markets. These countries have grown in economic power globally. Whereas the US as the world's largest economy was considered the dominant economic power in the decades following the Second World War, there are now multiple powerful players in the global economy, notably the emerging economies. None has yet taken over from the US as the world's dominant economic power. Globalization has led to greater interdependence among all players, but there remain huge divergences in economic power globally.

Economic conditions in one country impact on the economies of other countries with which it has ties, including its neighbours, home countries of inward investors and its trading partners. If a major economy stumbles, the ripples will extend around the globe. For example, the financial crisis in Russia in 2014 impacted on foreign manufacturers and retailers operating in the country, sending shivers through those companies' home economies. It also sent shivers through stock exchanges where Russian companies were listed, notably the London Stock Exchange. MNEs' global strategies have resulted in many countries gaining from global business ties. But poor countries that are not favoured miss out on the potential benefits of FDI, while having to rely on global markets for energy and commodities. In what might seem a paradox, economic inequality between countries can thus be exacerbated by globalization.

Moreover, inequalities have arisen within countries favoured by internationalizing firms. In these countries, globalized companies and appropriately-skilled workers have benefited. China, for example, has a growing affluent middle class, but it has seen growing income inequality (Xie and Xiang, 2014). These researchers highlight two factors in particular: large variations from region to region in China and the large gap between urban and rural inhabitants. Both are aspects of globalization. Export-oriented industrialization has favoured urbanized areas and **export processing zones** specifically set up to attract foreign investors wishing to export.

Political environment – National political systems around the world remain diverse, reflecting the fact that each country's politics is rooted in its own heritage and values. On the other hand, political co-operation across borders has taken place, largely as a result of the increase in economic and other ties between countries. Deeper political integration across borders has been fostered within the European Union (EU), which has EU-wide political structures, but this example is exceptional. Political integration, in general, has not followed from economic integration. But greater co-operation among sovereign states has progressed, largely through the **United Nations (UN)** and is agencies. The UN (www.un.org) was formed in the aftermath of the Second World War, chiefly to prevent future threats to global security and to promote peaceful co-operation among member states. It does not operate as a government, but seeks to achieve agreement among sovereign players. Some might lament that the UN cannot coerce members to come into line with resolutions which represent the majority of its members, but this limitation reflects a widespread wariness among national governments to cede powers to supranational organizations. On the other hand, international public opinion – as well as long-term self-interest – can be effective in persuading governments to co-operate with others to solve global problems.

Also dating from the post-war period, the **General Agreement on Tariffs and Trade (GATT)** has sought, through successive rounds of negotiations, to promote agreements among countries to dismantle trade barriers. The **World Trade Organization (WTO)** (www.wto.org), created in 1995, became a successor to the GATT, re-enforcing the belief that freer trade benefits all countries, both large and small. The WTO's banner of freer and fairer trade has become somewhat tattered, however, as many governments have tended to pay only lip service to its goals, putting national economic and political concerns first. It is perhaps mainly in the dimension of the political environment that the contentions of the hyperglobalization advocates, noted earlier, are not being borne out in reality.

Legal environment – National legal systems are closely connected to sovereign national political systems. In countries where there is a strong sense that the law should operate independently of political influences, an independent judicial system open to all is considered an important institution in the safeguarding of civil and political rights. In countries where the legal system is controlled by political élites, the legal system lacks independence. This is considered a significant risk factor for firms doing business in these locations. Firms doing business in China, where legal institutions are weak and politicized, are well aware of the risks. However, there is a growing body of international law, to which countries willingly commit themselves in a process which is inching towards global legal standards. Central to this process is the **International Court of Justice (ICJ)** (www.icj-cij.org), founded in 1920, which is headquartered in The Hague, in the Netherlands. In the area of human rights, in particular, international law is the benchmark, and is now incorporated in the national law of many countries, as well as the EU. Regional lawmaking in many areas, most developed in the EU, is also influential for cross-border businesses, affecting numerous areas of law, including employment, competition and consumer rights. Microsoft and Intel, two giant American companies, have both been fined by the EU court for breaches of competition law. Google has also been found to be in breach of EU competition law and privacy law. A global company would be unwise to believe that because it is large and dominates its sector worldwide, it is somehow above national and EU law.

Ecological environment – Globalization is often blamed for environmental degradation, but the processes taking place are complex. Industrialization, which got under way long before the current era of globalization, is a direct cause of pollution, the depletion of natural resources and destruction of natural ecosystems. Industrialization is itself associated with urbanization, industrialized agriculture, the growth in transport and growing need for energy, all of which contribute to environmental degradation. Where globalization comes into play is in the mounting speed of these destructive processes in the post-war era. China's rapid industrialization, driven by an insatiable appetite for energy and natural resources, has resulted in a particularly woeful toll on the environment, with record levels of air pollution and dangerous depletion of water supplies. China is now the world's largest emitter of greenhouse gases, which are largely responsible for climate change (see Chapter 10). Climate change is a global issue, and the UN's Climate Change Panel (www. ipcc.ch) has been active in urging all countries to sign up to emissions reductions through global agreements, first in the Kyoto Protocol of 1998, and now in the 2015 Paris accord. However, as in other dimensions highlighted in this section, governments are slow to commit their countries to emissions reductions and other measures which they perceive could damage national interests. Again, we find that global problems have local impacts, and governments tend to see global issues through national lenses.

Technological environment – It was once assumed that technological advances, especially in high-tech industries, would come from America and be diffused through the rest of the world. Much innovation *has* emanated from America, and American entrepreneurs have stood out in exploiting new ideas. However, as other countries have improved scientific education and technology infrastructure, technological excellence has become more widespread. A factor has been the diffusion of technology through FDI, whereby local workers gain skills through technology transfer, which can boost domestic firms. Technology transfer has been a major positive aspect of globalization, benefiting developing countries. Internet technology has facilitated the operation of extended supply chains. Technological innovations have transformed much manufacturing, often leading to greater automation. But while the disruptive effects of technology are beneficial in terms of production, they raise issues for societies and governments, who must adapt to rapid technological change and, if need be, devise regulatory frameworks that take account of new technology. The worker who has suffered from redundancy and the town whose obsolete factory has closed are likely to view globalization in a negative light. So, too, is the traditional taxi driver who has lost business to the driver utilizing Uber's ride-hailing software (see the opening case study in Chapter 6).

Financial environment – Globalization of financial markets has progressed swiftly due to advances in communications technology and the liberalization of national financial systems. Banks and other financial services companies became global players, prospering from innovative financial instruments, a liberalized financial sector in many countries, and light regulation in key financial centres (discussed further in Chapter 8). While governments welcome capital flows, many have become susceptible to the risks of liberalization, highlighted in recurring financial crises since the 1990s. The Asian financial crisis of 1998 showed the risks of opening up fragile domestic financial systems to volatile capital flows from foreign investors. A mismatch emerged between huge globalized financial markets and the predominantly national structures which regulate finance in each country. Excessive risk-taking, especially in investment banking, led to a global financial crisis in 2008, which saw some large banks fail and others, deemed to be too big to fail, bailed out by the governments of their home countries, even though the banks had larger operations abroad than they did at home. The **International Monetary Fund (IMF)** (www.imf.org) and **World Bank** (www.worldbank.org), both established in the aftermath of the Second World War, aid countries in financial distress and maintain international financial stability (see Chapter 8 for a further discussion). Their roles could be enhanced but, as with international bodies generally, this would require agreement by sovereign member states to give oversight roles to supranational bodies – a step many are reluctant to take.

Cultural and social environments – Distinctive cultural identities, especially national cultures, seem to be at odds with globalization. A growing 'global middle class' which shares similar tastes and lifestyles might seem to be oblivious of national borders. These new, mostly urbanized, consumers are changing from traditional cultures, based on rural and family ties, towards a culture based more on material consumption and individualist values. A fear is that people are becoming 'rootless', disconnected from traditional attitudes and values which have ensured stability and observance of norms of social behaviour within societies over the centuries. An undercurrent is disquiet that the new consumer society is essentially shaped by American culture. The growing middle class in emerging economies is taking on characteristics of an American lifestyle, notably greater consumption of meat and processed foods. The international expansion of companies such as Coca-Cola and McDonald's can be perceived as Americanization, which is a more culture-laden concept than globalization. On the other hand, traditional cultural values can persist even though people acquire the trappings of consumer society. Certainly, global companies now aim to satisfy differing consumer needs and tastes in different countries, implying that localization is an adjunct of globalization.

Many societies in today's world have become multi-cultural, largely through immigration. And many people travel to other countries for temporary work. Cultural minorities, whether residents or visiting workers, are at risk of discrimination and

GLOBAL BUSINESS IN ACTION

Reaching consumers in global markets

JR Little

JR Little is the Global Head of Innovation at Carat (www.carat.com), a media marketing firm going back to 1968 that is now part of the Dentsu Aegis Network. Carat's 8,000 staff worldwide provide marketing consultancy services for a wide range of companies globally with diversified media solutions. Client companies include manufacturing companies, banks and healthcare companies. Among them are General Motors, Mondelez, Johnson & Johnson and Bank of America. The government of Abu Dhabi is also among Carat's clients. JR holds a Bachelor of Science degree in Human Development and Family Studies, Sociology; and his Masters of Science degree was in Strategic Communications. He has been involved in a wide variety of business environments, including rapidly changing emerging markets. The diversity of Carat's clients and the global breadth of its marketing expertise give JR Little a unique insight into global marketing challenges.

The interview with JR focuses on reaching consumers in the era of globalization, where changing markets and rapidly improving digital media are reaching greater numbers of consumers in both developed and emerging markets. Still, local nuances in marketing messages can be key to reaching consumers in diverse markets. Consumers in all markets now have unprecedented access to information – good and bad – about companies whose products they buy. The reach of digital technology has empowered consumers to an unprecedented extent. Companies must now be aware that they need to be truthful and transparent in communicating with consumers and other stakeholders. In this context, JR stresses that ethics and CSR must represent real commitment rather than just publicity.

Before watching the interview with JR, look again at the section on 'Globalization across key dimensions of the environment'. It will also be helpful to look at Chapter 9, on technology and innovation.

Visit www.palgravehighered.com/morrison-gbe-4e to watch the video, then think about the following questions:

1. Despite its greater resources and familiar logo, the global brand might face stiff competition from local brands in many markets. How does he advise a global company to handle these competitive situations?
2. In what ways do country differences still matter in consumer markets? Why do General Motors sell the same car under different brand names in Germany and the UK? In your view, would it be better to simply market the same car as a 'GM' car in both markets?
3. Governments can turn to marketing tools to 'brand' the companies that they either run or heavily invest in. JR finds that governments of emerging countries, such as Abu Dhabi, are perhaps keener to do this than western ones. Why? In your mind, is Etihad 'just another airline' or a limb of government?
4. For brands associated with products such as fizzy drinks and sweets, what are the ethical challenges for marketers? To what extent do you go along with JR's approach to the health issues in these situations?

exploitation. The enjoyment of cultural rights is recognized as a human right, and is reinforced by the UN's cultural conventions under the authority of **UNESCO** (the UN Educational, Scientific and Cultural Organization, at www.unesco.org). Migrant labour is often organized along lines of ethnic or cultural groupings. Such workers, typically working in factories, mines, agriculture and construction sites far from their homes, are vulnerable groups. An alarming development has been the growing number of Syrian refugees, including children, working in Turkey's booming textile factories, which manufacture goods for global brands. These workers are not legally entitled to work in Turkey, and are particularly vulnerable to exploitation. They highlight an aspect of globalization that places human rights at risk. There is a sad irony here, as the idea of human rights is inherently global, pertaining to human beings wherever they are and whatever their culture.

The tensions between global and national or local forces are evident in each of these dimensions. But these are not simple 'either-or' choices in many cases. A government might open its borders to global companies, encouraged to think that foreign investment is in the country's best long-term interest. Growing integration into the global economy, it is encouraged to think, will bring growth and prosperity. But it involves risks that sometimes harm local interests, including domestic industries, local workforces and the natural environment. The global company might be expected to think in terms of higher international labour standards, as befits the idea that it is 'above' national jurisdictions. But the opposite is more likely: the global company seeks out particular countries for location advantages, including lower costs, weak employee protection laws and weak regulation.

Global versus local

In which of the dimensions of the environment discussed here are global regulatory mechanisms most relevant, and why?

Globalization: challenges and responsibilities

Challenges arise in connection with globalization, particularly in contexts of negative impacts on societies and individuals. Globalized production, aided by accommodating governments, has led to wealth creation and economic growth. But, as we have seen, income growth in a national economy does not automatically translate into improved well-being in society. A major challenge is therefore harnessing globalization processes to improve well-being for all. Figure 2.7 shows the interlocking challenges of globalization. Issues of sustainability have become more urgent as industrialization has touched more countries, driven largely by FDI and global supply chains. Where do responsibilities lie? Some people might argue that it is for businesses to pursue corporate goals that benefit shareholders, and that this constitutes the limit of their responsibility. As we have noted in Chapter 1, however, companies taking a purely economic view of their responsibilities are now finding this stance evokes increasing criticism among stakeholders and in international public opinion generally. Most would now conceive of their goals in terms of sustainability, wider values to societies and ethical concerns. Sustainability is also an urgent issue for governments, especially in the context of sustainable development. But for many, development equates to economic development measured by growth figures. As we have seen, there has been a congruence of interests between MNEs and governments: governments prioritize economic growth over environmental concerns, which encourages companies to expand in ways that risk environmental damage.

Interlocking challenges and responsibilities

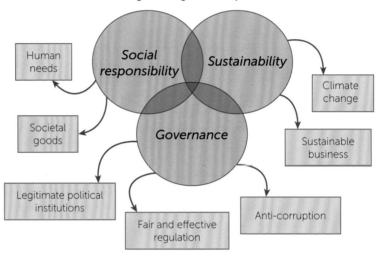

Figure 2.7 Globalization: challenges and responsibilities

The second group of challenges falls under the broad heading of 'governance'. While we might consider these to be entirely matters of government policy, this is not the case in today's world. Governance responsibilities fall on both governments and businesses. Weak and opaque governance in many developing countries has opened the way for businesses to do deals that benefit insiders and neglect wider interests, including those of society. Blame for corruption lies with both the businesspeople and the government agents they deal with. Most people would consider it unethical of a businessperson to negotiate a deal with a government official if it involves personal gain. The defence that the deal was deemed to be legal within the country would not convince many people that it is legitimate. But the fact that the company adhered to national law at the time is a standard response of companies accused of ethical wrongdoing. National law, and the people who administer it, are continually changing, especially in unstable political environments in which rulers have little claim to legitimacy. A stable political and legal environment is in the interests of all parties, and this is best achieved by transparent mechanisms of accountability. Foreign investors would benefit, as would responsible governments. In such a situation, societal goods are more likely to be achieved as well.

The last of the spheres in the figure is social responsibility. Companies are part of every society in which they are active, but how far does this responsibility go? MNEs have contracts with suppliers for the manufacture of their branded products, often at short notice and in large quantities. Their demands impact on the labour conditions in supply chains, and they thus share responsibility for mistreatment. The rise of outsourced manufacturing in developing countries has contributed to altering the economic landscape in these societies. While growing numbers of wage earners would seem to be a step on the way to economic development, insecure jobs, poor working conditions, risks to health and social upheaval have led to hardship, undermining the potential of burgeoning industries to fulfill human needs. MNEs that rely heavily on outsourcing are now likely to suffer reputational damage when the conditions of workers are revealed. MNEs are not lone actors: affiliate companies and governments must share responsibility.

As we have seen, despite resource riches and healthy economic growth, Mozambique is near the bottom of the UN's human development rankings. Workers in factories and in extraction industries in developing countries tend to be poorly protected in terms of employment rights and regulation of health and safety. While these operations provide jobs and salaries, lifting many out of rural poverty, they often involve harsh conditions for workers, many of whom are migrants working far from their homes. Millions of workers in China's export-oriented factories are migrants from distant rural areas, housed in dormitories that form part of the factory owner's complex. Mineworkers around the world live and work in similar environments, far from home. Such workers are vulnerable to human rights abuses and have few means to vent grievances. Achieving improvements in their conditions and recognition of their rights as workers is a major challenge. National governments are sometimes reluctant to intervene with legal safeguards, as they wish not to criticize the companies involved. Moreover, politicians often have links with the businesses that invest in the country. MNEs themselves are focused, above all, on financial priorities, to keep shareholders happy. MNEs can argue that they abide by national law and that, if there are questions about issues such as excessive overtime, nonpayment of wages, and child labour, these are matters controlled by the factory owner. In many cases, national laws are in place, but they are weakly enforced. Regulatory authorities with limited resources struggle to bring illegal activities under control. In these situations, companies and national authorities share responsibilities.

Conclusions

Companies have been drivers of globalization through their global strategies, but other factors, including the role of governments, have also been influential. Seeing the economic potential of opening their economies to foreign investors, governments have played crucial roles, interacting with MNEs to facilitate the deepening ties and interconnections that we witness in today's world. The post-war boom in FDI was initially dominated by developed countries, where western consumer societies, especially the US, became the aspirational example for others to follow.

As the focus of FDI strategies shifted to developing countries, impacts have been dramatic. Location advantages such as low-cost labour and natural resources have attracted MNEs. The large emerging economies have been at the forefront of this shift. As these economies have grown, emerging MNEs have themselves become FDI investors in both developing and developed countries. The globalization of production has seen supply chains reaching a growing range of countries. The impacts in societies have been uneven. Developing countries have seen dramatic changes, enjoying rising incomes and economic growth. In many poor countries, large numbers of people have been lifted out of poverty. The growing middle classes in many countries are testimony to the benefits of globalization, but the persistence of rural poverty and poor quality of life, including poor health provision and education, are indicators of the negative side of globalization. So too are the poor working conditions for low-skilled, low-paid workers. Moreover, many millions of people that are now part of the growing lower middle class in emerging economies are still teetering on the edge of poverty, as expectations of further upward mobility recede. Also adding to globalization's negative impacts are the detrimental effects to the environment of rapid industrialization.

For developed economies, globalized production has brought a flood of imported consumer products from low-cost manufacturing centres. But, while this is good news, it is clouded by the effects of de-industrialization in former manufacturing strongholds. For many people in developed countries, disappearing jobs are what they think of when the word 'globalization' is mentioned. At the same time, the poor working and living conditions of many low-paid workers in developing countries are increasingly being blamed on corporate behaviour. Corporate profits have grown for successful globalized MNEs, that are able to offshore operations and reduce tax exposure by choosing advantageous locations.

Companies are now in the spotlight for social responsibilities. Governments in host countries that have welcomed FDI are now seeing the risks of social unrest from poor labour conditions. A country's inhabitants expect the government to regulate fairly the activities of globalized companies within their territories. Equally importantly, governments are expected to ensure that the benefits of globalization are translated into well-being for all. However, the reality is often growing inequality and instability. There are growing pressures from consumers bearing down on both companies and governments to become more socially responsible in their behaviour. In addition, international pressures can be influential. The mismatch between powerful globalized businesses and relatively weak global governance is often observed (UNDP, 2014). Moves towards greater international co-operation among companies and governments are enhancing the roles of international bodies that focus on raising labour standards and achieving societal goals.

☐ References

Anderlini, J. (2014) 'China flexes its economic muscle', *Financial Times*, 23 October, at www.ft.com.

Buckley, P. and Hashai, N. (2009) 'Formalizing internationalization in the eclectic paradigm', *Journal of International Business Studies*, 40: 58–70.

Crowe, D. (2012) 'China Labor Watch criticizes Mattel', *Los Angeles Business Journal*, 30 November, at www.labusinessjournal.com

Dunning, J. (1993) *Multinational Enterprises and the Global Economy* (Wokingham: Addison Wesley).

Euromonitor International (2014) 'China overtakes the US as the world's largest economy', at www.euromonitor.com

Friedman, T. (2000) *The Lexus and the Olive Tree* (New York: Anchor Books).

Friedman, T. (2016) 'The age of protest', *New York Times*, 13 January, at www.nyt.com

Hymer, S. (1975) 'The multinational corporation and the law of uneven development', in Radice, H. (ed.) *International Firms and Modern Imperialism* (Harmondsworth: Penguin).

Mattel (2013) '2013 Annual Report', at www.corporate.mattel.com

OECD (2015) 'About the OECD: Members and partners', at www.oecd.org

Ohmae, K. (2000) *The Invisible Continent: Four Strategic Imperatives of the New Economy* (London: Nicholas Brealey Publishing).

Rodrik, D. (2011) *The Globalization Paradox: Democracy and the Future of the World Economy* (Oxford: OUP).

UN (2014) *World Investment Report* (Geneva: UN).

UNDP (2014) *Human Development Report 2014* (New York: UNDP).

UNECA (United Nations Economic Commission for Africa) (2013) *Africa-BRICS Cooperation: Implications for Growth, Employment and Structural Transformation in Africa* (Addis Ababa: UNECA).

Waters, M. (2001) *Globalization*, 2nd edn (London: Routledge).

Wells, L.T. (ed.) (1972) *The Product Life Cycle and International Trade* (Boston, MA: Harvard Business School Press).

World Bank (2013) 'New country classifications' at www.worldbank.org

World Bank (2014) 'World Development Indicators, World Bank Data', at data.worldbank.org

Xie, Y. and Xiang, Z. (2014) 'Income inequality in today's China', *Proceedings of the National Academy of Science of the USA*, 111(19): 6928–6933.

☞ Multiple choice questions

Go to the companion website: www.palgravehighered.com/morrison-gbe-4e to take a quick multiple choice quiz on what you have read in this chapter.

⑦ Review questions

1 What are the defining characteristics of globalization?
2 What are the leading schools of thought on the extent and depth of globalization?
3 What is the Human Development Index, and why is it an important indicator in international business?
4 What is distinctive about emerging economies as compared to those that are simply designated 'developing' economies?
5 What are the main motives behind MNE internationalization strategies?
6 Compare modes of internationalization in terms of degrees of involvement in the host country.
7 What are the advantages of FDI as an entry mode?
8 What is greenfield investment as a mode of FDI, and what are the benefits to the foreign investor?
9 Explain the position of the brand owner who opts for outsourced production?
10 How have the post-war shifts in international power led to (a) growing FDI; and (b) changing patterns of FDI?
11 What does the product life cycle theory contribute to our understanding of FDI?
12 What are the elements of Dunning's eclectic paradigm of FDI?
13 Looking at the impacts of globalization in differing dimensions of the international environment, which are the most globalized, and why?
14 To what extent has the legal environment become globalized?
15 How are MNEs rethinking supply chains in terms of social responsibility?

✓ Assignments

1 Examine the major globalization processes at work in today's world economy, and assess their impact on the international business environment.
2 Assess the extent to which MNEs' FDI strategies have generated re-thinking of global and local factors in terms of sustainability.

📖 Further reading

Dicken, P. (2014) *Global Shift*, 7th edn (London: Sage).

Eriksen, T. (2014) *Globalization: The Key Concepts*, 2nd edn (London: Bloomsbury).

Hirst, P., Thompson, G. and Bromley, S. (2009) *Globalization in Question*, 3rd edn (Cambridge: Polity Press).

Keane, J. (2010) *Global Civil Society?* (Cambridge: Cambridge University Press).

Lechner, F. and Boli, J. (2014) *The Globalization Reader*, 5th edn (Oxford: Wiley-Blackwell).

Roberts, J., Hite, A. and Chorey, N. (eds) (2014) *The Globalization and Development Reader: Perspectives on Development and Global Change*, 2nd edn (Oxford: Wiley-Blackwell).

Rodrik, D. (2011) *The Globalization Paradox: Democracy and the Future of the World Economy* (Oxford: OUP).

Sklair, L. (2004) *Globalization: Capitalism and Its Alternatives* (Oxford: Oxford University Press).

🌐 **Visit the companion website at www.palgravehighered.com/morrison-gbe-4e for further learning and teaching resources.**

Is India the new manufacturing superpower?

India's government is seeking to attract foreign investors, who will provide economic opportunities for people like this Indian engineer on a construction site.

Source: iStock.com/szefei.

India is an established global leader in computing services, but its manufacturing sector has lagged behind. A consequence has been lacklustre economic growth, along with increasing imports of consumer goods, to satisfy its huge population of 1.2 billion. Manufacturing's share in the economy is only 15%. India's major advantages as a location for manufacturing are its huge working-age population and low-cost labour. Each year, 12 million young people enter the labour market, and the medium-skill jobs offered by manufacturers could significantly help to ease this pressure. However, lack of education and vocational skills has been a factor in holding back the country's manufacturing investment. Most workers are in the informal sector, working for unorganized enterprises and simply gaining knowledge on the job. Equipping workers with relevant vocational skills is one of the prerequisites for increasing manufacturing jobs. In the general election of 2014, the overwhelming win of Narendra Modi of the BJP (Hindu Nationalist Party)

was based largely on the promise of economic reforms to open up the economy to investors and to pursue programmes of 'employability'. But turning campaign rhetoric into reality was to prove a challenge.

India's position as an emerging economy is often compared with that of China, whose stunning economic growth has been built on export-oriented manufacturing. India has excelled in some sectors, such as pharmaceuticals, which have global markets, and it also has a growing garment manufacturing sector. However, it has missed out on the global supply chains that have contributed to China's growth. Restrictive labour laws and bureaucracy are deterrents to investors. In the World Bank's 'ease of doing business' rankings, India ranks a lowly 142 out of 189 countries (World Bank, 2014). Investors are also discouraged by India's shaky infrastructure, poor roads and rail transport, and inadequate port facilities. One of Mr Modi's first policy announcements on taking office was to invite foreign companies to invest in much-needed modernization of India's state-run, largely colonial-era rail network. Big infrastructure projects take time, but reforming the labour laws and making it easier for companies to acquire land for factories are measures that can have immediate impact. For example, the prime minister introduced a policy to make it easier to convert farmland for factories. India's commerce minister has said that the country's notorious reputation for 'red tape' must shift to the 'red carpet' (Kazmin, 2014).

This positive message to foreign investors is now seeing results, with a 46% rise in FDI over the two years, 2014 and 2015. Some of these companies are relocating from China, where there are labour shortages and rising wages. The demographic advantage now lies with India, where the working-age population is growing more rapidly than the total population. Hasbro, the toy maker, is now manufacturing its Play-Doh and Monopoly in India, as well as in Vietnam and Indonesia. The attempts to lure manufacturers in global supply chains are now seeing fruit. Foxconn, the Taiwanese company well known for its factories making iPhones in China, is opening plants in India to make smartphones for the growing Chinese company, Xiaomi. Car manufacturing is also on the rise in India, with manufacturers mostly eyeing India's domestic demand. General Motors has increased its production of cars for the Indian market. Volkswagen,

too, is manufacturing cars for Indian buyers, but has found that these models are also appealing to buyers in other emerging markets, such as Mexico and South Africa. Volkswagen's India president says, 'Positive sentiment has been created but they have to create a positive environment ... If the government creates the environment, industry will do the rest' (Kazmin, 2014).

The sale of farmland for factories was halted by the prime minister, largely because it was proving politically damaging. Regional election results in 2015, in which the BJP's support slumped, was an indication that not everyone is happy with the promotion of 'made in India'. India's democratic system is sometimes pointed to as country advantage, in contrast with China's authoritarian communist rule. But Indian democracy tends towards the turbulent. Modi himself, as a Hindu nationalist, is a divisive political leader, with a poor record in respect of handling India's cultural diversity. Political pitfalls lie in the way of his plans to make India a manufacturing hub, despite the overwhelming need for sustainable employment among its vast population.

Sources: Bradsher, K. (2015) 'India's manufacturing sector courts world but pitfalls remain', *New York Times*, 14 October, at www.nyt.com; Kazmin, A. (2014) 'Modi seeks to change fabric of economy', *Financial Times*, 26 September, at www.ft.com; World Bank (2014) 'Doing Business 2015', at www.doingbusiness.org; EY (2013) 'Reaping India's promised demographic dividend', at www.ey.com.

Questions for discussion

- What are India's advantages as a host country for manufacturing FDI?
- What factors act as deterrents to would-be investors?
- What is the reasoning behind the prime minister's push for 'made in India'?
- In your view, would India be better advised to pursue its excellence in computing services and pharmaceuticals, rather than manufactured goods, where it is competing against numerous other countries for relatively low-skilled jobs?

PART 2 FRAMING THE BUSINESS ENVIRONMENT

In Part 2, we shift from the enterprise in a globalized world to dimensions of the international environment relating to societies – their cultures, how they are governed and how their legal systems impact on people. The first is Chapter 3, *Culture and societies*. For most businesses, as for people, a national culture is an anchoring point, but in today's globalized world, companies are constantly encountering new cultures, whether in markets or in new production locations. MNEs are becoming enmeshed in the societies in which they operate, facing stakeholder challenges in employment relations and community impacts. Understanding underlying values and norms in differing national environments helps international managers to respond to these challenges.

Chapter 4, *The global economic environment*, introduces national economies and economic systems. Understanding global forces depends crucially on grasping how national economies function, along with the ways in which decision-makers form policies. Global economic integration is proceeding apace, but there remains huge diversity among national economic systems. Although the spread of market values has seemed pervasive, market reforms are themselves taking on distinctive national characteristics, reflecting divergent histories and values. Understanding the dynamics of national environments and their interactions is essential for today's international manager.

In Chapter 5, *The political environment: state and business actors*, we look both at formal institutions and the changing roles of businesses in governance. Political institutions change over time. The adoption of democratic institutions has been a trend in the post-war period, notably in the post-colonial and post-communist countries. But democratic setbacks and the strengthening of authoritarian governments have led to a rethink of democratic values and institutions. Political stability is valued by businesses as well as by individuals. Is democracy the most stable government? A turbulent democratic system can be unstable, but businesses have cause to be wary of the stability offered by repressive authoritarian regimes, where tensions exist under the surface. The chapter also examines the widening scope of inter-governmental institutions, in which governments and businesses take on responsibilities.

These considerations are taken up again in the following chapter, Chapter 6, *The legal environment*. Here we focus first on national legal systems, and their differing approaches to civil and criminal law. For international businesses, legal risk arises in numerous types of activity, including contracts with suppliers and customers, dealing with governments and dealing with affiliate companies in differing environments. As in the political environment, legal considerations are increasingly taking on an international dimension. MNEs must now adapt to the obligations recognized in international law, notably in areas of human rights and the environment. Stakeholders increasingly expect corporate leaders to abide by both the letter and the spirit of the law.

CULTURE AND SOCIETIES

Outline of chapter

This chapter will enable you to

- Understand the nature and origins of cultural diversity in societies
- Identify cultural dimensions as an aid to comparing national cultures
- Assess the role and impacts of different organizational cultures in the business environment
- Appreciate the ways in which societies change over time, together with the implications for international managers

The golden arches lose their shine

From its modest beginnings as a hamburger restaurant in the 1950s, McDonald's pioneered the fast-food restaurant, its golden arches becoming a familiar feature of the American landscape. Offering standardized menus, consistent quality, low prices, and quick service, it seemed to have hit on a formula that could not fail with consumers. The McDonald's business model in the US is based on franchising. The franchisee is an independent business, whose owner agrees terms with McDonald's as the franchisor, to run the business on the company's terms. The number of stores multiplied across the US, and the company went on to expand globally, adapting menus to local tastes. The winning formula seemed secure. But faltering sales in the US in recent years, where 12,000 of its 35,000 stores are located, have caused shockwaves within the company. Changing consumer preferences in the US have seen customers turning their backs on McDonald's, and international sales have also stuttered. A new CEO, Steven Easterbrook, who took over in 2015, had to admit that competitors, notably 'fast casual' restaurants, were offering menus perceived as healthier, authentic and less formula-driven than McDonald's. McDonald's has been slow to react to these newcomers, even though it had been a shareholder in one of them: Chipotle, the Mexican-style chain which is growing in popularity.

Chipotle's Mexican menu of tacos, burritos and fajitas features fresher ingredients, often organic and locally sourced. This approach is succeeding with consumers in the US who are becoming increasingly conscious of where their food comes from, and how it is produced. Although McDonald's seems to have been caught napping as the market shifted, the trend towards healthier eating is not new. McDonald's was an early investor in Chipotle, helping it to get started in 1998. It grew quickly, growing from 14 to 500 outlets in just 7 years. By 2005, McDonald's held a 90% stake in Chipotle, but sold out one year later. At McDonald's 2015 annual shareholders' meeting, one unhappy shareholder queried the CEO about the sale. Easterbrook, who had not been in charge at the time of the sale, said that Chipotle was a 'distraction' at a

time when it needed to concentrate on building its core brand (Peterson, 2015). McDonald's and Chipotle had differing ideas about Chipotle as a restaurant. McDonald's had wanted Chipotle to offer 'drive-thru' and breakfast menus. The founder of Chipotle, Steve Ells, sums up the reasons that the two companies parted: 'What we found at the end of the day is that culturally we're very different. There are two big things that we do differently. One is the way we approach food, and the other is the way we approach our people culture. It's the combination of those things that I think make us successful' (Peterson, 2015).

McDonald's has attracted criticism for its employment policies, notably low pay and poor conditions. Concerns over inequality and low pay have become more widespread in the US since the financial crisis, and big companies such as McDonald's and Walmart have come in for criticism for their low pay. Jobs in fast food are among the worst paid in the US. Employee activism has drawn attention to these issues. A number of McDonald's workers have complained of retaliation by the company for their raising issues about working conditions and taking part in demonstrations for higher wages. A potentially important ruling by the National Labor Relations Board (NLRB), which has oversight of labour rights, has held that McDonald's is a 'joint employer' of these workers, along with the franchisee. McDonald's and other franchise-based businesses have long operated on the principle that the franchisees are not under the control of the company, but this ruling would make them equally responsible for wrongs in the workplace. In 2015, the NLRB launched investigations into 181 alleged cases of unlawful labour practices against McDonald's. Mr Easterbrook could well need to rethink employment policies as part of his strategy for revamping the company.

The new fast casual chains are gaining business from fast-food outlets like McDonald's largely because people are doubtful about the health aspects of the typical McDonald's burger meal. Some of the new competitors are in fact burger restaurants, but trading on a more healthy and upmarket offering.

McDonald's is responding with more choices of burger toppings and all-day breakfast menus, attempting to lure customers back to the golden arches. But Mr Easterbrook has a tough job ahead, rebuilding a tarnished brand in the perceptions of consumers.

Sources: Munshi, N. (2014) 'Eating their lunch', *Financial Times*, 25 October, at www.ft.com; Munshi, N. (2015) 'New McDonald's chief faces tough test over stalling sales', *Financial Times*, 31 January, at www.ft.com; Stangler, C. (2015) 'McDonald's considered "joint employer" as landmark National Labor Relations Board hearings begin', *International Business Times*, 30 March, at www.ibtimes.com; Peterson, H. (2015) 'The ridiculous reason McDonald's sold Chipotle and missed out on billions of dollars', *Business Insider*, 22 May, at uk.businessinsider.com.

Questions for discussion

- Why did McDonald's not spot the changes taking place in consumer tastes?
- Why are the 'fast casual' restaurants proving more popular than fast food?
- McDonald's has had a poor reputation in employee relations. Why?
- What changes should Mr Easterbrook introduce that would win customers back and improve employee relations?

Introduction

Globalization has brought people from different parts of the world and from different cultural backgrounds into routine contact with each other, and with each other's cultures. Greater interaction suggests increasing understanding across cultures, but for international business, cultural differences remain significant. Despite globalization, products are designed for cultural preferences of particular markets. And managers involved in cross-border business activities must be sensitive to differences in languages, value systems and norms of behaviour. In short, being attuned to cultural differences is a vital aspect of doing business in a globalized world.

This chapter has two broad aims. The first is to gain an understanding of how culture influences business activities and organizations across the globe. While globalization is seen as giving rise to a global culture, local cultural identities are not withering away, but are adapting and persisting in the new global environment. The second aim is to understand how societies are changing, especially due to the impacts of globalization. Globalization is now increasingly affecting developing countries, where economic development is taking wing. But globalization's societal impacts in developing regions are uneven, raising concerns for well-being among weaker groups of people, such as migrants and minority cultures. We begin by defining culture, looking at the dimensions of culture in society, and the makeup of specific cultural identities among the world's peoples.

What is culture and how is it relevant to business?

Culture has been defined in many different ways, reflecting the variety of cultural phenomena that can be observed. Language, religious ritual and art are just a few examples of cultural symbols whose shared meanings form the unique fingerprint of a particular society. **Culture** can be broadly defined as, 'a shared way of life of a group of socially interacting people, transmitted from one generation to the next, via acculturation and socialization processes, that distinguish one group's members from others' (Ronen and Shenkar, 2013: 868). Culture denotes a cohesive social group, which could be a whole society or a smaller group such as a tribe or ethnic group. Inevitably, we all view and interpret the world around us through a cultural 'filter' to some degree. Ethnocentrism denotes the inflexible approach of relating to the world only in terms of our own culture, while polycentrism is the approach of attempting to overcome our own cultural assumptions and to develop an openness and under-standing of other cultures. Successful international business relationships depend in large measure on developing a polycentric approach in situations where cross-cultural issues arise, such as joint ventures.

To bow or to shake hands? Cultural misunderstandings often arise over how to greet people.

Source: ImageSource.

Figure 3.1 presents key aspects of culture. Culture includes values and beliefs shared by a group, and also norms of behaviour expected of group members. Values relate primarily to notions of good and evil, right and wrong. Values also include notions of the individual in relation to the group, as will be discussed in the section on culture theories. Norms relate to patterns and standards of behaviour. They shape what is considered normal and abnormal behaviour within the group. Manner of dress, food and the etiquette associated with eating and drinking are also obvious distinguishing features of a culture. Norms within societies relate to the role of the family, education and gender roles. Norms often reflect values, and, like values, can derive from religious beliefs and take on religious significance in many societies. Norms may also reflect customs that distinguish societies one from another. For businesspeople in a foreign environment, an understanding of local culture is needed not just in the context of doing business, but in general social relations with hosts. Indeed, in Asian cultures, doing business is not confined merely to working hours, but blends into social occasions such as meals together. Here the bonds of trust are sown which are crucial to a successful business relationship. Globalization of supply chains has highlighted the cultural tensions that can arise when migrant workers, commonly from rural communities or from other countries, are employed in production. Understanding and responding to cultural issues should be a part of supply chain management. However, the reasoning behind recruiting these workers is overwhelmingly to reduce costs, and the economic benefits tend to outweigh concerns about their social well-being.

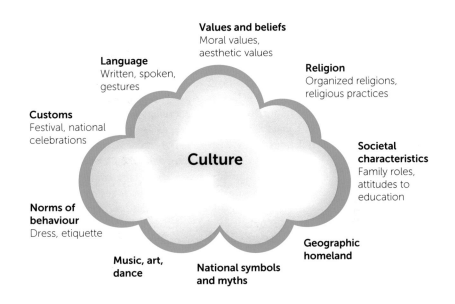

Values and beliefs
Moral values, aesthetic values

Language
Written, spoken, gestures

Religion
Organized religions, religious practices

Customs
Festival, national celebrations

Culture

Societal characteristics
Family roles, attitudes to education

Norms of behaviour
Dress, etiquette

Music, art, dance

National symbols and myths

Geographic homeland

Figure 3.1 Aspects of culture

Values and norms of behaviour are learned in a social context—we are not born with them. For this reason they are not fixed and static, but are capable of change. Societies evolve over time, and individuals may change when they move to a new environment. Organizations, too, change over time, and they are likely to change as they expand internationally. One of the themes of this chapter is the extent to which growing interactions between cultures are leading to cultural convergence. The growth of international markets and global brands such as McDonald's and Nike seem to indicate convergence towards a global or 'cosmopolitan' culture. Certainly, this is the view of the more ardent advocates of globalization (Bird and Stevens, 2003). At the other extreme, some commentators, pointing to the persistence of differing national cultures, assert that cultural divergence remains a reality, despite globalization processes (Berger, 2002). A more moderate view is that 'cultural learning' through interaction is leading to cultures being 'globally interwoven', acknowledging the potential of culture change from globalization (Bird and Fang, 2009: 141). In this vein, Ralston proposes the idea of 'crossvergence' as a continuum between the polar opposites of convergence and divergence, reflecting gradual processes of cultural integration (Ralston et al., 2008).

The fact that companies design products and communications for particular cultural preferences in different markets is an indication of persisting cultural diversity. The Big Mac and Coca-Cola epitomize the uniform standard product for all markets that is commonly used as an example of globalization. But in fact, the companies behind both these products have offerings for different markets, and also products that aim to reflect culture change. McDonald's has long been sensitive to differing local tastes, offering the teriyaki burger in Japan, for example, although relying on its core brands as the mainstay of the business. As the opening case study showed, waning enthusiasm for McDonald's hamburgers in mature markets has given impetus to changes in strategy. Coca-Cola, too, has revised its global strategy, offering different products to suit consumers in different markets, under a variety of brand names (see opening case study in Chapter 12). However, in a trend that reflects globalization, both companies are responding to concerns about healthy eating and sustainable sourcing being voiced by consumers everywhere, in emerging and developed countries alike.

National cultures

Peoples or nations are distinguishable from each other by language, religion, ethnic or racial identity, and, above all, by a shared cultural history. Together, these distinguishing characteristics blend into a national culture. Hofstede (1994) was largely responsible for highlighting national culture as a key concept in explaining cultural dimensions, and his framework remains influential (Stahl and Tung, 2014). Hofstede's research has shown that people have acquired their basic value systems by the age of ten (Hofstede, 1994). It is during these formative years that national culture exerts its strongest influence, through family and early schooling. National culture influences family life, education, organizational culture, and economic and political structures. The sense of belonging to a nation is one of the most important focal points of cultural identity. In the course of time, myth mixes with historical events in the collective memory, and the associated symbols serve as powerful emotive links between present and past, and even future.

The nation-state combines the concepts of cultural bonds created by the nation with the territorial and organizational structures of the state. The world's peoples comprise many more nations than states, and hence most states contain multiple cultural and national identities. There are two main reasons. First, through immigration, people move to other countries, usually in search of betterment and security. Second, in many countries there are indigenous peoples whose communities pre-date the arrival of colonizing outsiders who later founded the state. Historically, nations have sought self-determination for their own people. New nation-states thus represent the culmination of national aspirations. Largely as a result of the break-up of colonial empires, the number of nation-states has grown dramatically since the end of the Second World War. However, many of these states have proved to be ill-fitting administrative containers for the multiple social and ethnic groups within their borders.

Internal social tensions characterize many of the world's states, especially where minority ethnic groups feel disadvantaged by the state's institutions and laws. In times of economic stress, these tensions can come to the fore, as minority groups are typically poorer and less well educated than fellow citizens in mainstream groups associated with the national culture. Members of ethnic minorities are typically employed in low-skill, poorly paid jobs in manufacturing, mining and agriculture. As these industries have become globalized, labour needs have grown, often leading to the use of migrant workers, including indigenous peoples. They are vulnerable to exploitation and risks to health. The UN has long focused attention on the rights of minorities, including indigenous peoples, who are at risk of forced labour and other breaches of human rights (UNIASG, 2014). The UN highlights that the discrimination and harsh treatment endured by indigenous peoples in these industries are not only harmful to the people involved, but jeopardize 'social cohesion and inclusive development' in the countries where they take place (UNIASG, 2014: 1).

When an MNE (multinational enterprise) invests in a country that is culturally very different from its own, it is sometimes said that cultural distance can be a negative factor (Stahl and Tung, 2014). Similarly, cultural distance can come into play where there is a cultural gap between the MNE and a joint-venture partner or affiliate. Globalized production and supply chains lead to cultural learning through interactions and a growing appreciation of the cultural environment in different countries. At the same time, MNEs face challenges over human rights. Discrimination on grounds of race, ethnicity, gender or religion exists in many cultures. Companies are challenged to take an ethical stance, upholding human rights in these situations where they are at risk.

There are thus tensions between global and local influences. Moreover, just as individuals experience culture change in their lives, national cultures, too, change over time. Cultural changes take place within societies, but national cultures remain foundation stones (Inglehart and Baker, 2000). A national culture in which a deep sense of history permeates identity can evoke a sense of deep meaning in life that is remarkably durable. This is evident in countries which have gone through processes of industrialization. Traditional rural ways of life give way to urban living and salaried work, but national cultures persist.

Identifying with the nation-state

Think of a nation-state which you are familiar with. Does it have a strong national culture, or is there a mixture of diverse cultural identities within its borders? If the latter, explain what they are.

Languages

Language is the basic means of communication between people, which facilitates social interaction and fosters a system of shared values and norms. Language is much more than the vocabulary and grammar that make up written and spoken expression. E.T. Hall distinguishes between 'low-context' and 'high-context' cultures (Hall, 1976). In a low-context culture, communication is clear and direct; speakers come straight to the point and say exactly what they mean. America is a good example of a low-context culture. In the high-context culture, much goes unsaid; depending on the relationship between the speakers, each is able to interpret body language and 'read between the lines'. In this type of culture, ambiguity is the norm, and directness is avoided. Asian cultures fall into this type. For Americans, meeting with people from high-context cultures can seem frustrating, as they are unsure where they stand, while their Asian counterparts are unsettled by Americans' directness of approach, which may come across as insincerity.

In terms of numbers, the linguistic family of Chinese is spoken by the largest numbers of people, as Figure 3.2 shows. The figure indicates the number of speakers of each language as a first language. It is notable that five of the ten most widely spoken first languages are from the BRIC countries. The large numbers of Spanish and Portuguese speakers are due mainly to prevalence of Spanish in Latin America and Portuguese in Brazil. Hindi and Bengali are both Indian languages. Javanese is one of the main languages of Indonesia, another of the major emerging countries.

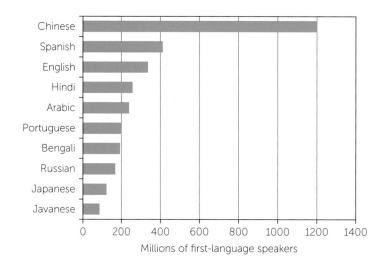

Figure 3.2 The world's ten most widely spoken languages

Source: Data from Lewis, M., M. Paul, G. Simons and C. Fennig (eds) (2014) *Ethnologue: Languages of the World*, 17th edn, Statistics, Table 3 (Dallas, TX: SIL International). Used by permission, © SIL.

In most countries, one or more dominant languages exist alongside minority languages, which may be concentrated in specific geographical regions. Canada has two official languages (English and French), and the minority French speakers have a history of separatist activism. Switzerland, by contrast, has four official languages (German, French, Italian and Romansh) which co-exist in harmony. Linguistic diversity within a state may arise in several different ways:

* A minority language may represent a native culture, such as the Indian nations which inhabited North and South America before the arrival of European settlers. The US, Australia and South Africa are all settler societies, where tensions erupted between the new arrivals and existing native cultures. These tensions are still observable today, as evidenced by the second-class citizen status of which native Americans complain.

* Colonizing states introduced their own language into their colonies. The western imperial powers of the sixteenth to the nineteenth centuries included the British, French, Dutch, Belgians, Spanish and Portuguese. All left their national languages in their colonies, where the colonial language became that of the élites, as well as that of government and administration. The many indigenous peoples spoke native languages, but struggled to maintain their cultures in the tide of colonialism. Brazil has a large indigenous population. These indigenous peoples face issues of discrimination, land rights and environmental degradation in the Amazon areas which they inhabit.

* Immigration can create linguistic diversity. Immigrants are faced with the difficulties of assimilation in a new culture, or maintaining a separate identity. Where immigrants are concentrated geographically, they may form a subculture in which they speak their home language.

Governments' education policies regarding minority languages are often contentious. They can be directed towards protecting minority cultures or, alternatively, compelling schools to teach the dominant language in order to facilitate the assimilation of minority cultures into the mainstream culture. In countries that have decentralized authority in regions or provinces, the regional authorities may wish to maintain the local language in the school system as a means of maintaining the local culture. In Spain, there are several 'autonomous regions', where regional languages, such as Catalan, predominate. Catalonia has seen a rise in separatist nationalist sentiment in recent years, encouraged by separatist politicians who point to the economic prosperity of Catalonia, which contrasts markedly with the recession that has deeply affected other Spanish regions.

English has gained an importance as a global language that extends far beyond the number of native speakers. It is the commonest second language globally and the dominant language in international business. Although English is the commonest language for the global media and the internet, its dominance is now challenged by the rise of Chinese, due to the rapid increase in Chinese internet use (see Table 3.1). The UN has highlighted a 'linguistic shift taking place online', predicting in 2012 that the number of Chinese language internet users would probably overtake those accessing the internet in English in 2015 (UN Broadband Commission, 2012).

Table 3.1 The top ten internet languages

Language	Number of users (millions)
English	800.6
Chinese	649.4
Spanish	222.4
Arabic	135.6
Portuguese	121.8
Japanese	109.6
Russian	87.5
German	81.1
French	78.9
Malaysian	75.5

Source: 'Internet World Statistics', 31 December 2013, at www.internetworldstats.com.

For the many people who travel internationally, English is a recognized means of communication, often when neither of the parties speaks English as a first language. These globetrotters include not only businesspeople and diplomats, but also tourists, sportspeople, academics and students. The English language in these contexts is an intercultural means of communicating. Businesspeople are likely to use English in their international business activities, but speak their own first language at home. By the same token, while Hindi is the official language of India, English as an associate national language facilitates communication between the many non-Hindi-speaking groups. India is one of the world's most multi-lingual countries, with fourteen major languages, and many more minor ones. English is spoken by about 50% of India's population. Moreover, in the country's booming IT sector, the use of the English language is proving a location advantage. India's executives are highly travelled. As of 2015, CEOs born in India headed two American technology giants, Google and Microsoft.

English, the global language?

English-speaking businesspeople sometimes say that there is little point in learning a foreign language, as everyone nowadays speaks English. Do you agree or disagree, and why?

Religions

In many cultures, values and beliefs are determined by religion. There are many thousands of distinct religions and religious movements among the world's population. They range from simple folk religions to highly refined systems of beliefs, with set rituals, organized worship, sacred texts and a hierarchy of religious leaders. A religion calls on its followers to believe in supernatural forces which affect their lives, and to follow prescribed moral rules. Religion may exercise considerable secular and political influence, and can form a major unifying force in society. Religious divides, both within states and between states, can also be a source of friction According to research published in 2014, hostilities involving religion increased globally between 2007 and 2012, encompassing 33% of countries in 2012. The regions which saw the largest increases were the Middle East and North Africa, and Asia-Pacific (Pew Research Center, 2014). Because of the large populations in these regions, the chances are that most people in the world live in countries that are affected in some way by religious hostility.

Religious freedom is a human right, and is reinforced by UN conventions, notably the International Covenant on Civil and Political Rights (ICCPR) which most countries have ratified. Even those that have not ratified, such as China, often recognize freedom of religion. In practice, hostilities against religious groups, consisting of intimidation and violence, can arise in societies where there are religious tensions, often where government restrictions are in place, but also in countries where freedom of religion is recognized in law. Government restrictions on religion exist in about one-third of the world's countries, among them some of the world's most populous. These are countries where social hostilities involving religion are also high. They include Egypt, Indonesia, Pakistan, Russia, Burma, China and India. Overall, 76% of the world's population live in places where social hostilities involving religion and government restrictions on religion are high (Pew Research Center, 2014). Also of concern is the rise in incidents of abuse against religious minorities in society, which occur in 47% of the world's countries. An example is Muslim attacks on Christian-owned businesses in Egypt in 2013.

Religions with the largest following globally are shown in Figure 3.3. The two major religions are Christianity and Islam (whose adherents are called Muslims). Both are 'monotheistic', that is, believing in one God, in contrast to polytheistic religion such as Hinduism, in which there is a panoply of gods. Christianity and Islam are both 'proselytizing religions', which means that they deliberately aim to expand numbers and convert new followers. Both are organized religions. Folk religions, including indigenous religions and traditional African religions, comprise numerous types of religious groupings, often tribal and highly local, lacking the organizational structures of the major religions. They are widespread, their followers numbering 405 million globally, mainly in the Asia-Pacific region, India and Brazil. Over a billion people worldwide, or 16% of the global population, are considered unaffiliated to any particular religion. Nonetheless, many of those in this category believe in a supreme being or spiritual dimension, and many engage in some religious practice, such as occasional religious services. We look at the major organized religions in this section.

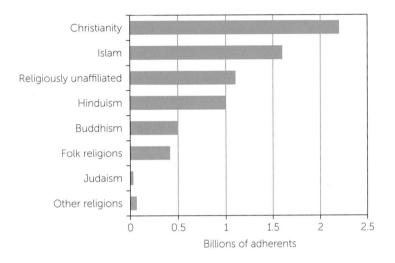

Figure 3.3 Religious affiliation in the world

Source: Data from Pew Research Center (2012) 'The Global Religious Landscape', at www.pewresearch.org.

Christianity

About 2.2 billion people, or 32% of the world's population, identify with Christianity in some way. Through missionary activity, Christianity has spread from Europe and America to all parts of the globe. While all Christians believe in the divinity of Jesus Christ and regard the Bible as authoritative, differences of interpretation have led to a great deal of fragmentation among Christians. The first of Christianity's major splits occurred in the eleventh century, between the Orthodox Church and the Roman Catholic Church.

The second major split in the Christian world occurred in the sixteenth century, when the Protestant Churches separated from Rome. Protestants went on to establish themselves throughout Europe and America, through different denominations, such as Methodists and Baptists. Protestantism is associated with the principle that individual salvation is achievable independently of the institutional Church. The Roman Catholics are now by far the more numerous Christians, numbering about 1.2 billion people (World Christian database, cited in BBC, 2013a). Followers of the Orthodox rites, numbering some 300 million, are still very influential in many countries, such as Greece and Russia.

Recent trends in both Protestantism and Roman Catholicism have been the growth of more evangelical groups outside traditional centres. Numbers of Catholics and Protestants have risen substantially in Latin America and Africa. Christianity, mainly Protestantism, is also on the rise in China, despite government restrictions. There are estimated to be 100 million Christians in China, making them more numerous than members of the Communist Party (Anderlini, 2014).

Islam

Muslims number about 1.15 billion globally, spread among many different countries, ranging from the Middle East and Africa to areas of Russia, and extending as far as China and Malaysia in East Asia. They make up a majority of the population in over thirty countries, and large minorities in others. Of these countries, Iran stands out as an Islamic Republic (see the case study that follows). Most of the other predominantly Muslim countries have secular governments that operate alongside the religious establishment. Through immigration, Muslims now form significant minorities in most European countries. Founded by the prophet Muhammad in the seventh century, Islam unites its followers through shared faith, shared ritual in everyday life, and belief in the words of the Koran, the sacred book. Of the two major branches of Islam, Sunni and Shi-ite, the Sunnis are far more numerous. For the Muslim, religious ritual is part of everyday life, not confined to worship on a particular day of the week. While codes of conduct form part of the values of all religions, Islam is particularly endowed with formal prescriptive guidance in all aspects of life, including social relations, social behaviour, rules for the consumption of food and drink, and the role and appearance of women in society. Religious leaders play an important guiding role, and are influential, particularly in education.

An enterprise culture is fostered in Muslim societies, and economic development is promoted. However, it is forbidden to earn a profit based on the exploitation of others. Interest payments are forbidden, and as a result, banking has developed systems complying with Islamic law. Islamic banking and finance show the adaptability of religious institutions to modern business conditions. Similarly, state courts have grown up in Muslim countries, where traditionally there were only religious courts. State courts can apply both religious law and also western-style commercial law, signifying an accommodation with western legal forms.

Religious practices are important in Islam, as shown by these Muslims praying.

Source: Photodisc.

CASE STUDY ON THE CHANGING BUSINESS ENVIRONMENT

Are social and cultural changes transforming Iran?

Iran has been isolated globally for decades as a result of a series of sanctions that prohibited trade and other dealings with the country and its businesses. The sanctions were imposed by leading western nations, primarily the US. Iran's Islamic revolution of 1979 created a strict religious state, the Islamic Republic, overthrowing the pro-western rule of the Shah. The westernization that had been occurring under the deposed Shah was abruptly halted, and morality police imposed strict Islamic rule. The system operates under the ultimate authority of the supreme leader. An elected president presides over the political system, under the oversight of the supreme leader. Iran's Muslims are Shia Muslims, who are generally perceived as more moderate in their religious practices than the Sunni Muslims that predominate in Arab states.

There are many in Iranian society who remain deeply conservative and feel that Islamic rule has been a good force against the negative influences of westernization. But these Iranians are now becoming less in evidence. Tensions between the religious establishment and groups in society that want more freedom have been ongoing, at times erupting into violent protests. Despite the constraints imposed by the leadership, Iranian society has been continuing to shift to more open ways of thinking. For many years, Iran's nuclear programme, which western countries feared was being pursued for military purposes, remained an obstacle to the country being able to enjoy open trade relations with western countries. After protracted negotiations, an agreement was reached in July 2015 that paved the way for the sanctions to be lifted, with the prospect of free movement of goods. Iran stands to benefit economically, especially from the exports of oil that suffered during the period of sanctions. Businesses that import consumer goods, from cars to televisions, are also hoping for a bonanza. What are the likely impacts on Iranian society?

Iranians have long been keen consumers of western culture, even during the dark period of the sanctions. Computer games, film, satellite television beamed from expatriot TV stations based in Los Angeles have all flourished, especially among the younger generation of Iran's 80-million population. Education, which has been a priority of the Islamic Republic's leadership, has provided one of the brightest prospects for young people to pursue personal goals and independent thinking. This has been especially true for women, for whom education has had an empowering effect, with the number of university-educated women continuing to rise. About 55% of the relevant age group go to university, placing Iran on roughly the same level as western societies. Iran is a young society, with the under-40s accounting for 60% of the population. As women are becoming better educated, they seek greater independence. They are also enjoying much more freedom than the religious leadership would like to see. Among younger women, black Islamic dress is giving way to bright colours and fashionable outfits, while the mandatory headscarf (the hijab) is becoming less prominent and worn further back on the head. Interest in cosmetics, hairstyles and fashion accessories is growing, to the horror of religious leaders, but they are becoming resigned to the fact that they can do little to stop these trends.

People are constantly aware of the powers of the morality police, who can step in at any moment. And the state has been highly repressive in stamping out protests, as happened in 2009. However, the new generation of Iranians, born since the Islamic revolution, are pressing for greater freedom. They are much less religious than their leaders, and are keen to assert their individuality. There are restrictions on the internet, and the social media are banned, but there are ways of getting round the bans. The social media have become highly popular among the 20 million Iranians who now own smartphones. This trend is perceived as a threat by the religious leadership, but it is virtually impossible to stop. Government leaders use Twitter, even though it is officially banned.

The election of the moderate political leader, Hassan Rouhani, as president in 2013 was a step forward for those who seek greater freedom and social change. He promised, above all, to negotiate a nuclear deal to end the sanctions. But he also promised better relations generally with western countries, improved access to the internet, and cultural freedom for the press, music and the arts. While he has often been at odds with the religious leadership, he made progress in negotiating the nuclear agreement, although it took two years to achieve. Iranians are impatient for their other freedoms to materialize. When a 30-year-old engineering graduate and her friends were asked how they saw the future for Iran, they replied that the Islamic revolution set them back as a society. She said she believed in reform as the way forward: 'In 2009, we gained a voice .... But we're not looking for revolution – we know revolution gets you nowhere. Only reform takes you forward' (Khalaf, 2015). She added that the priority for most Iranians is economic well-being.

Sources: Khalaf, R. (2015) 'Iran's "Generation Normal", *Financial Times*, 30 May, at www.ft.com; *The Economist* (2014) 'The revolution is over', 1 November, at www.economist.com; Beeman, W. (2015) 'In Iran today, little changes mean a lot', *The World Post*, in partnership with the Huffington Post and the Berggruen Institute, 2 July, at www.huffingtonpost.com; Wilkin, S. and Sharafedin, B. (2015) 'Iran's economy stagnates as shoppers wait for foreign brands', Reuters, 22 September, at www.reuters.com.

Questions for discussion

- In what ways has the changing role of women been important in Iranian society?
- Which of the social and cultural changes mentioned in this case study are the most significant for Iran, and why?
- What are the political implications of the social changes for the future of Iran?
- Professor Beeman, whose article is one of the sources of this case study, is in no doubt that the social changes taking place are transformational: '... the cumulative effect of these behavioural and cultural changes is a transformation of Iranian society ...' Do you agree with him?

The issue of westernization divides Muslims. 'Westernization' refers to a society's adoption of western culture and values, and is associated with processes of modernization, while 'Islamic fundamentalism' refers to maintenance of the supremacy of Islam in all aspects of society. Some militant Islamic fundamentalist groups, mainly Sunnis, have become major destabilizing forces in Middle Eastern countries. They are considered jihadists because of their fundamentalist view of a duty to fight for the supremacy of their version of Islam. Among them is al-Qaida, a loose grouping that is associated with terrorist activities, notably the attack on the World Trade Center in New York in 2001. More recently, the rise of the Islamic State of Iraq and Syria (or ISIS), also referred to as ISIL (the Islamic State of Iraq and the Levant), has become prominent. The Islamic State, as its name suggests, aspires to territorial control, and has made inroads in Syria and Iraq, seeking to overthrow existing social and political structures. It has built up a significant military force. Its brutal tactics have led to condemnation internationally. ISIS views not just western sympathizers and Christians as enemies, but also other Sunni fundamentalist groups, including local Sunni tribes in the regions they target. The growth in extremist religious groups such as ISIS highlights that religious hostilities often come mixed with other social and cultural dimensions, including ethnic divisions. A worrying aspect of the rise of ISIS has been its adept use of social media to spread its influence and recruit new followers.

Asian religions

Asia has been a rich source of some of the world's oldest religions. Hinduism, Buddhism, and Confucianism, among many others, originated in Asia, and still have millions of followers.

Hinduism

Unlike either Christianity or Islam, Hinduism is polytheistic, its believers worshipping many different gods through many different rituals. The sheer diversity of Hinduism is a major feature, despite the fact that geographically Hindus are mostly concentrated in the Indian subcontinent. Hindus make up 80% of the population of India. Hinduism is an ancient religion, older than all other major world religions. In keeping with its ancient origins, Hinduism resembles a folk religion, associated with rural communities and accessible to illiterate as well as literate followers. An important social and economic aspect of Hinduism is the caste system of rigid social stratification. It holds that a person is born into a particular station in society's hierarchy, which is fixed for life. For example, those at the bottom, the 'untouchables' have no prospect of rising out of this group into a higher caste. Numbering an estimated 160 million people, India's untouchables often suffer discrimination. This system, while officially abolished in the modern state, is still a force in Indian society, as is Hinduism itself. The Hindu nationalist party, the Bharatiya Janata Party (BJP), won a decisive victory in 2014. However, the return of a BJP government raised concerns among India's Muslims, who number 172 million people and constitute 14% of the population. The ascendency of Hindu nationalism has also led to fears that media freedom and freedom of expression generally could be curtailed, undermining India's democratic values.

Buddhism

Like Hinduism, Buddhism originated in India, where it has some nine million followers. Buddhism has also been an important religious influence in China and Japan. A feature of the Buddhist heritage in all these countries has been its assimilation with other religions: in Indian temples Buddhism and Hinduism mingle; in Japan, Buddhist temples and Shinto shrines rub shoulders. Buddhism does not recognize the many gods of Hinduism, nor does it subscribe to the caste system. The Buddha's teachings form the basis of the religion. They centre on the 'eight-fold-path' whereby the individual goes through a series of rebirths before reaching *nirvana*. As the Buddha's teachings were never written down, Buddhism split into a number of different schools. The two major ones are the Hinayana, which subscribes to a more ascetic lifestyle, and is followed mainly in Sri Lanka, Thailand, and Burma; and the Mahayana, which is less austere, and is followed in China and Japan. From this latter school arose Ch'an Buddhism, or Zen Buddhism, which became a quite distinctive sect, highly influential in the cultures of both China and Japan. Zen's attraction has been its simplicity and directness, with its emphasis on meditation and rejection of dogmatic teaching. Most Buddhists live in countries where Buddhism is a minority religion. An exception is Burma, but Burma's recent emergence from military rule has given way to a rise in religious and social hostilities, especially involving the suppression of minority groups (Pew Research Center, 2014).

Confucianism

Confucianism is often considered the cornerstone of Asian values. Founded in the fifth century BC by the Chinese philosopher, Confucius, Confucianism is more a set of moral precepts than a religion. Simon Leys, the modern translator of the *Analects of Confucius*, describes it as 'an affirmation of humanist ethics ... the spiritual cornerstone of the most populous and oldest living civilization on earth' (Leys, 1997: xvii). At the heart of Confucianism is the family and 'filial piety', the paramount value of family loyalty. The countries with a strong Confucian heritage – China, Korea and

Japan – have in common the prevalence of family-based social organization. In China, Confucianism was rejected by the communist revolution of 1949, but nationalists fleeing to Taiwan maintained Confucian beliefs, evidenced in temples and religious practices. Confucian heritage links many Asian economies, including Japan, South Korea, Taiwan and Hong Kong, where Confucian values have been adapted to the needs of modernization.

Many religions, including the Asian religions, Christianity and Islam, can be found in China and India, the two largest emerging economies. In both, cultural identity and religion are closely linked. China has long had a tense relationship with Tibet, with its own distinctive culture and Buddhist religion, and central government authorities.

Culture theories

Differences in national values and attitudes have been the subject of considerable research. We consider two main theories here, those of Geert Hofstede and Fons Trompenaars.

Hofstede's cultural dimensions

Hofstede developed a theory of culture which holds that cultural and sociological differences between nations can be categorized and quantified, allowing us to compare national cultures. Hofstede's research, which goes back to the 1970s, was carried out in fifty countries, among IBM employees in each country. An obvious weakness of the research is its reliance solely on IBM employees, who are a special group in themselves, and need not be representative of the countries in which they live. However, his research does yield interesting comparisons between national cultures, and has served as a benchmark for cultural research.

Hofstede distinguishes four cultural dimensions in his initial research. He later added a fifth, although this additional dimension has been queried, as noted below. He uses these dimensions to compare value systems at various levels: in the family, at school, in the workplace, in the state, and in ways of thinking generally. The cultural dimensions are:

1 **Power distance**, or the extent to which members of a society accept a hierarchical or unequal power structure. In large power distance countries, people consider themselves to be inherently unequal, and there is more dependence by subordinates on bosses. The boss is likely to be autocratic or paternalistic in these countries – a situation to which subordinates may respond positively, or negatively. In small power distance countries, people tend to see themselves more as equals. When they occupy subordinate and superior roles in organizations, these situations are just that – roles, not reflecting inherent differences. Organizations in these countries tend to be flatter, with a more consultative style of management. Asian, Latin American and African countries tend to have large power distance, while Northern Europe has relatively small power distance.

2 **Uncertainty avoidance**, or how members of a society cope with the uncertainties of everyday life. High levels of stress and anxiety denote high uncertainty avoidance countries. These cultures tend to be more expressive and emotional than those of low uncertainty avoidance countries. The latter have lower anxiety levels,

but their easy-going exterior may indicate simply greater control of anxiety, not its non-existence. High uncertainty avoidance countries are the Latin American, Latin European and Mediterranean countries, along with Japan and South Korea. Ranking relatively low are other Asian countries and other European countries.

3　*Individualism*, or the extent to which individuals perceive themselves as independent and autonomous beings. At the opposite extreme to individualism is collectivism, in which people see themselves as integrated into 'ingroups'. High individualism scores occurred mainly in the English-speaking countries, while low individualism was prevalent in Latin American and Asian countries. Hofstede remarks that management techniques and training packages, which almost all originate in the individualist countries, are based on cultural assumptions which are out of tune with the more collectivist cultures (Hofstede, 1994).

4　*Masculinity*, or the extent to which a society is inclined towards aggressive and materialistic behaviour. This dimension tends to present stereotyped gender roles. Hofstede associates masculinity with assertiveness, toughness, and an emphasis on money and material things. At the opposite extreme is femininity, which denotes sensitivity, caring, and an emphasis on quality of life. Conflict and competition predominate in more masculine environments, whereas negotiation and compromise predominate in more feminine environments. According to Hofstede's results, the most masculine countries are Japan and Austria, while the most feminine are Sweden, Norway, the Netherlands and Denmark.

5　*Long-term vs. short-term orientation*, or people's time perspectives in their daily lives. Hofstede added this dimension as a result of work by another researcher, Michael Harris Bond, who found different time orientations between western and eastern ways of thinking. Short-term orientation stresses satisfying needs 'here-and-now', and is more characteristic of western cultures, whereas long-term orientation stresses virtuous living through thrift and persistence, and is prevalent in eastern cultures (Hofstede, 1996). Later scholarship suggests that this dimension is problematic, as these two orientations are not polar opposites. Research indicates that both are present in Asian cultures (Fang, 2003). The different methodology underpinning the fifth dimension is also questionable. Unlike the original research based on IBM employees, the fifth dimension was based on surveys of students. For these reasons, the original four dimensions are treated as the key variables in Hofstede's theory.

Hofstede was able to make correlations and group countries together in clusters, as shown in Table 3.2. For countries in Group 1, high power distance combines with low individualism, suggesting that where people depend on ingroups, they also depend on power figures. Conversely, in cultures where people are less dependent on ingroups, shown in Group 2, they are also less dependent on powerful leaders. There are some anomalies, however. France seems to have high individualism, but also medium power distance. Japan seems to be roughly in the middle in both power distance and individualism. Japanese companies are usually depicted as collectivist ingroups, akin to family relationships. This apparent contradiction in the research could reflect the nature of Hofstede's survey sample, which focused on employees of a large American multinational company. However, the anomalies could also reveal a shortcoming of the methodology, which is that the dimensions are all set out along bipolar lines, each dimension expressed in terms of polar opposites. This type of analysis tends to classify cultures in an 'either-or' way: a culture is individualist, or it is collectivist. This rather oversimplifies how people behave. People might behave as

Table 3.2 Ranks of selected countries on four dimensions of national culture, based on research by Hofstede

	Power distance rank	Individualism rank	Masculinity rank	Uncertainty avoidance rank
Group 1 (high PD + low individualism)				
Brazil	14	26–27	27	21–22
Indonesia	8–9	47–48	30–31	41–42
Malaysia	1	36	25–26	46
Mexico	5–6	32	6	18
Group 2 (low PD + high individualism)				
Finland	46	17	47	31–32
Germany	42–44	15	9–10	29
Netherlands	40	4–5	51	35
Sweden	47–48	10–11	53	49–50
UK	42–44	3	9–10	47–48
USA	38	1	15	43
Group 3 (varying patterns)				
France	15–16	10–11	35–36	10–15
Greece	27–28	30	18–19	1
Japan	33	22–23	1	7

Note: Rank: 1 = highest; 53 = lowest

Source of data: Hofstede, G. (1994) *Cultures and Organizations* (London: HarperCollins), various tables.

individualists in some respects, but as collectivists in others (Williamson, 2002). In other words, in many cultures 'both' is more accurate that 'either-or'. This might help to explain why France and Japan show what look like contradictory results.

Trompenaars' theory of relationships

More recent research by Fons Trompenaars also used the individualism/collectivism continuum as a key dimension. Dating from the early 1990s, Trompenaars' research involved giving questionnaires to over 15,000 managers in 28 countries (Trompenaars, 1994). He identified five relationship orientations. These are:

1 ***Universalism vs. Particularism***. In cultures with high universalism, people expect to be valued in accordance with the same criteria and rules that apply to all. The more particularistic cultures value relationships more than formal rules. Western countries such as the UK, Australia and US, Trompenaars found, tend to rate highly in universalism, whereas China rated highly in particularist relationships. Equality of opportunity is associated with a universalist society, in which each person feels more encouraged to pursue personal goals than would be the case in a particularist society (Cullen et al., 2004). Universalism is thus linked to individualism.

2   **Individualism vs. Collectivism**. This relationship mirrors one of Hofstede's four dimensions, but the findings were somewhat different. Trompenaars found Japan to be much further towards the collectivist extreme. On the other hand, Mexico and the Czech Republic, which Hofstede had found to be more collectivist, now tended to individualism. This finding could be explained by the later date of the research data, reflecting the progress of market economies in both regions: the impact of the NAFTA (North American Free Trade Agreement) in the case of Mexico, and the post-communist transition to a market economy in the case of the Czech Republic.

3   **Neutral vs. Emotional**. In a neutral culture, people are less inclined to show their feelings, whereas in an emotional culture, people are more open in showing emotion and expressing their views. In the findings, Japan has the most neutral culture, and Mexico the most emotional.

4   **Specific vs. Diffuse**. In a specific culture there is a clear separation between work and private life. The notion of 'work-life balance' reflects this thinking. In diffuse cultures, 'the whole person is involved in a business relationship' (Trompenaars, 1994: 9). Doing business in these cultures, therefore, involves building relationships, not simply focusing on the business deal in isolation. The US, Australia and the UK are examples of specific cultures, while China is an example of a diffuse culture.

5   **Achievement vs. Ascription**. In an achievement culture, people derive status from their accomplishments and record. In an ascription culture, status is what matters, which could relate to birth, family, gender or age. The US and UK are achievement cultures, whereas China and other Asian cultures are ascription cultures. In business dealings in an Asian context, therefore, the key individual is invariably the person of the highest status.

The research of Trompenaars showed correlations similar to those found by Hofstede. Individualist cultures are associated with high universalism and also high achievement orientation. We find these characteristics in western countries where the individual pursuit of self-interested goals is strong. This view of the individual is at the heart of capitalist economic theory, and also democratic political systems (as discussed in the next two chapters). But it would be an oversimplification to view east-west divergence along bipolar lines. The tendencies of Asian cultures are towards collectivism and high power distance. However, this should be interpreted as a more nuanced view of the individual in society, rather than as a polarized view of the individualist/collectivist dichotomy (Fang, 2003).

Theories regarding clusters of countries with similar cultures contribute to the convergence/divergence debate. While geographic proximity tends to suggest cultural similarities, other aspects of culture, such as language and religion, are also influential. Ronen and Shenkar, who carried out research on cultural clusters in the 1980s, repeated the research two decades later. They found that, despite the march of globalization, cultural divergence remains a reality, as do clusters of cultures identified in their original research (Ronen and Shenkar, 2013). The research of Hofstede and Trompenaars shed new light on the diversity among national cultures, dispelling the assumption that there is 'one best way' of managing and organizing people. International companies had assumed the universal application of management theories, but theories of organization and management have evolved in the era of globalization. Just as standardized products do not suit all markets, organizations cannot be standardized, but must adapt to local social and cultural profiles.

All individualists now?

Individualism was firmly associated with western cultures in Hofstede's analysis, but later research suggests the individualism/collectivism dichotomy is not so clear-cut. How is this relevant to international business?

Organizations and management: cultural dimensions

Organizations have the attributes of culture, but not necessarily those of a single national culture. Organizations evolve as entities in their own right, interacting with differing cultural environments that influence how they are managed and the roles they play in society.

Organizations through cultural lenses

Organizational culture or 'corporate culture', like national culture, focuses on values, norms and behavioural patterns shared by the group, in this case, the organization. Elements of organizational culture include the following:

- Common language and shared terminology
- Norms of behaviour, such as relations between management and employees
- Preferences for formal or informal means of communication within the company and with associated companies
- Dominant values of the organization, such as high product quality and customer orientation
- Degree of empowerment of employees throughout the organization
- Systems of rules that specify dos and don'ts of employee behaviour

The organization, however, unlike the nation, is an artificial creation, and a corporate culture is one that is deliberately fostered among employees, who may have come to the company from a variety of different cultural backgrounds. Companies tend to reflect the national culture of their home country, despite globalization of their operations (Ronen and Shenkar, 2013). However, MNEs take different approaches to organizing and managing activities that span different continents.

Some multinational corporations see a strong corporate culture as a way of unifying the diverse national cultures represented by employees. Others evolve different organizational cultures in different locations, in effect incorporating a multiculturalism within the company. The need to manage cultural diversity may arise through a number of routes: the acquisition of a foreign subsidiary, a merger with another company, or a joint venture. In joint ventures, in particular, the need for co-operation and trust between partners is the key to long-term success.

Bartlett and Ghoshal devised a typology of international companies that highlights the extent of localization and the importance of the firm's own corporate culture. Their four models are as follows (Bartlett and Ghoshal, 1989):

- **The multinational model**, or 'multidomestic' model – This is a highly decentralized model. Subsidiaries are managed as autonomous units, with strategy-making powers for their areas.
- **The international model** – In this model, operations are decentralized and local managers have considerable latitude, but the firm's headquarters formulates overall strategy.

- **The global model** – This model features global strategy and centralized management. This system is a one-size-fits-all approach to both strategy and management. It has proved inflexible in changing markets and ill suited to adapting to diverse consumer tastes.
- **The transnational model** – This model represents a balance between central control and local responsiveness. This is achieved through networks based on supply chain configurations, which can be continually reconfigured to adapt to changing consumer demand.

While globalization might seem to point to the global model, in fact, the transnational has gained ground in recent decades. This is largely because of the balance between globalization and localization that has evolved in supply chains. But with the evolution of supply chains, organization and management have also evolved. We noted in Chapter 2 that MNEs select locations for their comparative advantages, leading to uneven development both within and between countries.

Changing managerial cultures

The global company is typified by a system known as Fordism, derived from the system implemented in the factories of the Ford Motor Company. Its founder, Henry Ford, pioneered the use of the moving assembly line to produce standardized products in large volumes. Formerly, cars were craftsmen-made vehicles: a single craftsman might spend a long time building just one engine. Prices were high, and volumes low. Fordism revolutionized car production, meeting growing consumer demand in America. On the moving assembly line, the production process was broken down into small tasks, each timed down to the second and each performed by a different worker. The worker had no control over the process: the job had become simply one of repeating the same task over and over. This was the key to mass production. It was welcomed by consumers, but was monotonous for workers.

The employer

- Belief that there is one best method for every task
- Methodical breakdown of each task
- Achieve maximum output and efficiency
- Close control of workers

Taylorist scientific management in theory

The employee

- Trained to perform a task in the most efficient way, timed by management
- Viewed as a pair of hands – absence of individual involvement
- Monetary compensation deemed to be sufficient motivation

The firm

- Maximum prosperity
- Cooperative relations between employers and employees

Figure 3.4 Taylorist scientific management

Source: Inspired by Taylor, F. ([1911] 2004) *The Principles of Scientific Management* (New York: Harper and Brothers); ebook published by Project Gutenberg eBooks, 2004.

Ford adopted principles derived from theories of scientific management, devised by Frederick Taylor in the early 1900s, and usually referred to as 'Taylorism' (Taylor, 2004). The main aspects of the theory are shown in Figure 3.4. In a Taylorist system, the worker's task is strictly defined and is part of a production process that is controlled in minute detail (Pruijt, 2000). While there seems to have been no explicit aim on the part of Ford to adopt Taylor's principles, there were clear similarities in practice. Workers had become 'replaceable cogs' in a production machine (Krafcik,

1988: 43). This resulted in greater efficiency, higher production and lower prices for consumers. But for workers on assembly lines, repetitive monotonous work offered little personal satisfaction. All control rested with the management, and workers' tasks were equivalent to tasks done by machine. Paying workers higher wages was seen as a way of compensating them for the absence of any sense of personal involvement in the job. Taylor believed that money was the worker's sole motivation: greater output would lead to greater monetary reward, and this would be sufficient to satisfy workers. Taylor criticized 'sweat-shops', and stressed the importance of workers' health, but mainly in the context of productivity gains (Taylor, 2004). Although the Taylorist vision was one of mutual self-interest between employer and employee, confrontational relations between trade unions and management became associated with Fordist operations. Fordism's inflexibility and lack of innovation also proved to be shortcomings.

Improved manufacturing processes, such as this conveyor belt in a biscuit factory, transformed industrial efficiency, but often to the neglect of the human dimension.

Source: Getty Images/Cultura RF/Array.

Innovations for which Japanese companies, notably Toyota, can take credit brought about a rethinking of mass manufacturing, taking into account the human element. Toyota looked back to the 'minds + hands philosophy of the craftsman era' (Krafcik, 1988: 43). If workers are given responsibilities and a variety of tasks, their working lives would be improved – as would operational quality. Workers were organized into teams, where ideas could be exchanged, and continuous improvement would be facilitated. We would now refer to such innovations as **empowerment**, bringing individual responsibility into the frame. Toyota pioneered systems of **lean production** and **just-in-time (JIT)** supply of components, enabling companies to reduce the huge inventories of stock that had characterized mass manufacturing in the past. Toyota's production system did not totally reject either Fordism or Taylorist principles. It simply adapted them to more flexible production. The firm was able to reduce the time taken to complete each product, while maintaining continuous flow. The Toyota system was also better adapted to satisfying consumer tastes and fostering innovation.

It has been highlighted in Chapter 1 that employees as stakeholders have direct influence on a firm's ability to achieve its goals. There is thus a practical reason for adopting a co-operative approach to employee relations. But the principles associated with Taylorism have retained an attraction in environments of low trust between managers and workers, where tight control is perceived to be needed. The Soviet Union was attracted to Taylorism in its drive to industrialize, but its industrial legacy was one of failing to modernize and innovate. We might not expect this type of system in the modern globalized economy but, in truth, globalization has seen a resurgence in Taylorist management, often in the outsourced manufacturing of products such as electronic gadgets and apparel. Manufacturing has gravitated to developing countries where labour costs are low, as are the skill levels of available workers. Factory owners such as Foxconn run highly regimented factories, demanding long hours and strict discipline. Owners of these outsourcing factories would say that such regimes are necessary in order to fill huge orders at short notice, as demanded by the global companies they supply. But the work is unpleasant, and in areas where other types of jobs are available, factories find it difficult to recruit. Wage rises inevitably follow. The workers in these complexes are in some ways more exploited than those who worked in America's large car factories. Today's electronics and apparel workers, mainly in Asia, tend to be migrants, often from rural regions (see next section in this chapter). They have little voice in the workplace and little access to representation of their interests, unlike the powerful trade unions that existed in Fordism's heyday.

Taylorism is not confined to outsourced manufacturing. Nor is it confined to developing countries. Other types of workers in the global economy work in similarly harsh and dehumanizing conditions. Among them are workers in the warehouses of Amazon, the internet retailing giant, who complain of excessive pressures to achieve continuous flow in fulfilling orders (BBC, 2013b). We might think that all firms now recognize more humane values than Henry Ford saw in workers, but Amazon is closer to some of the harsher aspects of scientific management.

The way I see it ...

'... to work in — and I find it hard to type these words without irony seizure — a "fulfilment centre", is to be a tiny cog in a massive global distribution machine. It's an industrialised process on a truly massive scale, made possible by new technology.'

Carole Cadwalladr, on work in Amazon's warehouse in Swansea, Wales; in *The Observer*, 1 December 2013.

How would Amazon justify its high-pressure, regimented system? Do you agree with the company's approach, and why?

Franchising, which has also flourished in the era of globalization, lends itself to scientific management principles, sometimes referred to as 'McDonaldization'. McDonald's is an example of the global model in Bartlett and Ghoshal's typography. McDonald's traditionally delivers a standardized product that is the same in all of its outlets, no matter where in the world (Pruijt, 2000). McDonald's has been criticized as an employer on numerous grounds, including low pay, sex discrimination, penalizing workers who voice grievances and banning trade union activities (recall the

opening case study). The US has seen manufacturing jobs shift to other (cheaper) countries. As factory jobs disappeared, jobs in services, such as fast-food outlets, have taken their place. Shifting patterns of employment have impacts on society.

Culture of the workplace: have we moved on?

The Fordist factory was not a very pleasant place for workers. What lessons can be learnt from the shortcomings of Fordism?

Changing societies

Societies are constantly changing, some in dramatic ways and others in ways that are scarcely perceptible. Industrialization, which has taken place rapidly in some countries, brings changes in people's livelihoods and style of life, which becomes urbanized as people move from the countryside to cities. Mobility also encompasses the movements of people to other countries, usually for the hope of a better life. Economic development generally brings growing prosperity, improvements in health and longer life expectancy. However, rapid urbanization in the absence of supportive infrastructure and services can result in poorer healthcare and well-being. Moreover, changes such as urbanization and industrialization often have detrimental impacts on social and cultural aspects of people's lives. People wish to make a good living for themselves and their family, but money alone does not lead to well-being. Figure 3.5 sets out the elements that make up the well-being of the person in society.

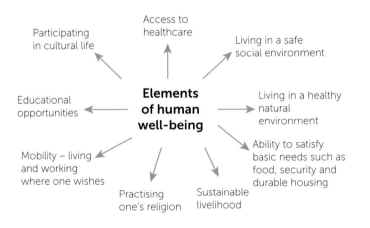

Figure 3.5 Elements of human well-being

As Figure 3.5 shows, well-being is multi-faceted. Each of us wishes to make a living, but a livelihood is something more: it encompasses the capacity – involving both assets and social relations – to achieve a viable living into the future (de Haas, 2010). While these elements centre on the individual person, they also entail responsibilities which rest with the governments and the organizations that interact with governments. For example, the practice of religion and participation in cultural life require an environment where there is freedom for multiple cultures and religions to exist, without fear of suppression or harassment. Education, healthcare and a healthy natural environment are desired by everyone, but these are more often aspirations than reality. Governments bear much responsibility for policies and programmes, through legislation and public spending. Businesses also bear responsibilities. They are creators of economic activity that hold out the potential for the prosperity of whole societies. They offer employment and provide the services communities need. However, these activities can be instrumental in negative ways too. Negative impacts are environmental degradation, pollution, utilization of water and displacement of people and wildlife. In this section, we look at key trends in changing societies, highlighting their impacts.

Migration

The urge to move to 'greener pastures' is not a recent phenomenon. People have been on the move throughout history. These movements are broadly referred to as migration. Migration can be internal, from one place to another within the same country, or it can be international, from one country to another. Many people simply set out on their own, but many, especially people in poor countries, are more likely to turn to agents who organize groups of migrant workers for particular locations. In these instances, migration is voluntary. However, much migration is not. People are sometimes compelled to leave their homes because of circumstances, or find themselves in a grey area between moving voluntarily and being forced to move. People can be driven out of their homes by fear for their security, such as religious persecution or the eruption of violent conflict. Forced migration can occur following natural disasters, when people move en masse away from the disaster zone. We tend to think in terms of 'immigrants' referring to people coming into a country, and 'emigrants', referring to people leaving a country. These terms suggest a straightforward permanent move, but migration in today's world is more complex than these terms imply, and also more nuanced.

Much migration is temporary, or intended to be temporary. A person might envisage a temporary stay in another country, but decide to stay there. If people are forced to leave their homes due to conflict or disaster, they probably wish to return if it is feasible. Although globalization has brought greater mobility, people seeking work abroad find there can be steep administrative hurdles in cross-border movements. Many people on the move lack the official documents required to work in another country. For those who are lucky and find work in the new country, the move can be fruitful. Migrants typically send money in the form of remittances back to relatives in their home country, where they retain family ties. New and old 'homes' can be seen as complementary to each other, as part of a whole family's 'household livelihood strategy' (de Haas, 2010: 244). 'Push' and 'pull' factors are involved, and tend to operate in tandem. Economic opportunities are among the main pull factors (IOM, 2013). Moving from a low-income country to a high-income one is the traditional route taken by migrants looking for employment and a better life. However, many migrants fall outside this pattern, sometimes moving from one high-income country to another in hope of better economic opportunities, or from one low-income country to another for similar reasons. 'Push' factors include poor or precarious livelihoods, poor healthcare and low levels of well-being. Climate change is now a major push factor in regions prone to drought or flooding. These factors all pertain in developing countries, such as those in Asia and Africa. A household in a poor country might well decide that, if a member can secure work elsewhere, it will add another source of valuable income.

For migrants, life can be a struggle, both to get to the new country and to carve out a life there. The well-being of migrants comes well down the list of priorities in the political perspectives of many of the world's governments, even though migrants fill vital roles in their societies. Those who flee their home countries out of desperation often suffer the most. The deaths that occur among desperate people who attempt precarious journeys, across militarized borders or in small boats, remind us of the human suffering that drives people to leave intolerable situations in their home countries. Migrant labour is in demand in many countries, mostly in unskilled work. The oil-rich economies of the Middle East rely almost entirely on migrants in their construction industries. These workers are mainly from India, Nepal, Pakistan and Bangladesh. Organizations of middlemen play a significant role in the migrant labour market, which is now globalized. While legal in theory, there is a fine line between legitimate employment agencies and people traffickers. An inhabitant of Nepal, for example, will turn to agency middlemen for work abroad, such as building work in the Middle East. They will probably demand large payments, often taking the form of long-term debts that become a burden on the worker and his family. These workers are in a vulnerable position from both the viewpoint of the poor conditions they endure, and their subservient status in relation to the firms that control their movements. As globalization has reached deeper into developing economies, human rights and well-being of migrants have become global issues.

Also of major concern is forced migration, which occurs when people are displaced in large numbers due to conflict or disaster. Natural disasters include floods, hurricanes, tsunamis and earthquakes. Other types of disaster bear the stamp of human intervention, and can be equally devastating. They include environmental disasters, famine and chemical spills that can involve the displacement of whole communities. Forced migration is on the rise. It affected more than 73 million people in 2013 (World Bank, 2014). Of these, 51 million were displaced by conflict. Roots of conflict can be political, religious, ethnic, communal or simply criminal activity. Violent conflict is most likely to flare in countries where there are tensions between ethnic and religious groups, political insurgency, terrorist activity and organized crime. Some of these causes overlap, such as terrorism by extremist religious groups.

People affected by conflict might move to other areas of their country, but when a whole country descends into violent conflict, people are driven to other states. In 2013, over 16 million refugees entered other countries, many of which were already sheltering large numbers of refugees (World Bank, 2014). Whereas in the 1980s, most refugees were located in developed countries, by 2013, 86% of the world's refugees were seeking haven in developing countries. Afghanistan, Syria, Sudan and Somalia are some of the main countries from which people flee conflicts, and the main host countries include Pakistan, Iran, Lebanon and Jordan. Basic humanitarian needs are a priority for these refugees, but in host countries that are already struggling to provide adequate infrastructure and health services, the tasks are all the more challenging, placing strains on the receiving countries. More than a million refugees arrived in Europe in 2015, nearly half of them from Syria (IOM, 2016). UN agencies help to provide humanitarian aid, as do non-governmental organizations (NGOs). But these bodies cannot resolve the underlying conflicts that lead to forced migration. There are about 3 million Afghan refugees living in Pakistan, some of these having been there since the Russian invasion of their country in 1979. The numbers have grown over the years, most recently during Afghanistan's civil war. These refugees have only limited rights in Pakistan, but for many, this is the only 'home' they have known. Their presence is a source of tension in Pakistan society and is also a challenge for the country's fragile government.

The way I see it ...

'Everything is done through favouritism. We Afghans seem to be worthless. What is it that we have done wrong? We are also humans. Our country is burning in the fire of war.'

An Afghan refugee who landed on a Greek island, having travelled from an Afghan province where ISIS is active. He is complaining that the Greek officials are giving priority to Syrian refugees fleeing from civil war. His comments are reported in *The Guardian*, 21 November 2015.

What are the dilemmas posed by refugees like this Afghan? What should be done from a humanitarian point of view?

Historically, many countries have welcomed immigrant workers, particularly during periods of rapid growth. Post-war economic development in France and Germany depended in large measure on immigrant labour. In Germany, many of these immigrants came as 'guest-workers', on short-term contracts. Millions of these workers, a large proportion of whom were Turkish, stayed on and have become settled. Indeed, during Turkey's recent economic development, its government has sought to encourage Turks who had settled in Germany to return to Turkey to impart valuable know-how they had gained from their years in Germany. The resource-rich countries of the Persian Gulf region, including Kuwait, Dubai, Qatar and Saudi Arabia, depend on migrant workers. At the higher levels, many are skilled and professional people offering vital services in these economies. These 'ex-patriots' see this work as temporary, and, in any case, are not legally entitled to remain indefinitely in these countries. At the opposite end of the spectrum are the migrant labourers on construction sites, mentioned above. These workers are also crucial to these countries' development plans. The many global companies who drive investment in these countries also benefit.

Migration impacts on both the sending and receiving countries. Professional people from developing countries, such as scientists, doctors and engineers, have long travelled to industrialized regions for self-betterment. Their departures can be seen as a 'brain drain' which deprives their home countries of their skills, but their presence is welcomed in host countries. Unskilled migrants are a different story. They tend to take jobs that citizens of developed countries are disinclined to do. Agricultural work, construction work and domestic service are typical jobs filled by migrants. These people pose a number of issues for both government and society in recipient countries. Employment, housing, healthcare and education are some of the main areas where they have particular needs, often because of language difficulties. However, governments can be reluctant to provide them the services that local people are entitled to. Indeed, in many countries, immigration has become a political issue: local people sometimes take exception to the idea of immigrants taking jobs and using services such as the health services.

Remittances sent by workers back to their home countries contribute to the economies of many developing countries, as shown in Figure 3.6. The money sent by

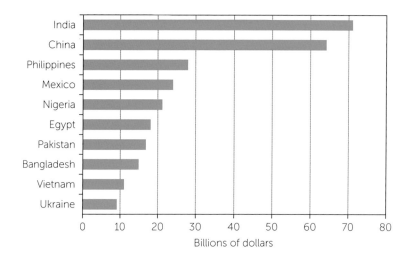

Figure 3.6 Countries in receipt of the largest remittances from migrant workers

Source: Data from World Bank (2014) *Migration and Development Brief,* 6 October, p. 5, at www. worldbank.org

each might seem to be too small to matter, but, cumulatively, these sums add up to improving life in villages, larger communities and ultimately the whole society. Total remittances to developing countries amounted to $400 billion in 2013. India and China are the leaders in the amount remitted by their citizens from working abroad. There are estimated to be 14 million Indians born in India but living abroad. Among the most illustrious are the CEOs noted earlier in this chapter, but Indians work abroad in a huge variety of jobs. The $71 billion in remittances flowing into India is still only 3.7% of India's GDP, while the much lower remittances sent back to small countries are more important in the overall economy, amounting to 29% of Nepal's GDP, for example. While these flows are a help, there are inherent limitations in the effects of remittances on achieving development goals. Ultimately, government direction and funding programmes are required to build the infrastructure, provide health services and promote universal education that is needed to achieve sustainable development.

Globalization's impacts: migrant workers

Who should bear responsibilities for the well-being of foreign migrant workers in low-skilled employment, such as construction?

Urbanization

Migration from rural areas to cities was commonplace long before industrialization. People were 'on the move' not just for economic motives, but for social and cultural reasons as well. The process by which a growing proportion of the population shifts to the cities is termed urbanization. In 1950, 70% of the world's people lived in rural areas, and the urban population globally numbered 746 million people. By 2014, that number had risen to 3.9 billion. More than half the world's people now live in urban environments. However, there are stark contrasts between developed and developing regions. Developed countries in North America and Europe are now over 75% urban, while developing countries in Africa and Asia are still predominantly rural, home to most of the world's rural inhabitants, who number 3.9 billion people. In Asia, 48% of people live in cities, and in Africa, the percentage is 40%.

Urbanization is generally associated with industrialization and economic development. This was the pattern of urbanization in today's developed countries, and it has been the pattern in China, which was transformed from being only 26% urban in 1990 to 54% urban in 2014 (UNDESA, 2014). In China, urbanization and economic development have contributed to poverty reduction and improved well-being, including better healthcare. However, rapid urbanization can be detrimental to sustainable development. China's urban residents suffer from poor air quality, which impacts on long-term health. Sustainable development should include economic development, social development and environmental protection (UNDESA, 2014). However, China's development model has focused mainly on economic development driven by industrialization.

The urbanization taking place in poorer developing countries also gives rise to concern in terms of sustainable development. But there are big variations across Africa, as shown in Figure 3.7. Algeria, in Northern Africa, is 70% urban, while Ethiopia in Eastern Africa is only 19% urban. As the figure shows, Eastern Africa, which is the least urbanized and least-developed African region, is experiencing the most rapid urbanization.

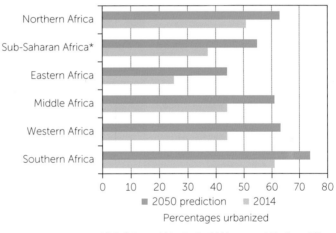

Figure 3.7 Urbanization in Africa

Source: Created using data from UNDESA (UN Department of Economic and Social Affairs) (2014) *World Urbanization Prospects: The 2014 Revision* (New York: UN), Table I, p. 20. Reprinted with the permission of the United Nations.

*Sub-Saharan Africa is all of Africa except Northern Africa

African economic growth has been impressive in recent years, but the prevalence of urban poverty has led to a questioning of the assumption that growing cities would lead to economic growth and human development going hand in hand (UN Habitat, 2014). In Africa, people tend to move to the cities from poor regions because rural livelihoods cease to be viable. This can be because of drought, environmental degradation or simply because precarious agriculture can no longer support their families. The movement of rural inhabitants to cities in the least-developed countries creates huge challenges. These cities struggle to provide infrastructure, safe water, electricity and other services. Effects of climate change and resource scarcity are issues in these fast-growing urban areas. Newcomers often concentrate in sprawling slums. Housing shortages, health risks and unemployment create urban insecurity. In particular, the levels of youth unemployment in the slums raise concerns over security. At the opposite end of the housing spectrum, recent urbanization has seen new urban areas springing up outside the main cities, many designed as residential areas for the growing number of affluent people, benefiting from Africa's globalized economic and financial activities. However, these serve to highlight the inequality associated with urbanization on the continent, where the affluent are improving their lifestyles and the slums suffer from high unemployment. Whereas forward-looking policies could be directed towards urban job creation and sustainable development, African cities tend to suffer from weak governance, allowing situations to worsen (UN Habitat, 2014).

The world's largest cities were once concentrated in the developed world, but now cities in the emerging economies predominate in the top ten largest cities, as shown in Figure 3.8. Five of the ten are in the BRIC countries. Only three cities – Tokyo, Osaka and New York – are in developed countries. Most of the world's urban population live in Asian cities, accounting for six of the top ten. Two are in China and two in India. These are countries where populations are still predominantly rural, and rapid urbanization is taking place. The challenges for cities to develop sustainably now focus particularly on cities in the emerging and developing world.

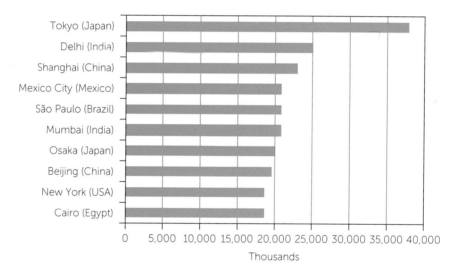

Figure 3.8 The world's top ten most populous cities

Source: Created using data from UNDESA (UN Department of Economic and Social Affairs) (2014) *World Urbanization Prospects: the 2014 revision* (New York: UN), Table II, p. 26. Reprinted with the permission of the United Nations.

Urbanization in the developing world

In urban areas, it should be easier than in the countryside to deliver health services, organize education and build durable housing. But urbanization in developing countries often turns into slums. What role can businesses play in improving living conditions?

Changing populations and ageing societies

The world's population in 2013 stood at 7.2 billion, 5.9 billion of whom live in developing countries. Most of the population growth now occurring is in developing countries (see Figure 3.9). Two countries – China and India – are home to 37% of the world's population. This percentage is likely to decrease slightly in future years, mainly because the most rapid population growth is occurring in the least-developed countries. These societies are becoming more urbanized, and they are also younger than societies in developed regions.

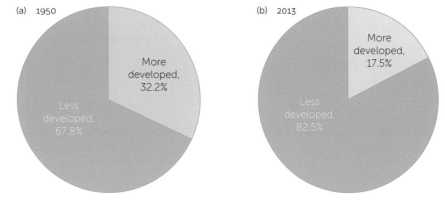

Figure 3.9 World population in more developed and less developed regions: 1950 and 2013

Source: Created using data from UN Population Division (2013) *World Population Prospects: The 2012 Revision* (New York: UN), Table 1.2, p. 2. Reprinted with the permission of the United Nations.

The most common way in which populations grow is increase in the number of births over deaths. Populations change constantly. They change naturally over time and across space. **Demographic change** refers to these population changes. They include births, deaths and migration. Demographic changes, while they take place at a slow pace, can have profound long-term effects on societies. **Ageing** is the rising proportion of older people in the total population. Improved health and living conditions result in lower mortality rates and greater life expectancy than earlier generations. Other important factors are declining fertility rates and improvements in the treatment of diseases. These processes differ between developed and developing regions of the world. Developing countries have younger populations than those in the developed countries. In developing regions, children under the age of 15 form 28% of the population, and young people aged 15–24 account for a further 18%. These percentages are at an all-time high, posing challenges for these countries in terms of needs for education and jobs (UN Population Division, 2013). Perhaps more alarming is the fact that the percentages for the least-developed countries are even bigger: 40% of their populations are under the age of 15, and another 20% in the 15–24 age group. To put these percentages in perspective, the equivalent figures for developed regions are 16% and 12%. Ageing populations have been a trend in developed countries for many years. Here, people aged 60 or over form nearly 23% of the population (as shown in Table 3.3), and that figure is predicted to rise to 32% by 2050. But while the developed countries have the greatest proportion of older people, the developing countries have the largest numbers (see Table 3.3).

Developing countries are now rapidly ageing, and the rates at which the older populations are growing are much higher than in the developed regions. The number of people aged 60 or over is expected to triple by 2100, rising from 841 million in 2013, to 2 billion in 2050 and to 3 billion by 2100 (UN Population Division, 2013). By that time, the 60+ age group will be 34% of the world's population. Nearly 80% of these older people will be living in the developing countries. Already, two-thirds of the world's older people live in developing countries. As Table 3.3 shows, the number of people aged 60 or over in the developing regions of the world is nearly double the number in the developed regions, but they are a much smaller share of the population – for the time being.

Governments in developed countries have long been aware of the challenges posed by ageing populations. And their counterparts in developing countries are now facing similar challenges, only with considerably larger populations of retired

Table 3.3 Where the world's older people live, 2013

	People aged 60 or over	People aged 65 or over	People aged 80 or over
More-developed regions	287,020 (22.9%)	211,052 (16.8%)	56,879 (4.5%)
Less-developed regions	533,608 (9.4%)	354,409 (6.1%)	63,321 (1.1%)
Least-developed regions	48,580 (5.4%)	31,654 (3.5%)	4,515 (0.5%)

Note: Numbers of older people in thousands, followed by the percentage of the total population in that region

Source: Created using data from UN Population Division (of the Department of Economic and Social Affairs) (2013) *World Population Ageing* (New York: UN), Table A, III, 1, p. 90, and Table A, III, 2, p. 91. Reprinted with the permission of the United Nations.

people. Many older people continue to work, either out of financial necessity or simply to keep active. This is particularly true in developing countries, where state support schemes are fewer than in developed countries. Still, the numbers of older men in the workforce is declining in developing countries, while it is rising in developed regions, partly because of rises in the statutory retirement age and partly because of financial need. While it is good news that people are increasingly fit and able to work for longer, it is a concern if the numbers of older people living in poverty are rising. Whereas levels of old-age poverty are roughly similar to those in the rest of the population in developing countries, there are variations among countries. In sub-Saharan Africa, old-age poverty is higher than in the general population, largely due to factors such as the incidence of HIV-AIDS, conflicts, shocks such as droughts and rapid urbanization. Old-age poverty is generally higher than poverty in other age groups in the richer countries of the OECD (UN Population Division, 2013). However, there are variations among OECD countries. In the UK, the level of old-age poverty is roughly similar to the rate of poverty in the overall population. In some countries, such as the Netherlands, France, Italy and Norway, old-age poverty is less than the national average. By contrast, the incidence of old-age poverty in the US, Australia and New Zealand is higher than the national average, largely because of rising average incomes in these countries. For governments, this is a growing concern.

Developed countries have varying state-supported pension schemes. Where pensions are funded simply as part of public spending, as in Italy, there is a risk of financial unsustainability as pressures on public spending mount. Where governments aim to fund pensions through investment and contributions by earners, as in the UK, there are risks that pensions will be inadequate to maintain well-being (OECD, 2013). Also coming into the equation are the savings and assets of older people. Healthcare expenses invariably rise for older people, placing strains on health systems, and funding healthcare for ageing populations is a sensitive issue for governments. They are entrusted with ensuring intergenerational fairness among all in society. While we tend to think of older people mainly as recipients of transfers from public support schemes, in fact, they are net givers in terms of their own families, who can benefit from their accumulated savings and assets such as houses (UN Population Division, 2013). And these private transfers often continue into the adult lives of their children. In extreme circumstances, as has happened in Spain's recent recession, an elderly parent might have to support a whole family from meagre pension income, including unemployed children, their spouses and grandchildren. This desperate situation gives rise to numerous challenges for policymakers, not just in the area of pension provision. It reminds us that well-being in old age is part of the overall picture of human development that an economy should be directed towards sustaining.

Old at 50?

Marketing departments tend to feature younger people in their advertisements, as a youthful image is presumed to be better for selling a product than a picture of someone over the age of 50. To what extent are they contributing to 'ageism' in society?

Challenges and responsibilities in the socio-cultural environment

Whereas international businesses have long focused their attention on the more developed regions of the world, they now set their strategic sights more and more towards developing countries, extending globalization's reach. Along with this expansion and deepening of engagement has come greater involvement in a wide range of cultures and societies. These emerging countries are not simply less industrialized versions of the developed countries most are familiar with. They present whole new sets of challenges: social unease among diverse ethnic, cultural and religious groups; weak governmental institutions; widespread poverty; low levels of human development; and vulnerabilities to adverse social and economic impacts of climate change. Businesses can offer much in terms of investment, jobs, improved technology and improved infrastructure. But they also bear much responsibility for the more problematic impacts their activities have in society. A new factory, for example, can contribute jobs and skills, but if it displaces a whole community or pollutes a river that a community relies on, its social impacts can outweigh the benefits. It might be argued that these are matters for governments, but the governance of foreign direct investment (FDI) projects involves a range of stakeholders: governments, communities and companies. For economic development to be directed more broadly towards human development, the challenges of social cohesion and meeting human needs (see Figure 2.7) fall on all the stakeholders.

This chapter has highlighted the changes taking place in societies globally. They include rapid industrialization, rapid urbanization, impacts of migration and ageing populations. These changes offer opportunities to improve human well-being in many ways. New industries bring employment; urban environments are generally able to provide better services; and migrant workers are grateful for jobs. Ageing populations, too, offer opportunities. They form a growing market for products and services directed towards their needs and desires. Many older people continue to remain active economically. However, in the workplace, older workers are often perceived as a liability, as organizations opt to hire and promote younger people (Altmann, 2015). This is especially the case for older women. The right not to be discriminated against on grounds of gender has long been recognized as a human right, and is established in the laws of most countries. However, discrimination on grounds of age, or 'ageism', is commonly tolerated. There are numerous business activities that can benefit from the experience that older workers can contribute, and businesses could potentially benefit greatly from tapping this growing source of talent (Altmann, 2015).

Much of the employment associated with globalized industries has brought exploitation to workers, many of them migrants. Unregulated urban sprawl, as happens in many of the least-developed countries, is detrimental to health and well-being. Rapid urbanization, with its potential for unrest, has become one of the major challenges faced by governments in developing regions. These challenges are not insoluble. Governments engaging with companies can plan business activities that provide employment, build social cohesion and serve human needs. However, such a vision requires businesses to focus on social responsibilities rather than short-term profits. The good news for such businesses is that socially responsible projects are more sustainable, and generate greater value in the long term.

Conclusions

The cultural environment presents a paradox for international business. While globalization has extended supply chains that knit businesses ever closer together, differing cultural outlooks among companies and societies remain potent. Research on cross-cultural management is not likely to become redundant anytime soon. On the other hand, the cultural dimensions highlighted by Hofstede now seen to be more blurred than his research suggested. The individualism/collectivism dichotomy, which is appealingly simple, no longer seems to reflect the way cultures evolve and people behave. All of us, whatever our cultural background, have individualist leanings to some extent, while at the same time desiring to be part of something bigger – and also more meaningful – in our lives. All of us also wish for improved well-being in our lives. But in the many diverse societies that make up the global economy, cultural differences remain potent, as do variations in human well-being.

The internationalized business seeks to satisfy the needs and wants of consumers in all its markets. Its managers dream of a global product that appeals universally, but they know that sales depend on attracting and pleasing consumers in different markets. The goal of success in all markets is brought closer by globalization. The global company has become adept at maximizing location advantages at every stage in a supply chain. Efficiency gains are maximized, and costs are minimized, typically through manufacturing in developing countries and choosing other locations for their specific advantages in other respects. It is in the supply chain that the negative impacts of globalized production on societies comes into focus. Poor working conditions, exploited labour, poor living conditions for migrant workers and displacement of families are commonplace in global production. Governments have been slow to react to these conditions, largely because they are keen to attract global companies. Companies have long recognized the importance of consumers as stakeholders, but have tended to see workers in terms of costs of production, rather than as stakeholders whose well-being matters in terms of achieving corporate goals. This is now changing, as a critical focus on the impacts of globalization becomes part of mainstream thinking in international business.

References

Altmann, R. (2015) *A New Vision for Older Workers: Retain, Retrain, Recruit*, independent report published by the UK Department for Work and Pensions, at www.gov.uk/government/publications

Anderlini, J. (2014) 'China's other leader', *Financial Times*, 9 November, at www.ft.com.

Bartlett, C.A. and Ghoshal, S. (1989) *Managing Across Borders: The Transnational Solution* (Cambridge, MA: Harvard Business School Press).

BBC (2013a) 'How many Roman Catholics are there in the world?', BBC News, 14 March, at www.bbc.com/news

BBC (2013b) 'Amazon workers face increased risk of mental illness', BBC News, 25 November, at www.bbc.com/news

Berger, P. (2002) 'The cultural dynamics of globalization', in Berger, P. and Huntington, S. (eds) *Many Globalizations* (New York: OUP), pp. 1–16.

Bird, A. and Fang, T. (2009) 'Cross cultural management in an age of globalization', *International Journal of Cross Cultural Management*, 92(2): 139–143.

Bird, A. and Stevens, M. (2003) 'Toward an emergent global culture and the effects of globalization on obsolescing national cultures', *Journal of International Management*, 9: 395–407.

Cullen, J., Parboteeah, K.P. and Hoegl, M. (2004) 'Cross-national differences in managers' willingness to justify ethically suspect behaviors: a test of institutional anomie theory', *Academy of Management Journal*, 47(3): 411–421.

de Haas, H. (2010) 'Migration and development: a theoretical perspective', *International Migration Review*, 44(1): 227–264.

Fang, T. (2003) 'A critique of Hofstede's fifth national culture dimension', *International Journal of Cross Cultural Management*, 33(3): 347–368.

Hall, E.T. (1976) *Beyond Culture* (New York: Doubleday).

Hofstede, G. (1994) *Cultures and Organizations: Software of the Mind* (London: HarperCollins).

Hofstede, G. (1996) 'Images of Europe, past, present and future', in Joynt, P. and Warner, M. (eds) *Managing Across Cultures: Issues and Perspectives* (London: International Thomson Business Press), pp. 147–165.

Inglehart, R. and Baker, W. (2000) 'Modernization, culture change and the persistence of national values', *American Sociological Review*, 65: 19–51.

IOM (International Organization for Migration) (2013) 'World Migration Report 2013', at www.iom.int

IOM (International Organization for Migration) (2016) 'Migration Flows – Europe', at www.iom.int

Krafcik, J. (1988) 'Triumph of the lean production system', *Sloan Management Review*, 30(1): 41–52.

Leys, S. (trans. and ed.) (1997) *Analects of Confucius* (New York: W.W. Norton & Co.).

OECD (2013) *Pensions at a Glance 2013: OECD and G20 Indicators*, OECD Publishing at www.oecd.org/publications/oecd-pensions-at-a-glance

Pew Research Center (2014) 'Religious hostilities reach six-year high: Report', 14 January, at www.pewresearch.org

Pruijt, H. (2000) 'Repainting, modifying, smashing Taylorism', *Journal of Organizational Change Management*, 13(5): 1–11.

Ralston, D., Holt, D., Terpstra, R. and Kai-Cheng, Y. (2008) 'The impact of national culture and economic ideology on managerial work values: a study of the United States, Russia, Japan and China', *Journal of International Business Studies*, 39: 8–26.

Ronen, S. and Shenkar, O. (2013) 'Mapping world cultures: cluster formation, sources and implications', *Journal of International Business Studies*, 44: 867–897.

Stahl, G. and Tung, R. (2014) 'Towards a more balanced treatment of culture in international business studies: the need for positive cross-cultural scholarship, *Journal of International Business Studies*, 1–24.

Taylor, F. ([1911] 2004) *The Principles of Scientific Management* (New York: Harper and Brothers).

Trompenaars, F. (1994) *Riding the Waves of Culture* (New York: Irwin).

UN Broadband Commission (2012) 'The state of broadband 2012 report', at www.un.org

UNDESA (UN Department of Economic and Social Affairs) (2013) World Population Ageing (New York: UN).

UNDESA (UN Department of Economic and Social Affairs) (2014) *World Urbanization Prospects: The 2014 Revision*, at esa.un.org/unpd/wup/

UN Habitat (UN Human Settlements Programme) (2014) 'African urbanization', at unhabitat.org

UNIASG (Inter-Agency Support Group on Indigenous Peoples' Issues) (2014) 'Thematic Paper, Indigenous peoples' access to decent work and social protection', June, at www.un.org

UN Population Division (of the UN Department of Economic and Social Affairs) (2013) *World Population Prospects: The 2012 Revision* (New York: UN).

Williamson, D. (2002) 'Forward from a critique of Hofstede's model of national culture', *Human Relations*, 55(11): 1373–1395.

World Bank (2014) 'Migration and Development Brief', 6 October, at www.worldbank.org

☞ Multiple choice questions

Go to the companion website: www.palgravehighered.com/morrison-gbe-4e to take a quick multiple choice quiz on what you have read in this chapter.

⑦ Review questions

1 What are the main elements of culture?
2 Explain the essential aspects of national culture. How can they change over time?
3 What is 'cultural distance', and how does it affect the MNE?
4 What are the differences between a 'high-context' and 'low-context' language? Why do these differences matter in business negotiations?
5 What are the divergent currents in predominantly Muslim societies?
6 What has been the impact of Confucianism on firms in Asia, including their organizations and ways of doing business?
7 What are the essential cultural dimensions described by Hofstede in his research?
8 How do the rankings of national culture produced by Hofstede shed light on international management practices in different locations?
9 List the main elements of organizational culture. Why is 'culture clash' a common problem in mergers between large companies?
10 What is Taylorist scientific management? In what ways is it continuing to be influential?
11 What are the challenges posed by ageing populations in developed countries, from government and business perspectives?
12 Why has international migration become an increasingly important social issue?

13 What ethical issues arise for migrant workers who travel to other countries for work?

14 What are the problems associated with urbanization, and why have they become most acute in developing countries?

15 What are the challenges posed by ageing populations, and what are the responsibilities of governments and businesses in adjusting to them?

✓ Assignments

1 Assess the social and cultural aspects of the use of migrant labour for manufacturing companies involved in global supply chains.

2 Assess the impact of demographic changes on the business environment in (a) advanced economies, and (b) developing economies.

📖 Further reading

Bartlett, C., Ghoshal, S. and Beamish, P. (2007) *Transnational Management: Text, Cases and Readings in Cross-border Management*, 5th edn (Boston, MA: McGraw-Hill).

Berger, P. and Huntington, S. (eds) (2002) *Many Globalizations: Cultural Diversity in the Contemporary World* (Oxford: Oxford University Press).

Hofstede, G. (1994) *Cultures and Organizations: Software of the Mind* (London, HarperCollins).

Pugh, D. and Hickson, D. (2007) *Writers on Organizations*, 6th edn (London: Penguin).

Schein, E.J. (2010) *Organizational Culture and Leadership*, 4th edn (London: John Wiley & Sons).

Schneider, S., Stahl, G. and Barsoux, J.L. (2014) *Managing Across Cultures*, 3rd edn (Harlow: Pearson Education).

Thomas, D. (2014) *Cross-cultural Management: Essential Concepts*, 3rd edn (London: Sage).

Trompenaars, F. (1994) *Riding the Waves of Culture* (New York: Irwin).

Usunier, J.-C. and Lee, J. (2009) *Marketing Across Cultures*, 5th edn (London: Financial Times Prentice Hall).

🌐 **Visit the companion website at** www.palgravehighered.com/morrison-gbe-4e **for further learning and teaching resources.**

Domestic workers, lesser people

Domestic work provides vital employment worldwide, but these workers are often exploited and poorly treated.
Source: iStock.com/GeorgePeters.

Domestic service tends to conjure up images of maids in period dramas such as portrayed in the popular UK TV show *Downton Abbey*. But the reality in today's world is far removed from costume drama. The world's estimated 53 million domestic workers are some of the most exploited, vulnerable and ill-treated of all workers. Yet their plight generally goes unnoticed. Hidden behind the closed doors of private homes, their lives revolve mainly around cleaning, cooking, laundry and looking after children. Long hours and harsh conditions usually come with the job, and employers have little fear that they will be held to account. About 90% of domestic workers are outside the protection of national labour laws. This means that they have no set hours, no written contract of employment and no guarantee of rest days. Making matters worse, in the privacy of a domestic environment, these workers often suffer verbal and physical abuse, but have nowhere to turn for help.

Domestic workers make up 4% of the global workforce in total, and 7.5% of global female employment. Human rights organizations and the ILO

(International Labour Organization) have been instrumental in drawing attention to these workers. There is an ILO convention on domestic work, dating from 2011, which aims to ensure that domestic workers have the labour rights that other workers have. As of 2015, only 22 countries had ratified this convention. Domestic work is recognized as important economically in national economies. However, the social and cultural environments in which domestic work has become entrenched are resistant to change. Domestic workers are somehow not seen in the same light as employees in factories, but as 'lesser people'.

Domestic work is often carried out by migrant workers. Within countries, women in poor rural areas have long sought domestic work for well-to-do families in cities. This phenomenon is more prevalent in societies with high levels of economic inequality and extremes in social classes. In Mexico, it is common for indigenous women from rural areas to seek domestic work in Mexico City, many of them under the age of 16. For example, one such worker, from Veracruz, came to Mexico City as a 13-year-old, speaking the native language of Otomí and knowing no Spanish. She faced not only the harsh conditions of overwork, but ridicule for speaking her native language. Years later, she is still trapped in this type of work, insecure, isolated from family, not knowing whether she will be paid, and feeling rootless. She has now lost all ability to speak her native language (Lakhani, 2015). Her story is similar to many others. Mexico is home to an estimated 2.3 million such workers. Mexico has signed the ILO convention, but not ratified it. These workers have now attempted to gain some voice by organizing a union, which is seeking social security protection, to provide rights to a basic pension and healthcare.

Globally, millions of workers travel to foreign countries to seek work for rich families. Many come from Asian countries such as the Philippines and Indonesia. High on the list of destinations are Saudi Arabia, Kuwait, Bahrain, the UAE, Qatar and Oman. In these countries, the workers come under the *kafala* sponsorship system, which ties them to the family that employs them. They are likely to have to give up their passports, and they cannot change employment without the permission of their employer. Their remittances provide valuable income for families at home, but at a cost in terms of the working conditions and vulnerabilities. Kuwait has been at the forefront in aiming to protect domestic workers, with legislation in 2015 that specifies a maximum 12-hour working day, paid annual leave and other rights (HRW, 2015). In Kuwait, migrant domestic workers constitute a third of the entire workforce in the country, but until now have had no recognized labour rights. This is a step forward, but there remain doubts about how well it will be enforced.

Inequality, both within countries and between countries, leads to situations in which the rich hire the poor to provide domestic services. In earlier eras, when inequalities were rooted in social class determined by birth, domestic service was seen as part and parcel of the social system. Nowadays, capitalist economies view waged labour in a different light: the worker is hired to do work under contract for a wage. There is a contractual relationship here, not a personal one. However, domestic workers, while performing vital roles in capitalist societies, are often not viewed in terms of waged labour, but in terms that suggest a throwback to earlier periods of personal control over the worker by a well-to-do family. The UK, which has not ratified the ILO convention, has a visa arrangement for migrant domestic workers, whereby the worker is attached to the family that hires her, usually through an agency. This makes it difficult for her to leave the employer in cases of unfair or abusive treatment. In the UK, 67% of domestic workers are required to work seven days a week.

In South Africa, one women in five is a domestic worker. Most are black or of mixed race and work for white families. Since the fall of apartheid, South Africa has introduced legislation specifying a minimum wage for these workers, but they often suffer discrimination. The rise to fame of a domestic servant on the popular television series, *MasterChef SA*, highlighted this 'forgotten army' of workers (Maclean, 2014). Ms Mdlankomo, despite her new-found fame, insists that what matters is that she is an 'ordinary person'.

Sources: Falconer, R. and Kelly, A. (2015) 'The global plight of domestic workers: few rights, little freedom, frequent abuse', *The Guardian*, 17 March, at www.theguardian.com; Lakhani, N. (2015) 'Mexico City's domestic workers: A life being treated as a lesser person', *The Guardian*, 10 November, at www.theguardian.com; HRW (Human Rights Watch) (2015) 'Kuwait: New law a breakthrough for domestic workers', 30 June, at www.hrw.org; Maclean, R. (2014) 'Domestic servant takes Masterchef by storm', *The Times*, 4 December, at www.thetimes.co.uk.

Questions for discussion

- What aspects of the social and cultural environment *within* countries lead to the vulnerable position of domestic workers?
- What aspects of the global environment contribute to the vulnerable position of migrant domestic workers?
- What are the best means for ensuring that domestic workers are given employment rights, and also ensuring that they are enforceable?
- What role is there for unions to play in achieving better conditions for domestic workers?

THE GLOBAL ECONOMIC ENVIRONMENT

Outline of chapter

This chapter will enable you to

- Define and apply the major concepts used to analyse the economic environment
- Identify divergent economic systems and their societal contexts
- Assess impacts of globalization on economic systems and in societies
- Appreciate economic issues that affect regional integration

OPENING CASE STUDY

Alibaba aiming to shape the world

Online sales amounting to the equivalent of $8 billion in 10 hours on 11 November 2015 gave Alibaba, China's ecommerce champion, a world record for a single day's trading. The news of the record made global headlines for its charismatic founder, Jack Ma, who received a congratulatory phone call from the office of China's president. For a private-sector Chinese company, global admiration combined with praise from the communist political establishment could be interpreted as the pinnacle of success. Certainly, achieving sales that exceeded the 'black Friday' record for equivalent sales in the US (falling the day after Thanksgiving) was an achievement that its billionaire founder could be proud of. But celebrations on the day should be tempered by consideration of where the company is going – and how. Only two months previously, when Alibaba was celebrating the first anniversary of its listing on the New York Stock Exchange (NYSE), doubts about its business, its governance, and the impacts of country factors associated with China were scattered across the world's media. Those reservations remain, despite the euphoria of 11 November.

Ma's Alibaba IPO on the NYSE in 2014 was indeed a success. The first day's trading valued the company at $235 billion, and the share price saw a 'pop' of a 35% rise in value on the listing price on the first day. US investors were keen to own shares in Alibaba, and the backing of large banks, such as JP Morgan, Goldman Sachs and Citi Group, reinforced their confidence. It seemed not to be misplaced: the shares soared 77% in the first two months after the IPO. But since then, the price has halved. Weakening economic data from China's economy have been a factor, and share prices on China's stock exchanges have tumbled. As a Chinese company, Alibaba would not be immune from these movements. Ma has grown the ecommerce giant in a business environment that has seen growing demand from Chinese consumers. Alibaba has had a dominant position in the Chinese market, with its Tmall business (similar to Amazon) and Taobao business (similar to eBay). Their popularity has risen among the middle-class consumers who have benefited from China's growing prosperity. Ma aims for global markets, but so far these have been limited, accounting for 9%

of overall sales. He has also been astute in catering to consumers who use smartphones for shopping, by increasing mobile sales and acquiring companies with expertise in mobile apps. By 2014, the time was ripe for listing Alibaba. But the method was unconventional, and Alibaba had had a previous listing that had misfired.

Alibaba was listed on the Hong Kong Stock Exchange in 2007, but the financial crisis soon followed, along with a corruption scandal that engulfed Ma. It was delisted five years later. In the meantime, Ma searched for another way to go public. He looked to Silicon Valley where, in companies such as Google and Facebook, the founders have relatively small shareholdings but retain control of the company. The Hong Kong Stock Exchange rejects such structures as a departure from one-share-one-vote. He turned to New York, which proved amenable to close control. The company, Alibaba Group, is registered in the Cayman Islands, an offshore Caribbean jurisdiction with light disclosure requirements. The ownership structure was to raise eyebrows.

Ma and 30 individuals have a partnership among them that gives them the right to name the people on the board of directors. These insiders, some of whom do not work for the company, own altogether only 13% of the shares. The investors who buy shares in the company have no say, and, what is more, their holding is not one of shares directly in the company, but in a number of offshore-registered intermediary entities that 'simulate' ownership. These are all private companies controlled by Ma. Critically, Ma also owns Aliplay, the payment company (similar to PayPal) that is the lifeblood of Alibaba. It, too, is a private company under his control. He justifies this arrangement on the grounds that Chinese law requires that non-bank payment systems must not be foreign owned. But there are clearly big risks for ordinary investors in these arrangements, as their ownership is indirect. Ma assures investors and consumers that he has their interests to the fore, but these promises have no force in terms of legal obligation.

Shares listed in New York are purchased by institutional investors such as pension funds. Although Alibaba shares were eagerly bought by investors and backed by prestigious institutions, there were risks. As an online company, Alibaba is particularly affected by internet controls and regulations imposed by government. Alibaba has encountered criticism for tolerating the sale of counterfeit goods and other goods of marginal legality. Although there are international agreements to control the trade in nuclear-sensitive materials that could be used to make bombs, active trading has appeared to be relatively unhampered on Alibaba's websites (Clover, 2014). Ma's warm relations with top political leaders are valuable. But when the leadership changes, new leaders might pose threats, especially if he has been associated with leaders that have fallen out of favour. China's market reforms have allowed talented entrepreneurs like Jack Ma to build empires and accumulate fortunes, but the ultimate control of the economic levers by authoritarian political rulers remains intact.

Sources: Clover, C. (2014) 'Weapons of mass ecommerce', *Financial Times*, 27 September, at www.ft.com; Pratley, N. (2014) 'Alibaba's stock market listing a risky prospect as insiders hold all the cards', *The Guardian*, 18 September, at www.theguardian.com; BBC (2015) 'China's Alibaba breaks singles day record as sales surge', BBC News, 11 November, at www.bbc.com; *Financial Times* (2014) 'How Alibaba turned itself into a different type of company', 19 September, at www.ft.com; Schaefer, S. (2015) 'On its first birthday, Alibaba's stock is a battleground', 17 September, Forbes, at www.forbes.com.

Questions for discussion

- What are the risks for private-sector companies in China's economic environment?
- What aspects of Alibaba's IPO in New York could be criticized, and why?
- Is Alibaba a good model for a modern Chinese company?
- Would you invest in Alibaba shares?

Introduction

The global economic environment reflects increasing and deepening globalization, and at the same time, diversity among national economies. The world's nearly 200 countries differ widely in their size, geography, population, climate and natural resources. These differences have direct effects on the types and intensity of economic activity that are viable. For example, trade is traditionally more likely to prosper in a coastal state than in a land-locked one. States rich in natural resources, such as minerals and oil, have developed national economies built around these natural endowments. In addition, each national economy exists in a cultural and political environment which influences policymakers' decisions on resources and public spending. Increasingly, the economic environment is seen in terms of impacts on societies.

This chapter will begin by looking at the tools with which economists measure and compare national economies. The data generated in these ways allow policymakers to assess economic performance and design national policies. We will examine the major types of national economic system which characterize most of the world's economies. They range from market capitalist models to those in which state controls predominate. These are not simply economic systems in isolation, but represent divergent pictures of societies. A trend observable across all continents in recent years has been the shift towards more open markets, bringing greater opportunities for business enterprises globally – and also greater impacts in societies, both positive and negative. In an economic environment which has become highly interconnected, the role of national governments has evolved, retaining a pivotal role domestically, and also taking on regional and international perspectives.

National economies: income and growth

The global economic environment is made up of economic activities conducted by individuals, businesses and governments within national frameworks. The aggregate of these activities form a national economy. In each of the world's countries, a range of economic indicators can be used to measure these activities, revealing the nature and vibrancy of the national economy. Is the economy growing? Are there enough jobs for those who want them? Where is public spending going? These are some of the many issues that affect the economy. Responding to these questions involves more than simply assessing available data in a vacuum. Economic data speak volumes about the nature of a society, its values and the way it is governed. This chapter will highlight these interactions between economic and social environments.

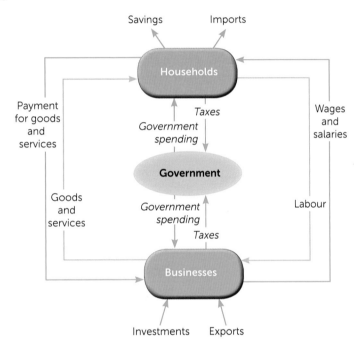

Figure 4.1 Circular flows of income in an economy

Economists study both the overall activity in the national economy and the lower-level economic activity which takes place between businesses and consumers. Macroeconomics is the study of national economies, while microeconomics refers to the study of economic activity at the level of individuals and firms. The two areas of economic study are related. Data compiled for each of the economic indicators at the microeconomic level are fed into macroeconomic analysis.

Flows of economic resources in the economy can be depicted as a model based on circular flows. While this type of model is greatly oversimplified, it does serve to show the interaction between the main groups, businesses and consumers, as can be seen in Figure 4.1. Businesses provide employment and wages to households, while consumers spend earned income on goods and services. At the same time, both businesses and individuals pay taxes to government, which are used to fund public spending and social security. By increasing or decreasing public spending or by altering the tax regime, it is possible for government to influence spending by firms and consumers. For example, public spending on government projects will provide firms with more orders and greater need for workers. These workers, in turn, will purchase consumer goods. Therefore, the 'injection' of government funds will have had a general effect on the economy, referred to by economists as a 'multiplier' effect, because of its ripple effects across the economy. It should also be noticed that effects of international flows are taken into account in Figure 4.1. Consumers buy imported products, which is depicted as a 'leakage' from the circular flow. Similarly, when firms export products, the income that arises is an injection, as is overseas investment.

Gross national income and gross domestic product

The economy of a country can be measured in a number of ways. One of these is Gross National Income (GNI). GNI represents the total income from all the final products and services produced by a national economy, including income that national residents earn from overseas investments, in a given year. It is the broadest measure of a nation's economic activity. Gross Domestic Product (GDP) represents the value of the total economic activity produced within a country in a single year, including both domestic and foreign producers. GDP and GNI vary enormously from one country to another. As can be seen in Figure 4.2, the US is by far the world's largest economy, with a GNI of nearly $17 trillion in 2013. The nine largest economies now include the BRICs, the large emerging economies, which are China, Brazil, Russia and India. China is rapidly catching up with the US.

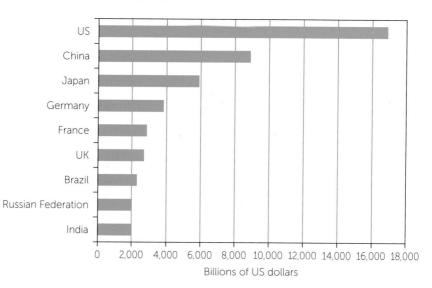

Figure 4.2 GNI of the world's largest economies in 2013

Source: Data from World Bank Data, GNI (PPP), at www.worldbank.org, accessed 27 April 2015.

The BRIC countries all have much larger populations than the US. For comparisons between countries, GDP or GNI per capita (per head) gives a better idea of a society's prosperity, as it takes the population into account. There are huge differences in per capita GNI across the world. US GNI per capita was $53,750 in 2013. The other advanced economies featured in Figure 4.2 had GNI per capita of between $38,000 and $45,000. These calculations are based on Purchasing Power Parity (PPP). PPP estimates the number of units of the foreign currency which would be needed to buy goods or services equivalent to those which the US dollar would buy in the US. The advantage of using PPP estimates to measure GNI per capita is that they more accurately reflect relative living standards in different countries. There is a wide gap between these countries and the developing and emerging countries. There is also considerable variation among the BRIC countries. China's GNI per capita of $11,850 in 2013, had more than tripled since 2000, marking a rapid rise in living standards, although the average income is still about one-fifth the income of a US citizen. India is by far the poorest of the BRICs, with a GNI per capita of about $5,000, less than half that of the Chinese citizen. African countries, especially those in sub-Saharan Africa, are among the world's poorest in terms of GNI per capita, which is in the range of just several hundred dollars.

GNI or GDP per capita represents an average figure. It does not take account of the distribution of wealth within the country. Some countries have extremes of wealth between the rich and poor while others are more egalitarian, although their GNI per capita could be similar. India has a low GNI per head, but is nonetheless seen as a huge potential market because of its large – and rapidly growing – middle class of an estimated 200 million consumers, eager to buy products such as televisions and mobile phones. This information is valuable for companies whose marketing strategy is targeted at emerging markets, as well as for foreign investors. When India's growing middle-class prosperity is placed in the context of Indian society overall, however, the picture is rather different. India has seen growing inequality and persisting high levels of poverty, indicating that economic growth is uneven.

Indian economic development presents a picture of contrasting fortunes: from growing middle-class affluence to the poverty of this Indian child, struggling to read by oil lamp.

Source: Getty Images/ iStockphoto Thinkstock Images\Trilok Singh Bangari.

Economic growth

Economic growth refers to a country's increase in national income over time, indicating expansion in the production of goods and services. The growth in GDP per capita is a measure often used by economists. A growing economy signifies improvement in material well-being, but this does not necessarily lead to overall improvement in well-being in a society. Societal well-being is broader than income and includes, for example, improvements in health and education, as recognized in the UN's concept of human development (introduced on p. 43). The OECD, a major source of economic data, also recognizes the limitations of economic indicators, and has devised a Better Life Index for assessing well-being across countries. That index covers eleven dimensions, including housing, income, jobs, education, environment and health (OECD, 2011). There is abundant evidence that economic growth leads to poverty reduction and is crucial to achieving development goals (Rodrik, 2011). Indeed, most of the dimensions of well-being just mentioned depend to some extent on economic growth. Despite its acknowledged limitations, it remains a key indicator (Aghion and Howitt, 2009).

Economic development depends on growth. Theories of economic growth have traditionally focused on external, or exogenous, factors, which were seen as given. Theorists now focus more on endogenous factors, which are internal to the economy. These include levels of technology, educational attainment and investment activities. They involve choices made by private individuals and also government policies. For example, government policies could encourage an entrepreneur to invest in technological innovation. A range of institutions, both formal (such as legal protections) and informal (such as a bureaucracy based on meritocracy) come into play (Rodrik, 2009). The level of technological innovation reflects a country's education policies and spending decisions (see Chapter 9). While government spending on primary and secondary education provides the groundwork, spending on higher education is seen as crucial to making the transition to a more technologically advanced economy (Aghion and Howitt, 2009).

National economies need to grow in order to create jobs and sustain livelihoods for growing populations. China's economy grew at annual rates of over 9% over the two decades from 1994 to 2014 (Giles, 2014). Historically, such growth rates are rare, and usually occur during phases of 'catch-up', when countries are aiming to catch up with richer, more technologically-advanced countries (Piketty, 2014: 97). China's growth has now slowed, as shown in Figure 4.3. Following the end of the Second World War, European economies grew strongly in the 1950s and 1960s. In the 1970s and 1980s, Japan underwent rapid industrialization in its efforts to catch up with the advanced western economies. As these economies became mature, growth slowed. In general, the advanced economies have relatively slower growth than emerging economies, as Figure 4.3 shows. Although world per capita GDP grew at a rate of 3% from 1950 to 1973, a normal rate of growth is closer to 1% (Maddison, 2007). But expectations rise during periods of prosperity, and many policymakers would now view a growth rate of 1% as disappointingly low.

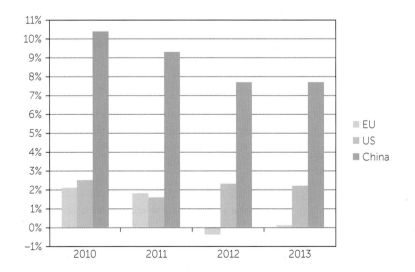

Figure 4.3 GDP growth in selected economies

Source: Data from World Bank Data, GDP growth, at www. worldbank.org, accessed 27 April 2015.

What propels economic growth? The classic picture of economic development is one of industrialization leading to economic growth. Apart from China, most of the countries with the highest growth over the last two decades do not fit this picture. The leading country in this group was Equatorial Guinea, and others include Qatar, Angola, Mozambique and Cambodia. Equatorial Guinea is an African country whose wealth is based almost entirely on oil and gas, but the wealth is very unevenly distributed. GNI per capita in 2013 was nearly $30,000. However, the country's human development ranking is a lowly 136 out of 197 countries (Bizimana et al., 2014), indicating a very low level of societal well-being. Over 70% of the population live in poverty, mainly in rural areas that depend on subsistence agriculture.

Equatorial Guinea is a stark example of a current preoccupation of international decision-makers, which is that headline economic growth can mask the realities of hardship for large portions of a society. Development should be inclusive, that is, bringing well-being to all in society. International organizations now look increasingly at the bigger picture of who benefits from growth (OECD, 2014). Inclusive growth involves improved living standards and greater economic security for all in society, along with social programmes to improve quality of life (ILO, 2014a). In a highly unequal economy dependent almost exclusively on oil wealth, growth is unlikely to bring the benefits of development to all. A particular weakness is the failure to diversify such economies in order to provide employment in non-oil activities. The consequences can be disastrous. A fall in global demand for oil, along with falling prices, hit Equatorial Guinea's economy in 2013, causing the country to plunge into recession, with a negative growth rate of −1.4%.

Fluctuations from periods of prosperity to downturn are part of what economists refer to as the business cycle. Longer cycles can be distinguished from shorter-term fluctuations, which are more closely identified with the business cycle. Although economists differ in their explanations of causes and indicators, four phases can be identified: prosperity, recession, depression and recovery. Prosperity is signified by healthy economic growth and rising standards of living. There are high levels of employment and wages, which lead to growing consumption. A recession can be narrowly defined as two consecutive quarters of negative economic growth, although economists prefer to look at the broader picture of the economy. Declining output in a recession is usually accompanied by rising unemployment and weak demand in the economy, as both consumers and businesses spend less. If these indicators continue to deteriorate, and the recession is prolonged, it can become a depression, which occurs when the economy has diminished by one-tenth in size. The Great Depression of 1929 provided a warning for later generations. Since then, financial crises, especially the financial crisis of 2008, continue to demonstrate that market instabilities can have damaging impacts on societies.

Economic growth in context

If inclusive growth is now seen as a surer indicator of sustainable development, why are governments in emerging economies still focused on headline economic growth?

Inequality

National economies of both developed and developing countries have seen rising inequality. Inequality as an economic indicator refers to the difference in wealth or income between the richest and poorest in society. If this gap is widening, it means that the rich are capturing a larger portion of the wealth of the country, while the shares of the middle and lower income groups are stagnating or diminishing.

Although recognized as an important economic indicator, inequality is difficult to define precisely and also difficult to measure. Inequality of wealth differs from inequality of incomes. Wealth is highly concentrated globally. In 2014, the richest 1% of the world's population owned 42% of the world's wealth, and the share of the richest is increasing (Oxfam, 2015). Whereas in 2010, 388 people had wealth equal to the bottom half of the world's population, by 2015, this number had shrunk to just 62 people (Oxfam, 2016). Economists usually focus on inequality of household or individual income after tax to measure the 'net inequality' within a country. By contrast, 'market inequality' is based on income before tax. The traditional tool used to measure income inequality is the Gini index, which ranges from 0, where income is shared equally among all, to 1, where all income goes to one household or person. The UN presents the Gini index as ranging from 0 to 100. Some European countries, such as Norway (25.8) and Germany (28.3), have relatively low inequality (UNDP, 2013). The US (40.8) and UK (36) have higher inequality. However, it is in Latin America, Asia and Africa where some of the world's most unequal countries are located. Mexico (47.2), Brazil (54.7) and Colombia (55.9) are among the most unequal. Many African countries are also in this category, including South Africa (63.1) and Zambia (57.5). China's Gini index rose from 30 in the 1980s to over 50 in 2010 (OECD, 2014). In 2013, it was 42.1, which is still high.

Another way to measure inequality is to look at the share of income going to those at the top: the top 10%, top 1% or top 0.1%. A global trend has been the increase in the share of income of those at the top. Figure 4.4 shows this trend in the US from 1970 onwards, where the share of the top 1% grew from 7.80% in 1970 to 17.54% in 2013, while the share of the top 10% grew from 31.51% to 47.01%. The share of the top 1% more than doubled over these years. Over the same period, the average income of the bottom 90% declined from $33,621 in 1970 to $30,980 in 2013 (Avaredo et al., no date).

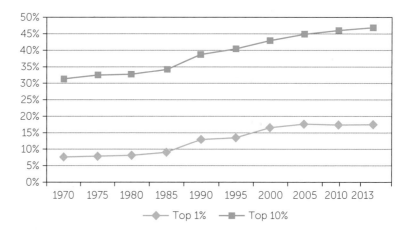

Figure 4.4 Income shares of the top 1% and top 10% in the US, 1970–2013

Source: Avaredo, F., Atkinson, A., Piketty, T. and Saez, E. The World Top Incomes Database, at http://topincomes.g-mond. parisschoolofeconomics.eu/, accessed 28 March 2015.

Unlike the Gini index, the top-income data give more of an indication of the power, real and potential, of the people with the largest incomes. The increasing share of the richest in the US has been reflected in a growth in lobby activity (Oxfam, 2015), aimed at influencing government policies (discussed in the next chapter). Democracy suffers if the rich are able to translate their economic power into political ascendency. But inequality is a concern for all governments, not just democratic ones. Inequality has not only economic implications, but also ethical, social and political implications.

The ethical aspects of inequality are capable of divergent viewpoints. Many economists would say that the inequalities associated with capitalism are part of its inherent dynamic, which, in general, has brought huge economic benefits to societies. Critics would argue that, where there is extreme inequality in society, the lack of opportunity for self-fulfillment suffered by those at the bottom constitutes injustice (Rawls, 1996; Sen, 2010). Inequality can undermine social cohesion and lead to political instability. These factors weigh especially heavily in developing countries, where they tend to occur alongside fragile institutions and weak governance.

A question that has exercised economists is whether high inequality, apart from its unethical connotations, adversely affects a country's economic growth. Widening inequality is increasingly associated with risks of crisis and threats to sustainable growth (Ostry et al., 2014). Underlying causes of the financial crisis of 2008 were the financial excesses of the very rich that had spiralled out of control, especially in countries where regulation was weak. This led to the collapse of companies exposed to the highest levels of financial risk, requiring bailout funds from governments. The crisis highlighted that the growing wealth of the rich is not solely an indication of economic power. It also signifies their growing ability to exert control of political processes, ensuring them light-touch regulation, low taxes and other policies that help to maintain their wealth – and power. However, social and political stability can be a consequence, which can in turn dampen growth.

Research suggests that high inequality adversely affects the sustainability of growth (Ostry et al., 2014). Expressed positively, lower net inequality leads to more sustainable growth. Redistribution is a way of compensating for high inequality. In highly unequal societies, governments can turn to policies that have a redistributive effect. Such policies include investing in education and healthcare, even though these benefit everyone, not just the poor. More targeted redistributive policies would be higher taxes for high earners and social spending aimed at the poorest. Some economists would argue that such measures adversely affect growth, as they can constitute disincentives. But others would advise a more nuanced approach, saying that investing in education and social insurance both aids growth and reduces inequality. The US has high market inequality and also high inequality of net income, combined with low levels of redistribution. Ethical arguments against inequality have met with little resonance in the US in the past. But redistribution policies might find more favour in the US if policymakers were persuaded that moderating inequality would contribute to sustainable growth.

Why does inequality matter?

Inequality is inherent in capitalism. Why do economists now see inequality as posing a danger to capitalism's long-term viability?

Unemployment

'Full employment', contrary to what it implies, is used by economists to refer to a country's natural rate of unemployment which exists in all societies. What we commonly refer to as **unemployment** reflects the percentage of people in the country's labour force who are willing to work but are without jobs. National governments use differing definitions of unemployment. There is a generally accepted definition which dates from the 1982 International Conference of Labour Statisticians and is recognized by the International Labour Organization (ILO). This 'ILO definition' (ILO, 2014b: 70) includes people who are:

a without work in either paid employment or self-employment;
b currently available for work, that is, available for paid employment or self-employment during a specific reference period; and
c seeking work (by taking specific steps, such as applications to employers or registering with an employment exchange) within a specific reference period.

Specific rules about who is included and excluded from national statistics differ from country to country, making comparisons hazardous. Moreover, in every country, there are probably significant numbers of people who are 'hidden' from the statistics, such as 'discouraged workers', who have ceased to look for a job, and casual workers who were not registered employees in the first place.

Unemployment may be 'structural', meaning that there are not enough available jobs in the economy to provide work for the people seeking employment. Often this occurs because of changing technology, which leaves behind workers with outdated skills. It can also occur when industries relocate to other regions or other countries. The shift of much manufacturing from developed to developing countries, especially China, represented a loss of jobs for manufacturing workers in western economies. A second type of unemployment is 'frictional', referring to the usual turnover in the labour force that happens, for example, when people are out of work looking for new jobs. When demand in an economy falters and economic growth slows, unemployment tends to rise, as firms lay off workers and cease hiring. Unemployment rose during the financial crisis of 2008–9, reaching levels of 9% or more in the advanced economies. Despite government policies and a fragile resumption in growth, unemployment seemed to remain stubbornly high, reminding governments that economic growth does not necessarily lead to significant job creation in the short term.

Government policies are influential in promoting job creation. Policies which promote innovation and training can help to mitigate the impacts of unemployment in particular sectors. Governments can also make it easier for new businesses to start up. If their businesses are successful, these self-employed people are likely to take on employees, but it can take years for start-up businesses to increase appreciably in size. Many start-ups, such as those in the high-tech sectors, commonly employ few full-time staff directly. They are likely to contract for specific services, and these activities generate work for suitably skilled people. Developing economies often encounter a dilemma. They need to create jobs to satisfy the demands of their growing populations, but at the same time, they wish to move up the technology ladder, which implies encouraging innovative companies that are likely to have fewer employees than the low-technology sectors which tend to predominate in developing economies.

Youth unemployment is a particular concern for governments, as young people aspire to embark on careers that will blossom over a lifetime. Young people who have never had a job find it increasingly difficult to obtain fulfilling work. The problem is acute in the young societies of Africa and Asia. In Morocco, the 15–29 age group constitutes 30% of the total population and 44% of the entire working-age population (15–64) (World Bank, 2012). The country has enjoyed healthy economic growth at rates averaging about 5% for the last decade, but decent job opportunities are scarce for the bulk of these young people. A World Bank study found that in the 15–29 age group, 90% of young women and 40% of young men were neither in education nor in work. They are, in effect, existing on the fringes of society at a period in their lives when they would expect to be setting out to realize personal goals and build careers. Moreover, those in work were mostly in insecure jobs in the informal sector, with no contract of employment and no job security. The World Bank gloomily observed that Morocco's young people were 'largely excluded from the sustained economic growth the country has experienced in the last decade', leading to feelings of 'failure and despair' on the part of those excluded (World Bank, 2012: ix).

High unemployment is a cause of social instability which can lead to social and political unrest. Extremist groups, including religious sects, are active in these uncertain environments. Along with inequality, unemployment has been highlighted as a source of risk in the global economy (WEF, 2015). Much of the tension in the rapidly-growing urban areas across the developing world stems from the presence in the streets of young people without work. These people, many of whom have educational qualifications, represent huge potential contributions to their societies, which could be turned into reality with appropriate responses from government and businesses. Morocco's Minister of Labour and Social Affairs has acknowledged the challenges, not just in his own country, but across the region, noting especially that youth unemployment has 'driven up poverty and inequality' (Young, 2014).

No job and no hope? Where jobs are scarce, sights like these young people in the street are indicative of simmering frustration.

Source: Photoalto.

While many governments provide state benefits and retraining for the unemployed, such schemes are scarce in developing countries. The ILO estimates that only 28% of the labour force worldwide would be eligible for unemployment benefit, either contributory or non-contributory (ILO, 2014a). There are big variations among countries. While 80% of the workforce is eligible in Europe, only 17% is eligible in Asia. In

China, where social programmes and employment protection are gradually being rolled out, migrant workers are excluded from these protections, leaving them without any income safety net if they lose their jobs (OECD, 2014). The growth in the use of migrant workers in supply chains is linked to globalization. While globalization has helped China to grow economically, the country has also seen rising inequality. China now faces the challenges of creating sustainable jobs and promoting social well-being in order to realize inclusive growth.

Other key economic indicators: inflation and balance of payments

In this section, we look at two further economic indicators: inflation and balance of payments. The indicators discussed so far are interlinked. In a healthy economy, we would expect to see low inflation, low unemployment and a positive balance of payments. In today's world, we find a rather more mixed picture among national economies.

Inflation can be defined as the continuing general rise in prices in the economy. Its effect is to make the country's currency worth less. The opposite phenomenon is 'deflation', or a general fall in prices. Deflation is likely to occur in periods of recession, reflecting falling demand.

The rate of inflation is expressed as a percentage rise or fall in prices with reference to a specific starting point in time. These rises and falls are tracked in the consumer price index for every country, usually making allowances for seasonal adjustments, such as seasonal variations in food prices. Each country has its own consumer price index, including a diversity of components in its calculations. For this reason, making comparisons between countries is imprecise and can give only an approximate picture of inflation. There is a single, harmonized Consumer Price Index (CPI) used within the eurozone, which enables more accurate comparisons between member states. The European Central Bank (ECB) set 2% as its target rate of inflation in 2004, when inflation was generally higher, but many EU states experienced inflation rates at near zero in the recession of 2008–9. Inflation has remained low, in line with weak recovery and falling fuel prices.

Rising inflation is a concern for governments. Economists point to a number of causes of inflation. 'Demand-pull' and 'cost-push' arguments are two of the most commonly advanced causes. The demand-pull explanation holds that demand in the economy is the key factor, which may be the result of cheap borrowing or tax cuts. It encourages producers to raise prices, and these then lead to rises in wage demands as workers strive to maintain their standard of living. The cost-push argument holds that rising costs drive up prices. As a significant element of costs is accounted for by wages, this theory becomes linked with the demand-pull argument. Rising wage costs tend to be passed on to consumers in the form of higher prices, thus creating what is known as the 'wage-price inflationary spiral'.

The damaging effects of high inflation can be widely ramified. A country's domestic producers will find their goods less competitive in global markets, and foreign investors may turn to countries where inflation is lower. High inflation tends to force up interest rates to enable investors to achieve a real return on their investments. However, high interest rates may adversely affect growth rates by reducing domestic demand.

The importance of energy costs as a driver of inflation was highlighted in the oil price shocks of the 1970s, which quadrupled the price of oil. Resultant increases in energy and transport costs affected all industrial sectors and sent inflation soaring in developed economies. To bring down inflation, governments can resort to imposing controls on prices or wages, but these measures can be damaging. In particular, they can lead to rising unemployment, as employers cut back on costs. In an environment of relatively low inflation, monetary policy seeks to prevent inflationary pressures arising.

The **balance of payments** refers to credit and debit transactions between a country's residents (including companies) and those of other countries. Transactions are divided into the current account and capital account. The **current account** is made up of trade in goods (the merchandise trade account), services (the services account), and profits and interest earned from overseas assets. The **capital account** includes transactions involving the sale and purchase of assets, such as investment in shares. If a country has a current account deficit, this means it imports more goods and services than it exports. If it has a current account surplus, it exports more than it imports. In Figure 4.5, we see that China has moved ahead of Germany to record the largest trade surplus. India and US have current account deficits, massive in the case of the US. Of course, the US economy is larger than any of the others in this chart, but the trade deficit is equivalent to about 3% of its GDP, whereas China's trade surplus is over 6% of GDP.

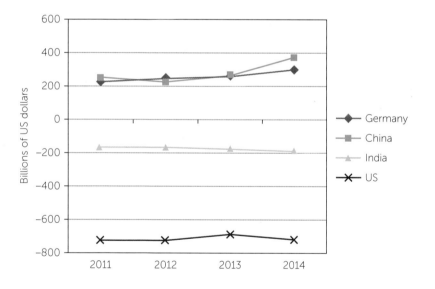

Figure 4.5 Balance of payments in selected economies

Source: Data from OECD Statistics: International trade and balance of payments, at www.oecd.org, accessed 1 April 2015.

The balance of payments reflects demand both at home and abroad. It also reflects exchange rates (which will be discussed in Chapter 8) and the relative costs of domestic production. Governments can exert influence by varying the exchange rate, raising interest rates (to slow down growth), or by imposing tariff barriers such as import duties and quotas. China is sometimes accused of keeping its currency low in order to aid exporters. India has been less successful than China in encouraging manufacturing and, as Figure 4.5 shows, has seen a growing trade deficit. The Indian government would like to redress this situation, promoting manufacturing investment (discussed in the closing case study in Chapter 2). The world's main trading countries are now linked in regional and multilateral trade groupings which, as will be discussed later, have brought down trade barriers, so that governments are no longer able simply to restrict imports. Nor would they be advised to do so, at the risk of retaliation by trading partners. On the other hand, WTO rules, discussed in the next chapter, allow a number of exceptions, permitting countries to restrict imports in their national interest.

Balancing the national economy

Governments seek policies which ensure economic growth, low inflation, and low unemployment, but there is considerable divergence of opinion on the extent to which they should intervene, or, alternatively, allow market forces to prevail. The role of government varies considerably between different types of economic system, which will be discussed in greater detail in sections to follow. For present purposes, we broadly define the ways in which governments act in the national economy. Governments may act directly as economic players, or indirectly in regulating the environment in which businesses operate. In Chapter 1, we noted that governments in many countries play a direct role in state-owned and state-controlled companies. Governments are also ultimately responsible for the legislative and regulatory systems with which businesses in the country must comply.

Policymaking falls under two headings. **Fiscal policy** refers to the budgetary policies for balancing public spending with taxation and other income, whereas **monetary policy** refers to policies for determining the amount of money in supply, rates of interest, and exchange rates. In many economies, a major role in monetary policy lies with the country's central bank, which is at the pinnacle of the country's financial system. It is responsible for issuing the country's notes and coins, and sets basic interest rates. It is also the banker to the government and the lender-of-last-resort. Most central banks, including the European Central Bank (ECB), are institutionally independent of government to help to ensure that policy will not be based on short-term political considerations.

At international level, the International Monetary Fund (IMF), which will be discussed further in Chapter 8, has oversight of international exchange-rate stability, and has also considerably expanded its role into areas of economic policy, once thought to be purely 'domestic' national policy. The institutional framework has thus become more complex as globalization has impacted on national economies. This intervention receives mixed reception in differing environments. IMF intervention in the Asian financial crisis of 1998 was widely perceived as misjudged (Stiglitz, 2002), whereas in the global financial crisis of 2008, several economies received emergency IMF loans. They included Iceland, Ireland and Hungary – all countries which had enjoyed considerable growth from globalization, but whose exposure to global capital flows put them at risk from sudden financial shocks.

Governments raise and spend huge sums of money. Their priorities and means differ according to the country's political system. Especially relevant is the concentration or dispersal of political power: in countries where political power is concentrated in an élite, priorities are likely to be different from countries where leaders are democratically elected. In democratic systems, governments must present annual budgets to elected legislators, who scrutinize how the money is being raised and how the government proposes to spend it. These can be heated debates! In every national economy, there are pressures to prioritize spending in one area over another, and there are also differences of opinion on how best to raise the money needed for public spending.

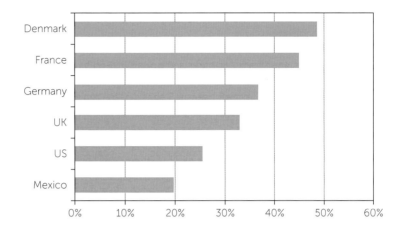

Figure 4.6 Tax revenues as a percentage of GDP, 2013

Source: Data from OECD Statistics, Tax revenue as a percentage of GDP, at www.oecd.org, accessed 4 April 2015.

Public spending is funded, in the main, from direct and indirect taxation, social security contributions and borrowing. Income tax is a direct tax, while taxes on goods and services, such as consumption tax and value-added tax (VAT), are indirect taxes. Money taken in by governments in taxation is often expressed as a percentage of GDP. This percentage can be high, and there are big discrepancies between countries, as shown in Figure 4.6. France and Denmark have the largest tax receipts of the countries featured, and, in general, developed countries have higher levels of taxation and public spending than developing ones. An exception is the US, where tax revenues are relatively low. The balance between direct and indirect taxation is a sensitive issue. Income tax falls on both individuals and companies, and most countries derive more income from individual income tax than from corporation tax.

Governments enjoy a budget surplus when they receive more in revenue than they spend. 'Good housekeeping' principles would suggest that governments, like households, should not spend more than they take in. It is common, however, for governments to be in deficit, spending more than they receive in revenue. The debt that accumulates over the years is known as the national debt. National debt, expressed as a percentage of GDP, can grow to large proportions, causing considerable problems for government finances and, in extreme cases, even the payment of interest becomes problematic. The national budget balance is the extent to which public spending exceeds receipts from taxes and other sources. Governments are more likely in today's world to have budget deficits rather than surpluses. Most economies saw a marked deterioration in government finances from the fallout of the financial crisis which started to bite in 2008–9.

Several factors can be highlighted. Tax revenues and revenues from other sources rise during prosperity, but diminish when incomes fall. In periods of recession, there are pressures on public spending, as the numbers claiming social benefits, such as unemployment and housing benefits, are rising. Tax revenues are falling due to weak productivity. The countries affected by the financial crisis were concerned about their high levels of government debt and, adding to their worries, a number were called on to bail out failed banks and other failing companies from public funds. Faced with the continuing need to make interest payments on government debt, some governments, including Spain and Italy, reduced social entitlements such as unemployment benefits and pensions in the years following the crisis. Ireland funded the bailout of its banks with money drawn from its state pension reserve fund (ILO, 2014a).

The economic indicators discussed here are intertwined, both in times of prosperity and times of downturn. Economic growth depends heavily on rising consumer demand, which helps to provide employment. When demand is low, businesses struggle and unemployment rises. In the economic upheavals of recession, governments reach for 'stimulus' measures to bring about recovery. Injecting public money into the economy, in the form of subsidies to particular industries or groups, is one. Another is maintaining low interest rates in the hope of encouraging investment.

Government support for banks has just been mentioned, and extends to other measures such as guaranteeing bank lending. Confidence in the banks is essential for any economy, and a banking collapse, as numerous financial crises have shown, can lead to economic recession in the wider economy. The need for government regulation in the financial sector rose to the top of the agenda following the global crisis of 2008. It also fuelled debate about the deeper issue of the role of government in the economy generally, along with the wider issue of international regulation, which might bring greater stability to the globalized financial environment. Differing economic systems offer differing perspectives, as we find in the next section.

CASE STUDY ON THE CHANGING BUSINESS ENVIRONMENT

Ethiopia's economic growth comes at a price

Ethiopia is now experiencing economic growth, but until just over two decades ago, it was grappling with recurring drought and famine, combined with violent ethnic tensions. The famine of the 1980s precipitated the fall of the communist dictatorship that had ruled since the 1970s; 1991 saw the overthrow of the communist dictator and the ushering in of a new era of hope for the economy and new constitutional democracy. Under the political leadership of the dominant party, the Ethiopian People's Revolutionary Democratic Front (EPRDF), which is still in control, the country's economic accomplishments have attracted praise from all parts of the world. Economic growth has been in region of 10%, an unusually high rate for an economy without large energy resources. The economy has diversified away from its primarily agricultural base. Flower growing has become an important industry. The availability of low-cost labour has attracted manufacturers, including textile and leather companies. H&M, the world's second-largest fashion retailer, is now manufacturing in Ethiopia. The government is spending public money on health, education, agriculture and roadbuilding. One of the biggest projects is a huge hydropower project, the Grand Ethiopian Renaissance Dam, which is government funded and will be the continent's largest such project. The government is both guiding development and becoming the largest investor in Ethiopia's future. The risks of drought remain, but it is hoped that there is now less risk of widespread famine. Ethnic tensions remain, and human rights issues are raising concerns.

With its strong state leadership driving economic growth, Ethiopia is an example of the development state, a model of development that has been successful among the emerging Asian countries, such as China. But China's development is guided by an authoritarian political system. Ethiopia has democratic political institutions, making its development policies potentially more accountable to a democratic electorate, while 'building capitalism from above' (KushKush, 2015). However, the formal democratic institutions are dominated by one party, the EPRDF; there is only one seat in the legislature held by an opposition member. The NGO, Human Rights Watch, has reported that political dissidents, such as bloggers, protesters and opposition parties, suffer from repressive tactics by the government (HRW, 2015). Moreover, the EPRDF is dominated by the Tigre ethnic group. The many other minority ethnic groups in the country are concerned about the authoritarian tendencies of the government.

Ethiopia remains predominantly a rural society. Four out of five Ethiopians live in rural areas, and agriculture accounts for half of the country's GDP. Despite the government's policies for improving well-being, its plans for regenerating agriculture have given rise to concerns of social justice. In southern regions of the country, where minority ethnic groups are prevalent, people have been moved away from their homes so that the land can be leased to foreign investors engaged in commercialized agricultural production. Some 1.5 million people have been forcibly moved to new 'model' villages in this process, which is effectively land clearance. The displaced groups complain that they have been moved to areas that are infertile and that have inadequate social services, schools and healthcare. They are left without their traditional agricultural livelihoods. These groups have little political voice and, although the constitution guarantees them the right to choose a livelihood, this seems to have been overridden in the interests of development at the national level. One displaced Ethiopian says of the new foreign investors, 'This is not the way for development. They do not cultivate the land for the people. They grow sorghum, maize, sesame, but all is exported, leaving none for the people' (Smith, 2015).

Despite its impressive economic growth, Ethiopia still has a lowly ranking of 173rd in the UN's Human Development Index (UNDP, 2015). Poverty remains an overriding issue. Although the percentage of people below the poverty line has fallen from 37% to 26% in the decade to 2014, the absolute number (25 million out of a total of 86 million people) is roughly the same, due to population growth. People hovering around the poverty line remain vulnerable to food insecurity. The UN has pressed for 'inclusive growth', but it finds that in Ethiopia, the benefits of growth have not been widely distributed throughout society. There are high rates of unemployment and under-employment in both urban and rural areas. Hence, poverty and international migration remain worryingly high. It urges policies that will promote private-sector economic activity, to create productive and sustainable jobs.

Ethiopia's GDP per capita is just $550. The government was aiming to raise Ethiopia to the level of a middle-income country by 2015. However, economic growth will not automatically resolve the inequalities: the people who are growing richer are mainly the business élites. The number of millionaires in Ethiopia grew 108% between 2007 and 2013 – the fastest growth in the number of millionaires of any African country. They are a tiny proportion of the population, only 2,700 people. For development to be sustainable, focus would need to shift to goals of raising levels of human development and inclusive growth.

Sources: UNDP (2015) 'National Human Development Report 2014: Ethiopia', at www.undp.org ; Dori, D. (2014) 'Ethiopia's "African tiger" leaps towards middle income', The Guardian, 22 October, at www. theguardian.com; KushKush, I. (2015) 'Ethiopia, long mired in poverty, rides an economic boom', New York Times, 3 March, at www.nyt.com; Smith, D. (2015) 'Ethiopians talk of violent intimidation as their land is earmarked for foreign investors', The Guardian, 14 April at www. theguardian.com; HRW (2015) 'World Report 2015: Ethiopia', at www. hrw.org.

Questions for discussion

- Summarize the main drivers of economic growth in Ethiopia's economic development model.
- What gains in social well-being are occurring in Ethiopia?
- In what respects are social goals being set back by government policies?
- Is Ethiopia's development model a good one for other emerging economies to follow, and why?

Classifying national economic systems

In the period following the Second World War, the major economic systems were classified as polar opposites, with capitalism at one end and socialism at the other. This view reflected political as well as economic views in the cold-war period, when economic systems were seen in the context of dominant ideologies – complete world pictures of societal structures and human values. The socialist states were the state-planned, collectivist economies, ruled by communist party dictatorships. The Soviet Union and China were dominant among the main planned economies. The capitalist states were free-market economies and also free societies. Among them were the US, European countries and Japan. With the crumbling of the Soviet Union and market reforms taking place in the other major socialist power, China, this polarized view has given way to a much more fragmented spectrum of contrasting economic systems. Post-communist countries are making the transition from socialism to capitalism. Cuba, whose communist revolution dates from 1959, has been one of the few avowedly communist states left. It has been subject to a US embargo, and has struggled to cope with deficiencies in its state-run agricultural sector. Cuba is now starting to open its economy, and relations with the US are thawing, opening the way for possible American food imports.

Cuba's capital, Havana, presents a picture of faded elegance and vehicles dating from the 1950s, but this could change with growing trade between Cuba and the US.

Source: © Stockbyte Royalty Free Photos.

While all systems now seem to have some elements of capitalism, there are significant differences between them, and market economies are themselves evolving towards a greater emphasis on regulation and social values. National economic systems are not static, but evolve over time, moving towards greater liberalization in some periods and shifting towards stronger government control in others. Nevertheless, there are conceptual differences underpinning the different types of economic system.

A national economic system is not just about a country's economic activities, but about its society. In any society, cultural values and social structures impact on economic activities. Therefore, in classifying economic systems, we are also pointing to the social and cultural aspects of a country. Figure 4.7 provides an overview of the

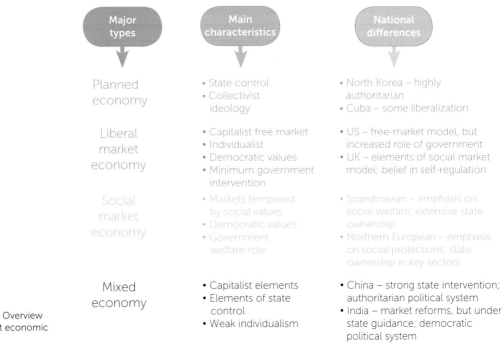

Figure 4.7 Overview of different economic systems

main types of economic system, along with the chief characteristics and examples of diverse countries within each. Note that the main characteristics highlight the role of the state and also the cultural values that support economic life.

As Figure 4.7 shows, the planned economy is probably the only distinctively 'pure' model, and even these closed economies are now opening up somewhat to outside influences. The two types of market economy have varying degrees of open markets and varying views of the role of government. The liberal market economies view state intervention as a necessary evil, while the social market economies take a positive view of the state's promotion of social cohesion. Note that all the market economies emphasize democratic values. It is common to define the mixed economy in the broad sense as one in which both state ownership and markets exist side by side. This definition is so broad that it would encompass just about every economy in the world, and is therefore not very helpful. Here, we take the view that the mixed economy is one in which capitalist elements, including free enterprise, competition and private property, are weaker than in the market economies. The mixed economy, while recognizing private enterprise, lays less stress on individual freedoms and democratic values. Some, such as China, retain the legacy of communist planned economies. India has a democratic political system and a vibrant market economy, but its roots in socialism have left a legacy of the strong state. Many countries, such as transitional economies and Latin American countries, fall into the same broad category, which can lead to some tension between the state's vested interests and newer market forces.

Market economies

Market economies encompass a wide range of systems with diverse cultural backgrounds. While they would all subscribe to capitalism in some form, they differ in the extent they would make market forces subordinate to other values, mainly through governmental regulation. Capitalism was the force behind nineteenth-century industrialization in Europe and the US, but their paths have diverged, reflecting differing cultural backgrounds.

The liberal market model

The liberal market economy refers to capitalism in what is considered to be its purest form, or *laissez-faire* capitalism. Commentators often refer to this model misleadingly as the 'Anglo-Saxon' model, but we opt for 'Anglo-American' here, in view of the fact that the US is the pre-eminent exponent. Capitalism rests on principles of private enterprise and freedom of individuals to pursue business activities as they wish. The underlying assumption of capitalism is that, through each individual's pursuit of self-interested economic activity, society as a whole benefits. The main examples of the *laissez-faire* model are Britain and the US. These economies are characterized by high individualism, following Hofstede's cultural dimensions (discussed in Chapter 3). Other examples are Australia and Canada, suggesting that the spread of this model in the English-speaking world was linked to shared historical roots. As Figure 4.7 indicates, democratic values go along with the individualist culture of these countries. In these societies, civil and political freedoms are commonly thought to be linked to economic freedom. This assumption has been questioned, however, in economies such as China, where market liberalization has proceeded independently of political liberalization.

The economist, Adam Smith, envisaged an 'invisible hand' guiding the market system in his *Wealth of Nations* (Smith, [1776] 1950), implying that markets are self-regulating. The principle that governments should refrain from intervention came to be enshrined in much economic thinking, but in practice, governments have frequently felt compelled to intervene on a number of public-interest grounds. Markets are deemed to be inherently competitive. Businesses compete on the basis of supply and demand: producers supply goods and services to satisfy consumer demand. It is well known, however, that if one supplier becomes dominant in a market, squeezing out smaller rivals, that firm, known as a monopoly, is able to dictate prices. Similarly, control by two or more firms, known as oligopoly, allows these firms to co-ordinate pricing. In these cases, most countries accept that regulation is needed to control market abuse and restore competition. In other words, governments intervene to *maintain* markets (Rodrik, 2009). Competition law (discussed in Chapter 6) has become integral to the smooth functioning of market economies.

Contrary to the image of stability implied by the invisible hand, markets can be volatile and unpredictable. Stock markets and individual companies are susceptible to swings in levels of confidence which can seem to verge on the irrational. Stock market crashes bring down the well-managed companies along with the reckless ones.

Capitalist systems have long acknowledged the need for government regulation. Indeed, Adam Smith himself recognized that markets cannot stand alone (Sen, 2010). Regulation is recognized as essential to ensure openness and fairness in markets, helping to retain public confidence and long-term viability. Concern has grown over the sustainability of any economic system in the long term. Sustainability as a concept includes not merely economic factors, but also issues such as whether the environment and non-renewable resources are being managed sustainably. It also concerns issues of social well-being. Is the economy creating enough jobs, and are there welfare safety nets for those stuck at the bottom? It is now recognized that the ecological environment is another priority. Governments in these countries prefer market mechanisms in principle over direct intervention. The US has no national health service, but legislation in 2010, the Patient Protection and Affordable Care Act (known as 'Obamacare' as it was a priority for President Obama), introduced a system of insurance intended to have universal coverage. Not everyone is covered, however. Illegal immigrants, as illustrated in the box below, have no entitlement.

The way I see it ...

'I went to the doctor once. He just made me lie down. He never gave me pills. But when I got the bill, I just freaked out because it was a lot of money [a week's wages for farm labour, her main source of income]. I was thinking, what did the doctor do for this money? Did he dress me in gold? So now I don't go to the doctor, even if I get sick. I just wait it out.'

Theresa Azuara, a 64-year-old Mexican who has lived and worked in Hidalgo County in Texas for 22 years, but has no right to legal residence or citizenship and therefore no entitlement to health insurance under Obamacare. Interviewed for *The Guardian*, 19 November 2015.

Theresa is convinced that, despite the hardship, poverty and insecurity, living in the US is better than life in Mexico. What humanitarian issues are involved? How could the US economic model take these more into account?

Social market models

The concept of the welfare state dates from the aftermath of the Great Depression of 1929, when western governments introduced systems of social security, unemployment benefit and other welfare programmes which are now perceived as necessary. To many, mainly those on the political right, these measures are seen as an essential social safety net in the market economy, while to those more to the left, social justice is seen as a goal in itself. The social market model gives a social-justice dimension to the capitalist model. Its main features are state ownership or control in key sectors and extensive social welfare programmes which reduce the inequalities inherent in the pure capitalist model. State ownership and private ownership exist side by side. Major enterprises such as heavy industry, banks, oil companies and airlines are likely to be state owned. Seen as national champions, they are naturally protected from takeover bids, making them less prone to the volatilities which private-sector companies experience. On the other hand, state-owned enterprises are a drain on the public purse, and have gained reputations as being less efficient than private-sector firms. A hybrid solution has been to 'privatize' public-sector enterprises by listing them as public companies in which the state retains a large shareholding and private investors are invited to take up a minority of 'floating' shares.

The social market model has evolved differently in the diverse societies which have adopted it. The Scandinavian countries have been grouped together broadly in what is often termed the 'Nordic' or just 'Scandinavian' social model. High taxes and high levels of public spending have characterized their extensive social support systems, and state ownership is part of this picture of social priorities. This social model has shifted in recent years, however, towards more market involvement, for example, in limited privatization of healthcare (see closing case study). These governments have reined in public spending and reduced budget deficits. They have also stressed transparency and accountability among providers of public services, whether they are public or private providers. Privatized healthcare providers in Sweden have faced criticism for handing the bulk of their profits to owners rather than reinvesting in their services to the public. In 2015, a Swedish council took a major step towards regulating these companies by imposing caps on profits (Orange, 2015).

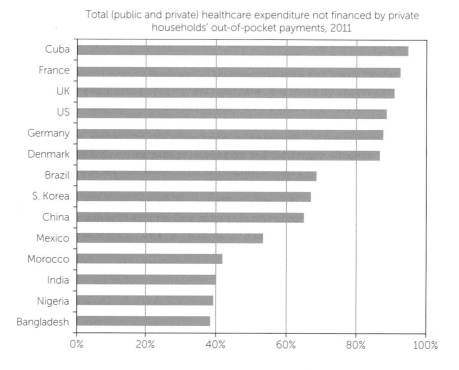

Figure 4.8 Funded healthcare: is everyone covered?

Source: Data from ILO (2014) *World Social Protection Report 2014/15*, June (Geneva: ILO), Table B10, pp. 280–284.

Healthcare is of vital importance in all countries, for both economic and social well-being. In developing countries, improvements in health are closely linked with the achievement of development goals (ILO, 2014a). Yet over 90% of the population in low-income countries have no right to healthcare provision, and must pay for each treatment or go without. Figure 4.8 shows the extent to which people can access healthcare funded by government schemes or private schemes such as pre-paid insurance. In the social market economies, health is traditionally a priority. Four European countries have among the highest levels of coverage. In France, coverage reaches 92.5% of the population. But the best performer is Cuba, where the state health system has delivered remarkable control of infectious diseases, improved life expectancy, and funded top-ranking medical research – all on a budget which is a fraction of that spent in richer countries. Cuba's achievements demonstrate that a state-directed health system can lead to substantial improvements in a population's health (Cooper et al., 2006).

The social market economies tend to have lower levels of inequality than the liberal market models. In France, the centralized state has created a more 'statist' model, while the German model values co-operation and consensus between the state, companies and workers. Market elements are moderated by government policies that stress the participation of social and trade union partners (Siebert, 2004). For example, workers in large German companies are legally entitled to a say in corporate governance (see Chapter 1). Germany thus contrasts with the *laissez-faire* model of the US and the statist model in France (Siebert, 2004). Many tiers of government in Germany, however, have tended to create complex regulatory regimes for businesses to navigate through.

The social market model is more attuned to issues of environmental protection and depletion of natural resources than the pure market economy, as these issues are encompassed in the model's recognition of ethical principles as an adjunct to market considerations. In liberal market economies, the 'business case' for environmental protection is that, ultimately, productivity and profitability will fall if environmental considerations are ignored, whereas the social market economy espouses action on the environment as an imperative on both ethical and business grounds.

Triumph of the social market model?

These systems achieve high rankings in human development, but at a cost in high social contributions and taxes. On the other hand, some countries with more liberal market models have larger budget deficits. To what extent does this suggest that more countries should shift to the social market model?

Asian capitalist systems

The East and South East Asian market economies are often grouped together as representing variations on the free-market model. Japan and South Korea can be highlighted as offering distinctive economic systems. Although different, they share key characteristics. Both were later to industrialize than the economies of Europe and America, and in both, economic development has been guided by the state. They also share a democratic political system, with civil, political and economic freedoms. For these reasons, we place these countries in the broad category of market economies. Although they share with the social-market economies a strong state perspective, theirs is not the western welfare-state model of the European countries. Both have far less developed welfare systems than would be the norm in western economies. In South Korea, only 67.1% of the population is covered by healthcare schemes. These countries are more in the collectivist than individualist cultural tradition. Their Asian cultural heritage emphasizes the role of the family and that of the company as a kind of family, looking after the whole person, rather than taking the narrow view of the worker as an employee.

Japan, like Germany, faced the task of rebuilding its industries after the Second World War. The state provided economic guidance, and hence Japan is looked on as exemplifying the 'developmental state' model (Johnson, 1982). The use of 'industrial policy', rather than outright state ownership, has been a chief feature of its economic development, relying on co-operation between the three centres of power – the bureaucracy, politicians and big businesses. Business in Japan has traditionally been organized around groups of companies, or *keiretsu*, linked by cross-shareholdings and informal networks with suppliers and customers. From a position of economic powerhouse in the 1980s the Japanese economy descended into stagnation in the 1990s, following a collapse in the banking and financial system brought on by a collapse in asset values and imprudent lending. Recovery came belatedly, in about 2004, but has been hesitant. Japan's leading companies, including Toyota and Sony, have remained globally competitive, despite newer competitors from South Korea, Taiwan and, of course, China. However, Toyota's reputation has suffered from high-profile quality problems entailing large recalls of cars in major markets.

South Korea, too, has taken its own distinctive development path. Here, economic development owes its impetus to the large family-owned conglomerates, or *chaebol*, which expanded aggressively overseas during the 1980s (see case study in Chapter 1). These groups include Hyundai, Samsung and LG. South Korean companies were severely affected by the Asian financial crisis of 1997–8, its companies having accumulated excessive debt, in a business environment where family considerations mattered more than objectively sound business practices. Restructuring these companies along more transparent lines of governance was one of the reforms that later governments have undertaken, although the strong cultural heritage has worked against radical reforms. On the other hand, a strong cultural heritage can be viewed as an 'anchor' against the more flamboyant characteristics of free markets (Mahbubani, 2009).

Lastly, China, the largest Asian country, is also undertaking market reforms, but still within the framework of the one-party state bequeathed by the communist revolution. We therefore classify China as a mixed economy, discussed in the next section.

Mixed economies: China and India

The mixed economy is the last category in Figure 4.7, combining market elements with institutional structures controlled by the state. China is the main example, with its embrace of two systems: capitalism as an economic system and an authoritarian political system controlled by the Communist Party. China's political leadership retains ultimate control of the economic levers that shape market reforms. By contrast, India has a democratically-elected government, but in a context of strong state guidance. Their development paths have been different, but both provide examples of state-led development which other emerging economies have emulated.

China

China covers a huge territory and is home to diverse peoples, the largest being the Han Chinese, tracing their roots to the ancient Han dynasty. China's long history revolves around successive empires that have subsumed regional minority groups and led to conflicts. These tensions, along with unity imposed from central authorities, give some indication of the social currents in China today. Although later than other Asian countries in economic development, China is now asserting itself as a regional and global power – economically, militarily and politically. The current state of China (its full name is the People's Republic of China) dates only from the communist revolution of 1949 led by Mao Zedong. The ruling party structures were roughly modelled on the Soviet system, and these remain the formal framework. However, the underpinning ideology has seen numerous shifts. The Maoism of the early years (based on the teachings of Mao Zedong), loosely based on Marxism-Leninism, has given way to a more nationalist perspective. It was only in 1979 that the shift towards and open economy began, under the leadership of Deng Xiaoping.

Thereafter, China's economy grew dramatically, achieving 10% average growth rates for the next two decades. The prosperity of its people has also grown, although there are wide variations between the rural standard of living and that enjoyed by the new urban dwellers. China's economic development has rested on globalization, but only in limited ways. As we found in Chapter 2, globalization implies an opening up to cross-border flows of capital and goods. China has been slow to open its economy in both these respects. China's development has rested on industrialization and improved infrastructure. Its leadership sought to benefit from its abundance of low-cost labour by aiding investment in export-oriented manufacturing. It welcomed foreign investors to Special Economic Zones, where they could import inputs duty-free, avoiding the usual import duties in place to protect state enterprises (Rodrik, 2011). The economic model relied on migrant workers travelling from rural areas to the urban manufacturing complexes. More than one-third of the country's entire labour force consists of migrant workers, numbering some 275 million people (Anderlini, 2015). Liberalizing reforms, including the introduction of private property, reducing quantitative restrictions on imports and allowing foreign financial institutions to operate in the country, have come about only slowly, and after the country's period of rapid growth. As Figure 4.9 shows, China's growth has now slowed, and the leadership is focusing on more sustainable growth.

Health risks from pollution are worries for people in China, especially in industrial cities.

Source: Getty Images/ iStockphoto Thinkstock Images/Barnaby Chambers.

China's state-directed economic development has been successful in transforming it into a manufacturing superpower. In the process, nearly half a billion people have been lifted out of absolute poverty (Rodrik, 2011). China ranked 91 out of 187 countries in the Human Development Index in 2013. But development remains uneven, and has been accompanied by rising inequality. Rapid development, including massive investment in fossil-fuel power generation, has resulted in detrimental impacts on the environment and societal well-being. Air pollution has become an urgent issue, leading to social tensions, which the leadership has cause to fear could boil over into political instability. Chinese people, while they have greater economic freedom, still enjoy little in the way of civil and political freedoms that are recognized as human rights and core social values. Although living and working in urban areas, migrant workers remain legally classified as rural. They have no right to settle permanently in the urban areas where they are working, or to access healthcare, education and pensions in those areas. They can feel caught in limbo: losing ties with their families in rural villages, but having no right to reside permanently in the city. This situation can impact on their health and well-being, casting doubt on the sustainability of an economy that relies so heavily on migrant labour.

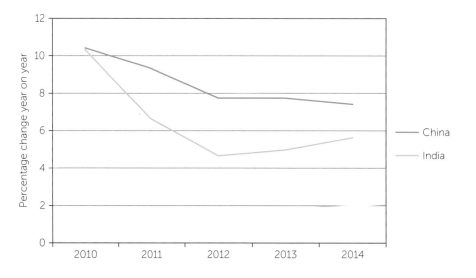

Figure 4.9 Economic growth in China and India

Sources: Data from World Bank, Data and Statistics, at www.worldbank.org, accessed 9 April 2015; IMF (2014) *World Economic Outlook*, October 2014, at www.imf.org.

The way I see it ...

'Migration of peasants to the cities is what created China's economic miracle.'

China's president, Li Kequing, in March 2015; quoted in *The Guardian*, 2 May 2015.

What are the negative impacts on society of this 'economic miracle'?

India

Like China, India has long historical roots and diverse ethnic groups. However, far from being an imperial power itself, India was subsumed into the British Empire, becoming an independent state in 1948. Partly because of its colonial legacy, India would seem to be closer to a market economy than China. There is considerable economic freedom, and its government is accountable through democratic elections. It has a legal tradition resting on the rule of law, also part of the colonial heritage. However, India was founded as a socialist state in 1948, and retains a legacy of the strong state prone to heavy-handed regulation. Its market reforms have been guided by government, which for many years was reluctant to welcome foreign direct investment (FDI). Since the mid-2000s, India has become more open to foreign investors, but the western investor must enter the market through a joint venture with an Indian partner.

India's economy benefited from growth in computing and high-tech service sectors from the 1990s onwards, but its manufacturing industries have been slow to expand, largely because of poor infrastructure and very restrictive employment protection laws that deterred companies from hiring workers (see the closing case study in Chapter 2). India's economic growth, shown in Figure 4.9, slowed following the global financial crisis, and then resumed its growth trajectory.

In comparison with China, India invariably looks the weaker in terms of development. The ruling Congress Party lost elections in 2014, and was replaced by the Hindu Nationalist party, led by Narendra Modi. Modi has sought to introduce business-friendly reforms, including eliminating many of the bureaucratic impediments to businesses and also investing in infrastructure. While welcomed by large companies, these reforms are met with more scepticism by many in India's society, fearful that profits will come before local concerns and social welfare. India remains a much poorer and less developed country than China. And inequality is growing. The Gini coefficient is up from 30.9 in 2005 to 32.3 in 2012 (World Bank, 2013). Its HDI ranking is 135 out of 187, and it is ranked below the average of other countries of medium human development. In terms of gender inequality, India's rank is a poor 127 out of 152 countries – below Bangladesh and Pakistan. Figure 4.8 shows that only 40.2% of the population is covered by any health scheme. The UN's Multidimensional Poverty Index, which covers health, education and living standards, finds that 55% of the Indian population live in poverty (World Bank, 2013). In terms of social well-being, India's economic development has been disappointingly uneven.

China versus India

China and India, both characterized here as mixed economies, are very different. In your view, which of the two is steering more convincingly towards sustainable development, and why?

The transition economies of Central and Eastern Europe

Many post-communist transition economies fall into the broad category of mixed economy, transforming state-dominated systems into market-oriented economies, accompanied by political democratization. Privatization, involving the conversion of state enterprises to privately owned and operated companies, was central to this process. Former state-owned firms were sold and new start-up enterprises were encouraged. These processes were put in motion when the Soviet bloc started to break up in 1989. East Germany was united with West Germany in 1990. New states were born in Central and Eastern Europe (CEE): Hungary, Poland, Croatia, the Czech Republic, the Slovak Republic, Slovenia, Romania and Bulgaria. These eight countries are now all EU member states. Croatia was the last of these to join the EU, joining in 2013. The Soviet Union itself broke up into 15 separate republics. The three Baltic republics – Estonia, Latvia and Lithuania – went their own way, eventually becoming EU member states in 2004.

To varying degrees, the eight CEE economies that have become EU members have sought foreign investors to drive economic development. While this might indicate their embrace of globalization through global supply chains, the reality is that these economies have mainly turned their sights towards Western European economies, notably Germany, which is the destination of 59% of their exports. 80% of the FDI flowing to the CEE countries has been from Western Europe. FDI has helped to promote investment and growth in sectors such as car manufacturing and business services, but the bulk of the FDI has targeted financial services. Between 2004 and 2008, one-fifth of the net FDI into these countries was in the financial sector (McKinsey Global Institute, 2013). In 2013, foreign owners held 85% of the equity of the top ten banks in the region. Car manufacturing also took off in the 2000s. Volkswagen took over the ailing Skoda company in the Czech Republic, and Renault transformed Dacia in Romania, the Dacia brand now contributing strongly to Renault's overall performance.

The CEE countries enjoyed economic growth averaging over 5% annually between 2004 and 2008 – not far beneath levels of the star emerging economies of China and India. These transition economies had much going for them. Workforces were skilled and well educated. The business environment was market-friendly, institutionally stable and less corrupt than China or India. Wages were about 75% lower than in Western European countries, and lower still in Romania and Bulgaria. Corporation tax was low. But there were risks lurking in the growth model of these countries. Investment and consumption were both heavily dependent on debt funding, and much of this debt was foreign, involving risky exposure to volatile financial markets. Domestic consumption was rising, and, although this contributed to growth, the low levels of domestic saving and rising consumer debt made these economies vulnerable to financial shocks. Rising property prices led to housing bubbles in several countries. When the financial crisis struck, immediate impacts were a dramatic drop in FDI inflows and in domestic consumption. FDI has recovered slowly. By 2010, FDI inflows were still only half those of the pre-crisis peak. The rapid growth of the 2000s has not returned. These economies are now looking to build sounder foundations through infrastructure investment, raising productivity and encouraging saving.

Russia's economic strength globally has rested on its rich natural resource wealth in oil and gas. Having been the largest of the Soviet republics, Russia privatized its large industries rapidly, unleashing a new powerful capitalist class, but without the regulatory institutions which are common in mature market economies. The gas ministry was transformed into Gazprom. A result was the growth of a class of powerful oligarchs in major industries, creating political tensions. Russia adopted a new constitution in 1993, but its democratic aspirations have only been partially fulfilled. The rise of Vladimir Putin was responsible for reining in the oligarchs and restoring stability following a financial crash in 1998, but this process resulted in a consolidation of leadership in the all-powerful ruling party. Gazprom's ownership reverted to the state in this process. Russia under Putin has continued to exert economic and political pressure in the former Soviet territories, despite their formal independence (see the opening case study in Chapter 5). Ukraine has been an example. The country has suffered divisive tensions between the more western-oriented region in the west of the country and the more Russia-leaning population of the east. Ukraine's government had aspired to EU membership, but these hopes became jeopardized when violent clashes led to Russia's annexation of the strategically important Crimean peninsula in 2014. This territorial incursion into a sovereign neighbour's territory met with international condemnation, prompting trade sanctions on Russia. Russia's economy, weakened from the fall in the price of oil in global markets, became further weakened by the imposition of sanctions. The Ukrainian instability affects the economic environment, in that both domestic and foreign investors are discouraged. Other post-Soviet states suffer similar tensions between continuing Russian influence and the desire to nurture closer ties with western countries.

Regionalization: focus on the EU

Regionalization has been taking place throughout the world, despite the forces of globalization. By regionalization, we mean growing economic links and co-operation within a geographic region, both on the part of businesses and governments. Economic ties, such as trade, can lead to what is termed 'shallow' integration, in that there need be little physical presence of the foreign company in its destination market. FDI, which entails establishing operations in the foreign location, represents a deeper involvement in local economies as stakeholders, although foreign investors, too, can withdraw from markets as their strategies change. Regionalization at a deeper level involves not just liberalized trade and investment, but deepening institutional ties and political co-operation. The extent of regionalization differs among the world's regions. In many, diverse economies and disparate cultural and political backgrounds tend to limit the deepening of ties. Regional trade agreements, discussed in Chapter 7, have sprung up in every continent. Examples include the North American Free Trade Agreement (NAFTA) and the ASEAN agreement of South East Asia. These agreements have focused mainly on reducing trade barriers between member economies.

The European Union (EU) (www.europa.eu), by contrast, has progressed beyond trade deals to take on regional governmental functions, becoming a supranational structure, potentially challenging the sovereignty of member states. However, the vision of the EU from its foundation in the 1950s, when the memories of the Second World War were still fresh, included creating a closer political union as a force for peace, co-operation and security. This was an ambitious project because, even among the original members (shown in Table 4.1), there was economic diversity. Diversity became much greater as more states joined, including poorer states and former communist states. Despite economic integration, the enlarged EU and eurozone have not brought economic convergence.

Table 4.1 Membership of the EU and eurozone

Date of EU entry	State
1957	Belgium*, France*, Germany*, Luxemburg*, the Netherlands*, Italy*
1973	Denmark, Ireland*, the UK
1981	Greece*
1986	Portugal*, Spain*
1995	Austria*, Finland*, Sweden
2004	Cyprus*, Malta*, Czech Republic, Hungary, Poland, the Slovak Republic*, Slovenia*, Latvia*, Lithuania*, Estonia*
2007	Bulgaria, Romania
2013	Croatia

Note: Members of the eurozone are shown by an asterisk (*).

The economies of the EU and eurozone

The EU encompasses a population of over half a billion people and, taken as a whole, it is the world's largest economy with a GDP of $18.51 trillion in 2014, coming ahead of the US in second place with a GDP of $17.42 trillion (World Bank, 2016). The EU now comprises 28 member states; of these, 19 are members of the single-currency eurozone (see Table 4.1). A turning-point came in 2004, when the union absorbed 10 new states, often referred to as the 'accession 10', distinguishing them from the pre-2004 states, which make up the 'EU 15'. As we have seen, most of these new states are transition economies.

The EU project aimed to create a single market in which goods, people, information and capital can move freely. The process has been mapped out in a series of treaties, beginning with the Treaty of Rome in 1956. The opening up of trade in goods and FDI among member states has been a success story, but other aspects of integration, such as services and transport across national borders, have not yet been liberalized. The free movement of people within the EU was curtailed by most member states in 2015, with the influx of refugees from wartorn countries such as Syria. The EU is committed to liberal goals of free markets and rolling back the state which, as we have seen, is a strong player in a number of European economies, notably those which fall within the broad category of social market systems. Any liberalization or harmonization of rules involves the co-operation of national governments, willingly ceding powers to EU structures. National governments are highly sensitive to the political power of groups and interests within their own countries and, despite wishes to commit to Europe-wide open markets, are constantly under pressure to protect domestic industries. The EU's history to date has been one of member governments pursuing domestic policy objectives within EU structures, rather than taking an EU-wide perspective.

In theory, governments remain responsible for the prudent management of their own economies, where national economic systems retain their distinctive characteristics. They retain control of fiscal policies such as spending and taxation, but in

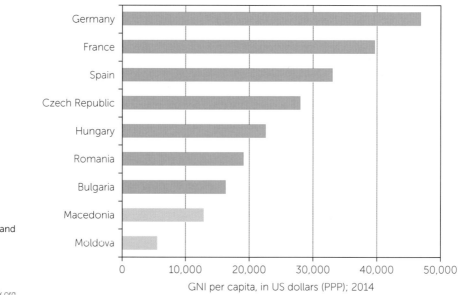

Figure 4.10 Income variations among a selection of existing and aspiring EU member states

Source: Data from World Bank database, GNI per capita, at www.worldbank.org, accessed 15 February 2016.

GNI per capita, in US dollars (PPP); 2014

Note: Aspiring member states (Macedonia and Moldova) are shown in a lighter shade.

matters of monetary policy, the EU plays an important role. All member states are members of the Economic and Monetary Union (EMU), which, although its name implies genuine economic union, is in practice well beneath this level of uniformity. The highest level of co-ordination is among the member states who have adopted the single currency, the euro. There are now 19 members of the eurozone, whose monetary policy is governed by the European Central Bank.

Central to the process of economic integration was the introduction of the single currency. The elimination of exchange-rate risk and reduction in transaction costs have contributed greatly to growth in trade and FDI. The euro as a currency came into existence in 1999, and went into use as a cash currency in 2002. Membership of the eurozone involves relinquishing power over exchange rates and interest rates to the European Central Bank (ECB). For eurozone member states, monetary policy is thus governed by the ECB, while fiscal policy continues to be controlled by national authorities. This apparent inconsistency has been highlighted as a weakness which contributed to the eurozone debt crisis that unfolded in the aftermath of the financial crisis (Lane, 2012).

Any EU member state wishing to join the eurozone must first fulfill a number of criteria, known as the Maastricht convergence criteria, set out in the Maastricht Treaty, which came into effect in 1993. A cornerstone of the Maastricht Treaty is the stability and growth pact which commits all EU governments, whether in the eurozone or not, to keep budget deficits in check. As budget deficits have mounted in most European countries, this is one of the important hurdles for prospective eurozone members. An applicant country must become part of the EMU, and comply with the Exchange Rate Mechanism (ERM) system, by which its currency is loosely pegged to the euro. This means that its currency fluctuation against the euro must remain within relatively tight bands. The EMU dates from 1979, and the ERM was updated in 2004, to become ERMII, with which current applicants must comply. The full convergence criteria are listed below:

- Price stability – The rate of inflation must be no more than 1.5% higher than the three member states with the lowest inflation rates.
- Sound public finances – The government's budget deficit must be below 3% of GDP.
- Sustainable public finances – National debt should not exceed 60% of GDP.
- Exchange rate stability – The country should have been in the ERM for two years without having devalued its currency within that time.
- Long-term interest rates – The country's interest rate must not be more than 2% higher than that of the three countries with the best performance in terms of price stability in the EU.

These criteria have been somewhat overtaken by events in recent years. A number of existing eurozone member states built up huge debt burdens in the 2000s. These burdens included corporate and household debt, in addition to sovereign debt. Greece and Italy both had national debt in excess of the 60% fiscal limit when admitted to the eurozone in the first place. Greece saw this debt burden swell to 175% in the following years. Ireland was weighed down by out-of-control household debt which, together with government and corporate debt, amounted to 400% of GDP. Radical cuts in public spending were introduced in these ailing peripheral eurozone countries, and bailout aid was organized by the IMF and EU. Greece has long teetered on the edge of sovereign default and forced withdrawal from the eurozone. By 2014, both Spain and Ireland were on the road to economic recovery, posting economic growth.

However, the fragility of the eurozone's mechanisms for ensuring financial stability had been exposed, leaving lingering concerns for the future.

Enlargement and the future of the EU

The process of enlargement has been at the heart of the EU since its inception, bringing the prospect of greater prosperity and stability to the wider region. However, the debate over the EU has gone on almost as long. Applicant countries face a long process of assessment, during which they must persuade the EU that their country is a market economy, a functioning democracy and an upholder of the rule of law. Questions over these issues have been raised in relation to some of the 'accession 10' countries. For example, Hungary's government has veered away from the rule of law and democratic values. Following the admission of Romania and Bulgaria in 2007 – both of which raised issues regarding corruption and the rule of law – there was a gap in new admissions. Croatia, formed from the former Yugoslavia, joined in 2013. Other states in the region have applied, including Kosovo, Serbia, Macedonia and Albania. In all of these countries, issues of corruption, organized crime and weakness of the rule of law are impediments. The largest of the applicant countries is Turkey, a Muslim country traditionally seen as straddling Europe and Asia, but whose secular and democratic constitution would seem to shift it closer into the European sphere. However, the increasingly authoritarian leadership of its former prime minister, now president, Recep Tayyip Erdoğan, suggests a shift away from EU criteria (see case study in Chapter 5).

Tension over future enlargement was one of the factors that delayed the Lisbon Treaty, which took effect in 2009. The treaty represents an amended version of a constitutional treaty that failed ratification hurdles in several member states. The difficulties encountered in securing ratification of the Lisbon Treaty reflect member states' scepticism about the benefits of the EU in terms of national interests. The spectre of national economic protectionism is one which has long haunted the EU, especially in the context of countries in which nationalist politicians have criticized the EU's liberal reform policies as threats to national sovereignty. EU enlargement has been about the prospects of economic gains winning out over these inward-looking forces. These gains have been real enough in new member states: businesses have flourished from greater cross-border activity, and governments have welcomed the structural funds which have flowed into poorer economies. The 'cohesion' funds, along with subsidies for agriculture, amount to a large proportion of the EU's budget, as Figure 4.11 shows.

The EU Commission has remained committed to market reforms, but these have taken place only very gradually, and governments have tended to retain a mindset which ranks countries as winners or losers in terms of EU funding. Poorer countries have been winners in this respect, as the lion's share of its budget is devoted to aiding poorer regions and vital sectors. The extent to which there is the basis of a definable regional capitalism is much debated. A model of European capitalism closer to the free-market model has been a beacon for many within the EU, but national governments have retained a strong grip on institutional direction within its structures. The fact that the financial crisis struck Ireland, a leader in market reforms, has clouded prospects of further market liberalization. Iceland, which in 2009 applied to join the EU, was also a casualty of the financial crisis, its banks having become vastly overstretched in global financial markets. Iceland's progress has been barred by its failure to reimburse the UK and the Netherlands, where governments compensated

Total budget is €161.8 billion.

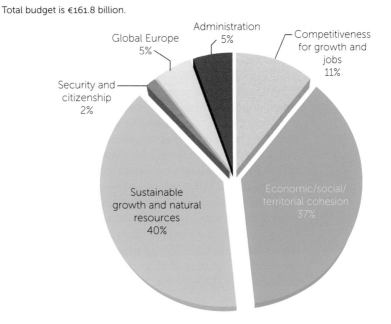

Figure 4.11 Breakdown of the EU's 2015 budget

Source: Data from EU Commission, Annual Budget life-cycle: figures and documents, at www. ec.europa.eu/budget/ annual, accessed 20 April 2014. © European Union, 1995–2016.

their own citizens who were victims of one of Iceland's failed banks. Another possible applicant is the former Soviet republic of Moldova, one of Europe's least-developed economies, with a per capita GNI of just $5,500 (see Figure 4.10). The country is now an independent republic, but, like neighbouring Ukraine, is heavily influenced by Russia.

The EU is unlikely to repeat the ambitious enlargement exercise that took place in the mid-2000s. Both the Netherlands and France voted 'no' in referendums on the constitutional treaty which preceded the Lisbon Treaty, largely for fear of paving the way for further enlargement. Inhabitants of the richer member states shoulder the financial burdens of the EU, which have grown to huge proportions. They question why they should be burdened with propping up member states which they feel have failed to act responsibly in managing their internal economies. They point to weak governance, out-of-control public spending, corruption and lack of transparency in some member states which, they fear, could threaten the whole edifice. In accordance with an election pledge made in the UK's general election of 2015, the Conservative government held a referendum on leaving the EU (known as 'Brexit') in June 2016. In a turnout of 72% of eligible voters, 52% favoured leaving, while 48% favoured remaining. The government was thus committed to negotiating the UK's exit, a process which could be economically and politically destabilizing, with ripples extending well beyond the UK.

The EU at the crossroads

Divergent national perspectives and goals have clouded the EU's future, causing many to predict its ultimate break-up. Is such a break-up likely, and what impacts would a break-up of the EU have on the business environment?

The economic environment: challenges and responsibilities

More than ever, businesses are now likely to take a global view of their strategies, singling out countries for location advantages. A country's economic environment is a key aspect of the PEST analysis (introduced in Chapter 1), which aids corporate strategists. A national economy will be targeted for advantages such as the availability of low-cost labour, resource wealth or a stage in a global supply chain. Similarly, a country such as a large emerging economy will be favoured for its large potential market. In India, healthy economic growth and a growing number of middle-class consumers attract numerous MNEs to its consumer markets. However, India's potential as a market must be tempered by a broader view of the social context. As we have seen, there are significant questions hanging over India's development model. Inequality is rising, gender inequality is a particular concern, and human development indicators are low. Rising average incomes point to improving standards of living, but form only part of the story for India, as for other countries. If growth is not sustainable, then there is a question mark over the direction in which the development model is heading. This chapter has argued that to be sustainable, growth needs to be inclusive. Growth that benefits the few and leaves behind the many is not sustainable.

China has been more successful than India in raising incomes, but in other respects still faces many challenges. Healthcare, education and a healthy natural environment are essentials of social well-being, but do not flow automatically from economic growth. Delivering these public goods presents responsibilities and challenges for governments. If a government attracts investment from global businesses, it does so mainly with a view to promoting growth and prosperity in the national economy. But prosperity for whom? If insiders, both in business and government, are the chief beneficiaries, then corruption sets in and social well-being is set back. The risks of social and political instability will rise, and economic growth itself can be undermined. The MNE is constantly on the lookout for more advantageous locations, and is deterred by instability that can jeopardize future growth. Governments that offer attractive deals to foreign investors can find that the negative impacts on society ultimately lead to their departure, resulting in economic worries that dovetail with deteriorating social well-being. To what extent are global companies themselves to blame?

Many would reply that the company exists to maximize its profits in each location, and social well-being is not its responsibility. However, as this chapter has shown, sustainable growth is in the interests of all concerned, including companies, governments and societies. Most companies now appreciate that their businesses must look beyond short-term profits, considering social and environmental implications of their activities in the locations where they operate.

As we have seen, the liberal market model in its pure form lacks a defined social-conscience dimension. Still, British and American companies have taken a lead in corporate social responsibility (CSR), even when their governments have shown only reluctant support for measures such as controlling greenhouse gas emissions. Would a company choose to invest in production in a developing country with weak environmental standards, over a costlier location with higher standards? Many would choose the former on economic grounds, but this could be rather short-sighted. Technological improvements could bring down costs, making the costlier country a more competitive location over time, whereas the operations in many developing countries might not be sustainable in the long term. Similarly, investing in a developing country where wages are low and social welfare is minimal might seem a viable cost-saving strategy, but is unsustainable as well as unethical. The investing firm is wise to look to the broader economic and social picture when surveying comparative economic environments. Companies play key roles in all national economies, their activities providing the jobs and income that generate prosperity in society as a whole. This role brings responsibilities to look beyond the interests of corporate owners to the broader interests of stakeholders, paramount among whom are employees and communities.

Strategy choices for MNEs

Emerging markets are now the focus of many MNE strategies, but they pose challenges in terms of sustainability. On what principles should today's MNEs design emerging-market strategies?

Conclusions

Expanding markets and deepening interconnectedness are hallmarks of globalization. Businesses have been drivers of globalization, pushing into new locations in terms of production as well as markets. Their activities bring societies and organizations closer together, facilitated by advances in communications technology. Markets in goods and services, notably including financial services, have expanded from national to global proportions, as countries have opened their economies to the potential benefits of globalization. Both business and state players have been active in this process. Companies see business opportunities, and states see opportunities for economic growth through investment and job creation. Thus, the interests of market players and states seem to coincide: companies and governments eye potential gains. But, with hindsight, governments and businesses alike have probably underestimated the risks in globalized markets and their impacts on national economies. Economists tend to view a market as inherently stable and self-adjusting, reflecting fluctuations in supply and demand. A national economy, however, can be destabilized by external shock, often revealing underlying internal weaknesses, as happened when the global financial crisis struck in 2008. A national economy requires governmental watchdogs and regulators to ensure that markets function effectively. But this still leaves many unanswered questions. How much government is too much; who is being served by markets; and if markets are now global, what can a national government do anyway?

Answering these three questions has been at the heart of this chapter. The liberal market model resists government intervention in principle, but this model took a knock in the financial crisis. The countries that have opted for more state-centred economic models were less affected by the global economic crisis and recession that ensued. States that advocate a social market model have long been sceptical of the impacts of markets in society, as profit-seeking firms naturally aim to generate wealth for private owners. Growing inequality, weak social welfare and resulting weak social cohesion can ultimately undermine stability in society. Advocates of the social market model demand that businesses operate in a regulatory framework that focuses on social goals. But in a globalized world, why would a foreign investor opt to invest in a country that has high corporate taxes and social charges, high levels of government regulation and requirements, for example, to provide social benefits for employees? All of these are costs that would deter any investor. The investor would surely prefer a country with low taxation, low wages, little regulation and no social agenda. Of course, the choice is not likely to be as crude as this. Most governments at least nod towards the need to pursue societal goals. However, the globalized economic environment has highlighted divergent national economic systems. It has become clear that some economic models, especially those focused on rapid development, are unsustainable and could undermine the very growth on which they are predicated. Inclusive growth, incorporating social goals, is thus the more trustworthy route to sustainable development, benefiting both societies and businesses.

References

Aghion, P. and Howitt, P. (2009) *The Economics of Growth* (Cambridge, MA: MIT Press).

Avaredo, F., Atkinson, A., Piketty, T. and Saez, E. (no date) 'The World Top Incomes Database', at http://topincomes.g-mond.parisschoolofeconomics.eu/, accessed 28 March 2015.

Anderlini, J. (2015) 'China's great migration', *Financial Times*, 2 May, at www.ft.com

Bizimana, G., Gallardo, G. and Pla, L. (2014) 'Equatorial Guinea', *African Economic Outlook*, published by the UN Development Programme, at www.africaneconomicoutlook.org, accessed 24 March 2015.

Cooper, R., Kennelly, J. and Orduñez-Garcia, P. (2006) 'Health in Cuba', *International Journal of Epidemiology*, 35: 817–824.

Giles, C. (2014) 'Productivity crisis haunts power league', *Financial Times*, 16 October, at www.ft.com.

ILO (2014a) *World Social Protection Report 2014/15* (Geneva: ILO).

ILO (2014b) 'KILM9: Total unemployment', in *Key Indicators of the Labour Market* (KILM), at www.ilo.org

Johnson, C. (1982) *MITI and the Japanese Miracle* (Stanford: Stanford University Press).

Lane, P. (2012) 'The European sovereign debt crisis', *Journal of Economic Perspectives*, 26(3): 49–68.

Maddison, A. (2007) *Contours of the World Economy, 1–2030AD* (Oxford: Oxford University Press).

Mahbubani, K. (2009) 'Lessons for the west from Asian capitalism', in the series, 'The Future of Capitalism', *Financial Times*, 12 May, at www.ft.com.

McKinsey Global Institute (2013) 'A new dawn: reigniting growth in Central and Eastern Europe', December, at www.mckinsey.com/mgi

OECD (2011) 'How's Life?: Measuring well-being', OECD Publishing, at www.oecd.org

OECD (2014) 'China: structural reforms for inclusive growth', March, at www.oecd.org

Orange, R. (2015) 'Swedish council becomes first to limit private profits in healthcare', *The Guardian*, 28 April, at www.theguardian.com

Ostry, J., Berg, J., Charalambos, G. and Tsangarides, G. (2014) 'Redistribution, inequality and growth', IMF discussion note, April, at www.imf.org

Oxfam (2015) 'Wealth: having it all and wanting more', Issue briefing, January (Oxford: Oxfam International).

Oxfam (2016) 'Billionaires who own the same wealth as half the world', Press release, 18 January, at www.oxfam.org.uk

Piketty, T. (2014) *Capital in the Twenty-first Century* (Cambridge, MA: Harvard University Press).

Rawls, J. (1996) *Political Liberalism* (New York: Columbia University Press).

Rodrik, D. (2009) *One Economics, Many Recipes* (Princeton: Princeton University Press).

Rodrik, D. (2011) *The Globalization Paradox* (Oxford: Oxford University Press).

Sen, A. (2010) *The Idea of Justice* (London: Penguin Books).

Siebert, H. (2004) 'Economic and political governance in Germany's social market economy', Kiel Working Paper No. 1207, Kiel Institute for World Economics, at www.ifw-kiel.de

Smith, A. ([1776]1950) *An Inquiry into the Nature and Causes of the Wealth of Nations* (London: Methuen).

Stiglitz, J. (2002) *Globalization and its Discontents* (London: Allen Lane).

UNDP (2013) 'Income Gini Coefficient', Human Development Reports Office, at www.undp.org/en/content/income-gini-coefficient, accessed 28 March 2015.

WEF (World Economic Forum) (2015) *Global Risks 2015*, 10th edn (Geneva: World Economic Forum).

World Bank (2012) 'Morocco: Promoting youth opportunities and participation', Report No. 68731-MOR, at www.worldbank.org

World Bank (2013) 'India Development Update', Report No. AUS5757, October, at www.worldbank.org

World Bank (2016) 'World Development Indicators', at www.data.worldbank.org, accessed 14 February 2016.

Young, H. (2014) 'In Morocco youth unemployment is driving up inequality', *The Guardian*, 20 August, at www.theguardian.com

☞ Multiple choice questions

Go to the companion website: www.palgravehighered.com/morrison-gbe-4e to take a quick multiple choice quiz on what you have read in this chapter.

⑦ Review questions

1 In what ways is the circular flow diagram useful to show overall economic activity in the national economy?

2 How are GDP and GNI per capita used to compare countries, and what are their limitations?

3 Define inflation, and explain what its damaging effects can be on a national economy.

4 Why is the balance of payments important to policymakers, and why are governments concerned if there is a current account deficit?

5 Why is economic growth an important indicator, and what are its limitations?

6 What is 'inclusive growth', and why has it become a concern of governments?

7 In what ways do governments control monetary policy, and how has their room for manoeuvre become more limited with economic integration?

8 What are the distinguishing characteristics of the liberal market economy?

9 What are the weaknesses of the liberal market economy in terms of societal well-being?

10 Which countries are considered strongholds of the social market model of capitalism, and how are their economies evolving?

11 What are the specific strengths of the Asian model of capitalism? In the case of Japan, how did these strengths seem to translate into weaknesses in the 1990s?

12 What are the elements of the transition process towards a market economy in (a) China; and (b) the transition economies of Central and Eastern Europe?

13 What are the implications of European Monetary Union (EMU)? Is EMU bringing about convergence between member states?

14 What are the sources of friction within the EU?

15 What are the challenges and responsibilities that fall on foreign companies investing in developing economies?

✓ Assignments

1 Looking at the key indicators of the macroeconomic environment, what policy instruments are available to national decision-makers, and to what extent are they now limited by factors beyond their borders?

2 Assess the potential benefits and drawbacks of the liberal market economic model. To what extent is China's state capitalism a valid alternative which can be emulated by other developing economies?

📖 Further reading

Acemoglu, D. and Robinson, J. (2012) *Why Nations Fail: The Origins of Power, Prosperity and Poverty* (London: Profile Books).

Begg, I. (2012) *Economics for Business*, 4th edn (New York: McGraw-Hill).

Bootle, R. (2010) *The Trouble with Markets: Saving Capitalism from Itself* (London: Nicholas Brealey Publishing).

De Grauwe, P. (2016) *Economics of Monetary Union*, 11th edn (Oxford: OUP).

Deaton, A. (2013) *The Great Escape: Health, Wealth and the Origins of Inequality* (Princeton: Princeton University Press).

Dunning, J. (ed.) (1997) *Governments, Globalization and International Business* (Oxford: Oxford University Press).

Fisher, M. (2009) *Capitalist Realism: Is There No Alternative?* (Ropley, Hampshire, UK: Zero Books).

Gros, D. (2009) *Economic Transition in Central and Eastern Europe: Planting the Seeds* (Cambridge: Cambridge University Press).

Landes, D. (1998) *The Wealth and Poverty of Nations* (London: W.W. Norton & Co.).

Maddison, A. (1991) *Dynamic Forces in Capitalist Development* (Oxford: Oxford University Press).

Morgan, M. and Whitley, R. (2014) *Capitalisms and Capitalism in the Twenty-first Century* (Oxford: OUP).

Parkin, M., Powell, M. and Matthews, K. (2007) *Economics*, 7th edn (New Jersey: Addison Wesley).

Piketty, T. (2014) *Capital in the Twenty-first Century* (Cambridge, MA: Harvard University Press).

Piggott, J. and Cook, M. (2006) *International Business Economics* (Basingstoke: Palgrave Macmillan).

Walter, A. and Zhang, X. (eds) (2014) *East Asian Capitalism: Diversity, Continuity and Change* (Oxford: OUP).

Yasheng Huang (2010) *Capitalism with Chinese Characteristics: Entrepreneurship and the State* (Cambridge: Cambridge University Press).

⊕ **Visit the companion website at** www.palgravehighered.com/morrison-gbe-4e **for further learning and teaching resources.**

Sweden: an economic model for others to follow?

Sweden, along with its Scandinavian neighbours, has become identified with an economic model that combines a market economy with social welfare. The thinking behind this combination acknowledges the benefits of the market, but recognizes that policies can be put in place to temper its inequalities and promote social well-being. The political underpinning of this thinking is most evident in the policies of the social democratic parties that have been at the forefront of politics in all the Scandinavian countries. To critics, there are inherent contradictions in these twin ideals. They maintain that high levels of social welfare inevitably entail high taxes, which discourage enterprises, while, at the same time, generous welfare benefits discourage people from seeking productive employment. The result can be increased public spending that spirals out of control, leading to possible economic crisis. The critics would note that this is roughly what happened to Sweden's economy in the 1980s. A financial crisis in 1991 saw the ruin of two banks that had to be nationalized. Economic recession and high unemployment led to growing pressure on public expenditure. The virtues of the so-called 'Nordic' model were looking more like myth than reality. It looked as if the critics had been right.

However, Sweden's government took a firm hand and guided the country out of its economic woes. Did this mean the old model would be abandoned? In fact, much of what the government did certainly seemed inconsistent with the old model (Stenfors, 2015). For example, privatization was introduced in many services, such as healthcare and education. And taxes were lowered. This did not seem to fit the picture of social-democratic orthodoxy, as markets appeared to be supplanting the state. However, in the Swedish context, the strength of the nation's cultural commitment to equality, full employment and individual freedoms remained the foundation for the reforms. Market forces and financial innovations were seen as means of restoring economic growth, not as ends in themselves. Hence, for example, privatization of services was introduced where efficiencies could be made, without sacrificing quality and without undermining the overall

system. Welfare spending was reduced after the crisis, but not drastically. Sweden remains essentially committed to social welfare. Government spending still accounts for half its economy.

Government efficiencies were an essential element of the newer version of the Swedish economic model, reining in the high levels of debt and strictly controlling public spending. Sweden was also alert to the changes taking place in a globalized economic environment. For businesses, Sweden has been a good deal more competitive as a location than might be imagined. Whereas corporation tax in the 1980s was 35%, it is now 22%, which is considerably less than in the US. Moreover, there are numerous tax exemptions. The company enjoys exemption from capital gains tax and from tax on dividends from shares held for business purposes, whether in a listed or non-listed company. These policies are favourable to the holding company structure, which is common among Swedish businesses. Sweden's economy is dominated by the large holding companies that are run as family dynasties, the most notable one of which is the Wallenbergs.

The Wallenberg family, now in its fifth generation, controls a huge array of businesses. Their holding company, Investor, controls a business empire worth in the vicinity of $250 billion. They are famous for their long-term perspective and for their active management of the many companies under their control. These include Electrolux, the white goods manufacturer; Saab, the aerospace company; and Ericsson, the telecoms equipment maker. Family members sit on multiple boards, and control board appointments. There are weighted voting rights held by family members, so that they can effectively control board appointments. It is sometimes said that this system creates too cosy an atmosphere between managers and the dominant shareholders (Milne, 2015). It could be argued that the system works in Sweden, where there is a high level of trust and those in charge feel a strong sense of personal responsibility. The family dynasty as it operates in Sweden is seen as a source of stability and long-term business strategy.

Sweden's economy suffered from the financial crisis of 2008, as did other European countries, which are the main destinations of its exports. However, it has been able to recover rather more strongly than its European neighbours, partly because its banks had been recapitalized after the earlier crisis, and its government had in place prudent policies to keep public spending under control. Is Sweden still enjoying the social stability that reflects its egalitarian values? Inequality is growing, and the rise of the anti-immigration political party, the Swedish Democrats, suggests that the consensus on the social aspects of the Swedish model could be coming under strain.

Sources: Stenfors, A. (2015) 'The Swedish model in 2015: A "safe haven" or a "Nordic Noir"?', *Global Labour Column*, No. 201, May, University of the Witwatersrand, at www.column.global-labour-university.org; Bergston, C.F. (2013) 'Obama should take lessons from Sweden to the G-20', *The Washington Post*, 29 August, at www.washingtonpost.com; Sanandaji, N. (2015) 'The end of Nordic illusions', *Wall Street Journal*, 24 June, at www.wsj.com; Milne, R. (2015) 'Meet the Wallenbergs', *Financial Times*, 6 June, at www.ft.com.

Questions for discussion

- What are the strengths of Sweden's economic model?
- How has Sweden's economic model changed since the 1980s?
- What criticisms could be made against the dominant family-run holding companies in Sweden?
- To what extent is Sweden's economic model a good one for other countries to follow?

CHAPTER

5

THE POLITICAL ENVIRONMENT: STATE AND BUSINESS ACTORS

Outline of chapter

This chapter will enable you to

- Appreciate the characteristics of nation-states and how they are evolving in the global environment
- Gain an understanding of sources of political legitimacy and authority
- Identify the dimensions of political risk in business decision-making globally
- Assess the extent to which democracy and authoritarian governments are evolving in the current global environment
- Evaluate the changing roles of business globally in political contexts, in light of ethical and societal responsibilities

The politics of gas in Russia

Russia's extreme Arctic conditions present challenges for the oil and gas industries.

Source: iStock.com/Berkut_34.

With claim to the world's largest gas reserves, Russia has huge potential for wealth generation from energy exports. The strong state tradition of its vast territory, along with satellite territories over which it has historically exerted control, has made the exploitation of gas pivotal in the eyes of rulers in Moscow. This was true in the former Soviet Union, and remains true today. The break-up of the Soviet communist dictatorship in 1991 marked the start of a period of political and economic instability. The sale of former state assets led to the rise of powerful business oligarchs, the leaders of newly privatized industries. New democratic political institutions promised accountability of government, but became mired in corruption and infighting among new business and political powerbrokers. The election of Vladimir Putin as president in 2000 promised to restore order and refocus the economy. His nationalist message was clear, and he intended to reassert Russian influence in former Soviet territories. This was a message that appealed to the Russian populace, boosting the popularity of his United Russia party. His success would depend heavily on the country's main source of wealth – its gas industry. Bringing energy under Kremlin control would be crucial to consolidating his political power. Political legitimacy and economic power seemed to go hand in hand.

Gazprom, the former Soviet gas ministry that had been privatized in the 1990s, was restored to state control, headed by a Putin associate. Other resource assets went the same way. Yukoil, the privatized oil company, was broken up and its owners imprisoned; the assets were awarded to Putin associates. In the Russia of Putin, Kremlin-linked individuals became the new oligarchs, able to gain rich rewards but on condition of loyalty to Putin. The economy became concentrated in the hands of these individuals, and, ultimately, under Putin's political control. In addition, Gazprom bought out Russian media businesses, helping to consolidate Putin's control of the media.

In a world of rising energy prices, the potential for wealth generation was seen as phenomenal. Russian optimists foresaw Gazprom overtaking companies like US giant, ExxonMobil. Global investors enthused, and

Russia was branded a BRIC economy, along with the fast-growing emerging economies of China, Brazil and India. But Russia was different, with a history of industrialization dating from the Soviet era, when its energy resources were a source of its power. In the post-Soviet era, however, the exploitation of Russia's gas has been dependent increasingly on partnerships with western oil companies. In particular, reserves in harsh locations, such as offshore and in Arctic locations, have seen the involvement of BP, Shell, ExxonMobil and the large service companies such as Schlumberger. In 2008, when Gazprom's confidence was high, it was valued at $367 billion, but the deterioration in the economic environment by 2015 saw its value slip to just $51 billion (Burke, 2015). The fall in energy prices globally was a big factor. The price of oil had fallen from $100 a barrel to $50 by 2015. The other big factor affecting Russia was sanctions imposed by the western countries whose companies had been active in Russia.

Russia sits on the world's largest reserves of shale oil, which make up 25% of its total reserves. The US has seen a boom in shale production, and Russia, which has greater shale reserves than the US, hoped to duplicate its success. Exploiting these resources, however, involves fracking technology, in which western companies have developed expertise. In the days of the Soviet Union, all the equipment used in the energy industries was Soviet manufactured. Nowadays, western oil-service companies hold the key, in fracking as well as in the technology to explore and tap resources offshore and in the Arctic regions. Without these companies, Russia's energy sector is vulnerable to dwindling production. These companies' activities were restricted by sanctions imposed on Russia when Putin ordered the annexation of Crimea in Ukraine in 2014. Although appealing to Russian nationalist sentiment, the move was damaging economically, and Ukraine became politically destabilized, with violent conflicts between Ukrainian and pro-Russian forces. Russian pipelines that had been delivering gas to European customers were vulnerable to disruption, and the volume of gas flowing through these pipelines declined rapidly. Gazprom's sales and profits were thus affected by the sanctions.

Gazprom has devised alternative plans for serving energy markets, but all seem to involve huge initial capital expenditure. Northern pipelines to avoid Ukraine are among these projects designed to serve European markets, but the new pipelines would be far more costly than the one through Ukraine. New customers for Russian gas are emerging in China, and, for these customers, too, a new pipeline can be built, but, again, the building of the new pipeline will add hugely to the costs for Gazprom. These costs would look more justifiable in an environment of high global energy prices, but if low prices persist, Russia's energy dependence creates risks for the economy, and for its political leadership.

It is often observed that the economic and political power concentrated in Putin and his circle of associates has created a system in which the institutions designed to be democratic have become transfigured into mechanisms to support what is effectively an authoritarian regime (Hille, 2015; Thornhill, 2015). Opposition politicians have little voice, and little scope to organize freely. Elections take place, but, in the eyes of one opposition campaigner, they are 'imitations of democratic institutions' (HIlle, 2015). The demise of the Soviet Union was seen as ushering in 'free speech, free markets and a free press' (Thornhill, 2015). Russia today seems to have none of these.

Sources: Hille, K. (2015) 'Russia's elections show Putin-style democracy in action', *Financial Times*, 10 September, at www.ft.com; Burke, J. (2015) 'How Russian energy giant Gazprom lost $300 billion', *The Guardian*, 7 August, at www.theguardian.com; Thornhill, J. (2015) 'Tsar quality', *Financial Times*, 7 February; Farchy, J. (2014) 'Between a rock and a hard place', *Financial Times*, 30 October.

Questions for discussion

- In what ways is Gazprom an example of subservience of a company to political leadership rather than business decision-making?
- How has the global political environment affected the Russian energy sector?
- What are the risks faced by western companies when working with Russian companies?
- How stable is Putin's rule in terms of political and economic conditions?

Introduction

From global corporations down to family-run enterprises, businesses desire a stable and reasonably predictable environment in which to carry on their activities. As interaction between government and business has grown, the importance of political stability has become more apparent. In the political dynamics of every society both internal and external factors come into play. Internal governmental structures and processes form a political system, responsible for containing and channelling conflict, and promoting the collective good of society. Just as no two societies are identical, no two political systems are identical.

People everywhere wish to see public order maintained, public services function efficiently, and government officers carry out their duties. But they want more besides. A police state can offer security, but it hardly offers a conducive environment for a happy life. People wish to have a good education, a good job and the prosperity it brings, not simply for material well-being but for a better quality of life in a society which values the dignity of every individual. Democracy has long been a beacon to peoples all over the world as a system in which governments are held accountable to the people, and every person's voice counts. But, although democracy as a system has spread across the globe, many nominally democratic systems fall short of the stability and legitimacy hoped of them. With large swathes of the globe under non-democratic systems, basic issues such as the merits of democracy are coming into question. Democracies, both established and fledgling, are undergoing changes that seem to undermine democratic values such as the dignity of the individual and political equality. Businesses are affected by the actions of all types of government, many of which fall beneath standards of the rule of law. The focus of much future business strategy is in emerging markets with authoritarian and semi-authoritarian leadership. Relations with governments raise ethical challenges in every country, but the challenges are greater in countries where political and legal institutions are weak and possibilities of corruption are high. This chapter will focus on political systems in a variety of states, and their implications for global business.

The political sphere

Politics has been defined in numerous different ways, but all highlight the function of conflict resolution in society. Broadly, politics refers to processes by which a social group allocates the exercise of power and authority for the group as a whole. Breaking down the definition into three elements, first there is the existence of a social group – the word 'politics' derives from the Greek word *polis*, meaning city-state, a political community. Conflict is inevitable within societies, and politics provides the means of resolving conflict in structured ways. Second, politics concerns power relations. The contesting of power in society arises from groups and individuals with a wide range of viewpoints — ideological, economic, religious, ethnic or simply self-interested opportunistic. In democratic societies political parties are the most high-profile players on the political scene, but political authorities interact with a range of interests in society, including businesses and numerous interest groups, in arriving at policy decisions.

The *third* element is the terrain of politics – the social group as a whole. While politics occurs in every organization, we are concerned here with agenda-setting for a society as a whole. Its scope is thus public life, rather than particular organizations.

For the citizen of ancient Athens, this distinction did not exist: participation in the city-state was both civic and moral in nature, the polis providing the means to the good life. Later developments, especially the growth of secular states in Europe and increasing emphasis on the worth of the individual, led to a separation between public and private spheres. The sphere of politics is public life, institutions of the state, governmental structures and the process by which individuals come to occupy offices of state.

The private sphere is often referred to as civil society, a term which covers the sphere in which citizens have space to pursue their own personal goals. Private individuals and businesses, trade unions, religious groups and the many sub-national associations which exist in pluralist societies are all part of civil society (Laine, 2014). Historically, civil society is a western concept, and is associated with states where national cultures value liberal principles, including pluralism – the presence of many different groups and interests in society. However, in recent years, the notion of civil society has broadened beyond the idea of groups within a state, to become a more globally-focused concept. It has thus broken out of ideas of national societies, and has gravitated more towards ideas and values that cross national borders (Laine, 2014). For example, volunteer groups such as NGOs are cross-border in their approaches to global issues. In some countries where civil society groups are perceived as threats to stability, NGOs and other groups face restrictions and even suppression.

Figure 5.1 Impacts of political policies on business

From a business perspective, the political sphere in any country is likely to be perceived as an obstacle to achieving its goals. Politics is often pictured as officials imposing bureaucratic requirements, rule changes that increase costs and growing statutory regulation in areas such as employment and consumer protection. All of these add to the burdens of doing business, which a businessperson is inclined to feel hampers the firm's ability to achieve its goals. But this represents a narrow view of the firm's purpose as one simply focused on financial goals. The firm's activities exist in a social environment where public goods are important for all concerned. These are not incompatible with private goals of enriching business owners, but can be seen as complementing each other.

The political sphere concerns policies on public goods that influence businesses and individuals. Public and private spheres, therefore, are not as easily separated as the theoretical distinction of liberal thinking suggests. Figure 5.1 shows a number of public policy areas where political decisions and government frameworks have impacts on businesses within the state's borders. In all these areas, governments aim to uphold public interest in some way, whether by promoting public goods or curtailing potential harm. Nowadays, most people would recognize the need for government intervention, while disagreeing on how much intervention is beneficial. Most people would say that the curtailing of activities such as unfair trade practices, exploitative employment practices or unsafe workplaces is justified. Others are more contentious. Businesses would probably highlight areas such as financial regulation, taxes and social charges, and rules for corporate governance as unwelcome constraints. Recall the markets-versus-state issues discussed in the last chapter. While businesses dislike government constraints on their activities, they welcome policies – and public spending – on research and innovation, education and helpful trade and investment policies. Businesses regularly interact with governments, and, indeed, take part in the formation of policies. Privatization of public services is now occurring in many different economies, even those that espouse the social market model. Similarly, public/private partnerships are being formed as means of financing investment and delivery of public services, including education, transport and healthcare. The simple dichotomy of public and private domains, therefore, is being replaced by a less polarized, more interlinking relationship between the state and business enterprises. This offers businesses opportunities, but, as these activities involve public-sector services, they demand a shift in corporate outlook towards social responsibilities. On the other hand, many governments now routinely enter negotiations with companies to entice them to invest in the country. Thus, a foreign company will be tempted by the prospect of lower taxes, government funding towards research, or the waiving of regulatory rules. Businesses are therefore more directly involved in the political sphere than the theoretical distinction between public and private sectors suggests.

Does politics have an image problem?

Businesses tend to have a negative view of politicians, as interfering too often in their activities, but taking the credit for business success when the national economy is doing well. Do you agree or disagree with this view, and why?

Nation-states: their scope and authority

The basic unit into which the world's peoples are divided is the nation-state. The concept of the nation-state combines the principle of a people's right to self-determination with the achievement of a territorial state ruled by its own government and subordinate to no higher authority. New nation-states are often born of nationalist movements within existing states. The dismantling of colonial empires in the years following the Second World War gave rise to newly independent states. Some 17 new states were born out of the break-up of the Soviet Union in 1990–91. Numerous new states seem to bring together social and cultural groupings that do not necessarily form a cohesive society. To many, the state is an embodiment of national aspirations. To others, it gets in the way of a people's aspirations. And to some, it is a tool of oppression, preventing people realizing their rights of self-determination.

Defining the state

The nation-state, or just 'state' for short, consists of the set of authoritative institutions that are responsible for lawmaking and governance over a defined territory, backed up by authorized powers of coercion. The definition highlights three defining principles of statehood: territoriality, sovereignty and the authorized use of coercive power. The state occupies a geographically-defined territory, within whose boundaries it has jurisdiction. Disputes over territory can be particularly bitter, and have led to innumerable wars. Maintaining border controls, all would agree, has become more problematic, as territorial boundaries generally have become more permeable with the processes of globalization. These developments are welcomed by firms, facilitating growth in cross-border business, but permeable borders are also seen by governments as a source of insecurity.

Although the state is still the legal gatekeeper controlling what crosses its borders, this role has become more daunting with the growing international flows of goods, people, information and money. Importantly from a national economic standpoint, the state also controls access to natural resources such as mineral reserves and oil in its territory. It is not surprising that countries such as Venezuela and Mexico, on gaining independence, nationalized their oil industries, but both later took steps towards liberalization and privatization. However, residual authority remains in state hands in the case of resource rights, giving governments the upper hand: a licence to mine granted to a private-sector firm is always at risk of being withdrawn at a later date.

The post-colonial states of Africa have generally followed inherited borders from the colonial period, which were artificially drawn and did not reflect ethnic groupings. Except for Rwanda and Burundi, none of the 34 modern African states corresponds to pre-colonial boundaries. Two consequences have followed: historic groupings are divided between states, and a state's population may comprise groups which are historic enemies (Hawthorn, 1993). Ethnic conflict has been an inevitable result. In these situations states struggle to maintain control and a sense of legitimacy over all their inhabitants. The pictures of flows of refugees from conflict into neighbouring countries have become a saddening feature of modern politics, highlighting the vulnerability and interdependence of states.

A second defining feature of statehood is sovereignty, which denotes the supreme legal authority of the state. Sovereignty has an internal and external aspect. A state has 'internal' sovereignty, in that it possesses ultimate authority to rule within its borders; all other associations within society are subordinate. In a unitary system, all authority radiates out from the centre. There may well be local and regional governments, but they lack autonomous authority. States where there are strong regional identities often choose constitutions based on a federal system, whereby authority is shared between a central government and regional governments. The US is an example, where the 50 individual 'states' have considerable legal and political authority. Nigeria is another example, where religious and cultural divides are recognized by the federal constitution. In federal systems, the central government of the state as a whole is the ultimate authority. The state's legal authority is supported by a monopoly of the legitimate use of coercive force, in the form of military and police forces. This is the third of the defining characteristics of states. There are many states where these institutions are imperfect or even failed. If an armed militia seizes power and ousts an established government, the new government has de facto power, but is not the legitimate sovereign.

'External' sovereignty refers to position of states in the international context, where all states recognize each other as supreme within their own borders. The principle of mutual recognition, known as the 'sovereign equality of states' has governed the conduct of international relations between states. This notion of sovereignty lies at the heart of the UN, forming the basis of international law. However, in practice, economic and political power are crucial in relations among states. The era of globalization has seen a questioning of the continuing autonomy of states in economic terms, and it is sometimes said that state sovereignty is an outmoded concept (Jackson, 2003). Economic globalization has increased rapidly, expanding the role of large global companies, which can seem to dwarf state authorities. In addition, companies have acquired deepening ties with governments, bringing their activities into the political spotlight and giving them a quasi-political role. Global politics remains dominated by state players, but corporate representatives are highly visible and active at international governmental gatherings on global issues. The principle of sovereign authority still underlies lawmaking authority within the state, as well as the authority to create international law, but inputs of business leaders are now commonplace in these processes.

Sources of authority in the state

In every viable state there is a source of legitimate authority. Some countries struggle to achieve viability, and where there is a complete breakdown of authority, the country is referred to as a 'failed' state. Here we examine the most common sources of legitimacy in states. In a traditional monarchy, such as the Arab state of Saudi Arabia, heredity in the royal lineage is the legitimating principle. The ruling family asserts absolute authority. In a 'theocracy', religious prerogative is the guiding principle. In Iran, an Islamic state, the supreme leader (the ayatollah) has ultimate authority over political institutions. Tensions inevitably arise between secular and religious authorities (see case study in Chapter 3).

Ideology as a source of legitimacy is based a system of beliefs which permeate the whole of society, not just the system of government. 'Ideology' is often used in a broad sense to refer to any set of political beliefs, such as liberalism or conservatism, but both these sets of beliefs embrace political pluralism, whereas the ideological state is monolithic, rejecting any competing belief systems. Fascism, an extreme nationalist ideology, reached its peak in the racist ideology of fascist Germany and Italy. While these states were defeated in the Second World War, fascist groups still form part of the political scene in many states. Historically, communism has been one of the most important ideologies. Communist revolutions take over the state, replacing existing governments with communist party dictatorships, as in China and the Soviet Union. After the Second World War, the assertion of power by the Soviet Union (USSR) under the dictatorship of Stalin sent alarm bells ringing in the US, leading to the so-called 'cold-war era', dominated by a clash of ideologies between communism and the American model of liberal democracy. This was a crude simplification of these two ways of political thinking, but nonetheless greatly influenced international politics between 1945 and 1991. Since the collapse of the Soviet Union, China has been the leading communist country, followed by a dwindling number of smaller states, such as Cuba and North Korea. China's leaders have embraced market reforms while maintaining the communist political system. Since its communist revolution in 1959, Cuba has more consistently maintained its communist system, but is now gradually initiating market reforms, helping to thaw relations with the US.

In most modern states legitimacy is founded on constitutionalism. **Constitutionalism** implies a set of rules, grounded in a society's shared beliefs, about the source of authority and its institutional forms. Constitutionalism stands for the **rule of law**, above both ruler and ruled. Its underlying principle is that the institutions of government derive their power from these pre-existing rules. Actual officeholders will change from time to time and, indeed, a vital function of a constitution is to provide for smooth change in the transfer of power. But the constitution, setting out the ground rules, provides continuity and legitimacy. Inherent in constitutionalism are the control by the civilian authority over the military and the existence of an independent judiciary (court system).

Most of the world's constitutions are written. The major exception is the British constitution. However, while the UK has no separate constitutional document, much legislation, which is contained in Acts of Parliament, is constitutional in nature. There are some states where, despite a written constitution, the rule of law is weakly established. In these countries, authoritarian rulers sometimes cloak themselves in the legitimacy of a constitution, although this device is simply a façade for autocratic rule. Former Soviet republics are among the countries with constitutional institutions that are subordinated to autocratic rule, usually bolstered by elections in which only the leadership's choice of candidates can stand. The mere existence of a constitution is thus no guarantee of accountable government. China's leaders broke new ground in 2014 by announcing at their party conference that they would henceforth embrace constitutionalism and the rule of law (BBC, 2014). While this gives the impression of veering away from party rule, it was probably prompted mainly by a desire to clamp down on corruption, which was felt by the leadership to have become excessive.

An absolute monarchy can give way to a constitutional monarchy, in which the monarch remains the formal head of state under a constitution that enshrines democratic institutions in government. Some examples are Britain, Japan and Spain. Other constitutional states are republics, where sovereignty rests in principle and in practice with representative institutions, usually headed by a president.

States in a globalized world

To what extent do state sovereignty and constitutional frameworks remain valid in the era of globalization?

Political risk: threats and uncertainties

In the aftermath of the Second World War, political leaders were anxious to put in place an institutional framework at the global level which would ensure peace and security. This was the impetus behind the setting up of the UN, as well as other international bodies such as the International Monetary Fund (IMF) and World Bank. The unfolding post-war period saw growing economic prosperity – a good indicator of the benefits of peaceful co-existence among nation-states. But in the decades that followed, has the world become a safer place in which to live and do business?

Political risk for businesses is the extent to which they are affected by uncertainties associated with the exercise of governmental power within a country, or from external forces. We look first at internal aspects of political risk, and then turn to external threats.

Internal risks

Changes in national law and policy that might adversely affect businesses, such as nationalization within a particular sector, are risks that have direct effects on a business. Venezuela's socialist government nationalized numerous assets in the 2000s, including oil assets, gas assets and a rice mill. All had been owned by foreign companies. Traditional views of political risk focus on four types of government action: confiscation, expropriation, nationalization and deprivation, known as CEND for short (Toksoz, 2014). In the broader context of the business environment, there are numerous sources of tension that can contribute to political risk. Social unrest, industrial unrest and dissatisfaction with the government are sources of political risk. Of course, these types of instability can occur anywhere. And government responses are crucial. The tensions are often resolved, but they can spill over into deeper instability. Generally, developed countries with more established political institutions, usually democratic, are more able to contain tensions than developing countries where political institutions are in the formative stages.

Globalization has seen economic integration among a wide variety of states, both developed and developing. Rising growth rates and economic development have placed many developing economies in the spotlight as new drivers of the global economy (see Chapter 4). We might assume that political risk is low where economic prosperity is high. If incomes and standards of living are rising, this contentment is good news for the government. In democratic systems, if the economy is suffering a downturn or recession, the electorate is inclined to vote out the governing party. On the other hand, a change of government in a stable, developed country is not seen as particularly destabilizing in terms of political risk. For developing and emerging countries, however, political risk looms much larger.

Globalization's star performers have been the BRIC economies, first highlighted in 2001, mainly for their impressive growth rates, which outshone those in the developed regions and suggested a shift in global economic power (O'Neill, 2001). This assessment, however, was one based mainly on the economic indicators. As we discovered in the last chapter, economic data give only a partial picture of a country's well-being. They give few clues about governance, political stability and sustainable growth policies. The BRICs all presented elements of political risk in the form of social and ethnic tensions, high levels of inequality and weak governmental accountability. These risks have largely been contained, but remain concerns. Two of the original BRICs, India and Brazil, are democracies, while China and Russia are not. China's leaders are concerned over potential unrest that could spill over into political opposition. They are improving wages and employment conditions on the one hand, and stamping out signs of public dissent on the other.

Meanwhile, other large emerging economies have come to the fore, including Indonesia, South Africa, Nigeria, Turkey and Mexico (Bremmer, 2015). Are these other emerging economies becoming more stable politically? Economic dependence on natural resources is an issue for many of the emerging economies. Brazil and Russia derive their prosperity mainly from natural resources. The same is true of Indonesia, South Africa, Nigeria and Mexico. Of the original BRICs, all but India have seen slowing growth, giving rise to political tension. Brazil has had serious corruption scandals involving government and state-owned companies (see the closing case study in Chapter 6); Russia's economy has suffered from falling oil prices and an embargo imposed for incursions into Ukraine; and China has seen slowing export sales.

Countries mainly dependent on resource wealth or commodities are inherently vulnerable to falling demand. With large populations and large numbers of poor people, these countries face challenges of creating jobs and improving well-being for all in society. But, while democratic institutions exist in all the newer emerging economies noted above, social and political tensions run high and can spill over into civil disorder and even violent clashes. This constitutes political risk. Nonetheless, companies seize opportunities for expansion that these countries present. But foreigners face high levels of political risk in entering these markets. The apparent flowering of liberal reforms might suggest that these countries are becoming more like western political environments, where democratization and constitutional governments took hold in the context of economic reforms. However, these large emerging economies have taken different development paths. Although they have democratic institutions, most are ruled by closed leadership groups. They are acutely conscious of threats to stability from within their countries, and they are also sensitive to regional instabilities that can boil over into hostilities. Spending on defence and national security has increased markedly in unstable regions of the world.

External threats

Although, in theory, sovereign states recognize the sovereignty of each other, in practice, wars and violent conflicts short of war have historically played a large part in politics at the global level. Following the Second World War, the setting up of the UN and the putting in place of negotiating processes to build a body of international law that would deter violations of sovereignty, the post-war period saw a build-up in military establishments by the chief players of the cold-war period, the US and Soviet Union (now Russia). The US is the world's biggest arms exporter, followed by Russia in second place (SIPRI, 2014). The US has by far the largest global military presence, and is the world's largest spender on military hardware and infrastructure. In 2014, the US spent $610 billion on defence, which is about three times the money spent by the country in second place, China (SIPRI, 2015).

Conflicts around the world ensure that military hardware, such as this Warrior armoured vehicle, which has been used by British forces in Afghanistan, will always be in demand.

Source: MoD/Crown copyright 2013.

The US accounts for 34% of global military expenditure, a percentage that is down from 46% in 2009. The extent of American military presence around the world is difficult to assess. In 2012, the US Department of Defense reported that it manages over 5,000 sites worldwide (US Department of Defense, 2012). It manages 28.5 million acres of land in total, the vast majority of which is in the US. These figures are likely to be underestimates of the real presence of the US military, which extends to many more countries than acknowledged in the official list. Many other installations, sites and assets come under its control or the control of subcontracted companies. The US relies heavily on the services of people working for private-sector contractors, in both combat activities and backup services. Although little information is made available, it is estimated that as many as half the American forces in the Iraq war were employed by private-sector companies (Isenberg, 2009). As the world's most pervasive military power, the US has a history of military interventions in other countries, and its military presence in states that are its allies is sometimes subjected to criticism; for example, in Spain, where the US is constructing a new base for operations against terrorists in the Middle East.

Globally, military spending reached a total of $1,776 billion in 2014 (SIPRI, 2015). This is 2.3% of global GDP. Following many years of rising expenditure, the global total in 2014 was slightly lower than the previous year. In the US and Western Europe, military expenditure has fallen slightly, but there have been significant increases in some countries, reflecting growing wealth and also rising regional tensions. China's military expenditure rose 167% from 2005 to 2014. The rise in 2014 was a 9.7% increase on the previous year. As a rising power globally, China is fearful of the threat posed by the extensive American military presence in Asian countries, including Japan, South Korea and the Philippines. Other countries with large annual increases were Russia (8.1%), Algeria (12%) and Saudi Arabia (17%). These countries are all oil producers, and their governments are concerned over regional instabilities. In 2015, Saudi Arabia, a predominantly Sunni Muslim country, launched airstrikes in neighbouring Yemen, where groups of Shia Muslim insurgents were active. A particular concern for Saudi Arabia was the possibility that these insurgents were being armed by Iran, a Shia Muslim state. Saudi Arabia's main outside support came from the US, which is its principal military supplier.

Figure 5.2 Military expenditure as a percentage of GDP in selected countries

Source: Information from the Stockholm International Peace Research Institute (SIPRI), www.sipri.org/, (2015), *Factsheet: Trends in world military expenditure: 2014*, Table 1, p. 2.

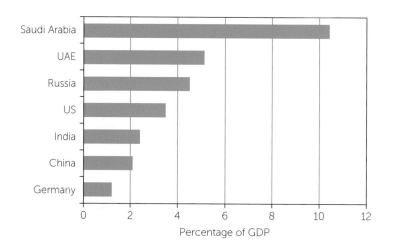

A significant trend has been the rise of military expenditure in Middle Eastern countries. Military spending as a percentage of GDP is an indicator used to compare countries' priorities. In general, countries would be expected to spend under 2% of GDP on their military establishment. In 2014, 55% of countries spent less than 1.5% of GDP on military budgets. But there are big variations, as shown in Figure 5.2. Twenty countries spent more than 4% of their budgets on their military establishment in 2014, and most of these were in Africa, the Middle East and Eastern Europe. These are all areas where political tensions are high. By comparison, the number spending over 4% in 2005 was 13. The big increase in military spending by countries in the Middle East is a worrying trend, reflecting both external threats from militarist Islamist groups such as the Islamic State, and internal social, ethnic and political instabilities. Traditional autocratic rule in many Middle Eastern Arab states started to crumble in 2011, in what was known as the 'Arab spring'. Uprisings in Egypt, Tunisia and Libya led to periods of political uncertainty and instability, the effects of which have lingered. Some of those protesting were calling for democracy, but many were inspired by Islamist groups, seeking to impose Islamic rule. In Egypt, an elected government was installed amid continuing turbulence, and it was soon displaced by military rulers. Tunisia has maintained its fragile democratic institutions, but is vulnerable to destabilization from terrorist activities.

Terrorism is a threat that raises concerns for all governments. Terrorist threats may emanate from numerous sources, including disenchanted groups within a society or from outside the state. Sometimes these two sources overlap. Terrorism has been defined broadly as action meant 'to inflict dramatic and deadly injury on civilians and to create an atmosphere of fear, generally for a political or ideological (whether secular or religious) purpose' (UN Policy Working Group, 2002). Terrorists have access to funding from sources such as illicit trading, and they can lay their hands on abundant weaponry. They have become adept at striking targets that achieve maximum impact. Terrorists are highly mobile, and they have become skilled at using the internet and social media for propaganda purposes. And they have developed abilities to target states and organizations with cyber attacks. Businesses and governments face considerable risks, not just in physical locations which have a history of terrorist attack.

Following the attacks on the World Trade Center and the Pentagon in 2001, the US set its sights against the threats of Islamic terrorists, notably, the Islamist group, al-Qaida. The then US president, George W. Bush, initiated a global 'war on terror' which attempted to legitimize pre-emptive strikes in other countries on the grounds that terrorism had become global and that any country could therefore be the target of a US strike for 'harbouring' terrorists (Wolin, 2008). But many questioned the legality of the invasion of Iraq in 2003, arguing that it lacked UN authorization and that there was little evidence that Iraq posed a serious threat to peace and security or that it had sponsored terrorist activities. The UK, which was America's main coalition partner in the invasion, encountered considerable anti-war public sentiment at home, helping to undermine the public's trust in its government. Between 2003 and 2006, some 151,000 civilians were killed in Iraq through violence, according to the WHO (Boseley, 2008). As an oil-rich country, Iraq has much economic potential. The region began to recover economically and politically, but is now being destabilized by the territorial ambitions of the Islamic State grouping of Islamists, an extreme Sunni group. Iraq is once again at risk of disintegration, and for its people, a humanitarian disaster is unfolding. This is also the case in Syria, where the civil war also has roots in Sunni-Shia conflicts.

The UN supports the provision of humanitarian aid, but armed engagement is in violation of international law. Nonetheless, the US has operated a programme whereby unmanned 'drones' fire at targets associated with al-Qaida in the areas where it is active. In American drone strikes in Pakistan and Yemen, 41 people have been targeted, but 1,150 people have been killed (Ackerman et al., 2015). Although some people associated with terrorism have been targeted in these attacks, the US military has acknowledged that in some cases they target an area, rather than particular individuals (Timm, 2015). These attacks, which have been operating since 2004, have aroused criticism for violations of human rights. The US has maintained that the drone strike programmes are in keeping with international law, stressing that the strikes take place in war zones. However, the justification put forward is a 'global war doctrine', which would allow it to target al-Qaida anywhere in the world (Boone, 2013). Such a sweeping doctrine on the part of the US flouts principles of state sovereignty and human rights, potentially sowing seeds of greater insecurity and mounting human rights violations. The US has asserted its global role in moral terms as grounded in values of democracy and due process. But the right it asserts to intervene militarily anywhere in the world suggests behaviour more associated with autocratic regimes, undermining its claims of moral leadership globally.

Worrying militarization of conflicts has seen links between internal instabilities and external threats. Military solutions tend to bring temporary peace only, and then hostilities are likely to flare up again. World Bank research finds that civil wars are almost all continuations of previous civil wars (World Bank, 2011). Longer-lasting solutions can only be found through political agreement. Where states reach accommodation among differing groups, it becomes possible to engage in a dialogue in which every group feels its legitimate interest is being served. It is only when tensions are thus contained that businesses can feel able to invest and contribute to a better society.

The way I see it ...

'The idea that a country can be united through its military might is a false one. Military might alone cannot unite people and may even lead to war and bloodshed.'

Myint Win Thein, speaking for Myanmar's military rulers after elections in which the National League for Democracy (NLD) won 77% of the votes in parliamentary elections; in the state-run newspaper, *The Global New Light of Myanmar*, 22 November, 2015.

Myanmar's military rulers expressed willingness to abide by the results of elections that showed overwhelming support for the opposition NLD. How does this represent an improvement in the business environment?

Businesspeople desire a stable environment, and some would argue that a stable authoritarian country is better for business than a turbulent democratic one. Many states under autocratic leadership maintain stability of a kind, through suppression of dissent and the use of coercive force. But tensions beneath the surface can give rise to uprisings, as happened in the Arab spring. Political risks arise in both autocratic and democratic states. In the former, a foreign company can conclude a contract with the current leaders, only to find it altered unilaterally by new leadership at a later date. In a democracy, a change of government usually takes place at regular intervals along constitutional lines, but policy changes can still happen at any time. Furthermore, ethical concerns weigh with many companies. Does the firm wish to be seen doing business in a country with a record of human rights abuses? A firm could well decide that its apparent acquiescence risks damaging stakeholder relations both within the company and in other markets.

Political risk

Assess the political risk for a foreign company in each of the following: (a) a military dictatorship; (b) a constitutional democracy; and (c) a monarchy where the ruling family asserts absolute authority.

Democracy and authoritarianism

Political systems are often classified along a continuum, with democracy at one end and authoritarianism at the other. Democracy broadly covers a range of political systems falling under the phrase, 'rule by the people', but popular sovereignty in theory can issue in a great diversity of institutional forms. In basic terms, **democracy** is rule by the people, through elected governments. **Authoritarianism** is rule by a single leader or small group of individuals, with unlimited power, usually dependent on military support to maintain stability.

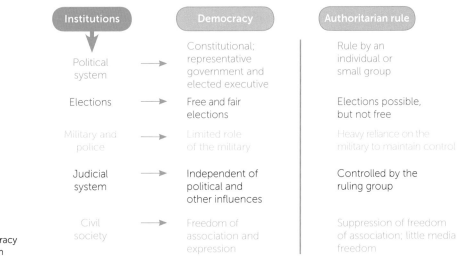

Figure 5.3 Democracy vs. authoritarianism

Figure 5.3 presents a comparison of democracy and authoritarianism. The political system in a democracy is based on representative institutions, which endure beyond the life of a particular government. Authoritarian rule is based on personal power, which is more precarious. Note that these two very different systems share many elements, including the military, police, justice system and even elections. The differences lie in their degrees of influence. The military and police elements loom larger in the authoritarian regime, where they are central to maintaining order. By contrast, the justice system and elections are of greater significance in the democracy. Elements of civil society represent a crucial difference. Whereas there is freedom of association and expression in a democracy, these rights are suppressed in the authoritarian regime.

Authoritarianism

In an authoritarian government, power is concentrated in the hands of the few, and this élite is largely unaccountable to the citizens for its actions. Authoritarian regimes vary from repressive military regimes to systems which have some democratic forms, such as elections to choose among state-approved candidates. In all these cases, personal rule by a single leader or small group of individuals is the norm. These leaders have usually come up through the ranks of the military or the party in a one-party state. All independent political forces are banned, and any opposition to the regime is seen as a threat, typically suppressed by military force. Freedom of expression, a free press and freedom of association are all restricted. The judicial system is not independent, but run as an administrative arm of the state. Although rule is personal to the leaders, the strong state is the dominant image that they wish to portray. They take care to keep secret the political infighting and disputes over succession issues which inevitably arise.

The economic success of China has led to a reappraisal of authoritarian governments. It might be thought that the authoritarian regime is inherently rigid, and that sooner or later it will topple. However, China's leadership has proved to be resilient, adapting to changing internal and external conditions, and using market reforms to boost economic growth. The Chinese leadership engages in a balancing act between freedom and control: balancing freedom of enterprise and state regulation, and balancing internet freedom and state censorship. It has been called an 'authoritarian capitalist' alternative to democracy (Plattner, 2010). While it had been assumed that authoritarian regimes inherently lack the moral credentials of legitimacy to govern that democratic systems offer, there is now a good deal of admiration for China's accomplishments, leading to a view that authoritarian governments are not as bad for societies as western political views have depicted them.

The 'economy first' view of development prioritizes economic development, implying that democratic reforms can be left until a later stage. This view is most notably exemplified by China, where the authoritarian regime has used oppressive means to retain its tight grip on power. Many developing countries now see this model as a legitimate alternative to received western views about liberal democracy, apparently unperturbed by the current lack of individual freedoms and weak human rights record. This view arguably rests on a mistaken conception of democracy as simply a set of formal mechanisms such as elections.

Democracy: in theory and in practice

Democracy is a system of government that is based on the principle of sovereignty of the people. This is rather an abstract idea, famously elucidated by Abraham Lincoln, who spoke of government 'of the people by the people and for the people' in his Gettysburg Address (Lincoln, 1863). Most definitions of democracy focus on the formal structural aspects of representative institutions, including elections and the right to vote. These institutions are grounded in principles that emphasize the equality of all under the law. Thus, where citizens are seen as equal before the law, all should have the right to vote. The following is a list of the identifying characteristics of democracy:

1 **Rule of law**, based on a constitution which establishes representative institutions, accountability of governments and an independent judiciary. Thus, executive power is kept in check.
2 **Free and fair elections**, at relatively frequent intervals. These must provide for a free choice of candidates and the peaceful removal of representatives from office when they fail to secure enough votes, in accordance with the constitution. Reports of outside monitors are usually seen as a guarantee that the election has not been tainted by fraud.
3 **Universal right to vote for all adults**. Voting alone is the most minimal form of participation.
4 **Freedoms of expression, speech and association**. These political rights are essential to ensure competitive elections in which all interests and groups may put forward their candidates. There should be independent media providing alternative sources of information to which citizens have access.
5 **Majority rule and minority rights**. Most countries have minority groups, who are often fearful that they will be oppressed by the majority. There must be safeguards to protect minorities as an essential element of civil society.

Most of the rights and freedoms listed above make up what is often called 'liberal democracy', focusing on the role of the individual citizen, in an analogous way to the notion that economic liberalism is rooted in individualism (see Chapter 4). Citizens have diverse interests and values. They have ideas about what policies they wish to see adopted by government, and they feel they have a right to make these preferences weigh with elected governments (Gilens and Page, 2014). This, after all, is what gives a democracy its legitimacy. However, in the pluralist political and economic environments that characterize democracies, numerous groups and interests, including business organizations, vie for political influence, raising the risk that the views of the average citizen are drowned out. It is not uncommon for citizens to feel disillusioned with politicians, who can often appear to serve their own interests rather than those of the electorate. Americans' trust in their government has fallen substantially in the last 50 to 60 years. Surveys by Pew Research Center show that in 1958, 73% of citizens expressed trust in the government, while in 2014, the percentage was down to just 24% (Pew Research Center, 2014). Is this just a sign that the political system cannot please everyone all the time, or deeper concerns about democracy?

Empirical academic research has concluded that in the US, economic élites and organized groups based on business interests have greater impacts on government policies than the wishes of ordinary citizens (Gilens and Page, 2014). These researchers found that on 1,779 public policy issues, where there is a proposed change, what matters is the support of the economic élites and organized business interests. They are likely to get their way when they support a proposed change, and also when they oppose one, even when the public is in favour. When there is an alignment on an issue between these two groups on a particular proposed change, 'it makes very little difference what the general public thinks' (Gilens and Page, 2014: 571). Even when 80% of the public favour a change, they get their way only 43% of the time, unless the business élites also support it. Moreover, the business-based groups, while they could possibly reflect citizens' wishes, in fact do not. Indeed, the research showed that the impacts on government policy of the most influential business-oriented groups were likely to be *against* average citizens' wishes (Gilens and Page, 2014: 276). The scholars who carried out this research concluded that, while Americans enjoy many of the features of democracy such as regular elections and freedom of speech, 'America's claims to being a democratic *society* are seriously threatened' [my italics] (Gilens and Page, 2014: 577).

A political system that is outwardly democratic can mask a society in which inequalities effectively deny a voice to ordinary citizens. Formal institutions are therefore necessary, but not sufficient, to construct a democracy. Minimal 'electoral democracy' can be distinguished from liberal democracy, which stipulates pluralism and political freedoms for individuals and groups (Diamond, 1996). Beyond liberal democracy, lies 'social democracy', which focuses on the broader social and economic spheres in society. Social democracy is concerned with the underlying social and economic conditions in a society which contribute towards deeper participation than just voting. A sharply divided or unequal society, in which power is concentrated in an entrenched ruling élite, is not a democracy in this substantive sense, even though it may have a constitution and regular elections. As the research by Gilens and Page suggests, however, liberal democracy, which enshrines political freedoms and equality, can itself deviate from its participatory roots if the economic élite wield decisive power over political institutions. Liberal democracy therefore risks slipping backwards towards a system more akin to a minimal electoral democracy (Wolin, 2008). When attempting to measure democracy, the principles of liberal democracy are generally accepted as the key criteria.

Is democracy retreating?

In what ways have the ideals of democracy been set back globally? Look at both established democracies and countries with limited democratic institutions.

Functions of government

A state encompasses people, territory and institutions, while **government** refers to the particular institutions by which laws are made and implemented. It can also refer to the particular individuals in office at a given time, as in 'the government of the day'.

It is customary to think of government as comprising three functions or branches: legislative, executive and judicial. The division of functions between the three is known as **separation of powers**, shown in Figure 5.4. The **legislative** is the lawmaking branch. The legislature is central in a democracy, as it represents the electorate. The **executive** is at the head of government, responsible for administration and policy. The **judicial** function, located in the court system, interprets the law and thereby keeps a check on the other two branches. The system thus functions through the principle of **checks and balances**. Law and policy therefore emanate mainly from legislative and executive branches, and more specifically from political interplay between the two, depending on the balance of power within the system. In practice, most systems have considerable overlap between these functions. We look at each branch in turn, beginning with the legislative.

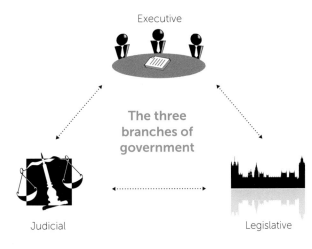

Figure 5.4 The branches of government

Most countries have a national assembly of representatives, whether elected or not. In authoritarian systems, the assembly is merely advisory, rubberstamping the decisions made by the ruling élite. This type of assembly has no actual lawmaking powers. In a democracy, the legislative assembly lies at the heart of the political system, representing the sovereignty of the people. It carries the main lawmaking function. Many countries have legislatures consisting of two houses (bicameral), where the lower house is the main lawmaking body. In the US, both houses, the House of Representatives (the lower house) and the Senate (the upper house) are directly elected. In the UK only the House of Commons (the lower house) is elected. The upper house, the House of Lords, has been a subject of much debate concerning its future composition and powers. Its role has been gradually reduced to one of a revising chamber.

Free and fair elections are a key element in political participation in a democracy. The electoral system may be the traditional first-past-the-post system or one of the more recent proportional representation systems (PR), which allocate seats in proportion to the votes obtained. The first-past-the-post system has predominated in the US and UK, although elections for devolved assemblies in Scotland and Wales are based on PR. Both these countries have a two-party system, whereby two mainstream political parties are politically dominant. A multi-party system, where there are numerous parties representing a variety of views and interests, is more likely to adopt PR. Most European countries (and also the European Parliament) have opted for PR. Outcomes in PR systems represent a broader political spectrum, giving small parties a greater prospect of winning seats than a first-past-the-post system, where they may win sizeable voter support but fail to win many seats.

The smaller parties in the UK are campaigning for PR reforms. In 2015, the UK Independence Party (UKIP) attracted 3.8 million voters (12% of the electorate), but gained only one Member of Parliament (MP) out of the total of 650 in the House of Commons. UKIP came second in 120 constituencies, but this support counted for nothing in terms of seats. Similarly, 1.1 million people voted for Green candidates, but only one Green MP was elected. In total, nearly 5 million voters supported UKIP and Green candidates, but this translated into only two seats. By contrast, the Scottish Nationalist Party (SNP), whose support is, by definition, concentrated in Scotland, received a total of 1.4 million votes (4.7% of the UK electorate), and won 56 seats. Smaller parties that have scattered support geographically are therefore disadvantaged in comparison to smaller parties that are concentrated in particular regions. This has also been the case in Spain, where a PR system operates (see a further discussion in Chapter 12).

PR systems are considered to be friendlier to women candidates. Women worldwide hold 22.1% of seats in national legislatures, up from 18.7% in 2010 (Inter-Parliamentary Union, 2015). There are wide disparities among countries, as Figure 5.5 shows. Scandinavian countries have relatively large percentages of women parliamentarians. In these countries, governments have introduced policies aimed at increasing the number of women candidates. While women hold 43.6% of the seats in Sweden, the percentage of women in other European countries is lower. The figure's data are taken for 1 April 2015. On that date, the UK had 23% women MPs, but the election one month later saw a significant rise – to 29%. Countries in the bottom half of Figure 5.5 cover a wide geographic area, a variety of cultural environments and differing political systems. They include advanced economies with democratic systems (the US and Australia), emerging economies with democratic institutions (Turkey, Nigeria and Brazil), and one Arab state with very limited representative institutions (Kuwait).

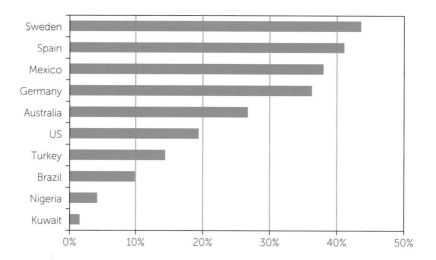

Figure 5.5 Women in national legislatures in selected countries (lower or single house)

Source: Data from Inter-Parliamentary Union, 'Women in national parliaments', as of 1 April 2015, at www.ipu.org, accessed 11 May 2015.

A drawback of proportional representation is that in a multi-party system, if many parties secure seats, it may be difficult to form a government, and political instability may result. In these circumstances, the largest party usually secures support from one or more smaller parties to form a coalition government. A **coalition government** is made up of two or more parties. This arrangement can lead to tensions in the tasks of legislating and forming policies. Aware of its power to bring down the government, a minor party in a coalition may demand a 'price' for its co-operation in terms of key policies, to keep it on board. It could be argued that coalition government is more representative of electoral support, and hence more democratic, but a major disadvantage is its potential instability.

The **referendum** is an example of direct democracy, and is used to complement the legislative function carried out by the assembly. In a referendum, voters are invited to approve or reject a question on a particular issue. In some states (such as

Italy) it is a constitutional requirement; in others (such as the UK) it is optional. Some examples of the varied uses of the referendum are:

- Devolution in Scotland and Wales, 1997
- Decision to join the UN by the Swiss in 2002, following earlier rejection in 1986
- The end of apartheid in South Africa, 1992
- The decision not to join the eurozone by Denmark (2000) and Sweden (2002)
- The decision of voters in Scotland to remain in the UK in 2014
- Vote in Britain in 2016 to leave the EU

The advantage of the referendum is that it acts as a check on elected governments, giving citizens an opportunity to express a view on an issue of the day. A drawback, however, is that citizens are typically asked to make a yes/no decision although the issues are complex. Moreover, ordinary citizens are not necessarily well informed of the ramifications of proposed changes. This was particularly highlighted in the context of Britain's vote to leave the EU.

The second branch, the executive, provides strong leadership in some systems, and only a co-ordinating role in others. We look at three types of system: presidential, parliamentary and 'hybrid'. A summary of their characteristics is shown in Table 5.1. These will now be discussed.

Table 5.1 Systems of government

	Presidential	**Parliamentary**	**Hybrid system**
Advantages	Strong executive based on popular mandate; fixed term of office	Executive reflects electoral support in parliament	Strong executive imparts unity; prime minister co-ordinates parliamentary programme
Disadvantages	Possible disaffection among electorate	Thin majority may lead to breakdown of government	Conflict between president and prime minister
Stability	Stable executive, but legislature may be dominated by the opposing party, stifling lawmaking agenda	Stable if prime minister has a large majority; coalition and minority governments can be unstable	Fixed-term president imparts stability; but successive coalition governments can be unstable in multi-party systems

A **presidential system** is thought of as producing a strong chief executive, as presidents are normally directly elected and thus have a personal mandate. The US is the leading example of a presidential system, although the president is technically elected by an electoral college to which each state sends delegates representing its voters' choice. Checks on executive power are provided by the constitution and also by a vigorous two-party system. The other main proponents of the presidential system have been Latin American countries, for whom a strong presidency is more grounded in political culture, in which nationalism and populism have been prominent features. Inherent drawbacks of the 'winner-takes-all' nature of presidential elections are that supporters of the losing candidates may feel alienated, while the winner may overestimate the popular mandate, 'conflating his supporters with the people as a whole' (Linz, 1993: 118). Supporters of minority parties are thus inclined to feel that their interests are not being served by the system. The president should focus on the public interest, but in practice, often focuses on promoting the interests of the majority party, including business interests. The case study on Turkey that follows highlights these risks.

Although the US presidential system exemplifies a strong executive, the US president's position is more complicated than might appear. As commander of the armed forces, the US president has enormous authority over military deployment, and presidents have expanded national security powers, such as mass surveillance. However, in many important areas, such as health, trade and justice, legislators in Congress are in a strong position to challenge the executive. The president's policies often face an uphill battle in Congress, where bargaining among the parties is the norm. Mr Obama prioritized healthcare reform during his presidency, aiming to extend health insurance to the many millions of Americans without coverage, but he struggled to steer these reforms through Congress.

In a **parliamentary system**, the voters directly elect members of parliament, from whom a prime minister and cabinet are selected, usually from the political party with a majority of seats. This is often called the 'Westminster model', as the leading example is the UK. The efficient running of a parliamentary system depends greatly on the nature and number of a country's political parties. It is usually felt that it works best in a stable two-party system of 'government' and 'opposition' parties, in which the opposition is, in effect, an alternative government. A coalition government of Conservatives (with 306 seats) and Liberal Democrats (with 57 seats) was the outcome of the UK general election in 2010. This partnership proved difficult to manage because of policy differences. The outright victory of the Conservatives in 2015 gave them the mandate that had eluded them in 2010.

Low turnout in democratic elections is a concern, as it indicates apathy or lack of engagement in the democratic process. Turnout in UK general elections was in the 70–80% region throughout most of the post-war period, and dived to a low of 59.6% only in 2001. It rose to 65.1% in 2010 and 66.1% in 2015. The turnout among the 18–25 age group reached a low of 38% in 2005, but had climbed to 58% in 2015, largely as a result of efforts to encourage people to register to vote. Still, the turnout among younger voters is disappointingly low. Disillusionment with politics and political parties is a factor, as we discuss in the next section.

The so-called **hybrid system** aims to achieve both a stable executive and maximum representation, with an independently-elected president and a prime minister selected by parliament to head the cabinet. The model for this system, also known as the dual executive, is the Fifth French Republic. Apart from Hungary, which has a parliamentary system, the post-communist states of Central and Eastern Europe have adopted the hybrid model. The theory is that the nationally-elected president can foster national unity, playing the role of head of state, while the prime minister plays more of a party-political role, maintaining support for the government in parliament. In practice, these systems may not run as smoothly as envisaged if the two executives are of different parties or, as is almost inevitable, each sees the other as a rival. In new democracies such as Poland and the Czech Republic, where politics tends to focus on personalities, the role of president can be seen as a strong political platform.

The third branch of government, the judicial, acts as a check on the legislative and executive. The legal environment in general will be discussed in the next chapter. Here we focus on the judicial function as a branch of government. The judicial function is carried out by the state's system of courts. In a constitutional system, the judges are tasked with ensuring that the country's laws passed by the legislature are consistent with the constitution. For firms and individuals, the way that the laws are applied in practice in the country's courts is of utmost importance. The rule of law and an independent judiciary are core to any constitutional system, and are crucial to

The consolidation of presidential power in Turkey: what are the risks?

Turkey presents a picture of an emerging economy with global ambitions, driven by a political leader, Recep Tayyip Erdogan, who aspires to consolidate his hold on the reins of power. However, the democratic political system which has framed Turkey's economic development and party politics now seems to be under threat from the forces of the country's strong-minded president and his Islamist political party. These developments would threaten not just its democratic institutions, but also the secular values that are established in its constitution of 1982. Turkey's constitution establishes a parliamentary system, in which the government is in the hands of a prime minister, with a non-partisan president as a figurehead. Mr Erdogan and his Justice and Development Party (the AKP) have enjoyed remarkable electoral success since 2002. Having served three terms as prime minister, which is the legal maximum, he shifted his ambitions to the office of president, which he wished to see transformed into a more active executive role – a role in which he would wield executive power. Winning the presidential election of 2013 gave him the political platform for a campaign to change Turkey's constitution to a presidential one with a strong executive. Changing Turkey's constitution would require the support of 330 out of the 550 members of Turkey's parliament in order to authorize holding a referendum. Would the country back the AKP to this extent, impliedly giving the voters' blessing to a new presidential framework?

Historically, Turkey stands at a cultural crossroads between east and west. Many of its inhabitants look more towards Europe, as evidenced by the fact that Turkey applied for EU membership in 1995. But Turkey today is far from leaning towards the values of democracy and freedom that the EU stands for. Culturally and politically, Turkey is highly divided. The majority party, the AKP, has a broad base in the Muslim population, and has been the force behind Erdogan's popularity. Its business leaders, many of whom are close to the president, have been the main drivers of Turkey's economic growth, which reached a high of 8.8% in 2011. Since then, growth has weakened, as export markets for the many consumer products that it produces have stalled.

Turkey has a large westernized population, concentrated in Istanbul. They lean towards more individualistic and liberal thinking, and they tend to see Mr Erdogan as a threat to democratic values, freedom of speech and the rule of law. They also fear that the president is introducing more conservative Islamist policies, despite the constitutional guarantees of secularism. Mr Erdogan has a record of suppressing the activities of the opposition parties and other dissidents, as well as curtailing freedom of speech. Another important cultural grouping in Turkey is the large Kurdish population, linked to the Kurdish militarist group known as the PKK (the Kurdistan Workers Party). A destabilizing factor in Turkish politics has been the civil war raging in neighbouring Syria. While Mr Erdogan has taken a stance against the Islamic State (ISIS) terrorists that are fighting to topple Syria's government, he was slow to come to the aid of Kurds being overrun by terrorists near the border in 2015. This event had the effect of alienating many of Turkey's Kurdish people.

Parliamentary elections in June 2015 were inconclusive, and new elections were then called for November, the AKP hoping for a big majority for changing the constitution. The AKP won 317 seats, representing 49.4% of the vote, but this was not sufficient in itself to call a referendum on the constitution. Importantly, the pro-Kurdish party gained 13.2% of the vote, and its members expressed willingness to consider a new constitution. Worryingly, the international monitors for the electoral process reported violent intimidation and arrests of opposition supporters. Mr Erdogan professed satisfaction with the result, and hopes to unite the country behind a new presidential constitution. But, in truth, the country remains highly divided. Polls show that some 57% of Turks prefer to keep the parliamentary system (Cengiz, 2015). Many opponents of constitutional change view the real motive behind Mr Erdogan's constitutional reform as wanting to increase his power over the system. His plans are for the president to be given powers to issue executive and legislative decrees, and to appoint half the members of the higher courts. It is usual in a presidential system to have separation of powers, along with a system of checks and balances. By contrast, Mr Erdogan seems to be planning to consolidate his power over all branches of government. The vision of Turkey's future projected by its president is one of strong national will and security. He is confident that his core Muslim electoral support will remain solidly behind him, but other groups in Turkey fear that democracy will suffer.

Sources: Shaheen, K. (2015) 'Turkey election campaign unfair, say international monitors', *The Guardian*, 2 November, at www.theguardian.com; Toksabay, E. and Aslan, M. (2015) 'Turkey's Erdogan calls for new constitution as EU frets about rights', Reuters, 10 November, at www.reuters.com; Cagaptay, S. (2015) 'Turkey's divisions are so deep they threaten its future', *The Guardian*, 18 October, at www.theguardian.com; Cengiz, O. (2015) 'Turkey's path to dictatorship', *Al-Monitor*, 12 November, at www.al-monitor.com.

Questions for discussion

- How has democracy lost ground in Turkey?
- To what extent has Turkey turned its back on possible EU membership?
- How is the rule of law being jeopardized in Turkey?
- How would a new constitution along the lines that Mr Erdogan envisages affect Turkey's business environment?

a functioning democracy. These principles imply that the law is above any individual, whether an officeholder or a rich and powerful private person. To be independent, the members of the judiciary should be seen to be impartial: a judge who is in the pay of an interest group is not suitable for office. In order for the judicial function to act as an effective check on the other two branches of government, procedures must be devised to call officeholders to account if they have acted unlawfully. The member of the legislature who takes money from a firm for helping to secure a government contract is acting unlawfully, although many firms seek such advantages through payment of politicians.

The president versus the prime minister

A stable and predictable political environment is desired by businesses everywhere. A presidential system would therefore seem to be more stable than a parliamentary system. But in practice, systems with strong executive presidents often unsettle businesses. Why?

Political decision-making in practice

Where do policies and proposed legislation come from? How do democracies differ from authoritarian regimes? And what is the role of business in these processes? These are the questions addressed in this section. Policies and new laws usually emerge in the context of groups, both formal and informal, that participate in political activities within a country. Political parties are the most high-profile of these groups, and they are active in both democratic and authoritarian systems. But other types of political grouping are also active, as are interest groups. Organized groups also include business interests. Businesses are highly sensitive to political decision-making processes, and play active roles. Conflicting interests and agendas thus make up the multifaceted scene of politics in practice.

Political parties and related groups

Political parties are a feature of political life in many kinds of political system, whether democratic or undemocratic. A political party is usually a voluntary organization whose members come together to promote their own political outlook and put forward candidates for elected office. These functions are central to the institutions of representative democracies. Political parties form the link between voters and legislative assemblies. In democratic states, they are essential to the pluralism which characterizes civil society. In authoritarian and semi-authoritarian states, political parties help to cement the ideology of the leadership, and mobilize public support. We look at democratic systems first.

In a pluralist society, parties perform several functions:

1 They provide candidates for public office, who rely on their organizational machinery and funding to get elected. The independent candidate faces an uphill battle, and needs to be very rich.
2 They provide a policy platform, on which voters can decide whom to support. Many voters traditionally are party loyalists, not bothered about who the individual candidate is.
3 When in office, they provide an agenda for government, against which performance can be judged.

Parties vary in their political agendas and in their views of society. Some embrace strong ideological positions, such as communist parties. Others are religious in origin, such as Muslim parties and Christian parties. Many countries have rural-based or peasant parties which exist mainly to foster rural interests. Parties may also emerge from interest groups, such as the Green Party, which concentrates on ecological issues. Most of the narrowly-based parties have little hope of gaining a majority of legislative seats and forming a government; instead, they seek publicity and political influence for their views. They are more likely to win seats in multi-party systems with proportional representation. In two-party systems, such as the US and UK, the trend has been towards the 'catch-all' party, with weaker ideological underpinning and greater direct appeal to voters via the media, in which personalities are as important as policies. Political parties depend on funding largely from supporters, and, although many states attempt to regulate funding, this area is a fertile one for corruption scandals, in which politicians and corporate donors can become enmeshed.

Political parties are usually described in terms of left, right and centre, with the modern catch-all parties falling somewhere near the centre. The modern Labour Party in Britain shifted from being a left-wing socialist party to a broader-based centre-left party. Historically, the Labour Party has been close to the large trade unions, but the influence of the trade unions has diminished in recent years. In general, pinning down what left and right stand for in terms of policy can be bewildering, especially as their meanings have shifted over time. Parties to the 'left' generally support high public spending on social services, protection of workers, and trade union rights; they tend to oppose privatization. The Democratic Party in the US falls broadly within this tradition. Parties on the 'right', known almost universally as 'conservatives', generally wish to see a minimum of government intervention in business, reduced public spending, and low taxes. They favour more privatization in the economy and reduction in government bureaucracy. The Republicans in the US fall into this broad category. However, all modern parties, including the British Conservatives, support the welfare state to some extent. Nationalist tendencies are associated with the right, but most parties of the right (except extremist right-wing parties) support multiculturalism.

In pluralist societies, numerous other groups exist to promote political agendas reflecting members of the group. Many of these are grassroots organizations, often focused on particular local issues. But they can also be entities established or funded by wealthy businesspeople who seek to influence political decision-making towards their own values and goals. Many groups loosely known as 'think tanks' fall into this category, often appearing to be quasi-academic, but established to promote particular political agendas. In the US, groups known as super-Pacs (political action committees) are formed to promote political causes favoured by their founders. The super-Pacs are legally outside the party system, and they are subject to no spending limits, so long as their activities are not co-ordinated with a political party. They raise large sums from wealthy donors to promote particular causes and are active campaigners on issues and during election campaigns. Recall from the opening case study in Chapter 1 that Google has launched a super-Pac. The position of super-Pacs was bolstered by the Supreme Court in a judgment in 2010 known as the 'Citizens United' judgment, which held that a company has a right to free speech analogous to that of the individual citizen. Individuals and companies can thus give unlimited amounts of money to their favoured political causes.

Wealthy donors also benefit from the legal framework on charities. A not-for-profit organization can be set up for welfare purposes, but US law allows it to raise money for political purposes in addition. The advantages of the not-for-profit organization or 'foundation' are that it is tax-exempt and need not disclose the identity of the donors. Much of the money flowing into political campaigns in recent elections is thus being channelled through these groups that are outside the formal parties, and that exist mainly to promote the interests of their wealthy founders and donors. The power of business élites has been the main factor in growing economic inequality, and this power now extends into the political sphere, resulting in widening political inequality. Many candidates for political office are now inclined more towards seeking the backing of wealthy donors than seeking the support of the electorate. The hallmark of democracy, the right of all to democratic participation, has arguably given way to élitist rule, the antithesis of democracy (Wolin, 2008).

Authoritarian states are typically one-party systems in which parties not approved by the leadership are banned. In China, the Communist Party is the dominant institutional force, in effect capturing the state. The state's institutions, while appearing to be autonomous, are in practice controlled by the party. Russia is a more complex example. Here there was a democratic transition and privatization of the economy, resulting in economic power concentrated in the hands of powerful oligarchs that controlled key industries. Russia under Vladimir Putin, who has been in control since 2000, has taken on the aggressive nationalist and authoritarian style of government that characterized the former Soviet Union. The oligarchs have been tamed by Putin, and the state has reasserted control over Gazprom, the gas giant (as discussed in the opening case study). Russia's annexation of parts of Ukraine, which became independent after the fall of the USSR, has indicated a resurgence of Russia's expansionist ambitions, and arguably rekindled cold-war attitudes. The dominant United Russia party is firmly in control, and other political organizations, as well as NGOs, have little freedom. With little press freedom and precarious freedom of association, elections fall short of being free and fair.

Business engagement in political processes

Companies, business interest groups, charitable foundations and think tanks: we have already seen the many organizational ways in which businesses can take part in political decision-making. But what are their aims? Businesses are highly sensitive to the political climate in every country where they are active or have active affiliates. They seek stability and certainty in both policy and governmental processes that affect their activities. Governmental organizations can be envisaged as important stakeholders. Positive stakeholder dialogue can contribute to business success in any location, as well as building relations with communities. However, the line between improving relations with governmental bodies and engaging in bribery and other corrupt activities can sometimes be blurred. Businesses routinely lobby governments to promote policies that favour their activities, including tax reductions and reductions in regulation. Lobbying is a broad term that covers the activities of business and other groups that seek to influence people in political decision-making offices. In the US, lobbying legislators in Washington, DC, is a multi-billion dollar industry. Lobbying is also big business in the UK, other European capitals and the EU. The risk of bribery and corruption is high: legislators can be offered money and other benefits by business interests for promoting an issue, voting a particular way on an issue, or hiring particular individuals. Lobbying is regulated in most of these jurisdictions, in that lobbyists are required to register and maintain transparency in their activities. However, much lobbying is carried on outside these regulatory structures by people not strictly classified as lobbyists. Thus, lobbying activities can be highly influential in accessing politicians while taking place underneath the radar of the regulatory mechanisms.

In the UK, business lobbying has tended to focus on Parliament, but lobbying of the devolved legislative bodies in Scotland, Northern Ireland and Wales, as well as government ministries, is also widespread. Lobbying in the UK has become big business, estimated to be worth £2 billion a year (Transparency International UK, 2015). Most of this activity is associated with legitimate democratic activities of providing information and accessing views of stakeholder parties. However, various lobbying scandals in the UK have brought to light the darker aspects of how decision-making is being influenced for promoting particular interests. Examples include MPs accepting money to lobby on behalf of a particular cause and officials taking jobs with companies that had been within their remit when they were in public office. It might seem incongruous, but MPs are allowed to have conflicts of interest so long as these are declared, apparently legitimating the practice of accepting benefits from a lobbyist. Political parties in the UK are allowed to accept donations without limit, and wealthy donors are typically rewarded with appointment to the House of Lords. In a survey, Transparency International has found that 59% of respondents in the UK think that the UK government is run 'entirely' or 'to a large extent' in the interests of large entities that push their own interests (Transparency International UK, 2015: 12). In this survey, 67% felt that political parties in the UK were 'corrupt' or 'extremely corrupt', and 55% expressed the same opinion about the UK Parliament.

Lobbying of governments and elected representatives by business interests is often depicted as two-sided: on the one hand, politicians who must focus on the public interest, and on the other hand, businesses that promote self-interested agendas. In fact, recent years have seen an increasingly active 'revolving door' between politicians and lobbyists (Wolin, 2008: 63). The politician is likely to see a lucrative lobbying role as a logical career step after serving in public office. A political career is more-than-ever entwined with a business one. The revolving door between business and politics in liberal democratic systems poses risks that the interests of ordinary citizens are being squeezed out.

Global politics

On the international stage, every sovereign state theoretically enjoys equal status with all others, now numbering over 200. But in practice, international politics revolves around power, both economic and military: the most powerful states in any historical period tend to be the richest and those with the most substantial military establishment. The weight of a country's military helps to ensure that it can assert its will over others, by force if need be. On the other hand, it is increasingly recognized by governments that states no longer have the means to deliver national security and material well-being on their own. By co-operating with other states, a government can boost its country's material well-being, for example, through trade, and also reach defence agreements with other countries for their mutual security. In this section we look first at some of the institutions which aim to channel sovereign states towards peaceful and prosperous co-existence. We then discuss the changing power relations which help to determine how these institutions function in practice.

Institutions

Interdependence and co-operation have generated numerous alliances and international organizations, dating mainly from the period following the Second World War. The main legally established institutions are governmental, but non-governmental organizations (NGOs) have gained in political influence and become part of the international institutional process in some areas of global concern. These include human rights (for example, Amnesty International, at www.amnesty.org) and the environment (for example, Greenpeace, at www.greenpeace.org). UN agencies feature regularly in this book, for the research they carry out and global issues they deal with at international level. Founded in 1945, the UN has grown from 50 to 193 states. It acquired 26 new members in the period 1990–95, mainly the post-communist states of the former Soviet Union. The authority of the UN's institutions derives from inter-governmental co-operation. They do not constitute a world government, but they do indicate the extent to which sovereign states are committed to abide by international conventions. The UN's Secretary-General, while having no executive powers that state leaders possess, commands considerable respect in the international community, and exemplifies the UN's aim of achieving peaceful negotiated settlement of conflicts between states. See Figure 5.6 for a summary of some of the main provisions of the UN Charter.

The General Assembly, in which all member states have one vote, contrasts with the Security Council, in which the major post-war powers – the US, UK, France,

The UN General Assembly, based at the organization's headquarters in New York City, enshrines the principle of one-country-one-vote.

Source: UN Photo/Sophia Paris.

China and Russia (formerly the Soviet Union) – were made permanent members and given the right of veto. The use of the veto – and threat to use the veto – has hampered the Security Council's effectiveness. The UN has provided a forum for international debate, and expanded its social and economic activities through its many agencies and affiliated bodies. The International Labour Organization (ILO) (www.ilo.org), which actually pre-dates the UN, has set standards for health and safety, workers' rights, and child labour. ILO conventions in these areas have been ratified by dozens of states, accepting responsibility for implementing them in national law. Similarly, the human rights covenants have been ratified by over 140 states (see Chapter 6). The acceptance by states of the principle that these conventions impose on them a 'higher' duty to comply is an indication of a shift away from the pure theory of state sovereignty.

The United Nations

To maintain international peace and security:

Collective measures to prevent and remove threats to peace, suppress acts of aggression

Settle international disputes which might lead to breach of the peace

To promote friendly relations among nations:

Principle of equal rights and self-determination of peoples

To help solve international problems:

Economic
Social
Cultural
Humanitarian
Upholding basic human rights

Figure 5.6 Main provisions of the UN Charter

Source: 'The UN Charter', at www.un.org

At its founding in 1945, the UN was envisaged as an overarching body that would ensure world peace, but it was a peace dominated by sovereign states, notably the major powers which emerged victorious in the Second World War (Mazower, 2010). This world picture was reflected in the composition of the Security Council, which had three western members out of the five with permanent seats (the US, UK and France). At that time, the UN had only 45 member states in total. The crumbling of empires, both political and economic, which occurred in the following years, creating dozens of new sovereign states, could hardly have been foreseen. These developments have transformed the world. The sovereign state is no longer the preserve of a minority of world powers, but claimed by countries large and small, located all over the globe. The bulk of the UN's current membership is made up of developing countries, representing an incredible shift. Many would argue that this broad base gives the UN a greater mandate to take action, for example, by intervening in situations of human rights abuses. On the other hand, its enshrining of the principle of sovereignty has led it down the path of persuasion and diplomacy, which in many situations appears to be ineffectual. The UN remains active in many spheres, notably peacekeeping and humanitarian aid, but in global politics, it now looks more like a debating forum: although it retains moral authority in theory, in practice it is unable to follow through with actions. One of its enduring accomplishments, which should not be underestimated, however, is its work in negotiating treaties (discussed in the next chapter). The role of facilitator in areas such as climate change is a worthy one, although many would see this role as second-best to the political role envisaged by its founders.

Focus on the European Union

Regional groupings of states have grown in numbers in the post-war period. Most of these are trading alliances, but the most advanced, the EU, represents much deeper economic, social and political integration. It is featured here because its political system has become integral to the national political systems of member states. This process has not been without controversy. Originally comprising a group of six states (Germany, France, Belgium, Luxembourg, the Netherlands and Italy) under the Treaty of Rome in 1957, the European Community, as it then was, envisaged a 'pooling' of national sovereignty. When Britain joined in 1973, the possibility of the erosion of parliamentary sovereignty was a major issue, and it has remained so, culminating in the vote to leave (see p. 147). Despite misgivings about national sovereignty, perceived economic benefits have made the EU more popular than ever, now comprising 28 members (see Chapter 4).

The EU's main institutions are the Council, which was envisaged as holding the main lawmaking authority; the Commission, through which much legislation originated; and the Parliament, which acted mainly as a check on the other two bodies. The enlargement debate has raised questions about the effectiveness and democratic credentials of these structures, perceived as unwieldy, over-bureaucratic, and lacking in democratic accountability. A proposed new constitution for the enlarged EU was put forward in 2004, but rejected in referendums in two countries (France and the Netherlands). A revised document was put forward as the Lisbon Treaty. A key aspect of the Lisbon Treaty, which took effect in December 2009, was to enhance the powers of the European Parliament. A summary of the constitutional proposals and Lisbon Treaty appears in Table 5.2. These will now be discussed.

Table 5.2 Comparison of the EU draft constitution and the Lisbon Treaty of 2009

Constitutional proposals of 2004	Lisbon Treaty of 2009
Enhances powers of the European Parliament over legislation and EU budget	Yes
Introduces new system of weighted voting in the Council of Ministers: a yes vote requires at least 55% of member states representing at least 65% of EU population	Yes
Reduces size of European Commission: members to be sent from only 2/3 of member states on a rotation basis	Not in force. All member states retain right to send commissioners
Creates new offices of president of the Council (serving a term of up to 5 years), and high representative for foreign affairs	Yes
Ends the 6-month rotating presidency of the Council	Not as yet. Rotating presidency retained in 2010, although the new president was in place
Incorporates an EU Charter of Fundamental Rights	Yes

Source: The European Parliament, at www. europarl.europa.eu.

The highest lawmaking authority in the EU is the Council of Ministers, renamed the Council of the European Union in 1993. Members are ministers in their own states. Under the Lisbon Treaty, a new president of the European Council was appointed. He was intended to replace the previous arrangement of a six-month rotating presidency among member states, but in fact, the rotating presidency continued. Originally, unanimity among council members was required for a proposal to proceed, but this requirement has been relaxed in some key areas (for example, agriculture, the environment and transport) by 'qualified majority voting' (QMV). A safeguard for small countries is the provision that a vote is carried if it is supported by at least 55% of member states representing 65% of the overall population of the EU. National veto is still retained on issues of tax, defence, foreign policy and financing the EU budget. A new office of high representative for foreign affairs has been created, to oversee the diplomatic service. The aim of creating the new foreign affairs post was to raise the EU's foreign relations profile.

The European Commission is composed of 28 commissioners, one from each member state. The Commission is headed by a President. The Directorates-General of the Commission are the heart of the EU's civil service, responsible for its day-to-day running. Importantly, in addition, the Commission takes the lead in proposing legislation, and thus enjoys considerable political power from its 'agenda-setting' initiatives, such as the Single Market and Monetary Union. The 2004 constitutional plan provided for a reduction in the number of commissioners to 18 from 2014. There have been objections to this streamlining of the Commission, and the proposed reduction in size of the Commission was shelved.

The European Parliament is composed of members from each state roughly in proportion to the state's population. The EU Parliament has grown in size from 78 to 736 members. Although Members of the European Parliament (MEPs) have been directly elected by EU citizens since 1979, the parliament does not play the pivotal role which is customary in national systems. The Treaty of Rome gave parliament little direct say in legislation, but with later treaties, it gained greater influence, with an increase from 15 to 38 areas in which has 'co-decision-making' powers with the

Council (amounting to two-thirds of all EU legislation). These reforms have come in response to criticism that EU institutions lack sufficient democratic accountability and that they are bureaucratic and inefficient. The new constitutional treaty also provides for increased scrutiny of proposed legislation by national parliaments.

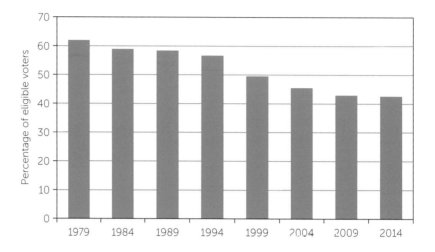

Figure 5.7 Voter turnout in European Parliament elections

Source: Data from European Parliament, 'Election turnout', at www.europarl. europa.eu, accessed 20 May 2015. © European Union, 1995–2016.

The European Parliament has not as yet resonated with voters to the same extent that national parliaments do. As Figure 5.7 shows, voter turnout has declined with each successive election, reaching a low of 42.61% in 2014. It had been hoped that the prospect of a greater role for the parliament in the new European constitution would persuade voters to take greater interest. However, the popularity of 'eurosceptic' parties in many countries suggests that national issues loom larger with the electorate than pan-European issues. The very low turnout in some new member states is a cause of concern. Turnout in the Czech Republic in 2014 was 18.20%, and in Slovakia, just 13.05%. Keen advocates of European political integration have seen a federal solution as strengthening EU institutions, but the electorate in many member countries do not share this European vision.

How the global balance of power is shifting

Global politics rests on power relations. Historically, the strongest states, economically and militarily, have expanded their reach, acquiring territory through empires and growing rich through distorted trade relations with subservient peoples. Imperial expansion can have numerous dimensions: economic, territorial, cultural and political. Empires rise and fall. The UK, France, Spain and Portugal are among many former imperial powers whose territories are now independent states. Legacies, such as the language of the imperial power, remain, and there is often a lingering sense of injustice associated with the destruction of local cultures. In today's world, the idea of imperialism thus bears a negative moral taint. The historical role of imperial powers has given way to today's 'superpowers'. The **superpower** is a state that is able to impose its power over other countries, which nowadays is likely to be mainly in the economic sphere.

In the cold-war period, the two strongest powers, the US and Soviet Union, took on the mantle of superpowers. The US, seeing itself as the champion of freedom and democracy, was driven by ideological abhorrence to the Soviet communist system, which was depicted as an embodiment of evil. China, also a large communist state, was perceived as a lesser threat, mainly because in this period it was still a relatively poor developing country and also lacked the military prowess of the Soviet Union. In these years, the US adopted an all-encompassing anticommunist mission, going so far as propping up dictators in Latin America and elsewhere who were felt to be bulwarks against the spread of communism. The US was at the centre of the group of advanced economies known as the **Group of Seven**, or **G7**, dating from 1976. The seven members were the US, Canada, the UK, France, Germany, Italy and Japan.

The collapse of the Soviet Union left the US as the one remaining superpower. Russia joined the G7 in 1998, creating the G8. However, in a sense, the ideological impetus that drove US foreign policy in the cold war remains strong, although the perceived threats, notably from terrorists, have become more diffuse. The US still sees itself as the world's moral policeman and sole superpower, reinforced by its continuing military reach and the power of its corporations. However, the rise of China as an economic and military power represents a shift in the global balance of power. In 1999, a grouping of countries known as the **G20** was launched by the IMF, bringing together a more diverse range of countries, in terms of both economic and political systems. Members of the G20 include the G7, but also the EU, Argentina, Brazil, Mexico, China, India, Australia, Indonesia, Russia, South Korea, South Africa, Saudi Arabia and Turkey. The G20 thus represents a number of key emerging countries that are taking on greater prominence in the global economy. The IMF envisaged the G20 as focusing mainly on global financial stability. However, the grouping has no permanent institutional framework or authority to bind member states. On the other hand, because it represents key global economies, including those with the largest populations, its policy initiatives are highly influential in global politics.

Since opening up to market forces, China has played a vital role in economic globalization, with growing foreign direct investment (FDI) helping to enrich American companies such as Apple. China has also been building up investments in the US through FDI, revitalizing companies and employing thousands of American workers. And US universities have welcomed Chinese students, among whom are the sons and daughters of China's communist leaders. Chinese students now form the largest group of foreign students at US universities. China is thus not an 'enemy' in the sense that the USSR was depicted in the cold-war years. Yet, China's leaders have hardly relaxed their political ideology. In 2015, the government reiterated an order to educational institutions, including universities, that 'western values' should not be taught, and that attacks on the leadership of the party would not be tolerated (Anderlini, 2015). Western businesses still look to China for production locations and markets. While it was long the case that Apple's iPhones were made in China but out of reach of the pockets of Chinese consumers, in the space of only a few years, Apple has gained significant market share among China's affluent urban consumers. Business ties thus seem to overcome political divides.

While both countries benefit from these economic ties, it would be a mistake to assume that political divides are melting away, or that China is on course to become a democracy. Economic integration can lead to more co-operative political relations, but political risk remains real, and underlying tensions can turn into hostilities. China's military and political leaders, while espousing socialist ideology and decrying western values, have long favoured the trappings of western lifestyles. These party leaders control not just political institutions, but large swathes of business activity.

Chinese students studying in the US: a sign that education is becoming globalized, or a sign that Chinese students are being attracted to western values?

Source: © Andersen-Ross/ Corbis.

The Chinese leadership sits atop a political, military and business hierarchy that has seen the rise of a wealthy élite. Their political ideology is the antithesis of democratic values and individual freedoms – values that would threaten the existing élites. China's citizens have themselves seen rising prosperity and aspirations for a better life. But worrying levels of pollution and other aspects of environmental degradation are the prices China is paying for breakneck development. These are political issues that are now foisting themselves on China's leaders, who fear that social unrest can lead to political uprisings (see the closing case study on Hong Kong).

The 'wave' of democratic transformations that followed the dismemberment of empires, as well as the fall of the apartheid regime in South Africa, has given way to a rise in development models. Despite democratic forms, many mix élitist political systems with greater economic freedoms. Political and business élites gain handsomely, while social goals take a back seat. At the same time, the leading western democracy, the US, has experienced a continuing rise in the political power of big business, while citizen participation in democratic processes has retreated, and along with it, the weakening of policies promoting social inclusion. A rather pessimistic view of today's global political powers – existing and aspiring – is that business and political élites are gaining, often in tandem with each other, but these gains are not being translated into a better societies or more accountable governance.

The way I see it ...

On political leadership in Africa, 'Insufficient care was taken to ensure that Africa's economic growth was inclusive, equitable and job-creating, particularly for young people ... Better governance is the only sustainable solution to our peace and security challenges.'

Mo Ibrahim, mobile communications entrepreneur from Sudan, writing in the *Financial Times*, 6 October 2014.

In your view, how can better governance meet the challenges identified by Mo Ibrahim?

The changing political environment: challenges and responsibilities

In the western countries that have been to the forefront in global political debate in the post-war era, it has been common to view the political environment in terms of external influences on businesses. This view holds that the political system is a given, and that business must adapt to the changing political makeup in a state, abiding by new policies and laws. The business is seen in this scenario as reacting to changes, including risks. This thinking rests on a conceptual view that there is a dichotomy between politics, which is about public goods, and business, which is essentially about private actors. This dichotomy has gradually become blurred as businesses have become more active in the formulation of political policies and more involved in government activities. Businesses now participate in broad processes of governance, involving them in dialogue with a range of governmental and quasi-governmental bodies, as well as civil society organizations. This is a more participatory concept than that of government, which implies distinct roles: governments make policy and businesses apply it.

Business participation in governance involves businesses reaching more deeply into societies. This has a positive aspect that is captured by the concept of corporate social responsibility (CSR), which focuses on the responsibilities of business in society. But greater engagement with officialdom also has negative implications. Businesses lobby politicians to promote policies that will favour them. As we have seen, dialogue with officials is constructive and legitimate, but this more engaged role in public policy implies responsibilities on businesses, and also invites critical assessment of their behaviour on grounds of public good. Where companies, such as large American banks, become closely associated with governments, they reap the benefits of policy decisions, but they can face criticism when evidence of corruption arises.

In many developing countries, companies take lead roles in negotiating with governments for advantageous terms in FDI and trade, often dealing with authoritarian leaders in situations which give rise to corruption. These activities often cast corporate executives in opportunistic roles that suggest private gain at the expense of public goods. Businesses are possibly uncomfortable in this new spotlight, and many would take the view that co-operation with autocrats or military leaders is simply a business deal, with no ethical overtones. Executives in these circumstances argue that the company's role is economic, and its managers rightly pursue goals of wealth creation for their corporate owners. But there is a fine line between legitimate ties with government and exploiting ties with government for private gain. China ranks in the bottom half of Transparency International's Corruption Perception Index. Opaque government, party influence (both structural and informal) and state-controlled entities with opaque governance are all aspects of a shadowy system in which political and business actors have ample scope for exerting power through corrupt practices. This is in an environment where there are few effective regulatory checks, especially in a context of weak rule of law and regulatory bodies that lack independence.

Many companies nowadays deliver public services. A company that runs schools or hospitals wishes to make profits, but is also fulfilling a role in serving the public. Thus, there arises a responsibility to society, not just to its owners. If it takes an aggressive profit-seeking approach, for example registering the company in an off-shore tax haven, it is not behaving illegally, but it is engaging in unethical practices. Citizens criticize politicians for self-interested behaviour. Elected politicians who claim excessive expenses or take money from lobbyists are roundly criticized. But, of course, corruption is facilitated by unethical business practices, not just greedy politicians. The political sphere can serve society well, through honest and accountable governance, but only if all players, including businesses as well as politicians, carry out their roles and responsibilities with a view to societal well-being.

Conclusions

The political sphere can be identified with structures and processes by which power and influence are allocated, whether among groups in a state or among states in the global political sphere. But an organizational view of politics is only part of the story: the undercurrents of where power lies in society are also influential. As this chapter has shown, structures form the framework of political systems, which aim to ensure stability of governance over whole societies. Often set out in written constitutions, political systems should ideally represent an enduring set of institutions that stands above the people in office, and to which they must adhere. All systems change over time, usually incrementally, but sometimes by violent overthrow of an autocratic regime. Democratic systems are by definition responsive to the citizenry as the source of their legitimacy. When there are grassroots pressures for change, this thinking should be part of the democratic responsiveness of the system, although the voices of ordinary people do not always weigh with politicians in the corridors of power. Democratic values are closely associated with western political thinking. They have taken root roughly alongside the rise in capitalism, although capitalist development preceded democracy. Freedoms of the individual are aspects of both developments: freedom of expression and association are linked to economic freedoms. But democracy claims a broader perspective which is ethical and social. Democratic thinking asserts that human dignity matters, whatever the country, and that governmental legitimacy must ultimately rest with the people on ethical grounds, whatever the cultural values of the society.

Democratic values have become enshrined in political systems across the globe, particularly on the dissolution of empires in the last two centuries. But the formal installation of elections and universal suffrage goes only part of the way towards achieving democratic values. Constitutional systems are formal. To work in practice, they must be nurtured through the cultivation of values of civil society, pluralism and responsiveness to societal needs. The leaders that emerge in a political system, however, are more likely to be those who have become adept at cultivating personal power bases within parties and other political groupings in national contexts. A political outlook, while ideally focused on the good of society, is more often focused on the pursuit of particular interests. Those interests in today's world are likely to be linked with powerful businesses. This can be a positive relationship. Businesses, after all, provide employment, generate wealth and drive development goals. They also provide many public services such as health, education and utilities. But business goals almost invariably clash with the egalitarian goals inherent in democracy.

Businesses have become highly successful at cultivating ties with political leaders, in both democratic and non-democratic systems. Indeed, in some they have become established in the governmental structures. Moreover, business leaders have moved from national political stages to the global stage, as globalization has transformed business relations. A globalized business élite has enjoyed not just greater wealth and an ability to manipulate that wealth globally, but an ascendency over numerous political leaders, who remain focused on their national interests. In the US, the business élite, largely made up of global companies and wealthy donors, has found allies in politicians who share their corporate values. These clash with the democratic goals of empowering ordinary citizens and building an inclusive society. In authoritarian states, business interests have also found favour, but on terms laid down by dictatorial leaders. Political risks abound in both environments, whether ostensibly democratic or autocratic. Businesses desire a stable environment, but in taking on quasi-political roles, they inevitably court risks that they will be subject to greater scrutiny, and will be associated with particular political interests that could prove damaging to them in the long term. In engaging with political actors, they are taking on responsibilities that are rooted in social and ethical considerations. The company that takes a 'business as usual' approach to activities with corrupt overtones can find itself out in the cold when the winds turn, as they almost inevitably do. By contrast, the company that focuses on a balance of business and social goals, treating every government as a stakeholder among other stakeholders, is likely to tread a more sustainable path through an increasingly complex global political environment.

☐ References

Ackerman, S., Siddiqui, S. and Lewis, P. (2015) 'White House admits: we didn't know who drone strike was aiming to kill', *The Guardian*, 23 April, at www.theguardian.com

Anderlini, J. (2015) 'Beijing blocks "western values" in classrooms', *Financial Times*, 31 January, at www.ft.com.

BBC (2014) 'China media back discussions on judicial reforms at party summit', BBC News, 17 October, at www.bbc.com

Boone, J. (2013) 'US drone strikes could be classed as war crimes, says Amnesty International', *The Guardian*, 22 October, at www.theguardian.com

Boseley, S. (2008) '151,000 civilians killed since Iraqi invasion', *The Guardian*, 10 January, at www.theguardian.com

Bremmer, I. (2015) 'The new world of business', *Fortune*, 22 January, at www.fortune.com

Diamond, L. (1996) 'Is the third wave over?', *Journal of Democracy*, 7(3): 21–39.

Freedom House (2015) 'Freedom in the world 2015', at www.freedomhouse.org

Gilens, M. and Page, B. (2014) 'Testing theories of American politics: elites, interest groups and average citizens', *Perspectives on Politics*, 12(3): 564–581.

Hawthorn, J. (1993) 'Sub-Saharan Africa', in Held, D. (ed.) *Prospects for Democracy* (Cambridge: Polity Press), pp. 330–374.

Inter-Parliamentary Union (2015) 'Women in national parliaments, as of 1 April 2015', at www.ipu.org

Isenberg, D. (2009) 'Private Military Contractors and US Grand Strategy', Report: PRIO 1/209, International Peace Research Institute, Oslo, at www.prio.no

Jackson, J. (2003) 'Sovereignty-modern: a new approach to an outdated concept', *American Journal of International Law*, 97: 782–802.

Laine, J. (2014) 'Debating civil society: contested conceptualizations and development trajectories', *International Journal of Not-for-profit Law*, 16(1): 59–77.

Lincoln, A. (1863) *Gettysburg Address*, transcript, at www.ourdocuments.gov

Linz, J. (1993) 'Perils of presidentialism', in Diamond, L. and Plattner, M.F. (eds) *The Global Resurgence of Democracy* (Baltimore, MD: Johns Hopkins University Press), pp. 108–126.

Mazower, M. (2010) *No Enchanted Palace: The End of Empire and the Ideological Origins of the United Nations* (Princeton: Princeton University Press).

O'Neill, J. (2001) 'Building better global economic BRICs', Goldman Sachs Global Economics Research Group, Global Paper No. 66, at www.gs.com

Pew Research Center (2014) 'Public trust in government: 1958–2014', 13 November, at www.people-press.org

Plattner, M. (2010) 'Populism, pluralism and liberal democracy', *Journal of Democracy*, 21(1): 81–92.

SIPRI (Stockholm International Peace Research Institute) (2014) *SIPRI Yearbook 2014: Armaments, Disarmament and International Security*, at www.sipri.org

SIPRI (Stockholm International Peace Research Institute) (2015) 'Trends in World Military Expenditure', SIPRI Fact Sheet, April, at www.sipri.org

Timm, T. (2015) 'The hostages killed by US drones are casualties of an inhumane policy', *The Guardian*, 15 April, at www.theguardian.com

Toksoz, M. (2014) 'Investors must prepare for worst case scenarios', *Financial Times*, 29 September, at www.ft.com

Transparency International UK (2015) 'Lifting the lid on lobbying: the hidden exercise of power and influence in the UK', February, at www.transparency.org

UN Policy Working Group (2002) 'Report of the Policy Working Group on the United Nations and Terrorism', Ref A/57/273, at www.un.org/terrorism

US Department of Defense (2012) 'US Base Structure Report Fiscal Year 2012 Baseline', at www.acq.osd.mil/eie

Wolin, S. (2008) *Democracy Incorporated* (Princeton: Princeton University Press).

World Bank (2011) 'World Development Report 2011', at www.worldbank.org

☞ Multiple choice questions

Go to the companion website: www.palgravehighered.com/morrison-gbe-4e to take a quick multiple choice quiz on what you have read in this chapter.

⑦ Review questions

1 What are the defining characteristics of the nation-state? How is globalization threatening state sovereignty?

2 Give some examples of internal political risk for businesses.

3 What are the main external threats to states that present political risk in today's world?

4 What are the characteristics of a constitution, and why is it felt to be stable in the long term?

5 What are the differences between authoritarian states and democratic ones? Why is the line between them becoming blurred?

6 In what ways does a democracy promote social and ethical values?

7 What are the risks where electoral outcomes can be influenced by the richest in society?

8 What is proportional representation in electoral arrangements, and does it make outcomes more democratic?

9 How do presidential systems compare with parliamentary systems of government? The hybrid system is said to combine the best of both worlds, but does it?

10 What is the role of political parties in democratic systems, and in authoritarian ones?

11 What are the roles of businesses in lobbying?

12 Looking at the main institutions of the European Union, how democratic are they?

13 Corruption is a problem in political and business relations in most countries. What can be done to curtail corrupt practices?

14 What institutional mechanisms exist at international level, and what are their limitations?

15 Is China becoming a global 'superpower', and, if so, what impact will it have on global business?

✓ Assignments

1 For a company considering a new FDI project, assess what aspects of the country's political structure and processes it should it take into account when assessing political risk.

2 Discuss the extent to which democratic institutions can promote inclusive growth in a national political environment.

📖 Further reading

Bale, T. (2013) *European Politics: A Comparative Introduction*, 3rd edn (Basingstoke: Palgrave Macmillan).

Baylis, J., Smith, S. and Owens, P. (eds) (2013) *The Globalization of World Politics*, 6th edn (Oxford: Oxford University Press).

Deaton, A. (2013) *The Great Escape: Health, Wealth and the Origins of Inequality* (Princeton: Princeton University Press).

Goldin, I. (2012) *Globalization for Development: Meeting New Challenges* (Oxford: OUP).

Hague, R. and Harrop, M. (2013) *Comparative Government and Politics: An Introduction*, 9th edn (Basingstoke: Palgrave Macmillan).

Held, D. and McGrew, A. (2007) *Globalization/Anti-globalization: Beyond the Great Divide*, 2nd edn (Cambridge: Polity Press).

Heywood, A. (2013) *Politics*, 4th edn (Basingstoke: Palgrave Macmillan).

Heywood, A. (2014) *Global Politics*, 2nd edn (Basingstoke: Palgrave Macmillan).

🌐 **Visit the companion website at** www.palgravehighered.com/morrison-gbe-4e **for further learning and teaching resources.**

The promise of democracy in Hong Kong

Hong Kong's legacies from its days as a British colony were centred on its vibrant market economy and on its constitutional political system, designed by its British administrators. When Hong Kong was handed over to China by Britain in 1997, these legacies were part of the agreement for the former colony's future. From now on, it would be a 'special administrative region' (SAR) of China, and it would be governed under the principle of 'one country, two systems', that would preserve its cultural and political heritage. Hence, freedom of speech, freedom of assembly, an independent judiciary and recognition of the rule of law were to be guaranteed. These guarantees were contained in its constitutional document, the Basic Law, and it was assumed that these safeguards were sufficient to assure Hong Kong society that there would be no radical crackdown by the Chinese government. There was no democratic government put in place, but there was a promise of universal suffrage in the future.

Although tiny in size geographically, Hong Kong has been a highly important element in China's overall economic environment. Its market freedoms, stock exchange and financial centre provided a convenient gateway for western and Chinese businesses. In the 1990s, 20% of China's trade passed through Hong Kong. That share is now down to 2%, but the importance of Hong Kong as a financial centre, with access to international capital, has grown over that period. Both Hong Kong companies and mainland Chinese companies have prospered through its open-market financial framework. These companies, along with their wealthy owners, now have considerable vested interests in the continuation of Hong Kong's relatively independent status. But, for the people of Hong Kong, numbering some 7 million in total, the picture looks different. Property prices have rocketed with the spread of luxury developments for the few, contrasting sharply with those that ordinary residents can afford. Hong Kong has become a highly unequal society. Its Gini coefficient has risen to an estimated 0.537, close to the 0.55 estimated for mainland China (Chen, 2014). The Forbes Billionaires List of 2014 recorded 35 billionaires in Hong Kong, with a combined wealth of $214 billion, which was the equivalent of 80% of Hong Kong's GDP in 2013 (Chen, 2014). At the bottom, there are 1.3 million inhabitants living beneath the poverty line. Those down the social ladder are likely to feel stuck in cramped housing, with poor social services and little economic opportunity. Would a democratic election of the leader offer some prospect of a government more focused on social well-being?

Hong Kong is led by a chief executive who is elected by an election committee of 1,200 members, the majority of whom are Beijing oriented. The Chinese government in Beijing held out the prospect that direct elections by Hong Kong's 5 million eligible voters would be held in 2017. In 2014, however, Beijing proposed that the candidates would be 2 or 3 people chosen by a nominating committee, which would be roughly the same as the pro-Beijing election committee at present. Hong Kong's democracy activists complained that the screening of the candidates meant that the election would not be free. Pro-democracy demonstrators, who were mainly students, gathered in the streets for a rally. They were met by police with tear gas and pepper spray. Putting up umbrellas against these onslaughts, they soon became known as the 'umbrella' movement. They gathered support from a public who were appalled by the use of repressive tactics. After this initial rally, protesters stationed themselves around the city, while the police changed their tactics and simply looked on. Although the protesters maintained their presence in the streets for 75 days, the impetus eventually fizzled out, and residents tired of the continuing obstructions. The police eventually cleared the streets.

The pro-democracy protests achieved no breakthrough, and there is now little prospect of direct elections. A reform package based on the Beijing proposals failed to secure the two-thirds majority needed in Hong Kong's legislature, the Legislative Council, in 2015. The existing system of indirect election of the chief executive therefore remains in place. The 'one country, two systems' principle has come under strain. The protests were perhaps a 'wake-up' call to the Chinese government, but the messages are blurred. Beneath the calls for democracy lie issues of social injustice that remain unresolved.

Sources: Chen, L. (2014) 'Beyond the Umbrella Movement: Hong Kong's struggle with inequality in 8 charts', Forbes, 8 October, at www.forbes.com; Pilling, D. (2014) 'Hong Kong's special status is stretched to its limit', Financial Times, 2 October, at www.ft.com; Pilling, D. (2014) 'Protesters take solace in public "awakening"', Financial Times, 13 December; Sevastopulo, D. and Mitchell, T. (2014) 'Hong Kong power play', Financial Times, 4 October; BBC (2015) 'Hong Kong's democracy debate', BBC News, 18 June, at www.bbc.com.

Questions for discussion

- What are the contradictions in the 'one country, two systems' principle?
- How has Hong Kong evolved economically since the handover by the British in 1997?
- In what ways is inequality impacting on the political situation in Hong Kong?
- What are the risks that there will be a crackdown by the Chinese government on the freedoms that have existed in Hong Kong?

THE LEGAL ENVIRONMENT

This chapter will enable you to

- Understand the interrelationships between national, regional and international legal frameworks in their impact on the international business environment
- Appreciate the divergence in structures, processes and content between national legal systems
- Identify the ways in which legal frameworks impact on cross-border business activities
- Assess critically the role of multinational companies in relation to issues of law and society in diverse locations

Outline of chapter

OPENING CASE STUDY

Is Uber transforming the world's taxis?

Under threat: Uber challenges traditional taxis – and regulatory systems – but who are the winners?
Source: BRAND X PICTURES.

Uber was launched in 2010 as a start-up business in San Francisco, where its founders first offered a luxury, chauffeur-driven taxi service under the name of UberCab. But, noticing a shortage of ordinary taxis in the city, they soon came up with the idea of a low-cost alternative to the conventional taxi, which became known as a 'ride-sharing' service. The idea behind it was that anyone with a car could offer a ride to passengers as a one-to-one transaction. Drawing on his technology background, co-founder and CEO, Travis Kalanick, devised a convenient app that could be downloaded by anyone, allowing the driver to offer rides to customers, whenever and wherever needed. The fares were set by Uber, and the driver would hand over a percentage of the takings to the company. This formula could easily be rolled out in any city in the world. In the post-crisis economic environment of 2010, the low-cost ride was sure to be attractive. However, Kalanick's global aspirations would come up against legal and regulatory hurdles in most cities, where frameworks for licensed taxi operators are the norm. Mr Kalanick would say these are too restrictive, but local authorities are conscious of public safety

factors. Licensed taxi drivers usually face background checks and other legal requirements, whether they are self-employed or are employed by a company.

Undeterred, Uber has expanded rapidly, from operating in 9 cities in 2012 to 311 in 2015; 170 of these are in the US. In many of these cities, including the US locations, Uber faces legal challenges. Its start in San Francisco was indicative. A cease-and-desist order was issued by the San Francisco Transport Agency in 2010, which drew public attention to Uber, and also attracted public support for the company, seen as the victim of bureaucratic interference. Kalanick has adopted a combative approach to these legal hurdles, trying to navigate around them and also launching lobby campaigns to get the law changed. He has expanded aggressively, sometimes going ahead with expansion plans in cities where the regulatory environment is hostile. Despite these challenges, he can claim considerable success for Uber's rapid rise as a global business. He sees himself as championing the consumer, who wants a good service at a low price; and also benefiting the drivers, who are able to make money as and when they please. To aid in his lobbying activities, in 2014, he hired an expert in political communication, the man who led President Obama's presidential campaign in 2008.

Is the business able to navigate the legal challenges? Uber refers to drivers as 'partners', which is ambiguous. In California, Uber drivers have been held by the courts to be employees rather than self-employed people. The courts in most countries look at the degree of control the company exerts over the worker, to determine whether the driver is an employee or self-employed. Uber controls the driver's fares and monitors the car's movements, but does not control the driver's hours. If a driver is an employee, Uber as the employer would have to pay employment taxes. Alternatively, if the driver is self-employed, the driver would be responsible for acquiring a licence. In Germany, UberPop was banned, and the company then launched UberX as an alternative, paying the 200-euro licence fee for each partner driver. In France, UberPop was fined for running an illegal minicab service in Paris in 2014, and was banned in 2015. This led to violent clashes with licensed taxi operators, who are highly regulated in Paris. Two of Uber's senior executives were arrested and brought to trial in France for running an unlicensed taxi service and holding private data illegally. While they could have faced prison sentences, prosecutors instead sought fines and a ban on company office-holding. The company has faced legal problems in a number of other countries, including Spain, the Netherlands, China and India. In most of its locations, Uber faces local competitors, keen to have a share of the ride-sharing business, especially if the legal climate thaws.

Despite the legal and competitive challenges, Uber has been popular with large investors, attracting backing estimated to be over $50 billion, an extraordinary achievement for a young private company. It is likened to other companies in the 'sharing economy', such as Airbnb, with which it is often compared. But the two companies differ markedly, and not just in the more conciliatory approach to lobbying adopted by Airbnb's CEO, Brian Chesky. Mr Kalanick insists that Uber is an innovative 'platform' rather than a taxi business. But the essence of the service is that a driver is paid to carry the passenger, which makes it closer to the traditional business transaction of hiring labour. Labour laws and employment protection are put in place by governments everywhere in the public interest. Uber as a company has set out to evade them or override them as part of its business model. This approach has aroused critics as well as admirers.

Sources: Ingham, E. (2014) 'Start-ups take note: Uber made it big, but did they get it right?', *Forbes*, 5 December, at www.forbes.com; Herne, A. (2015) 'Why the term "sharing economy" needs to die', *The Guardian*, 5 October, at www.theguardian.com; Waters, R. (2014) 'Uber is leading the battle of the taxi apps into a war of attrition', *Financial Times*, 17 October, at www.ft.com; Bremner, C. (2014) 'Uber chiefs held by police as war on app accelerates', *The Times*, 30 June, at wwwthetimes.co.uk.

Questions for discussion

- How does Uber differ from a conventional taxi business?
- Summarize Mr Kalanick's approach to the legal and regulatory environment in the cities where Uber is launched.
- Suggest ways that Uber might have approached a launch in Paris so as to avoid the bitter relations with the authorities and the court cases.
- Should Uber be allowed to operate freely in cities using its present business model? Why?

Introduction

The legal dimension of international business has become more pertinent as business relations across national borders have expanded. This might seem like a paradox: if businesses are more mobile than ever, then the significance of borders might be expected to diminish. This chapter will explain the ways in which borders do still matter, and also how businesses are now becoming adept at skipping over borders. Historically, the legal environment has been determined by national legal systems. Businesses are traditionally advised that obeying national laws in each location is the overriding guide they must follow. But the legal environment is now much more complicated than this rule-of-thumb suggests. Globalization of markets and production has provided scope for companies to do business in a variety of national legal environments, but in many the rule of law is weak and legal risk is a major factor. Moreover, international law, which invokes higher standards than much national law, is increasingly becoming the benchmark for global businesses. The legal environment can be divided into three interacting spheres, as shown in Figure 6.1: national legal systems; regional lawmaking authorities, of which the European Union is the major example; and international law, sponsored by international bodies such as the United Nations and its agencies. This chapter will explore the ways in which these overlapping spheres of law impact on international business.

Figure 6.1 The international legal environment

For international businesses, national law remains the primary legal backdrop for cross-border transactions. The chapter looks at relevant areas of the law, including contract law, liability for accidents and competition law. Businesses do not just watch from the sidelines as laws are framed and implemented. Increasingly, they take on roles in advising governments and international bodies. They also spend money on lobbying lawmakers around the world. As technological innovation alters business models, lawmakers are called on to respond with regulatory changes. The speed of some developments such as ecommerce has far outpaced the development of the law to cover them. While governments have slowly woken up to the legal implications of advances in technology, they have also realized the limitations of national law in areas such as data protection and privacy, which have become global issues.

All countries appreciate the need for an efficient, modern, impartial legal system, to attract enterprises (both local and overseas investors) and to retain their confidence in its processes. They also see the benefits of harmonization of laws to facilitate international transactions. Governments are aware that relations with businesses, domestic and foreign, offer opportunities to fund investment, provide jobs and promote economic growth. They are also aware that the legal environment plays an important role in ensuring that societal well-being is prioritized. Businesses now have extensive ties with governments, and also deepening roles in societies that involve responsibilities to multiple stakeholders. As the last section of this chapter will show, these evolving roles present a blend of legal and ethical considerations much more complex than the traditional view of law as rules that simply have to be obeyed.

Classifying law

Law refers to the rules identified as binding because they emanate from state authorities. Groups within a society, such as sports bodies, create rules for their own participants and members, but the distinguishing feature of law is that it creates obligations for society as a whole. Law touches on almost all aspects of business. While businesspeople are inclined to see legal rules in a negative light, constraining their activities (for example, an application for planning permission), in fact, much law is of an enabling nature (for example, eligibility to apply for public funding). Market-driven economies aim to strike a balance between freedom of enterprise and sufficient regulation to safeguard the public interest. In the post-war era, with an upsurge in welfare-state provisions, the law has extended to areas such as employment protection, consumer protection, and health and safety in the workplace. A more recent concern is data protection of individuals' personal data.

A number of the main areas of legal obligation are shown in Figure 6.2, showing each of the three spheres. There is overlapping jurisdiction in some of these areas, such as competition and environment. For sheer scope of jurisdiction, the national legal system is the most relevant for any business. However, the regional and international spheres cover some of the global issues which are becoming increasingly important for business, and there is now greater co-ordination between the three sets of authorities.

Law may be broadly classified into two categories: public law, which concerns relations between citizens and the state, and civil (or private) law, which concerns relations between individuals (including companies). Tax and social security fall within public law, whereas contract law and employment law are areas of civil law. The state plays a significant, although less direct, role in the civil law. Legislatures enact law regulating employment relations, for example; and the state's courts may be called on to settle disputes between the parties. In a dispute over a contract or an accident at work, the person who has suffered loss or injury (the 'plaintiff') may bring a claim for money compensation ('damages') or a range of other remedies against the 'defendant' in the state's courts. The use of the courts to bring claims for damages and other remedies is referred to as litigation. Litigation can be costly and time-consuming. Companies generally prefer to settle disputes 'out of court', saving costs and achieving an agreement more quickly than in judicial proceedings. There are now many mechanisms available which help to facilitate settlements through mediation and negotiation short of full court proceedings. One mechanism is arbitration (see p. 221), whereby the parties agree to allow a third party to step in to settle disputes. An arbitration clause can be included as part of a contract. On the other hand, some companies routinely engage in legal proceedings as an integral part of their global business strategy. Uber, discussed in the opening case

International jurisdiction, e.g. UN-sponsored international conventions

- Environment
- Human rights
- Labour standards

Regional jurisdiction, e.g. the EU

- Consumer protection
- Environment
- Competition

National jurisdiction, e.g. Austria

- Contract
- Employment
- Crime
- Environment
- Intellectual property
- Negligence and product liability
- Competition
- Company

Figure 6.2 Summary of major areas of law affecting business and relevant authorities

study, is an example. Litigation is also commonplace in the high-tech and pharmaceutical sectors, where disputes arise over intellectual property rights.

A major body of public law is the criminal law, under which certain types of wrongdoing are designated by the state as criminal offences. In these cases, state authorities initiate proceedings, known as a 'prosecution', in the criminal courts, which, on conviction, will lead to a fine or imprisonment of the offender. In Italy in 2014, the captain of the Italian cruise ship, *Costa Concordia*, was found guilty of manslaughter when the ship ran aground and sank, causing the deaths of 32 people. Sentenced to 16 years in prison, he launched an appeal, but that appeal was turned down by the court in 2016. Was the cruise company partly to blame? Victims of the disaster are suing Costa Cruises for damages in civil courts, but, as we will see, it is not clear-cut where or against whom to pursue such claims. Some are suing Costa Cruises, an Italian affiliate of Carnival Cruises of the US, for damages in the civil courts in Florida, in the US, where Costa has an office. Others are suing Costa in Italy, where the company is registered. These civil claims are separate from the criminal proceedings.

While we tend to think of crime in terms of individual crimes, such as assault and theft, companies, as well as their directors and employees, can be guilty of criminal offences, as the opening case study showed. Breaches of health and safety law are a common type of corporate crime. In Britain, corporate liability has been extended by a new offence of corporate killing, following unsuccessful prosecutions for manslaughter in relation to ferry and train disasters, including a crash at Paddington, London, in 1999, in which 31 people died. Directors cannot hide behind the façade of the company: they may be held personally liable for its crimes. On the other hand, enforcement of the criminal law, which is mainly rooted in national systems, poses major challenges, as many criminal activities have become globalized and also highly organized. Fraud is an example of a 'white-collar' crime which has been greatly facilitated by global financial networks. See Table 6.1 for a breakdown of the distinctions between civil and criminal law. Note that the 'burden of proof' is higher in a criminal case, which means that a greater degree of certainty is required for criminal guilt than for a judgment as to which party succeeds in a civil case.

Table 6.1 Outline of civil law and criminal law

	Criminal law	Civil law
What is it about?	Offences against society	Disputes between private individuals or companies
What is the purpose of the action?	To preserve order in the community by punishing offenders and deterring others	To seek a remedy for the wrong which has been suffered, usually money compensation
Who are the parties?	A prosecutor, usually representing the state, prosecutes a defendant, the accused	A plaintiff sues a defendant
Where is the action heard?	State, regional or local criminal courts	Civil courts, at local, regional or state level
Who has to prove what?	The prosecutor must prove a case against the defendant beyond all reasonable doubt	The plaintiff must establish a case on the balance of probabilities
What form does the decision take?	A defendant may be convicted if found guilty, or acquitted if found not guilty	A defendant may be found liable or not liable
What remedies are handed down by the court?	Imprisonment, fine, probation, community service	Damages (money compensation) to the successful plaintiff is the commonest
What are some common types of legal action?	Offences including theft, assault, drunken driving, criminal damage	Actions for breach of contract; actions in negligence for breach of a duty of care owed to the plaintiff

Legal risks for international business

For a business, the bulk of the relevant law stems from national lawmaking authorities. Each of the world's sovereign states has its own legal system, which has both lawmaking capacity within its territory ('jurisdiction') and capacity to apply its law to organizations and individuals within its jurisdiction. Legal systems do not exist in a vacuum, but are influenced by the society's social, political and cultural environments. The legal environment, including the content of law and legal processes, is an indication of attitudes to law in general, as well as the wider values of a society. It also reflects the historical development of the country's institutions.

Legal risk confronts all businesses to some extent, but is more likely to arise where a firm engages in business across national borders. Some of the main areas of risk are shown in Figure 6.3. The degree of risk depends on the extent and nature of the firm's involvement in the foreign location. Contracts are often the first area in which the firm encounters a foreign legal system. If disputes arise with suppliers or customers, then foreign courts could be involved. The multinational enterprise (MNE) which manufactures in a foreign location incurs several types of legal liability. Its operations are affected by local environmental and employment law, and its products are subject to the law on product liability in each country. For a global company, the impacts can be widely ramified. In 2015, Toyota, Nissan and Honda were compelled to recall an estimated 6.5 million cars due to faulty airbags. Although the airbags were made by a supplier to these car companies, the three carmakers were nonetheless liable to customers for the faults.

Figure 6.3 Legal risks in international business

A firm's patents and trademarks, which are areas of intellectual property law, can be difficult to enforce in some locations, even leading companies to exit particular markets. The food company, Danone, is an example of a company which engaged in a long legal battle with a Chinese partner, Wahaha, in a soft drinks joint venture, and eventually decided to sell out its 51% stake. It accused Wahaha of running parallel businesses which infringed its trademarks. Had Danone taken a 60% stake, giving it greater control, it might have been able to prevent the activities which led to legal action.

Although functioning in an authoritarian environment, China has adapted its legal system since the 1980s to accommodate business transactions, including contract law and intellectual property law. A new competition law (discussed later) is based on the EU model. However, despite western forms, the workings of the legal system lack the transparency and independent judiciary that would be expected in western contexts. In 2014, the Chinese subsidiary of global pharmaceutical company, GSK, was found by a Chinese court to have engaged in bribing doctors and hospitals (see the closing case study in Chapter 9). GSK was fined a sum equivalent to nearly $500 million, but, more significant than the large fine was the prosecution of GSK's country head of operations, who was British, and four other company executives, all Chinese nationals. These GSK executives were tried in secret and faced potential prison sentences of four years. All were found guilty and were given suspended sentences; the country head of operations was deported. Although GSK could feel relieved that its employees were not imprisoned, being embroiled in opaque legal proceedings in a country that is known for corruption was a warning to the company that it must assess its management systems in light of legal risks and ethical principles (Pratley, 2014).

In its Worldwide Governance Indicators, the World Bank assesses the depth of the rule of law in the world's countries. Included in its assessment are the quality of property rights, the police, the courts and the risk of crime. A range of countries spanning five continents is given in Figure 6.4. Denmark stands out as the highest example of the rule of law, and this standing has been consistent over a long period. The US also has a high ranking, but with recent slippage. In the US, the use of a secret court, the Foreign Intelligence Surveillance Court (FISA Court), which is outside the public court system, to authorize the bulk collection of data on members of the public can be criticized as undermining the rule of law. The other three countries shown are emerging economies. Of these, South Africa, where there is a legacy of an independent judiciary, has been reasonably consistent, but it might have been expected to show more improvement as its democracy becomes more established. Brazil has shown improvement, but China has seen slippage.

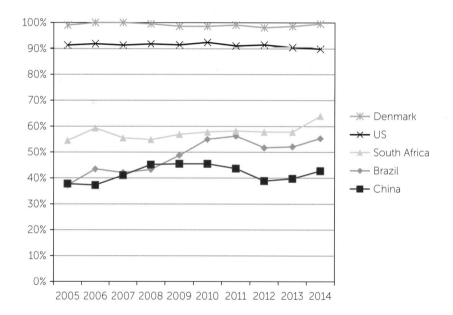

Figure 6.4 The rule of law rankings of selected countries

Source: Data from World Bank (2014) Worldwide Governance Indicators 2014 (Rule of law), at info.worldbank.org, accessed 25 May 2016.

The rule of law

The emerging economies tend to show weaker protections for the rule of law. What would you recommend foreign businesses to do in handling the legal risks in these situations?

National legal systems

The pre-eminence of national legal systems derives from the theory of the sovereign state. Every legal system may be divided into two main sets of functional institutions. These are legislation (lawmaking) and adjudication (the settlement of cases). Legislation, or statute law, is enacted by the authorized bodies in the state, often under a constitutional framework. In a democracy, the elected legislature is a key lawmaking body. Much lawmaking follows the social and political agendas of elected governments. Legislators can get it wrong, of course. In 1920, the US passed a constitutional amendment prohibiting the manufacture, sale and transport of alcoholic beverages. It proved to be unpopular and virtually impossible to enforce, and was overturned by a later constitutional amendment in 1933.

The system of courts, or judicial system, interprets and applies the law in particular cases. Judges thereby play a role in shaping the development of the law – a role that differs from one legal system to another. As will be seen below, 'case law' (judge-made law) is more important in some countries than in others. A general rule is that legal systems attempt to draw a line between lawmaking and judicial functions. But tension inevitably arises between the judicial institutions and the lawmaking branches, which are the executive and legislative. Court systems are designed to prevent the intrusion of political and personal considerations, and judges should be seen to be fair and impartial. The judiciary often finds itself influencing policy although, in theory, judges are meant simply to apply the law rather than make it. If judges become 'politicized', this is seen as eroding their independence. On the other hand, justices of the US Supreme Court are openly categorized as 'conservative', associated with Republican Party values, or 'liberal', closer to Democratic Party values in their thinking. It is generally accepted that presidents seek to appoint justices to the Supreme Court who have similar values to themselves, thus ensuring a perpetuation of their political vision in the judicial sphere long after they have left office. Antonin Scalia, a Supreme Court judge who had been appointed by Republican president Ronald Reagan in 1986, died in 2016, leaving a significant legacy in numerous spheres, including the controversial Citizens United judgment (discussed in Chapter 5) which gave the green light to unlimited corporate financing of political campaigns.

The world's legal systems can be classified in terms of legal traditions or legal families. The two major western historical traditions are the civil law tradition and the common law tradition. The civil law tradition, prevalent in continental Europe, is founded on a comprehensive legal code, whereas the common law tradition, English in origin, emphasizes case law. Both have been adopted in a variety of non-western contexts, as part of modernization processes (see Table 6.2). Newly independent states have tended to adopt the legal tradition of their former colonial power. For this reason, a lawyer from Ghana will find it much easier to understand a lawyer from Kenya or England than one from the Ivory Coast just next door, which falls within French colonial influence (Zweigert and Kötz, 1998).

Civil law tradition

The civil law tradition is by far the older of the two, originating in the ancient Roman *ius civile*, which in the sixth century was codified in the Justinian Code. Civil law relies on a legal code for the basic groundwork of the system on which further lawmaking is built. The legal code is a comprehensive, systematic setting out of the basic law for a country. The modern models of codified law are the French Civil Code of 1804, known as the Napoleonic Code, and the German Civil Code of 1896. Codified law is in fact divided into a number of different codes, depending on the subject matter. The civil code, which contains the body of private law (that is, between citizens), is complemented, for example, by a Commercial Code and a Criminal Code. These codes have demonstrated their adaptability by providing models for numerous

Table 6.2 Selected civil law and common law countries

Civil law	Common law
Argentina	Australia
Brazil	Bangladesh
Chile	Canada
China	Ghana
Egypt	India
France	Israel
Germany	Jamaica
Greece	Kenya
Indonesia	Malaysia
Iran	Nigeria
Italy	Singapore
Japan	England
Mexico	United States
Sweden	Zambia

other countries in Europe, Latin America, Africa, Asia and the Middle East (see Table 6.2). In the UK, Scotland falls within the civil law tradition. Japan's choice of the civil law model coincided with the country's initial industrialization and modernization policies in the late nineteenth century.

The attraction of the civil law model lies in the supremacy of the single authoritative source of the law. The principles and concepts contained in the codes form the basis of legal reasoning. Although the accumulated decisions of judges are useful as guidelines, they are not in themselves a source of law. This is the major distinction between the civil law and common law systems, shown in Table 6.3. The distinction has been described as one between different legal styles. The urge to regulate and systematize has dominated continental legal thinking, whereas English lawyers have tended to improvise, not making a decision until they have to, on the view that 'we'll cross that bridge when we come to it' (Zweigert and Kötz, 1998: 70).

Table 6.3 Outline of civil law and common law traditions

	Civil law tradition	Common law tradition
Sources of the law	Comprehensive legal codes	Judge-made law and statutes
Role of case law	Guidance, but not binding	System of binding precedent
Legal style	Systematized application of principles	Pragmatic and piecemeal

Common law tradition

The common law system originated in England some 900 years ago – long before Parliament had become the supreme lawmaking authority. Common law is essentially judge-made law, known as case law. In deciding a particular dispute, the judge creates a precedent to be followed in similar cases in the future. The body of law builds up through the accumulation of precedents in decided cases. The system has both flexibility and rigidities in practice. Precedents may be applied more loosely or more strictly in later cases, lending flexibility. However, as the court system is hierarchical, the decisions of higher courts form precedents which must be followed by lower courts. Faced with what seems to be a bad precedent, the judge in a lower court has little choice but to follow it. The growth in statute law in the form of Acts of Parliament, mainly in the last hundred years, has come about mainly in response to the complexities of economic and social changes. Modern judges spend a great deal of their time interpreting and applying statute law. The growing importance of statute law (also referred to as enacted law) suggests a convergence with the civil law tradition, although when it comes down to interpreting the law in particular factual situations – which is what matters to litigants – the judge still holds a good deal of power.

Common law systems have been transplanted to countries as diverse as the US and India. Like all legal systems, the tradition has been adapted to the local environment. The US, with its division between federal and 50 state jurisdictions, has evolved a particularly complex system, with overlapping jurisdictions that can be confusing to outsiders (and even insiders). Each state constitutes a system within a system – Louisiana even has remnants of French codified law from its own colonial past. The individual states have made efforts to achieve consistency in the law in key areas that affect business, notably through the Uniform Commercial Code, which has been adopted by all the states (although only partially in Louisiana). The American Law Institute has spearheaded the efforts to bring about consistency by producing its Restatements of the law in areas such as contract, tort and product liability. These restatements resemble codified law in all but name, but they do not have the status of a statute as they are not passed by Congress. Their aim is clarify the law and they act as guidance to lawyers and judges. In matters that raise issues of constitutionality, federal courts, and ultimately the US Supreme Court, are the ultimate authorities.

Non-western legal systems

The growth in commercial law has reached almost all countries, aware that economic development depends on a sound legal framework and an efficient and accessible court system. As has been seen, the groundwork for modern legal systems in much of the world was the legacy of colonial regimes. Legal traditions in many countries, which are based on customary law, pre-date western systems, and continue to form an important part of the overall legal environment. In many countries, therefore, we now find a mixture of pre-modern customs, colonial forms, and newer codes designed to keep up to date with business needs. The study of evolving legal systems in developing countries reveals much about the relationship between law and social change.

Non-western legal traditions include Islamic, Chinese and Hindu law. Of these, Islamic law, called the *Shari'a* (or God's rules), is perhaps the most highly developed. Islamic law can have a direct impact on the way business is conducted in Muslim countries, such as Saudi Arabia and Sudan. Because the *Shari'a* prohibits 'unearned profits', the charging of interest is forbidden. Financing through banks can still be arranged by

Towards open accessibility of research and data

Mark Hahnel

Mark Hahnel is the founder and CEO of Figshare (http://figshare.com), a web-based platform that makes scientific research openly available to the wider public. The company's services provide a means for individual researchers to publish their data, and for academic institutions to manage, publish and disseminate their data and research outputs in a professional manner. Mark gained firsthand knowledge of managing research outputs from his own academic background, having completed his PhD in stem cell biology at Imperial College, London. In carrying out his own research, Mark saw the huge potential benefits of making data openly available, both for the researcher to reach the widest possible public and for other researchers to benefit from shared data. Restrictive laws relating to copyright and ownership of data and outputs had meant that owners were in a strong position to charge for access: researchers unable to pay could be effectively barred from access. However, the atmosphere was changing. Founding Figshare in 2011, Mark was able to gain momentum early on, as open content was becoming more widely available. Figshare has gone on to develop numerous tools used by researchers and institutions globally for dissemination and management of shared data.

As the interview with Mark shows, he is a fervent believer in the open science movement and in a sharing research community. These ideals underline the growth of Figshare as a company, having been one of the first companies to take advantage of this growing trend. In the interview, he notes the challenges in the regulatory environment, as technological changes move more rapidly than the legal regulation in areas such as data security. Such issues are of the utmost importance to researchers, and Mark is keen to stress the importance of legal compliance and differing international jurisdictions, especially in the context of maintaining client trust.

Before watching the interview, look again at the opening case study on Uber, and read the section on 'Legal risks for international business'. It will also be helpful to look at the section on challenges and responsibilities of the technological environment in Chapter 9.

Visit www.palgravehighered.com/morrison-gbe-4e to watch the video, then think about the following questions:

1. The interests of researchers are uppermost in Mark's priorities for Figshare. In what ways is this reflected in the company's thinking and the ways it goes about its engagement with clients?
2. How is the competitive environment changing in this fast-moving area? In particular, what impacts might there be with 'low-cost' and outsourcing as possible trends?
3. In what ways does Mark see social responsibility as important for Figshare?
4. Figshare has been disruptive in its approach. How does Mark view the impacts of Uber in this respect? What are his reservations about Uber as a business?

devising alternative legal forms to cover transactions, such as profit-sharing and loss-sharing by a lending bank. Islamic countries have introduced codes for the secular regulation of activities such as the formation and enforcement of contracts, and foreign investment. Accordingly, most now have secular tribunals for these areas.

Both western and non-western legal traditions have evolved and adapted to different cultural contexts in response to two related forces. First, there has been a perceived need to modernize national legal structures as societies have become more complex, and legal relations, such as consumer and employment contracts, have become more common. Most of this development has come through legislation. In the UK, the Consumer Rights Act 2015, which covers the sale of goods, digital content and services, consolidated a number of existing statutes. Second, the growth of global markets has led to increasing international efforts to achieve uniformity and standardization of laws across national borders. Much of the latter effort has come through multilateral international conventions. These are signed and then ratified by national authorities, ultimately taking on a status similar to the domestic law of the state. In particular, international conventions have played an important role in bringing common legal frameworks for international trade in goods (as will be discussed below). Within the European Union harmonization has gone further, putting in place supranational legal structures for both lawmaking and adjudication.

National legal systems

Which of the types of national legal system described here is most likely to be accessible, fair and efficient, from a business perspective?

Legal framework of the European Union

For each member state, the EU is a growing source of law, which has become intertwined with national law. The foundation treaty, the Treaty of Rome of 1957, and later treaties have created supranational institutions, that is, institutions above those of domestic law. Under the Maastricht Treaty of 1992, three pillars were designated: the European Communities, the Common Foreign and Security Policy, and the Police and Judicial Co-operation in Criminal Matters. The first of these was supranational, and the other two represented inter-governmental co-operation. The law of the EU was technically referred to as EC law, as it fell under the first pillar. With the Treaty of Lisbon of 2009, the three-pillar system was abolished, subsuming the second and third pillars. The EU itself now has legal personality: the EU can now make treaties in its own name, and its law is now 'EU law'.

EU lawmaking now extends to a wide range of areas, although not as yet taxation and defence. The legislative function is divided between the Commission, the Council and the European Parliament, through the co-decision procedure (see Chapter 5). EU law falls into two main types. 'Regulations' are directly applicable throughout the EU, becoming incorporated automatically into the law of each member state. They create individual rights and obligations which governments must recognize. 'Directives' require member states to implement their provisions, usually within a given period of time, such as two years. In some cases, the directive may have direct effect, allowing individuals to enforce rights directly, if the member state does not implement the law in the required time limit. For businesses, competition law is an area with growing implications for MNEs (see later section). In competition law, high-profile cases have involved the Commission taking legal action against a company in the European Court of Justice.

The judicial function centres on the European Court of Justice (ECJ) (curia. europa.eu). It is the sole interpreter of EU law, and can override national legislation in cases of conflict. Although national supreme courts have ultimate authority in domestic matters, in issues involving EU institutions and EU law, the ECJ is the ultimate authority. The ECJ interprets the treaties and other legislation. It is modelled on courts in the civil law tradition, in that it is not bound by its previous decisions, but its case law has in fact shown consistency. The ECJ is now divided into sections which hear cases at first instance and those which hear cases in an appellate capacity, that is, on appeal.

Cross-border transactions

Laws covering trade between businesses in different countries have existed since the medieval period, when the *law merchant* was born of customary rules used by the merchants of the period. These rules, relating to sale of goods and the settlement of disputes, were gradually incorporated into national bodies of law, codified in the case of the civil law countries, and part of the common law in common law countries. In England, the law became enacted in the Sale of Goods Act 1894 (now superseded by the Consumer Rights Act 2015), and in the US the Uniform Commercial Code (1951) harmonized the law between the 50 states. Impetus to achieve international harmonization has come from a number of initiatives.

International codification of contract law

Set up in 1966, the UN Commission on International Trade Law (UNCITRAL) (www. uncitral.org) attempted to devise a framework to satisfy the needs of businesses in trading nations of all continents. The result was the Convention on Contracts for the International Sale of Goods (CISG) of 1980 (the Vienna Convention), which came into force in 1988. The CISG does not apply automatically to international sales. The convention must be ratified by individual states, becoming incorporated in their domestic law. The number of countries which have ratified the convention (83 by 2014) continues to rise, accounting for the bulk of the world's trade. Among major trading nations, the US, Germany, France, China, Brazil and Japan have ratified. Notable among those which have not yet ratified are India, South Africa and the UK. The convention applies to contracts falling within its scope that are concluded by firms in countries which have ratified, or to contracts whose performance is carried out in a country which has ratified. For transactions between firms in non-ratifying countries, the rules of private international law apply (discussed below).

The CISG makes a major contribution in harmonizing rules to do with the formation of contracts for the sale of goods, obligations of the parties and remedies. It attempts to bridge the gap between civil and common law jurisdictions on questions such as the 'meeting of minds' between the parties over the existence of an agreement and its particular terms. These are the key areas in which disputes arise, and the CISG attempts to encourage compromise between countries which require certainty and those which allow greater flexibility. For example, the requirement that a contract must be in writing is traditional in the common-law countries (although of diminishing importance), whereas civil law countries tend to have no writing requirement. The CISG allows ratifying countries the option, in keeping with their own national law. China, for example, has preserved its writing requirement.

The International Institute for the Unification of Private International Law (UNIDROIT) has complemented the CISG, and approached the need for unification from a different perspective. The UNIDROIT Principles of International Commercial Contracts, published in 1994 and revised in 2004, offer general rules for international contracts, and are broadly similar to the CISG, but of wider application. The Principles are not confined to the sale of goods. Moreover, as they are not embodied in any binding international convention, they can be incorporated into contracts by firms from any country, not just those that have ratified the CISG. It has been suggested that they come closest to 'the emerging international consensus' on the rules of international trade (Moens and Gillies, 1998: 81). Because the Principles do not themselves have any force of law, they can be adopted and modified as needed, and have even provided models for legislators as diverse as Mexico, Québec and the Netherlands. In particular, they have facilitated the growing trade between Australia and its Asian neighbours.

Cultural factors in international contracts

Negotiation of international contracts usually involves the use of a foreign language for at least one of the parties. Apart from problems of translating technical terms, the cultural context of negotiations varies considerably. High-context and low-context languages will have different styles of negotiation. Attention to detailed terms and confrontational bargaining are far more significant in the Anglo-American context than in Asian contexts, for example. The formally-agreed contract may be in one language, with an unofficial translation in another, which clarifies the terms. Alternatively, the contract may have two official versions in two different languages. An inescapable difficulty is possible misunderstandings in the translation process. Interpretation of terms, even between speakers of the same language, can differ from country to country. Hence, it should be remembered that while the contract creates legal obligations, these are not necessarily interpreted in exactly the same way by all parties, and, in case of dispute, an arbitrator or judge faces an unenviable task of finding out what the parties intended in a particular situation.

The role of the contract itself is viewed differently in different cultures. In individualistic cultures the detailed formal contract governs business relationships, whereas in the more group-oriented societies, such as Japan and South East Asia, business relies more on informal, personalized relationships. Relational contracting, as the latter is known, is rooted in societies where personal ties built on trust, often over a number of years, matter more than formal written documents. In these societies, the preferred method of settling disputes is out of court, rather than through litigation. In China, this cultural approach is known as *guanxi*, which simply means 'relationships'. In more individualist societies, arm's length contracting (in which the agreement is paramount) is more the norm. With the growing numbers of joint ventures and expanding markets across cultural boundaries, an understanding of cultural sensitivities is essential in cross-border contracts. While written contracts are now part of the modern legal systems that have been adopted in non-western societies, the underlying cultural environment is still influential in their negotiation and interpretation. It goes without saying that a 'meeting of minds' over both the terms and the working relationship that flows from the agreement is good insurance against a breakdown which could lead to the courts.

The Philippines: a good place to do business?

This poor neighbourhood on the outskirts of Manila contrasts with the modern tower blocks in the background.

Source: iStock.com/Marco Richter.

In May 2015, a fire in a slipper factory in Valenzuela, a northern suburb of Manila, caused the deaths of 74 workers. Ignited by sparks flying from welding operations into unlabelled chemicals nearby, the fire lasted for seven hours. Of those in the building, only 45 came out alive. The workers in the building had little hope of escape. Fire exits had been blocked or locked, and metal grilles had been placed on windows. The factory was owned by Kentex Manufacturing, a local company. The fire occurred on the second anniversary of the Rana Plaza textile factory disaster in Bangladesh, in which over 1,000 workers lost their lives. The Rana Plaza disaster was viewed as a turning point for health and safety in Asian factories, prompting concerted efforts by businesses and governments to improve building and fire safety. However, the Philippines blaze suggested that much still needs to be done. Investigations were launched, but the victims' families were doubtful that anyone would be held accountable.

The jobs Kentex provided were the type of low-skilled factory employment that developing economies rely on. They were poorly paid, but in a country of high unemployment, jobs such as these are valuable, and have been encouraged by the government. President Benigno Aquino, who was elected in 2010, had promised to transform the country, once known as 'the sick man of Asia', into a thriving economy. Reducing poverty and corruption, he felt, went together. He promised to 'transform the government from one that is self-serving to one that works for the welfare of the nation' (Southgate, 2015). Encouraging foreign direct investment (FDI) was a key policy. As the end of his six-year term approached, the Philippines had made impressive strides, with growth rates over 6%. The rate of growth peaked at 7.2% in 2013. FDI increased 60% from 2013 to 2014. But most of this growth has been in the fast-growing service sector, especially business process outsourcing (BPO). BPO comprises call centres and back-office activities for large investors such as Morgan Chase and HSBC. This sector was expected to bring in an estimated $25 billion in revenues in 2016. Aiming to attract these investors, the government sought to raise the country's ranking in the influential 'ease of doing business' index published by the World Bank. This has meant cutting red tape and bureaucracy, and has also involved offering investors incentives such as tax holidays and freedom to employ foreign nationals. The ranking of the Philippines rose impressively, from 136 (out of a total of 189 countries) in 2012 to 103 in 2015 (World Bank, 2015). However, one of the reforms was a less strict enforcement regime for factory safety.

Not all Filipinos are feeling the benefits of economic success, and living standards have hardly risen over the last six years. In 2015, 28.8% of the population were living beneath the poverty line, which was an improvement of just 0.5% on 2009. The revenues from BPO, while impressive, are still not as much as revenues from remittances from migrant workers, which are estimated at $27.4 billion. Despite its economic growth, the Philippines is not creating enough jobs to sustain households and raise living standards in places like Valenzuela. Attracting manufacturing FDI would help in this regard. But, arguably, the government's policies of reducing red tape contributed to the Valenzuela fire.

Kentex Manufacturing has strongly asserted that it had all the necessary permits for its operations, but relevant government offices have denied this. The Bureau of Fire Prevention said it had not issued a fire permit, and indeed, had found failings in the building. But a business certificate was issued to the company by local government officials, who seemed not to know of the problems with the fire permit, even though the fire permit was a prerequisite for getting a business certificate. Each set of officials has blamed the other.

Valenzuela is a rundown area where fires are common, usually in slum dwellings. Kentex workers were exposed to chemical fumes that present health risks, and they also complained of excessive hours and wages below the legal minimum. The majority worked on a piece rate, and were treated as casual workers. They described lax fire safety precautions. About 35 families of victims are now suing the factory owners and the government office that issued the business certificate. One survivor said, 'There were no fire escapes and no storage for the chemicals, no labels on the chemicals' (van der Zee, 2015). President Aquino laid the blame on the local mayor who issued the business certificate. The mayor strongly denies responsibility.

The president had promised to curb corruption, but the country's politics are dominated by family dynasties that are associated with corrupt practices. President Aquino, himself a member of one of these dynasties, oversaw a period of growth, but did not transform the system in the way he had wished. All the candidates to succeed him are connected to dynasties; they include three members of the family of former dictator, Ferdinand Marcos. Investors are likely to be wary.

Sources: Pietropaoli, I. (2015) 'Philippines factory fire: 72 workers need not have died', *The Guardian*, 8 June, at www.theguardian.com; van der Zee, B. (2015) 'The inside story of the Kentex disaster: "74 people died, but no one is in prison"', *The Guardian*, 20 July, at www.theguardian.com; World Bank (2015) 'Ease of Doing Business Rankings', at www.doingbusiness.org; Southgate, L. (2015) 'The legacy of Philippines president Benigno Aquino', *Global Risk Insights*, 25 August, at www.globalriskinsights.com.

Questions for discussion

- What were the legal failings that caused the fire in Valenzuela?
- What legal reforms would be needed to prevent future disasters such as this?
- What are the underlying political and social issues in the Philippines?
- What are the legal risks for FDI investors in the Philippines?

Negligence and product liability

Whereas obligations under contracts are defined by the particular agreement, obligations in tort arise from a range of broadly-defined obligations owed by those in society to fellow citizens generally. The plaintiff may suffer personal injury or damage to property in an accident caused by the activities of the defendant. If the plaintiff's reputation has been damaged by something the defendant has said publicly, the claim is in libel. There are many different areas of tort law, but the areas which are of greatest relevance to business are negligence and product liability. In a negligence claim, the defendant is alleged to have failed to take reasonable care and so caused the plaintiff's injuries or loss. Negligence can cover injury from defective products, and it can also cover situations where there is a service provided, such as professional services. Product liability claims impose a duty which is much nearer to 'strict' liability, in which the defendant (usually the producer) is made liable for defective products that cause harm to consumers. The development of tort law in these areas parallels the growth of modern consumer society. Factory-produced goods, mass transport, advanced pharmaceutical products, medical procedures, and industrialized food production all carry risks of accidents and injury, sometimes on a wide scale. All industrialized countries have in place laws protecting consumers and other victims in these cases. In the EU, product liability laws were harmonized by a directive in 1985, which has been incorporated into national law (in the UK, by the Consumer Protection Act 1987). The directive, which includes a 'development risks defence', providing an escape route for producers who have achieved an industry-standard level of product testing, is perceived to be less consumer-friendly than US law.

In the US, tort litigation, particularly product liability, has developed into a booming industry. While product liability laws vary from state to state, the legal climate has facilitated litigation in three key ways: (1) the use of the 'class' action, whereby a group of plaintiffs may come together to bring legal proceedings; (2) the award by courts of 'punitive' damages (intended to punish the defendant for the wrongdoing) to plaintiffs, in addition to compensatory damages. Huge sums have been awarded by American juries as punitive damages (although often reduced on appeal, and punitive damages are capped in some states); and (3) the 'contingency' fee system for lawyers' fees, also known as the 'no-win-no-fee' system, whereby the legal fees are an agreed percentage of the damages. With this prior arrangement, the potential plaintiff without huge resources can bring a claim.

In Bhopal, India, in 1984, a chemical disaster resulted in the deaths of 8,000 people in the immediate aftermath, and injuries to several hundred thousand others, including long-term health problems. The victims attempted to sue the parent company, Union Carbide, in New York, arguing that negligence in the design of the plant caused the accident, in which a massive escape of poisonous gases occurred. Their claim failed, as much of the design and engineering that went into the plant was carried out by local engineers in India. The plaintiffs then sought damages in India. A settlement was reached with the Indian government, which took over the case, but where payments were made, they were inadequate, and many victims received no compensation. Meanwhile, contamination remains a blight on the area, over three decades later. Criminal cases against those held responsible were also a story of too little, too late, from the point of view of victims. Seven former employees of Union Carbide, all Indian, were found guilty of criminal negligence in 2010, some 26 years after the explosion. They were given prison sentences of two years each, the maximum possible for criminal negligence, as the original charges of culpable homicide had been reduced by a previous court. There was a public outcry at these light sentences, but they were upheld by India's Supreme Court.

In light of the Bhopal disaster and the legacy of protracted civil and criminal cases, the Indian government was concerned about the legal implications of purchasing equipment for nuclear power generation from foreign suppliers, who would be deterred by legal uncertainties following Bhopal. A new law on civil liability for nuclear damage was enacted in 2010, raising the possibility that the supplier of nuclear reactors and parts would incur liability for nuclear accidents. The US expressed concerns about possible liability, as one of its companies, General Electric (GE), is a major global supplier in the nuclear industry. A clarification agreement between India and the US was reached, reiterating the principle usually accepted as the international norm, which is that the operator bears all the liability and the suppliers bear none. However, this agreement between governments on the interpretation of the new law might well fail to provide the assurance that companies such as GE seek before selling equipment in India.

A GE Mark 1 model of reactor was involved in the Fukushima nuclear disaster in Japan in 2011, in which a major earthquake and tsunami caused meltdown in the six Fukushima reactors. Radiation was released over a large area, affecting hundreds of thousands of people. Blame fell on the power company that operated the plant. It was unable to pay the huge sums involved in dealing with the damage, and the Japanese government was compelled to make up the shortfall. There was arguably negligence in the operation of the plant, and three former executives of the power company were charged with professional negligence, a criminal offence, in 2016 (see Chapter 10). Were there problems with the GE Mark 1 reactor? Dating from the 1960s, the Mark 1 was known to have safety weaknesses, but GE faced no liability (Zeller, 2011). Critics of this situation point out that the nuclear industry is allowed to escape liability for the damage caused by its products, whereas companies in other sectors are made to pay under laws of product liability (Naidoo, 2013). The British oil company, BP, faced huge liabilities for lack of oilrig safety over the Deepwater Horizon oil spill in the Gulf of Mexico in 2010, in which 11 people lost their lives. By 2014, the sum had reached about $58 bn, and was still potentially rising. The payments included $27 bn on cleanup, $13 bn in damages and $18 bn in fines. If global suppliers in the nuclear industry were to incur liability for damage caused by their faulty products, they would arguably devote greater attention to improving safety in their designs.

The way I see it …

On India's nuclear civil liability law, 'We are not comfortable with it … We are a private enterprise, and we just can't take that kind of risk profiles.'

John Flannery, CEO of GE, in an interview with *Forbes India*, 9 March 2013.

How do you see it? Should GE be liable for accidents caused by its reactors?

When a consumer suffers harm as a result of a product defect, a manufacturing company can find itself on the end of product liability claims, where the damage may be multiplied, depending on the number of consumers affected. The large corporation which manufactures for global markets may face claims from millions of consumers worldwide. The **product recall** is a means of limiting the damage. It is recognized by the global companies as part of their legal obligations and is also important in maintaining their reputations. Still, there are many companies that sell unsafe and substandard products globally. These companies calculate that the risks of being caught are low. And, even if caught up in legal proceedings, their legal teams are likely to find ways to avert liability and contest claims.

The EU has operated the Rapid Alert System on product safety since 2003, which applies to dangerous products with the exception of food. As Figure 6.5 shows, there has been a marked increase in notifications of unsafe products since it was launched. In large part, this is due to improvements in the mechanisms for detecting risky products and tracing where they have come from. The majority of unsafe products notified are in the areas of clothes and fashion items, toys, electrical appliances and motor vehicles. An issue in the EU has been the proliferation of consumer goods manufactured in low-cost locations where quality standards are weak or not enforced. The bulk of unsafe products notified originate in China, and this preponderance of Chinese products seems to be rising, standing at 64% in 2014. The manufacturer of unsafe products is often listed as 'unknown'. However, authorities are improving their ability to trace goods, and the rise in numbers of Chinese manufacturers recorded probably reflects this improved traceability. China and the EU form the world's largest trading partnership: China is the EU's biggest supplier of goods, and it is the EU's largest export market after the US. Co-operation with Chinese authorities is a priority for the EU Commission, to trace the origins and stem the flow of unsafe products.

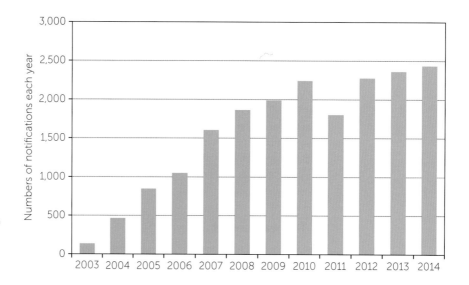

Figure 6.5 Product safety notifications in the EU

Source: Data from European Commission (2014) *Keeping European Consumers Safe: Complete Statistics*, p. 9, at ec.europa.eu/consumers/consumer_safety.

Competition law

Where companies compete fairly and are not allowed to manipulate markets, it is assumed that consumers will benefit in terms of price, value for money and innovation. Most governments would probably prefer that markets remain fair and competitive, but history has shown that unfair practices, such as price-fixing, can occur, either between companies which are ostensibly competitors or where one firm has a dominant market position. Governments step in to regulate uncompetitive behaviour in these situations. This body of law is known as 'antitrust' law in the US, where the large business empires which dominated at the end of the nineteenth century relied on the trust as a legal device in corporate ownership. The number of countries introducing competition law frameworks has grown from about 20 in the 1990s to 130 in 2015 (Vestager, 2015).

Competition law can be divided into distinct areas, each targeting different types of anti-competitive activity:

- Prohibition on agreements which amount to restrictive practices, such as a price-fixing agreement. This prohibition is aimed at cartels, that is, groups of firms which come together, often informally, to restrict trade or engage in anti-competitive behaviour.
- Oversight of mergers, to prevent the creation of a monopoly in a particular market.
- In cases where a firm already has a dominant market position, prohibition of behaviour that constitutes abuse of a dominant position in that market.

In every country that has competition law, the government sets up specialist agencies to handle competition matters, including investigation and enforcement of the law. There are wide variations in the size and approach of these bodies. Agencies in some countries consist of only a handful of people on a very limited budget, making it difficult to carry out extensive investigations. In others, competition authorities have greater resources and an ability to take on large MNEs such as Microsoft, which themselves are able to spend large sums on defending anti-competitive cases brought against them. The vigour with which cartels and monopolists are pursued differs from country to country, and over time. Although legislation tends to be worded in a similar way in every jurisdiction, interpretation can vary: a merger could be viewed as compliant in one country, whereas in another, one of the firms might be asked by the authorities to divest itself of some parts of its operations. In Mexico, in 2007, Telmex, part of Carlos Slim's empire, was cleared of antitrust allegations despite its 90% domination of the fixed-line telephone market. Historically, competition law has developed in market economies. US and European national competition authorities are examples, as is the EU. The EU has widened its perspective, taking in cases involving state aid to companies, which violates EU competition law.

For international managers, competition law can be an important determinant of strategy. If a firm wishes to take over another in a country where it already has a sizeable market share, the takeover would look attractive from the firm's point of view, but the country's competition authorities might take a dim view. Moreover, it might be many months before the firms are given the decision of the government agency. When the decision does come, it might state conditions which must be met before the merger can go ahead. A competition authority's jurisdiction is ostensibly its own territory, but decisions can compel a firm to divest activities in another country. Although this extra-territorial aspect might seem strange, it is being actively used by Chinese competition authorities.

China introduced competition law only in 2008. The law covers acquisitions, mergers and anti-competitive agreements. It has caused considerable stir among foreign companies due to its aggressive approach. Coca-Cola was among the first western companies to feel the force of it, when its proposed acquisition of China Huiyuan Juice Company in 2008 was blocked. As well as blocking acquisitions, Chinese competition authorities can compel foreign companies to dispose of assets in China, on the grounds that, without the disposals, the company would have a monopoly position. The most aggressive of Chinese policies is to compel foreign companies to dispose of businesses outside Chinese territory. In 2009, when deciding on whether Panasonic, a Japanese company, should take over Sanyo, a Chinese company, they cleared the deal, but ordered Panasonic to dispose of production capacity in Japan, and to reduce its stake in a joint venture making car batteries with Toyota from 40% to 20%.

In the era of globalization, companies are often involved in mergers and acquisition activity that straddles multiple countries. While there is no global competition agency, there is now considerable co-operation among national and EU competition authorities. EU competition authorities, for example, co-operated with non-EU agencies in 62% of their decisions in the years 2012 and 2013. There now exists an International Competition Network that brings together representatives of competition authorities in 132 member states. All share the same goals of promoting procedural fairness, impartiality, transparency and co-operation (Vestager, 2015). Co-operation among them can help to ensure consistency and fairness in the legal hurdles that are associated with mergers and acquisitions. These developments can benefit companies planning mergers, helping to resolve the complexities and introducing a global – rather than simply national – perspective.

International law framing the business environment

International law covers the body of rules recognized by the international community as governing relations between sovereign states. It is also referred to as 'public international law', to distinguish it from the rules of private international law discussed in the next section. The world's sovereign states, while recognizing international law, have not (as yet) created a supranational legal system with enforcement mechanisms mirroring those at national level. The functions of lawmaking and dispute settlement, therefore, rely on the co-operation of states and the willingness of state authorities to submit to international law as a matter of obligation. Since the Second World War there has been an accelerated growth in international law, coinciding with processes of globalization. The vibrancy of international law depends on states recognizing that, in the long run, national interests are interdependent. International law has been a means of facilitating cross-border activities of MNEs, and, on the other hand, it has been seen as a tool of international co-operation for mitigating some of the negative impacts that have accompanied globalization. These functions can be seen in Figure 6.6, which shows key areas in which international law affects businesses.

Figure 6.6 Areas in which international law affects business

International businesses have benefited from trade liberalization through international agreements, as Figure 6.6 shows. This has facilitated the growth of global supply chains and has formed the backbone of globalization. But international law also focuses on obligations that fall on companies as well as states. In the areas of environmental protection, global security and human rights, international law now impacts on companies. In these areas, international law often sets higher standards than national law in many countries, guided by ethical principles, as in human rights law. It thus imposes obligations on states to bring national law up to international standards. Most international law comes about through treaties and conventions, and most of these are the result of initiatives by UN-affiliated bodies. Treaties may be multilateral, involving many countries, or bilateral, between two countries. An extradition treaty is an example of a bilateral treaty, requiring states to co-operate on the handing over of persons accused of crimes. Major multilateral treaties may take years in the drafting stages, and do not become law until ratified by a given number of individual states specified in the treaty itself. There is no cut-off date – additional states may ratify indefinitely. When a state ratifies, it is obliged to bring national laws into conformity with the treaty provisions. However, states are sometimes slow to respond and slow to enforce international law, especially if national interest seems to conflict. It is in these circumstances that the effectiveness of international law is tested.

At the International Court of Justice, pictured here, any UN member state is able to bring a case against another for violation of international law.

Source: UN Photo/Andrea Brizzi

An international court, the International Court of Justice (ICJ) (www.icj-cij.org) hears a limited range of international cases. Based in The Hague in the Netherlands, the ICJ is a UN body, whose authority derives from its governing Statute, attached to the UN Charter. While the ICJ's prestige is acknowledged, its effectiveness is limited by the restrictions to its jurisdiction. The major one is that it hears only disputes between sovereign states. A non-state organization cannot apply to it, although cases can involve activities of individuals and companies. The Hague is also home to the International Criminal Court (ICC) which was established by the Rome Statute in 1998, a time when reports of the genocide in Rwanda were raising questions about the weaknesses of international responses. As a supranational court, the ICC aims to prosecute leaders responsible for crimes against humanity, genocide and war crimes, in situations where national authorities have failed to act. This presents a formidable set of challenges. The ICC has no police powers itself, and must rely on the co-operation of national legal authorities, in, for example, arresting those who it has charged with crimes. There are now 123 member states, newer members including Bangladesh, Chile, the Philippines and Tunisia. The US, Russia and China have not ratified the treaty, but the US government has expressed approval of its aims. Although the ICC faces challenges in attaining its goals, it can be encouraged by the fact that the membership of 123 countries indicates an acknowledgement of international legal obligations in the area of human rights. These two major international courts have established a forum in which to bring sovereign states – and, in the case of the ICC, their leaders – to account for breaches of international law, exerting moral as well as legal pressures on states to conform.

International public opinion, encouraged by the many non-governmental organizations (NGOs), plays an important role in putting pressure on governments. In areas such as climate change (discussed in Chapter 10), many businesses have gone further than national lawmakers, and have taken their lead from international law, often working with NGOs on initiatives.

The way I see it ...

'The ICC is not mission impossible; it is just mission difficult.'

Sang-Hyun Song, ICC President, in an interview with the *Financial Times*, 14 March 2015.

What are your views on the ICC's aims, and why they are difficult to achieve?

International dispute settlement

Every international business, sooner or later, becomes involved in a dispute with a foreign dimension. The exposure to legal risk is greater for international businesses than domestic ones, mainly because of multiple jurisdictions. Disputes are likely to arise over contractual terms, licence agreements and in the area of tort, in which the firm either alleges wrongdoing or becomes the defendant in a negligence or product liability claim. The area of the law concerned is private international law, which determines which national law pertains between individuals and firms in more than one country. Also referred to as 'conflict of laws', private international law seeks to establish rules for deciding which national law to apply to a particular situation. The rules of private international law give guidance on three broad issues: (1) the choice of law governing transactions; (2) the choice of forum, that is, the country in which a case should be heard; and (3) the enforcement of court judgments. The harmonizing of private international law has been an important aim of international conventions. The Rome Convention on the Law Applicable to Contracts 1980 and the Brussels Convention on Jurisdiction and Enforcement of Judgments in Civil and Commercial Matters 1968 have both been incorporated into English law.

In the basic transaction of buying or selling goods, at least one of the contracting firms is likely to find its rights governed by foreign law, thereby adding to the legal risk in a number of ways. First, there is the question of what contract law in the foreign jurisdiction actually stipulates. Then there is the possibility of having to go through the courts in that country to obtain redress. Finally, the firm may face problems of getting a judgment of the foreign court enforced in its own country.

Contracts between firms based in different countries may specify a 'choice of law' to govern their contract. This choice will also normally govern the forum in which any disputes will be heard. Most countries recognize choice-of-law clauses. For EU member states the Rome Convention provides that, if the parties have not made a clear choice of law, the contract is governed by the law of the country with which it is most closely connected. In practice, this is likely to be the law of the party who is to carry out performance of the contract. The Brussels Convention provides that jurisdiction depends on whether the defendant is 'domiciled' in the EU (which, for a firm, means that it must have a 'seat' of business there). In employment contracts, the employee can sue where his or her duties are carried out. In consumer contracts, the Brussels Convention (now an EU regulation) gives the consumer the right to sue in local courts. This regulation has profound implications for online traders, who may be liable to be sued in national courts of any EU member state where their business activities are directed. For enforcement of judgments, most states will recognize the judgment of a foreign court if the foreign law and procedure are broadly compatible with their own. Within the EU this recognition is automatic, as it is between states within the CISG.

Litigation is costly, time-consuming, and may bring unwanted publicity if the case is a high-profile one. Added risks in international disputes are the distance, unfamiliarity of the law, and unfamiliar legal cultural environment. While US businesses have become accustomed to a culture of litigation, the costs in damages can be astronomical, and the high cost of liability insurance is a consequence. In contract disputes, the incentives to find other means of dispute resolution are therefore strong. Practising lawyers, far from suggesting litigation in all cases, emphasize the benefits of 'alternative dispute resolution'. Alternatives to litigation are:

- **Settlement** by the parties 'out of court'.
- **Mediation**, in which the parties agree to bring in a third party, who attempts to settle their differences.
- **Arbitration**, the submission of the dispute to a named person or organization in accordance with the agreement.

Arbitration has grown in popularity in recent years. It is usually thought to be cheaper and quicker than litigation, but can still be costly, as both legal fees and arbitrators' fees have to be taken into account. Major arbitration centres in the US and London have seen increases in workload in the last decade. Only about 18% of the cases handled by the London Court of International Arbitration originate with parties from the UK. So strong is its global reach, its caseload involves businesses from every continent. In many cases, legal services at this level of expertise are not available in the parties' home countries. In Asia, the Singapore International Arbitration Centre (SCIA) has seen a remarkable rise in workload, as shown in Figure 6.7. In comparison to courts, arbitration processes are informal. They also offer flexibility and privacy which court-based litigation does not. On the other hand, the settlement of disputes out of court, often cloaked in secrecy, contributes little to the development of a body of commercial law. Danone's dispute with Wahaha, its joint-venture partner, discussed earlier in this chapter, is one of many cases settled by arbitration.

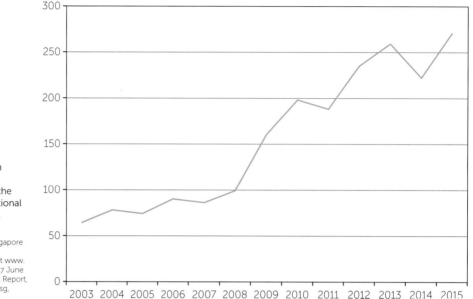

Figure 6.7 Growth in number of new cases handled by the Singapore International Arbitration Centre, 2003–2015

Source: Data from Singapore Court of International Arbitration, Statistics; at www. scia.org.sg, accessed 17 June 2015; and SCIA Annual Report, 2015, at www.scia.org.sg, accessed 3 June 2016.

A growing area of arbitration is that involving companies suing sovereign states for compensation in cases where a foreign investor feels its economic interests are jeopardized. The legal basis on which it can bring a case is the inclusion of a clause in a treaty between the two countries that incorporates **investor-state dispute settlement (ISDS)**. These treaties are often trade agreements between two or more partners (see discussion in Chapter 7). There are now some 3,000 such treaties in existence. Arbitration tribunals facilitate the resolution of these investor-state disputes, the numbers of which have grown dramatically. The system dates from 1960s, when there were concerns that foreign companies would be reluctant to invest in developing countries because of the risks involved, including economic and political uncertainties such as possible nationalization of the investor's assets. The **International Centre for Settlement of Investment Disputes (ICSID)** was set up as a limb of the World Bank Group at a World Bank meeting in Tokyo in 1964. At the time, 21 countries, mainly Latin American, objected that the process would undermine state sovereignty. But the World Bank pressed ahead with the system, feeling it would be necessary to encourage the foreign investment that drives development. The dispute settlement system was little used for three decades, but as Figure 6.8 shows, it became much more popular from 2000 onwards. As of 31 December 2014, the ICSID had 497 cases registered in total.

With the rise in the number of cases, the ISDS has given rise to renewed debate. The US government has pressed for its inclusion in both the Trans-Pacific Partnership (TPP) and the Transatlantic Trade and Investment Partnership (TTIP), but objections have arisen among partner countries and also from legislators in the US Congress. A system that was envisaged as giving legitimate assurances to investors seems to have been transformed into a system that is increasingly weighted towards large multinationals, to the detriment of public interest in the countries where they do business. In some cases, the sums of money being demanded run to billions of dollars.

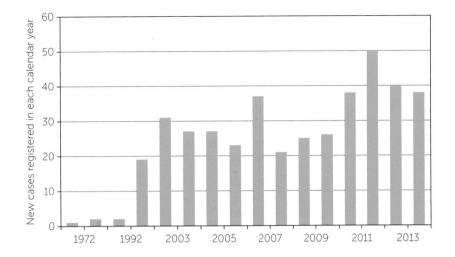

Figure 6.8 Cases registered by the ICSID

Source: Data from ICSID (2015) *The ICSID Caseload – Statistics (2015-1)*, p. 7, at https://icsid.worldbank.org, accessed 17 June 2015.

The system of tribunals and compensation cases now envelops about half the world's countries, both developing and developed. The scope for companies to take cases to tribunals has expanded to include actions for future loss of profits from changes in environmental law, employment protection law and other social legislation. For example, foreign investors in some Central and Eastern European countries provided private healthcare in the early years of post-communist independence, but changes in the law later introduced national health services, reducing the role of private medical services. The foreign companies involved sued for compensation amounting to billions of euros. In 2012, Ecuador was ordered by a tribunal to pay $1.8 billion to an American oil company for cancelling an oil exploration contract. This is roughly the equivalent of the country's entire health budget for a year (Provost and Kennard, 2015). There is no appeal process against the decision of the tribunal, and if a state does not pay up, its assets can be seized in any country through local courts.

Reform proposals for ISDS have been put forward by the UN Conference on Trade and Development (UNCTAD), targeting specific areas of concern. The areas of concern are summarized below (UNCTAD, 2013: 110–112):

- **Legitimacy** – The private individuals who sit on ISDS arbitration tribunals are appointed ad hoc. It is questionable whether they should be taking decisions affecting public interests, including development goals of sovereign states.
- **Transparency** – Proceedings can be held entirely in secret. This seems inappropriate where issues of public interest are being decided.
- **'Nationality planning'** – A company can restructure to establish a subsidiary in a country where it can make use of the ISDS to bring a case against a country that it would not otherwise be able to do.
- **Consistency of arbitration decisions** – Arbitration tribunals decide each case individually, and there are inevitably inconsistencies, including divergent interpretations of treaties. This gives little guidance as to how treaties would be interpreted in future.
- **Erroneous decisions** – Where a substantive mistake has occurred, there is no process for putting it right. There is a provision for annulment of a particular decision, but an appeals process would be preferable.

- **Arbitrators' independence and impartiality** – Arbitrators are recommended by the parties. The individuals appointed as arbitrators can serve as lawyers representing parties in future cases. The system, which is very lucrative for specialist lawyers, thus allows them to 'change hats', exerting considerable influence over outcomes.
- **Financial stakes** – The ISDS process has become very expensive. When a state wins against an investor, it is common for the arbitrators to award no costs to be paid by the losing party. The costs of arbitrators and lawyers is, on average, $8 million per case, making these proceedings a significant burden on public finances in the country.

UNCTAD has proposed a number of possible reforms (UNCTAD, 2013: 113-116). Among the main ones are introducing an appeals procedure. A second is requiring documents to be available for public access, to increase transparency. On the investor side, companies could be restricted in their use of corporate restructuring to bring an investor within a treaty. They could also be required to exhaust the national legal system in the country before launching an ISDS claim. A long-term possibility would be a standing international investment court. This would replace ad hoc arbitrators with a court staffed by tenured judges who have no ties with interested parties.

When companies sue countries

Compare the legal and ethical considerations for companies that pursue claims for compensation against countries in international tribunals.

The global legal environment: challenges and responsibilities

Globalization has had contrasting impacts on the ways companies view the legal environment. Corporate decision-makers now routinely devise tax arrangements to minimize their companies' liabilities, making use of tax havens with little or no tax and few rules requiring public disclosure of financial information. Global manufacturers have gravitated towards countries such as China where they have encountered few environmental regulations and weak employment protection. But China is now imposing stronger legal obligations on firms, as concerns about societal well-being rise up the agenda. Another consideration for foreign firms is that China's legal system poses risks that a firm could be targeted for wrongdoing, often in a context of accusations of corruption, as was seen in the case of GSK. Where the rule of law is weak, it is often due to the opaque workings of an authoritarian regime that subordinates law enforcement to political considerations. A multinational company faces challenges such as this in many emerging markets. Figure 6.9 shows that the large emerging markets are some of the most corrupt in the world, according to Transparency International's Corruption Perception Index. All the emerging economies shown in Figure 6.9 scored less than 50%. China is ranked 100 out of 103 countries in total.

Where bribery is commonplace, the foreign company is alerted to the risks, and must examine the ways it does business in the country, in light of the legal risks and also its ethical principles. Companies must ultimately face their shareholders

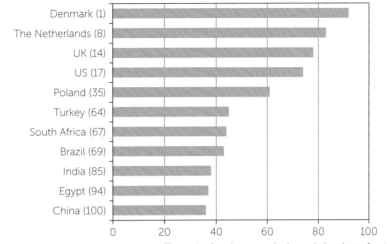

Figure 6.9 Transparency International's Corruption Perception Index: findings for selected countries

Source: Data from Transparency International (2015) Corruption Perception Index for 2014, at www.transparency.org/cpi2015, accessed 20 June 2015.

Note: Country scores are percentages. The rank of each country is shown in brackets after the country name. There are 103 countries overall in the ranking.

and other stakeholders, who are concerned not just that the business makes profits, but *how* those profits are made. The attraction of locations that impose weak obligations on businesses has been one of the hallmarks of globalization, but national laws often lag behind higher international standards. Vodafone, the global telecommunications company, has introduced mandatory maternity leave for employees in all 30 countries where it operates. These new rules provide for 16 weeks' fully-paid maternity leave, followed by a 30-hour-per-week period of six months on full pay. These rules will be of particular benefit to employees in African countries, India and the US, where legal entitlements are not generous. In the US, there is no legal entitlement to maternity leave at all. Significantly, Vodafone sees the new rules as cost-cutting measures in the long run, as these employees are likely to be retained by the company. Research carried out for the company found that the costs of paid maternity leave are far less than the costs of recruiting and training replacement workers (Hooker, 2015).

We have seen that global companies are making increasing use of treaty provisions to pursue claims against states. The traditional views of market entry are that any company enters a new market on the basis that it is subject to national law, and that national law might change. The rise of ISDS, however, seems to dilute this principle. Where it applies, the global company bringing a claim for compensation against a country can justify its action as entirely legal in international law, but often its claim is criticized on ethical and social grounds. Ironically, these claims are sometimes launched in contexts where the country is raising legal standards to conform to international law in areas of global concern, such as environmental protection. The foreign company that wins compensation for loss of future profits due to a change in the law is gaining a distinct advantage over domestic companies in the same sector. In effect, it is above the law. Local companies must abide by the changed law, and must also abide by the country's tax laws. In these cases, the global company appears to be able to escape both.

Global companies have thus benefited from differing national laws and from international law. Some companies have become adept at devising financial arrangements that conform to the letter of the law in areas such as taxation, while flouting the spirit of the law by paying little or no tax. They are able to take advantage of local laws in some countries and lobby governments in other countries for changes in the law that would favour their businesses. Such an opportunistic approach is increasingly unlikely to be welcomed by governments and societies where, after all, companies must engage positively with stakeholders in order to achieve business goals.

Conclusions

A system of laws that is legitimately authorized and fairly enforced serves all within the borders of a state, including individual people, civil society groups, businesses and governments. A legal system that enjoys the confidence of those in society is vital to people's sense of security and to a firm's confidence in conducting business activities within the country. In countries where laws go unenforced and corruption is rampant, it is sometimes said that the 'law of the jungle' prevails, implying that the only rule is one of 'might is right'. There is little security in such an environment, and little sense that it is worth planning for the future. Few businesses are attracted to such a location. While businesses often complain about too much regulation, too little regulation – or unpredictable regulatory interference – is also a disincentive. The world's legal systems vary greatly, and governments are increasingly conscious that the legal environment of their country is a factor in attracting businesses, whether in developed countries or developing ones. Governments, especially in developing economies, must look to a range of goals beyond simply presenting a seemingly attractive package to would-be investors, notably featuring light regulation. Development provides opportunities for investors, but also must serve societal goals. Otherwise, development hopes can turn to disillusionment for many in society.

Opportunities for international expansion and growing financial returns attract businesses to foreign investment. This has been a driver of globalization. Does the business see a foreign location merely as a source of short-term profits, aiming to move on to a more advantageous location in a few years' time? Some firms might profess not to take this view, but in practice are constantly looking for new locations from a mainly cost-cutting perspective. This is feasible in some cases where there is little capital invested. But the commitment of capital involved in a large FDI project usually suggests that the firm takes a longer view, as do governments of host countries. Firms cultivate relations with governments, and, in many cases, with civil society groups. Their activities contribute to development, but for businesses in today's world, the focus should be on sustainable development, involving all in society. International law now plays a growing complementary role to national lawmakers, highlighting global issues from a perspective of higher ethical standards, and becoming a beacon guiding both governments and businesses.

References

Hooker, L. (2015) 'Vodafone offers global maternity equality', BBC News, 5 March, at www.bbc.com/news

Moens, G. and Gillies, P. (1998) *International Trade and Business: Law, Policy and Ethics* (Sydney: Cavendish Publishing).

Naidoo, K. (2013) 'Fukushima disaster: holding the nuclear industry liable', *The Guardian*, 11 March, at www.theguardian.com

Provost, C. and Kennard, M. (2015) 'The obscure legal system that lets corporations sue countries', *The Guardian*, 10 June, at www.theguardian.com

Pratley, N. (2014) 'GSK still has questions to answer over bribery case in China, *The Guardian*, 19 September, at www.theguardian.com

UNCTAD (2013) *World Investment Report 2013* (Geneva: UN).

Vestager, M. (2015) 'Enforcing competition rules in the global village', speech delivered in New York, 20 April, at www.ec.europa.eu/commission/2014-2019/vestager

Zeller, T. (2011) 'Experts had long criticized potential weakness in design of stricken reactor, *New York Times*, 15 March, at www.nyt.com

Zweigert, K. and Kötz, H. (1998) *Introduction to Comparative Law*, 3rd edn (Oxford: Clarendon Press).

Multiple choice questions

Go to the companion website: www.palgravehighered.com/morrison-gbe-4e to take a quick multiple choice quiz on what you have read in this chapter.

Review questions

1. What is meant by the interlocking spheres of national, regional and international law? Which is the most important in the business environment, and why?
2. What are the differences between civil and criminal law? Give an example of each.
3. What are the legal risks in countries where the rule of law is weak?
4. What are the main functions of a national legal system?
5. How do codified legal systems differ from common law systems?
6. How can non-western and western legal systems be designed to function in the same country?
7. What are the difficulties facing a defendant company in a federal system such as the US?
8. What international conventions exist for harmonization of national commercial law?
9. Distinguish between arm's length contracting and relational contracting. What are the factors to consider for joint ventures across the two cultural approaches?
10. What factors account for the global growth in product liability claims?
11. What are the difficulties for plaintiffs in claims for damages following disasters in which there are multiple possible defendants, including parties in other countries?
12. What are the alternatives to settling legal disputes in court?
13. Why is national competition law inadequate to deal with global takeovers and mergers?

14 What is provided by an investor-state dispute settlement (ISDS) provision in treaties? What criticisms has it incurred?

15 In what ways is the International Criminal Court relevant to enforcing legal obligations on international businesses?

✓ Assignments

1 Compare the legal risks that arise for businesses in countries where the rule of law is established with those that arise in countries where the rule of law is weak.

2 In what ways does international law impact on businesses? Discuss both the enabling aspects and those that constrain or impose liabilities.

📖 Further reading

Adams, A. (2014) *Law for Business Students*, 8th edn (Harlow: Pearson).

August, R., Mayer, D. and Bixby, M. (2012) *International Business Law: Text, Cases and Readings*, 6th edn (Harlow: Pearson).

Bell, S., McGillivray, D. and Pedersen, O. (2013) *Environmental Law*, 8th edn (Oxford: OUP).

Harris, D. and Sivakumaran, S. (2015) *Cases and Materials on International Law* 8th edn (London: Sweet & Maxwell).

Schaffer, R., Augusti, F., Dhooge, L. and Earle, B. (2011) *International Business Law and its Environment*, 8th edn (Boston, MA: Cengage Learning).

Shaw, M. (2014) *International Law*, 7th edn (Cambridge: Cambridge University Press).

Wild, C. and Weinstein, S. (2013) *Smith and Keenan's English Law*, 17th edn (Harlow: Pearson).

> 🌐 **Visit the companion website at** www.palgravehighered.com/morrison-gbe-4e **for further learning and teaching resources.**

CLOSING CASE STUDY

Brazil's Petrobras: the fallen star

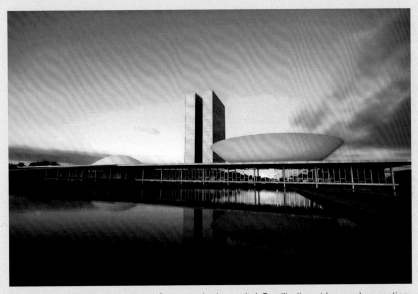

Behind the impressive buildings of Brazil's National Congress, in the capital, Brasilia, lies widespread corruption, undermining the public's faith in political and business leaders.

Source: iStock.com/VelhoJunior.

Petroleo Brasileiro, usually referred to as Petrobras, was a star performer among emerging economies in the 2000s. Although listed on the New York Stock Exchange, two-thirds of the shares are controlled by the Brazilian state, and the board is dominated by government-appointed directors. Nonetheless, private investors bought shares and expected strong growth. Petrobras' success derived from the global commodity boom, which saw rising demand for energy and other resources. The political leadership of Brazil viewed Petrobras as central to government policies. The socialist president, Luis Inacio Lula da Silva of the Workers' Party (PT), elected in 2002, promised to improve living standards for Brazil's many poor people. His two four-year terms of office were noted for lifting millions out of poverty. Creating jobs was a priority. Building refineries in poorer regions of the country, such as the northeast, was envisaged as aiding development efforts. The government imposed a cap on fuel prices for domestic consumers. New discoveries of oil off the coast of Brazil in 2007 seemed

to assure a bright future for Petrobras. When President Lula de Silva left office in 2010, he was succeeded by Dilma Rousseff, who had been chairman of Petrobras from 2003 to 2010. Her Marxist background seemed to ensure the continuation of socialist policies. However, Brazil's opposition centre-right parties were concerned that Petrobras had become too politicized and should be run more on principles of what was best for the company.

The years following 2010 saw slowing economic growth in Brazil, as global demand for commodities weakened and prices fell. Petrobras had overindulged in borrowing in the boom years, and was becoming weighed down with debt, estimated to be a staggering $137 billion by 2013. Among global oil companies, Petrobras had a reputation for being inefficient. While the expertise of foreign oil companies was needed for exploiting the offshore oilfields, the government had effectively frozen them out, restricting them to financial investment only. Petrobras was not producing the amounts of oil anticipated, and its debt burden became worrying. With its history of close political ties, the company was also mired in a corruption scandal involving allegations of bribes and inflated contracts, by which money due to Petrobras had been channelled into the private accounts of political and business leaders, many of them associated with construction companies. Money was said also to have flowed into the campaign funds of the Workers' Party. The scandal went back to Lula da Silva's presidency.

The money siphoned off by the corrupt deals, much of it flowing to offshore bank accounts, was estimated to have been as much as $10 billion. When the scandal broke, investigations were launched and prosecutors expressed determination to spare no one involved, however rich or politically powerful. There have been over 100 people arrested or charged, and 30 convictions. Some leading industrialists have been among those arrested. In some cases, those accused have become informants in order to be given lighter sentences. The police have called the investigation *Erga Omnes*, meaning 'towards everyone' in Latin, to indicate that all are equal under the law (Leahy, 2015). Corruption is a familiar phenomenon in Brazil. Indeed, President Lula da Silva became president on the heels of a corruption scandal that had brought down the previous government.

Ms Rousseff claimed to know nothing of the corrupt payments, but, as the accusations swirled around leading politicians, she was inevitably in the firing line. Ms Rousseff only narrowly won a second term as president in 2014, signalling that the corruption scandal was undermining the Workers' Party. The disquiet was compounded by the fact that by 2015 the economy had slumped close to negative growth. For Petrobras, the situation had become perilous. There was fear that an inability to service its debt could lead

to a default. And its debt was relegated to 'junk' status by global rating agencies.

Petrobras has had to sell assets and reduce costs. The main trade union of oil workers organized strikes from the beginning of November 2015, angered by the fallout from the corruption scandal. They complained that complicit executives have been enriching themselves personally for years, and now workers were being laid off, although they had committed no wrong. The laying off of workers has extended to construction workers on sites in poor regions where refineries were being built. On one site, construction workers' salaries were stopped, and the company ceased to make social security contributions, with the result that workers were unable to claim unemployment benefits.

Valued at $228 billion in 2011, Petrobras had fallen to $30 billion in 2015. Minority shareholders were angry, having seen their shares lose most of their value. Many are pension funds in US states. Some investors have launched lawsuits against Petrobras, alleging that it misled investors over the depth of the corruption scandal. Those who suffered, including the workers who lost livelihoods and the minority shareholders, had no say in company decisions. Ms Rousseff faced impeachment proceedings in 2016, but many of the political leaders seeking to impeach her were themselves accused of corruption. Reforms were urgently needed, focusing on transparency, accountability and corporate governance, but these seemed unlikely to materialize in a context of endemic corruption.

Sources: Davies, W. (2015) 'The real losers in the Petrobras scandal', BBC News, 23 April, at www.bbc.com; Pearson, S. (2015) 'At breaking point', *Financial Times*, 21 March, at www.ft.com; Watts, J. (2015) 'Brazil elite profit from $3bn Petrobras scandal as laid-off workers pay the price', *The Guardian*, 20 March, at www.theguardian.com; Leahy, J. (2015) 'Top industrialists arrested in Petrobras probe as police vow no one is immune', *Financial Times*, 20 June, at www.ft.com.

Questions for discussion

- What are the weaknesses in the way Petrobras was controlled by the government?
- What are the deficiencies in the legal environment in Brazil?
- How should corporate governance be reformed in Brazil?
- To what extent has the corruption scandal damaged Brazil as a location for investment and doing business?

3

SHAPING INTERNATIONAL BUSINESS ACTIVITIES

Chapter 7, *International trade and globalization*, takes us more broadly into the international environment, looking at the ways in which competitive forces, many of them from emerging economies, are shaping the business landscape. We examine the nature and patterns of international trade from a range of perspectives, including nation-states and business organizations. Economic integration, at global and regional levels, is creating greater interdependence among economic actors, but we find that national forces are still powerful influences, both in the developed and developing parts of the world. The WTO has sought both to liberalize trade and achieve fairness in trade practices among the many differing national perspectives. Global concerns about trade impacts on societies and the environment have become more pertinent as trade and FDI have deepened.

In Chapter 8, *Global finance*, we explore a sphere of business activity which has seen rapid growth, but which has also seen increased risks. All businesses rely on financial transactions, not just those in the financial sector. Smoothness and efficiency of cross-border finance has been one of the prominent features of globalization. MNEs have been aided by a liberalization in national financial systems which has opened opportunities for raising capital in different locations. However, the risks have multiplied with the broadening opportunities. Successive financial crises have pointed to a need for greater regulation, but national governments are aware that regulation needs to facilitate markets, not stifle them, if enterprises are to thrive. Similarly, international financial institutions such as the IMF are looking at regulatory reforms in the global arena. Internationally, players are looking towards the emerging economies, where new national forces are counterpoised against trends towards greater global outreach.

Chapter 9, *Technology and innovation*, also examines the impact of globalization, this time in the changing technological environment. Innovation has long been recognized as a key to competitiveness, and with more and more countries building greater technological capacity, the scope for innovation now encompasses a wide range of countries, notably the large emerging economies. Transforming a novel idea into a successful product requires a range of skills spanning entire organizations. Environmental factors, including the legal protection of intellectual property, are crucial. So too is the need for a business climate in which entrepreneurs can obtain the resources needed to pursue their ideas. Technological innovation provides a route towards economic development, notably illustrated by the emerging economies. Governments of both developed and developing economies also look to innovation in meeting environmental challenges such as climate change, the subject of Chapter 10.

CHAPTER

7

INTERNATIONAL TRADE AND GLOBALIZATION

Outline of chapter

This chapter will enable you to

- Appreciate the contributions of theories of international trade to an understanding of the ways in which companies, industries and nations compete in the global environment
- Understand the rationale and mechanisms of national trade policies
- Understand the workings of the multilateral trading system
- Assess the impacts of trade on societies in developed and developing countries

Global mining and the rise of BHP Billiton

Mining iron ore has brought rich rewards to BHP Billiton, mainly from Chinese demand, but mining sites also bring risks to communities and the environment.

Source: iStock.com/John Kirk.

The origins of BHP Billiton lie in Australia, in the silver, lead and zinc mines of Broken Hill, and in the iron and steel works that employed thousands of people in the early years of the twentieth century. From its founding in 1885, BHP's mining and manufacturing activities spread across Australia, providing employment and consolidating a strong position in the economy. The company was shielded from foreign competitors by the Australian government, allowing it to prosper in the domestic environment from the 1960s to the 1980s. It became Australia's largest manufacturing employer, employing 60,000 people at its peak. But mining was becoming globalized, and exports were becoming more important. BHP began exporting from the 1960s. It also started acquiring foreign companies. The sale of its Australian steel works in 2000 marked a turning point, as it exited Australian manufacturing. The merger with Billiton of South Africa in 2001 resulted in the company's current name. By 2010, only 15,000 people were employed by BHP Billiton in Australia.

Mining is a hazardous industry, often involving large-scale sites in sensitive geographies, in which BHP Billiton has invested heavily. These activities have impacts far beyond the sites, extending to communities and the ecological environment. Mining iron ore involves many risks. BHP Billiton is one of the world's three largest iron ore exporters, the other two being Vale of Brazil and Rio Tinto of Australia. Mainly in response to Chinese demand, all three have greatly increased productive capacity. Two-thirds of the world's iron ore exports go to China's steel industry, generating handsome profits for the exporters during China's period of rapid growth. As a result, they have invested in further huge mining projects, ramping up production in recent years, even as the indications of a slowing down were evident in China. Oversupply of iron ore has been a consequence, and with it, falling prices. Iron ore fell from $135 per tonne in 2013 to $43 in 2015. The clear signal from the market was that miners should reduce supply, but they have been reluctant to do so. Even at low prices, iron ore remains profitable for them. And low prices globally deter new competitors from entering the market. However, by 2014, BHP Billiton was becoming convinced that the boom period was over, and output needed to fall. The company froze the pay of its CEO, Andrew Mackenzie, and senior managers in 2014.

Mr Mackenzie has sought to streamline the structure of the company, selling off non-core businesses (Wilson, 2015). This runs counter to BHP Billiton's history of acquisition, but reflects the new reality of the market. The company would remain committed to iron ore, copper, coal, oil and gas. Coal, oil and gas – all fossil fuels – have become controversial in view of climate change implications. Mackenzie, himself a scientist, has written on business ethics. He has urged that multinational corporations should work in partnership with stakeholders, including 'communities, customers and societies' (Mackenzie and Rice, 2001: 4). He has also said that multinational corporations (MNCs) should be powerful exemplars of human rights and environmental protection in a co-authored article that was written when he was employed by BP, an oil giant that has a poor record for environmental protection. BHP Billiton has encountered allegations of human rights breaches in its iron ore activities. It has faced litigation in Papua New Guinea for polluting rivers with waste from iron ore mining. A mining disaster in Brazil on 5 November 2015 brought BHP Billiton under the spotlight again.

Samarco, the owner of the Brazilian mine, is a joint-venture company owned by BHP Billiton and Vale of Brazil. In the accident, an earthwork dam that contained mining waste burst and sent flows of waste into the Rio Doce. A number of people were killed or recorded as missing, including Samarco employees. The mud flow from the burst dam destroyed homes, killed fish hundreds of kilometres away, and contaminated the water supply for hundreds of thousands of people. The potential liability for compensation is huge, beyond the limits of Samarco's insurance. BHP Billiton and Vale are both being targeted, as they are the ultimate owners, but they were not in operational control themselves. Experts have observed that monitoring of the dam did not use the latest technology. The dam posed additional risk as it had been raised in 2013. Brazil's inspection system is weak, and the dam was considered low risk (Phillips, 2015).

The communities around the Brazilian mine disaster are stakeholders, but for BHP Billiton, the link is tenuous, as Samarco is legally a separate company. Decades ago, when BHP was mainly Australian, its employees and communities were clearly visible and close to the heart of the company. What about poor communities, often inhabited by indigenous peoples, in remote locations of the world? They are likely to be off the radar of shareholders. BHP Billiton's shareholders have been accustomed to generous dividends, but their shares lost 25% of their value in trading on the London Stock Exchange in November 2015, following the disaster, contributing to a total of a 50% slide for the year.

Sources: Wilson, J. (2015) 'Monday interview: Andrew Mackenzie, BHP Billiton CEO', Financial Times, 22 March, at www.ft.com; Mackenzie, A. and Rice, D. (2001) 'Ethics and the multinational corporation', The Moral Universe, Demos Collection 16/2001, at www.demos.co.uk; Phillips, D. (2015) 'Brazil's mining tragedy: was it a preventable disaster?', The Guardian, 25 November, at www.theguardian.com; Wilson, J. and Hume, N. (2014) 'End of the Iron Age', Financial Times, 30 September.

Questions for discussion

- What are the characteristics of the global market for iron ore, and why has supply greatly outstripped demand?
- How has globalization changed the business of BHP Billiton?
- How has the configuration of BHP Billiton's stakeholders changed as a result of globalization?
- If you were a shareholder in BHP Billiton, what message would you send to the company following the Brazilian mining disaster?

Introduction

Across the ages, businesses have looked to trade beyond their home country. Growth in international trade has been a major contributor to the rise of the industrialized countries, stretching back to the Industrial Revolution. Indeed, when we look at the flourishing trade between Asia and Europe as far back as the medieval era, we are tempted to think that globalization has been happening for a long time. However, both the volume of trade and the patterns of trade between nations have changed greatly over the years. In the decades following the Second World War, the dominant trading powers were the US, Japan and Europe. From the 1990s and into the twenty-first century, there has been a shift towards Asia. Two major factors can be high-lighted: globalization of supply chains by multinational enterprises (MNEs) and the opening up of national economies. Understanding the impacts of these factors on the global trading system, including particular regions and national economies, is key to formulating business strategies in the changing environment.

We begin this chapter with an overview of international trade, highlighting shifts in trading relations now taking place. We look at the major theories which help to explain changing patterns of world trade. We then analyse the divergent views on the issues of free trade and protectionism, which have shaped national perspectives. Trade policies go beyond economic considerations, extending to impacts on socie-ties, including issues such as employment, food security and the use of natural resources. While these have economic dimensions, they also have important social dimensions that governments must take into account. Belief in the benefits of free trade has underpinned agreements to open markets, guided particularly by the World Trade Organization (WTO). We examine the role of the WTO as trade envelops more developing and emerging economies. Each has a range of goals in relation to national needs and priorities. These concerns are increasingly part of the backdrop for companies wishing to create trade links with the newer trading nations.

Trends in world trade: impacts of globalization

Trade involves the exchange of something of value, usually goods or services, for a price, usually money. **Exports** are products leaving a country, and **imports** are prod-ucts entering a country. Trade in physical goods (merchandise), which amounted to over $18 trillion globally in 2013, is greater than trade in services, which totalled $5 trillion (UNCTAD, 2015: 1). Goods traded are classified as 'primary' and 'secondary' products. Primary goods include natural resources and agricultural produce, while manufactured goods are secondary. The 'tertiary' sector covers services. Histori-cally, thriving trade has aided countries in becoming economically powerful, espe-cially following the transformation of national economies by industrialization. In the eighteenth and nineteenth centuries, Britain imported cotton from India, to be processed and made into clothing in the newly industrialized cities in the north of England. The textile industry transformed the economies of these northern cities, and also brought about changes in society due to the rise in industrial employment. Since the end of the Second World War, trade has grown at a remarkable rate. From 1950 to 2002, the volume of world exports tripled, while production doubled. In the 1990s, world trade grew on average 6.5% annually, while output grew at 2.5% annu-ally. The following decade showed similar growth, but the global financial crisis of 2008 precipitated sharp declines in both world output and the global volume of trade. Global trade shrank by over 10% in 2009, but rebounded the following year (IMF, 2015). Since then, growth in world output and in global trade has hovered around 3.4% annually.

Developed countries have long been the main forces in global trade. Their dominance is now receding, but they still account for about half of global merchandise exports and two-thirds of exports of services. The balance in global trade is now shifting towards greater participation by developing countries, as shown in Figure 7.1. This shift, perhaps paradoxically, is being driven largely by the globalizing production chains of the world's MNEs, most of which originate in developed countries. The leading developed countries in trade are traditionally known as the '**triad**' countries of Europe, North America and Japan. Japan was the last of these economies to experience industrialization (in the 1970s and 1980s). The triad countries have now experienced shrinking manufacturing sectors and a growing emphasis on high technology and services, while developing economies have experienced growth in manufacturing. Figures 7.1 and 7.2 show this shift. In Figure 7.1, we see the trade performance of the developing countries closing the gap on the developed countries. Developing countries suffered less from the financial crisis than developed countries. Since then, developing countries have moved ahead more decisively.

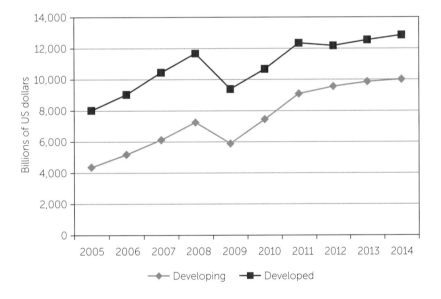

Figure 7.1 Comparison of developed and developing countries' trade

Source: Created using data from UNCTAD statistics, 'Exports and imports of goods and services', at www.unctad. org, accessed 24 June 2015. Reprinted with the permission of the United Nations.

Figure 7.2 shows the shift that has taken place in world merchandise exports in the post-war period. We see that North America's share of total merchandise exports has more than halved, from 28.1% to 13.2%. Asia's exports are the mirror opposite, having risen from a global share of 14% in 1948 to 31.5% in 2013. European countries continue to hold a prominent position, while the exports of African countries, mainly primary goods, have halved. The contrast between Asia and Africa highlights that developing countries represent a mixed picture of trade performance.

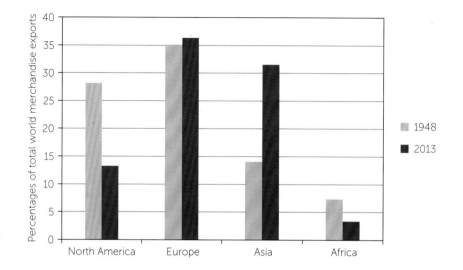

Figure 7.2 Merchandise exports from selected regions, 1948 and 2013

Source: Data from WTO, *International Trade Statistics 2014*, Table 1.5, p. 24, at www. wto.org, accessed 21 July 2015.

Behind the growing integration of developing countries in world trade lie divergent national scenarios. East Asian economies, particularly China, emerge as outstanding performers, whose development has been based on export-oriented manufacturing industries. These countries' trade, including both imports and exports, increased by 40% between 2008 and 2013. Globally, trade in manufactured goods far exceeds that of natural resources and agricultural products, as shown in Figure 7.3. Developing countries that mainly export natural resources and commodities have seen weaker growth. Many sub-Saharan African and Latin American countries fall into this category. In general, developing countries' exports make up three-quarters of global trade in natural resources. The critical difference between the two groups of countries is the rise of global supply chains.

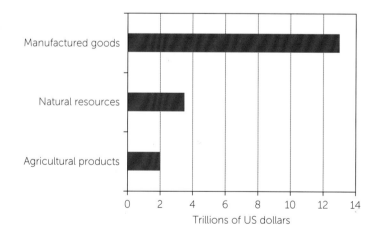

Figure 7.3 Categories of world merchandise trade by value, 2013

Source: Created using data from UNCTAD (2015) *Key Statistics and Trends in International Trade 2014* (Geneva: UN), p. 4, Figure 4(b). Reprinted with the permission of the United Nations.

In today's world, most trade is determined by production supply chains. These are often referred to as 'global value chains', highlighting the fact that value is added at each stage in the chain. Through these supply chains, goods and services are provided in diverse locations, co-ordinated by MNEs. Over two-thirds of world trade is accounted for by **intermediate goods**, consisting of components which might cross national borders more than once before being made into final products. These goods are counted each time they cross national borders, leading to 'double counting', which is estimated to amount to about 28% of total trade (UNCTAD, 2013). Trade in intermediate products rose from $2.5 trillion in 2002 to $7 trillion in 2011 (UNCTAD, 2014). MNE strategies co-ordinate a variety of linked firms, including affiliate companies, licensed or contract manufacturers, and arm's-length contractors. A complex product like a car is likely to contain numerous imported components, amounting to 50% of the value of each finished vehicle.

Participation in global value chains has benefited those developing countries that have focused on attracting foreign direct investment (FDI) in export industries. Electronics and textiles are examples of industries transformed by global supply chains. Asian emerging economies have been particularly successful in this respect. Differing trade profiles are shown in Figure 7.4. In the figure, Country B is analogous to a developing country such as China that imports intermediate goods, incorporates them into finished products, and exports them to other countries. Destinations typically include countries like Country C, from which Country B has sourced intermediate goods, including high-value components. Country B thus benefits from the foreign value added to its exports. Country C in Figure 7.4 is mainly an importer, and is likely to be a developed country like the US. It imports manufactured goods from Country B and also goods from Country A, which are likely to be natural resources and energy. Country A is indicative of developing countries that depend on exports of primary products. These countries, which include many resource-rich African countries, must import manufactured goods, and must also import commodities and energy that they cannot produce. Their position is more precarious than Countries B and C, as they are highly vulnerable to swings in prices in commodity markets, affecting both their revenues from trade and their ability to import the goods they require. For such countries, diversifying their economies into manufacturing would contribute to sustainable growth, but these economies often struggle to convert this advice into practice.

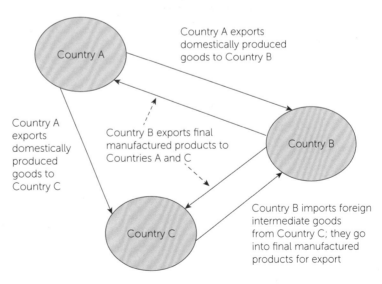

Figure 7.4 Trade profiles of contrasting countries

Transition economies, notably the post-communist countries of Central and Eastern Europe, bear similarities to Country B in Figure 7.4. Their manufacturing industries have grown from FDI, increasing their integration into the EU economy. Germany has played a key role in driving this growth. Its large industrial companies have invested heavily in productive assets in these newer EU member states, whose exports are mainly destined for other EU member countries, notably Germany itself. Germany has also remained a major exporter of domestically produced goods, and has retained a large manufacturing sector. Germany's trade is thus more evenly balanced between exports and imports than that of the US, which has a huge trade deficit.

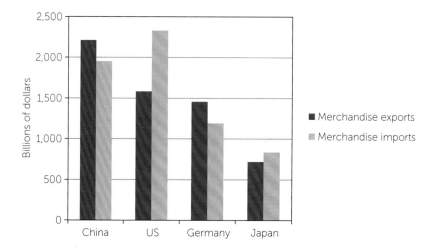

Figure 7.5 The world's four leading trading countries in 2013

Source: Data from WTO, *International Trade Statistics 2014*, Table 1.7, p. 26, at www. wto.org, accessed 24 June 2015.

Figure 7.5 shows the world's four leading countries in global trade. China is the world's largest exporter of merchandise, and also the world's second largest importer of goods. Favourable tax treatment of foreign investors, including tax-free export zones, has helped to turn the country into a powerhouse for exports of consumer goods globally. About half of China's imports *and* exports are made up of intermediate goods. Of the four leading traders, the US stands out as being the largest importer by far, but the US has the greatest imbalance between exports and imports. The US trade deficit with China rose to a record $343 billion in 2014, mainly because of rising imports (US Census, 2015). Consumer electronics and clothing are among the many goods imported from China. Most of these goods bear the brand names of American companies, who have their products manufactured in China to benefit from low labour costs, often using raw materials shipped from the US. Germany exports more goods than it imports. US exports, valued at just over $1.5 trillion, are only slightly in front of those of Germany (at $1.45 trillion) – a country whose GDP is less than a quarter that of the US.

Value-added trade can contribute greatly to a country's GDP, more so in developing countries than in developed ones. Economic growth per capita flows from a developing country's participation in global value chains. While this is good news on the face of it, there are wider concerns that pose challenges for governments that wish to become more integrated in global value chains. For many, that involvement can lead to the nurturing of domestic enterprises and technological development. For others, dependence on low-tech manufacturing activities can set in, delivering few technological spillovers. In these circumstances, it could be argued that globalization is not contributing to development goals to the hoped-for extent. Indeed, globalization poses risks that MNE strategists will shift activities to other locations, adversely affecting the economies of communities where its activities had provided employment. By the same token, the shift of large swathes of manufacturing to developing countries has posed problems for the developed countries now importing goods that they once produced domestically. The decline of manufacturing has brought economic hardship throughout much of America's former industrial landscape, with repercussions in communities. Following the collapse of Detroit's motor industry, the city declined rapidly, becoming the largest municipal bankruptcy in US history. MNEs have realized the benefits of scanning the globe to achieve lower-cost production, while consumers rejoice in lower prices on goods, from clothes to televisions. The benefits of globalized production must be weighed against the negative impacts in societies, in both developing and developed economies.

Trade and development

Although trade is boosting growth in developing countries, often in conjunction with FDI, these economies can become entrenched in low-cost manufacturing activities which can damage growth prospects in the long term. How does this happen, and what can be done about it?

Theories of international trade

Theories of trade have emerged with the rise in industrialization because of its potential to expand trade on a large scale. The first major theorist of international trade, Adam Smith, believed that all countries benefit from unrestricted trade. Free trade is said to exist where citizens can export and import without restrictions or barriers imposed by the governments of either the exporting or importing country. In his book, *The Wealth of Nations* (published in 1776), Smith argued in favour of the 'the invisible hand' of market forces as opposed to government intervention. When countries produce the products in which they are the most efficient producers, they are said to have an **absolute advantage** in these products. A country may then sell these goods overseas, and purchase from overseas goods which are produced more efficiently elsewhere. Thus, both countries benefit from trade.

The theory of comparative advantage

Starting from the principle of absolute advantage, David Ricardo ([1817]1973), writing some 40 years after Adam Smith, developed his theory of **comparative advantage**. His theory contends that, if Country A is an efficient producer of wheat and Country B an efficient producer of clocks, it pays A to purchase clocks from B, even if it could itself produce clocks more efficiently than B. According to Ricardo, if countries specialize in the industries in which they have comparative advantage, all will benefit from trade with each other, consumers in both countries enjoying more wheat and more clocks than they would without trade. According to Ricardo's theory, therefore, trade is not a 'zero-sum' game, i.e. where one side's gain is the other's loss, but a 'positive-sum' game, i.e. one in which all parties benefit.

In reality, most countries do not specialize in ways envisaged by Ricardo's theory. Further, the model does not allow for the dynamic changes that trade brings about. Economists base the benefits of free trade on 'dynamic gains' that lead to economic growth. Free trade leads to an increase in a country's stock of resources, in terms of both increased capital from abroad and greater supplies of labour. In addition, efficiency may improve with large-scale production and improved technology. Opening up markets and creating more competition can provide an impetus for domestic companies to become more efficient. Trading patterns are also influenced by historical accident, government policies and the importance of MNEs in the global economy – all of which have been incorporated into newer trade theories.

Product life cycle theory from the trade perspective

Raymond Vernon's theory of the international product life cycle was introduced in Chapter 2 for its early contribution to our understanding of FDI and the location of production. The theory also helps to explain trade from the perspective of the firm (Wells, 1972). It traces a product's life from its launch in the home market through to export to other markets and, finally, to its manufacture in cheaper locations for import into its original home market. The theory observes that, over the cycle, production has moved from the US to other advanced countries, and finally to developing countries where costs are lower.

This simple interpretation of the product life cycle rests on a view of manufacturing which has been rather overtaken by globalization. In modern supply chains, a firm may use components from various locations, and choose yet another for assembling the final product. Because of the rapid pace of technological innovation and short product life cycles, a company in an industry such as consumer electronics may well introduce a new product simultaneously in a number of markets, wiping out the leads and lags between markets. Vernon's model is useful in explaining production patterns for some types of products, such as standardized consumer goods, but is less useful in predicting future patterns, especially in industries dominated by a few global players. Moreover, the theory takes little account of trade barriers and government trade policies. Trade barriers of various kinds (discussed later in this chapter) are typically imposed to block imports or protect local industries.

Newer trade theories

More recently, theorists have turned their attention to the growing importance of MNEs in international trade, taking into account the globalization of production and trade between affiliated companies (see Chapter 2). Krugman, in his book, *Rethinking International Trade* (1994), emphasized features of the international economy such as increasing returns and imperfect competition. More precisely, he said, 'conventional trade theory views world trade as taking place entirely in goods like wheat; new trade theory see it as being largely in goods like aircraft' (Krugman, 1994: 1). For companies, innovation and economies of scale give what are called **first-mover advantages** to early entrants in a market. This lead increases over time, making it impossible for others to catch up. For firms able to benefit in this way, the increased share in global markets has led to oligopolistic behaviour in some industries, such as the aircraft industry. For countries, there are advantages to be gained from encouraging national firms which enjoy first-mover advantages. There are clear implications here that government intervention can play a role in promoting innovation and entrepreneurship, thereby boosting the competitive advantage of nations.

Porter's theory of competitive advantage of nations

In his book, *The Competitive Advantage of Nations*, published originally in 1990, Michael Porter develops a theory of national **competitive advantage**. He attempts to find out why some countries are more successful than others. Each nation, he says, has four broad attributes that shape its national competitive environment. Porter envisaged the four attributes as forming the four points of a diamond. Assessing each of these attributes gives a picture of the country's competitive advantage.

The first two attributes relate to the national environment. The first, factor conditions, is about the nation's factors of production, such as skilled labour, infrastructure and natural resources. The social and cultural environment is also relevant to this analysis. The second attribute, demand conditions, refers to the nature of home demand, relating to the nature and depth of home demand for particular goods and services. In emerging economies, the rise of the middle class is a strong indication of rising demand in consumer products and services. The third and fourth attributes concern the country's firms and industries. The third attribute is related and supporting industries, which contribute to competitive advantage. If the country is home to a host of supporting industries, including innovative entrepreneurial businesses, this is a good sign of growing national competitiveness. The fourth attribute is firm strategy, structure and rivalry. This includes the conditions in the nation governing how companies are created, organized and managed. It also involves the nature of domestic rivalry (Porter, 1998a: 71). Where firms are focused on innovation, sensitive to changing demand and continually rethinking quality improvements, there are advantages to be reaped in international markets.

Porter stresses that the four determinants are interdependent. Favourable demand conditions, for example, will contribute to competitive advantage only in an environment in which firms are able and willing to respond. Advantage based on only one or two determinants may suffice in natural resource-dependent industries, or those with lower technological input, but to sustain advantage in the modern knowledge-intensive industries, advantages throughout the model are necessary.

Porter adds that there are two additional variables in his theory. They are chance and government. Chance can open up unexpected opportunities in a variety of ways: new inventions, external political developments and shifts in foreign market demand. He cites the fall of communism, which resulted in the opening of Central and Eastern Europe, as an example. His categorization of these occurrences as happening as if by chance is perhaps unfortunate, and it would be preferable to see them from the business perspective as simply opportunities. On the other hand, government policies can be highly influential.

The government policies highlighted by Porter include a strong antitrust policy, which encourages domestic rivalry, and investment in education, which generates knowledge resources. Government policies can play a crucial role in building national competitive advantage. Porter stresses that this role, however, is indirect rather than direct (Porter, 1998b). Government remains an 'influence' rather than a 'determinant' in his model. However, it is arguable that government policy has had a larger direct role than his model suggests. Governments in market economies have taken on a more directly interventionist role, including ownership stakes in companies, in addition to a regulatory role. This has been particularly noteworthy since the financial crisis of 2007–8. In countries climbing the economic ladder, the role of government has been a key to international success.

Government guidance was critical in Japan's economic development, but was indirect, as Japan's large companies were mostly private sector. By contrast, in the more recently emerging economies, such as China, the state has played an active role in the development model, leading with large state-owned companies. Schemes to attract FDI, business-friendly taxation regimes and the setting up of special economic zones are aspects of government policy that have become common in emerging economies that seek to build competitive advantage. In addition, government policies are instrumental in the development of infrastructure. China and India provide contrasting examples. Transport and other infrastructure have developed rapidly in China, but have progressed slowly in India, largely because of lack of government impetus and complex rights over land. On the other hand, the Indian government has prioritized investment in high-technology education in order to attract computing and IT services industries, which have driven the country's economic growth.

Porter's theory is useful in demonstrating the interaction between different determinants of national competitive advantage, but it probably under-emphasizes world economic integration and the role of production supply chains.

Competitive advantage

Which aspects of Porter's theory of competitive advantage of nations have retained validity, and what aspects have not? How would you modify Porter's theory?

National trade policies

National economic prosperity for almost all countries is more than ever tied in with international trade. But, as we have seen, all countries are not equal in building prosperity from trade. Richer countries are in a stronger position than poorer countries to use trade to foster national goals, such as food security, or to benefit particular industries, such as the car industry. Governments face innumerable political and social, as well as economic, pressures to intervene in trade. **Protectionism** is the deliberate policy of favouring home producers, for example by subsidizing home producers or imposing import tariffs. Figure 7.6 summarizes the pros and cons of free trade which are discussed in this section. The term 'free trade' is misleading. There has never been 'free' trade in the sense of no cross-border barriers at all. 'Trade liberalization' is therefore more accurate, to indicate measures *towards* free trade which involve reducing border controls and reducing governments' scope for curtailing imports. Trade liberalization has been an important contributor to globalization, facilitating cross-border movements of goods. As we saw earlier in this chapter, benefits of greater integration in global supply chains come mixed with risks of negative impacts that are of concern to national decision-makers. In this section, we look first at national priorities and then at policy tools for promoting them.

The free trade debate

In favour of free trade:

- Free trade benefits all countries.
- A country risks falling behind if it is isolated from global markets.
- Costs of protecting industries can be high, and tend to go to uncompetitive industries.

In favour of protectionism:

- Protection of national industries promotes independence and security.
- It protects domestic employment.
- It supports national industries, allowing them to compete globally, and adding to national wealth.

Figure 7.6 The pros and cons of free trade

Government perspectives on trade

Governments are perceived as ultimately responsible for the safety and well-being of those within its borders, including individual citizens, groups of people, industries and companies. We highlight below four major policy areas in which trade policy is shaped by national interests.

Promoting industrialization

Industrialization may be promoted by restricting the flow of imported products, thereby encouraging domestic manufacturing. We have seen that industrialization in many countries, such as Japan and the later industrializing countries of South East Asia, has been guided by government, through industrial policy. These countries have made rapid transitions from mainly agricultural to industrial economies. The 'infant industries' argument holds that developing countries should protect infant industries in which they have potential comparative advantage until they are strong enough to survive when protections are removed. Japan is an example of both successful infant industry support and industrial policy (Gilpin, 2000). For Singapore and other Asian economies, foreign direct investors provided the impetus for development. Industrialization may focus on **import substitution**, that is, producing goods for domestic consumption which otherwise would have been imported. India is an example. Domestic industries nurtured through protective measures in this way do not always become competitive in world markets. Export-led development, by contrast, focuses on growth in export-oriented goods. Industrialization in China has taken this route.

Protecting employment

By restricting imports, governments aim to safeguard domestic jobs. However, the situation is seldom as simple as this. Many US manufacturing jobs have been transferred to lower-paid overseas workers. Work in lower-skilled jobs, as in the textile industry, is particularly vulnerable to being lost to low-cost imports. Propping up uncompetitive domestic industries is costly and leads to declining competitiveness in the long term.

Workers in industrialized countries who are displaced by global competitive forces are usually those without the skills to benefit from the newer job opportunities. Payments to displaced workers fall on the public purse, and whole regions can suffer decline as a result. In the long term, it could be argued, governments need to look at the education and training needs of the economy to enhance competitive advantage. Nonetheless, protectionist pressures are very strong, and special interests' regional strongholds are often effective in mobilizing political support.

Protecting consumers

Conventional wisdom holds that consumers benefit from free trade in that competition in markets brings down prices and increases choice among all products, from agricultural commodities to televisions. Both agriculture and consumer electronics have become global industries. The industrialization and globalization of the food chain have resulted in agricultural produce and livestock being transported hundreds – even thousands – of miles to markets. An outcome is that any health and safety concerns, such as contamination from BSE in beef, can have wide ramifications.

Governments have at their disposal a variety of regulatory measures in respect of consumer products such as food and medicines, whether produced at home or abroad. However, levels of regulation and quality controls differ from country to country. Governments that take a stance against genetically-modified organisms (GMOs), for example, are often accused of using safety as a barrier to keep out legitimate goods. American pharmaceutical companies and agribusiness companies are active in lobbying, pressing their cases to the US government to seek greater access to foreign markets. Their interests are often reflected in US trade policy.

Promoting strategic interests

Strategic interests cover a number of considerations. It is often thought that the strategic sensitivity of defence industries dictates that domestic suppliers are preferable to foreign ones, and thus should be protected. The strategic necessity argument can be extended to a great number of products. It was used to provide federal funding for the semiconductor industry in the US in the 1990s, as semiconductors are crucial to defence systems. Food production is one of the most heavily protected industries because of the strategic importance of safeguarding food supply and also agricultural employment. On this reasoning, subsidies and import restrictions have long benefited Japanese farmers, while Japanese consumers have paid well above world prices for their food. These barriers are only slowly coming down. However, after 20 years of stability, sharp rises in global prices of basic commodities, such as wheat and rice, in 2008 caused shortages around the world, leading to food riots in some countries. As a result, food security has become a greater preoccupation of governments.

Strategic industries are also a target of policymakers. Strategic trade policy holds that governments can assist their own firms in particular industries to gain competitive advantage. This theory mainly applies to oligopolistic industries such as the aerospace industry, in which the US helped Boeing (www.boeing.com) by providing it with lucrative defence contracts, while European governments helped Airbus (www.airbus.com) through subsidies. Both sides have accused each other of breaching WTO rules restricting state aid, resulting in a long-running legal action under the WTO's dispute procedure.

Trade policies may be linked to foreign policy objectives, as was clearly demonstrated during the cold war, when trade followed political and military alliances. Government overseas aid packages to developing countries may be tied to trade. Trade policies are often based on historical relationships between countries, such as those between the former colonial powers of Europe and their former colonies. This resulted in another long-running dispute between the EU and US. The so-called 'banana dispute' had its roots in the preferential treatment that former colonies in the Caribbean received, which were found to contravene WTO rules.

Protecting national culture

For governments, maintaining national culture and identity is an important aspect of social stability. This covers cultural products such as literature, film and music. The growth of the internet and global media has led to fears of cultural globalization, prompting some national authorities to limit foreign content and foreign ownership in these sectors. Internet censorship, which has become highly elaborate in some countries, such as China, is based in some measure on the perception by the government that the free flow of content from abroad can undermine national cultural and social values.

Tools of governmental trade policy

Government policies affect trade in numerous ways, both directly and indirectly. Of direct impact is the manipulation of exchange rates. Devaluing a country's currency will have the immediate effect of making exports cheaper and imports more expensive (see Chapter 8). However, governments now have less scope for manipulating exchange rates in increasingly interlinked currency markets. Similarly, most governments are now party to multilateral, regional and bilateral trading arrangements which curtail their ability to control trade. We will therefore look at government policy options in the context of changing global and regional contexts. The traditional tools for controlling trade are tariffs, quotas, subsidies and other non-tariff barriers to trade.

The classic tool of trade policy is the **tariff**, or duty payable on goods traded. Tariffs are usually imposed on imported goods, but they can also be imposed on exports. When we think of protectionism, we think naturally of tariff barriers. The tariff raises the price of an imported product, thereby benefiting domestic producers of the same product. Japanese whisky producers have been protected in this way by huge import duties levied on foreign whisky. The sums collected also swell government coffers. The main losers are the consumers, who pay higher prices for the imported product. While tariffs on manufactured goods have diminished dramatically, thanks to the multilateral GATT (discussed later), tariffs on agricultural products are still common.

The **import quota** limits the quantity of an imported product that can legally enter a country. Licences may be issued annually to a limited number of firms, each of which must stay within the amounts specified in its import licence. Limits are set so as to allow only a portion of the market to foreign goods, thus protecting the market share of domestic producers. Restricting supply in this way is likely to result in higher prices for consumers. Import quotas are sometimes evaded by companies shipping goods via other countries with quota to spare when their home country's quota is used up. An exporting firm may ultimately set up production in a country to avoid the imposition of quotas.

An alternative to the import quota is the **voluntary export restraint (VER)**, which shifts the onus on the exporting country to limit its exports, or possibly risk the imposition of quotas or tariffs. A leading example of the VER has been Japanese car exports to the US. In the 1980s, when the Japanese motor industry was growing apace and making rapid inroads in the American market, the US government persuaded Japan to agree to a VER. To sidestep these restrictions, Japanese manufacturers set up local operations in the US through FDI. Governments can introduce **local content requirements**, to ensure that local component suppliers gain. Japanese motor manufacturers have responded by locating associated Japanese component manufacturers near to assembly plants in overseas locations, thus facilitating just-in-time operations while maintaining high local content.

Local content requirements can be viewed as a type of **non-tariff barrier** to trade, which has indirect impacts in keeping out imports. As we noted earlier, rules regarding product safety and public health are also sometimes viewed as similarly deterrent. American agribusiness giant, Monsanto, along with the US government, extols the safety of food products containing GMOs. Research carried out by Pew Research Center found that, while 88% of scientists consider GMOs safe, 57% of ordinary American consumers disagree, considering GMOs unsafe (Funk and Rainie, 2015). There have been calls for compulsory labelling of food products – a move which the large companies in the US have strongly opposed. Cargill, one of the world's largest agricultural traders, has been vocal in its opposition to compulsory labelling (see quote below), although it is increasing its range of products labelled 'GMO free' in response to consumer demand. Some 64 countries require GMO labelling, including many European countries, Japan, Brazil and Russia. Monsanto and other agribusiness companies have targeted African countries as lucrative new markets, where they are pressing the virtues of GMOs in obtaining higher crop yields in harsh conditions. However, the control exerted by the agribusiness company over smallholders engaged in GMO farming raises concerns that farmers and farming will become subordinated to corporate goals rather than national development priorities (see Chapter 10). African governments are in a relatively weak position to resist the strong overtures of the agribusiness industry and their US government backers.

The way I see it ...

'... the mandatory labelling of GM foods does not provide consumers with meaningful information. Mandatory labelling can actually be misleading to consumers who interpret foods produced, either in whole or in part, from or with biotechnology, as unsafe.'

Cargill's views, in 'Does Cargill support mandatory labelling legislation for foods containing GM ingredients?', at www.cargill.com, accessed 27 July 2015.

Do you go along with Cargill's views, and why?

Government **subsidies** can also amount to non-tariff barriers. These are payments and other financial support from public funds to support domestic producers. Governments often justify subsidies to domestic producers, such as farmers, as a strategic need, to ensure livelihoods of farmers, who provide basic domestic food supplies. This can be distinguished from the argument used to justify programmes to boost farmers' incomes for the purpose of enabling them to export cheaply. The latter line of reasoning is that the extra funds, which are export subsidies, will boost the local producers' competitive position in global markets. Export subsidies are against WTO rules as they distort markets. Some types of state funding fall into a more nebulous, 'grey' area. For example, R&D grants, viewed as legitimate, help local producers indirectly. Funds to promote green technology are similarly viewed as legitimate. There are other types of state aid, including loans at preferential rates and tax concessions.

Advocates of trade liberalization criticize subsidies on several grounds. They argue that subsidies work against a 'level playing field' for trade, as unsubsidized firms face unfair competition. When rich developed countries pay local producers subsidies, those in poorer developing countries that trade in the same product markets are disadvantaged. The impact on markets is likely to be a downward movement of prices.

The EU has provided substantial subsidies for farmers since 1962, creating considerable trade friction with other nations. The extent of EU support diminished in the 1990s, but agriculture continues to be a highly politically sensitive sector. EU subsidies to farmers in 2013 amounted to 19.8% of gross farm receipts (OECD, 2014). Still, in France, one of the EU's main agricultural producers, farmers' livelihoods are precarious, due to falling returns to producers from the large food processors and retailers combined with rising costs.

Although poor countries derive much-needed export revenues from growing cotton, the realities of global markets can be stacked against them.

Source: © Royalty-Free/Corbis.

Cotton is one of the world's most widely grown and traded agricultural products. Most of the world's cotton is grown in developing countries, but it is the US that has the greatest impact in world markets. The world's third largest producer (behind China and India), the US is by far the largest exporter of cotton, accounting for about one-third of global cotton exports, as shown in Figure 7.7 About 75% of its crop is exported, its main destination being China's large textile manufacturing sector.

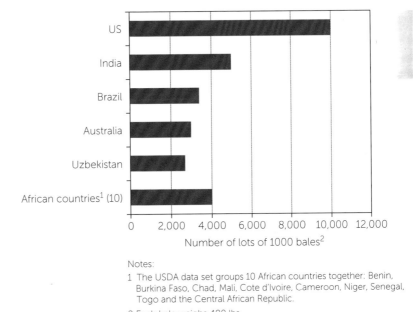

Figure 7.7 World's leading cotton exporters

Source: Data from USDA/ Economic Research Service, *Cotton and Wool Yearbook* data, Table 1, US cotton supply and use 1965–2015; and Table 17, Cotton exports: major foreign exporters, at www.ers.usda.gov/data-products/cotton, accessed 15 July 2015.

Notes:

1 The USDA data set groups 10 African countries together: Benin, Burkina Faso, Chad, Mali, Cote d'Ivoire, Cameroon, Niger, Senegal, Togo and the Central African Republic.

2 Each bale weighs 480 lbs.

Both China and the US heavily subsidize their cotton growers. China's crop mainly supplies local factories, whereas most of the US crop is traded in world markets. US export subsidies, mostly in the form of insurance payouts that violate WTO rules, help to keep global prices low. Using the WTO's dispute resolution procedure (discussed below), Brazil has won cases against the US for unfairness suffered by Brazilian cotton producers. But instead of changing the non-compliant subsidy regime, the US offered money compensation of several hundred million dollars to Brazilian farmers, and Brazil agreed. Two such deals have been approved by the WTO, the latest in 2014. Although settled between the two parties, bilateral settlements such as these do not resolve the overall unfairness from the perspective of other developing countries that depend on cotton exports. In four poor West African countries alone (Benin, Burkina Faso, Chad and Mali), 10 million people depend on revenues from cotton (Pelc, 2014). These countries cannot afford the costs of bringing WTO legal actions. Nor do they have influence in the corridors of power in Washington, DC. By contrast, farming in both the US and Brazil is dominated by large agribusinesses that have considerable influence on political leaders. US agribusinesses and insurance companies that handle the payout schemes have been highly effective in lobbying politicians to perpetuate subsidies from public funds, despite their illegality under WTO rules (Pelc, 2014). Farmers in Africa would have hoped for an outcome from the WTO that focused on justice for all stakeholder countries involved in cotton trading.

International regulation of trade

The Brazilian cotton farmers' deals with US authorities resolved trade disputes between the two countries only in the short term. Continuing subsidies to US cotton growers will probably prompt Brazil to launch new claims for redress. Meanwhile, the distortions in global markets remain. This unsatisfactory situation highlights the need for multilateral agreements to promote fairness in world trade for member countries – large and small, rich and poor. The WTO's predecessor framework dates from the immediate aftermath of the Second World War. The preceding era, scarred by the Great Depression of the 1930s, had seen protectionism and a decline in world trade. Indeed, it was in that period that that the US government began its farm subsidy programmes to support farming communities in hardship. Under the **Bretton Woods agreement** reached at a conference of the allied nations in 1944, exchange rate stability would be achieved by pegging every currency to gold or the US dollar (see Chapter 8). It also envisaged **multilateral** treaties as a means of dismantling barriers to trade. Negotiators laid plans for an international trade organization (ITO) to bring down tariff barriers, but the charter eventually drawn up in 1948 met with little enthusiasm from nations still reluctant to endorse free trade. Instead, a more modest set of proposals for a weaker institutional framework was formulated – the **General Agreement on Tariffs and Trade (GATT)**.

Under the GATT, successive rounds of negotiations brought about global trade liberalization, leading to the establishment in 1995 of the WTO, which is reminiscent of the stronger body envisaged in the early days after the war. The WTO now has 161 member states. Building on the GATT, the WTO oversees a global framework for multilateral agreements.

GATT principles

The GATT provided the principles and foundation for the development of a global trading system which were carried forward into the WTO. Perhaps the most important of these is non-discrimination, or the **most-favoured-nation (MFN)** principle. There are two aspects to this principle:

1 Favourable tariff treatment negotiated with one country will be extended to similar goods from all countries.

2 Under the principle of 'national treatment', imported goods are treated for all purposes in the same way as domestic goods of the same type.

MFN status is negotiated between countries, and while it is the norm among trading partners, there are exceptions. US legislation has linked MFN treatment with human rights records. Because of its poor human rights record, China was granted only temporary MFN status from 1980 onwards, which was renewed annually. Unconditional MFN status came in 2000, paving the way for China's WTO membership. After years of negotiation, Russia joined the WTO only in 2012, becoming the last of the BRIC countries to join.

Other GATT principles include reciprocity, requiring tariff reductions by one country to be matched by its trading partners; and transparency, ensuring that the underlying aims of all trade measures are clear. The principle of fairness allows a country which has suffered from unfair trading practices by a trading partner to take protectionist measures against that country. Defining fair practice is at the heart of many trade disputes, as countries naturally have differing perspectives on what is and is not fair. An example is **dumping**, or the sale of goods abroad at below the price charged for comparable goods in the producing country. The GATT **anti-dumping agreement** of 1994 allows anti-dumping duties to be imposed on the exporting country by the importing country in order to protect local producers from unfair competition. The country which makes allegations of dumping against another asks the WTO to investigate the matter. The annual number of investigations initiated by the WTO reached a peak of nearly 300 in 2013, but fell back to 200 in 2014, which was roughly the norm for the previous decade (Global Antidumping, 2015). China is by far the most frequently cited country alleged to be engaged in dumping, and the countries which launched the most anti-dumping complaints are India and Brazil, not – as one might expect – the advanced western economies.

The Uruguay Round, culminating in the GATT 1994, laid the groundwork for future trade liberalization, while allowing countries to take limited steps to safeguard national industries. It resulted in worldwide tariff reductions of about 40% on manufactured goods. Less spectacularly, it made strides in the more difficult areas of reducing trade barriers in agricultural products and textiles. It also initiated agreements on intellectual property rights and services, both crucial areas in growing world trade. The agreement on **Trade-Related Aspects of Intellectual Property Rights (TRIPS)** was a landmark agreement designed to provide a framework by which developing countries would implement stronger IP laws while also having the right to issue a 'compulsory licence' to use medicines under patent. The compulsory licence would be appropriate when the society's public health is at risk, and the country is unable to afford the prices charged by the global pharmaceutical companies. Finally, the GATT 1994 created the WTO as its successor institution.

WTO and the regulation of world trade

Whereas in 1947 the GATT created only a weak institutional framework, the WTO, which came into being in 1995, was designed on firmer legal footing, with a stronger rule-governed orientation. This approach is reflected in its organizational structure. A Ministerial Conference, consisting of trade ministers of all member states, is the main policymaking body, which meets every two years. Under the **Dispute Settlement Understanding (DSU)**, the WTO oversees a dispute settlement procedure for specific trade disputes between countries. This new legal procedure for resolving disputes marks a departure from the GATT procedure, which had no power of enforcement.

The WTO procedure aims to resolve trade disputes through impartial panels before they escalate into damaging trade wars in which countries take unilateral action against each other. A country which feels it has suffered because of another's breach of trading rules may apply to the WTO, which appoints an impartial panel for hearing the case within a specified timetable. A country found to be in breach of trade rules by a panel may appeal to the Appellate Body. If it is again found to be in the wrong, the WTO may authorize the country whose trade has suffered as a result to impose retaliatory trade sanctions.

For the WTO's procedure to succeed, countries must adhere to its decisions even when they disagree with them. All countries enjoy a recognized right to safeguard national interests, but this principle, as well as interpretation of WTO rules themselves, is subject to considerable latitude in interpretation. If countries impose unilateral sanctions, bypassing the WTO, then WTO procedures, and the authority that underlies them, could be eroded. The US law known as Section 301 is such a provision. Originally enacted in the Trade Act 1974, it was strengthened in 1988 to 'Special 301'. It authorizes the US Trade Representative (USTR) to identify the policies or practices of countries that are considered unreasonable in their interpretation of WTO rules and that restrict US trade. A country singled out is placed on a 'watch list' or a 'priority watch list', leading to the possible imposition of unilateral sanctions by the US. A country could lose access to the entire US market, not merely that of the offending product.

The legislation has been criticized for its aggressive unilateral approach, which flies in the face of WTO rules. A country could be in compliance with all multilateral and bilateral agreements to which it is bound, but nonetheless be targeted with US sanctions. Monitoring by the USTR has focused on intellectual property (IP) rights, relevant to medicines under pharmaceutical patents and copyright material. The TRIPS agreement specifies that parties are obliged to use the WTO's dispute settlement procedure in case of disputes, and unilateral sanctions such as the Special 301 procedures are prohibited (Flynn, 2010). Indeed, it is arguable that the watch lists themselves are in breach of WTO rules, notably the GATT's most-favoured-nation principle. However, the US has continued to use Special 301 procedures, and indeed, the number of actions increased following the TRIPS agreement. India, which has a thriving generic medicine sector, has particularly been targeted, although it is in breach of no treaties. The aggressive US stance stems in large part from the power of the country's large pharmaceutical companies, who feel threatened by generic producers (see Chapter 9). The targets of US unilateral actions over IP rights are invariably developing countries, highlighting the truth that in trading relations, the rich and powerful usually get their way against the weaker countries.

The way I see it ...

'Trade policy done right now is how we protect American workers and jobs, create a more fair and level playing field, and ensure that is the United States that leads in defining the rules of the road.'

US Trade Representative, Michael Froman, in a statement on the *President's 2015 Trade Policy Agenda*, Press Release, March 2015, at www.ustr.gov

How might countries that trade with the US react to this statement of official US trade policy?

The WTO's multilateral system was designed to offer a level playing field for all developed and developing countries. However, we have seen how the multilateral system is undermined in a number of ways. The example of the Brazil cotton settlement is one. The unilateral imposition of sanctions by the US is another. And, finally, there is the growing use of the investor-state dispute settlement process (the ISDS), discussed in Chapter 6. There, we noted concerns over the legitimacy, transparency, consistency and impartiality of these arbitration processes. The US has pressed for the ISDS process to be included in two plurilateral treaties – the Trans-Pacific Partnership (TPP) and the Transatlantic Trade and Investment Partnership (TTIP). Countries in both the Pacific and European negotiations have raised criticisms of this process, discussed in a later section. The ISDS is the subject of the case study that follows.

CASE STUDY ON THE CHANGING GLOBAL ENVIRONMENT

The fuel additive that sparks international controversy

Fuel additives go back a long way – to the 1920s, when new models from Ford and General Motors were shaping the American market. The chemical company, Ethyl Corporation of the US, in conjunction with General Motors, introduced lead as an additive to petrol (gasoline), to reduce 'knock' in the more powerful car engines, making them run more smoothly. Even then, lead, a heavy metal, was well known to be poisonous and harmful in engine exhausts, but in tiny amounts performed a useful function. The use of lead in petrol became widespread by the 1940s. By the 1980s, evidence of the risk of lead poisoning had grown, and the US Congress imposed a ban on lead in petrol. Meanwhile, Ethyl had shifted its sights to marketing its lead additive in developing countries. It had also developed another additive, MMT, as a substitute for lead in the US market. MMT was widely sold from the 1970s onwards. Based on another heavy metal, manganese, MMT was also controversial, as it is considered to be a neurotoxin. Like lead, MMT poses particular neurological health risks for children. MMT is also highly pollutant in the atmosphere, raising the level of emissions from car exhausts. Ethyl persisted, marketing its lead additive in developing countries and pressing the case for MMT in developed countries. It had mixed success in the US, where there was resistance to it. California banned it in 1976; in most places it was legal, although not widely used. Ethyl also exported MMT to Canada.

In 1997, Canada passed a law banning MMT. This move might have put a definitive block on its sale. However, the creation of NAFTA (the North American Free Trade Agreement) in 1994 offered Ethyl Corporation an opportunity to effectively overturn the legislation. Ethyl launched proceedings under the investor-state dispute settlement (ISDS) provision of NAFTA, suing the Canadian government for damages for lost income. Ethyl's case was based on the potential loss of profits due to the ban on sales of MMT in Canada. The case would be heard by a tribunal convened under the treaty provision.

The Canadian government, conscious of rising legal costs, concluded that Ethyl was likely to win its case in the tribunal. The potential loss of sales would be the key issue for the tribunal, and matters of public health would not be considered. The Canadian government thus backed down, and agreed to pay US$13 million in compensation to Ethyl. The government repealed the ban, and issued a statement that the fuel additive was not a risk to human health or the environment. Ethyl was, in effect, able to veto legislation of the Canadian parliament that had been passed in the interest of public health. This backdown encouraged Ethyl to continue marketing MMT worldwide. By the time of the Canadian ban, MMT had long been banned in California and much of the Eastern US. Most US oil refiners were not using MMT, pointing out that there were cheap, safe and less pollutant alternatives available, such as ethanol. Motor manufacturers, too, were concerned that MMT caused damage to engines, hampering the electronic systems that monitor exhaust gases, therefore increasing emissions of harmful greenhouse gases (Minjares and Walsh, 2009).

Ethyl Corporation was renamed Afton Chemical in 2004. Afton has continued to pursue a strategy of marketing MMT aggressively. The company states that the product is legally sold in 53 countries, but does not publish their names on its website (www.aftonchemical.com, accessed 2 December 2015). Research has indicated that, like lead, manganese entering the bloodstream can cause brain damage. Afton points to numerous studies on MMT, but these often tend to be written by researchers with links to Afton, and therefore are not independent. There is a consensus among carmakers, refinery companies and public health bodies, all of which raise objections to MMT. Carmakers say it is damaging to catalytic converters in car engines. Oil refiners exclude manganese additives in most of the developed world. Afton has unsuccessfully challenged an EU directive, losing its appeal in the European Court of Justice. Afton was aided by the US government, which, in a diplomatic initiative, urged the EU Commission not to impose a ban on MMT. This was despite the fact that MMT is banned in reformulated gasoline in the US, which comprises two-thirds of the fuel market.

In South Africa, MMT and lead were banned in petrol in 2006. Nonetheless, the Department of Energy announced in 2012 that MMT would be approved from 2017. However, a draft standard prepared in 2014 did not mention MMT, urging the adoption of bioethanol as a substitute which would serve the same function. The Department of Energy maintained that both MMT and bioethanol would be allowed. Motor industry and oil executives in South Africa expressed disappointment at this ambiguity, having hoped for the introduction of international vehicle emissions standards. They had prospects of increasing the market in premium models with the highest levels of technology. There are also concerns over public health and vehicle emissions. Despite the tide of objections from motor manufacturers, oil companies and public health officials, it seems certain that Afton will do its utmost to sell MMT wherever it can.

Sources: Traynor, K. (1998) 'How Canada became a shill for Ethyl Corporation', Canadian Environmental Law Association, 23(3), July–September, at www.cela.ca; Monbiot, G. (1998) 'Running on MMT', *The Guardian*, 13 August, at www.theguardian.com; Furlonger, D. (2014) 'Hazardous fuel additive raises its head', *Business Day*, 5 May, at www.bdlive.co.za; Minjares, R. and Walsh, M. (2009) *Methylcyclopentadienyl Manganese Tricarbonyl (MMT): A Science and Policy Review*, January, International Council on Clean Transportation, at www.theicct.org.

Questions for discussion

- What are the objections to MMT as an additive in petrol?
- What are the lessons of the Canadian case for other countries involved in trade and investment treaties, such as the Transatlantic Trade and Investment Partnership, which include ISDS clauses?
- How has Ethyl, now Afton, managed to spread the use of MMT in numerous markets, despite the known risks?
- Assess Afton Chemical in terms of corporate social responsibility.

Multilateralism in crisis

The WTO has made a dramatic impact in focusing international attention on issues of world trade, and it has also sparked considerable controversy. Since its creation in 1995, issues of globalization and the rise of developing nations have come to the fore, involving WTO in wider debates. Its meetings have been targeted by demonstrators, from anti-capitalist protesters to environmental activists. In addition,

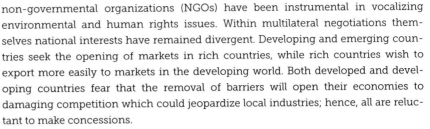

non-governmental organizations (NGOs) have been instrumental in vocalizing environmental and human rights issues. Within multilateral negotiations themselves national interests have remained divergent. Developing and emerging countries seek the opening of markets in rich countries, while rich countries wish to export more easily to markets in the developing world. Both developed and developing countries fear that the removal of barriers will open their economies to damaging competition which could jeopardize local industries; hence, all are reluctant to make concessions.

An ambitious round of multilateral trade negotiations, known as the Doha Round, commenced in Doha, Qatar, in 2001. Negotiations continued at several ministerial conferences which followed, but the major policy areas which had been carried forward from the Uruguay Round generated a sharp divergence of perspectives, mainly between developed and developing countries. It was intended that the Doha agreement would be in place by the end of 2008, but negotiations faltered once again, and the deteriorating global economic situation at the time seemed to dampen national leaders' appetites for further multilateral talks. Areas in which agreement was sought included agriculture, rules for trade in services, and access to patented drugs. Other issues were labour standards, environmental protection, and competition policy. Doha was described as a 'development' round, focusing on issues central to developing countries. These countries have been firm in their view that progress must be made by rich countries in reducing farm subsidies and tariffs. However, it became clear that the interests of the large emerging economies, such as Brazil, diverged from those of the smaller and poorer developing countries, as we saw in Brazil's dispute with the US on cotton subsidies.

The appointment of a Brazilian, Roberto Azevêdo, as director-general of the WTO, in 2013, seemed to confirm the growing voice of developing countries in global trade policies. However, the hoped-for conclusion of the Doha Round, in December 2013 in Bali, rapidly turned into disappointment. The Bali meeting focused on a Trade Facilitation Agreement (TFA), designed to cut the red tape required of businesses when sending goods across national borders, including goods in transit, which are crucial to global supply chains. The TFA was particularly championed by the US, mindful of the globalization strategies of America's large multinationals. The TFA had wide support, but was blocked by objections from India, which refused to agree unless the US dropped objections to India's system of subsidies and price support for farmers. These are based on concerns for food security, and help to guarantee food for the country's poor. These policies are criticized by the US, but through a 'peace clause' due to expire in 2017, the US has refrained from challenging them through a WTO dispute process. In November 2014, India and the US struck an accord, India agreeing to the TFA, and the US withdrawing its threat to initiate a formal complaint on the expiry of the peace clause. India had been accused of trying to wreck the Bali agreement by raising an objection which, on the face of it, had nothing to do with reducing red tape. In a seemingly ironic twist, US objections to India's subsidies are echoed by governments of some of the world's least-developed countries. Thanks to farm support programmes, India began producing more commodity grains than it consumed, and became the largest exporter of cereals to the least-developed countries of Africa. In these agrarian economies, cheap imports from India make it difficult for domestic farmers to compete.

The India-US conflict had highlighted the difficulties that had troubled the Doha Round for over a decade. The WTO has focused on trade liberalization as the primary goal, assuming it to be beneficial to all countries. This assumption underlies its approach to both trade negotiations and dispute settlement. However, as the Doha Round foundered, it became clear that countries have divergent interests economically, and that broad issues such as societal goals and environmental concerns should also be taken into account.

The liberalizing of trade in services has been an aspiration of multilateral talks, but the Doha Round made no progress. An initiative from the US has seen the coming together of 23 parties, including the US and EU, in negotiations for a Trade in Services Agreement (TiSA). This covers services like financial services, ecommerce and health. It also covers the industrial sector, including mining services such as fracking. Although talks have taken place behind closed doors, it has emerged that the draft agreement provides for 'technological neutrality', which is equivalent to a level playing field (Inman, 2015). The implication is that fracking companies or others in fossil-fuel extraction would be able to bring a case to a tribunal under the ISDS process if a government subsidizes renewable energy investment. The TiSA would thus seem to be striking a blow against efforts to combat climate change.

India and the US: trade clashes reveal differing national priorities

Look at arguments on both sides in the trade positions of India and the US. Can they be reconciled, and how?

Regional, bilateral and plurilateral trade agreements

Running in parallel with the WTO's activities, countries have been active in making their own agreements with trading partners, both within their own geographical regions and beyond. It is common to make a distinction between a **bilateral** agreement, between just two countries, often just called a **free trade agreement (FTA)**, and a **regional trade agreement (RTA)** among a number of countries in the same broad geographic region. However, from the WTO's perspective, both types of agreement, which lie outside the multilateral system, are treated broadly as regional trade agreements. The RTA is often referred to as a 'preferential trade agreement' (PTA), reflecting the fact that its terms give preference to goods and services from countries which are parties to the particular agreement. The number of RTAs (including bilateral agreements) notified to the WTO has grown dramatically in recent years. In 2015 the total number of RTAs in force was 262, and the total number notified to the WTO was 406 (WTO, 2015). Member countries are highly likely to also be WTO members, creating overlapping ties, as shown in Figure 7.8. What is more, the prospect of new **plurilateral trade agreements**, between many countries, such as the proposed Trans-Pacific Partnership (TPP) and Transatlantic Trade and Investment Partnership (TTIP), constitute further overlapping obligations. The overlap is particularly evident in dispute resolution, as shown in Figure 7.8. In any dispute, there could be three or more routes available, which could be pursued simultaneously. They include national legal systems of member countries, ISDS and the WTO's dispute settlement system.

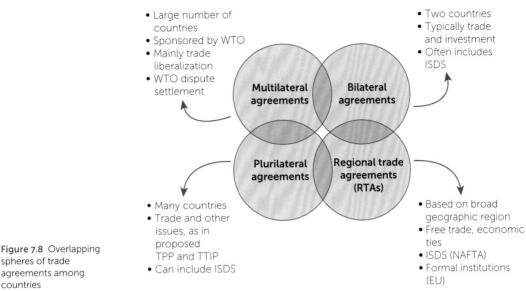

- Large number of
  countries
- Sponsored by WTO
- Mainly trade
  liberalization
- WTO dispute
  settlement

- Two countries
- Typically trade
  and investment
- Often includes
  ISDS

Multilateral agreements

Bilateral agreements

Plurilateral agreements

Regional trade agreements (RTAs)

- Many countries
- Trade and other
  issues, as in
  proposed
  TPP and TTIP
- Can include ISDS

- Based on broad
  geographic region
- Free trade, economic
  ties
- ISDS (NAFTA)
- Formal institutions
  (EU)

Figure 7.8 Overlapping spheres of trade agreements among countries

Categories of regional trade agreement

Countries look naturally to trade with their neighbours. Not only does regional trade make sense in terms of costs, firms are likely to have greater familiarity with firms and industries in their own region than with those oceans away. RTAs are designed to bring down trade barriers among their member states, thus opening up regional markets for national producers. A group of countries which have joined in an RTA are sometimes referred to as a **free trade area** or bloc. The RTA can cover a range of issues besides trade, including investment, intellectual property protection and environmental protection. Political considerations can play a key role, as economic integration is inseparable from the political power balance within any region, and regional trading blocs are influential in global politics. We begin by looking at the categories of regional groupings, expanded from the one originally devised by Bela Balassa in *The Theory of Economic Integration* (Balassa, 1962). They can be categorized accordingly:

- **Free trade area** – Member states agree to remove trade barriers among themselves, but keep their separate national barriers against trade with non-member states.
- **Customs union** – Member states remove all trade barriers among themselves and adopt a common set of external barriers.
- **Common market** – Member states enjoy free movement of goods, labour and capital.
- **Economic union** – Member states unify all their economic policies, including monetary, fiscal and welfare policies.
- **Political union** – Member states transfer sovereignty to the regional political and lawmaking institutions, creating a new 'superstate'.

Most of the world's nations belong to at least one regional grouping, the vast majority of which fall into the first two categories – free trade area and customs union (see Table 7.1). The categories can be seen as successive steps towards deepening economic integration. Only the EU has reached the stage of economic union. Political union is still some way off, but reforms in 2009 enhanced the role of the European Parliament, discussed in Chapter 6. Free trade areas are now in place in all the world's regions, although with less regional economic integration than in Europe.

Table 7.1 Regional trade groupings

Region	Group	Current member countries	Date of formation	Type of agreement
South America	Mercosur (Southern Common Market)	Argentina, Brazil, Paraguay, Uruguay, Venezuela	1991	Common market
South America	Andean Community	Bolivia, Colombia, Ecuador, Peru	1969	Customs union
Asia-Pacific	APEC (Asia-Pacific Economic Cooperation)	21 countries: Australia, Brunei, Canada, Indonesia, Japan, South Korea, Malaysia, New Zealand, Philippines, Singapore, Thailand, US, China, Hong Kong, Taiwan, Mexico, Papua New Guinea, Chile, Peru, Russia, Vietnam	1989	Co-operation group
South East Asia	ASEAN (Association of Southeast Asian Nations)	Indonesia, Malaysia, Philippines, Singapore, Thailand, Brunei, Cambodia, Laos, Myanmar (Burma), Vietnam	1967	Free trade area
Caribbean	CARICOM (Caribbean Community)	15 Caribbean nations: Antigua, Bahamas, Barbados, Belize, Dominica, Grenada, Guyana, Haiti, Jamaica, Monserrat, St Lucia, St Kitts and Nevis, Trinidad & Tobago	1973	Common market
Europe	EFTA (European Free Trade Area)	Iceland, Switzerland, Norway, Liechtenstein	1960	Free trade area
Europe	EU (European Union)	Austria, Belgium, Denmark, France, Finland, Germany, Greece, Ireland, Italy, Luxembourg, the Netherlands, Portugal, Spain, Sweden, UK, Czech Republic, Poland, Hungary, Slovenia, Slovakia, Estonia, Lithuania, Latvia, Cyprus, Malta, Romania, Bulgaria, Croatia	1957	Economic union, moving towards political union
North and Central America	NAFTA (North American Free Trade Agreement)	Canada, Mexico, US	1994	Free trade area
Africa	ECOWAS (Economic Community of West African States)	15 members: Benin, Burkina Faso, Cote d'Ivoire, Gambia, Ghana, Guinea, Guinea Bissau, Liberia, Mali, Niger, Nigeria, Senegal, Sierra Leone, Togo, Cape Verde	1975	Customs union
Africa	EAC (East African Community)	Kenya, Tanzania, Uganda, Rwanda, Burundi	2001	Common market

Regional trade groupings – and beyond

The world's large geographic regions differ in the extent to which regional neighbours trade with each other. RTAs are intended to foster intra-regional trade, and in some notable cases, such as the EU and NAFTA, they have been effective. In other regions, such as Asia, intra-regional trade thrives, although the causes are more to do with supply chains. The extent of intra-regional trade is shown in Figure 7.9.

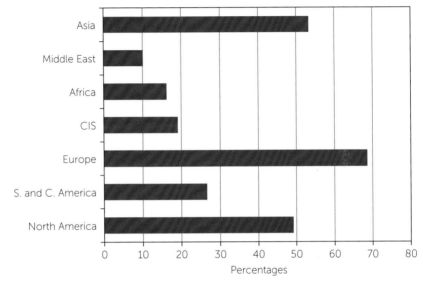

Figure 7.9 Share of regional trade flows in each region's total merchandise exports, 2013

Source: Data from WTO (2014) *International Trade Statistics 2014*, Table 1.4, p. 23, at www.wto.org.

Note: CIS is the Commonwealth of Independent States (including Russia).

As Figure 7.9 shows, Europe is the region with the largest intra-regional trade flows, facilitated by the **European Union (EU)** (http://europa.eu). The second most integrated region in terms of trade is Asia, home to the manufacturing powerhouses of China, Japan and South Korea. Intra-regional trade in North America has been dominated by the large US market for goods from Mexico and Canada. The other three regions shown in Figure 7.9 have low levels of intra-regional trade, despite the existence of numerous RTAs. In this section we look in turn at the major geographic regions, describing the free trade groupings in each, along with regional variations and prospects for the future. We begin with Europe.

European countries trade mainly with each other. In the EU, the Single European Act of 1987 aimed to dismantle internal barriers and establish a single market by 1992. Businesses would be able to move seamlessly from one member country to another, without bureaucratic frontier procedures. Product standards would be recognized between member states. Financial services would be liberalized, so that firms such as banks and insurance companies could compete across national borders.

In reality, progress in internal liberalization has been neither as swift nor as easy as many predicted back in 1987. Legacies of protected industries and varying degrees of state ownership have slowed progress. Deeply-rooted national cultural differences were underestimated, and domestic political considerations have loomed large. The latter have sparked continuing debate on principles of sovereignty and national identity, and also the economic interests of groups of workers affected by liberalization.

As Table 7.1 shows, Europe has long had a free trade area co-existing with the EU. The **European Free Trade Area (EFTA)** was formed in 1960 by countries not signed up to the Treaty of Rome. They were Austria, Denmark, Norway, Portugal, Sweden, Switzerland and the UK. They were later joined by Iceland and Finland. As most of these countries joined the EU, EFTA has four remaining members, as shown in Table 7.1. With the exception of Switzerland, EFTA members have joined the EU in a wider **European Economic Area (EEA)**, which is a free trade area. The UK could conceivably become part of the EEA following its exit from the EU.

In the Americas, the Andean Pact, later changed to the **Andean Community** (www.comunidadandina.org) is the oldest of the regional trade groupings. Political instability in the 1970s set back plans to establish a customs union. With the upsurge in global commodities markets that occurred in the 1980s, South American countries saw economic gains from commodity exports. The two largest traders, Brazil and Argentina, joined forces in 1988 to form a grouping which became **Mercosur** (www.mercosur.org) with the addition of Paraguay and Uruguay. These countries are all associate members of the Andean Community. Similarly, Andean Community member countries are associate members of Mercosur. Venezuela, one of the continent's largest trading nations, and also an oil exporter, applied to join Mercosur in 2006, and is now a full member.

The **North American Free Trade Agreement (NAFTA)** (www.naftanow.org/), which came into effect in 1994, comprises the US, Canada and Mexico. While NAFTA does not envisage the degree of economic integration of the EU, its provisions and future developments raise similar issues, including political concerns and the question of sovereignty. Elimination of tariffs on manufactured goods were at the heart of NAFTA. NAFTA's investment rules allow investors from any of the three countries to be treated in the same way as domestic investors. These rules apply to both FDI and portfolio investment. For settling disputes, NAFTA introduced the investor-state dispute settlement (ISDS) (discussed in Chapter 6), which, it was thought, was needed to protect US and Canadian investors in Mexico. Over time, the dozens of cases launched, mainly by US corporations, have frequently targeted Canada, which has been compelled to pay out large sums in compensation.

Unlike the EU, NAFTA operates no common external trade policy. Also in contrast to the EU, it has no formal institutions. At its inception, NAFTA aimed to increase exports between partners, who already traded heavily with each other, and to create jobs in all three countries. The trade is uneven, however. In 2013, 80% of Mexico's exports went to the US, but only 14% of US exports went to Mexico. Mexico is thus vulnerable to any economic downturn in America. Mexican GDP per capita has doubled since NAFTA came into effect, but in 2013, was still only one-fifth that of the US. In the US there is a perception that US jobs have been lost to cheap labour in Mexico. The US has had 'Buy American' laws on the statute books since the protectionist era of the 1930s, and these laws, both at federal and individual state levels, have seen a resurgence (Ikenson, 2014). Such laws are unsettling for Mexico and other trading partners of the US. Moreover, in the world of global supply chains, finding the pure American product can be frustrating for authorities determined to strictly implement such laws.

Asia's economies vary from the small city state of Singapore to the industrial giants, China and Japan. Despite some cultural affinities among the many Asian countries, they are diverse in their economies and political systems. The

Association of Southeast Asian Nations (ASEAN) (www.asean.org) brings together ten South East Asian countries (see Table 7.1). Even among these economies, there is considerable diversity and differing levels of economic development. Singapore has developed as an FDI-oriented market economy with rather autocratic political rule, while Vietnam is a poorer country, whose communist leadership is keen to foster economic growth and market reforms. For these countries, links in global supply chains are key to development. A new free trade agreement has been made between China and the six founder members of ASEAN (Brunei, Indonesia, Malaysia, Philippines, Singapore and Thailand). This agreement, which came into effect in January 2010, is the world's largest free trade agreement, covering a population of 1.9 billion people. It eliminates tariffs on 90% of imported goods.

The **Asia-Pacific Economic Cooperation (APEC)** (www.apec.org) is the other large regional grouping, although it lacks the coherence of most free trade areas. It is hardly regional, as its members, all bordering the Pacific, are located on three different continents. As yet, it does not function as a free trade area, and its large size, encompassing more than half of the world's economic output, makes it rather different from regional groupings. Its members attend regular summits at which bilateral agreements are negotiated. A proposed Free Trade Area of the Asia-Pacific (FTAAP) was endorsed in 2014. The FTAAP is being supported by China, giving rise to potential conflict with the US, which is pressing for conclusion of the smaller Trans-Pacific Partnership (TPP), an overlapping plurilateral agreement that would exclude China.

African countries, many of which are rich in oil and other natural resources, are becoming increasingly important in world trade. Co-operative agreements focusing on regional trade, in the western, southern and eastern regions, have not as yet led to deepening regional integration (see Figure 7.9). Poverty and poor governance have combined with internal instability in many countries, which has spilt over into regional conflicts. These have all been factors in slowing the economic development that Africans had hoped for as post-colonial independent states. A number of regional co-operative agreements have been entered into, often with overlapping membership. One of the oldest and most developed at the institutional level is the **Economic Community of West African States (ECOWAS)** (www.ecowas.int), which has a Commission, Parliament and Court of Justice. The Commission's specialized agencies focus on development projects in areas such as health and sport. The **East African Community (EAC)** (www.eac.int), which started as a free trade area, became a customs union and is now being transformed into a common market. From mid-2010, goods have flowed tariff-free across the national borders of five of its member countries (Burundi, Kenya, Rwanda, Tanzania and Uganda). Kenya is the largest of these economies, with well positioned retailers, manufacturers and banks which hope to gain from the common market. The smaller countries also stand to gain, with better transport and the opportunity to build more competitive manufacturing industries than they could achieve individually. By coming together, these countries' manufacturers could begin to compete with imports from China. In 2013, EAC members signed a protocol to set up a monetary union to be implemented gradually over the next ten years. It would create a common currency, harmonize monetary and fiscal policies, and be overseen by a common central bank.

By 2014, the shine might have worn off the idea of monetary union, in light of the problems experienced in Greece, a eurozone member on the verge of sovereign default. However, there are only five countries in the EAC, and there is nothing like the economic and political divergence that prevails in the EU. The EU is the world's largest trading bloc, with considerable political integration. Each member state's sovereign status is overlaid with the legal recognition of the EU itself as having status to negotiate trade deals, raising the potential for policy disagreements among member states. These have come to the fore in talks with the US over a **Transatlantic Trade and Investment Partnership (TTIP)**. This would be considered a plurilateral agreement, covering many states, although in practice, there have been only two sets of negotiators: the European Commission and the US Trade Representative. The precedent for the TTIP is the US initiative for the Pacific countries, to which we turn first.

Talks to create the **Trans-Pacific Partnership (TPP)** go back to 2010. They involved 11 countries at that time: Australia, Brunei, Canada, Chile, Malaysia, Mexico, New Zealand, Peru, Singapore, the US and Vietnam. Japan joined the talks in 2013. These countries overlap with the two Asian regional groupings and with NAFTA. Negotiations have been classified as secret. US corporations have been involved, but not members of Congress. The officially secret status of the talks has raised suspicions among members of Congress and civil society organizations. While trade issues, such as reducing barriers to imports, are involved, it has become clear that priority is being given to enhanced protection for IP rights, which would mainly benefit the large US companies in the pharmaceutical, software and entertainment sectors. These extra protections would exceed those in existing trade agreements, and have been a cause of concern for the smaller countries, especially over access to medicines. Also adding to their fears is the inclusion of a clause providing for the ISDS mechanism. Many bilateral negotiations have taken place under the broad TPP umbrella. Talks between the US and Japan over trade barriers in food and motor vehicles continued into 2015. The TTP was finally agreed and signed in October 2015, but would need to be ratifed by all the participating countries.

The TTIP has been more ambitious in its scope, talks having begun in 2013. Trade in goods and services are only one aspect of the talks. Another is known as 'regulatory co-operation', including non-tariff barriers to trade in respect of both goods and services (EU Commission, 2015). The EU has strict regulatory regimes in a number of areas, including employment rights, labour rights, human health and the environment. In all these areas, US laws are less stringent, and there has been a fear that the US position would prevail, weakening much EU protective legislation and undermining the social priorities of many member governments. There are fears among EU countries that any deal would allow imports of food containing GMOs and hormone-treated beef. Other issues in this category are environmental rules and rules on animal health and welfare. In the area of services, health services and education are areas in which the US would see opportunities for its companies to make inroads in EU countries as public services become increasingly privatized. The secrecy of the negotiations has added to public concerns, notably voiced by Members of the European Parliament. They have also objected to the inclusion of the investor-state dispute settlement (ISDS). The possible dilution of much regulatory legislation, combined with advantages to investors from the ISDS, suggest that the US position is based on facilitating the expansion of its large corporations. For many in the EU, opposition to the TTIP has rested on the view that facilitating the ascendancy of American corporate interests risks undermining democracy.

Concerns over food safety and animal welfare have turned many European consumers against the TTIP.

Source: Photoalto.

Globalization and world trade: challenges and responsibilities

Changing patterns in world trade have accompanied the global shift in manufacturing towards Asia. China stands out as the leading new trading power, and other developing countries are following its example of attracting export-oriented manufacturing. In China, economic growth has rested on rapid industrialization and urbanization, which has seen rising GDP per capita, but also high levels of pollution and increased risks to health. Economic data look flattering, but daily life for millions of workers has not matched expectations of continuing improvement that China's market transformation had promised. The rise of Asia as a force in global trade has been associated, above all, with global supply chains. Political leaders in China take credit for their development model delivering rising prosperity, but on them falls the main responsibility for dealing with the social challenges of improving well-being in a society where people now aspire to a better quality of life, not just in economic terms, but in terms of meeting human needs. This is, of course, a goal of development in the broad sense. It has proved more elusive to attain than China's economic goals and growing role in world trade. Can trade and sustainability be conceived as going hand in hand?

A challenge for both companies and governments is to meet human needs and sustain development goals in the context of growing corporate power in supply chains in which global companies are in a position to dictate their own terms – terms that are likely to be profit-oriented above all. Developed regions of the world, including the US and UK, have mourned the loss of manufacturing jobs, while global companies based in these countries have profited hugely from outsourced production to Asia and other developing regions. The global brands that have driven the rise in trade in intermediate goods have benefited from location advantages of low-cost labour, weak employment protection laws, and numerous policies instituted by governments to smooth the flow of cross-border trade. In the sector of resources, global trading companies in commodities, mining and financial services have benefited from surging Chinese demand for resources and energy. With that growth now slowing, new challenges of sustainability and public expectations are becoming more urgent, for governments and for businesses.

Resources are often seen as a 'curse' in developing countries, with rewards flowing to corporate and sectoral interests rather than towards providing public goods. In the best scenario, countries manage resource wealth responsibly, looking to share wealth with all in society. Trade can, and should, follow sustainable development goals. But this is an ideal, rather than reality, requiring governments to focus on public goods rather than political self-interest. And it also requires the large companies, that are essential to the dynamics of world trade, to shift from a focus on corporate profit maximization towards social goals and human needs. Most MNEs nowadays speak of sustainability and corporate social responsibility (CSR) as part of their global outlook, but how far does this go? Large trading and mining companies typically include CSR projects such as education and training in their investment projects in developing countries. However beneficial, these projects are ultimately in the hands of corporate providers who, if business conditions deteriorate, exit the country, setting back development goals. Cargill had been active in Zimbabwe since 1996, largely in cotton farming and cotton processing, involving CSR training schemes for the cotton farmers with whom it had contracts. When returns fell, the company exited these activities in 2014, but continued trading activities in grains. Although exports in agriculture and mining (including gold, platinum and diamonds) would potentially provide the country with the basis of sustainable development, Zimbabwe is one of the world's poorest countries, dependent on food imports. It has been ruled for 35 years by a repressive president, Robert Mugabe, who has presided over continuing high levels of poverty and setbacks in human well-being, dimming aspirations for legitimate democratic government. The example of Zimbabwe shows that responsibilities for broad goals of accountability and sustainable development from trade must be shared by both governmental and corporate actors.

The resource curse and developing countries

To what extent does responsibility lie with large foreign investors when the resource curse strikes developing countries?

Conclusions

A country with no trade at all would be a distinctly dismal place to live. No country is self-sufficient in the many areas that make up what we would consider essential to minimal living standards, including food, natural resources, manufacturing capacity and energy. The closed economy would inevitably be poor, probably relying on subsistence agriculture, with little scope for human development. But it does not follow from this depressing picture that free trade is unqualifiedly good. Zimbabwe, as we have seen, enjoys the benefits of trade, but life for the average Zimbabwean is hardly better than what we have just described. Cargill's executive chairman extols the merits of Ricardo's theory of comparative advantage: countries should produce what they are best at, using the revenues from exports to import other goods (Page, 2014). However, we no longer live in the nineteenth century. Globalization has opened up wide inequalities in trade, and, indeed, in the nineteenth century, trade was controlled by imperial powers. Those in the driving seat nowadays are global companies from the large trading nations, presiding over complex supply chains through which they are able to extract value. They are usually aided by the trade policies of the governments in their home countries, and by compliant co-operation in partner countries keen to attract investment. The smallholder in Africa is likely to be tied into a deal with a large foreign agribusiness company that exerts decisive control over not only production, but all processing and transport. Increasingly, through the global strategies of MNEs, foreign investment has been the facilitator of trade, aided by governments of both investing and host countries.

Trade liberalization, sponsored by the WTO and its predecessor, the GATT, aspired to bring the benefits of trade to all countries and all peoples. Multilateral agreements would remove barriers to trade, allowing access to markets for all on equal terms, as enshrined in the most-favoured-nation principle. However, in reality, trade is dominated by the rich and powerful, be they countries or companies. The WTO recognizes, at least in theory, the equal voice of each of its 161 members. Through its regulatory structures, including the dispute settlement process, it aspires to ensure that global markets retain a level playing field. However, the ambitious Doha Round of multilateral negotiations, ostensibly focusing on development goals, failed to resolve differences between developed and developing countries. The governments of emerging economies, Brazil and India, both growing in influence, reminded the world that national social priorities must be accommodated.

National decision-makers and regulators hold legal authority over trade policies within their borders – a reality acknowledged by the WTO. Governments see trade policies as an aspect of national security, employing protectionist measures as they deem necessary, despite commitment to WTO principles. The WTO, for its part, has tended to focus on markets in the product traded rather than on *how* the product is produced. Hence, issues such as environmental practices and food safety tend to be treated as simply barriers to trade. This approach is considered a shortcoming by many people concerned with broader societal issues, but is widely supported by the global companies who view national regulations generally as unjustifiable barriers to trade. National priorities, such as food subsidies to the poor, are also viewed as critical in developing countries, although seen as trade-distorting by the WTO. The failure of Doha can be depicted as failing the needs of developing countries. Unable to negotiate multilateral solutions, the WTO appears to have acknowledged its own shortcomings. Faltering multilateralism has provided an opening for economic superpowers to design their own plurilateral agreements. A consequence has been the creation of the TPP and TTIP, both initiated by the US, and both aiming to pave the way for trade and investment policies that favour US corporate interests.

References

Balassa, B. (1962) *The Theory of Economic Integration* (London: Allen & Unwin).

EU Commission (2015) 'TTIP: Basics, benefits, concerns', at ec.europa,eu/trade/policy/, accessed 24 July 2015.

Flynn, S. (2010) 'Special 301 of the Trade Act of 1974 and global access to medicine', *Journal of Generic Medicines*, 7: 451–472.

Funk, C. and Rainie, L. (2015) 'Public and scientists' views on science and society', Pew Research Center, 29 January, at www.pewinternet.org

Gilpin, R. (2000) *The Challenge of Global Capitalism: The World Economy in the 21st Century* (Princeton: Princeton University Press).

Global Antidumping (2015) *Antidumping Statistics*, 20 April, Global Antidumping Publishing, at www.antidumpingpublishing.com, accessed 15 July 2015.

Ikenson, D. (2014) 'New Jersey seduced by the false promise of "Buy American" laws', *Forbes*, 18 December, at www.forbes.com

IMF (2013) 'Trade interconnectedness: the world with global value chains', 26 August, at www.imf.org

IMF (2015) 'World Economic Outlook', April, at www.imf.org

Inman, P. (2015) 'Secret talks could weaken climate targets set in Paris, warn campaigners', *The Guardian*, 3 December, at www.theguardian.com

Krugman, P. (1994) *Rethinking International Trade* (Cambridge, MA: MIT Press).

OECD (2014) *Agricultural Policy Monitoring and Evaluation 2014: OECD Countries*, OECD Publishing, at www.oecd.org

Page, G. (2014) 'Choices in food security', speech at the University of Michigan, 14 March, transcript at www.cargill.com (under News Center), accessed 28 July 2015.

Pelc, K. (2014) 'Why the deal to pay Brazil $300 million just to keep subsidies is bad for the WTO, poor countries, and US taxpayers', *The Washington Post*, 12 October 2014.

Porter, M. (1998a) *The Competitive Advantage of Nations* (Basingstoke: Macmillan).

Porter, M. (1998b) *On Competition* (Boston, MA: Harvard Business School Press).

Ricardo, D. ([1817] 1973) *Principles of Economy and Taxation* (London: Dent).

Smith, A. ([1776] 1950) *An Inquiry into the Nature and Causes of the Wealth of Nations* (London: Methuen).

UNCTAD (2013) *World Investment Report 2013* (Geneva: UN).

UNCTAD (2014) *Key Trends in International Merchandise Trade* (Geneva: UN).

UNCTAD (2015) *Key Statistics and Trends in International Trade 2014* (Geneva: UN).

US Census (2015) 'Foreign trade data', at www.census.gov/foreign-trade, accessed 26 June 2015.

Wells, L.T. (ed.) (1972) *The Product Life Cycle and International Trade* (Boston, MA: Harvard Business School Press).

WTO (2015) *Regional Trade Agreements: Facts and Figures*, at www.wto.org, accessed 20 July 2015.

☞ Multiple choice questions

Go to the companion website: www.palgravehighered.com/morrison-gbe-4e to take a quick multiple choice quiz on what you have read in this chapter.

? Review questions

1 How relevant is the theory of comparative advantage to modern trade patterns?
2 What are the main contributions of Porter's theory of competitive advantage?
3 What is meant by strategic trade policy?
4 Outline the motivations underlying government trade policy.
5 Summarize the arguments for and against free trade.
6 What are the main tools of government trade policy?
7 Define the GATT principles of most-favoured-nation and national treatment.
8 In what ways does the WTO represent a step on from GATT?
9 What did the Doha Round of multilateral talks accomplish?
10 Identify the main groupings that represent distinctive interests in multilateral trade talks.
11 What is the Trade in Services Agreement, and why is it significant?
12 Why have regional trade groupings become popular, and in what ways, if any, do they undermine multilateral trade liberalization efforts?
13 Who stands to gain from the TPP and the TTIP?
14 Contrast the European Union and NAFTA in terms of regional integration.
15 Why do developing countries have ambivalent feelings about trade liberalization?

✓ Assignments

1 Assess the contrasting perspectives and interests of developed countries, the large emerging economies and the weaker developing countries with respect to global trade liberalization.
2 Assess the extent to which the two ambitious trade partnerships, the TPP and TTIP, could transform world trade.

📖 Further reading

Baldwin, R. and Wyplosz, C. (2015) *The Economics of European Integration*, 5th edn (New York: McGraw-Hill).
Beckett, S. (2015) *Empire of Cotton: A Global History* (New York: Vintage).
Feenstra, R. and Taylor, A. (2014) *International Trade*, 3rd edn (New York: Worth Publishers).
Gilpin, R. (2001) *Global Political Economy: Understanding the International Economic Order* (Princeton: Princeton University Press).
Goldin, I. and Reinert, K. (2012) *Globalization for Development: Meeting New Challenges* (Oxford: OUP).
Gallagher, K. (2014) *The Clash of Globalizations: Essays on the Political Economy of Trade and Development Policy* (London: Anthem Press).
Krugman, P., Obstfeld, M. and Melitz, M. (2014) *International Trade: Theory and Policy*, 10th edn (London: Pearson).
Oatley, T. (2013) *International Political Economy*, 5th edn (New York: Routledge).
Ravenhill, J. (ed.) (2014) *Global Political Economy*, 4th edn (Oxford: OUP).

⊕ **Visit the companion website at www.palgravehighered.com/morrison-gbe-4e for further learning and teaching resources.**

CLOSING CASE STUDY

Stormy outlook for Glencore

Who are the winners in large-scale grain production? All stages of production and transport are dominated by a handful of large companies, among them, Glencore.
Source: BRAND X.

The global trading company, Glencore, is accustomed to sailing close to the wind. Originally, the company was Marc Rich & Co, a private company founded in 1974 by Marc Rich, known as the 'godfather' of modern commodity trading. Traditionally, the large trading firms are closely run and secretive. Rich was controversial in that he traded with regimes such as the apartheid regime in South Africa, Libya during its military dictatorship and Iran, in breach of a US embargo. Pursued by the US Justice Department, he was indicted in 1983 on 65 criminal counts for tax evasion, racketeering and trading with an enemy country. He was on the FBI's wanted list and became a fugitive from US justice, fleeing to Switzerland, where he carried on the business. Ivan Glasenberg, another trader, joined the firm in 1984. In 1994, Glasenberg and other senior traders led a buy-out of the business from Rich, who, from then onwards, played no role in the firm. It remained based in Switzerland, which has historically been favoured by trading firms, with minimal regulation and tolerance of the secrecy they

value. It was renamed Glencore. Glasenberg became its CEO in 2002. He is known as a competitive, round-the-clock trader who invariably plays to win, and the Glencore culture reflects his personal drive. He has said, 'Glencore does not do work life balance' (Hume and Sheppard, 2015).

The growth in commodities trading in the 2000s brought unprecedented profits to the world's large trading companies, in many cases outshining the financial performance of the Wall Street banks such as Goldman Sachs. In contrast to the bankers, the trading companies were operating in unregulated markets. The large trading companies seized opportunities to expand into production and other activities, giving them a grip on supply chains in commodities. The returns enjoyed by the traders in these years were the envy of other businesses, including the banks. After 37 years as a private company, Glencore went public in 2011, and listed in London and Hong Kong simultaneously. By then, it was the world's largest commodities trader, although its name was hardly known outside commodities trading circles. The London debut promised to make the six traders at its heart all billionaires. As in most trading companies, senior employees hold most of the shares – and take most of the risk. Glasenberg himself had a stake of 16% at the time of the initial public offering (IPO), which was then worth $9.6 billion. Glencore's stock exchange debut was not the runaway success that many had expected, but, valuing the company at £38 billion, it was still a huge IPO. And it opened the way for Glencore to do more deal-making.

The commodities boom had lifted mining companies as well as traders, and Glencore eyed the miner, Xstrata, as a takeover target. The takeover of Xstrata would cost $30 billion, but by the time it was completed, in 2013, the slowdown in global demand for commodities was already evident. Xstrata, moreover, had borrowed heavily to fund investment projects aimed at boosting mine production, and was saddled with debt of $15 billion, which Glencore inherited. Glencore had envisaged that trading activities would be consistent performers financially, compensating for the fluctuations in fortune that affect mining operations. After the takeover, however, the company found itself heavily dependent on mining, and also carrying a worrying level of debt. The timing of the Xstrata takeover was unfortunate, and critics have said that Mr Glasenberg and his fellow traders probably made a strategic mistake in purchasing Xstrata (Hume et al., 2015). Has the business model turned out to be misconceived?

Mr Glasenberg, who now owns a stake of 8.4% in the company, has been of the view that the combination of trading and mining is working, and said in 2015 that there were no plans to break up the company. By 2015, he had seen Glencore's share price tumble 82% since the London listing. The company had been through dark periods before in its history, and the fortitude of its workaholic chief executive would again be called into play. The regulatory environment in Switzerland has cooled towards the large commodities traders, and some have shifted headquarters to Singapore or Malaysia. Glasenberg is a trader by nature, but he is now the head of a mining company that is suffering from just the volatility of global markets that he had hoped to avoid. Mick Davis, the former CEO of Xstrata, who lost his job at the time of the takeover, said the two companies would be difficult to meld together. He felt that Glencore had a different view of how a company should be run: 'Trading is about managing risk, making sure your traders don't create more risk than you're comfortable with. It lends itself to a centralized approach .... Running an asset-rich company like ours means the people who actually take the decisions must be where the action is, and they must have ... discretion to get things wrong – otherwise, how do they learn?' (Hill and Thomas, 2013).

Sources: Hume, N. and Sheppard, D. (2014) 'Steely hard charger who trades to win', *Financial Times*, 12 September, at www.ft.com; Hume, N., Wilson, J. and Sheppard, D. (2015) 'Glencore scrambles to halt downward spiral', *Financial Times*, 3 October; Schaefer, S. (2015) 'Glencore's crashing stock sends CEO Glasenberg tumbling down billionaire ranks', Forbes, 28 September, at www.forbes.com; Hill, A. and Thomas, A. (2013) 'The dealmaker's dealmaker', *Financial Times*, 28 January.

Questions for discussion

- What does the history of Glencore reveal about the rise in commodity trading as a globalized activity?
- Was the takeover of Xstrata by Glencore misjudged, and why?
- It is common for trading companies to own productive assets, but Mick Davis was sceptical about such deals. Why?
- Should global commodities trading be subject to greater regulation and greater requirements for transparency? Why?

GLOBAL FINANCE

This chapter will enable you to

- Gain an overview of the elements that make up the international financial system, including the extent and implications of financial globalization
- Analyse the ways in which shifting patterns of global finance have impacted in diverse economic environments, including developed, industrializing and developing countries
- Understand the diverse causes of financial crises and roles played by reforms and regulation
- Appreciate the current challenges for global finance in building more sustainable and socially responsible businesses

Outline of chapter

HSBC and banking nightmares

Switzerland's secretive banking system has attracted customers from around the world, many wishing to hide money from authorities in their home countries.

Source: iStock.com/assalve.

In November 2015, a former IT employee at HSBC's subsidiary bank in Switzerland, Hervé Falciani, was sentenced by a Swiss federal criminal court to five years in prison for industrial espionage, data theft and breaches of banking secrecy laws. Falciani, by then well known as a whistleblower, was not present to hear the verdict. In the largest data leak in banking history, he had downloaded the banking details of 130,000 of the Swiss subsidiary bank's clients between 2005 and 2007. Most were people who simply wished to hide their wealth from tax authorities, but among them were arms dealers, drug dealers and money launderers. The massive amount of data was released to the media and

to tax authorities in the relevant countries, who could then investigate the individuals.

HSBC is listed in London, but a large proportion of its business is in Asia. The bank started life in Scotland in 1965, and set up in Hong Kong and China soon thereafter, providing trade finance in the British colonial era—hence its original name, Hong Kong and Shanghai Banking Corporation. In Hong Kong, it has become one of the dominant financial institutions, but it moved its base to London in the 1990s, in anticipation of Hong Kong's handover to China. Its Swiss bank was acquired in the course of HSBC's global expansion strategy. Dating from 1999, it aimed to cater for very wealthy individual clients. But the bank had veered away from traditional banking services towards a model that had systematically allowed the thousands of account holders to hide money and evade taxes. Some clients were even given 'bricks' of untraceable banknotes on a regular basis. In the year Falciani was tried, HSBC was fined 42 million Swiss francs for facilitating money laundering at its Swiss subsidiary. Did HSBC's head office knowingly acquiesce in the Swiss activities, or did it simply fail to notice? Either way, it was clearly failing to exert proper control.

HSBC said the federal structure of the bank allowed the various businesses to operate independently under country managers, arguing that senior executives knew nothing of the wrongdoing. Executives, it insisted, cannot know what everyone is doing in a bank with 240,000 employees. This explanation sounded thin to the various forums in which HSBC was having to answer searching questions. Stephen Green, the CEO at the time of the leaks, was in the firing line. As an ordained Anglican priest, he was noted as a spokesman for high moral principles, going beyond simply abiding by the letter of the law. But the culture of the bank, and the lax oversight, suggest that there were serious failings in the way the bank was run. Green was CEO from 2003 to 2006. He became chairman in 2006, and in 2010, he was appointed trade and industry minister in the Conservative government, becoming Lord Green. This period saw the emergence of damaging evidence that international branches of HSBC in Mexico had been involved in money laundering by drug cartels. The US fined the bank $1.9 billion in 2012.

The UK tax authority, HMRC (Her Majesty's Revenue and Customs), had evidence on wrongdoing at HSBC's Swiss bank at the time that Green was appointed trade minister. The current CEO, Stuart Gulliver, took over in 2010. He has admitted that there were failures in controls during Green's tenure. HMRC had also received the names of the British holders of HSBC Swiss bank accounts, but was noticeably reluctant to take action in the way that other countries had. HMRC's head of tax retired from the service two years after the leaked data were handed over – and went to work as a consultant for HSBC. Senior executives from both HSBC and HMRC were questioned before the parliamentary public accounts committee. The committee's chairman, Margaret Hodge, expressed the view that that there appeared to be 'a systemic policy to support hundreds of people in avoiding paying their tax' (Leigh et al., 2015). She urged that tax authorities in the UK should pursue possible legal action against HSBC.

Stuart Gulliver has stressed that the bank has been completely transformed since 2008. While the global financial crisis brought other British banks to their knees, HSBC did not have need of a government bailout, its strong Asian business helping to bolster its financial position. But its shares have suffered, and many shareholders criticized executive remuneration in 2015. In 2016, leaked documents known as the 'Panama Papers' implicated HSBC in Panamanian offshore firms designed to hide clients' wealth. Even the CEO was found to have used an offshore firm in Panama to hold £5 million. In 2016, the board bowed to shareholder criticism, and reduced executive pay.

HSBC considered moving its headquarters from London to Hong Kong, where much of its business is located. However, the political tension with China posed a risk. Under the handover agreement with the UK, there are 32 years left before Hong Kong loses its current status and becomes part of China. The bank announced early in 2016 that it would not be moving.

Sources: Leigh, D., Ball, J., Garside, J. and Pegg, D. (2015) 'HSBC files: HMRC had data on misconduct before bank boss made trade minister', *The Guardian*, 9 February, at www.theguardian.com; Ratcliffe, R. (2015) 'HSBC boss: we failed to live up to the standards expected of us', *The Guardian*, 13 February; Farell, G. and Kocieniewski, D. (2016) 'UBS, HSBC offshore dealings thrust into Panama Papers spotlight', Bloomberg, 5 April, at www.bloomberg.com.

Questions for discussion

- Where does the blame lie for the massive tax avoidance operations that flourished in HSBC's Swiss bank?
- The CEO said he cannot know what everyone in the bank is up to, and therefore cannot be held liable. Do you agree?
- What regulatory weaknesses were there in Britain?
- Why was HSBC tempted to leave London and go back to Hong Kong, and why did it reject this idea?

Introduction

Finance is among the most globalized of all international business activities, largely thanks to technological advances. With globalization, many more firms, including SMEs, are internationally active in a diverse range of countries. Many of these are in developing regions that are becoming integrated in global financial networks. Growing trade and overseas investment have led to the growth of global capital markets and global financial institutions. This expansion has been made possible, first and foremost, by the opening of national economies to financial flows. National financial systems have become more deeply enmeshed than ever before in global financial networks. For companies, governments and individuals, opportunities for accessing financial markets have expanded. However, these opportunities have also given rise to risks, as evidenced by the recurrence of financial crises around the globe.

Global financial markets are now 24-hour-a-day, fast-moving and complex processes, whose operations are on a scale which dwarf many national governments. This chapter will attempt to demystify these processes as they impact on businesses. A major aim is to explain in relatively simple terms how international financial institutions interact with businesses, investors, and national financial systems. As will be seen, sharply differing perspectives have emerged between enterprises, consumers and governments. The growth of international financial institutions, raising broad questions of stability and control in financial markets, has drawn both praise and criticism. From the business point of view, there are huge benefits from integrated markets, which have been particularly evident in emerging markets, but there are also risks of instability and vulnerability to financial shocks. MNEs have been major drivers of financial globalization. Shifting patterns of corporate control, now evident on a global scale, have revealed the differing perspectives of corporate management, shareholders, lenders, consumers and governments. With globalization has come greater awareness of the interactions between markets.

Evolution of the international monetary system

The foundations of the international monetary system have formed the backdrop of global finance. International institutions aim to provide stability and guidance to the governments of sovereign states. However, national interests and perspectives vary, and stability ultimately rests on co-operation between governments and international institutions. In order to understand the challenges currently confronting international financial institutions, we will look briefly at how the international institutions have evolved. Currencies are generally controlled by national central banks and, in the case of the EU, the European Central Bank (ECB). But central banks cannot always ensure exchange-rate stability against other currencies. Currencies are linked in global financial networks, which have become more integrated as trade and foreign direct investment (FDI) have grown.

The gold standard

The rise in trade and financial flows from the late nineteenth century onwards led to the growing internationalization of finance. To facilitate these movements, the world's major trading nations adopted a global **gold standard** system, which lasted from the 1870s to 1914, a period in which Britain was the strongest trading nation. Under the gold standard, all currencies were 'pegged' to gold, which removed the uncertainty of transactions involving different currencies. For each currency, a conversion rate into gold ensured stability. The system required countries to convert their currency into gold on demand, and did not restrict international gold flows. Governments willingly endorsed the system even though, in theory, it reduced their control over their own economic policy. In practice, governments did not always play by the 'rules of the game,' and there was more national monetary autonomy than supposed (Eichengreen, 1996: 28).

Significantly, national interest rates, while they showed some convergence, were largely influenced by domestic conditions. The gold standard period none-theless represented the emergence of a global financial order. The maintenance of the gold standard depended on central banks' continuing commitment to external convertibility. This system broke down with the First World War when governments used precious metal to purchase military supplies and restricted movements in the gold market, thus causing currencies to float. The system collapsed despite efforts to resurrect it in the inter-war period, during which government priorities had shifted from exchange-rate stability to domestic economic concerns. Moreover, the domination, or hegemony, that Britain had exerted over capital markets had declined. American commercial and financial power had grown, but this did not lead to its taking on a similar role in the international system (Eichengreen, 1996).

Bretton Woods Institutions

The **Bretton Woods agreement**, dating from the close of the Second World War, created a broad institutional order to restore financial stability. The GATT, which was the fore-runner of the World Trade Organization (WTO), dates from this agreement (see Chapter 7). The two major financial institutions created were the **International Monetary Fund (IMF)** (www.imf.org) and the International Bank of Reconstruction and Development, better known as the **World Bank** (www.worldbank.org). We will look first at the institu-tions, which have endured, and, in the next section, the agreement itself, which did not. The IMF aimed to maintain global financial stability by helping out countries with balance-of-payments difficulties and providing assistance to heavily-indebted poor countries. The IMF is now more known for its loans to countries suffering from finan-cial crisis. The World Bank was intended from the outset to be more development-oriented, beginning with post-war reconstruction. Money would be channelled through governments towards specific development projects. As the organization has evolved, however, it has shifted towards the financing of broad programmes.

The membership of both financial organizations has grown to 188 countries, the majority of them developing economies. While the WTO was established on the basis of one-country-one-vote, the voting structures of the World Bank and IMF are more like corporations. They allocate voting rights that reflect the share ownership stakes of member countries. This system greatly favours the US and other advanced economies. The US holds 16.74% of the voting rights in the IMF. The UK's voting rights amount to 4.92%, and China's, 3.81%. As voting on important issues requires an 85% majority, the US can singlehandedly block any measure it does not favour. Both organizations are based in Washington, DC, which has given its name to their broad outlook: the **Wash-ington consensus**. The IMF, in particular, has been criticized for imposing conditions on recipient countries that are dictated by American thinking on free markets and minimal government. The Washington consensus was originally conceived by econo-mist John Williamson, who focused on the countries of Latin America. He set out ten principles that represented the Washington consensus. These are shown in Figure 8.1.

Figure 8.1 The Washington consensus in John Williamson's original formulation

Source: Inspired by Williamson, J. (2004) 'A short history of the Washington Consensus', Paper given at the conference, 'From the Washington Consensus to a new global governance', Fundación CIDOB, Barcelona, 24–25 September, at www.iie.com/publications, pp. 3–4.

10 Property rights

1 Fiscal discipline – reduce large deficits

2 Reordering public spending priorities – towards 'pro-growth' and 'pro-poor'

9 Deregulation

The Washington consensus: 10 principles

3 Tax reform

8 Privatization

4 Liberalizing interest rates

7 Liberalization of inward FDI

6 Trade liberalization

5 A competitive exchange rate

The ten principles can be seen as an approach to economic development generally. It is striking that the principles as presented by Williamson are balanced between market reforms and considerations of public goods (Williamson, 2004). Fiscal discipline involves reducing budget deficits and trade deficits, which can lead to high inflation and cause the most harm to the poor in society. Taking a 'strictly neutral' view of how big the public sector should be, he says the priorities for public spending should be pro-social investments, including education, health and infrastructure (Williamson, 2004: 2). While Williamson emphasizes deregulation, he explains that this relates primarily to entry and exit barriers, not regulations that, for example, protect public health and safety or the environment. The inclusion of property rights refers to the reforms needed in the large informal sector in many developing countries to help poor people to become part of the mainstream economy, as advocated by the Peruvian reformer, Hernando de Soto (see Clift, 2003). While many of the ten principles are plainly market-oriented, it is clear that market reforms are intended to be moderated by social needs. However, as interpreted by the Bretton Woods institutions, the Washington consensus was translated into a rather doctrinaire, one-size-fits-all set of market reforms. They came in for particularly sharp criticism during the Asian financial crisis, discussed later.

The Washington consensus: room for divergence?

To what extent would you agree with Williamson's outline of the Washington consensus? In your view, would the IMF be a more relevant institution today if it had taken Williamson's approach?

The Bretton Woods legacy

In the immediate aftermath of the Second World War, the IMF sought to restore a stable foreign exchange framework, but could not turn the clock back by re-introducing the gold standard, given the huge development goals. The US was the dominant economy in the world. It had been spared the devastation of war, and was by far the world's richest economy. It owned 60% of the world's gold. Under the

Bretton Woods agreement, currencies were pegged to the dollar, with the dollar fixed in terms of gold at $35 an ounce. This was an 'adjustable peg'. A country could alter its currency only if it was in 'fundamental disequilibrium', which was not fully defined. Controls were permitted, to limit private financial flows. The agreement aimed to liberalize world trade, but also took into account governments' wishes to maintain systems of social protection and other domestic objectives. This meant that governments had considerable autonomy to pursue domestic economic policies.

In the post-war period, the priority for many economies, including those in Europe and Japan, was getting industries back on their feet. The US embarked on a huge aid programme – the Marshall Plan – that aimed to fund redevelopment in Western Europe, notably West Germany (as it then was). The period 1945–73 is sometimes referred to as the 'golden age of capitalism', characterized by healthy economic growth, relatively full employment and financial stability (Glyn et al., 1992). In the world as a whole, output of manufactured goods quadrupled from the early 1950s to the early 1970s. Exports of manufactured goods rose, mainly from developed countries to other developed countries. Corporate gains were impressive, enabling companies to invest in future expansion. But alongside corporate profitability, there was a bigger picture of social and political contexts. Employees saw rising wages, feeding through into rising consumption. Employee protection and labour rights were consolidated in this era, including rights of collective bargaining and the minimum wage. Governments played active roles in many areas, including the expansion of welfare-state measures. Spectacular economic growth in Japan, at rates around 8% in the 1960s and 1970s, rested in large part on guidance from the Japanese state (Ito, 1996). State-owned enterprises in a number of European countries (including France, Norway and Austria) contributed to high growth. In the UK, where more free-market thinking had hitherto prevailed, the post-war Labour government created the National Health Service (NHS). In the US, government funding flowed into key strategic industries, including aircraft and pharmaceuticals. For many developing countries, this period was marked by optimism, with the birth of new independent states following the departure of colonial rulers. These countries, too, enjoyed steady growth. The US did not see economic growth on the scale experienced in Western Europe and Japan, and its growing imports and balance-of-payments deficit became contributors to global financial instability.

Even in the 1960s and 1970s the Bretton Woods system was coming under strain. Three factors can be highlighted. First, the US in the 1960s was gripped by inflation and a mounting trade deficit fuelled by increasing imports, largely from the growing economies of Europe. Second, there arose the 'Euromarkets', which were systems for taking foreign currency deposits, such as dollar deposits in European banks (Kapstein, 1994). The source of the dollars could be individual investors, central banks or firms. From the 1950s, a Eurocurrency market grew, as funds flowed into European banks, and European economies were growing. European banks were able to expand their Eurocurrency business, unrestrained by the national regulations and capital controls. Third, the 'oil shock' of 1973 saw a sudden quadrupling of the price of oil. This was brought about through the price co-ordination of member countries in OPEC (the Organization of Petroleum Exporting Countries) (www.opec.org), which were able to control the supply and price of oil. These oil-rich countries, which accumulated large sums from higher oil prices, invested in international money markets, swelling the funds of international banks. Large sums flowed from the oil-importing countries to the oil-exporting countries, many of

them developing countries, thus contributing to the expansion of global financial flows. The effects of a booming Eurocurrency market, combined with US inflation and a growing trade deficit, led to speculative activities against the US dollar, the linchpin currency of Bretton Woods. In 1971, President Nixon announced that the dollar would no longer be convertible to gold, heralding the collapse of the Bretton Woods system of fixed exchange rates. This brought about extreme volatility in exchange rates.

Instilling stability in the exchange rate system

Post-Bretton Woods, the IMF was concerned with curbing volatility, opting for a policy of greater exchange rate flexibility. This recognizes several means by which governments and central banks can determine exchange rates, ranging from a fixed rate to a free-floating currency. The key free-floating currencies are recognized by the IMF as reserve currencies for the purposes of their 'Special Drawing Rights' (SDR). These have been the US dollar, the Japanese yen, the UK pound and the euro. The Chinese currency, the yuan, was added to this basket of currencies by the IMF in 2015.

Many countries adopt a middle position between market valuation and a fixed rate, known as the 'managed float' of the currency. This allows the currency to fluctuate within a band. Another option is the **'pegged' exchange rate**. It has the benefit of a peg to a 'harder' currency, usually the US dollar or euro. The peg is intended to act as a stabilizing factor. It is often seen as an advantageous policy by governments of developing and transitional economies, as it attracts foreign investors. The currency peg helps to facilitate economic growth, but when an economic downturn occurs, the policy can have a deleterious effect on the currency, leading to pressure to devalue. In currency markets, as in financial markets generally, confidence is a crucial element. When a national economy appears to be in trouble, the currency comes under pressure, but when a whole economy is in trouble, the government bailout is likely to be beyond the means of a country's national reserves. Sound policies can help to prevent a crisis arising, but with the opening of national financial systems, risks can arise from external as well as internal vulnerabilities.

If a country's currency is perceived to be undervalued, its exporters enjoy an advantage in global markets. China's currency, the yuan, has been pegged to the dollar since 1994, but its economy has slowed, wages have risen, corporate debts have grown (see next section), and its exports are struggling to compete with those of other Asian emerging economies. These factors combined with a strong dollar brought the currency under pressure in 2015. China dipped into its huge foreign currency reserves to prop up the currency. These reserves are still high, estimated to be $3.7 billion, down from $4 billion in 2014. There followed a policy shift, in which the dollar peg was effectively dismantled and replaced with a mechanism that was more market-oriented to a mix of currencies. The result was akin to a de facto devaluation, seeing the currency fall some 3% in a few days. As a policy measure, the currency devaluation is a boost for the country's exports, but critics would say it is a manoeuvre to undercut competitors, which could lead to 'currency wars'. It would also lead to even more anti-dumping actions against Chinese goods in the WTO (see Chapter 7). An alternative explanation for the devaluation was that China was becoming more market-friendly, seeking the status of reserve currency from the IMF, which it would consider only if the currency is close to a free-floating one. These policies proved successful from this point of view, with the recognition of the yuan as a reserve currency late in 2015.

Governments desire exchange-rate stability, and they share this broad goal with the IMF. But the IMF sees markets as the best long-term means of ensuring stability. Pegged and manipulated currencies have a poor record of precipitating financial crisis when the peg comes under pressure, and governmental efforts to prop up their currencies from accumulated foreign currency reserves usually fail. A conundrum for governments is that they wish their economies to be attractive to foreign investors, but they also wish their currency to be shielded from destabilizing shocks that occur in global financial markets.

International capital flows

Access to capital is essential for every business. Firms may turn to banks and other institutions for loans, raising capital by **debt financing**. Or they may raise capital through share offerings, known as **equity financing**. In practice, companies rely on a combination of equity and debt financing, which are discussed in this section. Capital markets handle flows of capital, including equity investments (portfolio investment) and also bonds, which are loan instruments. Students of international business might expect that the biggest and most influential players in equity and debt markets are the large multinational enterprises (MNEs), but this would be only partially true in today's world. Some of the largest players are governments, which are active in many global markets, and some of the more influential players have been the world's private investment funds, which act as catalysts in both debt and equity markets. This section sheds light on the interactions among these diverse players.

Equity markets

When a company is publicly 'floated', it is listed on a stock exchange, and its shares are offered through an **initial public offering (IPO)** (discussed in Chapter 1). Founders of private-sector companies typically take the decision when to 'go public' and list the company, inviting the public to subscribe for shares in the new PLC (public limited company). These companies, such as Google or Microsoft, it will be recalled, are still private-sector companies. The 'public' aspect refers to the offer of shares to the general public. When governments wish to privatize an organization in the public sector, such as the post office, for example, they typically create a PLC, listing the company on a stock exchange and offering a portion of the shares to the public (often retaining a large stake in state hands). The government-controlled PLC is not uncommon in many countries, especially those that tend towards a more statist model of capitalism. The share offerings that attract media attention are often those of companies, such as Alibaba, in which a charismatic founder seeks a greater presence on the global stage (see the opening case study in Chapter 4).

Shares in listed companies are traded on the world's **stock exchanges**. A rise in the value of a company's traded shares is an indication of market sentiment towards the company, and also towards the sector and the general economic environment. When the investment climate is buoyant, shares can trade at many times their nominal value, but when sentiment declines, corporate values can decline sharply. This is what happened to the Royal Bank of Scotland (RBS). It grew spectacularly in the decade leading up to the 2008 financial crisis, its shares trading at £60 in 2007, but their value had plunged to just over £1 by 2009.

Since then, stock markets have enjoyed impressive rises in value, and this optimism has encouraged increased numbers of IPOs. Total IPO activity in 2014 amounted to $256.5 billion globally, and the number of IPOs that year was 50% up on the previous year (Ernst & Young, 2014). The number and size of IPOs is a good indication of the investment climate. When share prices are rising generally, a company is confident that its IPO will find subscribers, and its value will rise in subsequent trading. Nonetheless, market volatility has led many companies to be cautious. Each year, hundreds of IPOs in the pipeline are withdrawn, indicating a nervousness to take the plunge and possibly suffer deteriorating share prices following the launch. The collapse of high-technology shares in the dotcom crash of 2000 affected numerous sectors, and the recovery in share prices was slow to gain momentum. The largest IPO globally in 2014 was that of Alibaba, the Chinese ecommerce company, on the New York Stock Exchange. This huge cross-border IPO contributed to the general rise in cross-border IPO activity, which accounted for 11% of all IPOs, the highest percentage since the pre-crisis year of 2007. Although Alibaba chose a US listing, IPOs in China have shown impressive rises: 45% of all IPOs were in Asia-Pacific exchanges in 2014, compared to 25% in North America. Still, the US remains the largest centre by far in terms of value of IPOs.

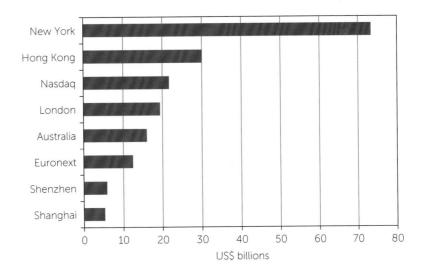

Figure 8.2 Value of IPOs on selected leading stock exchanges, 2014

Source: Data from Ernst & Young Global Limited (2014) *EY Global Trends 2014*, at www.ey.com

As Figure 8.2 shows, the main US exchanges, the New York Stock Exchange (NYSE) (www.nyse.com) and the Nasdaq (National Association of Securities Dealers Automated Quotations) (www.nasdaq.com) dominate global equity markets. The Nasdaq is the younger of the two, founded in 1971, and aiming to trade mainly in technology and other 'new economy' stocks. In the year following the crash in dotcom stocks of 2000, shares traded on the Nasdaq lost half their value. The London Stock Exchange (LSE) (www.londonstockexchange.com) is not far behind in attracting IPOs, with new listings valued at $19.4 billion in 2014. Asia is how home to some of the exchanges with the strongest growth. The Hong Kong, Shanghai and Shenzhen exchanges have benefited from the effects of Chinese growth. However, these exchanges are also volatile. While Hong Kong, with its long tradition of attracting Chinese companies, is well established, the mainland Chinese exchanges of Shanghai and Shenzhen are more prone to swings in value, especially in a context of slowing growth in the Chinese economy. The Shanghai market soared 150% in just 12 months to June 2015 but, in the following three weeks, fell 30%, raising fears that a financial crisis could be brewing. The downswing shook stock markets globally. After further falls and signs of a flight of capital, the Chinese central bank announced a slight lowering of interest rates, to help steady the economy and assure investors of continuing good returns.

Most of the shareholders in listed Chinese companies are small investors. These small retail investors, numbering over 90 million people, hold 80% of listed shares. The low interest rates paid to savers in China's regulated banking sector have had the effect of sending private investors to look for greater returns on stock markets. Many of these investors do not simply invest their savings, and have turned to borrowing to fund investment. But risks abound in equity markets, especially when investors are also indebted, and it is a concern of the Chinese government that millions of small investors are taking risks that impact on household finances.

The trend in capital markets generally in the developed economies has been in the opposite direction. Individual investors are investing less in specific companies, and opting instead for investment funds and other vehicles that spread risks. In these markets, there has been a growth in institutional investors such as pension funds and other investment funds. These institutional investors deal in huge share transactions, and often have substantial holdings in key companies. They value stability as well as financial returns from their investments, targeting companies that are considered well-governed and transparent. Also important in equity markets are the sovereign wealth funds that operate under the control of state authorities. These investors, too, look for stability and good returns. But many investors, particularly some types of investment fund, take an altogether different view of equity markets, looking for short-term gains that can be rapidly re-invested in other equities. This type of investor has come to the fore in recent years, facilitated by advances in the technology that drives trading platforms.

From the mid-2000s some of the major stock exchanges saw rapid growth in 'high-frequency trading', whereby large numbers of trades take place in fractions of a second, programmed by algorithms. The software decides when, what and where to buy and sell, without any human intervention. Each trade is designed to generate a profit from the tiniest movement in prices; although each trade is small in itself in terms of value, the volume of trades is immense. It is estimated that about half the trades on the New York exchanges are from high-frequency traders (McCrank, 2014). These traders, who pay to have their servers located inside the data centres of the exchanges themselves, are sometimes criticized because they receive key data on shares ahead of ordinary users of the exchange, thus gaining an advantage. The banning of high-frequency trading has been considered by regulators in New York, but rejected in 2014. The traders themselves argue that they are in fact improving the efficiency of the exchanges for all users, not just themselves. Nonetheless, the risks of system overload that can cause systems to crash are a concern for the exchanges, as any breakdown in trading systems can cause losses to participants and damage to the reputation of an exchange for dependability.

Public companies and their investors depend on the smooth running and prudent administration of stock markets. Stock exchanges are subject to national regulation, and differ in their rules for corporate listing and for trading of shares. Regulatory systems aim to maintain confidence in their fairness, integrity and transparency. Just as there are different national approaches to regulatory issues in general, financial regulation differs from country to country. Many exchanges are themselves listed companies, and compete with other exchanges to attract listings. If the listing rules of a particular exchange are more generous in respect of insider-dominated companies,

that exchange is likely to attract such companies, as noted in the opening case study. However, public companies that are controlled by insiders, with only a small portion of free-floating shares, are not in keeping with the values of transparency and fairness that stock exchanges aim to uphold.

The US regulator, the **Securities and Exchange Commission (SEC)** (www.sec.gov), was founded in 1934, in the reforms that followed the stock market crash of 1929. The SEC's role includes protecting investors, maintaining fair and efficient markets and also serving the companies that come to the market to raise capital. In the UK, the regulation of financial services was reformed by the Financial Services and Markets Act 2000, which set up the Financial Services Authority (FSA), under the oversight of the Bank of England. Its philosophy of light-touch regulation, rather than direct oversight, reflected the free-market thinking that has contributed to the UK's rise in attractiveness for financial services. However, the financial crisis of 2008 dealt a blow to the UK's reputation as a financial centre, when regulatory failures were seen as partly to blame for the banking collapses that ensued (discussed later in this chapter). The banking crisis, which saw RBS effectively nationalized, with 79% of its shares owned by the UK Treasury, led to a rethinking of the UK's financial services regulatory framework generally. The FSA was replaced by new regulatory frameworks, including the Financial Conduct Authority (FCA), to oversee financial market behaviour. The Bank of England took over direct supervision of the banking system, and the Prudential Regulation Authority (PRA), part of the Bank of England, took over the oversight of financial services firms.

Global equity markets

Share ownership and corporate IPOs are no longer predominantly national phenomena. As they become increasingly globalized, what are the new opportunities, and threats, for companies contemplating listing on a stock exchange?

Debt financing

People, companies and governments borrow money to pay for assets and services that they need. They must pay off the debt, of course, and also pay interest on the loan. But if the interest payments are manageable, borrowing can be a good way of financing big expenditures. Exchange risk often comes into the equation: if the money owed to the creditor is in US dollars, for example, and the debtor is relying on income in local currency to make payments, then the debtor is at risk when the local currency falls in value against the dollar. In a period of just five months between October 2014 and February 2015, the dollar appreciated 14% in nominal terms against a range of foreign currencies, causing consternation for anyone holding dollar-denominated debt (IMF, 2015: 42). When credit is easy and interest rates are low, the temptations to borrow seem irresistible. But how much debt is too much? This is a question often posed for governments and companies, as well as for individuals. The three categories of borrower are interrelated. If households take on huge debt burdens, this is a concern for governments, not just because of the risks to household finances. Much of this debt is probably owed to banks, which could see a rise in bad loans if householders default in large numbers. The same is true of companies, who also tend to borrow from banks. When a government becomes heavily indebted and struggles to service its debts, it could be facing sovereign default.

Loans are a class of asset, and can be traded. Debt financing has given rise to an international bond market which facilitates trade in a variety of loan instruments. A **bond** is a loan instrument which promises to pay a specific sum of money on a fixed date, and to pay interest at stated intervals. Bonds are marketable securities that can be issued in different currencies. An 'external bond' is one issued by a borrower in a capital market outside the borrower's own country. The external bond may be a foreign bond, which is denominated in the currency of the country in which it is issued. **Eurobonds**, by contrast, are denominated in currencies other than those of the countries in which they are issued. Dollar-denominated bonds issued outside the US are examples of Eurobonds. Their attraction has been that they escape official regulation. Global bonds are the most flexible of bonds, as they may be sold inside as well as outside the country in whose currency they are denominated. Dollar global bonds are regulated by the SEC in the US. The World Bank is the leading issuer of global bonds. Governments have also raised money in this way, with the practice recently spreading to governments of developing countries.

Government debt, or 'sovereign debt', has grown to huge proportions in some countries, as we noted in Chapter 4. Governments have tended to rely on borrowing, feeling confident that economic growth would follow, and that the debt burden would be manageable. However, the economic recession following the 2008 financial crisis put extra strain on governments, leading to increased borrowing. This was mainly due to a combination of decreasing revenues from taxes and increasing social payments, including unemployment benefits and housing benefits. It is also the case that ageing populations, especially in the advanced OECD countries, are contributing to increases in money needed to pay for pensions and healthcare. Government debt varies greatly from country to country, and the most indebted are not always, as one might expect, the ones that have the most expansive social welfare systems.

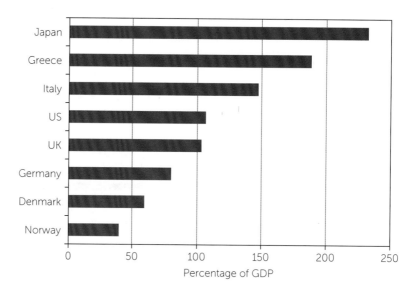

Figure 8.3 Government debt as a percentage of GDP in selected OECD countries

Source: Data from OECD, 'Economics Tables, Number 21: Government Debt', 6 May 2014, at www.oecd.org, accessed 5 August 2015.

Government debt is often expressed as a percentage of GDP. Looking at Figure 8.3, Norway and Denmark, both countries with among the highest rankings in human development, have relatively low government debt. These countries have relatively balanced economies, with adequate revenues to fund social programmes. Recall Figure 4.6 (p. 129), which showed that Denmark's tax revenues amount to nearly 50% of GDP. Tax revenues in the US are much lower, and US government debt, in terms of

percentage of GDP, is nearly double that of Denmark. The worrying examples in Figure 8.3 are Italy, Greece and Japan. Italy struggles to collect tax revenues, but has generous social programmes and a generous pension system – one the country probably cannot afford. Greece has been on the verge of sovereign default for several years, and is surviving on a lifeline of loans from the IMF and EU. But what about Japan, which looks in worse shape? Japan's huge government debt has mounted over two decades of deflation and a stagnating economy, combined with the burdens of an ageing population. However, Japan is a rich country, with growth potential, and is not perceived as likely to default despite the massive government debt. Another factor is that Japanese people, like Asians generally, are frugal and have not accumulated huge household debts.

On the other hand, *companies* in Asian emerging economies, along with those in emerging economies in other regions, have turned to debt financing as a means of generating rapid growth. From 2007 to 2014, debt grew faster than GDP in all of the major emerging markets, and also in the smaller economies of Hong Kong (a special administrative region of China) and Singapore. This growth mainly reflected the rising debt burdens of non-financial companies, as shown in Figure 8.4. In most emerging markets, bank loans are a major source of funding for companies. High levels of corporate debt present risk to the banks, which can set back the achievement of development goals. Over half the total bank lending in emerging economies is commonly to private-sector companies (IMF, 2015: 43). In Hungary and Turkey, the level of dollar-denominated debt is high, leaving borrowers exposed to exchange rate risk. Risk also arises from the growing participation of foreign investors in local bond markets. If a domestic currency weakens suddenly, foreign investors are likely to react by reducing their holdings. This can be significant if these investors hold domestic currency government debt, as public-sector finances can be jeopardized. Many emerging economies are dependent on sectors such as commodities (for example, Brazil) and energy (for example, Russia). These sectors are subject to price volatility in global markets which, in turn, can adversely affect domestic companies' capacity to repay debt. The price of oil was relatively stable at about $110 a barrel from 2010 to 2014, but fell sharply thereafter, and by 2015 was less than half that price. Russia's dependence on oil exports leaves it vulnerable, and its currency, the rouble, has come under pressure as a result.

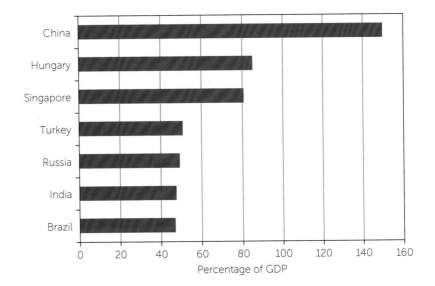

Figure 8.4 Debt of non-financial companies as a percentage of GDP in selected emerging economies, 2014

Source: Data from IMF (2015) 'Global Financial Stability Report', April, Table 1.5, p. 46, at www.imf.org, accessed 5 August 2015.

China is the most spectacular – and disquieting – country shown in Figure 8.4, with non-financial corporate debt standing at nearly 150% of GDP. China's level of government debt, at 64% of GDP, is not unduly high; nor is its level of household debt. But the debt burdens of its private-sector companies pumps up the total debt burden in China to 280% of GDP (Curran, 2015). Given China's key role in the global economy as the major source of demand for raw materials and energy – and also the largest manufacturing superpower – this possible source of economic instability is troubling. Much of this debt is owed not to official banks, but to financial institutions in the 'shadow' banking sector. Chinese companies and banks have also taken advantage of the near-zero interest rates available in the US since the financial crisis. Reliance on debt is referred to as **leverage**. In China, construction and real estate are sectors in which debt has dramatically accumulated and firms are likely to be highly leveraged. China's political leaders have tightened credit, but face a balancing act in wishing to maintain strong growth.

Global financial risks and their consequences

A number of financial risks have been highlighted in this chapter. They include volatile stock prices, foreign exchange risk and excessive reliance on debt financing, especially when coupled with exchange risk. All companies that engage in cross-border activities are subject to some of these risks, including both non-financial and financial firms. But globalization has greatly ramified the sources of risks and the extent of the damage when market volatility undermines financial planning. Financial experts have become highly innovative in seeking new opportunities for gains, but these come with greater risks. The aura of gambling has thus crept into finance. With the possible risks extending to whole sectors, whole economies and societies, the potential for disasters has risen markedly. In this section, we look at the sources of risk, the broader consequences that lead to financial crises, and the possible ways in which global finance can be reformed.

How globalization has increased risks

Interconnectedness, liberalization and the deepening integration of markets have become hallmarks of globalization, as we have seen in sectors such as manufacturing. The global company typically seeks to have its product manufactured in a place that offers location advantages. For societies in the host country, this can be a mixed blessing: jobs are on offer, but the employer could pull out if conditions become adverse. In finance, we see an analogous pattern. Liberalization and deregulation have contributed to encouraging cross-border finance. Opportunities for investment are rapidly multiplying, investors often taking advantage of factors affecting different locations, such as currency fluctuations and interest rates. Capital flows benefit individual countries, but investors can exit if internal fundamentals deteriorate. A financial crisis can develop relatively quickly. The consequences of a generalized exit by investors, known as a 'flight of capital', are far more serious for an economy than the exit of a global brand's manufacturing operations.

International business is traditionally built on trade in goods. An exporter or importer is directly affected by foreign exchange rates. To protect it from adverse currency fluctuations, it may turn to trading in currency markets. The currency **futures contract** allows a business to buy or sell a specific amount of foreign

currency at a designated price in the future. They are therefore said to have a **hedge** against future fluctuations which can adversely affect their business. An example is the airline company that hedges future purchases of jet fuel for its fleet of planes. The company might also find the **option** a useful tool in hedging against currency risk: the option gives the firm the right, rather than an obligation, to purchase the currency in the future at a specific exchange rate. Some airline companies have taken advantage of low fuel prices by negotiating option contracts well into the future. Futures contracts and options are types of derivatives. For most non-financial MNEs, dealings on the currency markets are incidental to their main business. They see finance as a function that serves their main productive activities.

Banks traditionally shared this view of financial activities. They existed to serve customers, including individuals, companies and governments. Contrast this view of finance with one that sees finance as a business in its own right. The growth in global financial markets has come about largely as a result of this shift in the way finance is viewed. Finance is no longer a means to an end: it *is* the end. Finance thus became a significant sector in its own right – one that grew rapidly. As we have seen in the case of exchanges, technological innovation has played a big role. It is paradoxical that risks have multiplied partly due to innovative financial products that purport to offer new ways to spread risk. Banks once focused on traditional banking activities, but saw tempting opportunities for growth and globalization through these newer activities in global finance. They thus transformed themselves into 'universal banks', covering both retail operations and capital investment units. The latter, more risky operations were formerly required to be conducted via separate entities in the US, under the Glass-Steagall Act of 1933, passed following the Great Depression. That law was repealed in 1999, allowing the universal bank to flourish – and become highly globalized.

Central to these more ambitious activities has been the rise of new players such as hedge funds, whose businesses rest largely on the more risky types of investment. Derivatives trading brings together both of these trends.

Financial instruments broadly classified as **derivatives** have become a large market in their own right. Since 1998, primary securities have remained stable, at about double world GDP. But derivatives, amounting to two-and-a-half times world GDP in 1998, were twelve times world GDP by 2007 (Blundell-Wignall, 2012: 2). The value of any derivative depends on the value of some underlying asset, such as cash or property. Derivatives have facilitated growth in the securitization of debt, that is, the packaging of debt as securities which can be traded. There are many classes of securitized debt. The basic form is an 'asset-backed security' (ABS). The security lies in the repayment of the loans, which is a future event subject to the risk that the original debtors will default. There are many types of ABS. They can be mortgage-backed securities, either residential or commercial. As it is difficult to assess the value of derivatives, debt instruments thus came to be 'structured', packaging a range of assets, some higher risk than others. This was deemed to be a relatively safe strategy. The likelihood was that, if there was a fall in the value of one, the remainder would suffice as security. It was not thought likely that all could fall, but that is what happened when the housing market in the US collapsed in 2007.

Among the main new players in derivatives markets are investment funds known as **hedge funds**. They are considered short-term investors. Their speculative strategies are designed to generate short-term gains, but, in aggregate, can distort markets. This type of activity must be distinguished from the hedging which non-financial companies engage in on a daily basis in the course of business. Hedge funds are active in futures markets. We would expect the market in crude oil to be about the price of crude oil that obtains in physical cargoes, but in fact, the main forces in the crude oil market are the funds that trade in futures, speculating on a rise or fall in demand that would push prices up or down. Fund managers are active investors in equities, constantly seeking opportunities to generate profits. They are behind much high-frequency trading. They occasionally take stakes in companies they deem to be underperforming, with a view to shaking up the existing management.

Hedge funds are also investors in sovereign debt, many specializing in purchasing government bonds for a fraction of their face value on secondary markets. The owners of these so-called 'junk' bonds bet on their ability to pursue claims for their full face value, through the courts if need be. Funds that specialize in 'distressed' securities are usually called 'vulture funds' because of their aggressive strategies targeting poor indebted countries. They are the object of criticism on ethical grounds from both governments and corporate leaders, especially when they move, vulture-like, on weak targets, be they governments or companies. Argentina has been pursued for over a decade by 'hold-out' creditors who purchased Argentinian bonds at the time of its sovereign default in 2001 (see the case study in this chapter).

The vulture, a symbol of the predatory behaviour of hedge funds that relentlessly target indebted countries.

Source: Photodisc.

The funds have engaged in forum-shopping among legal jurisdictions, choosing the best location for launching legal action. In 2010, the UK passed legislation, in the form of the UK Debt Relief (Developing Countries) Act, to limit the scope of vulture funds to pursue such claims in its courts. Many funds then shifted their claims to the offshore jurisdiction of Jersey, a Channel Island legally independent of UK law. In 2012, Jersey's legislature voted to bring the island into line with UK law on debt relief, its government having been disquieted by the use of its courts for this type of litigation (Neate, 2012). Globally, there still remain alternative legal routes open to the hedge funds to pursue such claims. This type of litigation, while strictly legal, is generally perceived as unethical. Hedge funds have fully exploited the opportunities presented by global financial markets. However, the aggressive legal strategies of the funds have been associated with negative consequences that can result in enduring damage in poor countries.

Hedge funds: the unscrupulous face of finance?

Why are hedge funds criticized on ethical grounds? To what extent do you think the criticisms are unfair?

When financial crisis strikes nations

Individual people can go bankrupt, unable to pay their debts. Companies can default, failing to pay their creditors, and go into liquidation. National financial systems have in place legal frameworks that allow possible debt restructuring, and failing these attempts, an orderly way of winding up the company, ensuring that creditors are dealt with fairly. In the financial crisis of 2008, some companies, such as Lehman Brothers in the US, collapsed, while others in difficulties were bailed out with public money. These included those deemed to be 'too big to fail'. Most of these companies, including both financial and non-financial firms, had indulged heavily in derivatives trading. While regulators were highly critical of these companies' high-risk strategies, they nonetheless took the view that rescue plans for these major companies were integral to restoring order and confidence in financial markets.

When a whole country is on the brink of default, there is no international framework equivalent to national bankruptcy law, although there are now calls for such a system to be considered (Stiglitz, 2015). In these cases, too, decision-makers in government are usually at least partly to blame, like imprudent managers in a business. But, often, external shocks are a crucial factor for national economies, especially in the light of globalized markets. The IMF can organize rescue packages with short-term loans, but, of course, it is itself a creditor in many cases. Moreover, the IMF is often criticized for its recommended reforms that overemphasize policies such as austerity measures which, in many emerging economies, can lead to greater hardship. We look first at the Asian financial crisis that struck in 1997.

The Asian financial crisis spread from Thailand to South Korea, Malaysia and Indonesia. In each case, there are specifically national factors involved, but there are also issues of 'contagion', whereby the woes of one country spread to others in the region. In all these countries, policies of liberalization and deregulation in the 1990s led to inflows of capital, as investors were attracted to high rates of interest and trusted that governments would not allow their banks to fail. Net capital inflows more than doubled between 1994 and 1996 in the four countries (Singh, 1998). The investment boom, however, was largely financed by borrowed money, much of the borrowing in US dollars.

The crisis originated in Thailand. Thai financial institutions had engaged in imprudent lending on local property development, and found themselves at risk of defaulting on dollar-denominated debt to international financial institutions. The Thai government attempted to defend the currency, the baht, by increasing interest rates and buying baht with its own foreign currency reserves, but this effort exhausted the reserves of the central bank. Under increasing pressure, the baht was floated in 1997, and immediately dropped 20% in value.

A swift deterioration in confidence followed, causing investors to flee. Banks and businesses found the burden of dollar debts increasingly crippling. The banking crisis was thus directly related to the currency crisis, the combined effect of which was to send the economy into meltdown (Krugman, 1999). Contagion spread to other

Asian economies. Large sums by way of credits were made available by the IMF to South Korea and Indonesia, to support the currency and meet external debts. IMF conditions to strengthen fiscal and monetary stability were imposed in the hope that confidence in capital and foreign exchange markets would be restored.

In its Asian rescue packages, the IMF has been criticized for exacerbating the problems, rather than curing them. In particular, its one-size-fits-all market-oriented solutions, administered as shock therapy, have been criticized as not taking into account national conditions that vary from country to country. In giving assistance, it imposed strict monetary and fiscal conditions on recipient countries. This approach was held up as exemplifying the Washington consensus, but in fact, as we have seen, was motivated more directly by purely market values. This criticism is expressed by Joseph Stiglitz, former chief economist at the World Bank, who has pointed out that the IMF programme in Indonesia helped to cause a recession. Rocketing unemployment and economic hardship in ethnically-divided Indonesia contributed to social and political strife, causing the government to fall (Stiglitz, 2000). Since the crisis, the Asian economies have enjoyed a revival in economic growth, largely driven by China. In response to the continuing US dominance in the structures of the IMF and World Bank, China launched the **Asian Infrastructure Investment Bank (AIIB)** (www.aiib.org), envisaging an Asia-focused institution that would be similar to the World Bank, but with China as the main shareholder and India as the second-largest. Because of the pre-eminence of China in its governance, the US has objected to the AIIB. However, the AIIB's signing ceremony went ahead in 2015, with an initial 50 member states signing up, including Germany, the UK, Australia and South Korea.

The Asian crisis also impacted on Russia, where the 1990s did not bring the economic growth and prosperity that had been hoped for at the fall of the Soviet Union. The IMF was active in Russia in the 1990s, encouraging liberalizing reforms and the growth of the private market economy, which accounted for 70% of Russia's GDP by 1998. But Russia's prosperity depended on natural resources and commodities. When the Asian crisis struck and demand for oil fell, the Russian economy was threatened. The currency, the rouble, was subject to a 'floating peg' with the US dollar, which meant that it had to be maintained within a band of value. When the rouble came under pressure, the central bank intervened, using foreign currency reserves to buy roubles and thus try to sustain the peg. The IMF stepped in with loans, but with confidence in the currency draining away, the peg had to be abandoned in 1998. When the rouble was allowed to float, it lost two-thirds of its value against the dollar. The financial crisis soon translated into a political crisis, with the fall of the government. The new government which emerged, that of Vladimir Putin, took a more statist approach to the economy, in contrast to the market reforms sponsored by the IMF. A resurgence in the price of oil and other resources helped the Russian economy to recover, although it remains highly dependent on resource wealth.

Argentina, another resource-rich country, enjoyed strong economic growth in the 1990s, but Argentina's government had imprudently accumulated unsustainable levels of sovereign debt, leading to default in 2001, as discussed in the case study that follows. A number of hedge funds purchased Argentine debt in the form of 'junk' bonds, gambling on their ability to obtain full payment. As the case study indicates, Argentina has been embroiled in legal battles with creditors ever since, despite two deals in which the vast majority of creditors accepted a debt restructuring compromise deal. It has become apparent that the terms agreed with bondholders could have been designed more tightly to restrict the ability of a small minority to hold up a collective agreement. The IMF has now called for agreements to include such clauses, requiring just a simple majority vote to activate. Orderly debt restructuring should arguably be facilitated through international mechanisms that ensure fairness to all parties. In these cases, the losers are almost inevitably the poor, heavily-indebted countries.

CASE STUDY ON THE CHANGING BUSINESS ENVIRONMENT

Argentina's debt woes: lessons for other nations?

The 1990s were years of economic growth for Argentina, but much of the development was funded by overindulgence in borrowing in international capital markets. The country accumulated sovereign debt liabilities on a colossal scale, issuing over a hundred types of bonds in numerous currencies and in numerous jurisdictions. Some were issued to institutions, but many were issued to private investors, including ordinary Argentinians. Unable to meet repayments, Argentina defaulted on nearly $100 billion in sovereign debt in 2001, following which the currency was devalued. For millions of Argentinians, the consequences were disastrous: their savings were wiped out, poverty levels soared, and unemployment was in the range of 20%. The crisis was both economic and social (Stiglitz and Guzman, 2014).

Agreements with 93% of the bondholders were achieved in 2005 and 2010, by which they would receive about 30% of the face value, known as a restructuring, or 'haircut'. This could have led to a resolution of the country's debt problems. However, a number of 'holdout' creditors, amounting to about 7% of the total, were outside these agreements. These holdout creditors were hedge funds, led by NML Capital, which had bought Argentine bonds in the aftermath of the country's 2001 financial crisis. These creditors, often referred to as 'vulture' funds, mounted numerous legal battles for full payment. The holdouts were confident in the strength of their legal case. They obtained numerous awards of damages in the US civil courts, although these were not paid by Argentina. NML followed up with claims abroad to have Argentine assets seized, some of which seemed bizarre. In 2012, an Argentine three-masted sailing ship was detained in Ghana at the behest of NML. Argentina applied to the international tribunal of the law of the sea, which ruled that the ship should be released because of its sovereign immunity as a vessel in the Argentine navy.

In a court case in New York in 2014, the judge, Thomas Griesa, held that payments by Argentina to the holders of the restructured bonds was illegal, as the holdout creditors were entitled to full payment. By 2014, the full face value plus interest amounted to $1.5 billion. NML had bought $48 millions' worth of bonds in 2008, and stood to be paid $832 million: a return of 1,600%. Failing to pay the holdouts would mean that Argentina was in default. Argentina had attempted to pay the holders of the restructured debt their latest interest payment, but this was barred by Judge Griesa. Had Argentina paid the holdouts, it would have breached a clause in the restructured bonds, which states that Argentina cannot give a better deal to any creditors than the 30% deal that they had agreed. Triggering this clause would have involved paying the whole money due to all. The total could have amounted to $140 billion. Argentina's then-president, Cristina Fernandez de Kirchner, argued strongly against what she felt was the bias of the US court, maintaining her resistance to paying the holdouts. The country thus defaulted again, at a time when it needed to be able to access international credit in order to develop its huge shale gas reserves.

The political tide turned with the election in 2015 of a new centre-right president, Mauricio Macri, who wished to see settlement with the holdout creditors. An agreement with four leading holdout hedge funds was reached in 2016, which paved the way for an agreement with all of them. The deal was approved by Argentina's legislators, enabling the country to access international capital markets after the long period of legal battles with holdout creditors.

The experience of Argentina demonstrated the power of the hedge funds in pursuing sovereign borrowers. Sovereign borrowers would henceforth be keen to avoid US financial institutions, as bonds issued under US law would run the same risks as Argentina faced with holdouts. The IMF was concerned that the US judgment would make it difficult in future to restructure sovereign debt, and it proposed that a clause should be included in bond agreements to exclude the obligation to pay holdout creditors. It also recommended a 'collective action clause', which would compel all creditors to go along with a restructuring if 75% of them agree. The country issuing the bonds would have to incorporate these changes. These changes, while modest, would be a step forward. But why not create an international sovereign bankruptcy court? The IMF had suggested this in 2001, but met with lukewarm reception. Following the experience of Argentina, there could be more support.

In national law, businesses and individuals that fall deeply into debt can reach arrangements that allow them to get back on their feet. In principle, the same could apply to states.

In 2015, the UN General Assembly passed a resolution supporting a country's right to restructure its sovereign debt without fear of resistance from minority creditors and judgments in foreign courts. The resolution was an initiative by a group of 77 developing countries. Although non-binding, the resolution was approved by 136 countries. Among those that voted 'no' were the US and Britain.

Sources: Rathbone, J., Stocker, E. and Rodrigues, V. (2014) 'Argentina nears default as contest with holdouts enters endgame', *Financial Times*, 30 June, at www.ft.com; Allen, K. (2014) 'Argentina on brink of second debt default in 12 years', *The Guardian*, 29 July, at www.theguardian.com; Stiglitz, J. and Guzman, M. (2014) 'Argentina default? Griesafault is much more accurate', *The Guardian*, 7 August; Rogoff, K. (2014) 'Argentina is not solely to blame for its latest debt default', *The Guardian*, 1 August.

Questions for discussion

- To what extent did Argentina's government mismanage its sovereign debt?
- The hedge funds in the case study, led by NML, stood by their strict rights in contract law, but what is the ethical case against them?
- Should there be a new global framework for allowing the restructuring of sovereign debt?
- The US and UK voted against the UN resolution on sovereign debt restructuring in 2015. Why?

Has Greece fallen into the same debt mire as Argentina? Greece is a eurozone country, propped up by both the European Central Bank and EU Commission, which formulated rescue packages to restructure its sovereign debt of over €300 billion. About 13% of this debt is to private creditors, among whom are hedge funds, but Greek bonds, unlike those of Argentina, have clauses that restrict the blocking manoeuvres of holdout creditors. Hedge funds have been attracted to Greece, largely because there has been the perception that EU institutions would not wish to see the country exit the eurozone. Obstacles posed by the terms of Greek bonds have led the funds to look for other means to pursue claims.

One possibility is utilizing the ISDS process to claim for the full face value against the Greek government, as Greece is party to a number of treaties that would allow such claims (Geddie and Zaharia, 2015). In such a scenario, an ad hoc tribunal would be entrusted with deciding on the validity of the claims. This possibility would probably look depressing to most Greeks, who are struggling to cope with hardships such as shortages of food and medicines. The country has seen weakening economic activity, high unemployment and failing public services due to the government coffers simply running out of money. Of course, the Greek

economy did not get into these dire straits overnight. The country has long lived beyond its means. Successive governments have pandered to the business and political élites. A flourishing grey economy has been a factor in the country's poor record in collecting taxes. EU money, intended to fund public goods, has flowed into the country, but much of it has fallen into corrupt channels, often on ill-judged prestige construction projects. There is one aspect of the problems facing Greece that is similar to those faced by Argentina: the rich are able to shift their wealth out of the country, while most of the day-to-day hardship falls on the weakest in society.

The way I see it ...

On Greek debt as an investment opportunity, 'One of the reasons it's so attractive is everyone thinks it's as mysterious and dangerous as being in *Game of Thrones* or something.'

Hans Humes, founder of Greylock Capital Management LLC, a hedge fund, in an interview with Bloomberg news, 10 June 2015.

How do you view the opportunities as described by this hedge fund founder?

Incentives such as low taxes have lured rich American investors to Puerto Rico, where upmarket resorts and residences are transforming the island – and its population. The influx of rich Americans to the island, an unincorporated US territory, is being matched by an exodus of ordinary Puerto Ricans who are unable to find work in the island's shrinking traditional industries but able to settle in the US. A concern for the bulk of the mainly poor population is that the transformation of the island offers little prospect of sustainable development and little in the way of much-needed government revenues. To fund public spending, the government has actively sought to sell bonds to hedge fund investors, but this has resulted in a huge debt burden. The governor has threatened to stop making repayments on debts of $72 billion, and has sought to bring the country within the jurisdiction of the US bankruptcy laws, in much the same way that Detroit did when its industries collapsed. However, the hedge funds, many with recent expertise in Argentinian and Greek debt, have pressed for full repayment.

In 2015, a group of 34 hedge funds commissioned a report on how Puerto Rico should best deal with its debt crisis. The research was carried out by former economists at the IMF, who were working under the auspices of a Washington think-tank associated with lobby activities. The report, *For Puerto Rico: There is a Better Way* (Fajgenbaum et al., 2015), concludes that the government should raise taxes, privatize public buildings and cut social spending in areas like education and health. These recommendations look similar to the former policies of the IMF itself that proved disastrous in the Asian crisis.

The global financial crisis of 2008

The decade preceding 2008 seemed like a golden age for financial markets. Easy credit, high returns and stable markets provided ideal conditions for continuing growth – or so it seemed. However, two aspects of the boom in finance posed potential threats. First, there were the risks underlying derivatives trading, which included the securitization of debt. Banks, unshackled from traditional banking models, became skilled at repackaging their loans into bonds which could be sold on, thus removing them from the balance sheet. Banks took to funding lending through inter-bank borrowing. Banks were able to use short-term debt to fund further lending, thus enabling them to lend far more than would have been possible under traditional rules of capital adequacy, which required banks to have a substantial asset base. This type of trading was outside regulated exchanges, generating large sums of money for participants, which included not just banks but also firms in non-financial sectors that were drawn by the possibilities of greater profits from financial activities. Second, the appetite for risk that gripped the firms involved, and, in particular, the decision-makers within those firms, seemed to know no bounds. The idea that 'greed is good' implied that self-interested financial gain was the only goal to aim for, by whatever means that seemed likely to yield the most money. This approach led to excessive risk-taking.

The origins of the crisis go back to the boom in the US housing market from the early 2000s. Government policies encouraged home ownership, making it easier for people to obtain mortgages, which in turn led to a housing boom. But much of the growth in mortgage lending was in 'sub-prime' mortgages. These were loans to people who in earlier periods would have had little hope of obtaining a mortgage. These mortgages carried a high risk of non-payment, but as long as property prices continued rising, the risk seemed negligible. The market peaked in 2006, but risks lurked beneath the surface. The new sub-prime borrowers were vulnerable to interest rate rises and falling property values. For lenders such as banks, there is always a risk that borrowers will default, but default rates would normally be manageable, and traditionally, the property itself is 'concrete' security. With sub-prime debt, these assumptions became problematic. To alleviate the risks, sub-prime mortgages were repackaged with higher value assets and sold on as securitized debt. However, as noted above, valuing derivatives is not a science. When cracks appeared in the housing market, and defaults started to rise, the underlying riskiness of securitized mortgage debt became apparent. The housing boom collapsed, and uncertainty spread rapidly through financial markets, affecting the many financial institutions that had built businesses around derivatives trading.

What is this house worth? This scene became common in the US housing crash, when homebuyers fell into arrears with mortgage payments, and their properties were taken over by lending institutions.

Source: iStock.com/MCCAIG.

There followed falls in equities, as confidence in corporate finances was rapidly fading. Lending abruptly stopped, with devastating repercussions for activities in the wider economy. Banks were caught in a 'credit crunch', as their access to short-term lending, on which they had come to depend, was cut off. Their asset bases, which in earlier times would have held them in good stead, looked inadequate. Moreover, banks and other financial institutions had built up global operations, often inter-twined with each other. When losses mounted, it became clear that these banks were overstretched and overexposed in high-risk markets.

The aftermath of 2008: national authorities step in

The US and UK, both with large financial sectors, saw the most immediate impacts of the crisis, and also relatively quick policy decisions from their central banks, the US Federal Reserve and the Bank of England. Also affected were smaller countries that had opened their borders to global finance – and its attendant risks. These included Ireland and Iceland, both of which suffered financial crises. The banking systems in both countries were rescued through nationalizing the banks.

The UK government and Bank of England stepped in to rescue two major UK banks on the verge of collapse, Royal Bank of Scotland (RBS) and Halifax Bank of Scotland (HBOS). RBS had expanded rapidly through global acquisitions, acquiring 280 subsidiaries in 38 countries. As Figure 8.5 shows, its shares were just over £55 in April 2007, and fell to under £3 by April 2009. Its CEO was compelled to step down, and the bulk of the shares were transferred to the UK government in the years 2008 and 2009, with a view to selling them back to private investors in the future. As Figure 8.5 shows, the shares had hardly recovered by 2015. The company is now a shadow of its former self. Having exited 25 countries, it has become more like a national bank. In 2015, nearly 6% of the shares were sold off to private shareholders, although at a price about £1 less than the government had paid. While the sell-off was seen as a move in the right direction, the fact that taxpayers lost out suggested that the woes of the banking sector were not as yet resolved. Indeed, in the years following the financial crisis, evidence of further mismanagement and mis-selling of financial products and services revealed an even more widespread slippage in ethical standards than had emerged at the time of the bailouts.

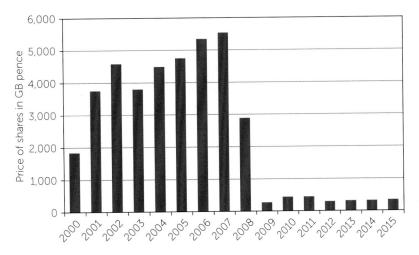

Figure 8.5 Movement of share price of Royal Bank of Scotland (RBS)

Source: Data from RBS (2015) Share price information for investors, at www.investors. rbs.com, accessed 23 August 2015.

Note: The price is the average for April of each year.

Along with several other major banks in the US and UK, RBS was implicated in scandals involving the concerted rigging of the interbank lending rate (LIBOR) and rigging of foreign exchange rates. Rates were rigged to ensure that the traders would always gain and the clients would lose out. Market rigging is a serious type of anti-competitive practice, subject to prosecution. For these malpractices, six banks (Barclays, JP Morgan Chase, Citicorp, RBS, UBS and Bank of America) received fines totalling $6 billion in the US. In addition, these banks face civil law-suits from the many investors, including pension funds and institutional investors, who suffered losses as a result of rigged rates. In the UK, banks have faced fines for mis-selling a range of financial products to retail clients, including insurance, structured investment products and pensions. In all these examples, banks have been compelled to compensate the customers who were misled about the nature of the products. These legal actions have targeted the banks themselves, not individuals within them. However, it has become clear that the culture of the banks themselves was a root cause.

A report on banking culture in the UK, published in 2014, revealed that an 'aggressive sales culture' had taken over from the traditional banking focus of serving clients' needs. This had been a major factor in the spate of bank failures (Spicer et al., 2014: 9). This aggressive culture was dictated from the top by the more recently-appointed banking executives whose focus was capital markets – the trading activities that have been likened to the 'casino' side of the business – which was the most profitable. Greed and bad practices had become so engrained that it would take years to bring about the culture change needed to restore to banks a sense of ethical principles and social purpose. Regulation has a role to play, but regulation alone cannot bring about the cultural transformation that is required. The Financial Services (Banking Reform) Act of 2013 (UK legislation, at www.legislation.gov.uk) has gone some way to addressing the regulatory issues, although this legislation has been subject to delays.

The way I see it ...

'Many people in the sector still believe they should be paid entrepreneurial wages for turning up to work with a regular salary, a pension and probably a health-care scheme and playing with other people's money.'

John Cryan, co-CEO of Deutsche Bank, describing what he feels is wrong in the banking culture, in an interview with Bloomberg, 23 November 2015.

Do you agree with John Cryan's remarks? How should bankers be paid? Is there a place for bonuses?

Under the 2013 legislation, retail banking would be 'ring-fenced', to make certain that the banking activities that serve ordinary customers and small businesses are separated from the investment activities that left the banks overexposed to risks. This structural change, which was intended to be effected by 2019, is more modest than a full-scale separation of these activities into separate entities. There is to be a new regime for senior managers in banks, aiming to uphold prudent banking standards and monitor culture within the organization. In respect of senior managers, there is a new criminal offence of taking decisions that are so far beneath what would be expected of a

reasonable person in that position that they caused a bank to fail. In effect, this provision criminalizes reckless management of a bank, and on conviction, the manager could face seven years in prison. An independent Banking Standards Review Council was set up, designed to monitor banking standards in practice. These regulatory changes would need to be followed up with commitment to enforce them in practice. The legacy of the UK's light regulatory approach could well preclude the stronger oversight envisaged by legislators.

Culture change derives in large part from the tone set by the senior executives, but must also engage employees, who are the crucial intermediaries in interacting with clients. The direction provided by the board of directors is central to bringing about culture change. Boards focused on maximizing shareholder value are associated with prioritizing short-term profits. In the decade leading up to the financial crisis, boards were highly unlikely to complain about corporate strategy and policies when members saw impressive growth in profits. As the Spicer report found, many in banking say that shareholder demands can act as a barrier to culture change in banking (Spicer et al., 2014). However, it became clear that the profits-above-all model had failed, and many shareholders now accept that a more sustainable banking model is better, serving a range of stakeholders. The regulatory reforms, especially the increased liability of senior managers, reinforces this culture change. The Spicer report found that the light-touch regulation that had characterized the more liberal market economies had proved insufficient to curb the market excesses.

In 2008, the US and UK governments focused on the broader issues of monetary policy in a deteriorating economic environment. In co-ordinated policies, the monetary authorities launched a series of measures designed to stimulate economic growth. Interest rates were reduced to levels under 1% to provide stimulus. This would be good news for borrowers, but not for savers, thereby encouraging households to spend rather than save. The unconventional policy of **quantitative easing (QE)** was introduced in both countries. In the UK, the Bank of England effectively created money electronically. Although this is often referred to as 'printing' money, no new notes are put into circulation. The money created was used to purchase assets, mostly government bonds, but also some corporate bonds, from private financial institutions such as banks and insurance companies. They could then use the money to lend to businesses or buy equities. The aim was to inject money into the financial system that would help to stimulate the economy. One of the results was a rise in equity markets. These measures were intended to be temporary: QE would come to an end when growth resumed in earnest, and the Bank of England would then raise interest rates. This process has been slower than anticipated. In 2009, the Bank of England purchased £200 billion in financial assets. Further purchases brought the total to £375 billion by 2012. In the US, a series of QE programmes continued for five years, and resulted in over $4 trillion being pumped into the economy. The US recorded improved growth rates, an indication that the stimulus had worked, although employment was slower to improve than had been expected. As of 2015, the US was considering raising interest rates, but raising interest rates would have repercussions around the world.

Emerging economies did not suffer the same meltdown in their financial systems as the more open free-market economies. The BRIC economies did feel the chill from the slowing exports to the advanced economies, but their financial systems had been less exposed to the riskier aspects of global finance. China's growth rate remained in the region of 7% from 2008 to 2014. While the advanced economies of North America and Europe were struggling to recover, healthy growth in emerging markets attracted the eyes of investors. Besides the BRICs themselves, other emerging economies, including Indonesia, Malaysia, Turkey and Nigeria, promised growth and were attracting investment. As a result, capital flowed into these economies. Cheap loans from US banks helped to fund development in these countries. The best prospects for many MNEs globally seemed to rest with emerging markets. However, as we have seen, emerging markets have had a propensity towards financial instability, including problems with falling currencies, excessive borrowing (especially in dollar-denominated debt) and weak banking systems. The Asian financial crisis exhibited all these frailties. In the years since 1997, these countries have become more significant players in the global economy, with large export sectors integrated in global supply chains that, it was thought, would shield them from financial shocks. At least, that was the hope.

However, export markets depend on demand from customers. Sluggish growth in the developed world has particularly affected China's exports of manufactured goods. Countries that export oil and iron ore rely mainly on Chinese demand, and when Chinese manufacturing shrinks, these countries feel the chill. In turn, they are unable to import as many manufactured goods from China. The fall in oil prices that occurred from 2014 onwards was considered good news in oil-importing countries, but not welcome in the countries that rely on oil exports. China's effective devaluation of its currency, discussed earlier in this chapter, was a sign that the country's export industries needed help.

The US Federal Reserve tightened monetary policy by raising interest rates very slightly in 2015. Emerging economies had cause to worry about this rise, depending on the proportion of their debt that was denominated in dollars. Unsustainable debt – whether by governments, businesses or individuals – is one of the recurring elements in financial crises. In this respect, the financial crisis that struck the advanced economies in 2007–8 was similar to the crises that have struck emerging economies (Reinhart and Rogoff, 2013). As a monetary policy designed to stimulate US recovery, QE had injected huge sums of new money into the economy – amounting to over $4 trillion. US central bankers perhaps underestimated the global impacts of this glut of money. Investors unhappy with the low returns from government bonds piled into equities, sending stock markets soaring. And the abundance of cheap money encouraged firms and households to take on debt. These trends were global in their effects. At the same time, concerns for national finances were growing, in a context of rising levels of national debt and increased calls on public spending. QE policies saw benefits flowing mainly to investors and businesses. It was hoped that economic recovery would generate new jobs and increase incomes. In reality, employment lagged behind while stock markets soared. Triggered by a slowing Chinese economy, stocks fell in 2015, raising a possibility that instabilities in emerging markets would once again be a prelude to financial crisis.

The impacts of QE policies: pros and cons

What are the pros and cons of QE, in your judgment, for the US, and for countries such as China and other emerging markets?

Global markets for corporate control

The globalization of financial flows has facilitated MNEs in their expansion strategies. Cross-border acquisitions and mergers, known generally as 'M&A' activities, forge ahead when markets are buoyant, but can slow down markedly when markets are weak. In this section we look at mergers and acquisitions from a financial perspective, and the impacts of the financial environment on current trends.

Mergers

A **merger** occurs when two or more companies agree to come together to form a new company. For example, GlaxoSmithKline (www.gsk.com) was formed by a merger between Glaxo and SmithKlineBeecham, the latter of which was a product of earlier mergers. Mergers are a feature of consolidation in an industry which has become globalized. Mergers can also be referred to as **horizontal integration** because the merger takes place between companies in the same industry. There have been waves of consolidation in the pharmaceuticals and chemicals sector, for example, in the late 1990s. In research-intensive sectors, a main rationale for consolidation is the increasing returns to scale in R&D. There are other reasons at work, too. Pharmaceuticals enjoy a lucrative global market. A merged company is in a stronger position in large national markets, having, for example, greater resources for marketing than the two firms would be able to access independently.

If mergers bring together two large players in a market, there are implications for competition policies in the countries where their businesses are carried out. Competition authorities can take an aggressive approach towards a proposed merger if they feel there is a possibility that the combined company will be in a dominant position from which it can act anti-competitively. Competition issues are now a major concern in global M&A strategies. In 2014, Holcim of Switzerland and Lafarge of France, two cement giants, proposed to merge in order to cut costs, due to the shrinking global demand for building materials. The merger looked destined to involve forced selling of assets in different locations that could amount to nearly $7 billion, in order to satisfy competition authorities (Winters and de Beaupuy, 2014). The combined company would constitute the world's largest cement company. Senior managers were expecting to have to present their case to regulatory authorities in 15 countries, in many of which sales of assets would be required.

Acquisitions

A favoured growth strategy of MNEs is acquisition (see Chapter 2). Acquisitions help to build market share quickly in new markets (discussed in the closing case study). The acquirer often benefits from the strengths of an existing business, shortening the timescale in which the profits from the acquisition start to flow.

In the case of an **acquisition**, or takeover, one company takes over another, often turning the target company into a subsidiary. The predator must pay for the firm it buys, which usually means raising money. How to finance the acquisition is a major concern, which can influence whether the purchase goes through at all. The acquirer can raise fresh capital through a rights issue, involving issuing more shares, to finance the acquisition. Alternatively, it can finance the deal through debt, issuing bonds or seeking loans from banks. The **leveraged buy-out**, financed through debt, is a favoured strategy of private equity groups. The **private equity** fund, which usually lasts for a fixed term of several years, invests on behalf of wealthy investors. Like hedge funds, private equity groups look for relatively short-term gains. Their strategies include buy-out activities, often buying companies which are then saddled with large debt burdens. Private equity groups, for example, looked to purchase productive assets cheaply in the event of sell-offs resulting from the Holcim-Lafarge merger.

Financing a takeover depends in part on the size and status of the target company. If the target company is a private company rather than a public one, the acquirer need only buy out the owners. If the target company is a public one, however, the shareholders become involved. The acquirer will make an offer to the board, which will then recommend it to the shareholders. If the board rejects the offer, the bid becomes 'hostile'. A hostile bidder must win over the owners of the majority of shares in order to succeed. In countries where the norm in corporate governance is to adopt a 'one share, one vote' policy, this can be relatively straightforward, assuming the shareholders find the offer appealing. The UK is such an environment. Shareholders are sometimes offered a combination of cash and shares in the acquiring company. In countries where companies operate weighted voting systems (in which a few dominant shareholders control most of the votes), there is an inbuilt barrier to takeo-vers. This situation prevails in many continental European countries. The takeover of Cadbury of the UK by Kraft of the US in 2009 was facilitated by the ease with which it was possible to accumulate shareholder support in the UK. In 2012, Cadbury was spun off into a new company, Mondelèz, bringing together numerous snack brands (www.mondelezinternational.com). Kraft was itself merged with Heinz in 2015 (www.kraftheinzcompany.com), in a takeover by Brazilian private equity investors and the famous US investor, Warren Buffet.

Trends in cross-border mergers and acquisitions

Historically, there have been periods of heightened merger activity generally, resulting in the rise of large conglomerates, as happened in the 1960s in the US and Europe. From the 1980s onwards, waves of privatizations in former state-owned industries, such as telecommunications and utilities, have accounted for much acquisition activity, attracting foreign investors, usually global companies keen to expand into new markets.

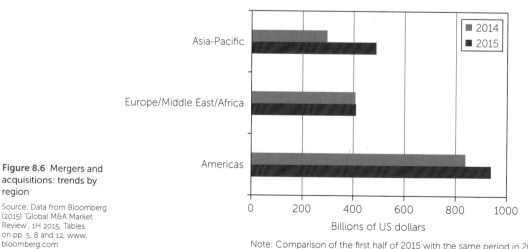

Figure 8.6 Mergers and acquisitions: trends by region

Source: Data from Bloomberg (2015) 'Global M&A Market Review', 1H 2015, Tables on pp. 5, 8 and 12, www.bloomberg.com

Note: Comparison of the first half of 2015 with the same period in 2014.

Rapid growth in emerging markets has driven much M&A activity since 2000. Among the more active acquirers have been Indian companies, such as Tata, which acquired British car manufacturers, Jaguar and Land Rover, purchasing the brands from Ford Motor Co. of the US in 2008. The Indian steel magnate, Lakshmi Mittal, achieved one of the more ambitious takeovers in the years between 2000 and 2010, by purchasing European steelmaker, Arcelor, to create ArcelorMittal, now the world's largest steel company. Mexican cement maker, Cemex, pursued a successful acquisition strategy, becoming a global force in the industry. It became the world's third largest building materials company, behind Holcim (first) and Lafarge (second) with the acquisition of Rinker Group of Australia in 2007. Cemex was expected to purchase some of the cement works that Holcim and Lafarge were being forced to sell. However, Cemex failed to secure these deals, and has fallen behind rival building materials companies globally, while remaining a strong force in Latin America. Chinese companies have focused more on acquisitions in the developing regions, pursuing resource-seeking strategies. As Figure 8.6 shows, M&A activity grew globally in 2015, although the growth in Europe, the Middle East and Africa was only 0.6%. The Americas are by far the most active of the regions, with a healthy 12% growth in 2015. However, the biggest rise was in the Asia-Pacific region, where there was a 65% increase on the first half of 2014. Most of this activity was in China, which saw a 91% rise. Easy access to debt financing has played a large part in driving acquisition activity in China. However, as noted above, the rise in corporate debt in China has become a potential source of instability.

A recent trend has been for large, highly-diversified companies, or **conglomerates**, to slim down to what is conceived to be their core business. This involves selling off, known as 'divesting', the non-core businesses. The urge to sell weakly-performing businesses can arise at any time, but is particularly associated with periods of economic downturn. In extreme cases, companies have felt forced to raise money by selling businesses even though they would have liked to keep them. In other cases, corporate executives conclude that it is best to reduce the number of brands on which to focus. From 2014, P&G (Procter & Gamble) (us.pg.com), the world's largest consumer goods company, has embarked on this strategy, aiming to sell 100 brands in all. In 2015, it sold 43 beauty brands, including Clairol, which it had purchased in 2001 when the company's thoughts were more on expansion. The beauty brands were sold to Coty, the cosmetics company, for $12.5 billion, effectively doubling the size of Coty's existing business. In the years following the financial crisis, competitiveness has been a challenge in the context of the multiplicity of brands that P&G had acquired. It has retained key brands, Pantene and Head & Shoulders, considered to be core brands in the company's hair and skincare portfolio. P&G has also sold the Duracell battery business, and other brands ranging from coffee to soap. P&G, like other large companies, aims to restore competitiveness by re-focusing on core brands.

GLOBAL BUSINESS IN ACTION

Cargotec pursues an M&A strategy to better serve global customers

Toni Rannikko

Cargotec (www.cargotec.com), a Finnish MNE, specializes in cargo-handling equipment that operates in hundreds of ports and terminals worldwide, facilitating the movement of goods that keep the global economy running. These goods cover a wide range, from raw materials to finished consumer goods, and mostly are transported in containers but also as bulk cargo. Cargotec was formed in 2005, from the demerger of Kone Corporation into two separate listed companies, KONE and Cargotec. Since then, Cargotec has grown to encompass operations in over 100 countries, with a workforce of over 11,000 people worldwide. It has grown largely by acquiring businesses that contribute to its aims of providing a full range of services for clients' needs. One in four containers that serve consumer markets globally is handled by a Cargotec business. It now comprises three main business areas, each with its own identity and history: Kalmar, Hiab and MacGregor. Kalmar specializes in cargo handling, and has been a frontrunner in automated handling in container terminals. Hiab specializes in handling equipment for road transport, an area in which it is a world leader. MacGregor's business focuses on marine cargoes and offshore load handling. MacGregor's roll-on-roll-off equipment can be found in most of the world's car ferries. Toni Rannikko is Director of Strategy and M&A at Cargotec. He is focused particularly on business development through acquisitions. Toni holds an MSc in Economics, and is widely experienced in finance, high-tech industries and engineering. He is thus well placed to appreciate the strategic challenges in the areas of shipping and logistics generally.

World trade has seen only modest growth since the financial crisis of 2008, and this has impacted on all the players in the transport sector. In the interview, Toni stresses that cargo-handling companies must adjust to this challenging environment by providing more efficient services to customers. While providing equipment has been a mainstay of the company's business, he sees this focus as shifting towards services and software, or 'intelligent' cargo-handling. In this way, the company is adapting better to customers' needs. Future acquisitions of companies would contribute towards these goals. He also stresses that this strategic outlook emphasizes sustainable solutions. It is notable that each of the Cargotec business areas has a strong innovation profile. For example, MacGregor's specialized winches are being used in an innovative project which aims to generate electricity from waves.

Before watching the interview with Toni, look again at the following sections in Chapter 2: 'Why do companies internationalize?' and 'Modes of internationalization'. Also look again at the section in Chapter 7 entitled, 'Trends in world trade: impacts of globalization'. It will also be helpful to look at Cargotec's website, which contains a wealth of information about its three distinctive business areas. There you will find a timeline that shows the pattern of acquisitions.

Visit www.palgravehighered.com/morrison-gbe-4e to watch the video, then think about the following questions:

1. How does Toni see the role of M&A in the development of Cargotec?
2. In terms of the push and pull factors that influence companies to internationalize (listed on pages 46–7 in Chapter 2), which ones are relevant to Cargotec, and why?
3. Why is the company shifting from a focus on equipment to one on services?
4. How does sustainability fit into Cargotec's corporate strategy?

Global finance: challenges and responsibilities

The bedrock of classical economic thinking has been the assumption that a free market, made up of individuals and firms pursuing self-interested goals, is inherently stable. This article of faith has been dislodged by market failures that have led to financial crises. 'Self-regulation' is the seemingly contradictory term often used in connection with market economies, suggesting that if governments refrain from mandatory regulation, markets will function more smoothly, and economic prosperity will be unleashed for the benefit of all. The implication is that the players themselves will behave in responsible ways. But, as we have seen, the financial sector has shown little sense of long-term responsibility for the consequences of their activities on stakeholders. The challenges for firms and governments are to allow an enterprise culture to flourish, but one that is coupled with a sense of broad responsibilities to stakeholders, including employees, customers and whole communities.

Finance as a business has long attracted the exuberant trader, but it has also had a long history of highly responsible and socially-focused corporate ownership. Most of the banks highlighted in this chapter have distinguished histories of serving communities in eras when bankers were respected members of society. Those times have given way to the image of the adrenalin-fuelled trader on the floor of the stock exchange. The evidence of illegal and unethical practices is testimony to the need for change in the culture of financial services generally – not just banking. Regulatory reforms are now under way at national level, but reforms do not take place in a vacuum. A long period of consultation preceded the Banking Reform Act in the UK, and there will be an even longer wait for implementation. The ring-fencing provisions would come into force over a decade after the banking meltdown. Moreover, these ring-fencing provisions are themselves a compromise: banks are not being required to restructure radically.

Financial services touch every member of society, either directly or indirectly: people need funds for housing, trustworthy banks for their household finances, pensions they can rely on, and many other financial services. The backlash against greedy bankers was widespread in 2008 when executives responsible for bank failures were paid generous rewards while ordinary employees lost their jobs. The new criminal offence of causing a bank to fail is largely in response to this situation. But culture change is as important as regulatory reform – and more difficult to bring about. The bigger challenge for firms and governments is to shift towards a more sustainable and stakeholder-focused business model. In theory, this should be uncontroversial, as the excesses of high-risk strategies had disastrous consequences that saw banking empires crumble. However, the culture of finance in the decade leading up to the financial crisis of 2007–8 tended towards the casino mentality, as trading activities became the big moneyspinners. The gambler persists in believing with every bet that this could be the big one that could win the jackpot.

Conclusions

Finance is essential to the functioning of whole economies, businesses, governments and households. Without well-managed financial systems, businesses would be fearful of investing, governments would be reluctant to embark on large projects and householders would face uncertainty in how to support families and cope with old age. Stability is perhaps the one feature most prized in the financial environment. But stability has become more elusive as finance has become globalized. Finance was once seen through the lenses of national financial systems, overlaid with co-ordination at international level to maintain exchange-rate stability, as in the era of the gold standard. The era of globalization has brought about dramatic changes in the way financial activities take place and in the kinds of transactions involved. While opening up new opportunities, global financial markets have also generated new risks. Innovation and computer technology have been instrumental, facilitating the growth of large financial sectors in countries such as the US and UK. At the same time, some of the most dramatic growth in financial markets has come in emerging markets, now increasingly involved in global capital flows. Global financial markets allow businesses everywhere to aspire to cross-border investing and borrowing. But the stability of these markets has raised questions for all participants. In particular, responsibilities have fallen on international businesses and governments.

Stability at the national level is almost impossible to attain unless there is a stable framework at the international level. The IMF and World Bank date from the late 1940s. The creators of these institutions could not have envisaged the challenges posed by the scale and complexity of today's global financial markets. Nor could they have envisaged the global roles now played by emerging economies, notably China. The creation of an Asian development bank (the AIIB), along the lines of the World Bank, is an indication that international institutions need to recognize these shifts in power. The IMF has been instrumental in co-ordinating the rescue packages of heavily-indebted countries and, despite its shortcomings, it remains the only inter-governmental institution fulfilling this role globally. However, rescue packages are put in place when financial systems have already failed, with the huge damage suffered by societies in the ensuing economic recession. Despite the abundant signs that financial globalization has spun out of control, there is no global regulatory framework analogous to the role played by national regulators. Taming markets to serve the goals of all stakeholders is perhaps not 'mission impossible', but very difficult.

References

Blundell-Wignall, A. (2012) 'Solving the financial and sovereign debt crisis in Europe', *OECD Journal: Financial Market Trends*, 2011(2): 1–23.

Clift, J. (2003) 'Hearing the dogs bark', *Finance and Development*, 40(4): 8–11.

Curran, E. (2015) 'China's very high mountain of debt', *Bloomberg News*, 8 May, at www.bloomberg.com

Eichengreen, B. (1996) *Globalizing Capital: A History of the International Monetary System* (Princeton: Princeton University Press).

Ernst & Young Global Limited (2014) *EY Global Trends 2014*, at www.ey.com

Fajgenbaum, J., Guzman, J. and Loser, C. (2015) *For Puerto Rico: There is a Better Way*, Centennial Group International.

Geddie, J. and Zaharia, M. (2015) 'Greek debt better shielded from vultures than Argentina's', Reuters, 3 July, at www.reuters.com

Glyn, A., Hughes, A., Lipietz, A. and Singh, A. (1992) 'The rise and fall of the Golden Age', in Maglin, S. and Schor, J. (eds) *The Golden Age of Capitalism: Reinterpreting the Postwar Experience* (Oxford: Clarendon Press), pp. 39–125.

IMF (2015) *Global Financial Stability Report*, April (Washington, DC: IMF).

Ito, T. (1996) 'Japan and the Asian economies: a "miracle" in transition', *Brookings Papers on Economic Activity*, 2: 205–272, at www.brookings.edu

Kapstein, E.B. (1994) *Governing the Global Economy: International Finance and the State* (Cambridge, MA: Harvard University Press).

Krugman, P. (1999) *The Return of Depression Economics* (Harmondsworth: Penguin).

McCrank, J. (2014) 'U.S. high-frequency trading ban unlikely: Nasdaq', 28 March, Reuters, at www.reuters.com

Neate, R. (2012) 'Jersey puts stop to vulture funds circling its courts', *The Guardian*, 20 November.

Reinhart, C. and Rogoff, K. (2013) 'Financial and sovereign debt crises: some lessons learned and those forgotten', IMF Working Paper, WP13/266, at www.imf.org

Singh, A. (1998) '"Asian capitalism" and the financial crisis', Centre for Economic Policy Analysis Working Paper Series III, No. WP10, August, https://mpra.ub.uni-muenchen.de/24937

Spicer, A., Gond, J., Patel, K., Lindley, D., Fleming, P., Mosonyi, S., Benoit, C. and Parker, S. (2014) 'A report on the culture of British retail banking', New City Agenda and Cass Business School (City University London) at www.newcityagenda.co.uk

Stiglitz, J. (2000) 'The insider', *New Republic*, 222(16/17): 56–60.

Stiglitz, J. (2015) 'Sovereign debt needs international supervision', *The Guardian*, 16 June.

Williamson, J. (2004) 'A short history of the Washington Consensus', Paper given at the conference, 'From the Washington Consensus to a new global governance', Fundación CIDOB, Barcelona, 24-25 September, at www.iie.com/publications

Winters, P. and de Beaupuy, F. (2014) 'Holcim to merge with Lafarge to form biggest cement maker', Bloomberg news, 14 April, at www.bloomberg.com

☛ Multiple choice questions

Go to the companion website: www.palgravehighered.com/morrison-gbe-4e to take a quick multiple choice quiz on what you have read in this chapter.

⑦ Review questions

1 How have capital markets become globalized, and what are the implications for listed companies?

2 How can a company benefit from the issuing of bonds, and how do bondholders differ from shareholders?

3 Explain the benefits that were enjoyed under the gold standard system.

4 What were the aims of the Bretton Woods agreement? What were the reasons behind its collapse in the 1970s?

5 What is the 'Washington consensus', and how has it been criticized?

6 Explain the differences between fixed, floating and pegged exchanged rates.

7 Summarize the initial aims of the Bretton Woods institutions – the IMF and World Bank. How have their roles evolved since their formation?

8 What are the problems faced by countries issuing sovereign bonds that can lead to national financial crisis?

9 What is the role of hedge funds in global finance?

10 What lessons could be learned from the Asian financial crisis of 1997–98?

11 How did global banking strategies contribute to the collapse of banks that had to be bailed out?

12 What was the sub-prime housing market in the US, and how did it contribute to the global financial crisis?

13 How have governments responded to the 2008 financial crisis?

14 How have banks changed their strategies since the 2008 financial crisis?

15 Mergers and acquisitions have become increasingly important in the markets for corporate control. What are the driving forces behind them?

✓ Assignments

1 Globalizing capital markets have provided investment opportunities for outside investors, but have also posed risks both for investors and for national authorities. Assess the lessons have been learned from the 2008 financial crisis.

2 Assess the ways in which banking reform can stabilize national and global financial markets.

📖 Further reading

Cable, V. (2016) *After the Storm: The World Economy and Britain's Economic Future* (London: Atlantic Books).

Eichengreen, B. (2008) *Globalizing Capital: A History of the International Monetary System*, 2nd edn (Princeton: Princeton University Press).

Eichengreen, B. (2015) *Hall of Mirrors: The Great Depression, the Great Recession, and the Uses – and Misuses – of History* (Oxford: OUP).

Kay, J. (2015) *Other People's Money: Masters of the Universe or Servants of the People?* (London: Profile Books).

Krugman, P. (2008) *The Return of Depression Economics and the Crisis of 2008* (Harmondsworth: Allen Lane).

Krugman, P. (2013) *End this Depression Now!* (London: W.W. Norton).

Martin, I. (2014) *Making it Happen: Fred Goodwin, RBS, and the Men who Blew up the British Economy* (London: Simon & Schuster).

Turner, A. (2015) *Between Debt and the Devil: Money, Credit and Fixing Global Finance* (Princeton, NJ: Princeton University Press).

Zestos, G. (2015) *The Global Financial Crisis: From US Subprime Mortgages to European Sovereign Debt* (London: Routledge).

> 🌐 **Visit the companion website at www.palgravehighered.com/morrison-gbe-4e for further learning and teaching resources.**

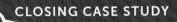

CLOSING CASE STUDY

The creation of a 'megabrewer'

At least one of the glasses on this table probably contains a beer whose brand is owned by AB InBev.

Source: PhotoDisc/Getty Images.

There are many hundreds of branded beers globally, but the number of companies making them has been shrinking. Larger beer companies grow by buying smaller ones, often to acquire a brand that looks to have potential in growing markets. This is the reasoning behind the takeover of SABMiller by AB InBev. AB InBev is the world's largest brewing company, and SABMiller lies in second place globally. Both have grown by acquiring other companies and their brands, totalling over 400. A merged company would produce one in every three beers bought by consumers globally, generating 47% of the profits made in the global beer market. Their combined revenues amount to $73 billion, which would make the new company bigger than Google. It is no wonder that industry experts call this merger 'Megabrew' (Daneshkhu, 2015). However, in an overall deal worth over $100 billion, there were numerous competition hurdles to be overcome in the markets where the two companies are dominant. And there were questions hanging over what brands would have to be sold to satisfy national regulators. Could AB InBev find that some popular brands would have to be sacrificed?

The driving forces behind the takeover were three Brazilian private equity financiers, known as 3G Capital, who built up the Brazilian brewing business, Ambev. Ambev merged with the Belgium brewing empire, Interbrew, maker of Stella Artois and Beck's, in 2004. In 2008, the Brazilians bought Anheuser Busch of the US, owner of the Budweiser brand, creating what is now AB InBev. Registered in Belgium, AB InBev is the dominant beer company in the US, where the most popular brand is Bud Light. AB InBev's Brazilian CEO, Carlos Brito, is known for cutting costs ruthlessly and seeking efficiencies in production. Reducing staff numbers and other cost savings are an important part of Brito's strategy. He would be aiming to apply this approach to SABMiller's operations. SABMiller's origins are in South Africa, which is still seen as its home market, even though the company was listed in London. The company has branched out into other African markets, and has been a major beneficiary of growing beer consumption in Africa. The Brazilian owners of AB InBev were particularly keen to access the growing market in Africa. However, the South African government is keen that employment in brewing is maintained, and would resist Brito's possible cost-cutting and slimming down of the workforce.

SABMiller can claim some popular global brands, such as Peroni and Grolsch. It successfully expanded into markets around the world. In China, it is involved in a joint venture with China Resources Enterprise, to produce Snow, China's most popular beer. However, combined with AB InBev's presence in China, the two would control more than 40% of the beer market. Under China's 2008 anti-monopoly law, SABMiller could be compelled to sell its stake in the joint venture. In the US, it entered a joint venture to form MillerCoors, maker of the popular Miller Lite. MillerCoors is the second-largest beer company in the US, behind AB InBev. This successful joint venture also looks to be at risk in the 'megamerger'.

AB InBev made numerous attempts to buy SABMiller. After four successive offers and a public appeal by Brito to the SABMiller investors, the two dominant shareholders in the target company agreed. The largest block of shares belonged to Altria, the American tobacco company that owns the Marlboro brand, and the other major shareholder was the Colombian brewing dynasty, the Santo Domingo family, who held out for a better deal. Eventually, Brito clinched the deal. While it brings AB InBev market opportunities outside the US, he maintains that the deal is good for consumers everywhere because it gives them more choice, as the brands of the combined companies will be sold in all markets. However, because of the dominant position of the two companies in the US, SABMiller was compelled to sell its interest in MillerCoors to its partner, Molson Coors. With the sale goes the Miller Lite brand, and the global rights to the Miller brand. Miller's popularity is growing globally, notably in Asia and Africa, where it will be competing with the new combined company. Also among the brands in the MillerCoors portfolio are Peroni and Pilsner Urquell. The MillerCoors brands will be imported into the US. Budweiser and other domestic brands have been losing ground in the US, as drinkers are increasingly turning to imported brands and craft beers. The merger of the two giant beer companies does not address this issue of changing tastes. However, in the tradition of acquiring competitors, the new company is already acquiring craft brands. This might seem a contradiction. The appeal of the craft brand is its local, small-scale production. A megabrewer is the 'antithesis of the craft brewer' (Ruddick, 2015).

Sources: Farrell, S. (2015) 'SAB Miller agrees AB InBev takeover deal of £68 billion', *The Guardian*, 13 October, at www.theguardian.com; Ruddick, G. (2015) 'Beer titans opt to merge as trend for small craft brews comes to a head', *The Guardian*, 17 October; Daneshkhu, S. (2015) 'Champagne on ice for AB InBev's "Megabrew"', *Financial Times*, 17 October, www.ft.com.

Questions for discussion

- What is the reasoning behind the takeover of SABMiller by AB InBev?
- Is the deal a good one for consumers worldwide, as the CEO claims, or is it a bad one? Explain.
- 3G Capital has a voracious appetite for deal-making and cost-cutting. The Brazilian private equity group also owns Burger King and Kraft-Heinz (another recent merger). How does their approach affect the competitive environment in the markets where their companies are active?
- Should there be a global competition authority to handle deals such as this one?

CHAPTER

9

TECHNOLOGY AND INNOVATION

Outline of chapter

This chapter will enable you to

- Appreciate the role of technological change in economic progress
- Gain an insight into the ways in which innovation is generated and diffused in different societies
- Understand the interactions between national systems of innovation and the diffusion of technology
- Assess the roles of governments and business in harnessing technological innovation to achieve qualitative benefits for all in society

OPENING CASE STUDY

ARM: the Cambridge start-up behind the smartphone

In the 1960s, IBM, the American technology giant, had plans to establish an R&D facility in Cambridge in the UK. In most countries, a foreign investor of the stature of IBM would be more than welcome, but the local authority in Cambridge refused planning permission, effectively blocking the investment. In the decades since then, Cambridge has become known as a technology cluster, sometimes called Silicon Fen, mirroring Silicon Valley in California. Local entrepreneurs, many linked with academic units in Cambridge University, have formed start-up companies that have flourished in a cluster-like environment. It has been argued that if IBM had been allowed to set up in the Cambridge area, it might have swept up local talent, squeezing out the new indigenous businesses that have emerged (Bolton and Thompson, 2004). In many places, foreign direct investment (FDI) acts as a catalyst to local innovators, but in others, the arrival of a large company from outside can stifle them. Since those early years, foreign companies such as AstraZeneca, the pharmaceutical company, have moved into the area, helping to make Cambridge a hub for medical research. And many local start-ups have become successful in the fast-changing world of computer technology. One of these, ARM Holdings, has emerged as a leader in its field of processors for small devices such as smartphones. Unlike its arch rival, Intel, which has a high-profile brand image, ARM is hardly known by consumers, although 95% of smartphones contain ARM processors. Users of iPhones and rival Samsung smartphones both rely on ARM's technology. How has ARM managed to become a global success in designing processing chips?

ARM has specialized in low-power computing. Engineers originally associated with Acorn Computers in Cambridge latched onto a simplified chip design which led to a partnership with Apple Computers in 1990, the aim being to make a handheld computer. But this was the era in which Microsoft's Windows operating system and Intel processors came to be dominant. As the Acorn ARM chips were not powerful enough to run Windows, its fortunes declined. However, ARM emerged as a separate company, aiming not to be a manufacturer, but a designer of low-power processing chips that manufacturers could utilize as they wished. Indeed, ARM considers its designs as essentially a layout in character, allowing the manufacturer's designer to adapt them, and giving the manufacturer maximum flexibility. ARM's innovations were also timely – coinciding with the rise of mobile technology. The first iPhone contained a chip manufactured by Samsung, but with a chip designed by ARM. ARM considers that the first of its two competitive advantages is low power and, hence, mobility. Lower power consumption enables batteries to be smaller and lighter, which is a priority for all the manufacturers of smartphones.

ARM considers that its second competitive advantage is the way it works with partner companies, providing processing units that allow the manufacturing partner to incorporate its own innovations. ARM's head of brand marketing says, 'Intel had too much control over innovation on their PCs. They left very little for the PC manufacturers to do other than slot their chips in. That's not a healthy environment, and the road to innovation will slow' (Hern, 2015). Apple has seen the advantages of ARM-based chips. Following their success with iPhones, Apple has considered using ARM chips in its laptops, PCs and workstations, all of which had been relying on Intel chips. This would seem to be a case of the successful iPhone processors showing the way forward. For Apple, there are advantages in switching to ARM for its microprocessors. Apple holds an 'architectural licence' to use ARM's microprocessor architecture. This means that it can give its designers free rein to design ARM-based chips for whatever device it wishes, be it a Mac or a watch.

ARM's revenues derive from the royalties it receives from the users of its patented technology. It has seen impressive growth in revenues from smartphones, but this growth has slowed due to the large proportion of low-cost smartphones that swell the global market. The lower the product's price, the smaller the royalties ARM receives for each unit sold. The company has thus continued to look for innovations in other areas, such as connected devices and the 'internet of things'. The company is already seeing a rising proportion of its royalties coming from the use of its processors in products other than smartphones. And it has started to increase the power of its processors in order to compete with Intel directly. The connected home of the future is likely to have a smart fridge powered by ARM.

Sources: Burton, G. (2015) 'Is Apple about to shift CPU architectures from Intel to ARM?' *Computing*, 18 June, at www.computing.co.uk; Hern, A. (2015) 'ARM: Britain's most successful tech company you've never heard of', *The Observer*, 29 November, at www.theguardian.com; Bolton, B. and Thompson, J. (2004) *Entrepreneurs: Talent, Temperament, Techniques*, 2nd edn (London: Routledge).

💬 Questions for discussion

- What factors contributed to the growth of the technology companies in Cambridge?
- How does ARM differ from its rival, Intel?
- What is ARM's relationship with Apple, and why has it been successful?
- What does the growth of ARM show in terms of innovation strategies?

Introduction

A new medicine, a smartphone, a cleaner fuel – technological innovation holds out the prospect of changes that will improve lives and benefit the environment. Businesses are at the heart of these processes, making technology a key driving force in the world economy. Technological innovation and the capacity to sustain a technological lead are crucial to success in the competitive environment, for both companies and countries. No longer the preserve of engineering and design departments, technology now penetrates every aspect of business, linking R&D, design, production and distribution, in global networks. In particular, advances in computing, telecommunications and transport have resulted in dramatic improvements in all sectors, from car manufacturing to vaccines to fight diseases. Technological changes have impacted on the ways in which organizations operate, both internally and, increasingly, in interdependent global networks. They have also transformed the daily lives of people around the world, as illustrated by the huge rise in internet and mobile phone use globally in the last decade. In 2000, there were about 400 million internet users in the world, mostly in developed countries. That number has risen dramatically, as shown in Figure 9.1. There are now estimated to be 3 billion people using the internet globally, and the steepest rise is among people in developing countries.

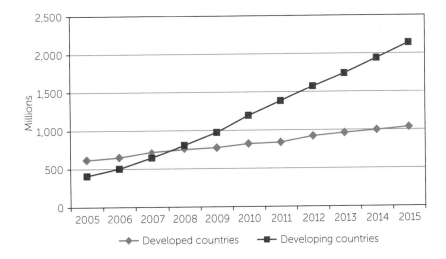

Figure 9.1 Number of individuals using the internet

Source: Data from ITU (2015), 'ICT Facts and Figures, Key ICT Indicators: Individuals using the internet', at www.itu.int, accessed 2 September 2015.

'Cutting edge' technology can be an important source of competitive advantage for businesses. There is hardly a company that would not welcome the competitive edge that developing its own new technology can deliver. However, the relationships between knowledge, technological innovation and markets are now recognized to be more complex than was once thought. The growth of international markets has focused attention on differences between national systems of innovation, as well as differences in organizational structures that can promote or inhibit innovation. Social, cultural and political factors in national environments can influence the creation and adoption of technological know-how. Globalization processes have raised these questions, particularly in relation to technology transfer and knowledge transfer. Thus, while organizations see the need for a strong focus on technological innovation, they are becoming increasingly aware that technology must be viewed in the context of the wider business environment. In particular, the regulatory environment in many countries impacts on multinational enterprise (MNE) strategies, reminding us that, even in this most globalized of areas, national forces remain potent. For countries, technology is directly relevant to development goals, and governments are keenly aware of the need to nurture education and technological innovation as part of their development agenda. Their hopes are that benefits will flow both to the domestic economy and society. This chapter aims to explain the broad processes of technological innovation and diffusion in the context of national environments, and to assess the changes that result in national economies and societies.

Concepts and processes

We begin by defining the basic terms which are used in this chapter. **Technology** can be defined as the methodical application of scientific knowledge to practical purposes. It is a concept at the intersection of learning and doing. Throughout history there have been talented, imaginative individuals, able to assimilate scientific knowledge and transform its principles into practical inventions. An **invention** is a product or process which can be described as 'new', in that it makes a significant qualitative leap forward from the state of existing knowledge. Inventions come under the broad heading of **innovation**. Innovation is a broad term, including improvements which are less radical but offer commercial benefits. The OECD defines innovation as 'the implementation of a new or significantly improved product (good or service), or process, a new marketing method, or a new organizational method in business practices, workplace organization or external relations'. It can be 'new to the firm, new to the market or new to the world' (OECD, 2010: 1). An innovation can be new to the firm, although having been adopted by other firms already. Similarly, it can be new to a particular market, although it already exists in other markets. If an innovation is new to the world, it has not been done before by any firms or in any markets. If a particular innovation proves successful, it is soon taken up by other firms and in other countries, and has the capacity to transform markets. While such transformation is seen as generally beneficial, a salutary lesson to bear in mind is that innovations in financial markets were largely responsible for the boom in global finance that led to the devastating crash of late 2007 (see Chapter 8). Innovations unlock opportunities for improvements, but they also entail risks. Key to harnessing their benefits is the responsible management of the development of new technologies, their applications and the rewards that flow from them.

R&D (research and development) is a function that covers the broad range of innovations, not just inventions. Larger firms typically have an R&D budget and employ specialist R&D staff. Governments in many countries help to fund R&D, often in conjunction with specific industrial sectors. While many inventions, including patented ones, are never commercially produced, innovations, by definition, are economically valuable. Technical innovation has thus been described as the matching of new technology to a market, or 'the first commercial application or production of a new process or product' (Freeman and Soete, 1997: 201). Inventions can be legally protected by a patent, which gives the inventor (or more often, a company) 'ownership' of its rights of exploitation. An innovation may be a less dramatic step forward, for example, an improvement that speeds up an industrial process. While not patentable, it is nonetheless significant in that it can lead to scale economies.

Scientific knowledge plays a crucial role in the genesis of technical innovation. But it is only the start of the process. As Figure 9.2 depicts, there are many steps along the way from turning a scientific discovery into a workable invention that can be commercially exploited. Figure 9.2, although highly simplified, shows the flow of ideas from science to applied research, and then to development for commercial application. Note that consumer feedback is integrated into the process, helping to generate improved products and further innovation. The successful innovator is not simply a person with a flair for coming up with a great idea. The innovator has a mixture of qualities, including knowledge and awareness of commercial opportunities – and perseverance. The process that appears in Figure 9.2 can take years to unfold, with mis-steps along the way. National and corporate environments can facilitate the bringing of innovative ideas to commercial fruition (Tellis et al., 2009).

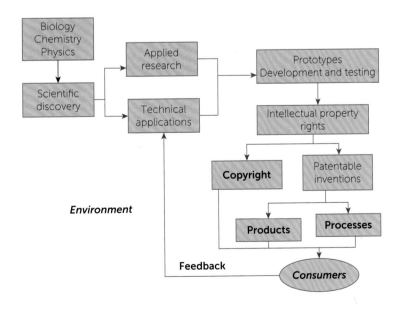

Figure 9.2 The innovation process for intellectual property

Historians puzzle over two key questions in relation to technology. First, why do science and invention flourish in particular societies during certain eras, but not in others? And second, why are some societies with high levels of learning, scientific knowledge, and creative inventors still not able to convert learning into invention, or invention into technological advancement at the level of society? David Landes points to two examples. Islam, in its golden age, 750–1100, 'produced the world's greatest scientists, yet a flourishing science contributed nothing to the slow advance of technology in Islam' (Landes, 1998: 54). More remarkable were the Chinese, with a long list of inventions, including the wheelbarrow, compass, paper, printing, gunpowder and porcelain. In the twelfth century, the Chinese were using a water-driven machine for spinning hemp, anticipating English spinning machines by some 500 years. Yet such technical progress made little impact on the Chinese economy. The Chinese, it seems, had the scientific knowledge to produce the steam engine, but for some reason that still baffles historians, failed to do it. Summarizing the debate, Landes points to China's lack of 'a free market and institutionalized property rights' as key factors that discouraged initiative (Landes, 1998: 56).

The magnetic compass was invented in China around 200 BC, but it was not until over a thousand years later that its use for finding direction caught on. Thereafter, it became widely used by western traders, who saw its potential to transform navigation.

Source: PhotoDisc/Getty Images.

We generally assume that in societies where learning is valued, a high level of science education will lay the foundations for people with technological talent to flourish. Their skills will feed into the country's industries, fostering economic prosperity. However, the relative importance of 'demand-pull' and 'science-push' is debated. Both forces play a role in technological innovation. The emphasis on demand-pull factors, as in product life cycle theory, has been criticized as one-sided. How, it might be asked, can consumers judge a revolutionary new product of which they have no knowledge (Freeman and Soete, 1997: 200)? Many of the early inventors, with their scientific backgrounds, had little idea of the economic potential of their innovations, or of the many possible applications of their technology. Science-push was clearly important among the early inventors and entrepreneurs, who formed new companies in order to exploit their inventions. However, there were instances where demand predominated, and these certainly became more prevalent when innovation became 'routinized' within large firms. Even today, whereas large firms with vast R&D expenditure account for the bulk of innovations, radical innovations often come from small firms. This is particularly the case in the rapidly growing digital sphere, in which the small start-ups are gaining competitive ground.

Theories of technological innovation

Theories of technological innovation start from the assumption that innovation is vital to economic progress. In terms of competitive advantage, technological innovation, as Porter has pointed out, can create first-mover advantages, which governments can promote (see Chapter 7). The importance of 'improvements in machines' was recognized by Adam Smith at the outset of his *Wealth of Nations*. However, for a long period, economic theorists tended to see technological change as an 'exogenous variable', that is, outside the traditional inputs of labour and capital. Against this background, Schumpeter stands out for his analysis of technological innovation as central to economic development.

Schumpeter's theory of industrial waves

Schumpeter's work spanned a long period, from 1912 to 1942. As industrial economies developed during that period, his analysis of the role of technological innovation evolved. From the outset in 1912, he stressed the importance of the individual entrepreneur in the innovative process. Schumpeter saw that innovation can encompass not just technical, but also marketing and organizational, innovations. The key actors in the Industrial Revolution were both talented inventors and entrepreneurs, who often went into production, making (and improving) their own inventions. The cotton-spinning industry, for example, was transformed by the inventions of Arkwright, Hargreaves and Crompton in the late eighteenth century. Richard Arkwright, for one, embodied important qualities as an inventor and entrepreneur, protecting and exploiting his patents, with a partner, Jedediah Strutt, providing needed capital for further investment. Large-scale machine production dramatically increased output and brought down prices.

Schumpeter saw the shift in technical innovation from the individual inventor to R&D specialist professionals within firms. Two developments were of particular importance. The first was the growing impact of scientific research as the basis of innovation, and the second was the growing bureaucracy of large organizations with their specialist R&D departments. He viewed the changes taking place within capitalism as involving 'creative destruction'. New products, new methods of production and new forms of organization emerge, 'revolutionizing economic structure, *from within*' (Schumpeter, 1942: 83 [Schumpeter's emphasis]).

He used the notion of business cycles, devised by the Russian economist, Kondratieff, to describe successive 'waves' of economic development in which technological innovation played a crucial role. The first long wave is the Industrial Revolution and the development of factory production (1780s–1840s). The second wave is that of steam power and the growth of the railways, lasting until the 1890s. The third wave, which lasted until the Second World War, was dominated by electricity and steel. Following Schumpeter's death shortly after the war, theorists have added a fourth wave, that of Fordist mass production (1940s–1990s) (see Chapter 2), and a fifth, that of microelectronics and computing, from the 1990s. Each Kondratieff wave is based on technological changes and their widespread diffusion in the economy, creating changes in investment opportunities and employment. While Schumpeter could not have foreseen the pace of technological change of recent decades, an enduring contribution of his analysis, which is echoed by more recent theorists, is the interdependence between technological innovation, economic progress and the social environment.

Technology and economic development

Technological innovation has long been recognized as key to economic development, but the processes involved are more complex than might appear (Lall, 1992). Although development is a broader concept than economic growth, the two are closely related. The technological advances described in the last section took place in developed countries, and involved qualitative changes in societies. There is a 'technology gap' between the developed economies and the developing ones, spurring the latter to 'catch up'. This is sometimes depicted in theory as a matter of convergence, but in practice, the process is uneven, combining periods of convergence and divergence. It might seem that this is just a question of the developing country simply replacing old technology with new (Fagerberg and Verspagen, 2002). However, while at firm level, a foreign investor in a developing country might well build a new factory with the latest technology, this need not contribute directly to achieving development goals: the investor is above all looking for cheap labour, and could well move on to another country. Technological changes take place continually in all industries, with considerable variation among industries. Firm-level factors and national environmental factors come into play. Moreover, technology does not stand still. It is constantly changing, so catching up is not simply a matter of bridging the gap in a simplistic way. Development is about qualitative changes in economies and societies (Fagerberg and Verspagen, 2002). The ways in which technology drives these processes are both direct and indirect. Firms in developing countries can draw on technology from both foreign and local firms. They are subject to both internal and external factors, public and private, as they evolve firm-level technology strategies (Lall, 1992). The process is incremental, dependent on a number of factors, including social systems, institutions and government interventions. Non-economic as well as economic factors play a part. This means that technological catch-up is more challenging than might appear, as it involves institutional contributors as well as technological capabilities.

Foreign direct investment (FDI) has brought about the globalization of production, but the diffusion of technology does not necessarily follow. Technology transfer from FDI has brought benefits in some national environments, but absorption depends on numerous factors, including technological and scientific capabilities in the host country. Industrialization driven by FDI can boost economic growth, as the experience of China shows. China's development model was based on FDI investment in mass manufacturing for export markets. The political leadership has faced greater challenges in fostering goals of nurturing domestic technological innovation which would contribute to more sustainable development. While technological innovation is recognized as a driver of economic growth, its contribution to development goals is more elusive. As we will see, governments look to technological innovation to contribute to improvements in society, including more and better jobs and higher living standards. These broader aims do not flow automatically, but depend on a range of national and firm-level contexts.

Technology catch-up: the elusive target

What are the disadvantages faced by developing countries in technological catch-up with advanced countries? In your view, have these disadvantages to some extent been alleviated in the digital era and with the rapid pace of globalization?

National systems of innovation

First Britain, then the US, and later Japan and Germany, have all been able to achieve high levels of technological innovation coupled with economic growth. It has long been recognized that the national environment is important in stimulating or inhibiting innovation. Writing in 1841, Friedrich List, in his *National System of Political Economy*, addressed ways in which Germany could catch up with England. Significantly, he emphasized the importance of social and cultural factors, and also government policy, in, for example, the protection of infant industries and the setting up of technical training institutes (Archibugi and Michie, 1997). Indeed, List anticipated many of the aspects of the national environment which were later to be grouped together under the term 'national system of innovation'. There is now a considerable body of literature on national systems, their different approaches to innovation and how they interact (see Tellis et al., 2009).

A national **innovation system** is broadly defined as the structures and institutions by which a country's innovation activities are encouraged and facilitated, both directly and indirectly. The term 'system' might imply that these institutions and policies are co-ordinated, when in fact levels of co-ordination vary between countries. The word 'network' has been used in to describe the relevant linkages between companies, disciplines and institutions (Patel and Pavitt, 2000). Summing up these threads, Mowery and Oxley define national innovation system as 'the network of public and private institutions within an economy that fund and perform R&D, translate the results of R&D into commercial innovations and effect the diffusion of new technologies' (Mowery and Oxley, 1997: 154).

A national innovation system consists of both institutions and interactions. Educational and government inputs are institutional in nature, while collaboration, scientific research and technology networking are more interactive. In practice, these dimensions are mutually reinforcing; for example, research institutions facilitate collaborations between education and industry.

Key aspects of a national innovation system

Five key aspects of a national innovation system can be highlighted (Archibugi and Michie, 1997).

Education and training

Achieving high rates of participation in education at all levels, from primary through to higher education, helps to promote economic growth, but there is no simple correlation. Educational attainment is one of the main ways in which citizens are able to acquire higher-skilled employment that offers more scope for personal development and satisfaction than the lower-skilled jobs that largely characterize developing economies. Governments of developing economies are also keen to see investment in education, whether public- or private-sector funded, in order to raise the level of technology and innovative capacity in the country. In general, spending on education in developed countries is much higher than in developing countries, but there are wide divergences, as Figure 9.3 shows. Denmark's pre-eminent position is consistent with its high levels of social spending. In the US, the share of national wealth spent on education has decreased since 2009, whereas in South Korea, it has increased, reflecting the importance of education in national cultural values. South Korea has one of the world's most highly-educated populations. Furthermore, its education system is strong in science and technology which is seen as key to competitive advantage. Note that Mexico's expenditure, at 6.2%, is relatively high, but this reflects in part the inefficiencies in Mexico's educational system. Germany's is lower, at 5.1%. The figure for Germany looks low for a major industrial power, but, in practice, much technological education takes place within corporate structures, rather than in educational institutions.

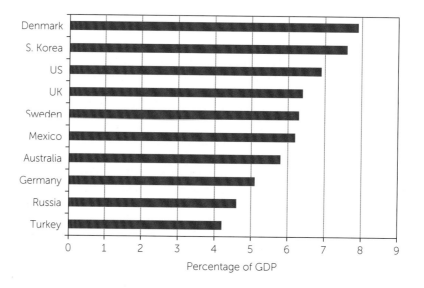

Figure 9.3 Proportion of national wealth spent on education (all levels)

Source: Data from OECD (2014) 'Education at a Glance 2014: OECD indicators', Table B2.1, p. 230, at www.oecd.org.

Spending on education does not automatically lead to the rise in technological capacity that South Korea has seen. China's leaders have taken note of the examples of South Korea and Japan, both of which successfully linked greater educational participation with development goals. This was true particularly in engineering technologies, such as automotive engineering, in which both countries are world leaders. China and India, two leading BRIC economies, are rapidly expanding their education systems, especially in university education. China now has over 2,400 universities, more than double the number a decade ago (Bandow, 2014). And graduates now number over 7 million a year, four times as many as there were a decade ago. However, the percentage of Chinese people with higher education remains low: only about 3% have some college education, and the government is hoping to raise this proportion to 15% by 2020 (Bandow, 2014). This would still be low by the standards of developed countries. In the US, 45.7% of 25- to 34-year-olds have experienced higher education of some kind, but this is lower than the percentage in Japan (58.6%) or South Korea (67.7%) (OECD, 2016).

As this classroom shows, computing skills can be acquired from an early age, laying the foundation for technological achievements in years to come.

Source: Fancy.

Of concern for China's leaders are the challenges associated with rapid growth in university education, especially in the context of a slowing economy (Bradsher, 2013). There is considerable diversity in quality among the many higher educational establishments, and there have been shortages of highly-qualified professorial staff. Courses in administration and finance have grown in popularity, while those in science and engineering, which would be of more direct relevance to industries, have not been as popular. Graduate unemployment is a growing phenomenon in China. Simply producing more graduates does not automatically translate into the type of technological innovation that will drive the country up the high-tech ladder. This has been an issue in both India and China. China has prioritized areas of technology, including alternative energy, environmental protection and clean energy. However, in the number of active researchers in employment, China still lags behind leading developed economies (see Figure 9.4). Vehicle manufacturing is looking to profit from new energy such as all-electric vehicles. China now produces more cars than any other country, but few are for export, and most of the production relies on technology licensed from western manufacturers.

Figure 9.4 Total researchers per thousand in total employment

Source: Data from OECD Statistics, Main Science and Technology Indicators Database, 2013, Excel tables at www.oecd.org, accessed 7 September 2015.

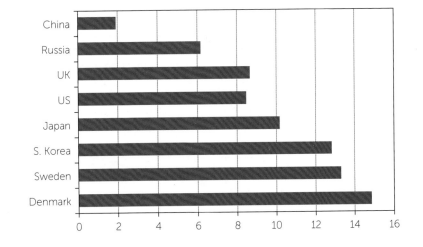

The way I see it ...

On the challenges facing India, 'The general education system is still too focused on grades and careers and is not oriented towards innovation and entrepreneurship .... While industry craves solutions to their problems, the academic institutions are generally too busy performing routine academic exercises, churning out educated manpower that is ill suited to either innovative industries or entrepreneurship.'

Ravindra Abhyankar, Advisor to the Indian government, August 2014, in 'The government of India's role in promoting innovation through policy initiatives for entrepreneurship development', *Technology and Innovation Management Review*, at www.timreview.ca

Reflecting on your own educational experience, is it similar to what is being criticized, or has it been more stimulating and intellectually challenging? What reforms would be needed in an educational system to bring in more of these latter qualities?

Science and technology capabilities

National authorities take decisions on what types of R&D to fund and how to meet the expenditure. Figure 9.5 shows comparisons of three leading countries in R&D expenditure. R&D spending is greater by far in the US than in any other country. The financial crisis took its toll, but spending grew again in 2011. China is the star newcomer globally, its R&D spending having risen from under $50 billion in 2001 to over $257 billion in 2012. The OECD estimates that China is on target to overtake the US in R&D spending in 2019 (OECD, 2014). In R&D spending globally, the share of the US stood at 37.7% in 2001, but this had fallen to 30.2% in 2012. Meanwhile, China's share rose from 6.3% to 19.5% over the same period. The richer countries tend to devote a higher percentage of GDP to R&D activities than the poorer ones. Despite China's huge increase in expenditure, the percentage of China's GDP devoted to R&D is relatively modest, at 1.98%, in contrast to 2.79% in the US. The country that ranks highest in R&D intensity on this measure is South Korea, where R&D expenditure is 4.36% of GDP. The bulk of funding for R&D is provided by businesses rather than governments. About 10% of R&D funding on average is provided by governments.

Figure 9.5 R&D expenditure: country comparisons

Source: Data from OECD, Main Science and Technology Indicators Database, June, 2014, Excel tables, at www. oecd.org, accessed 5 September 2015.

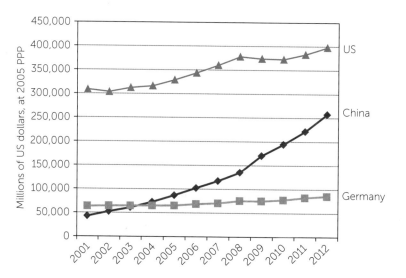

Industrial structure

Large-scale investment in R&D is borne mainly by a country's large firms, as only they are able to undertake the long-term R&D programmes and accommodate the accompanying risks. Of course, simply spending a lot of money on R&D does not ensure successful innovation. Inter-firm rivalry and competition in home markets can lead to 'imitative' increases in R&D in particular product fields (Patel and Pavitt, 1994). Small firms can play a role, as has been the case in high-technology areas. The small start-up is flexible and less bureaucratic than the large established firm, providing a fertile environment for innovation. Smaller, younger companies tend to grow more quickly, and can spur technological change. Where industrial structures have been dominated by large firms, as in the EU, the promotion of R&D-intensive small-to-medium-sized enterprises (SMEs) can help to revitalize innovation and improve competitiveness. In the EU, about one-third of business expenditure on R&D takes place in firms with fewer than 500 employees. Research suggests that policies such as R&D subsidies to SMEs are more fruitful in producing higher-quality innovations than those directed to large companies (Moncada-Paternò-Castello and Voigt, 2013).

Science and technology strengths and weaknesses

Countries differ in their areas of specialization and in the intensity of R&D activities. Where a country pursues a particular technological strength in an area of growing global importance, it stands to gain competitive advantage. Japan's intense investment in R&D in the fast-growing consumer electronics industry in the 1970s and 1980s is an example. Japanese electronics firms overtook both European and US firms in taking out patents, both at home and in the US (Freeman, 1997). Many of Japan's technology SMEs remain global leaders in specialized areas of technology. India has targeted computing and high-tech research as areas of competitive advantage, and its government has fostered the growth in educational institutions which excel in these areas.

Interactions within the innovation system

Interactions, whether formal co-ordination or informal networking, contribute to innovation activities within a country, and to their diffusion. Government guidance can be crucial in stimulating some industries to innovate – and discouraging others. The co-ordinating role of Japan's Ministry of International Trade and Industry is often cited for its crucial role in the country's economic development. Strong state guidance in the Soviet Union, by contrast, was much less successful. There, separate research institutes for each industry sector had only weak links with each other. The Soviet system's concentration of R&D expenditure on military and space projects, coupled with the rigid command economy, left little scope for civilian innovation links to develop (Freeman, 1997). A more recent trend globally has been growing interaction between academic researchers and firms, as scientific research is playing a more important role in the development of many new technologies, such as life sciences.

National innovation systems in context

There is no one model of innovation system that can be said to be superior in generating and diffusing technological innovation. While it is clear that technological change through innovation is linked to economic growth, countries display a good deal of diversity in their national innovation systems. Simple quantitative comparisons of R&D expenditure tell only a partial story. Social, cultural and historical differences have an influence on the ways in which learning, scientific curiosity and entrepreneurial flair are allowed to flourish in national environments. Government initiatives can be influential. Huge investment in industrial R&D in Germany and Japan in the post-war period was crucial in efforts to catch up economically.

The ability to assimilate and imitate innovations from elsewhere as the basis of further local innovative developments has been a particular feature of Asian economic development. This process of technology transfer (introduced in Chapter 2) holds out to all nations the possibility of benefiting from innovation. In theory, a country can benefit from the technology of foreign investors through technology transfer. However, technical change has proceeded unevenly among countries and among individual companies. Adaptation of technology and use in local environments still depends on diverse national systems. Why are certain countries and certain firms innovative when others are not? Tellis et al. (2009) highlight four factors:

- An educated and skilled workforce, especially in science and technology, at national and firm levels.
- The availability of capital and financial resources generally, within firms and within the country; includes banks, stock markets and private investors.
- The role of government and the national innovation system; includes protection of intellectual property and encouragement of collaboration between academic researchers and industry.
- The role of culture, including national culture and corporate culture in particular firms.

Of the four factors, Tellis et al. see convergence between developed and developing countries in the first three: skilled workers, capital and government policies. These developments are attributable largely to globalization. They include research links in integrated supply chains, global financial markets and the tendency for governments to use policies such as R&D tax incentives to gain national competitive advantage. Culture remains more rooted in national environments, and is a crucial factor in how a country's innovation system functions in practice. For example, relevant aspects of corporate culture that foster innovation include a willingness to take risks and to sacrifice profits flowing from established products in order to develop new ones. Also important is the empowerment of creative individuals within firms. This is more of a challenge in large companies. It is not difficult to see why policymakers stress the fostering of SMEs as a route towards enhancing a country's innovative capacity.

An innovation culture?

How can the cultural environment foster innovation – or discourage it? In which countries at present do you feel there is the best cultural environment for encouraging innovation, and why?

Patents and innovation

Patents are often referred to as a type of 'industrial' property, and patent activity is an indicator of levels of innovation. We should be cautious, though, not to read too much into patent statistics, as many innovations, such as informal and incremental improvements, fall outside patent activity. That said, patent statistics are an often-cited barometer of innovative activities.

Protection of property which exists in inventions and other products of human intellect has been the subject of heated policy debates from the days of the Industrial Revolution through to the present. Many would argue that technology should be freely available for anyone anywhere to use. Governments in industrialized countries, on the other hand, have legal frameworks for protecting intellectual property, in the belief that only by doing so will the incentive be provided for people to devote time and resources to innovation. Emerging economies are now following this example, with legal frameworks for the protection of IP.

From research and design through to testing, a new product can take many years before it reaches consumers. Companies, it is felt, would be unwilling to commit resources in the absence of a system for granting exclusive rights over the product for a reasonable period of time. It is acknowledged that limited monopolies are created, restricting competition, but is this a price that must be paid to ensure technical progress continues? Many in developing countries argue that they are effectively frozen out by these policies because of the concentration of intellectual property ownership in the industrialized countries. It is also the case that IP rights in developing countries tend to be weakly enforced, deterring innovators from seeking patents in the first place. In this section, we look at the nature of IP rights and how they come into being.

What is a patentable invention?

The **patentable invention** is a new product or process which can be applied industrially. These basic requirements are similar across most countries, with some variations. In Europe, the main source of law is the European Patent Convention 1973 (EPC), which EU member states have incorporated into national law. (This has also been adopted by Switzerland, Monaco and Liechtenstein.) A European Patent Office was set up under the convention. In the UK, the relevant law is the Patents Act 1977. US patent law requires that the invention be 'useful' rather than 'industrially applicable', as required by the EPC. The requirement that the invention must be an industrial product or process rules out discoveries, scientific theories and mathematical methods, as they relate to knowledge and have no technical effect. Mere ideas or suggestions are also excluded, as a complete description of the invention must be submitted with the patent application. Moreover, the invention must not have been disclosed prior to the patent application: once disclosed, it becomes 'prior art' and can no longer be said to be new.

Many inventions are not entirely new products, but improvements on existing ones. The threshold for a 'new' product differs from country to country. Where the threshold is low, it is possible for a pharmaceutical company to obtain a new patent on a medicine by, for example, changing the dosage to one-a-week from one-a-day. Known as 'evergreening', this can be a means of effectively extending the life of a patented medicine. While we tend to think of only the most formal inventions as patentable, in fact the scope of potentially patentable inventions is expanding all the time, extending to software, micro-organisms and business methods.

Computer software and business methods are both patentable in the US, but only to a limited extent in Europe. In Europe a software-based invention is patentable if it has a 'technical effect'. This means that a new program which affects how the computer operates is patentable, whereas a computer game is not. The game, like most software, is protected by copyright. The expansion of software patents has been a trend in the US since they were recognized as patentable by the Supreme Court in 1981. In the US, a 'way of doing business' is patentable. Amazon, the online retailer, was able to patent its 'one-click' shopping method in 1999. Since then, there has been a growth in business methods patents in the US, mainly in areas where new technology changes processes. However, in 2014, a judgment of the Supreme Court imposed a stricter interpretation of the law, disallowing a patent that simply used a computer for updating records

(Preston, 2014). In a unanimous decision, the justices held that to be eligible for a patent, the process would need to involve a more substantial role for the computer. The many business process patents that have been granted on a rather looser interpretation of the law since 1981 are not invalidated, but following this decision, future business methods patent applications will probably face a stricter test for eligibility.

Patent rights in practice

The **patent** gives its owner an exclusive right for a limited period to exploit the invention, to license others to use it, and to stop all unauthorized exploitation of the invention. Eighty per cent of patentholders are companies, not the actual inventors. The duration of a patent in the UK is four years, renewable up to 20 years. Renewal fees become steeper over time, and most inventions have been superseded by new technology long before the 20 years have expired. In the US, the normal duration is 20 years at the outset, with 'maintenance' fees payable at intervals. Any patentholder of a commercially valuable patent faces the prospect of legal challenges to the patent, sometimes by companies that exist simply for this purpose. Defending legal challenges is expensive, but probably outweighed by the earnings potential of the patent. When the patent on a drug has expired, 'generic' manufacturers are able to compete, but there are still profits to be made for the patentholder, as the original brand is a marketing advantage, especially in markets where counterfeit drugs are a problem. Being able to license the technology to other manufacturers entitles the patentholder to collect royalty fees agreed with the licensee. Much FDI relies on the licensing of technology. A patent may be sold outright ('assigned') to someone else who is then entitled to exploit it commercially. In common with other IP rights, 'exhaustion of rights' applies to patents. Under this principle, once the patentholder has consented to the marketing of the product in specific countries, he or she cannot prevent 'parallel imports', that is, importation of the product from another country, usually a lower-cost one. A consequence is that the owner of a patent for a product which is sold in a number of countries might find it difficult to maintain price differentials between them.

For an inventor, the process of applying for a patent can be complicated, long and expensive. The process of patent office 'examination' of a patent application typically takes from two to four years. The help of expert professionals is almost always needed, stacking the odds against the individual inventor-entrepreneur. The simplest route for the inventor is to apply for a patent in his or her home country, but in that case, the patent granted will cover only that country, which most nowadays would find inadequate. There is no such thing as a global patent! For the multinational company with global markets, there are means available to alleviate the need to make separate applications in every country.

The **European Patent Office (EPO)** (www.epo.org) in Munich was established by the European Patent Convention of 1977. A patent application to the EPO allows the applicant to designate particular countries, typically eight, in which the patent will be valid. However, the grant will be a bundle of individual national patents, each of which must be translated into the national language, and enforced in national courts. The expense of translation into several languages adds considerably to the overall expense, making European patents several times more expensive than US or Japanese patents. For many years, businesses have pressed the European Commission for a simplified system which would allow a single application submitted in one language, making the process much more efficient and cheaper. This 'unitary patent', which would be valid in 25 participating EU member states, is now close to being a reality (the three non-participating states are Croatia, Spain and Italy). Regulations governing the unitary patent took effect in 2013, and the final piece of the process will be the establishment of a European Patent Court, the agreement for which must be ratified by EU member states.

An alternative route is offered by the Patent Cooperation Treaty (PCT) procedure, which covers over 100 countries. Under the PCT, the applicant makes one application, to a regional office, and the process is divided into an 'international' phase and a 'national' phase. For the applicant with a global market in mind, there are considerable savings to be made in comparison with multiple individual country applications. The process is overseen by the World Intellectual Property Organization (WIPO) (www.wipo.int) in Geneva.

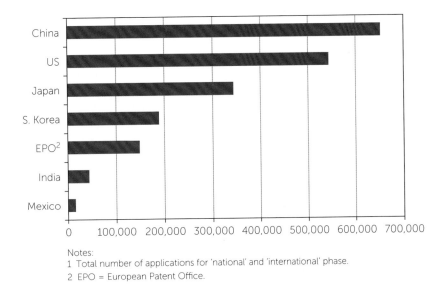

Figure 9.6 Patent applications[1] at patent offices in selected countries, 2012

Source: Data from WIPO (2013) 'World Intellectual Property Organization – IP facts and figures', Figure B.1.1, p. 11, and B.1.2, p. 12, at www. wipo.int.

Notes:
1 Total number of applications for 'national' and 'international' phase.
2 EPO = European Patent Office.

As Figure 9.6 shows, China is now the world leader in patent applications, with nearly 653,000 applications. This represents a rise of 24% on 2011, the steepest rise of any country. Asian patent offices received 55.9% of all patent applications made in the world in 2012. The majority of applications filed in each country's patent office are from residents of that country. China's surge in the number of patent applications does not necessarily indicate a substantial rise in the quality of patent activity, according to a report submitted to its main legislative body, the National People's Congress (*China Daily*, 2014). Despite the boom in patents, the quality of many Chinese patents appears to be poor, and there are only a few companies that are competitive globally in patenting. Mexico is the only country in Figure 9.6 that is in the category of middle- and low-income economies. Its filing activity totalled just over 15,000 applications, an increase of 9% on the previous year. Mexico is well ahead of the second country in this category, South Africa, which received 7,400, representing about half the patent activity of Mexico.

The US Patent and Trademark Office (USPTO) (www.uspto.gov) is the largest national patent office. It received over 600,000 applications for patents in 2014, and granted over 326,000 patents (see Figure 9.7). The percentages of foreign applications and grants to foreign residents have risen over the years, to about 51%, for both applications and grants. As Figure 9.7 shows, the presence of foreign patenting in the US has strengthened slightly since 2008. In 2014, the number of US applicants for patents stood at 285,096, down from 287,831 in 2013. This slight downturn is perhaps an indication of tightening R&D budgets.

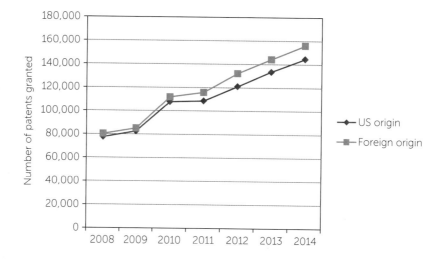

Figure 9.7 Grants of US patents to applicants of US and foreign origin

Source: US Patent and Trademark Office, U.S. Patent Statistics Chart (Summary Table), 1963–2014, at www.uspto.gov, accessed 11 September 2015.

Patent activity should be placed in perspective when looking at overall innovative behaviour. Patented inventions, however excellent, must be commercially viable and meet consumer needs. Capacity to build brands and reputation is as critical as winning products in achieving competitive advantage. Moreover, many innovations, such as new working practices, lie outside the category of patentable inventions.

The way I see it ...

'We needed to turn a profit on this drug ... The companies before us were just giving it away almost.'

Martin Shkreli, CEO of Turing Pharmaceuticals, in an interview with Bloomberg, September 2015.

The drug in question is Daraprim, a drug used by Aids patients. Turing acquired the rights to Daraprim in 2015 from a company that was charging patients $13.50 per pill. Turing raised the price per pill to $750, although the pill costs $1 to produce.

On what grounds could the CEO of Turing be criticized? What are the broader issues for pricing drugs?

Agreement on Trade-Related Aspects of Intellectual Property Rights (TRIPS)

There have been significant efforts to harmonize national laws on intellectual property rights through multilateral agreements. Following the Uruguay Round of GATT, the agreement on **Trade-Related Aspects of Intellectual Property Rights (TRIPS)** (www.wto.org/english/tratop) attempted to bring national legal regimes into harmony. Obligations of national treatment (equal treatment for foreign and domestic individuals and companies) and most-favoured-nation treatment (non-discrimination between foreign individuals and companies) apply. These provisions took effect from 1996 for most countries, with transitional periods allowed for developing countries to comply. Most developing countries had a further five years, but the least developed countries had until 2006. TRIPS does not aim to make all countries conform to a single system, but to set certain 'minimum standards', with latitude for national variations. It specifies 20-year protection of patents on both process and products. In the controversial area of plants and animals, TRIPS provides that plant varieties must be patentable, but members may exclude certain types of plants and animal inventions. The TRIPS

Council of the WTO monitors national laws for conformity. Disputes under TRIPS are settled through the WTO dispute settlement procedure.

TRIPS has come in for a great deal of criticism from developing countries. Critical areas for developing countries are new drugs to fight diseases and new seeds for crops. Both areas rely on research in biotechnology, or life science technology. In industrial countries, the trend away from publicly-funded research to private funding has brought the increasing domination of a few large multinationals in these areas. Many developing countries have become concerned about the grip of large MNEs in areas involving public goods.

PAUSE TO REFLECT

Patents: what are the benefits?

Patents are expensive to acquire, maintain and defend when legally challenged. Moreover, challengers are constantly at work, coming up with ways to reproduce the product or process without infringing the patent. Why do companies still believe the benefits outweigh the drawbacks?

CASE STUDY ON THE CHANGING BUSINESS ENVIRONMENT

The Czech automotive industry: motoring ahead?

Car manufacturing is an example of a globalized industry that has shifted increasingly to low-cost locations.
Source: Getty Images/iStockphoto Thinkstock Images\Stephan Jungck.

At the time of the fall of the Berlin Wall, the economies of Central and Eastern Europe (CEE) presented opportunities for economic development in these former communist states. The Czech Republic was well placed to take advantage. It had a proud tradition of higher education and excellence in science and technology. And its labour costs were much lower than those in Western Europe. At the time, the Czech Republic was best known for its Skoda car, a brand noted mainly for its outdated models and poor reputation for reliability. Skoda was transformed by Volkswagen, which eventually took over the company in 2001, and revived the brand. Car manufacturing grew into one of the Czech Republic's main manufacturing activities, benefiting from low-cost labour and proximity to Western European markets. Wages for a car worker in the Czech Republic are about half those of the equivalent worker in France. EU membership for the 11 CEE countries in 2004 meant that car exporters could take full advantage of the single European market. Economic growth from 2004 to 2008 averaged 4.6% across these countries. Yet, automotive FDI was sometimes criticized as being indicative of globalization strategies that seek out cost reductions above all else.

The financial crisis of 2008 saw the start of a series of layoffs and planned closures of car plants across France, as demand fell and costs remained stubbornly high. By then, PSA Peugeot-Citroen, one of France's leading carmakers, had already been active in investing in the Czech Republic. In 2003, construction of a new car factory was well under way in the industrial zone of Kolin-Ovcary. In a record investment of €1.5 billion, PSA Peugeot-Citroen had teamed up with Toyota in a joint venture, known as TPCA (Toyota Peugeot-Citroen Automobile), each partner taking a 50% stake. Commencing production in 2005, the new factory could boast the most up-to-date manufacturing technology. It offered jobs for 3,000 people, and it also set out to use local suppliers, thus adding about 10,000 jobs in the local supply chain. However, many of these companies are themselves FDI investors, attracted to the location by the car companies they supply.

TPCA produces small compact cars that are almost all exported to European markets. Only about 1% are sold in the domestic Czech market. The company produces the Peugeot 108, Citroen C1 and Toyota Aygo – all at the same time. About 80% of the components of these vehicles are from suppliers within the Czech Republic. While Western European plants have been struggling, TPCA has increased production, aiming to produce 220,000 vehicles in 2015. TPCA's executive vice president extols the competencies that exist in the country, making it a good location for motor manufacturing (Foy, 2014a). However, critics argue that foreign investors such as these are essentially creating assembly plants, and the jobs offered are only medium-skilled. Although jobs, local taxes and exports are beneficial, TPCA and other investors such as Hyundai have no R&D centres in the country. The manufacturing technology is all imported. As wages rise in the post-communist countries, the wage gap with Western European countries narrows, and the Czech Republic begins to looks less competitive.

Should sustainable development be focusing on promoting innovation and higher value-added manufacturing? R&D spending in the country is a lowly 1% of GDP, about half that of Western European neighbours. TPCA's vice president says that one must not overlook process R&D and organizational R&D, as these are important elements in the joint venture. The joint design of the latest versions of the three models is an example of this co-operation which has brought the company success to date. But without technological innovation, the business model, depending as it does on continued European demand, could see declining fortunes.

TPCA is aware that the company is competing against rivals in other CEE countries, whose car industries are also built on export-oriented FDI. There are 33 car factories in the Czech Republic, Slovakia, Hungary, Romania, Poland and Slovenia. These countries produced a total of 3.6 million cars in 2014, representing a doubling of output in ten years. In Romania and the Czech Republic, production tripled over that time. Competing against Romania, where wages are lower, Czech carmakers are seeking productivity savings, while their trade unions are seeking continuing improvements in pay and conditions. TPCA has sought greater flexibility in shift work, which was a contentious issue. Strikes were scheduled in 2015 as the prospect of successful negotiations looked dim, but a collective bargaining deal was struck following protracted negotiations, and it included the provision for flexibility in shift work.

Lower-cost locations further afield are now coming into focus as potential centres of car manufacturing. Renault has a factory in Morocco that produced 100,000 cars in 2013, 90% of them for export. The Czech Republic is sometimes described as an 'almost-emerged' economy: richer than a developing economy but not as rich as a Western European country (Foy, 2014b). Government policies to nurture a local innovative base that can promote R&D and entrepreneurship in engineering and car manufacturing would be a more sustainable way forward.

Sources: BBC News (2012) 'Peugeot Citroen plans 8,000 job cuts', 12 July, at www.bbc.com; Foy, H. (2014a) 'Carmakers speed ahead but country faces competition', *Financial Times*, 8 October, at www.ft.com; Buckley, N. (2014) 'From industrial dinosaurs to world-class growth rates', *Financial Times*, 2 October; Foy, H. (2014b) 'Hopes for a future built on technology', *Financial Times*, 8 October; Reuters (2015) 'Toyota-Peugeot Czech car plant raises production by 38%', 7 July, at www.reuters.com.

Questions for discussion

- In what ways does the Czech Republic possess competitive advantages in automotive manufacturing?
- Is TPCA a long-term investor, in your view, or one that is looking mainly for cost savings?
- What are the prospects for innovation that automotive FDI can bring to the Czech Republic?
- How could the Czech Republic transform itself from an 'almost-emerged' economy into a more advanced economy?

Technology diffusion and innovation

Technological diffusion was once thought to be the simple acquisition and adoption by developing countries of the technologies of developed countries, akin to adopting a set of 'blueprints', without any further creative contribution. It is now recognized that this view is oversimplified: the processes of diffusing technology are more dynamic, involving the spread of technical changes and adaptations to specific local conditions. Technological diffusion is likely to be a gradual process rather than an acquisition in the form of an event or transaction. When technology is acquired through a deliberate interaction between countries, it is known as **technology transfer**. The term usually refers to transfers from advanced economies to industrializing economies, but it also covers transfers between industrialized countries. Technology transfer has been crucial to the processes of industrial growth and global integration. It is now recognized that technology transfer is not a simple one-way process, but a more interactive and complex process of diffusion, both direct and indirect. The main means of technology diffusion are shown in Figure 9.8.

Figure 9.8 Technology diffusion in different contexts

FDI has been a major source of technology for developing countries. For the host country, the benefits derive from observing, imitating and applying the technologies, including the management methods. Spillover effects can include linkages developed with domestic suppliers, but to exploit spillover effects requires incentives for local firms to adopt the new technologies. Technological learning, or 'absorptive capacity', is at the heart of these processes. Formal education and training clearly play a part, but much learning is also acquired by doing, as in 'on the job' training. To benefit from technological accumulation, local firms need to develop skills and know-how to improve the technology acquired from abroad. Interactions with foreign investors can help to ensure that the investor sees the value of continued investment in the location. Where these links are weak, and local innovation capacities are low, the investor is less committed to the location (Lall and Narula, 2004). Japan and Germany are examples of countries that have combined imported technology with the development of local technological capabilities. On the other hand, foreign investors are often reluctant to incorporate the latest technology in foreign operations, for fear of 'leakage' of IP. This is particularly the case in countries that have weak IP legal protection, either through weak laws or lax enforcement.

Other sources of technology for developing countries include technology licensing. The owner of a patent may license a foreign manufacturer to produce the product under licence in return for royalties (see Chapter 2). Many late-industrializing countries have relied significantly on licences for technology, particularly from the US and Japan. South Korea's spending on licences increased tenfold in the period 1982–91 (Mowery and Oxley, 1997). Technology licensing is often combined with FDI. Crucial to China's manufacturing boom in electronic gadgets, such as Apple iPhones, was the influx of FDI from elsewhere in Asia, notably Taiwan. Global car manufacturers have flocked to China, often using joint ventures to manufacture vehicles under licence for the Chinese market.

Much acquisition of technology comes through less deliberate processes. Trade in goods is an example, as shown in Figure 9.8. Sometimes called 'embodied' technology transfer, imported machinery and equipment provide a means to assimilate the technology. By 'reverse engineering', discovering how a product has been made, it is possible to develop and refine the technology further. Japan's post-war industrial development is a good example of the benefits of imported technologies, which were assimilated and complemented by local R&D and engineering capabilities. Japanese firms similarly benefited from licensed technology, building on substantial investments in R&D and engineering (Bell and Pavitt, 1997). However, reverse engineering is not always as successful as the Japanese example. Machines can be reproduced, but this does not mean that local people have mastered the technology that went into making the machine in the first place (Fu et al., 2011).

Globalization has expanded the ways in which technology is acquired, both through formal mechanisms of technology transfer and through more nebulous means such as interactions with supply chain partners. R&D has become internationalized through alliances, allowing partners to share R&D. Less structured is the dissemination of knowledge from a variety of sources via the internet in unintended ways. These processes can provide the impetus for learning, whereby external knowledge becomes part of the innovation process. Much depends on the capacity of indigenous firms to absorb the technology available and to develop domestic innovation capabilities independently. However, indigenous firms in developing countries face challenges of developing innovative capacity that serves the needs of the country, in contrast to technologies that serve the interests of foreign investors in, for example, outsourced manufacturing.

The benefits of technology transfer and knowledge spillovers in any country depend to a great extent on the country's level of income. It is unrealistic to expect poorer countries simply to catch up with richer ones. The types of technology that many developing countries need are in low-skilled and low-tech operations, in which indigenous innovation is probably more relevant than imported technology from advanced economies. Some developing economies become locked into sectors where FDI has been targeted at low-wage production that depends on imported technology. This policy can lead to economic growth, but does not serve the long-term needs of the host country, which are to develop innovative capacity to lift it up to more knowledge-based sectors. Economies dependent on low-wage production are said to be 'path-dependent', and local R&D risks being 'crowded out' by imported technology. Building indigenous innovation capacity requires both domestic R&D and the institutional framework at national level that supports indigenous innovation.

Globalization and the diffusion of technology

How have evolving globalized value chains contributed more to the diffusion of technology in developing countries than the older pattern of specific FDI projects combined with technology transfer?

Technological innovation: challenges and responsibilities

Technological innovation is inherently disruptive. At its heart lies creative destruction: the old becomes obsolete and the new takes over. These processes are crucial to economic development, dramatically demonstrated by the Industrial Revolution. When looking back at technological advances, we tend to forget that change produces losers as well as winners, affecting individuals and societies. Industrialization brings the prospect of new jobs and earning capacity for those able to take up the opportunities, but many are left behind – without the skills or in the wrong place. Factory jobs bring in steady wages, but factory environments introduce new environmental risks and social upheaval. As we have seen, governments can promote these developments, but they can also do the opposite – reject them. This is what happened in the early nineteenth century, when the Industrial Revolution was in full swing in Britain. In swathes of Europe under Habsburg rule, the building of factories and construction of railways were discouraged, as they posed threats to the existing élites (Acemoglu and Robinson, 2013). In these traditional agrarian societies, where peasant workers were tied to landowners, the prospect of individuals given freedom to take up salaried employment of their choice posed a threat. Change had the capacity to empower people – and still does.

The digital era has seen an unprecedented growth in the ability of people to communicate, acquire knowledge from open sources and engage in social interactions. This empowerment has shaken the corridors of political power in just about every country, whether democratic or authoritarian. It is no wonder that controls of the internet are commonplace in many countries, usually held to be justified on broad-brush grounds of national security. While digital technology and the democratization of the internet are facilitating technological innovation, these innovations are also viewed as a source of disruption. Eager to catch up with advanced countries, emerging economies such as China face a dilemma. They are educating more and more people, whose expectations of rewarding jobs and personal fulfillment are overshadowed by the realities of clampdowns on individual freedoms and slowing economic growth. Could there be political dissent among these educated people? The social media have proved effective tools for much protest activity, giving authoritarian regimes good reason to be fearful of them. As with all technology development, a challenge facing governments is to channel the benefits towards goals of sustainable development, including social well-being.

Governments and companies value technological innovation for the benefits that flow from them. They can help solve the world's most difficult problems, such as curing diseases and protecting the environment. But an important technological innovation such as a new medicine will result in an IP monopoly for the corporate owner, whose profits will depend on steep prices that only the richest can afford. Governments everywhere face challenges in ensuring that the development associated with innovation is inclusive, benefiting all in society. For this reason, indigenous innovations in poor countries, such as encouraging entrepreneurs to find cheap and efficient ways of improving agriculture, are more likely to produce sustainable development than attempts to create centres of excellence in high technology. Poor infrastructure and unreliable electricity supply can sometimes frustrate these latter initiatives in any case. Inequalities within countries can be just as potent obstacles to boosting innovation as inequalities between countries. This need not mean that governments in developing countries should refrain from supporting high-technology innovation. Digital technology is a good example of the potential for inclusive innovation: it can aid the poor farmer or the scientific researcher. Businesses are crucial to these developments, not simply for economic opportunities, but because of their responsibilities towards sustainable development.

Conclusions

Technological innovation has the power to transform economies and societies. Companies that do not commit themselves to innovation will soon fall behind their competitors. And countries whose governments are reluctant to grasp the possibilities of innovative technology to fuel economic growth will fall behind. With hindsight, these might seem simple calculations, but all change brings risks that disruption of the old ways will be for the worse, or be perceived by ordinary people as devaluing their lives. Industrialization has been the major driver of economic and social change, the advanced industrialized countries setting the examples that others have followed. For developing countries, this has meant opening their economies to FDI and global MNEs as a route to rapid industrialization and, with it, rapid economic growth. But as we have seen, a risk has been the proliferation of low-technology operations and the reliance on low-skilled workforces, with little long-term prospect of climbing up the technological ladder. The expansion of supply chains in global production networks is now altering this path-dependent development. Developing countries have greater opportunities to engage in R&D, and there is greater scope for domestic innovation to find a wider stage. However, as we have seen, in issues of the absorption capacity for technological innovation, not all countries are equal.

National innovation systems present a range of divergences, from educational systems to industrial structures. While it has been thought that economic development based on industrialization would lead to convergence, it is now clear that catching up is not as simple as it seemed. The hope of acquiring technology through means such as FDI and technology transfer can prove a reality, but in many cases turns to disappointment. By contrast, a combination of foreign imports and local know-how can lead to innovation that is more in tune with development goals, and also more likely to be sustainable. At the heart of this process is the vital role of entrepreneurs. Entrepreneurial SMEs are rich sources of innovation in any country. An encouraging environment and the availability of funding are essential elements that can help domestic innovation. Governments are now aware of the need to encourage entrepreneurs and to target innovation policies in areas of social importance, such as biotechnology and clean energy. Profits are to be had, but so are benefits in which all can share.

References

Acemoglu, D. and Robinson, A. (2013) *Why Nations Fail: The Origins of Power, Prosperity and Poverty* (London: Profile Books).

Archibugi, D. and Michie, J. (1997) 'Technological globalization and national systems of innovation: an introduction', in Archibugi, D. and Michie, J. (eds) *Technology, Globalisation and Economic Performance* (Cambridge: Cambridge University Press), pp. 1–23.

Bandow, D. (2014) 'Transforming China from within: Chinese students head to American universities,' *Forbes*, 22 September, at www.forbes.com

Bell, M. and Pavitt, K. (1997) 'Technological accumulation and industrial growth: contrasts between developed and developing countries', in Archibugi, D. and Michie, J. (eds) *Technology, Globalisation and Economic Performance* (Cambridge: Cambridge University Press), pp. 83–137.

Bradsher, K. (2013) 'Next made-in-China boom: college graduates', *New York Times*, 16 January, at www.nyt.com.

China Daily (2014) 'High quantity, low quality: China's patent boom', 23 June, at www.chinadaily.com

Fagerberg, J. and Verspagen, B. (2002) 'Technology-gaps, innovation-diffusion and transformation: an evolutionary interpretation', *Research Policy*, 31: 1291–1304.

Freeman, C. (1997) 'The national system of innovation in historical perspective', in Archibugi, D. and Michie, J. (eds) *Technology, Globalisation and Economic Performance* (Cambridge: Cambridge University Press), pp. 23–49.

Freeman, C. and Soete, L. (1997) *The Economics of Industrial Innovation*, 3rd edn (London: Cassell).

Fu, X., Pietrobelli, C. and Soete, L. (2011) 'The role of foreign technology and indigenous innovation in emerging economies: technological change and catching up', *World Development*, 39(7): 1204–1212.

Lall, S. (1992) 'Technological capabilities and industrialization', *World Development*, 20(2): 165–186.

Lall, S. and Narula, R. (2004) 'FDI and its role in economic development: do we need a new agenda?', *European Journal of Development Research*, 16: 447–464.

Landes, D. (1998) *The Wealth and Poverty of Nations* (London: Little, Brown & Company).

List, F. ([1841]2005) *National System of Political Economy: History*, Vol. 1 (New York: Cosimo Inc.).

Moncada-Paternò-Castello, P. and Voigt, P. (2013) 'The effect of innovative SMEs' growth to the structural renewal of the EU economy', European Commission Policy Brief, September, EU Publications Office, at www.jrc.ec.europa.eu

Mowery, D.C. and Oxley, J. (1997) 'Inward technology transfer and competitiveness' in Archibugi, D. and Michie, J. (eds) *Technology, Globalisation and Economic Performance* (Cambridge: Cambridge University Press), pp. 138–171.

OECD (2010) 'Ministerial Report on OECD Innovation and Strategy', May, at www.oecd.org/innovation/strategy

OECD (2012) 'Innovation for Development', May, at www.oecd.org

OECD (2014) *Science, Technology and Industry Outlook 2014*, at www.oecd.org

OECD (2016) 'Population with tertiary education (indicator)', at data.oecd.org, accessed 28 May 2016.

Patel, P. and Pavitt, K. (1994) 'National innovation systems: why they are important and how they might be measured and compared', *Economics of Innovation and New Technology*, 3(1): 77–95.

Patel, P. and Pavitt, K. (2000) 'National systems of innovation under strain: the internationalization of corporate R&D', in Barrell, R., Mason, G. and O'Mahony, M. (eds) *Productivity, Innovation and Economic Performance* (Cambridge: Cambridge University Press), pp. 217 235.

Preston, R. (2014) 'Supreme Court toughens business process patents test', *Information Week*, 6 June, at www.informationweek.com

Schumpeter, J.A. ([1942]1975) *Capitalism, Socialism and Democracy* (New York: Harper & Row).

Smith, A. ([1776]1950) *An Inquiry into the Nature and Causes of the Wealth of Nations* (London: Methuen).

Tellis, G., Prabhu, J. and Chandy, R. (2009) 'Radical innovation across nations: the pre-eminence of corporate culture' *Journal of Marketing*, 73(1): 3–23.

☞ Multiple choice questions

Go to the companion website: www.palgravehighered.com/morrison-gbe-4e to take a quick multiple choice quiz on what you have read in this chapter.

⑦ Review questions

1 Explain science-push and demand-pull in the development of new technology.
2 What is Schumpeter's view of technological innovation and waves of economic development?
3 How should developing countries promote technological innovation in order to generate economic growth?
4 Outline the elements of a national system of innovation. How relevant is the educational and training environment of the country?
5 Which countries have evolved particularly successful national innovation systems, and why?

6 Why are patents crucial to technological lead?

7 What are the conditions which must be satisfied before a patent may be obtained for a process or product?

8 What is a generic medicine, and why are these medicines important in global healthcare?

9 Why is the TRIPS agreement said to be disadvantageous to developing countries?

10 How does FDI contribute to technology transfer?

11 In what ways has globalization impacted on technology transfer?

12 How can it come about that a country is 'stuck' in terms of technology, unable to catch up with more developed countries?

13 What is 'embodied technology', and why is it important for developing countries?

14 Why are some countries falling behind in the global diffusion of technology?

15 What are the benefits for an MNE in locating R&D activities in dispersed locations globally?

✓ Assignments

1 Assume you are advising a government of a developing economy. Report to the government on: (a) policies designed to bolster national innovative capacities; and (b) policies to gain maximum benefit from technology transfer afforded by its inward investors in manufacturing.

2 To what extent is R&D becoming 'globalized', and in what ways may developing countries reap R&D advantages which could spill over into their domestic companies?

📖 Further reading

Acemoglu, D. and Robinson, A. (2013) *Why Nations Fail: The Origins of Power, Prosperity and Poverty* (London: Profile Books).

Afuah, A. (2009) *Strategic Innovation* (London: Routledge).

Bently, L. and Sherman, B. (2014) *Intellectual Property Law* (London: Routledge).

Bessant, J. and Tidd, J. (2011) *Innovation and Entrepreneurship*, 2nd edn (London: John Wiley & Sons).

Castells, M. (2009) *The Rise of the Network Society*, 2nd edn with a new preface (Oxford: Wiley-Blackwell).

Freeman, C. and Soete, L. (2012) *The Economics of Industrial Innovation* (London: Routledge).

Landes, D. (1998) *The Wealth and Poverty of Nations* (London: Abacus).

Tidd, J. and Bessant, J. (2013) *Managing Innovation: Integrating Technological, Market and Organizational Change*, 5th edn (London: John Wiley & Sons).

Trott, P., van der Duin, P., Hartmann, D., Scholten, V. and Ortt, R. (2015) *Managing Technology Entrepreneurship and Innovation* (London: Routledge).

🌐 **Visit the companion website at www.palgravehighered.com/morrison-gbe-4e for further learning and teaching resources.**

CLOSING CASE STUDY

GSK seeks to restore reputation in global pharmaceuticals

Improvements in facilities and medicines in the Chinese healthcare system make this market potentially highly lucrative for global pharmaceutical companies, but they must be alert to the legal and regulatory frameworks.

Source: isisiStock.com/XiXinXing.

The image of a large pharmaceutical company that boasts of being research-led is one of an organization committed to finding new drugs to cure diseases and improve health. These laudable activities are expected to be its main purpose as a company. But the leading pharmaceutical companies' commitment to improving human well-being has been repeatedly questioned in recent years, as the rush for growth and profits appears to have got the upper hand. Scandals over improper marketing, bribery and misleading test results have swirled around the industry, giving the impression that, in reality, these companies are unethical in the ways they pursue profits. GSK (GlaxoSmithKline), Britain's largest pharmaceutical company, has been caught up in a number of these scandals. Restoring its ethical reputation has become a priority. It is seeking growth in emerging markets, but a scandal in China has affected its reputation there. At the same time, without innovative medicines, the core competencies that befit a research-driven company are threatened. In addition to these challenges, there is the likelihood of

a tightening of regulatory supervision in many markets, not just developed ones.

A research-led company could focus on developing new drugs and then wait to see whether there is a good take-up by health professionals, but this is not how the industry functions. In the early stages of the new drug's life, articles in academic journals are influential. We would expect an article in a medical journal to be independent but, in fact, the presentation of data and the writing of articles on a new drug are often done by 'ghostwriters' employed by the pharmaceutical company that developed the drug. Pharmaceutical companies spend billions annually on marketing, and some of these activities verge on bribery. Companies often pay doctors to go to conferences under the banner of 'medical education', when in reality the trips are closer to being luxury holidays. GSK was fined $3 billion in the US in 2012 for marketing abuses consisting of taking prescribers on trips to luxury resorts in Hawaii. This was a record fine at the time.

Much of this doubtful marketing takes place in emerging economies, where it is perceived that there will be lax regulation. However, GSK was in the mire in China in 2014, where it was fined the equivalent of $490 million for bribing doctors to adopt its drugs. This came after a 15-month investigation that was highly damaging for GSK's reputation in China, one of its major prospects for growing sales. The former head of GSK's China unit, along with four other senior employees, received suspended prison sentences. All had pleaded guilty. The case could have repercussions, as both the US and UK have anti-bribery legislation under which companies can be punished for committing corruption overseas. GSK has promised to change its sales practices, including reviewing its system of incentives to sales staff.

GSK's CEO is under pressure over ethical reform and revitalization of the business. Its shares did not suffer a downturn following the China prosecutions, but declining sales globally could have a greater impact on market sentiment. Respiratory drugs have been a profitable area for GSK, but its asthma drug, Seretide (known as Advair in the US), which is near the expiry of its patent, is facing competition from generic producers. The company needs to make good the slump in sales that is likely to occur, as this drug accounts for one-fifth of its revenues at present. A welcome boost in sales of its HIV drugs and flu vaccines has cheered executives and shareholders. In 2014, GSK carried out a minor restructuring with Novartis of Switzerland. GSK sold its underperforming cancer drug activities to Novartis, and acquired the vaccine business of Novartis, which was spun off into a joint venture between the two companies. GSK sells numerous consumer products, from Aquafresh toothpaste to Tums indigestion tablets, and even Horlicks, a powdered malted-milk drink. GSK took steps to sell off its older medicines that are now out of patent and have little growth potential. The company aims to offer these to

private equity groups. On the face of it, this would not be controversial, but private equity buyers are inclined to ratchet up the price charged to consumers, which can come as a shock to loyal customers of these products, reflecting negatively on GSK.

GSK announced in 2014 that, from 2016, it would stop paying doctors to go to medical conferences, and stop paying them to speak in support of the company's products. It also intended to stop setting sales targets for its individual salespeople, and stop offering bonuses to marketing staff that are linked to sales targets. Critics of the pharmaceutical industry are sceptical about such moves, observing that these practices are entrenched as 'a way of doing business' (Jack, 2013). They point out that prosecutions for marketing abuse in the US alone led to $20 billion in fines from 1991 to 2010, and in the following three years, another $13 billion. As the example of China shows, scrutiny is rising in emerging markets as well. Escalating fines would be a possible reform, if penalties were higher than current levels. The example of China shows that the risk of a jail sentence should be a warning to companies. The practice of industry-funded medical education breeds scope for abuse. Another possible reform would be the provision of continuing medical education by national healthcare systems.

Such regulatory reforms would lead to changes in pharmaceutical marketing, helping at least to prevent some of the more corrupt practices that have come to light. A refocus on innovation would be a more meaningful ethical shift, but the drive for growth is the major preoccupation of GSK's CEO.

Sources: Jack, A. (2013) 'End of the hard sell?', *Financial Times*, 27 December, at www.ft.com; Ward, A. (2014) 'Storehouse of trouble', *Financial Times*, 12 April; Ward, A. (2014) 'Overflowing in-tray awaits Hampton at embattled GSK', *Financial Times*, 26 September; Ward, A. (2014) 'GSK asks for bids on older drugs list', *Financial Times*, 30 May.

 ## Questions for discussion

- Has the drive for research excellence been lost at GSK? In reality, what does GSK exist to do?
- How have the marketing abuse scandals damaged GSK's reputation?
- What recommendations would you make to GSK's CEO to restore the ethical values that stakeholders expect?
- Should there be greater mandatory regulation of the pharmaceutical industry, or are voluntary initiatives enough? Explain.

PART

4 CONFRONTING GLOBAL CHALLENGES

In Chapter 10, *Ecology and climate change*, we take an overview of the impacts on the natural environment caused by human activity and, in particular industrialization and urbanization. Paramount among these impacts is climate change, a global issue, but one which can have devastating effects in local environments, especially severe in the poorest and most vulnerable countries. Combating climate change has become the focus of moves to achieve international agreement on limiting harmful emissions. However, achieving consensus has become more difficult in a world in which the developing economies are becoming the largest emitters. Closely intertwined are issues of scarce resources and the pressing need to shift to cleaner energy. Diverse national agendas and political sensitivity towards any measures which might dampen economic growth have affected the environmental policies of both governments and businesses. However, increasing awareness of the perils of climate change is shifting opinion among businesses and consumers towards sustainable solutions.

Chapter 11 is *Ethics and social responsibility*. Although distinguishing ethical from unethical behaviour might seem straightforward in principle, in practice, large areas of grey can make decision-making difficult. In many cases, a business might be faced with 'lesser evils', neither of which it would happily choose in an ideal world. In this chapter, we look at the foundation principles of ethical decision-making, taking the view that understanding how the definitions of good and bad behaviour have evolved aids in handling the practical situations which can arise. Ethics and CSR have become important elements of strategic decision-making for MNEs, not just because of high-profile corporate scandals. Certainly, CSR is compelling companies to look at their corporate governance and stakeholder responsiveness. But it is also leading firms increasingly to see the importance of *how* profits are generated in global operations, not just *how much* money they are making.

Chapter 12, *Challenges and responsibilities: towards a new perspective*, is the concluding chapter. It reviews the challenges of sustainability, governance and responsibility that have featured in earlier chapters. A highly focused discussion of global risks is presented, with examples from the ecological, economic, political and social dimensions of the environment. The chapter goes on to assess the responsibilities of both governments and businesses in terms of social and environmental goals. The chapter concludes by pointing towards a new, more responsible role for businesses in the global environment.

CHAPTER

10

ECOLOGY AND CLIMATE CHANGE

Outline of chapter

This chapter will enable you to

- Understand the nature and causes of the major environmental challenges, such as climate change and transboundary pollution
- Appreciate interconnections between local, regional and global concerns
- Gain insight into the role of governments and international co-operation in tackling environmental challenges
- Identify at a practical level the initiatives businesses can take in environmental management and sustainable development strategy

Solar power: Morocco leads the way

The harsh, uncompromising environment of the Sahara Desert has been the setting for a pioneering project in solar power.

Source: © Royalty-Free/Corbis.

Morocco is set to become a solar powerhouse through an ambitious desert project designed to bring electricity to over a million homes. Ouarzazate is the nearest city, located on the edge of the vast Saharan desert. This barren landscape has featured in films such as *Lawrence of Arabia*, but with its searing sun, arid terrain and risk of sand storms, this region is unsuitable for most purposes. Harnessing the abundant sunshine, however, is changing this image. Conceived on a vast scale, ultimately covering an area the size of 35 football pitches, the solar complex is based not on the familiar photovoltaic panels that are now common on rooftops, but on solar mirrors that move with the movement of the sun. This is known as concentrated solar power (CSP), a more expensive technology than solar panels. The advantage of CSP, however, is that it harnesses energy over a longer period in the day. The mirrors are focused on a pipeline that contains a heated solution that is carried to energy-generating turbines. This process allows the heat to be stored, so energy is being generated

even when the sun is not shining. The overall project has been conceived in phases. The first plant, Noor 1, which has 500,000 solar mirrors in 800 rows, opened in 2016, with two further phases due to open in 2017. The first phase will be able to generate three hours of energy after dark, and by the time the last phase is complete, the plant will be generating energy 20 hours a day. The government hopes that the solar power plants will help the country to achieve a target of 42% of its energy supplies from renewables. This would be a significant step towards energy independence.

For Morocco, completion of the three-plant Noor-Ouarzazate project has been a priority. The country produces no oil, relying on imported fossil fuels for 97% of its energy. Adding to costs from the public purse, the government subsidizes the energy used by consumers. The possibility of producing energy from solar power on a large scale thus has enormous appeal to the country's king and the government. The project has been conceived as a public-private partnership. The cost of $9 billion has been met by government funding, and also funds from the World Bank and the European Investment Bank. The World Bank's Clean Technology Fund contributed $3 billion. The plant's construction has been carried out by the Saudi company, ACWA Power Investment. The technology costs of the concentrated solar power plant are high. However, the learning experience gained from the Ouarzazate project helps to bring down the costs, and, if other countries build similar plants, these developments will also lead to valuable cost reductions over the long term. Such plants are being planned or constructed in Chile, South Africa, India and China. The World Bank urges that more such projects are needed in order to improve the technology and reduce costs (Duarte, 2015). Nevertheless, for many countries, especially emerging economies, the high technology costs are a deterrent when these projects are compared to fossil-fuel alternatives.

The benefits of the solar plant for Morocco do not stop at its borders. The Moroccan Solar Energy Agency has plans to export energy, first to neighbouring countries. High-tension lines are being built to transport energy to southern areas of Morocco and to Mauritania beyond. There are talks taking place with Tunisia, and energy could also be exported to countries of the Middle East. Morocco would like to export energy to Europe, but this will require interconnectors. The EU has aimed for each member country to be able to transport 10% of its power abroad by cable by 2020.

The advent of solar power on a large scale enabled Morocco to announce before the Paris climate change conference in 2015 that it was intending to reduce its CO_2 emissions by 32% by 2030. The country's environment minister has said, 'We are convinced that climate change is an opportunity for our country' (Harrabin, 2015). However, her government is looking for international funding at the same time, to help to achieve that goal. The shift to renewable energy requires technology and investment; many of the countries where such projects would be viable specify that international funding is a condition. This implies aid flowing from developed countries to developing ones, especially those most vulnerable to the impacts of climate change. Rising temperatures pose extreme risks for the countries of North Africa, where drought and desertification are affecting food and water security. The advanced economies have taken the view that all countries bear responsibility, not just the developed ones. After all, China is the world's largest emitter, and other developing countries are increasing emissions at significant rates. The Paris conference highlighted divisions among national perspectives that would be difficult to bridge.

Sources: Harrabin, R. (2015) 'Moroccan solar plant to bring energy to a million people', BBC News, 23 November, at www.bbc.com; Duarte, M. (2015) 'Morocco to make history with first-of-its-kind solar plant', World Bank, 20 November, at www.worldbank.org; Neslen, A. (2015) 'Morocco poised to become a solar superpower with launch of desert mega-project', The Guardian, 26 October, at www.theguardian.com.

Questions for discussion

- What are the benefits of solar power plants such as the Moroccan project?
- What are the specific benefits flowing to Morocco from the project?
- Why are other developing and emerging countries likely to be reluctant to follow Morocco's example?
- What global policies would encourage other countries to invest in solar power as Morocco has done?

Introduction

The challenges posed by the environment are increasingly impacting on societies, governments and businesses. They include global warming, depletion of natural resources and pollution. These and other processes are detrimental to human well-being, and they also harm plants and animals, both on the land and in the seas. While it is impossible to bring back species which have become extinct or replace resources which have become exhausted, it is possible to slow down and control harmful processes, and with the aid of research, to find ways of combating the harmful effects. Whereas environmental issues were once seen as mainly local, they are increasingly perceived in the wider context of regional and global implications. Similarly, because it is about the public interest, the environment was once seen mainly as a matter of government concern, whereas the role of businesses – whether for bad or good – is now attracting more attention. Governments and businesses now co-operate in environmental protection at national, regional and international level. Often, this co-operation includes international organizations, both governmental and non-governmental (NGOs). The role of specialist environmental NGOs has been important in raising awareness of 'green' issues and also in promoting green alternatives to environmentally damaging activities. Greater weight has been given to these efforts by advances in scientific research, which have shed light on trends affecting the planet as a whole and also provided details of the effects of different types of pollution in specific locations.

Much past and present environmental damage stems from the effects of economic development. These processes include industrialization, changes in farming methods, and depletion of natural resources. As has been seen in Chapter 3, industrialization leads to urbanization, as rural dwellers flock to urban areas in search of work in new industries. While these twin processes began two centuries ago in the advanced economies, the centres of today's industrialization are in the developing world, and the processes are taking place much more quickly than during the first wave of industrialization. Moreover, current environmental changes are occurring in a context of unprecedented population pressures, mainly in the developing world. Protecting the environment, therefore, is crucial to sustainable development, which takes a long-term view of development and its impacts. Sustainable development is increasingly incorporated in the strategic thinking of international managers.

This chapter will first highlight the major environmental challenges, including climate change and transboundary pollution. National regulation and international co-operation are explored, highlighting diverging national interests. The concept of sustainable development is discussed in the section on 'International frameworks to promote sustainable development'. Business responses and shifts in thinking on environmental management are highlighted in the following section. The last section discusses the challenges and responsibilities of both governments and businesses.

Environmental degradation in context

Ecology focuses on the interactions between living organisms and their habitats. Organisms range from plant and animal life to human beings, in a variety of habitats, including urban centres as well as rural areas, forests, waterways and the sea.

A change in any of these habitats impacts on the living creatures they support: the variety of living organisms (called **biodiversity**), their distribution and number are affected by even slight changes in environment. While environmental changes can occur naturally through changes in climate and weather, **environmental degradation** refers specifically to environmental change caused mainly by human activity. The development of agriculture in Europe and North America in the seventeenth and eighteenth centuries is an example, which saw a huge expansion in the area of cultivated land, technological innovations and the emergence of capitalist market relationships in agriculture (Maddison, 2001). Forests were cut down, heathland was cleared, and numerous species of wildlife declined as their habitats were destroyed.

With the Industrial Revolution, the capacity for environmental degradation started to grow dramatically, in both intensity and geographic scope. Factory production relying on power sources such as coal was joined by newer industries, such as synthetic chemicals, which generated a mixture of old and new pollutants. As urban areas grew up around these industries, environmental problems spread, posing threats to health associated with air pollution and poor access to clean water and sanitation. As Maddison points out, although city dwellers in the early period of industrialization enjoyed higher incomes than those in rural areas, their mortality rates were significantly higher, mainly due to the spread of infectious diseases which took their greatest toll among infants and recent migrants to the urban areas (Maddison, 2001).

As Chapter 3 highlighted, almost all the current population growth is now taking place in the developing world, especially in Africa. In general, these countries' economies are heavily reliant on agriculture, but agriculture can be precarious, and is unlikely to promote sustainable economic growth in today's world. Moreover, the effects of climate change, including extreme weather events and desertification, are taking their toll on agricultural production in the developing world. Meanwhile, there is growing demand for food from the large emerging economies, such as China and India, both of which are food importers. The world now faces stern challenges in growing enough food and managing its distribution.

Deforestation raises concerns over long-term threats to the habitats of human communities, animals and wildlife.

Source: Photodisc.

Although industrial development has brought much-needed employment and income, it has also led to environmental degradation, including resource depletion and pollution. Major causes of environmental degradation are shown in Figure 10.1. As the figure shows, urbanization and modern consumer lifestyles have been central to these processes, leading to increased needs for power generation and transport. Land is needed for factories, growing food, housing, roads and infrastructure. Deforestation, which is the felling of forests for fuel or to use the land for other purposes, has proceeded hand in hand with growth in the world's population. Historically, the need for food and fuel has driven much deforestation, which is known to increase in periods of rapid economic development (FAO, 2012). Forests cover about 4 billion hectares, or 31%, of the world's land surface, but this area is decreasing at a rate of about 5.2 million hectares annually (FAO, 2012). Latin America has seen some of the most extreme deforestation. About 9% of Latin America's forest area was lost between 1990 and 2010, mostly to clear land for crops and grazing. At that rate, Latin America would be totally without forests in 220 years. Deforestation and the degradation of existing forests present severe threats to biodiversity: many plants and animals are unique to particular areas and become extinct when their ecosystem is disrupted. Deforestation also leads to soil erosion, the capacity of the land to retain water and rising carbon emissions. Forests are, in effect, large stores of carbon, and the felling of trees releases emissions from stored-up carbon.

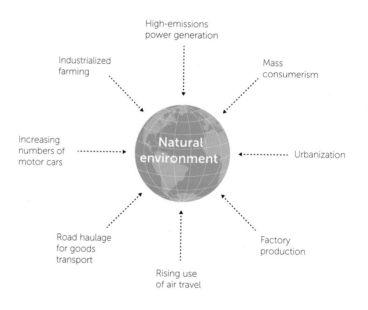

Figure 10.1 Causes of environmental degradation

'Global commons' refers to the resource domains that are not within the jurisdiction of any one country (UNEP, 2015). They include the high seas, the atmosphere, Antarctica and outer space. These areas are viewed as the common heritage of all humanity. With creeping environmental degradation caused by human activity such as pollution, as is happening in Antarctica, it is now recognized that international co-operation is needed to address the issues of degradation of the global commons. Interconnections between local, regional and global phenomena are increasingly being revealed. For example, air pollution or waste dumped into a river from a single factory may travel long distances, heedless of national boundaries. In the wider picture, air pollution generated by industrial agglomeration, we now know, depletes the ozone layer of our atmosphere.

Large emerging economies have enjoyed growing prosperity, both from growth in their home countries and in their outward foreign direct investment (FDI). Their expanding multinational enterprises (MNEs) have become enmeshed in the societies in which they operate, being called upon to take account of host societies' needs. Governments in the BRIC countries have tended to view economic development in their home countries as the top priority, and environmental damage, both at home and abroad, as a price worth paying. Now, as emerging economies have become global forces, and as the effects of decades of industrialization become apparent, they face environmental challenges. Action must be taken to safeguard societies – and plan for more sustainable growth in the future. Emerging economies face environmental pressures from three broad directions:

- From their own societies, where pollution threatens health and welfare.
- From societies in other countries where they operate, and where similar health and environmental concerns arise.
- From the international community, concerned that the developing countries take greater responsibility for global environmental damage.

The first two of these groups would broadly be recognized as stakeholders, and companies can see the direct links between their activities and social impacts. However, the third – international pressure – is more abstract and rests more on a sense of moral duty. As we will see in the next section, the climate change debate has brought out these differing perspectives.

The global commons are everybody's business

Companies perceive stakeholders typically in terms of interests such as suppliers and consumers. How can a company be persuaded that it should take action to preserve the global commons?

Climate change

Climate change covers any change in the climate over time, whether from natural causes or human activity. Climate experts generally believe that we are now experiencing a slow process of global warming, caused by the build-up of heat-trapping gases, or greenhouse gases (GHG), in the earth's atmosphere. In particular, carbon dioxide is to blame. Carbon dioxide (CO_2) emissions quadrupled over the second half of the twentieth century, a period of rapid economic growth in Europe, the US and Japan. The burning of fossil fuels, mainly in coal-fired power stations, is responsible for over half of greenhouse gas emissions globally. Factory production, with its accompanying needs for transport and energy, contributes to rises in emissions. These trends are pronounced in the world's large developing economies, where there is growing demand for the trappings of modern consumer lifestyles, such as cars and air travel.

Shares of greenhouse gas emissions by the countries with the highest levels of emissions are given in Figure 10.2. Global CO_2 emissions amounted to a record high of 35.3 billion tonnes in 2013, although this total represents a slowing in the overall rate of increase. China, the largest emitter, accounted for 10.3 billion tonnes of the total. China is also the country with the most rapid growth in CO_2 emissions, with an increase of 4.2% on the previous year, while in the US, the country with the second-fastest growth in emissions, the increase over 2012 was 2.5%. The rate of increase in emissions in China has fallen from rates of about 10% recorded in the ten previous years, largely because of economic slowdown. In general, emissions are rising fastest in emerging economies. CO_2 emissions grew at 6.2% in Brazil in 2013, and in India at 4.4%. China represented 60% of net global CO_2 increases in 2013. Coal consumption is responsible for 40% of global emissions, most of this emanating from China, but the US and India have also seen increases in coal consumption. India relies mainly on coal for power generation, and an increase of 7.9% in coal consumption was largely responsible for India's high level of emissions, at 2.1 billion tonnes. In the EU, greenhouse gas emissions have been falling since 2006, decreasing by 1.4% in 2013. The EU per capita emissions level of 7.3 tonnes is now less than that in China, at 7.4 tonnes, but both are less than half the per capita emissions in the US, which is 16.6 tonnes of CO_2. Per capita emissions rose in the US in 2013, mainly because of a shift from gas to coal in power production. The EU, US and China all have policies in place that seek to reduce emissions and shift to greater reliance on renewable energy.

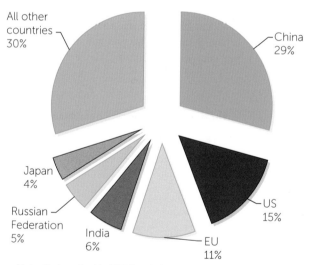

Figure 10.2 Global shares of greenhouse gas emissions by leading countries, 2013

Source: Data from Olivier, J.G.J., Janssens-Maenhout, G., Muntean, M. and Peters, J.A.H.W. (2014) *Trends in Global CO_2 Emissions: 2014 Report*, The Hague: PBL Netherlands Environmental Assessment Agency; Ispra: European Commission, Joint Research Centre, at www.pbl.nl. Published under a Creative Commons Attribution 3.0 licence: http://creativecommons.org/licenses/by/3.0.

Note: Carbon dioxide (CO2) emissions from fossil-fuel combustion and industrial processes (including cement and metal production).

What is known about climate change?

Theories of climate change have been around over a hundred years, but only since the 1980s have scientists been able to monitor the changes with precision in a variety of locations. It is impossible to measure directly climate changes which took place before human civilization, but climate scientists are able to study a range of phenomena, such as rock and ancient Antarctic ice, which give them data on the earth's climate history. These studies show them the changes brought about by natural variations in CO_2. They estimate that the last three decades have been successively warmer than any decade since 1850 (IPCC, 2014). This data helps them to assess current changes in the atmosphere, oceans, temperatures and rainfall. The UN established the Intergovernmental Panel on Climate Change (IPCC) (www.ipcc.ch/) in 1989, bringing together a panel of hundreds of scientists. Its aim was to consolidate the scientific evidence about what changes are occurring, aiding governments and other decision-makers. Their reports, beginning in 1990, have been influential in forming views about the nature and impacts of climate change. The research confirms the connection between increasing levels of CO_2 in the atmosphere and global warming.

The scientific data amassed by scientists show that global warming is a reality, and that it is happening because of human activity. In its fifth report, the IPCC finds that the evidence of human influence on global warming has strengthened in the years since its fourth report (IPCC, 2014: 5). Factors they highlight include the size of population, the types of economic activity, lifestyle, technology and climate policy.

The rate of increase in CO_2-equivalent emissions (CO_2 and other greenhouse gases) is the key factor in determining the extent of global warming. If there are no further measures to stop emissions growth than those in place now, temperatures by 2100 could have risen by 3.7 to 4.8 degrees C above the levels of 1850–1900. A rise on this scale would have severe impacts on ecology and human welfare. The IPCC estimates that limiting the rise to 2 degrees above pre-industrial levels would be an attainable target. This would require that emissions generated by human activity be reduced by 40–70% from their 2010 level by 2050, and to be reduced to zero by 2100. The concentration of CO_2 in the atmosphere is expressed as parts per million (ppm). Before the Industrial Revolution CO_2-equivalent concentrations in the atmosphere were 280 ppm. In September 2015, the concentration was 397.64 ppm (CO_2Now, 2015). To keep the rise in temperature to 2 degrees requires that greenhouse gas emissions must not exceed a concentration of 450 ppm of carbon in the atmosphere. Once released into the atmosphere, carbon dioxide can persist for a century, and there is no current technology to remove it on a large scale. This means that there is very little leeway for further rise, and action needs to be taken urgently to slow the rise in emissions.

The message of the climate scientists is therefore that urgent steps must be taken to reduce emissions. The IPCC stresses that there are multiple ways in which mitigation of warming can help to keep the rise to below 2 degrees, but no one method on its own will suffice. There is a good deal of technology for reducing emissions and utilizing clean alternatives in many spheres of activity. However, implementing changes on a large scale involves government action and regulation to compel businesses and individuals to change their behaviour. It also requires co-operation among national authorities. Among the many concerns highlighted by the IPCC is the persistent rise in the burning of fossil fuel for power.

The effects of climate change are complex, as climate is more than just temperature, but includes interactions of temperatures with winds and rainfalls in different locations. Heatwaves, droughts, floods and hurricanes are all associated with climate change. It is estimated that all continents can expect shifts in their climate, and thus their ecology, as a result of global warming. The IPCC says that it is 'very likely' that there will be more heatwaves and fewer spells of extreme cold over most land areas (IPCC, 2014: 10). Severe flooding is likely to occur in some places, and desertification in others. Arid and semi-arid areas in Africa and Asia will have higher temperatures, causing loss of vegetation and depletion of water sources. Because the polar ice caps are melting, sea levels are rising. Island nations and low-lying regions, such as

Bangladesh, risk becoming submerged beneath the sea, while the Sahara Desert in Africa is expanding. Subterranean aquifers are becoming depleted and rivers are drying up. Extremes of drought and flood, as well as extreme events such as storms, pose risks to agriculture and lead to insecurity of supplies of food and clean water. Agriculture is already becoming problematic in Australia because of drought, and agriculture in Spain, which supplies many European countries, would also be affected.

It has long been known that climate change poses serious threats to developing countries, mainly in Africa, which have limited resources to cope with natural disasters or to change existing agricultural systems. It is now becoming apparent that rich countries are also vulnerable to floods, droughts, severe storms and rising sea levels. Although technologies, such as flood defences, exist, costs are high, and hurricanes can wreak havoc in the most advanced economies. The IPCC says that the existing risks and new risks of climate change will impact more heavily on disadvantaged people and communities everywhere, not just in developing countries, but in countries at all levels of development (IPCC, 2014: 13).

Global co-operation to combat climate change

As in other spheres, such as trade, international co-operation relies on individual nations having the will and means to achieve goals which they share. The UN, like the WTO, can bring delegates to the negotiating table, but it cannot force them to make an agreement or, if agreement is reached, to stick to it. The first climate change treaty was the Kyoto Protocol, which was signed in 1998 and came into legal force in 2005, despite non-ratification by the US, which was then the world's largest carbon emitter. The Kyoto Protocol contained a framework for international co-operation to deal with the effects of climate change. The treaty specified goals of emissions reductions to be achieved by 2008–12, and laid the foundations for further treaty-making.

The Kyoto Protocol envisaged the world divided into developed and developing nations. Its targets for reduction in emissions were linked to these categories. This approach seemed appropriate at the time. Who in 1998 would have foreseen that China, a developing country, would become the world's largest emitter of greenhouse gases? Unfortunately, with hindsight, the treaty sowed the seeds of a rift among nations which has widened since then along political lines, making it difficult to bridge the gap in subsequent negotiations. Developing and emerging countries have pointed to industrialization in developed countries as the main historical cause of today's climate change crisis, and argued that these countries therefore should bear the main responsibility for measures to mitigate the impacts, including contributing financially to developing countries. India is a leading exponent of this argument. Although the world's fourth-largest GHG emitter, it has been reluctant to commit to reductions. Its government argues that its priorities must be relieving extreme poverty and providing electricity and sanitation for the millions of its inhabitants in need. It holds that, for these goals to be realized, economic growth based on industrialization and substantial reliance on coal-fired power stations is essential well into the future. On the other hand, India is committed to being part of the solution to climate change by expanding the use of renewable energy sources in the long term.

The Kyoto Protocol set 2008–12 as a target date by which developed countries would reduce their combined GHG emissions to 5% below 1990 levels. There were no targets for developing countries. It introduced the principle of emissions trading, in the Clean Development Mechanism, allowing polluting industries simply to buy emission 'credits' from other countries, in order to meet their national targets without actually cutting emissions in their domestic economy. The emissions trading principle now looks inadequate to bring about the reductions needed. But did the Kyoto Protocol succeed in reducing emissions, despite the abstention of the US and the non-inclusion of China? The EU more than succeeded in meeting its target of 8% reduction by 2008–2012. By 2013, GHG emissions had been cut by 18% below 1990 levels (European Commission, 2013). However, globally, emissions continued to rise, as the reductions recorded in the EU were outweighed by the growth in emissions from the US and from emerging economies, mainly China. Moreover, it should be borne in mind that the rise in emissions in China has been driven by demand for imported goods in the EU and other developed countries. This would contribute to the 'carbon footprint' of each of these countries (Clark, 2012). **Carbon footprint** thus gives a more accurate picture of impacts on climate change, as it represents both direct and indirect emissions. Hence, the carbon footprint of a toy includes the manufacturing process and also the process of making the plastics that go into the product (Berners-Lee and Clark, 2010).

Despite the inevitable conclusion that the Kyoto Protocol failed to achieve its goal of reducing global emissions, there were positive precedents set. It was the first international attempt to set mandatory targets for reducing GHG emissions, and it was also pioneering in its emissions trading scheme. These precedents have been important in follow-up meetings to continue the Kyoto process.

Negotiations to agree a follow-up treaty to the Kyoto Protocol included all the major emitting countries. Meetings in Copenhagen (2009), Durban (2011) and Doha (2012) made only limited progress in laying the groundwork for a new treaty. The Copenhagen meeting agreed the goal of limiting warming to 2 degrees. The Durban conference agreed that both developing and developed countries would be expected to take climate change action. And the Doha conference agreed the principle of funding poor countries for 'loss and damage' due to climate change. When the delegates of 195 countries met in Paris in 2015, there was considerable pressure to reach agreement on all major points.

Prior to the Paris talks, countries were encouraged to put forward their own 'intended nationally defined contributions' (INDCs), which included intended reductions in GHG emissions. By the start of the conference, 186 countries had submitted their INDCs. While this was a step towards committing both developed and developing countries, these targets were not legally binding, and, taken in aggregate, would reduce warming to 2.7 degrees, not 2 degrees. In an ambitious move at the conference, it was proposed to set the target at 'well below 2C and endeavour to reach 1.5C' (Vidal et al., 2015). This was accepted in the final agreement, but a good deal of negotiation was needed. It was felt that give-and-take was the key: each country would see some of its desired goals in the agreement, but not all it wished to see. China, formerly reluctant to accept targets, was now willing to accept them. It was reluctant to accept monitoring, but was persuaded to go along with the consensus in the end. The pledges contained in the INDCs are to be revisited every five years in a 'stocktaking', a review mechanism, the first of which under the agreement will be 2023. The stocktaking, which gives rise to setting stiffer targets, is a means of verification of each country's progress – or lack of it. Stocktaking at designated intervals offers a means of 'naming and shaming' countries that fail to live up to their defined contributions.

In recognition of the concerns of developing countries, especially poor countries that are vulnerable to the impacts of climate change, there was an agreement on assessing loss and damage in financial terms. This also includes prevention measures, but, at the insistence of the US, which was concerned about the legal position of its large corporations, the agreement specifically rules out any liability or compensation. Finally, there were the financial provisions, under which developed countries pledged $100 billion per year towards aiding developing countries to take measures to lessen the impacts of climate change and to make the transition to clean energy.

The financial provisions are set out in the preamble rather than the body of the agreement, signifying intention to pay, but not legal obligation. The other commitments made by the 195 countries in Paris are intended to be legally binding on each. However, countries must follow through with formal signing and ratification, as is the accepted procedure for treaties. Representatives of over 170 of these countries came together for formal signing at the UN's headquarters in New York in April 2016, signifying a high level of national commitment. At the point when it is ratified by 55 countries representing at least 55% of global greenhouse gas emissions, it will be recognized in international law. Ratification by large emitters such as China and the US would bring this target within reach. The Paris accord represents an agreement by the signatory countries to be bound to the processes and mechanisms, such as the setting of INDCs, stocktaking and monitoring, in good faith on the basis that all feel obliged to comply themselves; and all expect each other to comply.

The way I see it ...

'It's just worthless words. There is no action, just promises. As long as fossil fuels appear to be the cheapest fuels out there, they will continue to be burned.'

James Hansen, climate change scientist, commenting on the Paris accord, in *The Guardian*, 12 December, 2015.

Do you agree with this assessment of James Hansen, or not? Explain your reasons.

Climate change initiatives and business responses

No business is unaffected by climate change, just as no individual person is unaffected. Some sectors, such as those that use large amounts of energy or water, are more affected than others. But all must focus on issues like energy consumption and the carbon footprint of their products. Ideally, they would take initiatives on grounds of sustainability. But, in practice, they are inclined to wait for regulation to compel them to make changes in the ways they operate. Businesses in every sector have watched astutely the developments of climate change negotiations, knowing the outcomes will imply strategy shifts to more low-carbon alternatives in their operations. But uncertainties can arise following inter-governmental negotiations if they give no clear indications of new regulations or a detailed timeframe for changes.

Environmental regulations at the level of national law are likely to weigh more heavily with businesses than agreements of inter-governmental bodies. There is a long time lag before commitments are translated into law. National law is more immediate in its impact, and national regulators are able to impose legal penalties for breaches. Ideally, businesses would be pro-active, but in practice they take more notice of the impacts that affect their profits in the short term. This has been shown in an extensive survey carried out in the run-up to the Paris conference in 2015. In interviews with the CEOs of 142 of the world's largest companies, researchers found that only 46% said that a binding agreement in Paris would persuade them to prioritize climate change measures (PwC Global, 2015). In the view of the CEOs interviewed, the main influence on their climate change stance was public opinion, and the second greatest influence was national regulation. Business leaders are clearly sensitive to public opinion, as consumer perceptions of their activities affect sales and profits. The CEOs generally viewed climate change as having negative impacts on their businesses, rather than looking at the opportunities for innovation and sustainable solutions. Those that did embrace climate change initiatives mainly did so on the grounds of improving shareholder value, which represents an essentially economic perspective rather than an ethical one.

Large companies, especially in the energy sector, are among the groups lobbying against climate change measures. In 2015, major companies lobbied against EU measures to promote renewable energy, favouring instead greater use of gas, which is a fossil fuel (Nelson, 2015). The companies included oil giants, BP and Shell; BASF, a chemical company; and the steel producer, ArcelorMittal. These companies co-ordinate their lobby activities through organizations such as trade associations that specialize in lobbying decision-makers. One of these, Business-Europe, argues that EU climate targets damage the competitiveness of European companies (Fagan-Watson, 2015). Despite the strong objections of environmental groups, the EU Commission failed to endorse binding renewables targets, largely, it is felt, due to effective lobbying from the companies with direct interests in fossil fuels (Nelson, 2015). These companies all profess to take climate change seriously in their corporate strategy. A group of 25 large investors in many of these same companies (including BP, EDF, Total and P&G) wrote to the CEOs of the companies in which they have stakes, querying their membership of trade associations that pursue anti-climate change lobbying (Fagan-Watson, 2015). For these critical shareholders, the ethical case and the case based on long-term shareholder value are coming together.

Also indicative of the shifting views of shareholders is the move away from fossil-fuel investments by investors on ethical grounds. Many investors, including both institutional funds and private investors, have decided to sell their shares, or 'divest', in fossil-fuel companies. Among them are Norway's sovereign wealth fund and two large pension funds in California, whose policies are seen as indicative of broad shareholder thinking.

Projects to develop green technology and renewable energy can be costly. Businesses in these sectors often work closely with governments. Government incentives and funding can be crucial in encouraging investment. However, there are also likely to be policy shifts when governments change. In such an environment, companies are disinclined to commit resources, and CEOs are disinclined to take on big projects. Nonetheless, legal obligation is only one reason, albeit a strong one, for undertaking greener strategies. Companies with strong CSR and stakeholder commitments will proceed with their own targets for reducing emissions despite the slowness of governments to bring in legislation. Companies with weak environmental records face issues of stakeholder objections and reputational risk. Moreover, there are many areas of environmental regulation on issues such as pollution which are already subject to international law.

Transboundary pollution and energy strategy

Transboundary pollution refers to the transmission of pollutants through the water, soil and air from one national jurisdiction to another. The transmission may be intentional, as in the transport of hazardous waste, or it may be unintentional, as in an accident at a nuclear power plant.

Industrial enterprises commonly release waste into rivers and produce harmful emissions, such as sulphur dioxide, that are released into the atmosphere. Only in the twentieth century was there a dramatic increase in the capacity for pollution on a large scale, with potential for devastating environmental effects. In addition, industries such as nuclear power generation raised the possibilities of catastrophic accident. The cataclysmic event which is usually cited as causing a shift in the environmental paradigm was the meltdown of the nuclear power station at Chernobyl in the former Soviet Union in 1986 (Landes, 1998). The fire, which burned for five days, released more than 50 tonnes of radioactive poison into the atmosphere, affecting Belarus, the Baltic states, and the Scandinavian countries. The disaster and the inept handling of the aftermath are cited as factors which contributed to the eventual collapse of the Soviet command economy (Landes, 1998).

Less dramatic has been the quiet destruction that acid rain has caused in the environment, becoming visible only when rivers and forests appear to be dying. Acid rain is the term used to describe acid which falls out of the atmosphere. It may be wet, in the form of rain, fog and snow, affecting the soil on which plants and animals depend. Or it may be dry, in the form of acidic gases and particles, which may blow onto buildings and trees and into homes. Its main components are sulphur dioxide and nitrogen oxides. It causes trees to gradually wither, buildings to decay and aquatic life to die. Aquatic ecosystems are particularly endangered. The burning of fossil fuel such as coal for electricity is particularly blamed for acid rain. International co-operation for lowering acid rain emissions in Europe and North America has helped to reduce levels, but industrialization in the developing world has spread these problems to more countries.

Coal mines such as this are indicative of the world's continued use of fossil fuels in power generation.

Source: Getty.

Coal is the largest single source of carbon emissions, and is still the dominant fuel for power generation, accounting for 41% of the world's electricity generation. The use of coal for power generation continues to increase. Many countries in the developed world have policies to shift away from coal because of its carbon emissions and other environmental impacts, but in practice, there has been little reduction. The use of coal in the G7 industrialized countries decreased by less than 1% between 2009 and 2013, but this slight reduction was mainly because of the US increase in fracking to produce shale gas for power generation (Vidal, 2015). In five G7 countries (UK, Germany, France, Japan and Italy), the use of coal rose 13% during that period.

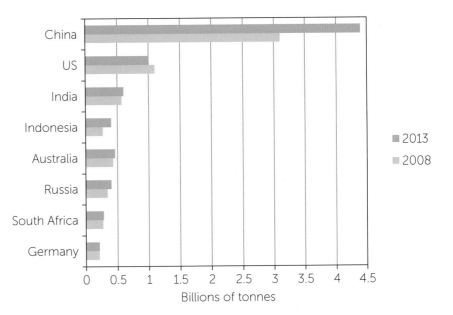

Figure 10.3 Coal production of major producing countries

Source: Data from US Energy Information Administration, *International Energy Statistics* (Tables), at www.eia.gov, accessed 23 September 2015.

The use of coal is greatest in emerging economies, particularly China and India, which are large producers for domestic use and also large importers. China relies on coal-burning power stations for 79% of its power, and India's power is 68% dependent on coal. The increase in coal consumption globally is due mainly to the increases in these countries. As Figure 10.3 shows, China is by far the world's largest producer of coal, but in the 2000s, the demands of its fast-growing economy outstripped supply, leading to a steep rise in imports. From imports of 44 million tonnes in 2008, China quickly became the world's largest importer of coal in 2011, with shipments reaching nearly 318 million tonnes in 2012. Since then, imports have slowed, falling to 291 million tonnes in 2014. Several factors are involved. Imported coal has tended to be cheaper than domestic coal, largely because of the costly transport bottlenecks within the country (Cornot-Gandolphe, 2014). As China's economic growth has slowed, the government has sought to re-balance supplies towards domestic production, imposing import tariffs on coal in 2014. The government is also seeking to improve standards for cleaner energy production in order to deal with high levels of pollution, especially the thick smogs that envelop eastern cities. More stringent anti-pollution standards have prompted the building of cleaner power stations in western regions, and also acted as a brake on low-quality imports.

By contrast, India's demand for coal continues to rise strongly, mainly to extend electricity to the one-third of India's population of 1.25 billion people who are still without. The government is hoping to meet most of this demand through new coal-fired power stations, but hopes of becoming self-sufficient seem a long way off. India, like China, has become a major importer of coal, importing over 240 million tonnes in 2014, mainly from Australia and Indonesia, whose miners are relieved that India's demand is now helping to make up for falling demand in China.

Governments are now focusing on renewable sources of power generation, such as wind turbines and solar power, offering opportunities for companies in these sectors. Investment in renewables is now one of the major drivers of growth in electricity generation (IEA, 2015). And much of this investment is in emerging and developing economies. With improving technology and falling costs, wind and solar power are expected to account for nearly half of new investment in global power capacity in the years to 2020. However, government policies and financial commitment are still holding back these developments, especially the continuing reliance on fossil fuels for power generation (IEA, 2015).

The case for nuclear power generation rests on its low level of emissions, combined with concerns over the depletion of non-renewable energy sources such as coal and oil. Some countries have invested heavily in nuclear capacity, as Figure 10.4 shows. Indeed, France's energy giant, EDF (Electricité de France), is in a strong global position in building nuclear power stations. However, the expansion of nuclear power has brought risks. Risks have emerged with the growth in the nuclear reprocessing and recycling industries, combined with the need for safe treatment and storage of nuclear waste. Further, the safe transport of nuclear waste across land and sea, to reach reprocessing sites, has created new concerns, not just because of the risk of accidents, but also from the fear of terrorist attack. The risks associated with nuclear-related industries have become dispersed

Figure 10.4 Share of nuclear power in electricity generation for selected countries, 2014

Source: Data from IAEA (International Atomic Energy Agency), Power Reactor Information System (PRIS), 'Nuclear share of electricity generation in 2014', at www.iaea.org/PRIS/WorldStatistics, accessed 29 September 2015.

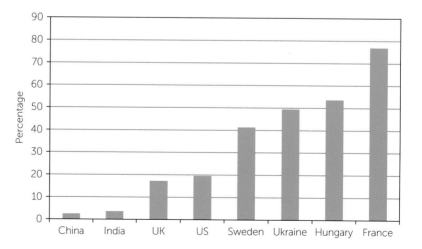

geographically as these industries have grown. China has become a major investor in nuclear, but its nuclear capacity in 2008 was only 1% of its overall power generation, although it is expected to rise to 8.9% by 2030. India pledged in 2015 to generate 40% of its electricity from renewable and alternative low-carbon sources by 2030.

The Fukushima disaster in Japan in 2011 has had a profound effect on the expansion of nuclear power. An earthquake and subsequent tsunami destroyed the Fukushima nuclear power plant, releasing massive radioactive contamination which rendered an area of 300 square miles of land unfit for human habitation. The overall death toll from the earthquake and tsunami was 18,000, and over 150,000 surviving victims were displaced. A larger area of 4,500 square miles was affected by long-lived radioactive caesium above Japan's legal limits. Radioactive caesium contaminates the entire ecosystem – water, soil, plants and animals. Decontamination has been unsuccessful. Homes and land can be decontaminated, but water flowing down the hills from melting snow soon contaminates an area again. The catastrophe resulted in the largest-ever radioactive discharge into the ocean. As noted in Chapter 6, the design of the nuclear reactor was considered problematic even at the time of its construction in 1970. Recent research highlights evidence that many mistakes and miscalculations were made by TEPCO (Tokyo Electric and Power Company), the operators of the power plant, who had failed to take account of the risks in areas prone to earthquakes and tsunamis, although these risks were known in other areas of Japan and internationally (Noack, 2015). Public prosecutors twice considered prosecuting TEPCO executives, but felt a prosecution would stand little chance of succeeding. However, this stance was overturned by an independent judicial panel, made up of 11 ordinary citizens, that ruled that three former executives should be prosecuted for criminal negligence (McCurry, 2016).

Damage caused by transboundary pollution, whether intentional or unintentional, may be long-lasting, and, in some cases, the full extent of the damage is not apparent for many years. How to apportion responsibility and compel polluters to compensate (insofar as possible) for the harm they cause is complicated by the fact that different legal jurisdictions are involved. Often, the victims are in developing countries, with little in the way of resources to seek legal redress, especially if they must resort to litigation in another country, as was seen in the example of the Bhopal explosion, discussed in Chapter 6. Co-operation between governments has led to numerous international regulatory regimes designed to monitor pollution and reduce the risk of accidents.

Is nuclear the answer?

The Fukushima disaster highlighted the risks of nuclear power. Do the benefits of nuclear still outweigh the risks?

Indonesia's fires: devastating ecological, economic and human impacts

Indonesia has been lauded as an emerging market. Following in the footsteps of the BRIC economies, it has maintained strong economic growth in the region of 5% annually since 2000. Like the BRIC economies, it is a populous country, its 250 million inhabitants making it the world's fourth-largest population. Indonesia's economy relies heavily on commodity exports. But behind the headline growth figures, there are doubts about the sustainability of the industries that produce forest commodities, including timber, pulpwood (used in the paper industry) and palm oil, on which the Indonesian economy relies.

Forest fires across Indonesia are a regular occurrence, but their effects vary from year to year, depending largely on the prevailing winds and the strength of the El Niño effect. In 2015, these factors had particularly severe consequences, as the devastation of the country's huge areas of tropical forests seemed to be uncontrollable. The damage took its toll on the economy, human life and the ecological environment. The pollutant smoke travelled to neighbouring countries, Singapore, Malaysia and even southern Thailand. The recurring fires, damaging though they are, have become systemic aspects of the Indonesian economy. The government, businesses and civil society groups are all agreed that the situation is intolerable. Apart from the physical destruction, the harmful emissions generated by the fires in 2015 came close to equalling the total annual emissions of Brazil (Harris et al., 2015). However, assigning blame and responsibility has become a case of many different interested parties blaming each other, rather than accepting responsibilities themselves. Surely, one might think, the government should take the initiative to stop the practices that lead to the fires. However, the government, which is closely tied to business interests, is reluctant to accept responsibility. Could it take a courageous stance and step in to halt the destruction?

The forests of Indonesia present economic opportunities for large companies involved in forest commodities. The easiest way to clear the land for new production is simply to burn off existing vegetation,

known as 'slash and burn'. Because of a covering of peat soil, which is highly flammable, fires are likely to get out of control. About one-third of the fires are on pulpwood plantations, and many of the rest are on or near palm oil plantations. The large agribusiness companies say that it is wrong to blame them alone. Some of the large companies support sustainable palm oil production, through the Roundtable for Sustainable Palm Oil (RSPO) certification, which opposes these practices. The agribusiness companies point to poor smallholders who expand their plots. They also point to groups that operate illegally to clear forests for land acquisition. There is a legacy of criminal activity carried out by gangs that have a quasi-political agenda, dating back to the era of the former dictator, Suharto, in the 1960s. The fact that the system of land title is inadequate makes it difficult to trace owners and identify boundaries. Small farmers say they are often not fairly paid by the large agribusinesses. Policies to encourage smallholders to reduce land clearance, including incentives and fair prices, would be the basis of a more sustainable approach to rural livelihoods. Fair prices to farmers are part of the commitment contained in the Sustainable Palm Oil Manifesto, which is more comprehensive than RSPO certification alone.

The damage to ecosystems and the hundreds of species that inhabit the forests is devastating. Many species are under threat, including orangutans, leopards, gibbons and tigers. The most visible evidence of risks to human health is the thick smoke that envelops the areas affected by the fires and can spread hundreds of miles. The smog containing smoke from burning peat is particularly toxic. In 2015, there were an estimated 500,000 cases of respiratory infections caused by the fires. Children are particularly vulnerable, and many have been evacuated from the worst-affected areas. The thick smog has caused six Indonesian provinces to declare a state of emergency. Indonesia has a poor record in child health as recorded in the UN's Human Development Index. Over 37% of children under five are stunted, meaning that they are too short for their body weight. This figure has increased from 28.5% in 2004 (Bland, 2014). Poverty and poor healthcare are largely to blame. The government devotes 16% of public spending to energy subsidies. Spending on social programmes, health and education are squeezed, jeopardizing the prospects for improved quality of life for the tens of millions of people in rural communities.

The government of Joko Widoko, elected in 2014, promised numerous reforms, including improvements in healthcare, acknowledging that this should be a national priority. But the political forces that prevail in the country are skewed more towards businesses than social needs. Concession licences and decision-making over land use are areas where corruption has been a recurring problem, resulting in continuing deforestation. Transparent procedures and enforcement would help to combat the corruption and keep track of authorized land use. The president has pledged to reduce deforestation. However, the government spends only modest amounts on prevention, while it promotes economic development through subsidies to companies that contribute to the deforestation. The Worldwide Fund for Nature (WWF) has concluded that the causes of the 2015 fires amounted to 'collective negligence' among the smallholders, the large companies and the government (Balch, 2015).

Sources: Harris, N., Minnemeyer, S., Sizer, N., Mann, S. and Payne, O. (2015) 'With latest fires crisis, Indonesia surpasses Russia as world's fourth-largest emitter', World Resources Institute, 29 October, at www.wri.org; Pilling, D. (2014) 'Indonesia's Jokowi should tread boldly', *Financial Times*, 30 October, at www.ft.com; Bland, B. (2014) 'Now for the hard part', *Financial Times*, 14 October; Balch, O. (2015) 'Indonesia's forest fires: everything you need to know', *The Guardian*, 11 November, at www.theguardian.com.

Discussion questions

- Of the several parties mentioned as responsible for causing the fires, which bears the greatest responsibility, and why?
- Reducing deforestation and improving social well-being would seem to go together. How?
- In what ways is the political leadership of Indonesia disappointing in terms of both environmental and social goals?
- How sustainable is Indonesia's development model?

International frameworks to promote sustainable development

The harmful effects of transboundary pollution on ecosystems and human well-being may emerge only gradually. By contrast, environmental disasters, such as the Exxon Valdez oil spill off the Alaskan coast in 1989 and the Chernobyl nuclear plant disaster in 1986, have an immediate impact, as well as lasting effects which can continue to harm the environment for many years. Such disasters have dramatically raised public consciousness of the need for co-operation between states. The United Nations Environment Programme (UNEP) dates from 1972. The UN Conference on Environment and Development (UNCED) produced a report in 1987, usually referred to as the Brundtland Report. It introduced the concept of sustainable development, which is 'development which meets the needs of present generations without compromising the ability of future generations to meet their own needs' (United Nations, 1987). This concept was at the heart of the Declaration on Environment and Development produced by the Rio Summit of 1992, sometimes referred to as the 'Earth Summit'.

The Rio principles

The main principles of the Rio Declaration appear in Table 10.1. The principles apply to a variety of activities and incidents, whether involving state agencies or commercial enterprises. Note that, although the principle of state sovereignty over resources is acknowledged, it is qualified by the principle of sustainable development. The 'polluter-pays' principle is acknowledged, although, when it comes to dispute resolution, the polluting state will seldom consent to international adjudication or arbitration. Principle 5 links sustainable development with poverty reduction. Critics have argued that this principle seems to indicate an underlying assumption of the Declaration that reducing poverty requires economic development, although the historical evidence suggests a more complex relationship than simple cause and effect (Castro, 2004). Poverty includes dimensions other than purely economic ones, especially in the context of sustainable development. Reducing poverty in economic terms can be short-lived, whereas sustainable livelihoods entail the capacity to provide for today's needs in an environmentally sound way that will continue into the future. As the benefits of market-based economic development are not spread evenly in societies, policymaking in relation to resource allocation, as well as social priorities, are factors in reducing poverty (Castro, 2004).

Table 10.1 The Rio Declaration on Environment and Development, 1992 – selected key principles

Principle 2	States have, in accordance with the UN Charter and the principles of international law, the sovereign right to exploit their own resources pursuant to their own environmental and development policies, and the responsibility to ensure that activities within their jurisdiction or control do not cause damage to the environment of other States or of areas beyond the limits of national jurisdiction.
Principle 3	The right to development must be fulfilled so as to equitably meet developmental and environmental needs of present and future generations.
Principle 5	All States and all people shall cooperate in the essential task of eradicating poverty as an indispensable requirement of sustainable development.
Principle 8	To achieve sustainable development and a higher quality of life for all people, States should reduce and eliminate unsustainable patterns of production and consumption and promote appropriate demographic policies.
Principle 13	States shall develop national law regarding liability and compensation for the victims of pollution and other environmental damage.
Principle 16	...the polluter should, in principle, bear the cost of pollution...
Principle 25	Peace, development and environmental protection are interdependent and indivisible.

Source: UN Environment Programme (1992) *The Rio Declaration*, at www.unep.org.

The Rio Summit of 1992 adopted the Convention on Biological Diversity and the Convention on Climate Change. The Biodiversity Convention aimed to protect and sustain biodiversity by a number of measures, including national monitoring of biodiversity, environmental impact assessments and national progress reports from individual countries. It re-enforced the principle of sustainable development. In 1992, the UN also adopted a Convention on the Transboundary Effects of Industrial Accidents, placing an onus on states to take preventive steps and also to respond responsibly when accidents occur. A Convention on Nuclear Safety followed in 1994. While these international instruments focus on state responsibility for the implementation of their provisions within their own jurisdictions, it should be noted that states vary in their commitment to prevent and control harmful activities. Developing countries, above all, may lack the resources to regulate environmental protection. Awareness of environmental implications by business enterprises is therefore a crucial factor in the environmental protection landscape. In particular, the responsibility of the large MNEs as important global players is increasingly recognized in environmental issues.

UN Sustainable Development Goals

In 2000, the UN Millennium Summit of world leaders introduced the Millennium Development Goals (MDGs) aimed at improving well-being over the following 15 years. There were eight MDGs, covering the following areas: poverty and hunger, education, child mortality, maternal health, disease, the environment and global partnership. Within these areas, specific targets were set, some quite ambitious. Although considerable progress was made over the 15 years, most of the targets were not met. The aim of halving the number of people living in extreme poverty (on less than $1.25 a day) was met: the number was reduced from 1.9 billion to 836 million. However, the aim of reducing hunger by half was not met. The proportion of people suffering from undernourishment fell from 23.3% in 1990 to 12.9% in 2015, leaving about 795 million people undernourished. Progress towards the target of halving the number of people without access to safe drinking water and improved sanitation was better. The number without safe drinking water was halved, but that still leaves 663 million people without (Galatsidas and Sheehy, 2015). The target for halving the number of people without improved sanitation was missed by nearly 700 million people (S. Jones, 2015).

In 2015, the UN launched the Sustainable Development Goals (SDGs), an even more ambitious set of goals for the following 15 years. This set of 17 goals is broader in scope, covering institutional and governance issues, as well as the basic goals of improving human well-being that were the focus of the MDGs. The SDGs are shown in Figure 10.5.

Figure 10.5 UN Sustainable Development Goals (SDGs), 2015–2030

Source: UNDP (UN Development Programme) (2015) *Sustainable Development Goals Booklet*, at www.undp.org, accessed 30 September 2015.

UN Sustainable Development Goals (SDGs)

1 End extreme poverty (less than $1.25 a day)

2 End hunger; achieve food security and sustainable agriculture

3 Ensure good health and well-being

4 Ensure inclusive and quality education

5 Achieve gender equality

6 Ensure safe drinking water and sanitation for all

7 Ensure affordable, clean energy for all

8 Promote decent work and inclusive, sustainable economic growth

9 Promote inclusive and sustainable industrialization, including infrastructure and innovation

10 Reduce inequality within and between countries

11 Make cities safe, inclusive and sustainable

12 Ensure sustainable consumption and production

13 Combat climate change

14 Conserve the oceans and seas

15 Promote sustainable use of land

16 Promote peace, justice and inclusive institutions

17 Strengthen global partnership for SDGs

The first six SDGs, like the MDGs, concern poverty, hunger, health and education, but with the more radical aim of wiping out extreme poverty and hunger everywhere. SDGs 7, 13, 14 and 15 directly address issues of climate change and the environment. Included are the need for clean energy that all can afford (SDG 7), sustainable use of the land (SDG 15), climate change (SDG 13) and conservation of the seas (SDG 14). Sustainable consumption, as well as production, is emphasized, reflecting the Rio Declaration (SDG 12). These are compatible with sustainable agriculture, which is part of SDG 1, forming a comprehensive set of goals relating to ecology and climate change. However, they are very broadly worded, articulating ideals rather than attainable targets. Remaining goals highlight the need for inclusiveness. Look at the numerous aspects of SDGs 8 and 9. These are broadly-worded goals related to a development agenda which raises questions for governments and businesses.

Sights of debris washed up on the beach should raise alarm over the risks to aquatic life posed by dumping waste into the sea, highlighted in SDG 14.

Source: iStock.com/Sablin.

What kind of development is being encouraged, how is it being financed, and who is benefiting? Economic development typically relies on foreign investors, with their capital and technology, which governments of developing countries are keen to attract. But the interests of investors and societies do not automatically coincide. For example, large agribusiness companies such as Monsanto base their business on the use of genetically-modified organisms (GMOs), which are plants and animals that have been altered genetically in ways that do not occur in nature. Monsanto presses for the adoption of GM crops in Africa, where drought and flooding can play havoc with traditional agriculture (see Chapter 7). However, GM crops are linked with damage to biodiversity and ecosystems. In addition, small farmers become tied to the company that provides the seeds and other products needed for GM production – a situation that involves not just being locked in contractually, but, for many, indebtedness caused by the loans they must incur. Included in the goal of sustainable economic growth (SDG 8) is the issue of debt relief for the many heavily-indebted developing countries. Most of the debt of these countries is owed to lenders in rich countries. There has been progress on a scheme of debt relief through the IMF and World Bank, but SDG 8 does not envisage any stronger mechanism (T. Jones, 2015).

Industrialization and infrastructure projects, highlighted in SDG 9, often serve mainly the interests of investors rather than all in society. As we saw in Chapter 9, governments play key roles in promoting domestic innovation that can contribute to sustainable development. SDGs 10, 11 and 16 specifically address the role of institutions and governance. SDG 11 refers to the growth of sprawling urban areas of mostly poor inhabitants in much of the developing world. Problems of health, clean water, employment, education and clean affordable energy are all associated with slums, setting back the prospects of improving human well-being. Indeed, these poor living and working conditions pose some of the greatest obstacles to achieving most of the other SDGs in this list. They also represent threats to social cohesion. SDGs 11 and 16 recognize the problems of huge disparities between the rich and poor, not just in terms of income, but in institutions that perpetuate inequality.

Are the new SDGs achievable, or simply a wish list? Like the MDGs before them, progress in achieving some of the goals, such as piped water, can be measured. But others relate to more fundamental aspects of economies and political systems. Governments of any hue, whether democratic or authoritarian, can promote universal education, but where power rests with political and business élites, often with corrupt links, the weak are likely to come off worst. This throws into doubt the hopes of achieving the more radical of these SDGs. The poor, whether in rural communities or precarious urban dwellings, remain most vulnerable to being exposed to environmental degradation and the ravages of climate change. Although they are perhaps too optimistic, the new SDGs do serve to draw attention to the importance of politics and institutions in achieving inclusive development.

SDGs: too ambitious?

Which of the SDGs are most crucial for achieving sustainable livelihoods among the world's poorest inhabitants? What are the difficulties lying in the way of achieving them?

Managing environmental impacts

Land, water and air are the components of the physical environment which have been affected by industrial processes associated with economic development. Managers have become accustomed to dealing with local pollution problems arising from their operations, entailing interaction with local community authorities. However, wider issues such as climate change and biodiversity, while nonetheless real, seem remote, complex, and not susceptible to the usual means of resolution. What is more, scientific evidence is not always clear-cut, and regulatory regimes differ in their monitoring and enforcement. NGOs such as Greenpeace and other 'green' groups have raised public awareness of environmental issues and climate change. As we have seen, the views of consumers and shareholders tend to influence corporate executives more than the more abstract arguments based on ethical principles.

Sustainable development in the business context

Businesses are becoming more conscious of the need for new, cleaner technologies, partly because of growing social and ethical considerations, and also because of international instruments that are gradually becoming part of national law. But how does a broad principle like sustainable development translate into a business strategy? The following statement from the International Institute for Sustainable Development (IISD) provides some indication:

> For the business enterprise, sustainable development means adopting business strategies and activities that meet the needs of the enterprise and its stakeholders today while protecting, sustaining and enhancing the human and natural resources that will be needed in the future. (IISD, 1992)

In terms of strategy, the statement is still rather general, but it does highlight the duty to stakeholders, and also the duty to both human and environmental resources. The IISD has revisited this definition in the light of Sen's concept of development as freedom of individual choice or capabilities (Sen, 1999). Development in this wider sense would reflect the perspective of human development articulated by Castro (cited above). This would apply not just in developing countries, but in any country where there are wide disparities in income and life opportunities between the rich and the poor. Where a business is party to environmental degradation, it can be impeding sustainable development in this wider sense. For example, eroding a resource such as a river on which a community depends will impair livelihoods and impact on future generations (Cosbey, 2003).

Companies are encouraged to take a broader view of their 'environmental footprint', looking at all phases of their operations, from production processes to the nature of the products they sell, to assess whether they can be made more environmentally friendly. Consumers have been a source of pressure, creating new demand, for example, for products which are recyclable. Environmental protection and economic efficiency, once seen as posing a dilemma of choice, could be seen as merging together. Protecting the environment should be at the heart of sustainable business strategy, viewed as value-enhancing, rather than as a constraint on business. Environmental issues are closely linked with social responsibility, and many businesses now publish sustainability reports on a regular basis.

Environmental management in practice

Environmental management, assessing environmental impact and devising suitable strategies, is now seen as central to companies' operations, especially in the industries which are by nature more polluting. These include chemicals, mining, pulp and paper, iron and steel, and refineries. For the large MNEs that use subcontracting and licensing arrangements, there is a question of how much control can be exerted on subcontractors in terms of environmental management. This question is often posed for MNEs operating in developing countries with weak environmental protection laws.

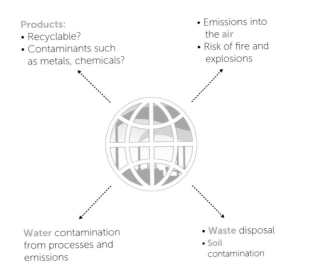

Products:
- Recyclable?
- Contaminants such as metals, chemicals?

- Emissions into the air
- Risk of fire and explosions

Water contamination from processes and emissions

- Waste disposal
- Soil contamination

Figure 10.6 Aspects of environmental management

Research and increased awareness of the damaging effects of climate change have impressed on businesses the need to look at the green implications of their operations, and especially their levels of emissions. One consideration is that reductions are likely to be legally required in the future, and it is preferable to get a head start. Another is that companies are in a position to take the lead in positive action to alleviate potentially harmful global warming, especially in industries that have high levels of emissions. Figure 10.6 shows the areas of environmental management in both processes and products. Industrial processes impact on the air, water and land, in the immediate vicinity of operations and often further afield. Emissions of gases, particle matter and chemicals can cause damaging air pollution. There are also risks of fires and explosions, which are high in some industries, especially in the energy sector.

The oil company, BP, has faced liabilities in the US for many billions of dollars following an oil spill at a rig in the Gulf of Mexico (see Chapter 6). These huge bills for damages, fines and clean-up activities that were incurred in the US are exceptional. Most companies that operate in sensitive environments are unlikely to face the years of litigation and punitive damages claims that BP faced. Contamination of water from industrial processes can affect all types of waterways, both surface and underground. Much of this contamination is hard to detect, and it can be difficult to prove who is responsible. In many cases, a fine payable under local law is the only penalty. But the effects can be long-lasting. Where water is becoming scarce, industrial use can be controversial, as whole communities can experience water shortages. Adapting processes to use less water, as well as reducing waste water, has become a priority in industries which are heavy users of water.

Soil contamination and degradation are more localized than emissions into the atmosphere, but can have long-lasting impacts on the land, affecting its use for human habitation and other uses such as agriculture. Waste disposal can be costly for firms, and in developing countries where environmental controls are weak, firms are more likely to be lax about how waste is disposed of than in more regulated environments. Ecuador is an example, where serious environmental degradation was caused by Texaco's operations between 1964 and 1992. Because environmental restoration requirements agreed by the company with the Ecuadorian government were minimal, there was little inhabitants could do to make the company clean up and restore sites when they left the country in 1992. Enduring contamination was impairing human health, leading to cancers and other illnesses. Legal claims to obtain redress have been staunchly resisted by Chevron, the company that now owns Texaco. Ecuadorian villagers initiated legal proceedings against Texaco in the US courts in 1993, which culminated in a judgment against the Ecuadorians in 2002, on the grounds that Ecuador would have been the appropriate forum. In 2003, the Ecuadorian villagers launched a class action in Ecuador against Texaco, which was by then part of Chevron. The decision of the Ecuadorian judge in 2011 was that Chevron should pay $8.6 billion in damages and clean-up costs, increasing to $18 billion if Chevron did not issue an apology. Chevron did not accept this ruling.

Meanwhile, Chevron had used the investor-state dispute settlement process (ISDS) to bring cases against Ecuador in 2006 and 2009, claiming Ecuador had violated a US-Ecuador bilateral investment treaty (see Chapters 6 and 7). The arbitration panel ruled in favour of Chevron, stating that Ecuador should suspend enforcement of its court's order against Chevron. Chevron has also filed legal actions in the US against Ecuador's lawyers, alleging conspiracy to extort billions of dollars from the company. In 2012, the Ecuadorian villagers initiated action in Canada to enforce the Ecuadorian judgment against Chevron's assets in Canada, and in September 2013, the Canadian Supreme Court held that this action could go ahead. The Ecuadorian villagers still have had no payment from the company, and Chevron acknowledges no liability for the contamination.

Surface disturbance, as well as waste disposal, is a factor in mining. Much of the world's coal reserves do not lie in deep mines but near the surface, in opencast mines. Extracting this coal despoils the land, and the operations can be widespread, affecting the ecology over large areas. Canada's oil sands are an example, where surface mining operations cover an area of 54,000 square miles. These mining operations to extract bitumen, a type of heavy petroleum, use large amounts of water and generate large amounts of GHG emissions. There are serious concerns about environmental damage from these operations. There are also concerns over the risks incurred in the transport of the fuel by rail and road to destinations in Canada and the US.

Cutting pollution, while it can be seen as a cost, is also a business opportunity. Much research is being carried out into changing the nature of consumer products, to make them less polluting. As Figure 10.6 highlights, recycling is one aspect of greener products. Products which have been designed to be environmentally friendly use fewer metals and chemicals, and are easier to recycle. The Global Commission on the Economy and Climate, headed by the former Mexican president, Felipe Calderon, makes the case that investments in cleaner infrastructure, transport and energy are affordable and cost-effective in the long term. The financial newspaper, the *Financial Times*, concludes that the 'greatest obstacle to sensible climate policies is the lobbying power of established interests, which resist change by conflating their own prosperity with that of the economy as a whole' (*Financial Times*, 2014).

The way I see it ...

'The structural and technological changes unfolding in the global economy, combined with multiple opportunities to improve economic efficiency, now make it possible to achieve both better growth and better climate outcomes.'

The Global Commission on the Economy and Climate, in its report, *Better Growth, Better Climate*, 2014, at www.newclimateeconomy.net

To what extent do you think that this view is realistic, or over-optimistic?

The extent to which businesses will voluntarily set targets for emissions reductions will affect global progress towards reaching national targets. Environmental reporting, detailing the ways in which a company's operations impact on the environment, has become an element in triple-bottom-line reporting. In addition to financial reporting, some companies report on the social and environmental aspects of their operations, making up the three elements of triple-bottom-line reporting. While the latter two impact reports are voluntary, they are increasingly viewed by shareholders and other stakeholders as indicative of good governance. The International Organization for Standardization, which produces ISO standards, has developed a certification for standards of environmental management. The initial standards were set out in ISO 14000, now updated to ISO 14001:2015 (ISO, 2015). Many MNEs are finding that, in the new context of social responsibility, it is advantageous to take a global approach to their environmental management, wherever the location.

Sustainable consumption

When we think of consumers and green issues, we tend to think mainly of recycling waste and buying organic produce. However, green consumerism covers a wide range of lifestyle decisions. Besides shopping for environmentally-friendly products and recycling, it covers using less polluting transport, using complementary medicine, exploring eco-tourism for our holidays, and investing our money in socially responsible funds. In addressing the role of consumers in environmental issues, the UNEP focuses on a broad notion of sustainable consumption, which covers the many lifestyle decisions made by consumers which impact on the environment over the long term, whether directly or indirectly. The Oslo Symposium of 1994 provided a broad definition of sustainable consumption as:

> the use of goods and services that respond to basic needs and bring a better quality of life, while minimizing the use of natural resources, toxic materials and emissions of waste and pollutants over the life cycle, so as not to jeopardize the needs of future generations. (Oslo Roundtable on Sustainable Consumption and Production, 1994)

The Oslo Symposium definition envisages a distinction between patterns of consumption and volumes of consumption. Substituting more efficient and less polluting products will improve environmental quality through changing patterns of consumption. Consumers will more readily adapt to changing patterns of consumption than reducing the volumes of consumption of a product or service. Typical measures that environment-conscious householders invest in are solar energy installations, energy-efficient boilers and lightbulbs, electric vehicles and bicycles. Cycling has grown in popularity in the UK, partly because of growing interest in professional cycling, boosted by interest in the Tour de France, which had its 'grand départ' in Yorkshire in 2014. Another important factor has been a government 'cycle to work' scheme that allows employees to use tax-free bicycles provided by their employer. However, whenever subsidies to encourage green alternatives are cut or reduced, the number of consumers attracted to the green alternative is likely to decrease.

'Green consumerism' has seen a rise in popularity of environmentally-friendly products, often at premium prices. In some instances, such as GM-free products, the reasoning is based on health fears as much as environmental concerns (see pp. 247–8 on GM labelling). Sceptics of green consumerism argue that, even if consumers in rich countries change their buying habits, the effects will be limited unless people are persuaded to consume less. The trend in the large emerging economies has been in the opposite direction. Development has tended to be equated with western consumer lifestyles, dependent on cars, cheap air travel and throw-away appliances, all of which are have been on the rise in developing countries, although they are recognized as problematical in today's ecologically stressed environment. Should western consumerism be held up as a model for developing countries? Global food and consumer products companies, such as Nestlé and P&G, whose operations are based on industrialized processes, now target developing countries as growing markets.

Development, both past and present, tends to mean economic growth, with little heed for environmental consequences. Carmakers are lured to the BRIC countries. Here, consumers are keen to acquire cars – and the new mobility they bring. With far fewer cars per inhabitant than the advanced economies, there is much scope for growth in these markets. Indeed, the BRIC countries are viewed by car manufacturers as their main source of future profits, but what about the environmental consequences? China is now the world's largest car market by volume, seeing a huge growth in sales of passenger cars in the past decade or so. In 2005, sales of passenger cars in China numbered about 4 million. This figure had more than doubled by 2010, and in 2014, nearly 20 million cars were sold in the Chinese market (*Wall Street Journal*, 2015). Since then, the growth in sales has slowed, largely because of the slowing rate of economic growth. However, other factors have been the government's policies of cracking down on corruption and measures taken in large cities to rein in car ownership to deal with traffic congestion and air pollution.

For businesses, especially manufacturing firms, the notion of defining sustainable consumption as reduced consumption meets with little appeal. Similarly, for governments, reduced consumption is not likely to find favour. Reduced consumer spending tends to pose headaches, as highlighted in Chapter 4: reduced output is linked to decreases in employment, falling tax revenues and weak economic growth. Governments, however, are in a position to promote changes in consumer behaviour and changes in manufacturers' approaches which fall within the notion of sustainable consumption.

Sustainable consumption – every day?

As consumers, we depend on a variety of industrialized products, from ready meals in packets to drinks in cans. To what extent would you be able and willing to give up these everyday products?

GLOBAL BUSINESS IN ACTION

Recycling solutions for a sustainable economy

Fabienne Pessayre

Fabienne has been involved in a number of businesses in the area of green technology, recycling, and creating new products from recycled materials. These research-oriented businesses are Hawthorn Research and Development (www.hawthornresearch.com) and Zembra Ltd. (www.zembragroup.com). Here, she speaks mainly about Zembra, which is focused on activities largely in the area of creating new, environmentally-friendly products from agricultural waste. Their underlying philosophy is based on principles of sustainability and protecting the natural environment. While the idea of saving the planet might seem rather abstract and idealistic, these business activities tackle down-to-earth issues that affect us all. Among the materials researched by Zembra are the residues of olive biomass left from producing olive oil. Compressed olive kernels, for example, can be used in the construction industry, and, when ground to a very fine consistency, can be used in cosmetics, to replace ingredients derived from plastics. Advances in recycling technology and scientific research are impacting in a wide variety of industries. Fabienne's academic and professional background includes both scientific and cultural achievements. She holds degrees in mathematics and physics, and in Islamic art. And her professional experience has reflected her diverse interests.

Fabienne has worked in a number of different countries, and has gained a unique perspective on the ways in which companies and individuals are now changing their views towards more ethical and sustainable business solutions. As the interview with her shows, these SMEs are for-profit enterprises – they aim to succeed in new competitive markets for sustainable products. She thus combines a strong sustainability perspective with a business orientation. Being first in the market with a new product that offers a green solution brings competitive advantage as well as a boost for sustainable business goals. Fabienne sees these issues in a moral context, noting that businesses and individuals are now more conscious of environmental impacts of everyday products.

Before watching the interview with Fabienne, look at the sections on environmental management and on sustainable consumption. There is a discussion of the use of antibiotics in animals in Chapter 12, in the section, 'Assessing the risks in the global environment'. Also in Chapter 12, in the section, 'Envisaging a new perspective', there is a discussion of the ethical dimension of investment.

Visit www.palgravehighered.com/morrison-gbe-4e to watch the video, then think about the following questions:

1. What new products does Fabienne mention specifically? What advantages do these products have over existing products that are less environmentally-friendly?
2. How has the supply chain become globalized in the case of Zembra?
3. Fish farming – a growing industry serving large markets – controversially involves giving antibiotics to the fish. What are the potential impacts of Zembra's development of replacement products based on natural extracts?
4. To what extent does she feel that businesses and individuals are becoming more conscious of environmental impacts? How important is the role of governments, in her view, in encouraging the promotion of sustainable solutions?
5. Fabienne mentions the success of 'moral stocks' – or ethical investing in shares – as an important trend. What does she see as the explanation?

Ecology and climate change: challenges and responsibilities

Economic development based on industrialization and exploitation of resources is an environmental issue for all countries, whatever their stage of economic development. Developed economies, which have long been more focused on services than manufacturing, continue to have high levels of carbon emissions, due in large part to consumer lifestyles. Emerging economies, where western consumer lifestyles are now spreading rapidly among the growing middle classes, are the sources of the biggest rises in carbon emissions. Urbanization in developing countries, where infrastructure is struggling to catch up, is causing problems for maintaining clean air, access to clean water and sanitation. Sprawling cities are also prone to suffer from food and energy shortages. Whereas these issues were once seen as matters of local concern, we now see them as part of a global picture. Similarly, in areas of the world where population pressures and depletion of natural resources are causing hardship to both humans and other sentient beings such as wildlife, the issues are of global concern.

Levels of pollution in the growing cities in developing and emerging countries have overtaken those in the developed countries. Air pollution is measured in terms of particulate matter (PM) per cubic metre. Particles smaller than 2.5 micrometres or microns, known as PM2.5 are found in emissions from vehicles, burning waste and metal processing. They present a serious risk to health, especially to people in the cities with the highest concentrations. The World Health Organization (WHO) has reported concentrations of PM2.5 in 1,600 cities, the most polluted of which was Delhi, in India (see Figure 10.7). Beijing's pollution has received much attention, due to the city's rapid industrialization and urbanization. Although not as widely publicized, the pollution problems in India's cities, as reported by the WHO, are worse. The WHO reports that 13 of the world's 20 most polluted cities are in India, whereas only three are in China. Pollution in Beijing has fallen by 40% since 2000, while Delhi's has risen by 20% (Chauhan, 2015). Since 2006, there has been an average annual rise of 15.7% in the number of vehicles in India's urban areas. While the new mobility is welcomed by vehicle users, grinding traffic congestion and toxic emissions have been the price.

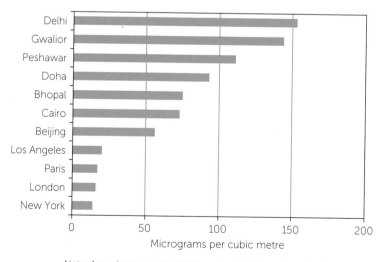

Figure 10.7 Air pollution in selected cities

Source: Based on data from WHO (World Health Organisation), Ambient (outdoor) pollution database, 2014, accessed 7 October 2015. www.who.int/phe/health_topics/outdoorair/databases/cities-2014/en/

Note: Annual mean concentration of particulate matter of a diameter of 2.5 microns or less.

Challenges and responsibilities for environmental damage and climate change are intertwined with other challenges, such as reducing poverty, improving food security and providing sustainable livelihoods. It is not difficult to see why governments of large emerging countries, such as India, seem ambivalent on responsibilities for the impacts of rising emissions. Improving human well-being, however, rests ultimately on sustainable development rather than unfettered industrialization. The Indian government wishes to be part of the solution to climate change, but has been reluctant to recognize that it has become part of the problem. India is seeing sustainable solutions springing up on a local basis, and its government is coming under pressure to take action at the national level to reduce emissions.

The UN has taken a lead in initiatives to report on the scientific findings of climate change, and also to promote co-operation among countries to reduce emissions. Challenges and responsibilities lie with governments, businesses and individuals. Governments subscribe to sustainable development goals in principle, but are inclined to prioritize economic goals. This has been true of both developed and developing economies. Climate change is now affecting all countries, but governments and businesses have been reluctant to accept the imperatives to change their policies. Governmental commitment to reductions in emissions has only recently been articulated by the US, on the one hand, and China, on the other. Accepting responsibility in principle is still a long way from legislating changes in behaviour, such as compulsory limits on emissions.

Businesses have also accepted sustainable development as a guiding principle, but have tended to wait for government regulation, rather than to pursue green initiatives on grounds of social responsibility. Uncertainty in regulatory frameworks is a complaint often heard from businesses, and companies have been able to justify weak responses to climate change on the grounds that the many rounds of intergovernmental negotiations on climate change in various cities around the world have produced few substantial outcomes that commit national authorities. At the same time, trade associations and think tanks engage in lobbying governments on behalf of large companies that perceive environmental regulation as a threat to competitiveness. Many companies see their future profits as linked to emerging markets, where economic growth has tended to take precedence over environmental concerns. But in these markets, as in the more established markets, questions of sustainable production and consumption are now on the agenda.

Conclusions

Industrialization, growing urban populations and changing patterns of consumption: these are all aspects of the effects of human activity on the environment. Industrial work and urban living present opportunities to improve human well-being through, for example, better housing, clean water and better healthcare. But urbanization that is haphazard and lacking sufficient infrastructure can be detrimental to humans – and the natural environment. Much of the human activity that has led to increasing economic development has also brought a downside of environmental degradation and risks to health and well-being – not just for the present generation, but for future generations, too. We now know far more about the impacts of global warming than earlier generations could have known. The case for making changes in behaviour is clear. But where does the responsibility lie? To say it lies with everyone on the planet is certainly true, but so abstract that no single person or organization actually feels responsible. Businesses have tended to take the view that environmental and climate change measures are for governments to legislate, and in the absence of regulation, there is no obligation to change their behaviour. But even if there is no legal obligation, there is moral obligation regarding impacts that are clearly known to be detrimental.

International agreements have made headway in urging governments to raise environmental standards, reduce levels of GHG emissions and slow deforestation, but national governments are ultimately the bodies that determine what regulations will apply. And, as we have seen, businesses look first to national laws as sources of obligation. If governments are slow to regulate, so too are businesses slow to make changes. The company whose activities pollute a river or emit toxic pollution into the atmosphere is often able simply to carry on. There might be no law against it, or, if there is, little likelihood of being caught. In some countries where enforcement systems are in place, the company can simply pay the fines that arise from time to time, considering the fines cheaper than cleaning up its operations. Whole communities and ecosystems can be at risk, with little realistic prospect of legal redress. Pressure on businesses to change their behaviour can seem weak in the absence of strict regulation. However, both governments and corporate leaders are frequently criticized by consumers and other stakeholders on grounds of ethics and social responsibility. These criticisms weigh with businesses which are part of the communities in which they operate. Cumulatively, the impacts of stakeholder voices, including those of shareholders, are helping to shift the thinking of corporate decision-makers from short-term economic goals to sustainable business practices.

☐ References

Berners-Lee, M. and Clark, D. (2010) 'What is a carbon footprint?', *The Guardian*, 4 June.

Castro, C. (2004) 'Sustainable development: mainstream and critical perspectives', *Organization & Environment*, 17(2): 195–225.

Chauhan, C. (2015) '13 out of world's top 20 polluted cities are in India, only three in China', *Hindustan Times*, 5 June, at www.hindustantimes.com

Clark, D. (2012) 'Has the Kyoto Protocol made any difference to carbon emissions?', *The Guardian*, 26 November, at www.theguardian.com.

CO_2Now (2015) Earth's CO_2 home page, at www.co2.org, accessed 10 October 2015.

Cornot-Gandolphe, S. (2014) 'China's coal market: can Beijing tame "king coal"?', Oxford Institute of Energy Studies, University of Oxford, at www.oxfordenergy.org

Cosbey, A. (2003) 'New views of trade and sustainable development: using Sen's conception of sustainable development to re-examine the debates', IISD, at www.iisd.org

European Commission (2013) 'EU over-achieved first Kyoto emissions target, on track to meet 2020 objective', at www.ec.europa.eu, accessed 22 September 2015.

Fagan-Watson, B. (2015) 'BP, EDF and Procter & Gamble face pressure over climate change lobbying', *The Guardian*, 10 September, at www.theguardian.com

FAO (Food and Agriculture Organization of the UN) (2012) 'The state of the world's forests', at www.fao.org

Financial Times (2014) 'Saving the climate need not destroy the economy', 22 September, at www.ft.com

Galatsidas, A. and Sheehy, F. (2015) 'What have the millennium development goals achieved?', *The Guardian*, 6 July, at www.theguardian.com

IEA (International Energy Agency) (2015) 'Renewables lead world power market growth', *Renewable Energy: Medium-term Market Report 2015*, at www.iea.org

IISD (International Institute for Sustainable Development) (1992) 'Business strategies for sustainable development', at www.iisd.org

IPCC (2014) *Climate Change 2014: Synthesis Report* (Geneva: IPCC).

ISO (2015) *ISO 14000 − Environmental Management*, at www.iso.org, accessed 10 October 2015.

Jones, S. (2015) 'UN: 15-year push ends extreme poverty for a billion people', *The Guardian*, 6 July, at www.theguardian.com.

Jones, T. (2015) 'Sustainable development goals promise little respite for indebted poor countries', *The Guardian*, 23 September, at www.theguardian.com

Landes, D. (1998) *The Wealth and Poverty of Nations* (London: Little, Brown & Company).

Maddison, A. (2001) *The World Economy: A Millennial Perspective* (Paris: OECD).

McCurry, J. (2016) 'Former Tepco bosses charged over Fukushima meltdown', *The Guardian*, 29 February, at www.theguardian.com

Nelson, A. (2015) 'BP lobbied against EU support for clean energy to favour gas, documents reveal', *The Guardian*, 20 August, at www.theguardian.com

Noack, R., (2015) 'The nuclear disaster at Fukushima didn't have to happen', *The Washington Post*, 22 September, at www.washingtonpost.com

Oslo Roundtable on Sustainable Consumption and Production (1994) 'The imperative of sustainable production and consumption: defining sustainable consumption', Oslo Symposium, Norway, January, at www.iisd.ca/consume/oslo

PwC Global (2015) 'CEO pulse on climate change', report at www.pwc.com

Sen, A. (1999) *Development as Freedom* (New York: Anchor Books).

UNEP (United Nations Environmental Programme) (2015) 'International environment and the global commons', at www.unep.org, accessed 20 September 2015.

United Nations (1987) *Report of the World Commission on Environment and Development: Our Common Future* (the Brundtland Report), at www.un-documents.net

Vidal, J. (2015) 'Five G7 nations increased their coal use over a five-year period, research shows', *The Guardian*, 8 June, at wwwtheguardian.com

Vidal, J., Goldenberg, S. and Taylor, L. (2015) 'How the historic Paris deal over climate change was finally agreed', *The Guardian*, 13 December, at www.theguardian.com

Wall Street Journal (2015) 'China car sales driven lower by slowing economy', 10 September, at www.wsj.com

Multiple choice questions

Go to the companion website: www.palgravehighered.com/morrison-gbe-4e to take a quick multiple choice quiz on what you have read in this chapter.

Review questions

1 In what ways do industrialization and urbanization impact on the environment?
2 What does environmental degradation refer to, and what are its effects?
3 What are the causes of climate change, and what are the effects of global warming?
4 What were the aims of the Kyoto Protocol, and why was the treaty significant in terms of progress towards international co-operation?

5 In the years following the Kyoto Protocol, how have the developed and developing countries diverged on climate change issues?

6 What did the Paris conference of 2015 accomplish?

7 Why has transboundary pollution become a global concern? Give some examples of transboundary pollution, and examine ways of dealing with it through collaboration between countries.

8 What are the benefits of nuclear energy, and why is it controversial?

9 Define 'sustainable development'. How does it differ from plain economic development?

10 What are the implications of sustainable development for business strategists?

11 What are the Sustainable Development Goals?

12 What is meant by environmental management?

13 How can environmental reporting contribute to sustainable business strategies?

14 What is meant by 'sustainable consumption'? Are consumer attitudes in rich countries changing as a result of green campaigns and greater availability of information on environmental issues?

15 What are the challenges posed by a sustainable development agenda in the developing world?

✓ Assignments

1 Assess the achievements of the Paris accord of 2015, and its likelihood of achieving real progress.

2 To what extent is sustainable development a realistic proposition for developing countries?

📖 Further reading

Bell, S., McGillivray, D. and Peterson, O. (2013) *Environmental Law*, 8th edn (Oxford: OUP).

Blewitt, J. (2014) *Understanding Sustainable Development*, 2nd edn (London: Routledge).

Dessler, A. (2015) *Introduction to Modern Climate Change* (Cambridge: Cambridge University Press).

Flannery, T. (2015) *Atmosphere of Hope: Solutions to the Climate Crisis* (London: Penguin).

Klein, N. (2015) *This Changes Everything: Capitalism vs the Climate* (London: Penguin).

Landes, D. (1998) *The Wealth and Poverty of Nations* (London: Little, Brown & Company).

Middleton, M. (2013) *The Global Casino: An Introduction to Environmental Issues*, 5th edn (London: Routledge).

Sachs, J. (2015) *The Age of Sustainable Development* (New York: Columbia University Press).

Stern, N. (2015) *Why Are We Waiting? The Logic, Urgency and Promise of Tackling Climate Change*, Lionel Robbins Lectures (Cambridge, MA: MIT Press).

🌐 **Visit the companion website at** www.palgravehighered.com/morrison-gbe-4e **for further learning and teaching resources.**

CLOSING CASE STUDY

Uruguay shines as an example for South Americans

Uruguay is South America's second-smallest country, with a population of only 3.4 million. Sandwiched between the continent's two economic powerhouses, Brazil and Argentina, it stands out as an example of how economic, social and environmental goals can be democratically implemented. It has enjoyed rates of growth of 5–6%, thanks in large part to the sound policies of its president from 2010 to 2015, José Mujica, who, despite his socialist background, embraced business-friendly policies and welcomed FDI. Mujica was known for his modest lifestyle, refusing to move into the presidential palace. As he departed from office, he said, 'I believe we have to favour capitalism, so that its wheels keep turning' (Gilbert, 2015). Strong economic growth has facilitated the government's expansion of social security, reducing the percentage of people living in poverty from 40% of the population to 12%. He says, 'We are very used in this world to seeing the economy and inequality grow together ... In Uruguay that has not happened. The economy grew and people were lifted out of poverty' (Gilbert, 2015).

Mujica's vision encompassed a shift to clean energy. In the run-up to the Paris climate change conference of 2015, Uruguay was highlighted for its strides in converting the country to renewable energy. Uruguay now produces 95% of its electricity from clean energy, including a mix of wind turbines, hydropower and solar, while renewables satisfy nearly 55% of its overall energy needs. This transformation, achieved in just 10 years, has not involved groundbreaking technology or huge debt financing. Much of the new power generation capacity derives from wind turbines, financed through public-private partnerships with foreign investors. For foreign energy companies, such as Enercon of Germany, Uruguay has presented an excellent opportunity. The country now enjoys stable democratic institutions and political leadership that is attuned to providing a good environment for investors. It also helps that, unlike Argentina, Uruguay has never defaulted on its debts. The country suffered a financial crisis in 2002, when demand for its commodity exports tumbled, but, with the help of the IMF and a restructuring package for its debt, it was able to recover, and it also withstood the effects of the global financial crisis of 2008.

The large windfarms now dotting the countryside are evidence of the country's long-term commitment, guaranteeing Enercon a fixed price for 20 years. With low maintenance and staff costs, profits are assured. Other foreign companies are now seeking to bid for these contracts, which is helping to drive down costs. A large windfarm now feeds into a hydropower plant, helping to offset the vulnerability of hydropower to drought, which was a problem before the advent of the windfarm investments. This makes Uruguay less vulnerable to climate change than countries that rely heavily on hydropower. Costa Rica is another country that has invested in clean energy, but relies 78% on hydropower. Uruguay has built no new hydropower plants, and there is no nuclear in the mix. Uruguay's industrial activities, which are mainly agricultural processing, are now run by biomass cogeneration plants. The transport sector remains dependent on oil, but the fossil-fuel proportion is now reduced to 45% of the total energy needs. Uruguay formerly imported electricity from Argentina, but now exports one-third of its power generation to its southern neighbour.

Uruguay's clean energy policies are part of an overall picture of progressive thinking, combined with social values and a welfare state. The country has had a state system of universal secular education since the nineteenth century. Recognition of workers' rights, universal suffrage and abolition of the death penalty go back to the early twentieth century. The government launched a crackdown on smoking in 2005, coinciding with the World Health Organization's framework convention on tobacco control. At the time, 40% of the adult population were smokers. That figure has now fallen to 27%. Importantly, young smokers, aged 12 to 17, have dwindled from 33% of the age group to 17%. However, in 2015, when the government introduced a larger health warning on cigarette packets, the tobacco company, Philip Morris International (PMI), sued Uruguay under the investor-state dispute settlement procedure (ISDS), for depriving it of potential profits.

PMI's parent company, Altria, is a US company, and Altria separated out the international business into Philip Morris International, registered in Switzerland.

Uruguay has persisted in its health policies, despite the millions of dollars it is having to spend to defend itself against the lawsuit. This is a 'David and Goliath' battle: Philip Morris International has annual revenues of $80 billion, whereas Uruguay's GDP is $55 billion. The government's defence is that it has 'the right and duty to safeguard the health and wellbeing of its citizens and is complying with international treaties on tobacco control' (Armitage, 2014). Nearly 200 countries have signed up to the WHO treaty. Philip Morris International has pursued similar claims against other countries, indicating its willingness to do battle against the countries that seek to control tobacco use. There is a persisting shadow over public-interest legislation in areas like health and climate change: which country will be the next to be targeted by global companies in industries like tobacco and fossil fuels?

Sources: Watts, J. (2015) 'Uruguay makes dramatic shift to nearly 95% electricity from clean energy', *The Guardian*, 3 December, at www.theguardian.com; Graham-Harrison, E. (2015) 'Where Uruguay leads, the rest of the world struggles to keep up', *The Guardian*, 6 December; Armitage, J. (2014) 'Big Tobacco puts countries on trial as concerns over TTIP deals mount', *The Independent*, 21 October, at www.independent.co.uk; Gilbert, J. (2015) 'Uruguay's most unexpected champion of capitalism', *Fortune*, 23 January, at www.fortune.com.

Questions for discussion

- What are the main factors that have determined the success of Uruguay's clean energy policies?
- What are the elements of Uruguay's model of capitalism under former president Mujica?
- How does the view of capitalism of Mujica differ from that of Philip Morris International?
- Why should governments be concerned about the lawsuits mounted by companies like Philip Morris International?

ETHICS AND SOCIAL RESPONSIBILITY

Outline of chapter

This chapter will enable you to

- Gain an overview of the foundations of ethical principles and how they are applied in business contexts
- Understand the legal and ethical dimensions of human rights, and how they affect corporate decision-making
- Examine the elements of corporate social responsibility in theory and practice
- Appreciate the impacts of CSR and stakeholder concerns on corporate governance

Apple: the world's most valuable company, but how ethical is it?

The popularity of digital devices such as this tablet has boosted Apple's profits, but Apple's profile as a respected company is a different matter.

Source: Getty Images/Hoxton/Tom Merton.

With a market capitalization of over $700 billion, Apple reached a market value in 2015 that no other company with publicly traded shares has reached. The oil company, ExxonMobil, which lies in second place, has a market value of about half that of Apple. Apple's rise to this unprecedented level has taken place in a relatively short time. Its shares have risen 120-fold since 2000, which marked the start of its recent successful spell, with the launch of a series of iconic gadgets, starting with the iPod and focusing primarily on successive models of iPhone. In 2015, it also reported the largest quarterly profits of any company in history – $18 billion. Apple's shares rose by 60% in 2014, with the launch of the successful iPhone 6.

Apple is ranked in first place in the annual rankings of the world's most respected companies, carried out by Barron's (www.barrons.com). This table is compiled from the views of institutional investors, and tends to reflect share performance rather than how the company is run. On the other hand, as Barron's points out, those criteria are

connected. Investors surveyed by Barron's took into account four criteria: ethical business practices, sound business strategy, strong management, and revenue and profit growth (Racanelli, 2015). In the 2015 survey, they felt ethical business practices to be the most important of the four, while revenue and profit growth were the least important. When corporate wrongdoing comes to light, a company's shares tend to plunge, affecting financial performance, which for investment managers is a central concern. Investment managers are highly sensitive to the opinions and values of the investing public whom they serve. And it is likely that corporate malpractice, for example offshoring profits to avoid tax, is now attracting greater criticism. Although Apple has attracted criticism on ethical grounds, its share price has remained strong, and one of the investors surveyed by Barron's summed up the reasons for Apple's Number 1 position: its innovative products, strong brand and financial performance (Racanelli, 2015).

For Barron's, 'respect' includes ethical practices along with other criteria. What would a multifaceted assessment of an ethical company include? There are issues relating to a range of stakeholders, not simply shareholders. It would focus on human rights issues in the supply chain. The use of outsourced manufacturing is one of the areas in which Apple has been vulnerable. Following attempted suicides in a Foxconn factory in 2010, Apple has introduced audits of supplier factories, but are these more about public relations than genuine improvement? There are hundreds of factories like Foxconn's, and many more that produce components for Apple devices. The electronics industry generally relies on ambitious production targets that have knock-on effects in terms of hours worked, equipment, pay and living conditions. Improvements in wages and conditions in China are derived not so much from changing the policies of brand owners as from reforms in protective legislation taking place, as China's economic development model evolves to take account of more qualitative issues.

Apple has a reputation for driving tough, uncompromising deals with suppliers, which is a contributory factor in poor working conditions. It is also accused of too much secrecy. These contracts are subject to comprehensive non-disclosure clauses, the terms sometimes coming to light only later in court proceedings. Greater transparency and flexibility in supply contracts would be a step forward. However, transparency and flexibility have not been values associated with Apple, either under its former CEO Steve Jobs, or its current CEO, Tim Cook. Cook has given greater attention to shareholder interests than his predecessor, introducing dividends. However, he faced criticism because the dividend payment was funded by a huge bond issue of $17 billion, to avoid a tax bill that would have arisen on profits brought back to the US.

Apple strenuously denies any wrongdoing over its offshore arrangements to channel profits away from the US tax authorities. Three Apple offshore units, facilitated by the Irish government, are used to hold money without any legal tax residence at all. This highly irregular arrangement is under investigation by the EU, and was also criticized by US Senators. The Senate Permanent Subcommittee questioned Tim Cook in a highly publicized hearing in 2013, accusing Apple of searching for the 'holy grail of tax avoidance' (Barker and Bradshaw, 2014). This hearing was seen as a pivotal moment, when the general public became more engaged with corporate tax avoidance issues. In 2015, Apple held $181.1 billion in profits offshore, which would lead to a tax bill of $59.2 billion if the money were returned to the US.

Apple's employment practices are also criticized on ethical grounds. Like other technology companies, Apple has a poor record on diversity as an employer: 70% of its employees are white and Asian males. Only 30% are women, and 7% are black. Tim Cook has been forthright in stating that there is much to be done to improve diversity. In 2015, staff in the Apple store in Melbourne, Australia turned away a group of black students on the grounds that 'they might steal something' (Rushe, 2015). Tim Cook has assured the public that this behaviour is contrary to the company's values and that staff would be retrained. As in other areas of ethical practices, Apple has appeared to respond when criticized, rather than establish a strong ethical stance in the first place.

Sources: Kopytoff, V. (2015) 'Apple: the first $700 billion company', *Fortune*, 10 February; Jeffries, D. (2014) 'Is Apple cleaning up its act on labour rights', *The Guardian*, 5 March, at www.theguardian.com; Racanelli, V. (2015) 'Apple tops Barron's list of respected companies', 27 June, at www.barrons.com; Barker, A. and Bradshaw, T. (2014) 'Apple braced for explosive Brussels probe', *Financial Times*, 29 September, at www.ft.com; Rushe, D. (2015) 'Tim Cook orders retraining for Apple store staff after Melbourne controversy', *The Guardian*, 13 November, at www.theguardian.com.

Questions for discussion

- What are Apple's ethical shortcomings?
- Is Apple's business model essentially unethical?
- Why have ethical shortcomings not appeared to adversely affect Apple's share price?
- Would you purchase shares in Apple, and why?

Introduction

At the start of this book, we posed some basic questions: 'What does the business exist to do?' and 'How should it go about achieving its goals?' We highlighted an obvious economic goal – to make money for the owners – but also suggested that businesses have a broader role in society. It is this broader role which is the focus of this chapter. It will be argued here that the business plays a multi-dimensional role in society, whether the firm's managers intend it to do so or not. This broader role can be seen through the eyes of stakeholder groups, such as customers and employees, and it can be viewed in even broader terms, such as the firm's role in respect of climate change. Although the planet is not a stakeholder in the traditional sense, we tend nowadays to see the business organization as having responsibilities and duties to take positive action to combat climate change. Where do these duties come from, and how should businesses respond to this range of duties, both to stakeholders and wider global concerns? Does this imply that the traditional economic goals are somehow less worthy? Many businesspeople would argue that social goals are for governments, and that the firm is best sticking to enterprise goals, such as selling goods and services.

This chapter clarifies these different threads of thinking on the role of business in society. We begin by looking at how ethics influences both individual and group behaviour, and how ethical considerations permeate business activities. We discuss different perspectives of corporate social responsibility (CSR), assessing both the 'business case' and the ethical underpinning for companies in global business operations. We look at the role of the social enterprise as an example of unequivocal commitment to social goals. For most businesses, CSR considerations are more peripheral. However, a shift in public expectations of businesses is taking place. In recent years, business ethics have come under the spotlight in a variety of situations, including corporate wrongdoing, such as breaches of human rights, and individual wrongdoing, such as bribery. What companies aim to achieve and how they go about it are coming more and more into the limelight, focusing on issues of corporate governance, executive rewards and political activities. In a final section, we look at the growing interactions between governments and businesses in both funding and carrying out social aims.

Ethics: theoretical foundations

Ethics focuses on systems of values by which judgments of right and wrong behaviour are made. Value systems are often termed standards of morality. As we found in Chapter 3, cultures involve value systems which dictate what is right and wrong within that culture. As businesses soon find when they become internationalized, values in one society may clash with those in another society. Google, for example, by complying with Chinese internet censorship, has been accused of acting unethically. This accusation was more pointed as the company has as its motto, 'Don't be evil'. This was a case of local law conflicting with ethical principles. The company could argue that acting morally in any location involves obeying the law, but accusations of unethical behaviour imply that there is some higher set of rules which should apply to individuals, companies and even governments.

Ethical principles and theories

Google's dilemma in China focused on the rights of the individual, including freedom of expression and association. The notion that respect for the individual human being is a source of ethical principles has deep historical roots, and is the foundation of theories of human rights (discussed in the next section). The foundation of the modern debate goes back to differing perspectives which emerged in the eighteenth-century Enlightenment. The individualist view that each person has wants and needs that are pursued in a self-interested way is at the heart of utilitarianism, which has been highly influential, especially in the English-speaking parts of the world. Based roughly on the ideas of Jeremy Bentham, utilitarianism focuses on the aggregate of individual goods. What is good overall is that which promotes the 'greatest happiness of the greatest number'. Sometimes referred to as the consequentialist principle, the test of the rightness or wrongness of an action depends on the results which flow from it (Quinton, 1989). The utilitarian favours minimal government interference in society, as the individual requires the maximum amount of liberty, defined as the absence of external constraints, to pursue his/her own goals. This view of human nature was taken up by the classical economists, notably Adam Smith, and has continued to underpin the thinking of economists. Free markets are assumed to be the best way to maximize the overall prosperity of a society, by facilitating as many individuals as possible in fulfilling their desires (Plamenatz, 1958).

We would now criticize this view of the individual in society on a number of grounds. First, it does not seem to take into account that different cultures have different views of the individual human being. Second, it takes a narrow view of what human beings desire in life, focusing exclusively on rational acquisitiveness. We look at each of these criticisms in turn.

First, we now realize that different cultures have different value systems. This view, sometimes referred to as ethical relativism, holds that principles are not absolute, but dependent on circumstances. Ethical relativism is perhaps a misleading term, as within a culture, right and wrong are clearly delineated. A more accurate term would be ethical contextualism, implying that ideas of right and wrong are real, but vary according to the particular belief system. That belief system can be a national culture, the culture of a distinctive people or, as is often the case, a religion.

In many national environments, acting morally is associated with membership of a nation or state. In ancient Greece, being a citizen involved the capability of acting morally: slaves, not being citizens, were viewed as outside the *polis*, or community, and thus incapable of attaining virtue. It is common among religious believers to hold that their religion alone is the path to a righteous life, looking down on non-believers. Similarly, some state ideologies, such as extreme nationalism and communism, see themselves as the determinants of a society's values. Adopting a moralistic tone, communist political leaders are prone to extol the superiority of their social perspective over the hedonist, individualist values of western cultures, viewed as decadent. Still, individualist values are permeating countries such as China, as market forces become established. The clash of cultures is exemplified by Google in China. Google has been more at home in the freer environment of Hong Kong, with its legacy of western individualism.

Second, utilitarianism reduces human motivation to the appetitive element, underestimating the complexities of people's sense of social values which influence their perceptions of right and wrong. Beliefs and feelings which people hold stem in large part from their interactions in society:

It is as social creatures that men acquire the standards and preferences out of which they build up for themselves images, however vague, however inarticulate, however changing, of what they are and would like to be, of how they live and would like to live. These are the images that give them a sense of position and of purpose in the world. (Plamenatz, 1958: 176)

We now appreciate the importance of community as a dimension of the individual's values and beliefs. European continental thinkers, notably Rousseau and Hegel, have long recognized the ethical dimension of the community. Contrasting views of liberty illustrate different concepts of the individual in society. Liberty in the negative sense, identified above in connection with the utilitarians, is about people having space to pursue their own personal goals. Liberty in the positive sense is about people being self-directed, each being one's own master: 'I wish to be somebody, not nobody' (Berlin, 1958: 16). As Isaiah Berlin points out in the essay, *Two Concepts of Liberty*, the two views of liberty would seem to be just two sides of the same coin. But historically, they have developed very differently. The theorists who emphasize self-realization have been accused of underestimating the dignity of the individual. They espouse a sense of community in which individual wills meld into a general will which is always right, even though individuals might not see it. This view of liberty is sometimes accused of opening the way for tyrants, and is at the base of much ideology that is reached for by authoritarian regimes to cloak themselves in legitimacy. Opposition to political tyrants has long rallied to the calls for freedoms of speech and association, famously articulated by one of the most notable of the utilitarians, John Stuart Mill, in his essay, *On Liberty* (1859).

Mill had difficulty in explaining how a sense of moral obligation arises from the greatest happiness principle, admitting that a person's conscience stems from education in the broad sense, and education can instill almost any values (Plamenatz, 1958: 139). Utilitarians have little interest in ethical principles, offering only general notions of feeling moral obligations towards others and also pointing to religious faith as a source of moral standards.

Do there exist ethical principles which aim to be universal, above national cultures and not dependent on religious values? Establishing how they arise and defining them has long been a concern of philosophers. They like to strip away religious, ideological, traditional and other sources of values, asking whether there is simply a 'human' basis for ethics. Immanuel Kant came closest to this approach with his postulate that 'every rational being exists as an end in himself, not merely as a means for arbitrary use by this or that will.' (Kant, 1785: 105) This notion of respect for every human being postulates human dignity as the guiding principle for behaviour. This principle is sometimes referred to as the categorical imperative. It holds that pure egoistic action, with regard only for oneself is unethical, and that one ought to behave in a way that takes the needs and wants of others into account. This ethical principle is aimed particularly at the personal morality of the individual, but how does it translate to organizations, governments and whole societies?

Ethical behaviour can be conceived in a variety of ways, including obligations, duties, responsibilities, rights and justice. A person has an overall responsibility to act ethically, which imposes particular obligations, such as the duty not to harm other people. An individual also has human rights, such as the right to life. There are many dimensions to human well-being, as this book has highlighted. Some of the main ones are food and shelter, education, health and a safe environment. In many societies, even these minimal requirements of a human existence are precarious. We would probably say that governments owe duties towards the population in respect of all these dimensions of human well-being. The leaders of a poor country which receives international donor funds for food, but spends the money on weapons, is acting unethically. Are firms which sell the weapons to such leaders also acting unethically? We examine the ethical context of business in the next section.

Definitions of freedom

Advocates of the negative definition of liberty tend to say that theirs is the true definition and that positive liberty is a contradiction in terms. Do you agree or disagree with them? Why?

Human rights

Human rights have become an important area of ethics, for both governments and businesses, involving a wide range of ethical principles, from freedom of speech to access to education. Here, we clarify how this rather 'umbrella' concept has evolved. Human rights may be defined as basic, universal rights of life which transcend social and cultural differences. The notion of human rights recognizes the inherent value of the human being. Most people, whatever their cultural background, would agree that slavery, torture and murder are wrong. The right to life is a basic human right, but the notion of human rights has been extended over the years to encompass many other rights, including spheres such as culture and extending to the rights of groups as well as individuals.

The origins of modern thinking on human rights lie in the eighteenth-century theorists of individual rights, notably Locke, who spoke of 'natural rights', rather than human rights. Locke saw natural rights as basic freedoms in the negative sense, focusing on life, liberty and property. These reflect western values of individualism, and are the underpinning of capitalist economic thinking. To these values were added rights of free speech and assembly, which we would consider civil and political rights. Locke's thinking was fundamental to modern democratic theory, in that people, he maintained, should have a right to overthrow tyrannical governments that violate individual freedoms. He was arguing, in other words, that despite what the law of the land says, a government trampling on natural rights is acting unjustly. The US Declaration of Independence spoke of 'inalienable rights' in 1776, and the French declaration of the 'rights of man' dates from 1789 (Sen, 2010: 355). These iconic statements have become touchstones for democracy campaigners around the world. They articulated the idea that law and justice are different: the law of the land can, and should, be judged by higher moral principles. It follows that, for the individual or organization, obedience to the law is only one kind of obligation – one that is subordinate to adhering to ethical principles.

The first general enunciation of human rights came in the Universal Declaration of Human Rights (UDHR), adopted by the UN General Assembly in 1948. A perennial dilemma in the area of human rights is that statements enunciating the principles are of limited benefit to the many victims of human rights abuse unless the principles are transformed into law that is enforceable. As we have seen in Chapter 6, international law in the form of treaties is enforceable in practice if sovereign states legislate accordingly. The UDHR did not have the legal authority of a convention or treaty, but it did provide a comprehensive view of human rights that builds on the earlier concepts of natural rights. It has grown in importance for this reason, and is now recognized as part of international law, giving it considerable authority globally. The UDHR reflected the divergent economic and political systems in the post-war world: the delegates from western countries and those from socialist and communist states. From the western tradition, the UDHR includes the fundamental freedoms of expression, assembly and religion. It also recognizes the basic right to life, including freedom from torture and forced labour. Finally, in this category, it recognizes civil rights, including freedom from arbitrary arrest, equality before the law, and the right to due process of law. From socialist countries, the UDHR articulates a group of rights known as social and economic rights, sometimes called 'second-generation' rights, that are more in the vein of positive liberty. These include rights to adequate living standards, employment, health and cultural participation. The social and economic rights are more about qualitative issues of human well-being.

The two rather different groups of rights took more concrete form with the adoption of two conventions in the 1960s: the International Covenant on Civil and Political Rights (ICCPR) and the International Covenant on Economic, Social and Cultural Rights (ICESCR) (see Figure 11.1). The two covenants and the UDHR are sometimes referred to as the International Bill of Rights. Article 1 in both covenants is identical, setting out the broad context of human rights. This is its first clause:

> All peoples have the right of self-determination. By virtue of that right they freely determine their political status and freely pursue their economic, social and cultural development.

The notions of self-determination and development in Article 1 echo a view of human dignity as self-fulfilment, in the tradition of positive freedom. But it is important to note the emphasis on the free choice and free pursuit of one's goals in the second sentence, emphasizing the importance of freedom from impediments in that pursuit – which originates in the tradition of negative freedom.

Universal Declaration of Human Rights (UDHR)

International Covenant on Civil and Political Rights (ICCPR)	International Covenant on Economic, Social and Cultural Rights (ICESCR)
• Right to life • Prohibition of torture, and cruel, inhuman or degrading treatment • Prohibition of slavery and forced labour • Prohibition or arbitrary arrest or detention • Freedom of movement, assembly, and association • Freedom of expression and religion • Right to privacy (family, home and correspondence) • All persons are equal before the law • Prohibition of discrimination on grounds of race, sex, religion, political opinion, etc.	• Right to work • Right to a fair wage that provides a decent living for the person and family • Equal pay for work of equal value • Right to paid holidays • Right to form trade unions that can function freely • Right to strike, in accordance with law • Adequate standard of living– freedom from hunger • Right to health • Right to education • Right to take part in cultural life

Figure 11.1 UN human rights law

Source: UN, International Human Rights Law, at www.ohchr.org, accessed 18 October 2015.

The two covenants can be seen as complementary: negative freedoms complemented by positive rights to fulfil personal goals. The ICCPR makes clear that not all rights are 'absolute'. Some are. The right not to be tortured is one: torture is never justified. However, freedom of assembly, freedom of expression and right to privacy are all qualified, in that they can be curtailed in the public interest and for security. But such encroachment must be done in accordance with the law. The rights spelt out in the ICESCR commit states to establishing laws and institutions that promote rights listed in Figure 11.1, including the right to work, health, education and housing. As part of international law, the two covenants commit ratifying states to implement them, bringing national laws up to these international standards. For example, ratifying the ICESCR would entail a government establishing the right in law to form independent trade unions. Despite the fact that a majority of the world's states have ratified both covenants, there are notable exceptions. China has ratified the ICESCR, but not the ICCPR, while the US has done the reverse, objecting to the idea of social and economic rights. The US does have laws recognizing many of the rights in the ICESCR, but some are only weakly established in practice. The right to join a trade union exists in law in the US, going back to the era of the New Deal legislation which bolstered labour rights following the Great Depression of the early 1930s. However, the growth in union membership that followed has now gone into reverse. Union membership in the private-sector workforce in the US fell from 30% in the 1950s to just 6.7% in 2014. Nowadays, anti-union stances among employers are common, discouraging union membership.

For all ratifying countries, subscribing to human rights goals in principle does not readily translate into practice. It is often the case that human rights, even when passed into national law, are curtailed in the broadly-framed interests of national security. In addition, corporate actors are often able to sidestep the law in practice. Child labour is tolerated in many developing countries, despite laws to the contrary. Large multinational enterprises (MNEs) which have affiliated manufacturers in these countries have been criticized for failing to take a stronger stand against the practice. Such criticisms have become increasingly voiced in today's globalized environment. There is now a means available for individuals and groups that are victims of breaches of economic, social and cultural rights to seek justice from the UN when their governments fail to enforce these obligations. This is through a new Optional Protocol to the ICESCR, which became part of international law in 2013 (www.ohchr. org). As of March, 2016, 21 state parties had ratified this optional protocol, and a further 26 had signed it. The new protocol is an important milestone in the legal recognition of economic, social and cultural rights globally, and in furthering access to justice for victims of human rights abuse.

The way I see it ...

'The only way you're going to end inequality is to give workers enough bargaining power that they can get a bigger share of the wealth and the value they produce.'

Richard Trumka, president of the AFL-CIO union federation in the US, in an interview in 2014, in Jopson, B. and Harding, R., 'US trade unionism views inequality as main fight', *Financial Times*, 1 July.

Mr Trumka laments the decline of trade unions in the US. Do you agree with him that trade unions can help to reduce inequality?

As human rights are essentially universal, would it not be logical to establish an international court to adjudicate in cases of alleged abuse? In fact, the authors of the UDHR proposed such a court, with access for states, organizations such as companies, and individuals. The idea was eventually rejected, mainly because of objections on the grounds that such a court would violate state sovereignty. There are some legal routes at international level, however. The International Criminal Court hears cases of crimes against humanity, war crimes and genocide. And in Europe, there is an established court, the European Court of Human Rights (www.echr.coe.int), which hears cases arising under the European Convention on Human Rights (ECHR), which came into effect in 1953. The ECHR mainly focuses on civil and political rights as set out in the first of the UN covenants in Figure 11.1. Of the rights spelt out in the ICESCR, it includes the right to join a trade union and the right to education. The latter right is expressed in negative terms, however. It is a right not to be excluded from the educational system as it exists in the country.

The countries within the ambit of the ECHR are members of the Council of Europe (not to be confused with the EU institution of a similar name). The Council of Europe comprises 47 countries altogether. It includes many countries, from Azerbaijan to Switzerland, which are not members of the EU. The court, which sits in Strasbourg in France, has seen a huge growth in its workload in recent years. The European Court of Justice, the highest court of the EU, also hears human rights cases, arising under its Charter of Fundamental Rights.

European countries are thus covered by several human rights legal instruments. There are statements of rights contained in national constitutions; national legislation on many issues; and the UN and European treaties at international level. The ECHR is incorporated in the national law of member states of the Council of Europe. The ECHR became part of UK law through the Human Rights Act 1998. However, the law has been criticized by some leading politicians in the Conservative Party, who have objected to the jurisdiction of the European Court of Human Rights, which they have argued undermines the sovereignty of the UK courts. Some leading Conservatives have thus supported repealing the Human Rights Act and substituting a British Bill of Rights. Lawyers and politicians concerned about civil rights safeguards urge that the Human Rights Act remains a valuable guarantee of the basic freedoms which underpin the country's values (Smith, 2015). Repealing it would seem to be a worrying step in the wrong direction.

Is the ethical tobacco company a contradiction in terms?

Source: PhotoDisc/Getty Images.

Ethics in business

Ethical principles arise in relation to both *what* the firm aims to do and *how* it goes about its activities. Many firms are successfully engaged in businesses such as gambling, manufacturing tobacco products and making alcoholic drinks, all of which can become addictive, and could be considered unethical. These areas, like many types of activity which involve ethical principles, are the subject of laws in most countries. The firm that abides by the regulations regarding gambling, for example, is engaged in an activity for which there is clearly consumer demand, and, as long as it abides by the regulations, is acting legally. Most companies that make addictive products, such as alcoholic beverage companies, are highly aware of the ethical dimension of their activities, and present themselves as promoting responsible drinking among consumers. In most countries, there are restrictions on selling alcoholic drinks to children, but inevitably some traders are prepared to do so, aware that they are probably not going to be caught.

Applying ethical principles

Much of the focus of ethics in business is on how the firm operates. Is it honest and fair in relation to stakeholders such as employees, customers, business partners and the wider community? Some of the major areas are set out in Figure 11.2. Major considerations are transparency and honesty in communications. Is it truthful in its advertising messages, and does it particularly target children? Note that the aspects of ethics highlighted in Figure 11.2 often overlap with the law. For example, there are laws on truthfulness in advertising. Many companies would say that if they abide by the law, that should be the extent of their obligation. But compliance with legal regulation is not as straightforward as it might seem. Many companies are careful to comply with the letter of the law while failing to comply with the spirit or intention of the law. This approach is generally considered unethical.

Figure 11.2 Ethical dimensions of business

Legal compliance can be a grey area in many contexts, including advertising, taxation, liability for accidents, and environmental management. Some companies, well aware of the law on advertising, draft messages which rely on half-truths and suggestions: they might well mislead the consumer, but the firm can argue that it abided by the law in the strict sense. In fact, in matters of advertising, truthful but misleading statements are often found to be in breach of the rules. In America, Volkswagen's advertised figures for its diesel cars' fuel economy and low emissions were found to be far too low, as the cars' engines were rigged to understate the results. Moreover, official tests of vehicles typically tolerate the use of techniques that reduce levels of emissions below those that would obtain in ordinary road use. This is standard in the industry, and is misleading, but has been tolerated.

In a second example, companies can go to great lengths, usually with the help of professional tax consultants, to devise methods of reducing their liabilities to tax. They can claim to be complying with the law, but their sidestepping devices could be seen as unethical. Moreover, pure tax evasion schemes are in breach of the law in many countries. Apple made profits of nearly £2 billion in the UK in 2014, which, at the corporation tax rate of 21%, should have led to a tax payment £400 million. But instead, it paid just £12 million to the UK tax authorities. Apple's subsidiaries set up in Ireland channel 65% of its worldwide income. By agreement with the Irish government, Apple pays tax at a rate of less than 2%, while Ireland's official corporation tax rate of 12% is itself well below international standards. Ireland's tax deals with Apple and other MNEs are criticized around the world (Thomas and Pfanner, 2013). The tax authorities in the many countries where Apple products are sold lose out, and US tax authorities are major losers. Apple is a US-registered company, and is obliged to pay tax on its global profits, but it holds $181 billion in overseas tax havens, thus avoiding a tax bill of about $59 billion to the US taxman.

Manufacturing and extracting industries are sectors where the risk of accidents is high, and where potential damage could be extensive. In all its operations, the business is obliged to observe the duty of reasonable care, which is the test for negligence. This can be interpreted in many ways, and in common law countries, there is a great deal of case law on what is meant by reasonable care. The firm is not expected to make operations 100% safe, which is impossible, but it is expected to take precautions which a reasonable person aware of the risks would take. There is a good deal of scope for differing interpretations of how safe an operation must be so as not to expose the employer to an accusation of negligence. Unfortunately, these issues are normally resolved after an accident has occurred, often in court proceedings. It is scant consolation for the victim or the victim's family that the employer was found to be negligent. Sometimes, safety devices would have incurred only small extra expenditures, but firms bent on cost-cutting would balk at the extra expense. By contrast, the firm with a strong ethical policy would take the view that the expense is justified, even if it eats into profits.

Environmental management is an area that also involves ethical and legal duties. Usually, duties are owed to a person or group, as in the examples just cited. But in the case of the environment, the case is less clear. As Figure 11.2 shows, firms owe a duty to protect the environment from harm that affects workers and local communities. But the principle of sustainability (discussed in Chapter 10) goes further, resting on what can be termed inter-generational justice. This means that firms owe moral obligations to later generations, as *their* standards of living could be at risk if *we* do not take steps to reduce emissions. There is a potential conflict between the needs and wants of today's inhabitants and those of future inhabitants, involving firms in calculations of a possible a trade-off between them. As we saw in Chapter 10, firms prioritize legal duties, but the law often lags behind the measures that a strong commitment to sustainability would recommend.

Human rights and the workplace

Legal duties written into national law underpin the protection of human rights. A number of the ethical dimensions highlighted in Figure 11.2 involve human rights. And many specific rights that feature in the UN covenants are relevant to the workplace. National laws and practice, however, can fall short of preserving these rights for workers. Migrant workers, in particular, are vulnerable to breaches of human rights. Specific areas of human rights that are relevant to the workplace include the terms of the worker's employment, health and safety in the workplace, the way workers are treated personally, and the rights of workers to organize in trade unions and bargain collectively. These will all be highlighted in this section. Labour rights are sometimes treated as separate from human rights, but labour rights are themselves human rights, and are important in the implementation of other human rights in the workplace.

People available for work should be able to choose freely the job they wish to do, and should be able to agree terms with an employer, which become elements in the contract of employment. That is the theory, but in practice, people seeking employment may have little choice of the job, the location or the terms. Factory workers in China's outsourced manufacturing, who are mostly migrant workers from rural regions, are likely to face a plethora of onerous terms: 12-hour working days, excessive overtime, few rest days, penalties such as withheld pay for discipline infringements. While China's employment laws provide that overtime should be limited to 36 hours per month, workers in many factories are effectively compelled to work over the legal limit. The death of a migrant worker in a Pegatron factory, where Apple iPhones are made, was reported in 2015. The worker had died after an 84-hour week (Fullerton and Chen, 2015). Apple's response was that it does more than most businesses to ensure safe working conditions. Apple was not the worker's employer, and had no contractual obligation towards him. But Apple has a 'Supplier Code of Conduct' which aims to uphold 'the highest standards of social and environmental responsibility and ethical conduct' (Apple, 2014: 1).

Large orders and tight delivery times are implicated in demands for excessive overtime, but the code allows this in 'unusual or emergency situations' (Apple, 2014: 3). Apple monitors these manufacturing operations, noting that in 2014 it visited 459 suppliers, who employ over 300,000 workers, checking for labour and human rights issues. While this sounds laudable in principle, the scale and spread of these operations across hundreds of factories suggest an almost impossible task. Moreover, there are a total of 1.1 million workers in Apple's supply chain. The claim to uphold the highest human rights standards throughout these operations is hardly tenable, especially in the context of Apple's demands on contractors for large orders to meet tight production targets. Two years before the death of the worker mentioned above, investigators from China Labor Watch, an NGO, found numerous violations of China's laws at three of Pegatron's factories, involving underage labour, excessive hours, poor living conditions, abuse by management and environmental pollution (BBC, 2013). Apple and Pegatron gave assurances that they would deal with the problems, but the problems seem to run to the heart of the exploitative system that characterizes the outsourcing model as practised by Apple. Samsung of South Korea, Apple's major competitor, has experienced similar criticisms for labour and human rights failings in its Chinese supply chain (Mundy, 2014). Samsung, too, has a code of conduct for suppliers, and it uses independent auditors, reporting their findings in a 'sustainability' report. Despite these third-party audits, China Labor Watch found children working 11-hour days in one of the factories making Samsung products (China Labor Watch, 2014). These global brand owners expend much energy in extolling their high standards of human rights in their corporate communications aimed at investors and consumers worldwide, but the reality would seem to be very different.

Would the right to join trade unions and bargain with management help workers in exploitative and unsafe work environments? Apple recognizes the right of Chinese workers to join a trade union, as is required by Chinese law. But, of course, Apple is not the employer of the workers who make their products. Walmart, by contrast, does employ workers in its retail outlets in China, and allows Chinese trade unions to operate. Unions are also recognized in its UK stores, but Walmart takes a strong stance against organized labour in the US. Walmart's perspective is that it goes along with the national environment of each country, but its position is ambivalent. Rights of workers to trade union participation are legally established in the US, but Walmart, along with many other employers, discourages trade union membership. Workers that engage in union activities, or even complain about conditions, are often subject to recrimination. Walmart has a poor reputation for low pay and discrimination in pay and promotion. While discrimination is in breach of labour laws, low pay is less clear-cut.

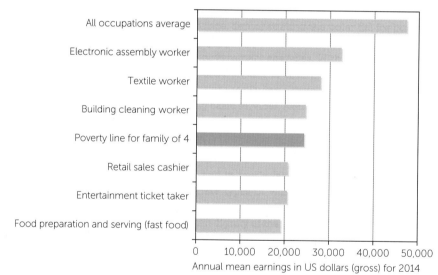

Figure 11.3 Comparative wages in the US

Sources: Data from US Government Bureau of Labor Statistics (2014) Occupational Employment Statistics, May, at www.bls.gov, accessed 22 October 2015; US Census, Poverty thresholds, at www. census.gov, accessed 22 October 2015.

International human rights law speaks of a fair wage that provides a decent living for a person and his/her family (see Figure 11.1). This is one of the economic and social rights, and is usually referred to as a 'living wage'. It is frequently held up as a demand by workers in low-pay environments, including fast-food outlets and retailing. The living wage is vague, however, and depends on the cost of living, which varies from country to country, and from region to region within a country. Minimum wage rates per hour are set by law in many countries, but the worker is unlikely to be able to support a family on these rates, especially if the work offered is not full-time. Figure 11.3 compares wages in a variety of occupations. Fast-food workers feature at the bottom of the figure, and, like retail cashiers, would fall beneath the poverty line for a family of four. The ticket collector is also poorly paid, but this job does not require as much skill and judgment as the cashier or the fast-food worker. The cleaner makes over $5,000 a year more than these other low-paid workers. Protests and strikes among low-paid workers in fast food and retailing have taken place across the US, targeting in particular large employers such as Walmart (see the closing case study in Chapter 12).

In 2014, the UK raised the minimum wage to £6.50 per hour, and has planned to raise it to £9 by 2020, thus achieving a living wage for the full-time worker. Although the hourly wage is important, so too are the terms of employment, and, in particular, the number of hours worked. Employers are now likely to favour hiring fewer full-time workers and more part-time workers, whose position is more precarious. Employers increasingly hire people without committing themselves to providing a minimum number of hours of work. There are estimated to be 1.5 million workers in Britain on such contracts (ONS, 2015). Within this category, workers can be hired on what is referred to as a zero-hours contract. There were over 700,000 employees hired on zero-hours contracts in 2015, 41% of whom would like to work more hours than they are offered (ONS, 2015). The worker is paid only for the hours worked, but must be available for work and is therefore not free to take other jobs. This arrangement is suitable for people who want only casual work, but not those in need of a regular income that is sufficient to live on. In many sectors, such as fast food, the zero-hours contract has become the norm. Such contracts are also being used increasingly in the health service and universities. While the zero-hours contract gives the employer the flexibility of being able to call on workers as and when they are needed, it provides no assurance to the worker of a steady income. Neither is the worker likely to receive sick pay or holiday pay. These contracts are one-sided and insecure, but the jobseeker might have little choice but to accept these terms.

The plight of garment workers in developing countries was highlighted by the Rana Plaza disaster in Bangladesh in 2013. There, the collapse of an unsafe garment factory left over 1,000 people dead, and over 2,000 injured. The factory, like thousands of others in Bangladesh, supplies many western brand owners such as Walmart, Gap, Tesco and H&M (see the case study in Chapter 12). The minimum wage for a garment worker in Bangladesh was the equivalent of $38 a month at the time, which was the world's lowest for textile workers, amounting to only just over $500 a year. By contrast, the average textile worker in the US makes nearly $28,000 a year (see Figure 11.3). Following the Rana Plaza disaster, the government of Bangladesh raised the minimum monthly wage to $68, representing a 79% rise. The steep increase in wages came at a time when factory owners were under increased pressure to improve safety in their buildings and reduce the risks of fire. This posed a dilemma: some felt that they would have to cut back on safety improvements in order to pay the increased wages. Some owners have shifted production to other countries, including India and Vietnam, where the same circumstances of poor working conditions and low wages obtain. Such moves are indicative of the setbacks to human rights that have characterized globalized supply chains. The fierce rivalry among western brand owners to reduce costs of production is partly to blame. These global companies are in a strong position to drive hard bargains with suppliers, using the threat to take their orders elsewhere. The owner of a typical garment factory in Bangladesh made a profit margin of 2% before the rise in wages, and now these businesses are facing losses. This is the position of the owner quoted below. Many western companies signed up to an accord to raise fire and safety standards in factories, and some, such as Tesco and Gap, have expressed support for higher wages, but many have chosen instead to re-locate.

The way I see it ...

'I approached one of my western buyers to raise prices, and the relevant company said, "It is your business and you have to manage it ... You cannot slip it to us".'

The chairman of a Bangladesh clothing company, Muzaffar Siddique, referring to a conversation with a western buyer, who he did not wish to name, following the rise in the minimum wage for garment workers, in Quadir, S. (2014) 'Rising wages squeeze Bangladesh garment makers as factories await upgrades', Reuters, 13 April, at www.reuters.com

How would the western buyer justify sticking to existing contract prices in this situation? Could this stance be defended on ethical grounds?

Garment workers in Bangladesh have a legal right to join trade unions, but the government has been restrictive on trade union activity in practice, in order to attract western brand owners. Repressive tactics have been used against protesting workers and labour organizers. Ties between the country's political leaders and the factory owners have also contributed to an environment in which labour rights are only weakly recognized. The recognition of an independent trade union, unconnected to owners, governmental agencies or political leaders, can play a positive role in industrial relations, helping to create a constructive dialogue between owners and workers. For workers, freedom of association can be crucial to gaining a voice and improving poor working conditions. Figure 11.4 shows the intensity of union membership in a variety of countries.

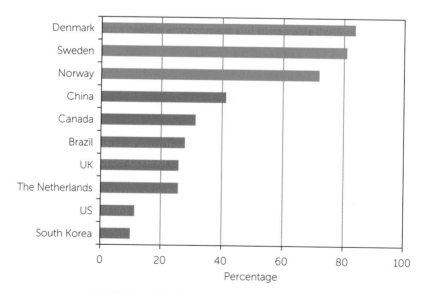

Figure 11.4 Trade union membership as a percentage of paid employment, 2014

Source: Data from ILO, Trade union membership statistics, Industrial relations indicators, at www.ilo.org, accessed 20 October 2015.

Note: Data are taken from national statistics, and include both independent and non-independent trade unions.

The countries that have the highest trade union density are those that also have high rankings in the UN's Human Development Index (HDI), which takes in income, education and health (see Chapter 2). The country with the least trade union penetration in Figure 11.4 (9.9%) is South Korea, which has a long history of acrimonious relations between managers and workers. The US, at 11.3%, is only slightly higher, and this figure is made up largely of public-sector workers. The percentage for the private sector is just 6.7%. China has a relatively high proportion of trade union members, but trade unions in China are not independent: they are connected politically to the Communist Party. In fact, this percentage has diminished as China's economy has become more market-oriented.

Benchmark international labour standards are set by the **International Labour Organization (ILO)** (www.ilo.org) through conventions that form part of international law. There are 95 of these, among which eight are considered fundamental. These are shown in Table 11.1.

Table 11.1 Fundamental ILO conventions

Convention	Year
Freedom of association and protection of the right to organize convention	1948
Right to organize and collective bargaining convention	1949
Forced labour convention	1930
Abolition of forced labour convention	1970
Minimum age convention	1973
Worst forms of child labour convention	1999
Equal remuneration convention	1951
Discrimination (employment and occupation) convention	1958

Source: ILO, Conventions and Recommendations, at www.ilo.org, accessed 26 October 2015.

Although most of the world's countries have ratified most of these conventions, the convention with the fewest ratifications is the first of those listed – recognizing freedom of association. Bangladesh has ratified this convention, but there are numerous countries that have not. Among them are Brazil, China, India, Iran, South Korea, Malaysia, Morocco, New Zealand, Oman, Qatar, Saudi Arabia, Singapore, Thailand, the UAE, the US and Vietnam. These countries present differing cultural and economic environments. There is a group of mainly Muslim countries, and there are large emerging economies. There are two western market economies: the US and New Zealand. European countries, including all EU member states, have ratified all these fundamental conventions. The US has ratified only two, while Russia has ratified all eight. Companies' legal obligations are dictated by national law predominantly, and those standards are weaker than international standards enshrined in ILO conventions. The US has historically been reluctant to recognize international human rights law, prioritizing the Bill of Rights in its own constitution. This seemingly parochial approach contrasts with the global reach of its large companies. Companies such as Nike and Gap adhere to national labour standards in their outsourced manufacturing in Vietnam and Indonesia, and questions arise about their moral responsibility for human rights breaches. Still, these companies maintain that they take social responsibility seriously.

The United Arab Emirates: the ambivalence of a rising power

Ambitious new developments in Abu Dhabi are seeking to enhance its global reputation, but questions over human rights in the emirate have clouded the picture.

Source: iStock.com/SisterSarah.

While the state of the United Arab Emirates (UAE) has become a leading Middle Eastern oil producer, Abu Dhabi, its capital, has become the focal point of cultural interest globally. Construction of the Louvre Abu Dhabi and the Guggenheim Abu Dhabi are prestigious projects on Saadiyat Island. This development appears to rise out of the sea, boasting luxury hotels, a marina, a sandy beach, two golf courses and other attractions. When complete, the art museums, which have been conceived in conjunction with their namesake western institutions, are intended to be beacons of cultural achievement. The UAE government paid nearly a billion euros for the use of the Louvre brand for a period of 30 years, and Paris is sending to Abu Dhabi many works of art. The UAE rulers, signing the deal in 2007, envisaged Saadiyat as a global cultural hub. Although the two sponsoring institutions evoke western art history, the curators of the Abu Dhabi establishments intend the new offshoots to be universal, blending civilizations and cultures in a new cosmopolitan environment. The University of New York has also set up a campus on Saadiyat Island, paid for entirely by the host country. Are these western-branded projects indicative of the new cultural horizons in this Gulf state? Or are they prestige projects designed to enhance the image of the country's rulers? National prestige does come into their calculations. In 2008, they acquired Manchester City football club in the UK, whose ground was renamed the Etihad Stadium after the country's national airline.

The UAE as a country is a relatively recent formation, bringing together seven sheikhdoms in 1971. Abu Dhabi is the dominant – and richest – emirate; and its ruler, Sheikh Khalifa bin Zayed, is the UAE president. The more flamboyant emirate, Dubai, without the oil wealth of its neighbour but with a penchant for luxury developments, stumbled in the global financial crisis and was helped out by Abu Dhabi. Abu Dhabi has pursued a more restrained path towards economic development. It sits at the crossroads of east and west. As a society, however, its model is one of conservative Islamic values. There is an apparent clash between the prevailing social and religious environment of the country and the overt acquisitions of western assets that are now catching attention.

The UAE is a highly divided and unequal society. Only about 11% of the population are citizens, forming the country's wealthy élite. The other 88.5% of UAE residents are foreign. Many are expatriate professional and businesspeople, but the largest group is migrant workers from countries such as India, who contract to work on construction sites. Migrant women are mainly in domestic service. Both groups are vulnerable. Under the *kafala* sponsorship system, they are tied to a particular employer. Common practices include confiscation of passports, withholding of wages, and substandard living conditions. They have no entitlements to social services such as healthcare. Human Rights Watch (HRW) reported in 2015 that, five years on from their first reporting of human rights abuses of workers on Saadiyat Island, these abuses were continuing. The treatment of domestic workers was of particular concern, HRW concluded that many were working excessive hours under conditions of forced labour (HRW, 2015). Women's rights in general are a concern highlighted by HRW. The UAE's personal law states that women must obey their husbands, and husbands are entitled to beat their wives (HRW, 2015).

The UAE is governed autocratically by the ruling dynasty, which allows no freedom of expression, association or assembly. Any evidence of political dissent is subject to repression by authorities. HRW has expressed concern over arbitrary detention, torture and unfair trials of those deemed to be a risk to national security. It also noted that trials were not fair, as the judges were effectively carrying out the orders of the executive. As tensions in the Middle East have risen, the UAE government has been forceful in its efforts to stamp out Islamic terrorist activity that could be destabilizing in the country. The government spends heavily on weaponry, buying extensively from western sources. There is an agreement for a new French military base, and there have been negotiations for the purchase of 60 Rafale fighter aircraft from the French government.

The Louvre, the Guggenheim and New York University have arguably been unsettled by the evidence of human rights abuses coming from Abu Dhabi. None of the three is directly involved in the construction work, but their names are inevitably highlighted in connection with the reporting of human rights issues. How will these edifices to culture blend in, and are we seeing the globalization of culture? The aims are to celebrate civilizations and cultures at a universal level, but the western influences that have been deliberately cultivated are high profile. The values of these institutions in France and the US include intellectual freedoms, human dignity and the pluralism of civil society. The UAE's rigid social system and denial of basic freedoms create an incongruous environment. There is little connection between Saadiyat Island and the lives of the majority of people who reside in the UAE. Will the New York University campus be allowed academic freedom? The UAE's rulers, looking beyond oil, are hoping to transform the country into a centre of arts and learning.

Sources: HRW (Human Rights Watch) (2015) 'World Report 2015: UAE', at www.hrw.org; Batty, D. (2013) 'Conditions for Abu Dhabi's migrant workers "shame the west"', *The Guardian*, 22 December, at www.theguardian.com; Tharoor, K. (2015) 'The Louvre comes to Abu Dhabi', *The Guardian*, 2 December.

Questions for discussion

- What human rights issues arise in connection with the Louvre and Guggenheim projects in Abu Dhabi?
- Explain the ambivalence of the UAE rulers in their embrace of western cultural icons while ruling a near-feudal society.
- What is your view of the ethical issues arising from the New York University campus on Saadiyat Island?
- To what extent is Saadiyat Island actually about vanity projects that exemplify the power of the rulers?

Social responsibility of the firm

Liberalization policies of national governments have attracted MNEs and drawn countries into global supply chains, often through FDI and outsourcing. An MNE's ties with the various countries involved in supply and production, however, can be tenuous. Some are inclined to see production of their branded products as simply a question of 'supply', denoting a rather neutral involvement, although there could be thousands of workers making a company's products in locations far from its home country. Hence the idea of supplier codes of conduct used by global brands. Other firms recognize a stakeholder relationship with these workers, acknowledging that they are morally responsible in areas of human well-being. Corporate social responsibility (CSR) refers to the role of the firm in society, which entails obligations to stakeholders in local communities and to the environment. Where the company is active in the place where it is based, and where it has a large number of employees, the concept of CSR seems more appropriate than it does in distant countries where workers making its branded goods are not its employees at all. Japan is an example of the first of these situations. Here, the firm has traditionally been viewed as being part of society and having a social role in addition to its economic activities. For the Japanese employee, the job is more than merely a way of making a living, but a way of life in itself, bound up the employee's sense of belonging.

In individualist western environments, the company has been viewed more narrowly, as performing an essentially economic role. Businesses have tended to feel that, so long as they adhered to existing legal obligations, they are free to focus on 'the bottom line', that is, profits and shareholder value. This simplistic view, which separates social responsibility concerns from business ones is increasingly untenable, for two reasons.

First, while markets have delivered economic results, they have left out of the equation considerations of human and environmental values. The insertion of these concerns in the social market economies is a recognition of market limitations. The human rights and environmental questions posed daily for large corporations, such as oil companies in developing states, also show the inadequacy of viewing business in isolation from the community. No longer can an MNE doing business in a developing country remain disengaged from the live community issues in the places where it operates or sources products. Moreover, as we noted earlier, a minimal policy of obedience to national laws can fall well short of ethical principles.

Second, the sheer size of the world's global corporations now dwarfs many national economies. Questions of how they are using this power in socially responsible ways are now being addressed to companies, as well as to governments. Theories of CSR have addressed both the normative and practical aspects of CSR.

Theories of corporate social responsibility (CSR)

Management theorists and corporate strategists for a number of years have been addressing the question of what the role of the company in society should be. While most now agree that its role extends beyond the purely economic dimension, there is much debate on the nature and extent of this expanded social role.

There is also a body of theory on social performance and how it can be measured (Wood, 1991). Adding complexity to the discussion is the reality that global companies operate in a number of different societies. Theories which attempt to define the company's responsibility to society are generally grouped together as theories of corporate social responsibility (CSR). These theories typically make reference to stakeholder groups, as well as to society in general. These concepts were introduced in Chapter 1. Here we look at theories of CSR in conjunction with stakeholder theories, which have been the subject of academic debate in recent years (Mitchell et al., 1997).

A 'weak' theory of CSR focuses on philanthropic or charitable contributions and activities, which the firm engages in as an adjunct to its business activities: any costs are weighed against the benefit to be gained in terms of the firm's enhanced reputation as a good corporate citizen. On this view, CSR 'is fine, if you can afford it' (Freeman, 1984: 40). The setting up of a charitable foundation has become a favoured philanthropic approach, often linked with the concept of corporate citizenship. Corporate citizenship visualizes the responsibility of the firm in the community as analogous to that of the individual citizen, entailing obligations to obey the law and pay taxes. As we have seen above, however, these obligations can be interpreted rather loosely. Obeying the law can involve following the letter of the law, but not the spirit of the law. A duty to pay taxes can translate into finding ways *not* to pay the country's taxes. Critics of this approach argue that it is 'skin deep', entailing no re-thinking of the firm's strategy and operations in terms of social issues. In theory, a company might be socially responsible in this limited sense, which would include setting up a charitable foundation, while allowing exploitation of the workers who make its products or tolerating damaging environmental impacts.

A stronger strategic approach to CSR is found in the work of A.B. Carroll. Carroll has devised a four-dimensional model of CSR (Carroll, 1991), which takes into account economic, legal, ethical and philanthropic dimensions. This model, which can be envisaged as a pyramid, places the economic obligations of the company at the base, recognizing that the business must be economically profitable in order to survive. Above economic activities are legal responsibilities. Legal obligations cover many areas, including employment law, environmental law, health and safety regulations. The law sets minimum standards, which differ from country to country. The firm with a strong CSR policy will aim to go beyond minimum legal standards. Carroll's model sees the need to rise above minimal legal requirements as an aspect of ethical responsibility, along with respect for ethical norms in the society in which the firm operates. The last element is philanthropy, such as charitable giving, which, while desirable, is less important than the other three — the icing on the cake. Carroll stresses that the model does not posit an inherent conflict between making profits and being socially responsible: for the manager, all four dimensions of the firm's responsibility should be central to corporate strategy.

While Carroll's model provides an overall framework, analysis of the 'social' component of CSR is provided by stakeholder theory. First developed by Edward Freeman, stakeholder theory points to the many different groups and interests that affect the company. Freeman defines them broadly as 'any group or individual which affects or is affected by the achievement of the organization's objectives' (Freeman, 1984: 46). In this broad category, some groups are clearly more influential than others. Stakeholders may be classified according to the strength of their influence on the company, and how critical they are to the company's operational success at any given time. Primary stakeholders are those that have direct impacts on the business. They include shareholders, lenders, employees and customers (see Figure 11.5). In terms of global supply chains, the licensed manufacturer that makes the MNE's branded products would be a primary stakeholder, with whom the MNE has contractual ties. The interests of secondary stakeholders have less direct influence on the business. They can be important influences over time, but in the short run, they do not directly affect the firm's performance. As Figure 11.5 shows, they include workers employed by manufacturers in the supply chain. Also included are interests impacted by the company's operations, including communities and the natural environment. These interests would come within the ambit of social responsibility.

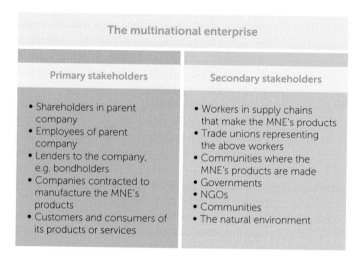

Figure 11.5 Primary and secondary stakeholders

Situations in which stakeholder interests conflict with each other pose particular challenges for managers. For example, the decision to outsource a particular operation to a low-cost location will save money, but cause loss of employment in the company's home country, where most of its shareholders are likely to be located. What do shareholders want? Shareholder value is often assumed to be just short-term profits, but shareholders also have views on long-term prosperity and sustainability. While shareholders would be expected to go along with the management's strategy, this should no longer be assumed. Following the financial crisis of 2007–8, in which significant blame attached to reckless corporate decision-making, shareholders are now more critical of senior managers.

CSR in practice

Many companies subscribe to the weak notion of CSR, equating it with charitable giving and corporate citizenship. On this view, the 'social' element resides in the notion that, once the company has made lots of money, it is in a position to give some of it 'back' to society. This approach rests on a view of CSR as being peripheral, not core to the business. However, many decisions a company takes, such as where to locate production, have both a strategic *and* a CSR dimension. Some theorists have combined CSR principles with a framework for applying them in practice. Theories of corporate social performance (CSP) reflect this approach, looking at the firm's social responses in differing contexts (Wood, 1991). This approach is akin to stakeholder management, but arguably more slanted towards applications, which would include processes such as monitoring and assessment of the company's stakeholder interactions. Codes of conduct would come into this outlook, as would sustainability reporting. From a managerial perspective, CSP and social responsiveness provide a process-oriented approach to CSR. The CSP approach can be seen is part of the business case for CSR, involving assessments of relations with various stakeholder groups. Central to this outlook are considerations of corporate reputation.

A number of stakeholder groups are involved, including investors, consumers, employees and the community (McWilliams, 2001). McWilliams argues that, analysed in terms of costs and benefits, a business case for CSR can be based on a differentiation strategy and can become a source of competitive advantage. Examples of CSR approaches in this context are:

- Products made from sustainable resources, such as recycled materials
- Products made through CSR-related processes, such as organic foods
- Advertising which provides information about CSR attributes, such as dolphin-free tuna labels
- Building brand reputation on CSR attributes.

The business case for CSR based on market considerations treats the choice of CSR attributes as analogous to the other strategic choices a firm makes, in terms of the demand for the attribute and the costs of providing it. This 'instrumental' view of CSR is akin to the weak version of the theory mentioned at the start of this section, in that the CSR case rests on business considerations rather than ethical ones. However, it does highlight the fact that demand exists and that it is coming from numerous stakeholder groups — an indication that social responsibility is one of the criteria guiding consumers and investors in their evaluation of corporate performance.

Many MNEs have in place voluntary codes of practice on CSR, ethical principles and environmental policies. These codes of practice contain stated aims which are not always carried through in practice, as we have seen. A way of assuring stakeholders of high corporate standards is third-party verification. Certification by specialist monitoring bodies is available across a wide range of industries, from organic produce to tourism. For example, the Fairtrade Foundation (www.fairtrade.org.uk) supports principles of sustainable agriculture and a fair return for farmers. Companies which sign up to these principles can use the Fairtrade logo, which signifies to consumers the product is produced according to fair trade principles. In some sectors, however, certification is less effective. Large food companies, including Unilever and Procter & Gamble, have committed themselves to using sustainable palm oil, but the Roundtable on Sustainable Palm Oil (RSPO) (www.rspo.org) has been only partially successful. It aims to assure consumers but, in practice, it is unable to guarantee sustainable supplies. Other global companies, including Pepsico and Kraft-Heinz, have been reluctant even to adopt the RSPO's certification system (Allen, 2015).

GLOBAL BUSINESS IN ACTION

Sustainable chocolate

Sophi Tranchell

Divine Chocolate (www.divinechocolate.com) grew out of a cocoa farmers' co-operative in Ghana, to become a successful Fairtrade chocolate company, selling its premium chocolate in markets around the world. Sophi Tranchell, Divine's CEO, who has been with the company for 17 years, emphasizes its mission as a social enterprise to promote sustainable livelihoods among the small-scale cocoa producers in Ghana, contributing to improvements in technology, education and healthcare that have been facilitated by the money flowing into these small, rural farming communities. In a unique ownership and governance structure, the cocoa farmers themselves own nearly half the company, and participate in corporate decision-making. Sophi points to the empowerment of farmers in determining their own futures, and also highlights, in particular, a focus on the empowerment of women in these processes. In the highly competitive global chocolate market, dominated by large multinationals, Divine has shown that there is 'another way' of doing business. Sophi has won a number of awards for her promotion of social enterprise goals, and in 2008, was awarded the MBE in the UK for services to the food industry.

Source: Copyright © Richard Nicholson, 2012.

The interview with Sophi ranges over a variety of issues, from the production of cocoa to the markets for Divine Chocolate's products. She emphasizes the roles of farmers as owners and stakeholders. As smallholders, farmers see the benefits of the Fairtrade premium that flows to their own enterprises, and they also share in the distributed profits of Divine, allowing them to choose how best to invest the money in their communities, in, for example, education and healthcare.

In addition to the material in this chapter on CSR and social enterprise, it will be helpful to look again at the discussion in Chapter 1 on stakeholders and stakeholder roles in corporate governance. Sustainable Development Goals (SDGs) are discussed in Chapter 10. Before watching the interview, look again at Figure 10.7 for the description of each of the 17 SDGs. There is further discussion of the SDGs in Chapter 12.

Visit www.palgravehighered.com/morrison-gbe-4e to watch the video, then think about the following questions:

1. What are the main ways in which the business model of Divine Chocolate and the farmers' co-operative deliver sustainable livelihoods for farmers?
2. Why has the empowerment of women been a priority for the company, and what are the challenges involved?
3. Consumer awareness of the Fairtrade ethos has been growing, and Divine has seen this happening in the US as well. How has Divine's experience in the two consumer markets diverged?
4. The chocolate industry is dominated by corporate giants that can look daunting for a small competitor like Divine. (As well as companies like Mars, that are familiar brands, Sophi mentions powerful less well-known companies like Cargill, the commodity trader, and Barry Callebaut, the world's largest chocolate company, that serves industry clients.) What are the challenges in the business environment that she highlights?
5. Sophi stresses the importance of the UN's SDGs, and highlights the ones that she would prioritize. Which are these? Looking at Figure 10.7, which other SDGs are also relevant to Divine Chocolate?

Reporting on social and environmental impacts is increasingly seen as part of the MNE's response to CSR concerns. There are different names and formats for this kind of reporting, many of which focus on sustainability as an umbrella category. Many MNEs adopt environmental, social and governance reporting (ESG), which covers a range of CSR issues, including human rights and responses to environmental pollution. By ESG reporting, the company aims to disclose information on its CSR performance generally, including how its decision-makers and governance structures are addressing CSR issues. ESG reporting has become widespread, and in many countries ESG reporting for listed companies is now compulsory (Baron, 2014). Among them are France, Norway, India and South Africa; the EU specifies categories of non-financial reporting along ESG lines. Research by KPMG in 2013 shows that, of the world's top 100 companies across 41 countries, 71% now report on ESG, whether this reporting is mandatory or not (KPMG, 2013). More than half of US companies listed on the S&P Index report on ESG, although there is no specific mandatory requirement to do so. Companies are now highly sensitive to reputational issues, and ESG reporting contributes positively to building a reputation for transparency and dialogue with stakeholders. At the same time, companies should be wary of using these reports simply as public relations exercises: stakeholders now expect concrete information on these issues, rather than abstract commitments to principles. On the other hand, presenting data on performance is only part of a CSR approach, and addressing normative issues which are not quantifiable is equally important.

CSR: more than skin deep?

A critical observer might say that MNEs are more than ever attuned to CSR issues, but this does not imply radical changes in business models, just more professional skill in handling reputational issues. To what extent do you think this a fair assessment, or not?

Reaching for international standards

There are now several sets of international CSR standards designed to guide MNEs in their international operations. Sponsored by inter-governmental organizations which enjoy wide participation by both developing and developed countries, these statements of CSR principles are increasingly recognized as setting the benchmarks in international CSR. We highlight several here, including those from the OECD, the ILO and the UN. These statements focus on broad principles, including human rights, working conditions, employment terms and environmental protection. Here is a brief summary of the main points of each:

OECD Guidelines for Multinational Enterprises – Issued first in 1976, this was among the first statements of principles of CSR. The fifth update of these principles was issued in 2011 (at www.oecd.org/corporate/mne). Participating in the revision were 11 non-OECD countries, mainly developing countries, in addition to the 30 OECD member states. Three areas are now highlighted. First, the responsibility of MNEs over the entire supply chain is highlighted as coming within the firm's sphere of influence, even though the companies are legally independent. Second, the guidelines stress human rights, addressing situations where host-country policies on human rights do not reach international standards, or where the host country has not ratified relevant UN human rights conventions. Third, the guidelines address new environmental issues, including 'green growth' of economies, eco-innovation, biodiversity and sustainability.

International Labour Organization (ILO) Tripartite Declaration of Principles concerning MNEs and Social Policy (MNE Declaration) – The ILO Declaration dates from 1977, and its 4th edition was issued in 2006 (www.ilo.org). It covers five areas:

1 General principles – These principles recognize the primacy of national law and urge respect for international conventions, for example, on human rights.

2 Employment – MNEs should provide employment for local people and not discriminate on grounds of race, colour, sex, religion, political opinion, national extraction or social origin.

3 Training – MNEs should provide appropriate training for local workers in their operations.

4 Conditions of work and life – MNEs should employ local people on terms not less favourable than those of local employers. MNEs should eliminate the worst forms of child labour, and observe international health and safety standards.

5 Industrial relations – MNEs should recognize freedom of association and the right to organize among workers. Collective bargaining should be allowed, and there should be consultation with workers' representatives, as provided by national law. There should be conciliation mechanisms for settling industrial disputes, involving equal representation of employees and employers.

The UN Global Compact – This compact (at www.unglobalcompact.org) between governments, corporations and NGOs lists nine key principles from the Universal Declaration of Human Rights, the core standards of the ILO, and the Rio Declaration. They include support of human rights, the elimination of child labour, free trade unions and the elimination of environmental pollution. These are 'aspirational' rather than binding in their effects. The significance of the initiative is the bringing together of the major players in a single forum for debate about the issues. Nike, Unilever and Royal Dutch Shell were among the corporations that signed the accord, as were Amnesty International and the World Wildlife Fund. By 2014, the number of corporate participants had risen to 8,000.

The International Organization for Standardization (ISO) (ww.iso.org) oversees quality and environmental standards recognized across industries. Its ISO 9000 is a recognized quality assurance standard, and the more recent ISO 1400 series applies to environmental standards. ISO has now produced ISO 26000, its first guidance on social responsibility, combining principles from the OECD, ILO and UN Global Compact. The guidance it contains is just that – broad guidance. It does not set out standards and certification in the way that other ISO standards do. Neither does it recommend specifically how CSR should be reported. Guidelines for ESG reporting can be found in the Global Reporting Initiative (GRI) (www.globalreporting.org), which goes back to 1997. Its focus was sustainability, owing much to the involvement of the UNEP (UN Environment Programme). The current guidelines are the 'G4 Sustainability Reporting Guidelines' (GRI, 2015).

CSR and corporate governance

In general, corporate boards are accountable to shareholders and other stakeholders through corporate governance mechanisms. However, as we highlighted in Chapter 1, every company is strongly influenced by the national environment of its home country and its own historical legacy. These factors are evident in its corporate culture, including perceptions of its role in society. Views of corporate governance reflect divergence in corporate cultures. Does the company view its primary duty as maximizing shareholder value or achieving wider goals associated with the stakeholder perspective? In countries where liberal market capitalism retains a grip, shareholder value is perceived as paramount, and CSR tends to be marginalized or conceived in terms of enhancing shareholder value. In countries where social market values have dominated, as in Western Europe, the stakeholder perspective is more prevalent. In these countries, especially under the guidance of the EU Commission, liberal reforms have made headway. The EU has been influential in promoting more competitive markets in member states, in reducing state subsidies to businesses and in encouraging the privatization of nationalized industries which have enjoyed monopolies in a number of sectors, such as telecommunications. That said, corporate governance in both the more shareholder-centred tradition and the stakeholder-centred tradition can be criticized on CSR grounds.

We found in Chapter 1 that even public companies can have ownership structures that concentrate power in the hands of a small group of insiders, often the founder's family and associates. Such power frequently stems from a dual-class share structure, in which the voting shares are concentrated in the ruling insiders. Ordinary shareholders may have little or no voting power on major issues. Insider control seems to be a phenomenon which crosses national borders. American, European and Asian companies, although divergent in corporate culture, have mechanisms which perpetuate a controlling group of shareholders. This control is typically exerted through appointments of executives and board members.

All company directors, whether executive or non-executive, owe a duty to act always in the best interests of the company. This is known as **fiduciary duty**. Fiduciary duty denotes a position of trust. It is owed to the company as whole, but differing interpretations of the nature of fiduciary duties lead to differing views of corporate governance. In the Anglo-American tradition, the primacy of shareholders over other stakeholders leads directors to think of their duties rather narrowly as maximizing shareholder wealth. Indeed, this principle became the beacon of American capitalism. The spread of market values around the world owes much to the success of American companies. But with the financial crisis of 2007–8, the assumptions about the stability of markets took a severe battering. Weaknesses in corporate governance are now held to bear much of the responsibility for the persistence of high-risk strategies in many companies, despite the risks to the very shareholder value that the system was meant to uphold. The following are some of the specific weaknesses which emerged:

- Corporate boards tend to go along with the strategic decisions of executive directors, rather than act in an effective monitoring role. Although most boards have independent, non-executive directors, these part-time directors, while legally bearing the same fiduciary duties as full-time executives, tend to be compliant with management rather than be seen to 'rock the boat'.
- In corporate governance best practice, the positions of chairman of the board and CEO should be separate, but in reality, the roles are often combined, especially in the US. An effect is to give executive managers greater control over boards.
- Dominant shareholders exert control in many public limited companies, often through dual share structures (as highlighted in Chapter 1). They are in a strong position to influence voting and dictate strategy, leaving 'minority' ordinary shareholders in a weak position. Although there are legal protections for minority shareholders, especially when their interests are at stake, they have little influence on boards, and are usually unable, because of procedural hurdles, to put forward candidates to become directors.

- Committees of corporate boards, such as the remuneration committee and audit committee, tend to be dominated by the insiders who control the company, despite having non-executive members. In theory, payments to managers through stock options and bonuses based on performance align managers' incentives more closely with owners', encouraging them to be more enterprise-minded. However, in reality, spiralling executive remuneration has come into the spotlight as an example of weak board oversight of managers.

The remuneration of executives, which is referred to as 'compensation' in the US, is typically made up of a number of elements. It includes annual salary, bonuses, incentive payments, and equity-based elements such as shares and share options. All of these elements can simply be considered 'pay'. The equity-based elements, in theory, align the executive's interests with those of shareholders. The steep rise in average executive pay in recent years, however, suggests that executives, rather than serving the aims of increasing shareholder value, have been able to extract personal gains at the expense of shareholders (EPI, 2015). Executive pay has become the focus of much attention in the critical evaluation of corporate governance. In the US, rises in executive pay from 1978 to 2014 (adjusted for inflation) were 997%, which is double the growth in equities in the same period, and contrasts with the 10.9% increase in the pay of the typical worker over that 36-year period (EPI, 2015).

The average pay of the CEO in the top 350 US companies in 2014 was $16.3 million, while that of the typical worker was $53,000 (see Figure 11.6). As the figure shows, the gap between CEO pay and that of the typical worker has ballooned since 1965, from a ratio of 20-to-1, to a ratio of 300-to-1. The gap has actually narrowed, from a peak of 376-to-1 in 2001. Comparing CEO pay with that of other top earners, top CEOs gained considerably greater rewards, receiving nearly six times more than the rest of those in the top 0.1% of wage earners. Top-paid CEOs tend to say that there is a global market for their skills and talent that justifies these huge pay packages. In reality, what drives these excessive rises has been the virtually unchecked ability of CEOs to get their way in dealing with their acquiescent boards.

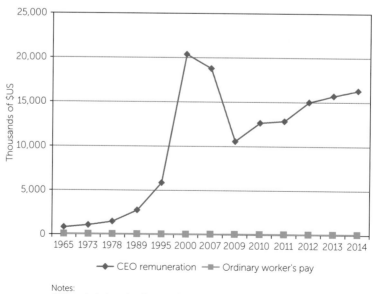

Figure 11.6 Annual pay for US CEOs versus ordinary workers

Source: Data from Economic Policy Institute (EPI) (2015) 'Top CEOs make 300 times more than typical workers', Issue Brief Number 399, 21 June, Table 1, p. 3, at www.epi.org.

Notes:
CEO pay includes salary, bonuses, long-term incentive payouts and stock options exercised in that year.

The ordinary worker is a private-sector production/non-supervisory worker.

Reforming corporate governance to promote greater accountability is a concern of governments, especially in sectors such as banking, which have received large sums of public money in some countries. But the questions remain: to whom is accountability owed, and how is it best achieved? Stakeholder interests are usually associated with theories of management rather than corporate governance. In continental European countries, employee representatives play a role in governance, but these employee representatives tend to speak for members in the home country. Other stakeholders, including workers in international operations, do not enjoy the same participative role. Contrast this stakeholder view with the wider perspective of CSR. CSR principles encompass all stakeholders, environmental concerns and ethical principles. Only CSR principles would cause executives to think twice about changing the company's registration to an offshore location for fiscal benefits such as lower taxes.

Procedural reforms of corporate governance, such as changing voting systems for directors, will go only a limited way in persuading the investing public that companies are being run soundly and sustainably. There have been weak reforms in the US on executive pay, requiring a 'say on pay' in the annual general meeting (AGM), but the vote is not binding. There is now legislation in the EU which requires the capping of executive bonuses at 100% of salary or 200% if shareholders approve. However, some companies have taken steps to sidestep these rules by making equivalent payments under other headings such as 'role-based allowances'. Such payments have been made in 39 banks in six EU member states. In 2014, ten executives of the UK bank, RBS, received a total of £5.5 million as allowances to sidestep the bonus cap (Treanor, 2014). This was in a bank that was bailed out with £45.2 billion of UK taxpayers' money. A corporate culture of responsiveness, transparency and fairness to stakeholders is now expected of MNEs. Shareholders increasingly look beyond short-term financial criteria to long-term value creation, in which CSR and stakeholder perspectives come into play.

CSR in the boardroom?

How would you respond to the CEO who holds to the view that shareholder value always comes before CSR?

The social enterprise

The social enterprise occupies the area between a for-profits business and a not-for-profits organization. Defined in Chapter 1, the social enterprise seeks to operate as a business and generate profits, but uses the profits for social causes. Its founders, known as social entrepreneurs, are committed to social causes, and see business activity as conducive to that end. The social entrepreneur typically combines a market orientation with entrepreneurial zeal and a commitment to a particular cause. In some cases, the social enterprise operates in an area between mainstream business and government services. These enterprises are active in social welfare sectors, delivering services and providing employment in local communities, often in areas of high unemployment. Housing, education, health and welfare advice for vulnerable groups are some of the sectors in which social enterprises operate in the UK. In many cases, they work alongside local and national government agencies. The social sector is expanding in many countries, as governments struggle to resource welfare needs, for example care for growing numbers of older people. Social enterprises, which are mainly SMEs, are not a way of outsourcing social services, but of offering complementary services, often working with government agencies.

The social enterprise as an organization can take several forms, from a registered charity to an ordinary limited company. There are also different types of charity, ranging from unincorporated associations to incorporated organizations. The UK government introduced the community interest company (CIC) (www.cicregulator. gov.uk) in 2004, allowing the social entrepreneur to form a limited company with strict requirements for adhering to social purposes. The Companies (Audit, Investigations and Community Enterprise) Act of 2004 provides a system of regulation of CICs, which assures the public that assets and profits are used for community purposes.

Social enterprises are popular choices for setting up new businesses. In the UK, the national body for social enterprises is Social Enterprise UK (www.socialenterprise. org.uk). Social enterprises compare favourably with mainstream SMEs in terms of generating income and longevity: 52% saw increased turnover in 2014, compared with 40% among mainstream SMEs (Social Enterprise UK, 2015). While we tend to think of social enterprises as mainly local, increasingly, they are branching out globally, especially through trade. And most of the profits are channelled into social and environmental goals. Social enterprises are also fulfilling needs in emerging economies, some providing simple, affordable solutions adapted to local conditions.

Micro-finance is an example. Micro-finance provides loans and other financial services to the poor, who, because they are perceived as being too high-risk, fall outside the mainstream banking system. Micro-finance has evolved from charitable organizations to social enterprises which are self-financing. Now, mainstream banks are also branching out into micro-finance, demonstrating the potential for business at the 'base of the pyramid'. In developing countries, social enterprises often work alongside NGOs, global charities and government agencies. With strained resources and uncertain funding in the form of aid from donor countries, the governments of developing countries see social enterprises as playing a development role, helping to promote social well-being in providing basic services, health and education.

Ethics and CSR: challenges and responsibilities

Work in mines, on construction sites and in textile factories around the world leans heavily on migrant workers. While these types of work rest, in theory, on the free choice of workers, in practice, migrant labour mostly involves one-sided, exploitative relationships that undermine the human dignity of the people who do these jobs, most of whom have no choice. Many migrants travel from rural to urban areas to seek work, but many seek work in foreign lands, facilitated by agents who demand substantial sums of money, often leaving the migrant worker burdened with a large debt to pay off. The worker is trapped in this relationship, in which poor conditions, poor treatment and long hours are inescapable. Human rights groups describe these relationships as forced labour, in breach of international human rights. Vast construction projects in the Middle Eastern Gulf states and elsewhere depend on workers from countries such as Nepal and Bangladesh. Working alongside them are other workers who are forced to work even longer hours, up to 20-hour shifts. These workers are from North Korea, whose government effectively sells the labour of some 50,000 of its citizens. The bulk of the 'wages' earned by these workers goes to North Korea's hardline autocratic government, generating the equivalent of an estimated billion dollars a

Migrant workers in dangerous industries, such as mining and construction, are among the world's most vulnerable workers, their situations made worse in the many countries that have poor records in enforcing international human rights law.

Source: BrandX Pictures.

year. UN human rights authorities have expressed dismay at this practice, stating that the North Korean government should be prosecuted by the International Criminal Court for crimes against humanity (Darusman, 2015). This would be highly unlikely, as China and Russia, both recipients of North Korean workers, are allies of the regime that exports their labour. The fact that even an extreme situation such as this has gone on for years highlights the precariousness of human rights in the business environment.

Most of the world's countries are parties to the UN's main human rights covenants, but how does this translate into human rights protection? Countries prioritizing development are often inclined to turn a blind eye to human rights. But what about companies and businesses in general? They are not covered directly by the covenants. They have moral responsibilities, but not legal obligations under the covenants, except in respect to those aspects of human rights that feature in national law. Hence, UN authorities can target a country, like North Korea, but cannot target a company specifically for breaches. Targeting a country, however, sends a strong persuasive message to governments, which usually have extensive business ties. The UN has endorsed a guideline document on Business and Human Rights, but these guidelines are voluntary, appealing to businesses to take human rights into consideration, but avoiding holding them liable for breaches of human rights, for example for abuses that take place in supply chains (Morrison, 2015). There is now a mechanism for victims of human rights abuse to complain directly to the UN, leading to UN pressure on governments to enforce human rights law.

MNEs view CSR as a voluntary approach to social responsibility. Companies sponsor numerous CSR projects, such as education and health services, often filling gaps left by cash-strapped governments. Brand owners took steps to set up fire and safety standards in Bangladesh following the Rana Plaza disaster, for instance. Should this have been the job of government? The company is not publicly accountable in these situations, and can walk away from the country if the business environment deteriorates. It is ultimately accountable to its shareholders. Indeed, businesses, including those with extensive CSR agendas, are likely to lobby governments for *less* legal regulation. Businesses genuinely wish to do good, but on their terms, not terms handed down by governments. Which is the more legitimate? Governments all extol their legitimacy in the eyes of the public. In many countries, such as Bangladesh, they are elected by their populations, with mandates for promoting social well-being and inclusive development. The MNE exists to enhance the wealth of its owners. Should its responsibility involve public accountability? MNEs and their directors can be held accountable for disasters that impact on societies, but it is rare. Hardly any banker has been prosecuted following the financial crisis. MNEs lobby for the inclusion of the ISDS in trade agreements, allowing them to escape public accountability.

Governments are rightly criticized for not upholding the human rights they have signed up to in the UN covenants. MNEs have no UN covenants to sign, but they nonetheless face the same challenges and responsibilities: to uphold human rights and to accept liabilities for breaches of those rights when their activities are implicated. Governments get away with undermining the human rights they officially subscribe to. So too, do businesses in many cases. However, just as public opinion criticizes the repressive policies of governments, people are coming to criticize the weak adherence to human rights of companies that wield economic power greater than many countries and exert increasing influence over the daily lives of all of us.

Conclusions

No one would doubt that the for-profit company has a role in society, but that role is now seen as multifaceted. The company's role is sometimes depicted as economic only, free to pursue business aims as it wishes as long as it stays within the relevant law. This simplistic view, although still articulated by some, is being rapidly overtaken by the interactions of companies in the societies where their activities impact. The notion of social responsibility recognizes this dimension, which involves ethical as well as legal obligations. We have seen that MNEs are now treated as responsible for impacts of their activities throughout supply chains. And these impacts extend to workers and communities as stakeholders. Consumers globally are increasingly concerned about the ethics of supply chains, including the human rights of workers. Western MNEs often include ethics and human rights in their annual reports. They point to their corporate citizenship profiles and hold up their codes of conduct in supply chains, but differences between the rhetoric and the reality continue to emerge.

Despite commitments to CSR, companies are ultimately serving goals of shareholder wealth maximization, which translates into seeking competitive advantage through profits. A shift in corporate culture towards a more balanced stakeholder perspective could well lead to a dip in short-term profits, but the shift to a more sustainable way of doing business would benefit shareholders in the longer term. MNEs from emerging economies, including both state-controlled and private-sector companies, are also facing greater scrutiny on social and environmental issues. Consumers have perhaps been more alert than executives to the multiple dimensions of social well-being: they seek improvements in material living standards, but they also think long-term about a healthy environment and sustainable livelihoods.

References

Allen, L. (2015) 'Is Indonesia's fire crisis connected to the palm oil in our snack food?' *The Guardian*, 23 October, at www.theguardian.com

Apple Inc. (2014) 'Supplier Code of Conduct', at www.apple.com/supplier-responsibility

Baron, R. (2014) 'The evolution of corporate reporting for integrated performance', OECD background paper for the 30th Round Table on Sustainable Development, 25 June, Paris, at www.oecd.org

BBC (2013) 'Apple faces new China worker abuse claims', BBC News, 29 July, at www.bbc.com

Berlin, I. (1958) *Two Concepts of Liberty* (Oxford: OUP).

Carroll, A.B. (1991) 'The pyramid of corporate social responsibility: toward the moral management of organizational stakeholders', *Business Horizons*, 34: 39–48.

China Labor Watch (2014) 'Another Samsung supplier factory exploiting child labor', 9 July, at www.chinalaborwatch.org

Darusman, M. (2015) 'Statement by the UN special rapporteur on the situation of human rights in the Democratic People's Republic of Korea, at the end of his visit, 6–10 September', at www.ohchr.org

EPI (Economic Policy Institute) (2015) 'Top CEOs make 300 times more than typical workers', Issue Brief Number 399, 21 June, at www.epi.org

Freeman, R.E. (1984) *Strategic Management: A Stakeholder Approach* (Boston, MA: Pitman).

Fullerton, J. and Chen, J. (2015) 'Chinese worker, 26, making Apple iPhones died after enduring 12 hour shifts, seven days a week, family claim', *The Mail Online*, 11 March, www.dailymail.co.uk

GRI (2015) 'G4 Sustainability Reporting Guidelines', 5 August, at www.globalreporting.org

Kant, E. ([1785]1948) *The Moral Law: Groundwork of the Metaphysic of Morals*, trans. H.J. Paton (New York: Routledge).

KPMG (2013) 'Carrots and sticks: sustainability reporting policies worldwide', at www.kpmg.com and www.globalreporting.org

McWilliams, A. (2001) 'Corporate social responsibility: a theory of the firm perspective', *Academy of Management Review*, 26(1): 117–128.

Mill, J.S. ([1859] 1947) *On Liberty*, edited by A. Castell (New York: Appleton-Century-Crofts).

Mitchell, R.K., Agle, B.R. and Wood, D. (1997) 'Toward a theory of stakeholder identification and salience: defining the principle of who and what really counts', *Academy of Management Review*, 11(4): 853–886.

Morrison, J. (2015) *Business Ethics* (London: Palgrave Macmillan).

Mui, Y. (2011) 'Wal-Mart works with unions abroad, but not at home', *The Washington Post*, 7 June, at www.washingtonpost.com

Mundy, S. (2014) 'Samsung fails to end labour violations in China', *Financial Times*, 1 July.

ONS (2015) 'Employee contracts that do not guarantee a minimum number of hours: 2015 update', 2 September, at www.ons.gov.uk, accessed 25 October 2015.

Plamenatz, J. (1958) *The English Utilitarians*, 2nd edn (Oxford: Blackwell).

Quinton, A. (1989) *Utilitarian Ethics* (Chicago: Open Court Publishing).

Thomas, L. and Pfanner, E. (2013) 'Even before Apple tax breaks, Ireland's policy had its critics', *New York Times*, 21 May, at www.nyt.com

Sen, A. (2010) *The Idea of Justice* (London: Penguin).

Smith, J. (2015) 'Human rights are at risk under our new Conservative Government', *The Independent*, 10 May.

Social Enterprise UK (2015) 'State of social enterprise report 2015', at www.socialenterprise.org.uk

Treanor, J. (2014) 'RBS gives 10 executives £5.5 million in allowances to sidestep EU bonus cap', *The Guardian*, 5 December, at www.theguardian.com

Wood, D. (1991) 'Corporate social performance revisited', *Academy of Management Review*, 16(4): 691–718.

☛ Multiple choice questions

Go to the companion website: www.palgravehighered.com/morrison-gbe-4e to take a quick multiple choice quiz on what you have read in this chapter.

⑦ Review questions

1 In what ways have utilitarian principles influenced ethical thinking, and what are their shortcomings?
2 What is meant by 'ethical relativism', and what is its relevance for international business?
3 Summarize the human rights that are relevant to a workplace environment.
4 What are the ethical foundations of current thinking on corporate responsibility in societies, and in what areas of business activity are they relevant?
5 Describe Carroll's theory of CSR, and explain the role of stakeholders in Carroll's thinking.
6 What is 'corporate citizenship', and what are its shortcomings in practice?
7 What are the weaknesses of corporate codes of practice in relation to CSR?
8 In what ways can the recognition of international guidelines for CSR make companies more responsible in their international operations?
9 What is the role of philanthropy in CSR?
10 Assess the differences between primary and secondary stakeholders.
11 What are the criticisms of the shareholder model of corporate governance, and how can they be remedied?
12 What is the 'business case' for CSR?
13 Why is executive pay perceived as an ethical issue, and what can be done to moderate it?
14 Why is the social enterprise perceived as a way of providing services which governments struggle to fund?
15 How is economic development contrasted with the broader concept of human development?

✓ Assignments

1 Firms which have seen weakening financial performance might argue that they can no longer afford CSR, and that they must revert to a 'back to basics' competitive strategy. Assess the extent to which this is a valid argument in the current global environment.
2 In what ways can the UN covenants on human rights and ILO conventions on labour rights be incorporated into CSR strategies, and become more observed in practice by international businesses?

📖 Further reading

Allen, T. and Thomas, A. (2000) *Poverty and Development*, 2nd edn (Oxford: Oxford University Press).

Amao, O. (2013) *Corporate Social Responsibility, Human Rights and the Law*, Routledge Research in Corporate Law (London: Routledge).

Collier, P. (2008) *The Bottom Billion: Why the Poorest Countries are Failing and What can be Done about it* (Oxford: OUP).

Deaton, A. (2015) *The Great Escape: Health, Wealth and the Origins of Inequality* (Princeton: Princeton University Press).

Dehesa, G. de la (2007) *What do we Know about Globalization? Issues of Poverty and Income Distribution* (Hoboken, NJ: Wiley-Blackwell).

Kotler, P. (2004) *Corporate Social Responsibility* (London: John Wiley & Sons).

Lomborg, B. (ed.) (2009) *Global Crises, Global Solutions: Costs and Benefits,* 2nd edn (Cambridge: Cambridge University Press).

Melé, D. (2009) *Business Ethics in Action* (Basingstoke: Palgrave Macmillan).

Morrison, J. (2015) *Business Ethics* (London: Palgrave Macmillan).

Stiglitz, J. (2002) *Globalization and its Discontents* (London: Allen Lane).

🌐 **Visit the companion website at** www.palgravehighered.com/morrison-gbe-4e **for further learning and teaching resources.**

The Volkswagen emissions scandal: what are the lessons?

'Made in Germany' has long signified quality and reliability in global markets. Motor vehicles are one of the main sectors in which the German pedigree is admired most strongly. But in 2015, that reputation at Germany's largest carmaker, Volkswagen (VW), suffered a dramatic blow, when news broke of a long-running practice of installing 'defeat devices' to understate diesel emissions in vehicle testing. The breaking story emerged only gradually, with alternating suspicions and denials part of the unfolding scandal. The depth of the engine tampering came to light only piece by piece, but in the end amounted to a full-blown nightmare that enveloped the company. How did it happen, and how can the company put right the damage, both in engineering terms, and in its corporate reputation?

From the outset of his tenure as CEO, Martin Winterkorn, who resigned just after the revelations broke, had been determined to see VW become the world's largest carmaker. When he took over as CEO, it was in third place, behind Toyota and General Motors, but in the first half of 2015, VW at last succeeded in toppling Toyota from the top position, to the huge satisfaction of its CEO. VW's array of 12 brands, ranging from Skoda and Seat at the lower end to premium vehicles, Audi and Porsche, have captured 25% of the European car market, but the company has had much less success in the US, where it had languished with only 3% of the market. In Europe, diesel vehicles are 53% of the market. Winterkorn's strategy for boosting US sales was to win over American customers to the virtues of VW's clean, fuel-efficient diesel engines.

The US has stringent emissions standards, which VW's Jetta, Golf and Beetle diesel models were able to meet – or so it appeared. VW's own clean technology, which differed from rivals', was introduced in 2008. As far back as then, rival manufacturers questioned how VW could achieve the low emissions that tests stated, but it was not until independent tests were carried out in 2012 by the International Council on Clean Transport (ICCT) that it was shown that the VW diesel cars in the US had excessive levels of nitrogen oxides. The ICCT tested the cars on ordinary roads, finding levels of Nox

15 to 35 times higher than the laboratory tests had stated. When VW was questioned, it pointed to 'various technical issues' (Sharman et al., 2015). The US Environmental Protection Agency (EPA) followed up, but it did not receive clear explanations from the carmaker. VW issued a voluntary recall of half a million vehicles in 2014. Eventually, VW admitted to the EPA that software installed in the vehicles, or defeat devices, gave understated emissions in laboratory tests. The company had engaged in evasive tactics with officials for over a year.

The number of vehicles distributed worldwide that were fitted with defeat devices could amount to 11 million, and these vehicles would need to be serviced. About half a million of the owners are in the US, where civil lawsuits, including class actions, have been launched. There are federal and state agencies investigating, and the EPA has proposed penalties of up to $18 billion on the company. The overall costs could be immense. In addition, the EU's anti-fraud authorities could claw back over €9 billion that were handed out to VW for R&D into clean technology. In the space of a week in September 2015, VW's shares fell 34%. VW's supervisory board moved quickly to appoint a new CEO, Matthias Müller, who pledged to do everything possible to win back confidence, looking to beef up compliance and also reform governance in the company. A nagging question in the minds of those who work for the company and the public in general is how deception on such a large scale could happen.

Martin Winterkorn has been firm that he knew nothing about the defeat devices, but the company recognized that there had been management failings. The company has admitted that there was a 'whole chain' of errors, facilitated by an unwieldy structure, in which there was a tolerance of rule-breaking (Ruddick, 2015). It was not simply a question of rogue engineers, but processes that allowed the cheating to take place. The timing of the introduction of the defeat devices coincided with pressures to meet the stringent US emissions standards. The management structure has now been streamlined into a new, leaner structure, and Müller has pledged to change the culture. Müller is himself an insider, having been head of the Porsche subsidiary. Corporate governance of VW has been dominated by family owners and the state of Lower Saxony, which owns 20% of the shares. There are calls for reforms from external shareholders.

Could regulators have caught the malpractices? EU officials were aware of defeat devices two years before the VW scandal, and such devices were made illegal in 2007. But officials did not investigate, and neither had national authorities discovered any. Experts have argued that diesel cars should be tested on real roads, rather than in labs. EU officials have tried to introduce legislation to this effect, but, in the view of environmental campaigners, the power of the diesel lobby has thwarted these efforts. The EU takes the view that the policing of compliance by companies is for national authorities (Oliver et al., 2015).

Sources: Ruddick, G. (2015) 'VW admits emissions scandal was caused by a whole chain of failures', *The Guardian*, 10 December, at www.theguardian. com; Oliver, C., Brunsden, J. and Vasagar, J. (2015) 'EU was warned two years ago over VW-type emission cheat devices', *Financial Times*, 26 September, at www.ft.com; Sharman, A., Bryant, C., Jopson, B. and Chon, G. (2015) 'Fuel for scandal', *Financial Times*, 26 September.

Questions for discussion

- What were the causes of the emissions scandal?
- What ethical weaknesses existed in the VW culture?
- What lessons are there in the wrongdoing and the way it was handled?
- Is VW doing enough to prevent future scandals?

CHALLENGES AND RESPONSIBILITIES: TOWARDS A NEW PERSPECTIVE

This chapter will enable you to

- Review challenges and responsibilities in the global environment
- Identify key areas of global risks confronting managers
- Assess overlapping responsibilities of governments and businesses
- Gain new perspectives on sustainable strategies for global business

Outline of chapter

OPENING CASE STUDY

Coca-Cola in Mexico: fizzy drinks at the centre of a health crisis

Coca-Cola's presence in Mexico goes back to 1898, when the American brand was first introduced in the Mexican market. Since then, it has grown to become virtually institutional in its influence in Mexico, reaching deeply into the economic, political and cultural life. There is no other country on earth in which Coca-Cola exerts the sheer power that it enjoys in Mexico. Mexicans drink more soda drinks that any other country, and Coca-Cola accounts for 73% of them (compared to its 42% share of the US soda market). Diabetes, which is closely associated with sugar consumption, is the leading cause of death in Mexico. The pervasiveness of Coke, often due to public distrust of tap water, is part of the explanation. In urban and rural areas alike, Coke is omnipresent, displacing local fruits and vegetables, as well as traditional fruit drinks, in the daily diet. The highest levels of Coca-Cola consumption are in the poor indigenous regions of Chiapas. Mexicans drink on average 163 litres of sugary fizzy drinks annually. Coca-Cola's dominance and the rise in health problems have been particularly marked in the last two decades. In a radical move, the country's political leaders have imposed a soda tax – vigorously opposed by the soda industry, which felt unjustly demonized. How did a country that had so wholeheartedly embraced Coca-Cola come to turn against the sugary drinks that had become a staple in people's diets?

Vicente Fox, a former head of Coca-Cola Mexico, was elected president in 2000. There followed Coke's growing power and influence in the country's political establishment, including influence in shaping health policies. Health officials and health foundations, many with links to Coke, have consistently argued that soda in itself is not a cause of health problems: the real cause is consuming too many calories. They advise a balanced diet and plenty of exercise, and refuse to single out sugar. However, in 2006, a national survey of Mexicans showed that diabetes had doubled from 1999 to 2006, and that obesity among children aged 5 to 11 had risen by 40%. The survey also showed that consumption of soda had doubled among adolescents over that period; and, among women, it had nearly

tripled (Rosenberg, 2015). The government became alarmed, especially at the implications for the health service. The Mexican diet had become increasingly based on sugary drinks and processed foods, especially snack foods, which had displaced traditional healthier foods. The influx of these products increased dramatically after the NAFTA (North American Free Trade Agreement) in 1994, which allowed American food and beverage giants open access to the Mexican market.

Following the alarm caused by the health survey in 2006, Coca-Cola stepped up its healthy-living campaigns, including increased sponsorship of sporting events. The company has been keen to counteract any link between sugary drinks and disease. It rejects comparisons with the tobacco industry, although tobacco companies have pursued similar tactics. In 2006, a civil society group was formed, to take aim at the soda industry. Known as El Poder del Consumidor (Consumer Power), this group, which had little money in comparison to the millions spent by Coke, started to make an impact. Funding from Michael Bloomberg, the former mayor of New York who supports controls of the soda industry, helped the organization to raise its profile. It was then able to buy television advertising. Success came in 2013, with the passing of legislation imposing a soda tax, which took effect on 1 January 2014. By the latter months of 2014, soda sales were 12% down on the previous year, and they were down 17% among the poorest consumers. The soda tax seemed to be working.

In 2015, Coca-Cola launched a campaign to promote Sidral Mundet, another fizzy drink, under a brand name that was originally Mexican. The brand dates from 1902, and was bought by Coca-Cola in 2002. The campaign ran into controversy over its advertising. Sidral Mudet is an apple-flavoured drink with 60 grams of sugar in a 600ml bottle. Coke's advertising campaign stated the drink is made 'with apple juice'. Many of the company's YouTube advertising videos feature fresh apples. In fact, the drink contains 1% 'juice from concentrate', which the US Food and Drug Administration (FDA) classifies as sugar.

Consumer Power accused Coca-Cola of misleading consumers. Mexican authorities asked Coca-Cola to clarify how much apple juice the drink contained. Coca-Cola then launched a lawsuit claiming a breach of its constitutional right to a fair trial. It also stated that the drink was a product of a subsidiary company, not Coca-Cola itself. Consumer Power accused Coca-Cola of using delaying tactics. The judge allowed Coca-Cola to carry on advertising, and, given the likelihood of a protracted legal process, the advertisements could continue for a long time. However, Coke removed the phrase 'with apple juice' from the advertisements. Meanwhile, the company was criticized for a Christmas advertisement showing light-skinned, affluent-looking young people handing out Coke as presents to indigenous Mexicans in Oaxaca state. The script referred to 'breaking down prejudice' (Blakinger, 2015). However, it was widely perceived as condescending, with colonial connotations that are culturally highly sensitive in Mexico. Coca-Cola removed the advertisement from its YouTube Channel.

Sources: Lakhani, N. (2015) 'Coca-Cola ads suggesting soda is made from apples lead to legal battles', *The Guardian*, 19 December, at www. theguardian.com; Rosenberg, T. (2015) 'How one of the most obese countries on earth took on the soda giants', *The Guardian*, 3 November; Blakinger, K. (2015) 'Coca-Cola pulls Mexican ad after accusations of rascism', *New York Daily News*, 7 December, at www.nydailynews.com.

Questions for discussion

- How did Coca-Cola succeed in growing into such a powerful force in Mexico?
- Coca-Cola has supported numerous health and sporting causes, but to what extent is this genuine CSR?
- How ethical is Coca-Cola in its approach to the Mexican market?
- Should other countries adopt the soda tax?

Introduction

What does the business exist to do, and how should it go about realizing its goals? These questions were posed at the start of this book, and the chapters that followed have revealed a wide divergence in outlooks, goals and business methods. Much of this divergence has derived from constrasting business environments – between countries, between industries, between companies and even between corporate leaders with diverging views of business in society. This chapter aims to highlight the divergent outlooks and environments in the contexts of the challenges that exist in the global business environment. A graphic showing the challenges at the start of the book has provided the framework for the many illustrations and case studies that have followed. By looking at how businesses pursue opportunities and deal with dilemmas, we have been able to assess the ways in which they are meeting these challenges – or failing to meet them. This chapter will not review all these cases. Rather, it will make comparisons and draw out insights, bringing in new examples where illuminating. The chapter number of each case example is given, and the list of case studies at the start of the book will be of help. The chapter begins with a review of those challenges and responsibilities. The focus then shifts to the risks arising in key dimensions of the global environment. There follows a critical assessment of where responsibilities lie, and how well notions of shared responsibilities and legal obligations deal with issues in practice. What should be changed, and what *could* be changed to bring about a more sustainable business environment? That is the ambitious question discussed in the last section.

Reviewing the challenges and responsibilities

Seven sets of challenges and responsibilities were listed at the beginning of this book. They were grouped under three broad headings, shown again in Figure 12.1.

Interlocking challenges and responsibilities

Figure 12.1 Challenges and responsibilities

The three broad headings cover business purposes and ways of carrying out both short-term and long-term goals. They involve contexts where legal, social and moral considerations arise, bringing in a range of stakeholders. Here, we bring together some of the points that have arisen under each of these headings.

Sustainability

Addressing climate change and adopting wider measures to achieve a sustainable business are the challenges highlighted under this heading. Every for-profit business needs to make money to survive. Looking for new sources of profits in, say, new markets and new products, is a preoccupation of businesses. Examples are AB InBev's launching a takeover of second-place brewer, SAB Miller, largely to gain access to new African and Asian markets, and Apple's launching new devices (case studies in Chapters 8 and 11). Efficiency gains in manufacturing and other operations are also sought. AB InBev has gained a reputation in this respect. Manufacturers of consumer products, from cars and clothing to electronics, have been driven by the allure of cost reductions, largely through global supply chains that benefit from low-cost labour in developing countries. Globalization has thus been a force in expanding markets and also production efficiencies. But the company that shifts locations to maintain and improve financial performance is not pursuing a sustainable business model – just a chase for short-term profits. Recall (in Chapter 9) the carmakers that have shifted from Western Europe to the newer Central and Eastern European countries, and from there to locations in North Africa – each move based largely on the attraction of lower wages.

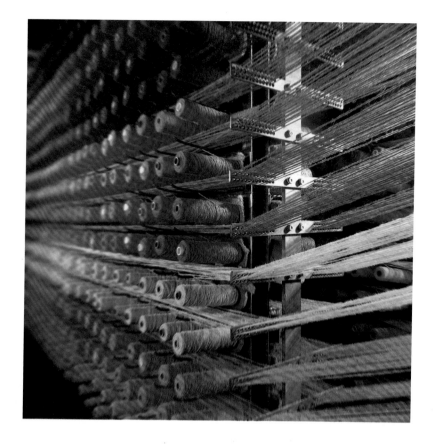

Improvements in machine technology transformed textile manufacturing, making large-scale production highly efficient, as shown in this textile factory.

Source: Getty.

Addressing climate change is one of the main challenges in building a sustainable business. This means minimizing emissions, seeking clean technology and minimizing the use of scarce resources or materials that cannot be recycled. These efforts all cost money in the short term, but as has been highlighted, are likely to bring benefits to both the environment and sustainable productive assets in the long term. The impacts of climate change have sometimes seemed remote, and, as has been highlighted in Chapter 10, businesses tend to give these risks low priority. They also tend to express the view that it is for governments to legislate. The notion of governments making the law and businesses complying with it is one that has been discussed in various other contexts including financial regulation (Chapter 8), company taxation (Chapter 11) and worker safety (this chapter). In each, it emerges that the regulatory framework involves *both* enterprise and government participation. And, indeed, businesses actively lobby governments and legislators. Many businesses support lobby groups that seek to thwart climate change measures proposed by governments, such as subsidies and quotas for renewable energy. The vested interests of the large oil and gas companies are among the main obstacles to progress in addressing climate change. Businesses play roles in governance that can be positive, helping to promote societal goals, but their activities in influencing public policy can also have negative impacts, setting back progress in combating climate change.

Governance

Businesses interact with national and local governments, and also with international bodies. Much that is positive can be accomplished through these relations. We have seen examples of public-private partnerships building solar plants in Morocco and windfarms in Uruguay (both in Chapter 10). In Scandinavian countries, the private sector has co-operated with public authorities in health services and education (Chapter 4). We have also seen, however, that close ties between businesses and politicians can have negative impacts when these ties become self-serving and corrupt. The three challenges highlighted in Figure 12.1 are fair and effective regulation, anti-corruption and legitimate political institutions. All three present challenges for businesses, not just for governments.

The spread of market economies has, perhaps paradoxically, given rise to increasing regulation. The purist advocate of free markets is now rare, following the market failures that led to the global financial crisis. And regulation serves not simply to maintain markets, but to promote other public goods, such as consumer safety and environmental protection. The challenges are to design fair regulation and to persuade all players to comply willingly. Many companies featured in this book demonstrate regulatory dilemmas. Uber, the ride-hailing company, is extreme, resting on a business model of defying regulation (Chapter 6). Coca-Cola, featured in this chapter, has used lobbying and lawsuits to thwart laws designed to promote public health. The global financial crisis is perhaps the most spectacular example of collective regulatory failure. Post-crisis regulation has been slow in coming, resisted by the financial services sector. It soon became apparent that devices to circumvent bonus caps, for example, were being used. A change in culture is hard to introduce, but is nonetheless essential to a regulatory regime. Moreover, in 2015, the Conservative government in the UK announced its intention to undo the 2013 legislation for making bankers responsible for failed banks (see Chapter 8). This had been one of the main pillars of banking reform, following the apparent ability of bankers to escape any liability for banks that had failed under their watch. Failure of regulatory oversight played a part in the housing market collapse in the US, and the collapse of the excessively-indebted UK banks in 2008.

Where regulation is fair and transparent, every party has an interest in supporting its mechanisms. It is an unfortunate reality that, in many places, relations between government and business descend into corruption. Often, political leaders are themselves linked to the country's large business interests, as in the Philippines and Indonesia (Chapters 6 and 10). In these situations, regulatory mechanisms that exist can be manipulated by those with vested interests, usually for short-term personal gain. The result is that societal well-being suffers. Both these countries have lowly rankings in Transparency International's Corruption Perception Index: Indonesia lies 107th on a score of 34 out of 100, and the Philippines lies 85th on a score of 38. Other selected rankings appear in Figure 12.2, which replicates Figure 6.9. In places where businesses routinely engage in undeclared payments to officials and others, corruption may become the norm. And in these situations, companies can take false comfort in the fact that others are behaving the same way. But a regulatory crackdown, as happened to the pharmaceutical company, GSK, in China, demonstrated that corrupt behaviour is still corrupt, whether widespread or a one-off example (Chapter 9). High levels of corruption are a disadvantage in assessment of a country's competitiveness. Corrupt behaviour is simply a risky way of doing business, dependent on personal ties rather than contractual terms, and liable to turn sour when there are changes in officialdom. One of the best safeguards against corruption is legitimate political institutions, the third of the headings under governance.

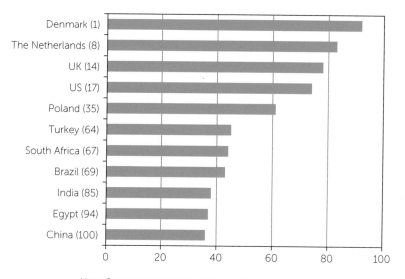

Figure 12.2 Transparency International's Corruption Perception Index: findings for selected countries

Source: Data from Transparency International (2015) Corruption Perception Index for 2014, at www. transparency.org/cpi2015, accessed 20 June 2015.

Note: Country scores are percentages. The rank of each country is shown in brackets after the country name. There are 174 countries overall in the ranking.

Countries with high levels of corruption are often authoritarian or semi-authoritarian political regimes. China's authoritarian system under Communist Party leadership has endured over half a century, continuity provided by a succession of leaders emerging from within the political élite. But this continuity does not bestow institutional stability to the entire political system. Government market policies have delivered economic development, but leaders fear any upsurge in dissent and protest. China's democracy protesters, many active since the 1989 Tiananmen Square protests, remind the world of the regime's lack of political legitimacy (Phillips, 2015). However, a constitutional system that formally guarantees democratic rights does not alone legitimize a government. A semi-authoritarian regime can overlay an electoral democracy. It has democratic forms, such as regular elections of a president and an elected legislature, but these processes are captured by political élites that are often linked to the country's largest businesses. Political legitimacy rests on democratic institutions that are supported by the rule of law, freedom of civil-society organizations and an independent judiciary.

A number of countries that have ostensibly democratic institutions are authoritarian beneath the surface. Among those that have featured here are Turkey (Chapter 5), Russia (Chapter 5) and Ethiopia (Chapter 4). Historically and culturally, they are all different, but there are similarities among them in terms of governance. All are emerging economies, and all have constitutions that should safeguard democratic institutions. But all are semi-authoritarian, ruled by political élites. These countries have prioritized development, but economic development in these systems tends to be uneven. Governments in all three have sought to realize the benefits of globalization. And, whereas all have enjoyed economic growth, their governments do not command the same legitimacy within all sections in society that a democracy should have.

Social responsibility

Social responsibility includes meeting human needs and societal goals. The first of these focuses on human well-being, including livelihood, housing, health and education. The second is broader, encompassing participation and engagement in communities and cultural life. It also embraces the notion of self-fulfilment that pertains to both individuals and societies. It is worth remembering that Article 1 of both the International Covenant on Civil and Political Rights (ICCPR) and the International Covenant on Economic, Social and Political Rights (ICESCR) is identical:

> All peoples have the right of self-determination. By virtue of that right they freely determine their political status and freely pursue their economic, social and cultural development. (at www.ohchr.org)

People everywhere look to governments to provide security and safety. But they also expect a conducive environment in which to pursue personal goals, start businesses, strive for educational achievement, express themselves freely, and join with others of similar beliefs and religious faith. People also expect government policies to promote these opportunities for all, not just the privileged and the rich. But there are marked divergences among countries in terms of social goods and social responsibilities. Recall the divergent views of human rights contained in the two foundation covenants noted above. One focuses on negative freedoms, the other on liberty in the positive sense of self-realization. Liberal political thought has traditionally held to the rights of the individual as freedom 'from' interference by the state, to pursue self-interested goals. But in countries where the poor lack opportunities through education, and suffer from inadequate access to healthcare, their 'freedom' has an altogether shallow ring. The welfare state, now recognized in the more free-market economies as well as the social market economies, is seen as essential in promoting social goods. But the welfare state steps in as an *adjunct* to the market economy, aiming to support market mechanisms. Within market economies, productivity is primarily driven by business enterprises.

Businesses provide jobs, incomes to employees, goods and services that people want, and much else that contributes to well-being. They fulfil a vital economic role, but they are also meeting human needs and influencing how societies function and change. The human and social dimension of business activities confers on them social responsibilities. These can be viewed as CSR, and can also be viewed in an ethical perspective. Companies are justifiably considered to owe obligations of adhering to human rights, not just those recognized in law, but also those recognized as ethical principles. The company that pays below minimum wage levels, as in the case study on the factory in the Philippines (Chapter 6), is operating in an environment where both legal and moral obligations are commonly avoided, and where the state also bears part of the blame.

Political institutions: how do they matter?

Why is political legitimacy a key for businesses in emerging economies?

Assessing the risks in the global environment

Uncertainties in the global environment cast a shadow over the hopes that many hold in the powers of globalization to bring about prosperity and stability. The positive side of globalization has been in evidence, lifting economies through growth and reducing poverty, but the negative aspects have highlighted risks. Among these are the rising concerns about climate change, especially in the light of rapid economic development. Slowing economic growth in both developing and developed economies, along with rising indebtedness, poses threats to economic and financial stability. Economic growth has often been accompanied by rising inequality. Furthermore, political leadership sometimes reinforces the inequalities rather than setting an agenda for inclusive development. In many countries, poor people have little or no hope of personal betterment. In others, such as China, many now have expectations of continuing improvement in their quality of life. The realities of unemployment, stagnant wages and poor social services can be destabilizing in society, and even divisive. The rise in ethnic and religious tensions in many countries compounds any economic uncertainties. These dimensions are shown in Figure 12.3. The figure shows three key sources of risk in each of these dimensions, which are discussed in turn.

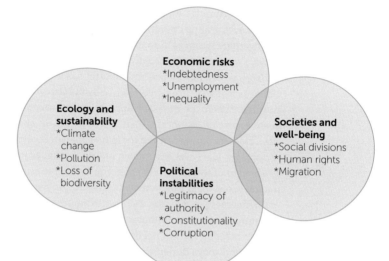

Figure 12.3 Risks in the global environment

Ecology and sustainability

The Paris conference of 2015 held out hope that an agenda supported by the 195 participating states would deliver the reductions in emissions that would hold global warming to a rise of 2C, or, more ambitiously, 1.5C. However, progress depends crucially on parties sticking to their promises on emissions reductions. It also depends on funds being channelled towards investments in developing countries. The two are linked. Vulnerable developing countries, especially those with low-lying areas and coastal communities, such as Bangladesh, could face the forced migration of millions of people. If temperature rises are kept at 1.5C, these countries would be able to avoid the worst impact of rising seas. These countries as a group pressed for the more ambitious target at the Paris conference. Also vulnerable are the states most prone to extreme weather events such as drought and flooding. Large swathes of land in Africa that support agriculture are fragile, prone to drought. The people face malnutrition, increased incidence of disease and displacement from lands that will no longer sustain farming and pastoral livelihoods. The effects of climate change accelerate these extreme conditions. African cities already struggle to cope with growing populations, and a rising influx of people driven from the countryside adds to the challenges of food security, safe housing and healthcare.

CASE STUDY ON THE CHANGING BUSINESS ENVIRONMENT

Bangladesh: a success story in achieving development goals?

In Bangladesh, low-lying communities such as this are at risk of flooding and, to make matters worse, are among the areas most vulnerable to rising sea levels associated with climate change.

Source: iStock.com/Sohel Parvez Haque.

Bangladesh is one of the world's poorest countries, and also one that is in the front line of damage from climate change. While negotiators met in Paris to address urgent issues of keeping rising temperatures to 2C, Bangladesh was already experiencing forced migration from flooded, low-lying areas, by 'climate refugees'. The country's population of nearly 160 million create enormous pressures on infrastructure, in both rural and urban environments. Daily, people are moving from coastal villages that are becoming submerged by the rising seas to slums on the outskirts of the capital, Dhaka, which struggles to cope with the influx. Ironically, although prone to flooding, Dhaka has a shrinking water supply, as underground water that serves the city is drying up. This is causing subsidence, adding to the problems of flooding. In rural areas, the incursion of sea water is threatening agriculture. Yet, Bangladesh has recorded progress in meeting the UN's Millennium Development Goals (MDGs) set out in 2000.

The main goals of the Bangladesh prime minister, Sheikh Hasina, have been to promote economic growth and make progress towards the MDGs of reducing poverty, and reducing child mortality and maternal mortality. Since 2000, the country has made progress in these goals, but levels of poverty and malnutrition are still high. Millions of people have been lifted out of poverty, but the World Bank estimates that 43% still live in absolute poverty, which is worse in rural areas. Growth rates that have consistently been in the range of 6% have been impressive, and she attributes much of this economic success to the garment industry, especially in terms of women's employment (Tisdall and Ridout, 2015). The government has made strides in providing primary-school education, but still only about half of children complete primary school. Bangladesh has a poor record in terms of women's rights, and improving the attendance of girls in primary schools has been a genuine accomplishment. There is legislation in place to protect women from domestic violence, but prosecutions have not been forthcoming. There are now 3.5 million women working in the garment industry around Dhaka, many of them migrants from rural villages affected by rising seas. Although work in the garment industry often involves unhealthy and unsafe working conditions, women tend to consider this employment better than work in domestic service in private homes, which is less well paid and has little legal protection from abusive or violent employers. However, the Rana Plaza factory collapse in 2013, in which over 1,100 people died, was a tragic reminder of the dangers involved.

The garment industry has been actively promoted by Sheikh Hasina. Over 5,000 factories producing garments, mainly for western brand owners, account for nearly $20 billion in export earnings. Many of the factory owners have links with the government, and, although there are construction and fire safety regulations, investigation and enforcement are weak. The Rana Plaza building was originally a six-storey building, approved for use as a shopping mall, but three floors were added and the building was converted to garment factories, for which it was essentially unsuitable. The workers trapped in the building had little hope of escape, but, despite the cracks appearing in the walls, were ordered to go back to their machines. In the aftermath of the disaster, western brand owners, including Marks & Spencer, Primark and H&M, took initiatives to set up a legally binding safety accord which provides for independent inspection of factories, backed up by paying for safety measures. American retailers, Walmart and Gap, did not support a legally binding agreement, and supported a voluntary agreement to help to provide safety training, along with 'worker participation committees'. Critics of this approach point out that it would lack the teeth of a legally binding agreement, and the worker participation committees would in fact be management initiatives that would stand in the way of workers exercising their legal rights to form independent trade unions.

After numerous delays, court proceedings in Bangladesh began in 2015 against 41 people charged with murder in the collapse of the Rana Plaza. Among the accused were Sohel Rana, the owner of the building, who had been kept in custody pending the trial. Seven owners of factories located in the building were also charged, as were 12 government officials responsible for carrying out inspections. Of the people charged, 24 did not turn up for the proceedings, and the court ordered their assets to be seized. The charge of murder against all these individuals would seem to be difficult to prove, and it is likely that these proceedings are envisaged essentially as a deterrent. Tightening up the operation of the official departments that inspect buildings would be of practical benefit to the millions in the garment industry who fear that their building could be the next one to collapse.

Sheikh Hasina has been active in the design of the new Sustainable Development Goals (SDGs) that are following on from the MDGs. In particular, she has been instrumental in having the climate change SDG (SDG 13) included. Whether Bangladesh will continue to make progress is questioned by critics. Sheikh Hasina has prioritized poverty reduction and encouraged economic growth, but on issues of human rights and security, her record has not been as impressive.

Sources: McPherson, P. (2015) 'Dhaka: the city where climate refugees are already a reality', *The Guardian*, 1 December, at www.theguardian.com; Tisdall, S. and Ridout, A. (2015) 'Sheikh Hasina: "I want to make Bangladesh poverty-free"', *The Guardian*, 25 September; *The Guardian* (2015) '24 Rana Plaza murder suspects abscond before trial', *The Guardian*, 21 December.

Questions for discussion

- What are the challenges facing Bangladesh in terms of climate change?
- To what extent should the global brands whose garments were being manufactured in the building be responsible for the Rana Plaza disaster?
- Were the actions taken by the western brand owners enough, in your view?
- To what extent is Bangladesh on course towards achieving sustainable development?

The WHO has emphasized the damage to human health caused by pollution, highlighting the toxic pollution caused by deforestation and burning of peatlands. As noted in the case study on Indonesia (Chapter 10), climate change is contributing to the rising incidence of disease in these areas. Deforestation is the world's second-largest source of emissions after the burning of fossil fuels, accounting for about 15% of global CO_2 emissions. Yet the tropical forests continue to be destroyed legally.

Large agribusiness corporations are the drivers. Globalized markets control the trading of food commodities, and large industrial processors have overseen the globalization of processed foods and other everyday consumer products. Increased demand for palm oil lies behind the clearing of forests for palm plantations, thereby devastating ecosystems, releasing pollution and destroying species. Palm oil is not just in processed foods – it occurs in 50% of the products consumers buy –from breakfast cereal to shampoo. The certification system of the RSPO (Roundtable for Sustainable Palm Oil) has attracted some large consumer products companies, but, even though founded in 2004, sustainable palm oil accounts for only 20% of the total. Moreover, RSPO-certified palm oil is not indicated on the brand's label. Palm oil production has doubled in the last decade, and is set to continue increasing, largely due to huge demand in Asian markets where awareness of sustainability issues is generally low.

Agribusinesses are active in promoting the virtues of technology as an answer to food security globally. However, their operations involve destruction of biodiversity and damaging social impacts on farming communities and livelihoods. The grip of a handful of agribusiness companies, such as Monsanto, on plant patents is an indication of increasing corporate control over crops and farm livelihoods. Although consumers in developed countries are now more aware of sustainability issues, these do not have the immediate impact of other issues, such as animal welfare in meat production. In animal agriculture, technology has driven the large meat companies towards increased production and efficiencies, but at what cost to sustainability? The pharmaceutical industry is increasingly active in animal husbandry. The use of antibiotics in animal farming has become widespread, especially in the US. The WHO has expressed alarm that the drug seen as the miracle cure of the twentieth century is now becoming overused in animals, mainly to improve growth. The result is that human resistance to antibiotics has grown, leading to higher mortality from diseases and greater risks to health in routine operations in hospitals. The non-therapeutic use of antibiotics was banned in the EU in 2006, but not in the US. The use of growth hormones in beef, banned in the EU since 1989, is also legal in the US. American consumer fears have led companies like McDonald's to restrict, although not eliminate entirely, the antibiotics used in their chickens (Thorsen, 2014).

Industrialized meat production has achieved greater efficiencies than traditional animal agriculture, but at what cost to health and safety – for both consumers and animals?

Source: Getty.

Economic risks

The global trend towards market economies has been a feature of the era of globalization. More freedom for all to pursue personal goals, everyone would agree, is a good thing. Market thinking has been embraced in communist China, and also now in communist Cuba. The percentage of people in the world living in absolute poverty (that is, on less than $1.25 a day) was 32% in 1990, and by 2010, was 16% (Wolf, 2015). This is a global percentage. The proportion is higher in many poor developing countries, and the halving of the percentage is largely accounted for by China's huge strides in reducing poverty. Over this same period, there has been a rise in inequality that has occurred in both developed and developing economies. China and the US are prominent examples, but there are many others. This trend has not been universal. Inequality has not increased in the Scandinavian countries or Germany, and it has narrowed in France. These are exceptions. How does inequality become a risk in economies? The free-market capitalist would consider that inequality is inherent in capitalism and is not a problem: 'If some people are made better off and no one is made worse off, the world is a better place' (Deaton, 2013: 207). Equality of opportunity is an assumption underlying this view. It holds that the rich earned their position at the top of the ladder, and those at the bottom, in theory, can climb the ladder as well. Improvement for those at the bottom would come with economic growth and rising wages. This assumption held true for the period of post-war growth in the US. The US example demonstrated to developing countries the benefits of market reforms, encouraged by the IMF and World Bank, notably through the Washington consensus (discussed in Chapter 8).

Economic growth has now slowed in the emerging economies, and growth is improving only slowly in the developed countries affected by the 2008 financial crisis. In the years following the financial crisis, other indicators have not looked very promising. High levels of household, corporate and sovereign debt create burdens verging on the unsustainable. Unemployment, especially acute among the young, remained relatively high despite a recovery in growth. Average wages are rising only modestly, if at all, in many of the countries affected by the financial crisis. But, tellingly, corporate profits, the wealth of the richest globally, and the salaries of executives, have soared ever upwards. Inequality has come to be seen from the economic perspective as hurting growth and posing a risk for long-term economic stability.

Two aspects of inequality stand out as undermining economic growth: health and education. A person's position in society and prospects of mobility depend heavily on good health and education. The adoption of universal public education in America's post-war years laid the groundwork for the economic growth that ensued. Where money is the key to accessing services, those without the means are likely to suffer poor health, low life expectancy and inability to pursue a job that offers enrichment in both income and personal fulfilment. This is detrimental not just for the individual, but for the economy as a whole. It means that much potential individual talent and ability to create wealth are not being tapped. Likewise, the growth in consumer spending power that leads to a growing middle class is held in check. A growing middle class that is healthier and better educated than previous generations is linked to economic development. It is happening in China now, and it was happening in the US in the decades following the Second World War.

The story in the US now, however, is of a declining middle class and backward trends in health and education. The Pew Research Center reported in 2015 that, following 40 years as the majority of the population, the middle class in the US is no longer the majority, having been overtaken by the growth in upper- and lower-income households (Pew Research Center, 2015). Moreover, middle-class income has fallen, as has middle-class wealth. This phenomenon can be envisaged as a 'hollowing out' of society, a description also applied to the de-industrialization that took place in the US as manufacturing jobs shifted to cheaper locations.

The US is the only high-income country in which those aged 25–34 have not overtaken the 55–64 age group in educational achievement. The reason is mainly the rise in costs that act as a barrier to those in lower income groups. In America's colleges, 74% of the students are from the top quarter of the population, while only 9% are from the bottom half (Stiglitz, 2013: 24). And those from poorer families are almost all funding their studies through student loans, with the lingering problems of paying off debt. For those without college education, the prospects of upward mobility are slim. Those with lower educational achievement and lower incomes are more likely to be black and Hispanic Americans. For the wealthiest in society, there was a 20% rise in the numbers of college graduates between those born in the early 1960s and those born in the early 1980s, but for the poorest households, that rise was only 4%. There are also wide discrepancies in life expectancy between rich and poor Americans. In 2010, a 50-year-old man who was in the top quintile of earners could expect to live to the age of 88.8, while, for one in the bottom quintile, life expectancy was 76.1 years. The top earner's life expectancy had risen from 83 in 1980, but the poorest earner's was one year *less* than in 1980 (Ehrenfreund, 2015). The figures for women were similar, except that the poorest women's life expectancy was down nearly two years over that period, from 80 in 1980 to 78.3 in 2010.

Inequality in society can be viewed as an ethical issue, on the grounds that it denies the equal moral worth of every human being. It has also been seen as undermining democracy and political legitimacy, as the few control power in society for their own gains, at the expense of the many (Reich, 2015). For the poor, the system no longer seems to be fair, either economically or politically. Poor health and educational outcomes for a large proportion of society augurs ill for an economy, and leads potentially to widening divisions between the haves and the have-nots. These trends are not inevitable. Where the system has become unfair, governments can devise policies to achieve a fairer distribution of wealth, by spending more on social services and raising taxes on the wealthy. However, where the institutions of government and the judiciary are controlled by the richest, such measures are unlikely.

Reducing inequality

Which is the more important justification for measures to reduce inequality: the ethical or the economic?

Societies and well-being

A society should provide an environment in which all have a feeling of belonging and a sense of participation. Divisions based on wealth, ethnic differences, religious conflicts and gender divides leave the disadvantaged groups behind, often feeling alienated and fearful of oppression from dominant groups. These divisions can be cross-cutting. The poorest are often those in ethnic minorities, such as indigenous people, as shown in the opening case study of this chapter. Broad-based and inclusive economic growth is an important source of stability in societies. Where growth has powered ahead, as in the resource-rich countries discussed in this book, and societal goods have been left behind, unfulfilled expectations can lead to flare-ups within society, ultimately even destabilizing the country. Research has shown that in 2013, there were four times as many big demonstrations in the world as in 2006. Many of these, such as the Occupy movement that spoke for the 99% who are outside the top 1% of earners, were rooted in the inequities of inequality (Dorling, 2015). Latin American countries, notably Chile, that have enjoyed prolonged economic growth due to Chinese demand for their commodity exports, have also seen social disruption, spurred by the perception that the vast majority of people are not sharing in the benefits.

As the world's largest copper exporter, Chile has enjoyed impressive growth in GDP, at 5% for over three decades, resulting in a quadrupling of per capita GDP. But protests starting in 2006, at the start of Michelle Bachelet's first term as president, reflected a deep sense of frustration over the lack of progress in tackling poor health and education. Students were in the forefront of the demonstrations. Protests became more intense during the presidency of the centre-right president, Sebastian Pinera, from 2010 onwards. Ms Bachelet was elected president for a second time in 2014, on the strength of promises to bring in reforms to the education system, which has historically been based on private means rather than public entitlement. Aiming to provide free and universal education was a radical goal in this most socially unequal country. The president hoped that improving education would lead to inclusive growth and greater productivity. Her policies included more public money for education, and higher taxes on companies. In the period between her two terms of office, Ms Bachelet was the executive director of UN Women (www.unwomen.org), and underlying her reforms lie principles of human rights. As many of the examples in the book have shown, the precariousness of basic human rights is associated with economic, social and political arrangements in many countries, contributing to the conflicts that threaten social cohesion and well-being.

It is estimated that a million migrants made their way through irregular means to cross into Europe in 2015. Almost all were fleeing from conflict and denial of human rights in their home countries. The largest group was Syrians, fleeing from civil war, but there were also Afghans, Iraqis and Eritreans. There are now 2.2 million Syrians living in Turkey, but these people are not allowed to work there (Kingsley, 2015), and most feel compelled to move on to countries within the EU. These movements of people are part of a record level of displacement of people globally. The UN estimates that the number of refugees and internally displaced people in 2015 reached 60 million. A UN convention of 1951 recognizes the rights of refugees. Those crossing into Europe through irregular routes should be entitled to rights as refugees and, in any case, they require humanitarian assistance. Migrants have multiple urgent needs, including food, shelter, health and, also, language assistance. However, the influx of migrants has become a contentious issue in both EU countries and those on the margins of the EU through which refugee families pass, many with children. Germany has been welcoming to these migrants, but cannot readily absorb the hundreds of thousands wishing to enter in the space of a few months.

Finance ministers of the federal states of Germany, estimating that the country received over 900,000 asylum seekers in 2015, have allocated nearly €17 billion for spending on refugees in 2016. Germany is unusual in its openness to refugees and the benefits they receive. But it should also be noted that there are extreme right-wing political groups in Germany who are hostile to immigration. Governments under pressure to provide social services feel their obligations are primarily to their own citizens. Immigration is a political issue, and parties to the right, which tend to be more nationalistic, are likely to be anti-immigration. There has also been a concern that among migrants making irregular entries there could be terrorists, taking advantage of the breakdown in border controls caused by the movement of refugees.

Societies: when divisions cause tensions

Most societies are home to diverse cultural groupings and classes based on economic status. In most, there are tensions between these groups. What should governments be doing to build social cohesion?

Political instabilities

The global risks highlighted so far in this section have all raised issues for political institutions, and posed challenges for political leaders. Businesses and individuals everywhere look to political leaders to address climate change, manage economic risks and promote social cohesion. These are daunting tasks in societies where divisions have widened, unemployment remains high and authorities struggle to deal with the effects of extreme weather connected with climate change. In authoritarian political systems, the signs of tension emerge in events such as protests, strikes, detentions and clampdowns on media that report unrest and criticism of the government. Under President Xi Jinping, China has become more authoritarian in these respects. The leadership is confronting slowing growth, pollution and other issues, such as the weakening of prospects of suitable jobs for 7 million college graduates each year. China's new urban middle classes expect improving living standards and health, including reduced pollution. How will continuing disenchantment show itself? They cannot vote out their leadership. Instead of crackdowns, further market reforms would probably be a better recipe for sustainable growth, but these would still be top-down measures, reflecting a political system with inherent instabilities and problematic political legitimacy in the eyes of much of the population. These were highlighted in the case study on Hong Kong (Chapter 5).

The way I see it ...

'The people are starting to realise that their rights have been taken away by the Communist party and they are feeling that they are being constantly oppressed.'

An anonymous anti-censorship protestor in China, reported in *The Guardian*, 27 November, 2015.

Are prospects for democracy likely to improve in China, or are Chinese authorities more likely to continue to suppress freedom of speech and association?

Democratic institutions provide the means for the electorate to hold political leaders accountable, at least at the time of elections. As we have seen, democratic systems are not necessarily stable, or, for that matter, very good at pursuing public goods. But they do contain an element of consent of the governed that authoritarian systems lack. Democratic institutions rest on freedoms of speech and association, giving voice to groups in civil society that governments should be listening to. Political parties are no longer necessarily the first choice of those seeking to voice concerns. Indeed, political parties in many places are seen as part of the problem of governance failings. Hierarchical organizations in their own right, they are often perceived as serving their own interests before the public interest. Corruption and business ties give them a poor reputation, undermining the trust that citizens would ideally hold in democratic institutions. We saw this in the case of Brazil (Chapter 6), Indonesia (Chapter 10) and the Philippines (Chapter 6). An established two-party system in Spain came under pressure from just these accusations in elections in 2015.

Spain's two main parties, the Socialists and the conservative Partido Popular (PP), were challenged in 2015 by new parties that have emerged rapidly and garnered surprisingly large voter support. The PP held a vast majority in the legislature going into December's election, having won a landslide victory against the Socialists in 2011, mainly on the strength of promises to guide the country out of a prolonged and damaging recession. The years of PP rule have brought economic growth, at an annual rate of 3% in 2015, but unemployment, which was 25% when the PP took office, was reduced only modestly to 21% in 2015. In the general election of 2015, the PP won the most seats in the parliament, but lost its absolute majority. It was snubbed by 3 million voters, and received 28% of the total. The Socialists fared poorly as well, receiving 21% of the vote. A new left-wing party, Podemos, founded on an anti-austerity platform in the aftermath of the Occupy demonstrations in May 2011, took over 20% of the total vote. Podemos considers itself more an anti-establishment party than a left-wing one: its leader says its philosophy is 'not left versus right but above versus below' (Buck, 2014). A fourth party, Ciudadanos, a right-wing party favouring business and taking a stand against corruption, received 14% of the total. The outcome was a strong sign of the disaffection of voters with the two established parties, both of which were perceived to be corrupt. Where there is no clear majority, parties can agree to govern as a coalition, but, if disenchantment is running very high, a stalemate results and new elections have to be called. This situation can lead to prolonged instability, with little prospect of positive policies to deal with the issues. One of these issues in Spain is continuing demands from regions seeking autonomy, including Catalonia and the Basque region. Spain has not been the only country to hold an indecisive election. Portugal experienced a similar pattern of voting behaviour earlier in the same year. There, the conservatives won the most seats, but not a majority, and the two left-wing parties that came second and third formed a coalition government.

Immigration is one of the issues that has sparked a rise in right-wing nationalist parties across Europe. These extremist parties are considered fringe parties, but in some countries, notably Hungary and Poland, these parties have gained political power and have shifted government policies towards their agendas. In Poland, the right-wing Law and Justice Party won an absolute majority in elections in October 2015. In November, laws were passed to reduce greatly the impact of the country's highest court, the constitutional court, and four new judges were appointed by the country's conservative president, the appointments taking place in the middle of the night. Both measures have raised concern over Poland's constitutional democracy, voiced by the EU and also by Lech Wałęsa, who led Poland's Solidarity movement in the 1980s. In December 2015, large demonstrations took place in the streets of War-saw, highlighting threats to democracy and human rights, including proposed curbs on the rights of women, and new 'anti-terror' laws that would restrict freedom of speech and right of assembly.

Questions of legitimacy and corruption are linked. A government that is duly elected in accordance with a country's constitution claims legitimate authority to rule. However, it is unfortunately not uncommon, as in the examples of Poland and Turkey (Chapter 5), for an elected government with an absolute majority to intro-duce constitutional changes that are designed to entrench its particular ideology. Introducing a constitutional amendment to repeal the limitation of two terms for a president is not unusual, and results in the deepening and extending of executive power. These moves undermine democratic values and shift a regime closer to authoritarianism, under the assumed cloak of constitutional legitimacy. Inevitably, the freedoms of speech and association are eroded away in these processes. An authoritarian political leader will thereby be able to manipulate both the functions of government and the judiciary. However, the appearance of unity under a strong executive is not indicative of enduring stability, as political tensions continue to exist beneath the surface.

Who bears responsibilities, and what should they be doing?

The discussion of global risks in this book has emphasized the responsibilities that fall on all players in the global environment. We have highlighted the failures of systems and individuals. To say that a system is to blame is not to exclude the blame that attaches to individuals: they are part of the system. The case study on Volk-swagen is an example (Chapter 11). That case also pointed to regulatory failures. Here, we draw out some points about how decision-making and the behaviour of multiple players can take on a greater sense of responsibility for outcomes that impact on societies.

Governments

Governments have their hands on a great deal of power, including that which is authorized by law and that which comes through economic and political influence. A government represents the sovereignty of the state. It has the capacity to make laws, enforce them, and use coercive powers as it sees fit. It has powers to run a military establishment and conduct foreign relations with other countries, including entering treaty agreements. Although the judicial system is deemed to be independent in most countries, governments in practice exert influence over it. When we take a look back at the risks identified in the last section, we can see that governments are in a strong position to act. They are entrusted with fostering public goods.

Governments have the policy tools to reduce damaging inequality and to ensure minorities have their human rights safeguarded. They can take steps to encourage entrepreneurs who could provide tomorrow's innovations and jobs. They can introduce measures to maintain fairness in market mechanisms, take action against anti-competitive practices, and impose fair regulatory regimes on busi-nesses. These policies must take account of societal goals and issues of sustaina-bility. For example, channelling money into industries that will provide jobs, but are heavy polluters, is not sustainable. Governments must now recognize the fact that economic growth must take account of a carbon-constrained future environment (Woodward, 2015).

The climate change agreement of 2015 is one example of international co-operation that holds out real prospects for reducing the impacts of climate change. But governments must carry out their intended reductions in emissions. This requires taking actions that many will resist, especially large companies with vested interests in fossil fuels. Before the Paris conference, ten global oil and gas companies, including BP, Shell, Total and Statoil, pledged to do more to reduce emissions, but the two American oil giants, Chevron and ExxonMobil, did not. This situation is indicative of the difficulties that arise when we expect governments to achieve social and environmental objectives, even when they have the policy tools to hand. These companies, and other American multinationals, also benefit from US trade policy and trade agreements, both bilateral and plurilateral. Incorporating investor-state dispute settlement (ISDS) clauses, these agreements facilitate American companies in over-riding environmental and social legislation in countries where they have invested, as the case study on the fuel additive MMT in Canada showed (Chapter 7). The US government has thus pursued positive policies to thwart legislation in other countries that attempts to raise standards of sustainability.

The holders of economic power in most countries, notably large businesses, whether in the private sector or state-owned, hold considerable sway over government policies. This is only partly because these companies develop the expertise to lobby effectively. It is mainly attributable to the fact that those holding economic power and those in the corridors of political power overlap to a great extent. Economic élites are the most forceful voices in influencing government policy in the US, as we saw in Chapter 5. A result is that public goods take a back seat to the interests of the country's big businesses. The so-called revolving door between business and politics is a source of corruption. Legislators who design laws at the behest of a large company can expect funding from the company for their next election campaign, and a board seat or consultancy when their term of office ends. Those legislators should be serving the public, but are more likely to serve the interests of those who fund their next political campaign. Companies commonly portray themselves in a compliance role as simply as abiding by the law of the land. This portrayal is disingenuous in many cases, as they actively seek to shape laws and fund friendly politicians' campaigns. Laws that would be unpopular with large companies are unlikely to reach the statute book in the US, and, if they do, could well be challenged through the courts in protracted lawsuits. The Affordable Care Act ('Obamacare'), creating a universal health insurance scheme, passed the two houses of Congress late in 2009, when there was a Democratic majority in the lower house, and a majority of just one vote in the Senate, the upper house. By early 2016, it would have stood no chance of passage, and it has been challenged repeatedly in the courts since it was signed by the president in 2010. It has been the subject of two Supreme Court rulings over this period, the latest in 2015, when, by a majority of 6 to 3, the highest court ruled that subsidies to the poor for health insurance were legal under the constitution.

Looking at the UN's Sustainable Development Goals (SDGs) provides an example of the contrast between expectations of government action and the realities that would seem to nullify those expectations. Figure 12.4 reproduces Figure 10.5. The SDGs are addressed to governments. There is no mention of what

1 End extreme poverty (less than $1.25 a day)

2 End hunger; achieve food security and sustainable agriculture

3 Ensure good health and well-being

4 Ensure inclusive and quality education

5 Achieve gender equality

6 Ensure safe drinking water and sanitation for all

UN Sustainable Development Goals (SDGs)

7 Ensure affordable, clean energy for all

8 Promote decent work and inclusive, sustainable economic growth

9 Promote inclusive and sustainable industrialization, including infrastructure and innovation

10 Reduce inequality within and between countries

11 Make cities safe, inclusive and sustainable

12 Ensure sustainable consumption and production

13 Combat climate change

14 Conserve the oceans and seas

15 Promote sustainable use of land

16 Promote peace, justice and inclusive institutions

17 Strengthen global partnership for SDGs

Figure 12.4 UN Sustainable Development Goals (SDGs), 2015–2030

Source: Data from UNDP (UN Development Programme) (2015) *Sustainable Development Goals Booklet*, 28 September, at www.undp.org, accessed 30 September 2015.

corporations should be committed to do, although all these goals involve business activities. The only reference to companies is in the global partnership mentioned in SDG 17. That refers to the UN Global Compact (www.unglobalcompact.org), whereby companies voluntarily sign up to principles of sustainability, anti-corruption and human rights. It involves no compliance obligations or responsibilities that commit corporate leaders. In Chapter 10, we queried whether the SDGs were just a wish list. Governments are in a position to deliver some of them, mostly those that involve public services such as education and health. But what about sustainable agriculture, industrialization and infrastructure? Should not companies bear at least some responsibility for these aspects of development? The assumption underlying the SDGs seems to be that companies essentially pursue profits, not social goals, so companies bear no responsibilities where there is hunger (SDG 1) or demeaning work (SDG 8). The goal in SDG 8 is to 'promote' decent work. But, as we have seen in the case study in this chapter, governments are loath to impose high standards of health and safety for fear of raising costs for companies that might shift production to other, less-regulated, locations. On these assumptions, businesses are grounded in corporate cultures that do not commit them to social and environmental goals. Many would now hold that this situation is unsustainable, and that businesses do have responsibilities, even if the SDGs do not recognize them.

Businesses

The question posed at the start of this chapter – What does the business exist to do? – raises more profound issues than simply those of making money to carry on producing goods and services. This narrow view of the business is purely economic, and is underpinned by a deeply-ingrained belief in the validity of self-interested profit-seeking. As this book has shown, however, businesses play roles in societies that go far beyond the economic dimension. Businesses are significant in influencing lifestyles and spending patterns. Their policies and activities are key to safe and healthy working conditions, standards of living, air quality, quality of healthcare, food safety, and adherence to human rights. The list could go on. These issues matter to people everywhere, and businesses are as instrumental as governments in determining how high, or low, the prevailing standards are. A business might take the line that its goal is to maximize wealth for its owners, and it abides by the national laws in place in each country. It would also probably claim that it is thus a good citizen in each. However, this minimalist approach does not translate into the company taking on a sense of responsibility to all the stakeholders in that society. Corporate strategy in the global environment typically includes seeking ways to divert profits to low-tax jurisdictions and doing deals with governments to obtain legal advantages, including tax advantages. For many companies, it also includes denying workers the right to organize, despite labour laws at national and international level. Typically, workers who organize into unions are fired for an unrelated disciplinary reason such as bad timekeeping.

Global brands that source products in developing countries regularly denounce the use of practices such as child labour, but those practices nonetheless continue. To disclaim responsibility in these circumstances is untenable. The companies whose brands appear on the products are responsible, but executives are well aware that they are never likely to be held liable for criminal wrongdoing. They are able to assert moral disapproval, confident that they will not be held to account. But this does not mean they are absolved of responsibility, only that they are not likely to be held accountable in the courts. Such an attitude to law and morals would probably strike most people as unworthy. In a society other than a police state, people obey the law because it is the right thing to do, and they expect others to do likewise. They expect companies to do the same. Companies do get caught on occasion, as the case studies in this book have shown. Examples include GSK in a bribery case in China (Chapter 9) and Volkswagen in the case of defeat devices that understate emissions (Chapter 10). In both, unethical corporate culture was partly to blame.

Consumers, employees and the public generally wish to see improved safety standards in products and workplaces, an end to tax evasion, and humane treatment of employees. Concern about business reputation is one of the means by which a company can be encouraged to engage with social responsibility. But many companies probably feel immune even from this negative publicity. In Italy in March 2015, the Milan prosecutor charged Apple with tax evasion, which is a crime (Agnew, 2015). Apple operated a scheme whereby Apple Italia directed money from its sales in Italy to Apple Ireland, as Ireland had a much lower rate of tax. Apple Italia was designated a 'consultant' for Apple Ireland. The prosecutors have alleged that this amounts to fraud, as Apple was in fact selling iPhones and other products in Italy. Two senior executives of Apple Italia and one at Apple Ireland have been notified by the Milan prosecutor that they could face trial and imprisonment. The EU Commission has long had Apple in its sights for tax avoidance arrangements in Ireland, to which Apple has responded, saying it wanted to be a 'good corporate citizen' (Agnew, 2015). Later in 2015, Apple agreed to pay the Italian authorities €318 million in back tax, but this payment did not halt the criminal proceedings by the Milan prosecutor against Apple's three executives. It will be recalled from the case study in Chapter 11 that Apple is rated the world's most respected company.

The way I see it ...

'I know I am not the first person to be injured. But more needs to be done to help the workers who are making the products that so many Americans buy. We don't ask for even a tiny share of the billions these companies make. We are just asking for enough to take care of our families and, when we are hurt, to take care of ourselves, too.'

Rosa Moreno, a worker in a flatscreen factory in Mexico, who lost both hands in a machinery accident. She was offered $3,800 by the company, HD Electronics, which was contracted to LG Electronics. With the help of lawyers who worked for no fee, she launched a lawsuit against LG Electronics in Texas, which failed on a technicality. Quoted in *The Guardian*, 11 June 2015.

What could be done to improve the situation for Rosa Moreno and the millions of workers who have had similar experiences?

Lexmark is an American printer and software company, with global revenues of $3.7 billion, making it one of the world's largest printer companies. It manufactures in the US and in Mexico, where wages and taxes are lower than in the US. Lexmark has been found guilty of 'wage theft' from its factory workers in California. Workers at its printer cartridge factory in Ciudad Juarez in Mexico complain of unhealthy conditions, as one records:

They didn't provide face masks or gloves to protect us, many people have injured hands. They cut our salaries for being even slightly late, even if our children were sick and we had to take them to hospital, and we had to put up with harassment from supervisors. (Lakhani and Thielman, 2015)

When workers at the factory asked for a pay rise of the equivalent of $.35 a day, Lexmark managers refused. Seven hundred workers went on strike. Of these, 78 had submitted an application to the state government to form an independent trade union to achieve better pay and safer working conditions. The company responded by sacking 120 workers, including all who had applied to form a union. The workers suspect that the sacking was co-ordinated with the government, which had a record of the names of the 78 applicants. Ciudad Juarez benefits from the provisions of the NAFTA, allowing access to US markets. A Lexmark spokesman said, 'We take our values of mutual respect and employee satisfaction very seriously' (Lakhani and Thielman, 2015). Given the evidence of the working conditions and the accusations of human rights violations, this hardly seems credible. In this case, Lexmark is the direct employer, not a contractor (as in the box above on 'The way I see it ...'). The record of wage theft in California was found to go back to 1991, when the company was separated off from its parent company, IBM. These companies, like others mentioned in this section, are not isolated rogue employers. They are well-known global brands whose products are bought by millions of consumers. Businesses like these are playing significant roles in societies, but in the cases cited here, they are not acknowledging the responsibilities that go with those roles. They are focused on profits above all, and, in the process, taking a risky approach towards compliance with laws. Such examples are not conducive to building a sustainable business.

Envisaging a new perspective

Companies are often said to be short-termist in their focus on profits and share price, and executives blame this preoccupation on the need to focus on shareholder value. Would a long-term approach be closer to one that encompasses social responsibility? Arguably, it would. But what would shareholders think? It is simplistic to assume that shareholders are interested only in short-term profits. Shareholders are interested, above all, in a viable business that can be sustained into the future. If the business is viable, then profits, it is often said, will look after themselves. And they are interested in other things besides. Institutional shareholders are now particularly aware of the ethical dimension of investments. Many are divesting shares in fossil-fuel industries. This is an ethical decision, but it is also a business-oriented one. The risks associated with fossil fuels are now a major consideration in light of the urgency of climate change. These businesses, including large oil and gas companies, will have to adjust to a carbon-constrained future, as a business-as-usual approach to oil extraction is no longer viable. In this instance, ethical and sustainability concerns point towards taking a longer-term approach, and also one that acknowledges the responsibility that falls on companies.

On other issues, too, the responsible approach and long-term business viability coalesce. Poor treatment of workers, as has been shown, is not confined to shady subcontractors, nor to developing countries. Global brands such as Amazon, operating in western environments, are accused of human rights breaches. It has been thought that the world has progressed beyond Dickensian workshop conditions, but modern methods, though more technologically advanced, are capable of imposing similar harsh conditions on workers. Many other practices, including zero-hours contracts, are also verging on human rights violations, but persist nonetheless. Improving conditions and pay, and offering genuine employment contracts for full-time commitment, would cost more, but, as long as the firm is making a reasonable profit, would reflect the responsibility that employers owe to employees, whether covered by specific national laws or not. The firm must be able to adjust to the idea of a reasonable profit that will sustain the business, in contrast to an obsession with maximizing profits ahead of all other concerns. Excessive greed was one of the aspects of the culture of banking that helped to bring down global banks in the financial crisis. They are timely examples of the perils of short-termism, and should be a lesson that prudent attention to serving the interests of stakeholders is the only way towards a sustainable future. That future will not bring in the mind-boggling profits that the pre-crisis banks were accumulating, or that Apple is currently accumulating. But executives would be more confident that when they claim to be socially responsible, it is not just rhetoric for media consumption.

Many companies, like technology giants Google, Microsoft and Facebook, make a point of emphasizing their CSR in the form of philanthropy. Their founders have accumulated billions of dollars in wealth, and they are prepared to create charitable foundations to 'give back' to society some of that wealth for good causes of their choice. These are worthy goals, although they come with provisos that the money is used as their owners see fit. However, philanthropy is only one small aspect of CSR. What matters more is how the wealth was accumulated in the first place. In this respect, these companies are not so socially responsible. Their owners' billions are derived from business empires that have more power than many states. Their

What springs to mind when Panama is mentioned? Until recently, the Panama Canal or the picturesque coastline shown here would probably have been the answer, but now, this small country has achieved notoriety with revelations from leaked documents of its role at the centre of massive tax-dodging networks.

Source: iStock.com/LisaStrachan.

businesses have profited from the mass collection of personal data, combined with weak privacy protection. Profits are channelled into offshore schemes that amount to systematic tax avoidance. The extent of offshored wealth, held by companies and individuals, is now gradually coming to light, highlighting the ways in which the rich and powerful are able to escape national tax frameworks. Lobbying and other types of political funding, as the examples in this book have shown, have been designed to maintain a business-friendly regulatory environment in which to maximize profits. These companies are also noted for their anti-competitive practices and employment practices that discriminate against women and ethnic minorities. Moreover, the creation of dual share structures and shares with no votes undermine any professed commitment to shareholder value. They, and others in the 1%, can make a difference in social outcomes with philanthropic initiatives, but their impacts are limited and piecemeal, given the scale of the problems faced by societies globally. These technology companies, through their profit-maximizing activities, continue to have huge impacts on societies. They extol the freedom of the internet, which empowers people globally, but the mass collection of private data poses threats to values of individual freedoms.

Technology companies would seem to have a bright future, as technological innovation races ahead. As we have seen, however, companies like Google make their profits largely from advertising and selling services to consumers. Competitors are continually threatening to topple those at the top in sectors such as social media, where continued popularity among consumers cannot be assumed. And consumers are now openly critical of unethical corporate behaviour, not to mention breaches of the law. The multiple dimensions of the environment that have featured in this book have shown that a business has numerous stakeholder concerns and responsibilities. Respecting and responding to them are part of what executives and managers should be doing. Shareholders would thank them, and so would those in societies. People are looking for companies to provide goods and services that serve social and environmental goals. Those that do will have a future. Those that do not will rue the missed opportunities.

References

Agnew, P. (2015) 'Apple Italy accused of using Cork affiliate to avoid tax', *The Irish Times*, 24 March, at www.irishtimes.com

Buck, T. (2014) 'Spanish upstart party challenges status quo', *Financial Times*, 22 November.

Deaton, A. (2013) *The Great Escape: Health, Wealth and the Origins of Inequality* (Princeton, NJ: Princeton University Press).

Dorling, D. (2015) *Inequality and the 1%* (London: Verso Books).

Ehrenfreund, M. (2015) 'The stunning – and expanding – gap in life expectancy between the rich and the poor', *The Washington Post*, 18 September, at www.washingtonpost.com

Kingsley, P. (2015) 'Over a million migrants and refugees have reached Europe this year, says IOM', *The Guardian*, 22 December.

Lakhani, N. and Thielman, S. (2015) 'Printer giant Lexmark fires Mexico factory workers demanding $.35 raise', *The Guardian*, 15 December, at www.theguardian.com.

Pew Research Center (2015) 'The American middle class is losing ground', Social and Demographic Trends, 9 December, at www.pewsocialtrends.org

Phillips, T. (2015) 'China democracy activist Guo Feixiong jailed for six years in Xi crackdown', *The Guardian*, 27 November.

Reich, R. (2015) *Saving Capitalism: For the Many, not the Few* (New York: Knopf).

Stiglitz, J. (2013) *The Price of Inequality* (London: Penguin).

Thorsen, O. (2014) 'Food, farming and antibiotics: a health challenge for business', *The Guardian*, 7 August.

Wolf, M. (2015) 'A world of difference', *Financial Times*, 2 May, at www.ft.com

Woodward, D. (2015) 'Incrementum ad absurdum: global growth, inequality and poverty eradication in a carbon-constrained world', *World Economic Review*, 4: 43–62.

Multiple choice questions

Go to the companion website: www.palgravehighered.com/morrison-gbe-4e to take a quick multiple choice quiz on what you have read in this chapter.

Review questions

1 What are the challenges to business associated with climate change?
2 What are the dilemmas faced by regulators in market economies?
3 In what ways does corruption undermine goals of sustainability?
4 On what grounds can businesses be held responsible for social impacts of their operations?
5 Why does large-scale agribusiness pose risks to sustainability?
6 Why are governments now increasingly concerned about inequality?
7 What is meant by the 'hollowing out' of society?
8 What are the issues involved for European countries receiving large numbers of migrants and refugees?
9 What are the risks to democracy when electoral institutions become simply formal exercises?
10 Political parties in many countries become bureaucratic and inward-focused. How does this harm democratic politics?

11 What are the risks to social and environmental legislation in the ISDS process that features in numerous bilateral and plurilateral treaties?

12 Why are the Sustainable Development Goals (SDGs) likely to be seen as difficult for governments to deliver?

13 How could businesses commit to relevant SDGs?

14 Why would a focus on stakeholder interests be more conducive to sustainable business than one on shareholder value?

15 How could institutional investors promote better adherence to ethical policies in the companies they invest in?

✓ Assignments

1 China has become a model for economic development that can boast impressive accomplishments, including rapid industrialization and significant reduction in poverty. Other emerging economies have thus been swayed towards the Chinese developmental approach, which diverges radically from the American model of a free-market economy. Assess how well the Chinese model of development is suited to promoting sustainable development.

2 Agriculture and food processing present some of the most significant challenges for human well-being. Both have become globalized, industrialized and dominated by a small number of companies. What threats are present in these trends, and how could they be controlled?

📖 Further reading

Aglietta, M. and Bai, G. (2015) *China's Development: Capitalism and Empire* (Rethinking Globalizations) (London: Routledge).

Collier, P. (2008) *The Bottom Billion* (Oxford: OUP).

Collier, P. (2014) *Exodus: Immigration and Multiculturalism in the 21st Century* (London: Penguin).

Deaton, A. (2013) *The Great Escape: Health, Wealth and the Origins of Inequality* (Princeton: Princeton University Press).

Dorling, D. (2015) *Inequality and the 1%* (London: Verso Books).

Roy, A. (2014) *Capitalism: A Ghost Story* (London: Verso Books).

Stiglitz, J. (2013) *The Price of Inequality* (London: Penguin).

Woodward, D. (2015) 'Incrementum ad absurdum: global growth, inequality and poverty eradication in a carbon-constrained world', *World Economic Review*, 4: 43–62.

🌐 **Visit the companion website at** www.palgravehighered.com/morrison-gbe-4e **for further learning and teaching resources.**

Wal-Mart: a story of the few and the many

Sam Walton, the founder of Wal-Mart, who died in 1992, was famous for his business approach focused on keeping down costs. He was also highly successful in managing the Walton family fortune. In 1953, he created his first trust fund in the name of his eldest daughter, who was 9 at the time. At that stage, he had only a modest retail business – the first Walmart store opened in 1962 (see Note). His early planning to avoid estate taxes and gift taxes has paid off handsomely. The Walton family is worth over $140 billion in total, more than the wealth of the bottom 42% of the US population. This money is protected in trusts that effectively pass on family wealth, tax-free, to later generations. The methods of charitable and estate planning are entirely legal. A former US Treasury Secretary, Lawrence Sumners, has expressed disappointment that the system of collection of estate and gift tax in the US raised just $14 billion in 2012. This is 1% of the amount passed on by the very rich to their descendants in a year – a sum that was then $1.2 trillion (Mider, 2013).

The Walton business empire is based in Bentonville, Arkansas, one of the mainly rural southern states where poorer families have been Walmart's main market over the years. Walmart aims to keep costs down so that customers pay less. This philosophy has proved highly profitable. Walmart's annual revenues amount to $476 billion. But low-cost policies have often stirred controversy. Walmart employs 2.2 million people worldwide, 1.4 million of them in the US, making Walmart the country's largest private-sector employer. These are overwhelmingly low-paid workers. Along with fast-food outlets like McDonald's, Walmart stands out as an exemplar of what many now see as the cause of poverty among America's low-paid workers. The US federal minimum wage, last raised in 2009, is $7.25 per hour. Many states have minimum wage thresholds slightly higher, but not as much as $10. Even at $10, workers are below the poverty line, and need to rely on government safety-net programmes in the form of 'food stamps' and Medicaid. Walmart employees, known as 'associates', form one of the largest groups or workers receiving federal aid.

Protests by employees and labour groups have become common in recent years, targeting Walmart not just for its low wages, but for practices such as sex discrimination and blocking the right of workers to join trade unions. Workers have called for a minimum hourly rate of $15 as a living wage. In 2015, Walmart announced it would raise the minimum to $9, in a move which would lift the pay of 500,000 workers, although it would hardly move most out of poverty. Walmart executives' deeply engrained cost-cutting and profit maximization have tended to prevail over considerations of employee welfare. However, worker protests, combined with lacklustre financial performance and low rankings in consumer satisfaction surveys, perhaps persuaded executives to take this initiative. It would help to reduce staff turnover and improve morale, which in turn would benefit the business numbers. Walmart has been criticized in other respects, such as animal welfare and supply chain safety issues. In both these areas, it has taken limited voluntary steps that stop short of binding commitment. Walmart is the largest gun retailer in the US. A proposal by a church group to have the shareholders vote on restricting gun sales was rejected by Walmart. The church group then applied to the court and won. But Walmart appealed, and the court of appeals ruled in favour of the company in 2015.

Walmart has sought to expand in emerging markets such as China, where it has operated stores since 1996. These stores have proved challenging, and local retailers, more attuned to Chinese customers' demands for quality rather than simply low price, have had a competitive edge over Walmart. It has had successful operations in the UK, with its takeover of ASDA, but UK supermarkets generally have seen weak financial performance in recent years. Walmart has no stores in Luxembourg. However, it has 22 offshore subsidiaries registered in Luxembourg, which are used to shelter profits amounting to $64 billion, on which it pays tax at a rate of 1%. The Walton family has famously kept the

Walmart empire in family hands, despite the fact that it is a listed company. Through charitable trusts, the family owns just over half the company. When a son-in-law took over from Rob Walton, a son of Sam Walton, as chairman in 2015, he said that Walmart was committed to 'long-term succession planning' (Whipp, 2015). This would be true of both the business and the family fortune.

Note: Wal-Mart Stores Inc. is the name of the listed company, and Walmart, without the hyphen, is now used as the trading name for the stores.

Sources: Crow, D. and Fleming, S. (2015) 'Walmart raises the bar for low-pay employers', *Financial Times*, 21 February, at www.ft.com; Mider, Z. (2013) 'How Wal-Mart's Waltons maintain their billionaire fortune: taxes', *Bloomberg News*, 12 September, at www.bloomberg.com; Whipp, L. (2015) 'Walton exit marks Walmart milestone', *Financial Times*, 6 June; Dewson, A. (2015) 'Wal-Mart does so much wrong, but the shame is that none of it is illegal', *The Independent*, 19 June, at www.independent.co.uk.

Questions for discussion

- What are the grounds for complaints by Walmart's low-paid workers?
- What impact will the rise in minimum hourly wage achieve, in your view?
- To what extent is Walmart a socially responsible company?
- What steps could be taken by the US government to rein in the inequality exemplified by the Walton family?

APPENDIX
ATLAS

THE WORLD

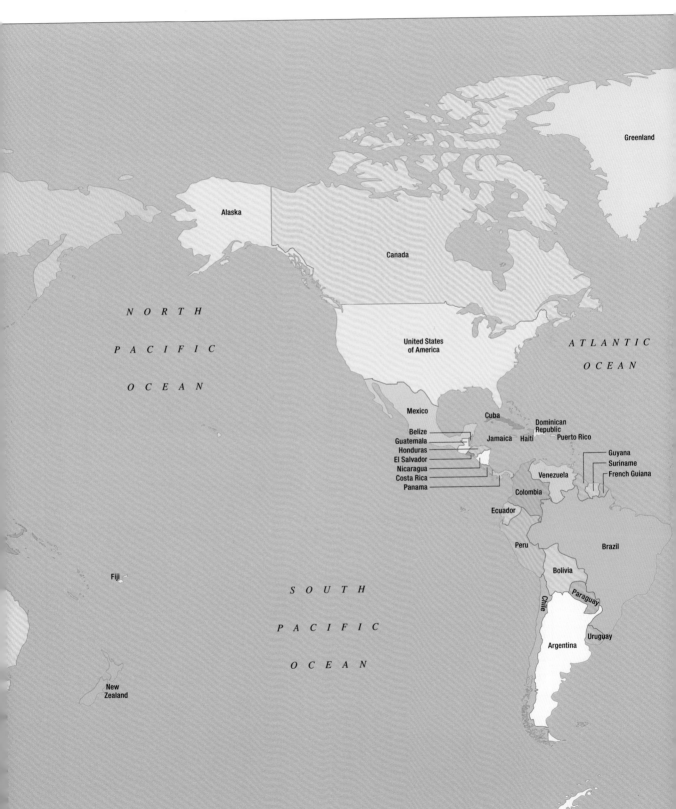

Greenland

Alaska

Canada

N O R T H

P A C I F I C

O C E A N

A T L A N T I C

O C E A N

United States
of America

Mexico

Cuba

Dominican
Republic

Belize

Guatemala   Jamaica   Haiti   Puerto Rico

Honduras

El Salvador

Guyana

Nicaragua   Suriname

Costa Rica   French Guiana

Panama   Venezuela

Colombia

Ecuador

Peru   Brazil

S O U T H   Bolivia

Fiji

Paraguay

P A C I F I C   Chile

Uruguay

O C E A N   Argentina

New
Zealand

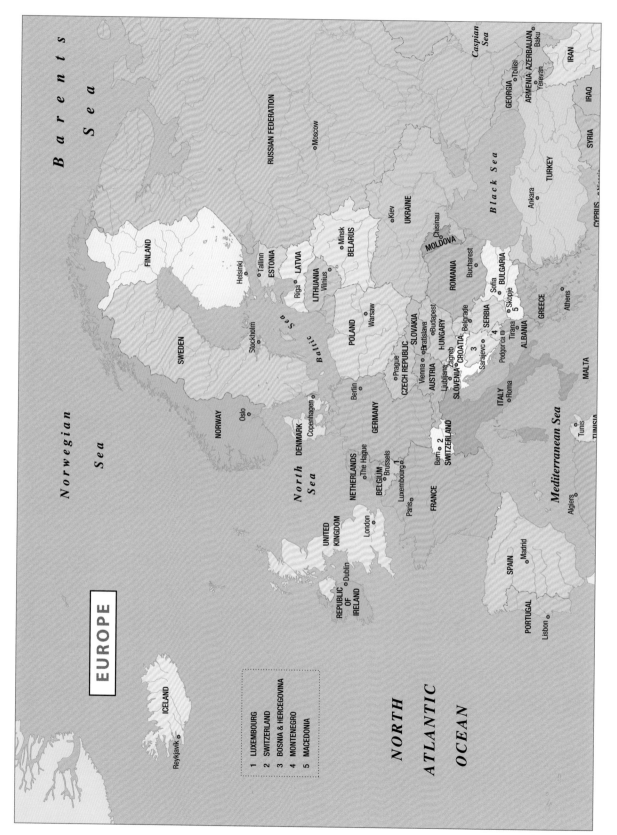

EUROPE

Barents Sea

Norwegian Sea

RUSSIAN FEDERATION

Moscow

FINLAND

Helsinki

ESTONIA
Tallinn
Riga
LATVIA
LITHUANIA
Vilnius

BELARUS
Minsk

Kiev
UKRAINE

Chisinau
MOLDOVA

Caspian Sea

GEORGIA
Tbilisi
ARMENIA AZERBAIJAN
Yerevan
Baku
IRAN

IRAQ

SYRIA

TURKEY
Ankara

Black Sea

ROMANIA
Bucharest

Sofia
BULGARIA
Skopje
5
GREECE
Athens

CYPRUS

SWEDEN

Stockholm

Baltic Sea

POLAND
Warsaw

SLOVAKIA
Bratislava
Budapest
HUNGARY
SERBIA
Belgrade
Zagreb
4
Tirana
ALBANIA
3
Sarajevo
Podgorica

NORWAY
Oslo

DENMARK
Copenhagen

Berlin
GERMANY

Prague
CZECH REPUBLIC
Vienna
AUSTRIA
Ljubljana
SLOVENIA
CROATIA

ITALY
Roma

MALTA

Mediterranean Sea

Tunis
TUNISIA

North Sea

NETHERLANDS
The Hague
Brussels
BELGIUM
1
Luxembourg
Paris
FRANCE

Bern
2
SWITZERLAND

UNITED KINGDOM
London

REPUBLIC OF IRELAND
Dublin

SPAIN
Madrid

PORTUGAL
Lisbon

Algiers

ICELAND
Reykjavik

NORTH
ATLANTIC
OCEAN

1 LUXEMBOURG
2 SWITZERLAND
3 BOSNIA & HERCEGOVINA
4 MONTENEGRO
5 MACEDONIA

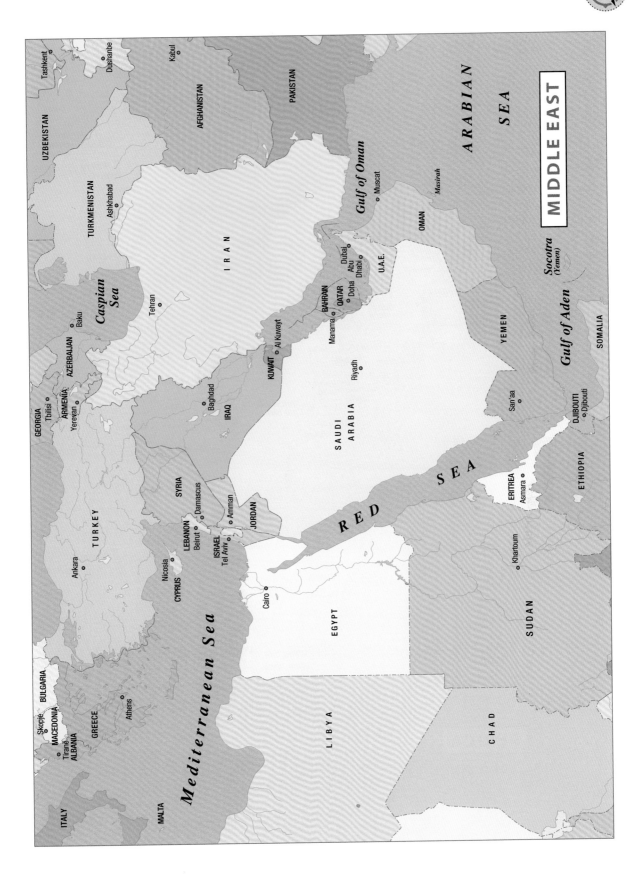

MIDDLE EAST

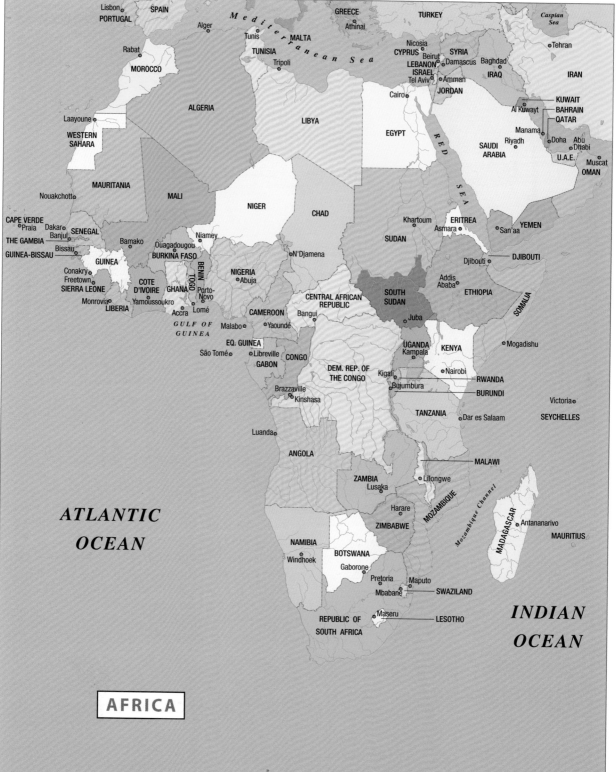

ATLANTIC OCEAN

INDIAN OCEAN

AFRICA

GUATEMALA
San Salvador • Tegucigalpa
EL SALVADOR
NICARAGUA
• Managua

CARIBBEAN SEA

ST. LUCIA
ST. VINCENT &
THE GRENADINES
GRENADA
Caracas

BARBADOS
• Bridgetown

TRINIDAD
& TOBAGO
Port of Spain

San José
COSTA RICA
Panama
City
PANAMA

VENEZUELA

Georgetown
Paramaribo
GUYANA
Cayenne
SURINAME
FRENCH
GUIANA

COLOMBIA
Bogotá •

Quito
•
ECUADOR

PERU

BRAZIL

Lima •

La Paz BOLIVIA
•
Sucre
(Legal Capital)

Brasilia •

SOUTH AMERICA

PARAGUAY
Asunción
•

SOUTH
PACIFIC
OCEAN

CHILE

ARGENTINA

URUGUAY

SOUTH
ATLANTIC
OCEAN

Santiago •
Buenos Aires •
Montevideo •

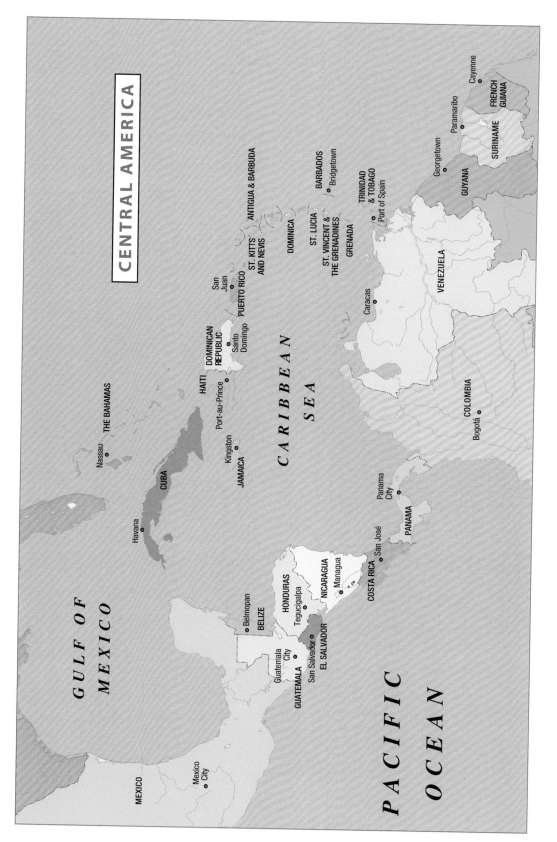

CENTRAL AMERICA

GULF OF MEXICO

PACIFIC OCEAN

CARIBBEAN SEA

MEXICO

Mexico City

THE BAHAMAS

Nassau

CUBA

Havana

JAMAICA

Kingston

HAITI

Port-au-Prince

DOMINICAN REPUBLIC

Santo Domingo

PUERTO RICO

San Juan

ST. KITTS AND NEVIS

ANTIGUA & BARBUDA

DOMINICA

ST. LUCIA

BARBADOS

Bridgetown

ST. VINCENT & THE GRENADINES

GRENADA

TRINIDAD & TOBAGO

Port of Spain

Caracas

VENEZUELA

GUYANA

Georgetown

SURINAME

Paramaribo

FRENCH GUIANA

Cayenne

COLOMBIA

Bogotá

BELIZE

Belmopan

GUATEMALA

Guatemala City

EL SALVADOR

San Salvador

HONDURAS

Tegucigalpa

NICARAGUA

Managua

COSTA RICA

San José

PANAMA

Panama City

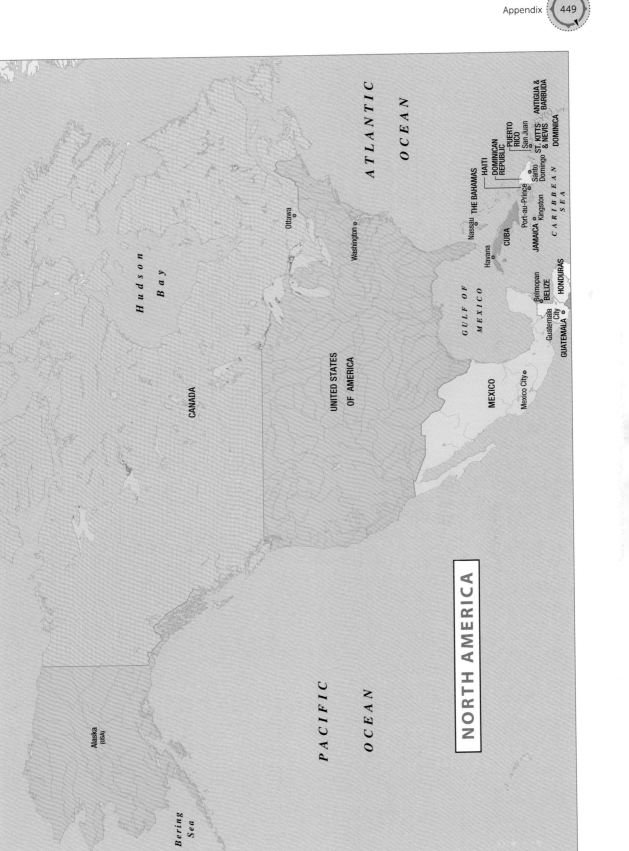

NORTH AMERICA

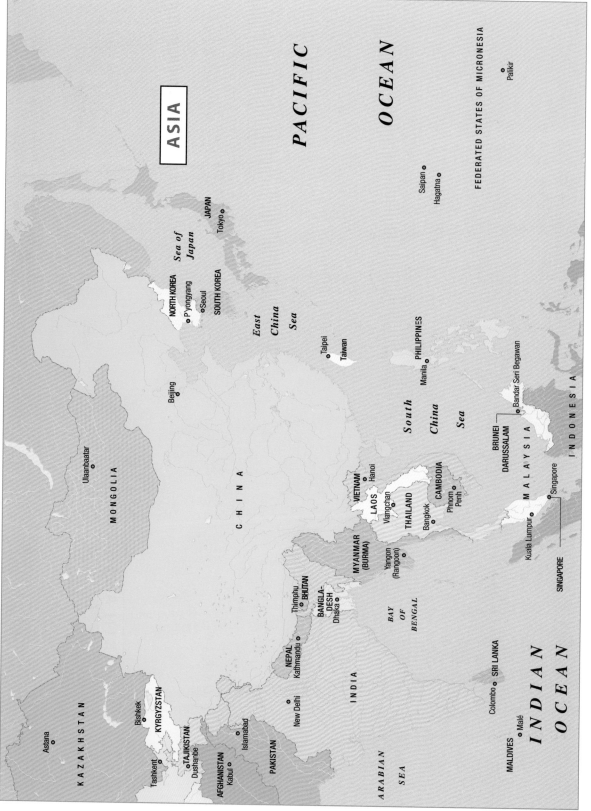

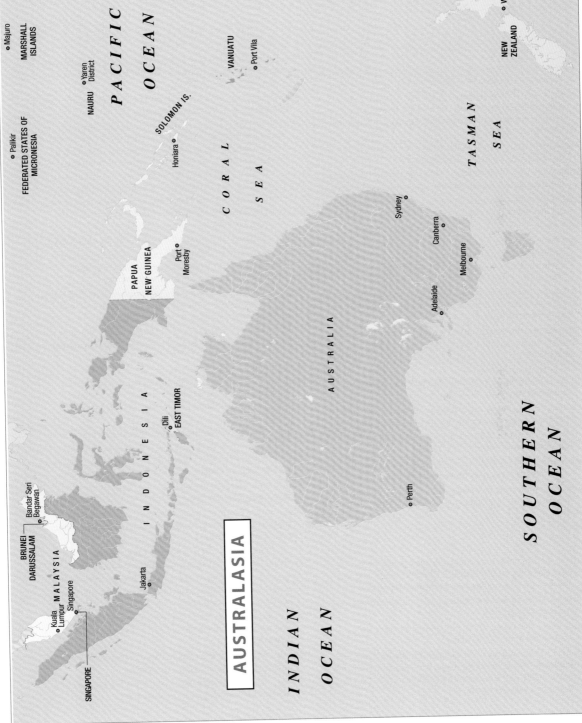

AUSTRALASIA

INDIAN
OCEAN

SOUTHERN
OCEAN

AUSTRALIA

• Perth

Adelaide
•

Melbourne
•

Canberra
•

Sydney
•

TASMAN
SEA

NEW
ZEALAND

• Wellington

CORAL
SEA

PAPUA
NEW GUINEA

Port
Moresby •

EAST TIMOR
Dili •

INDONESIA

Jakarta •

SINGAPORE

Kuala
Lumpur •
Singapore

MALAYSIA

BRUNEI
DARUSSALAM

Bandar Seri
Begawan •

SOLOMON IS.

Honiara •

VANUATU
• Port Vila

FIJI
Suva •

PACIFIC
OCEAN

FEDERATED STATES OF
MICRONESIA

Palikir •

NAURU • Yaren
District

MARSHALL
ISLANDS

Majuro •

KIRIBATI

TUVALU
• Fongafali

GLOSSARY

A

absolute advantage enjoyed by a country which is more efficient at producing a particular product than any other country

acid rain acid from greenhouse gases that falls out of the atmosphere, in the form of rain or wind-blown gases, causing environmental degradation, damage to buildings and risks to health

acquisition type of FDI in which an investor purchases an existing company in a foreign location

affiliate company organization connected through ownership or other strategic ties to an MNE, often in supply chains

ageing demographic trend characterized by a rising proportion of older people in a population

Andean Community South American free trade area

anti-dumping agreement WTO rules which allow anti-dumping duties to be imposed on the exporting country by the importing country in order to protect local producers from unfair competition

arbitration the submission of a legal dispute to a named person or organization in accordance with a contractual agreement; an alternative to litigation

arm's length contracting business dealings between people who interact only for the purpose of doing business with each other

Asian Infrastructure Investment Bank (AIIB) development bank launched by China, providing funding on a similar basis to the World Bank

assimilation of cultures process by which minority cultures become integrated into the mainstream culture of a nation

Association of South EAST Asian Nations (ASEAN) co-operation agreement of South East Asian countries

Asia-Pacific Economic Cooperation (APEC) co-operation agreement of economies bordering on the Pacific

authoritarianism rule by a single leader or group of individuals, often sustained by an ideology associated with a one-party state

B

balance of payments total credit and debit transactions between a country's residents (including companies) and those of other countries over a specified period of time

bilateral treaty agreement between two countries, often for reciprocal trade terms

biodiversity the variety of living organisms and species co-existing in the same habitat

board of directors body comprising all the directors of a company, including executive and non-executive, which is accountable to the company's shareholders; can be a single board or a two-tier board

bond a loan instrument which promises to pay a specific sum of money on a fixed date, and to pay interest at stated intervals

born-global firm SME which aims to become global from the outset, often in the high-tech sector

Bretton Woods agreement agreement between the allied nations in the aftermath of the Second World War which was intended to bring about exchange rate stability and foster multilateral agreements to dismantle trade barriers; established the IMF and World Bank

BRIC countries collective reference to Brazil, Russia, India and China, as a grouping of emerging economies; now extends to other emerging economies, such as Indonesia, South Africa and Nigeria

Buddhism Asian religion based on the teachings of Buddha

business any type of economic activity in which goods or services (or a combination of the two) are supplied in exchange for some payment, usually money

business case for CSR argument that business goals will be met more successfully in the longer term through CSR than through a narrow focus on economic goals

business functions activities of a business which form part of the overall process of providing a product for a customer

C

capital account in connection with an economy's balance of payments, account based on transactions involving the sale and purchase of assets, such as investment in shares

carbon footprint the amount of greenhouse gases produced either directly or indirectly by an organization or country

cartel group of firms that come together, often informally, to restrict trade or engage in anti-competitive behaviour

caste system social stratification system based on birth; associated with Hinduism

categorical imperative ethical principle put forward by Kant that respect for every human being should be the guiding principle for behaviour

chaebol family-dominated industrial conglomerate characteristic of business organizations in South Korea

checks and balances principle by which the three branches of government (legislative, executive and judicial) share legal authority and accountability

chief executive officer (CEO) a company's senior executive who oversees its management and is accountable to the board of directors

Christianity monotheistic religion based on belief in Jesus Christ, whose teachings are in the Bible

civil (or private) law in any legal system, the law pertaining to relations between private individuals and companies

civil law tradition legal system based on comprehensive legal codes which form the basic law

civil society sphere of activities in society in which citizens are free to pursue personal interests and form associations freely

climate change any change in the climate over time, whether from natural causes or human activity

coalition government government composed of two or more parties, usually arising in situations where no single party has obtained a majority of seats in legislative elections

codes of practice sets of rules which companies voluntarily follow to guide their CSR, ethical and environmental practices

co-determination principle of stakeholder participation in corporate governance, usually involving a two-tier board, with employee representation on the supervisory board

common law tradition legal system based chiefly on accumulated case law in decided judgments, through a system of binding precedents

common market regional grouping in which member states enjoy free movement of goods, labour and capital

community interest company (CIC) a limited company set up to function as a social enterprise which obeys strict statutory requirements for adhering to social purposes

company a legal form of organization which has a separate legal identity from its owners; also called a 'corporation'

comparative advantage enjoyed by a country where production of a particular product involves greater relative advantage than would be possible anywhere else

competitive advantage theory (devised by Porter) that international competitiveness depends on four major factors: demand conditions, factor conditions, firms' strategy and supporting industries

competition law area of law which concerns rules against abuse of a dominant market position and unfair trading practices by one or more firms

Confucianism ancient Chinese ethical and philosophical system based on the teachings of Confucius

conglomerate large, diversified company, in which there is no single identifiable core business

consequentialist principle utilitarian principle that the test of the rightness or wrongness of an action depends on the results which flow from it

constitutionalism set of rules, grounded in a society's shared beliefs, about the source of authority in the state and its institutional forms

consumer price index (CPI) index which tracks the percentage rise or fall in prices, with reference to a specific starting point in time

contextualism in ethical thinking, the principle that ideas of right and wrong stem from specific cultural environments

corporate citizenship concept which visualizes the social responsibility of the firm in the community as analogous to that of the individual citizen, entailing obligations to obey the law and pay taxes

corporate governance a company's structures and processes for decision-making at the highest level

corporate social performance (CSP) concept associated with CSR in practice which focuses on responses to stakeholders and broader issues of business in society

corporate social responsibility (CSR) an approach to business which recognizes that the organization has responsibilities in society beyond the economic role, extending to legal, ethical, environmental and philanthropic roles

criminal law laws that designate offences and set out the legal procedure for prosecution of those charged with breaches; can be contained in a criminal code

cultural convergence diverse cultures gradually becoming more alike through increasing interactions

cultural distance in cross-border business relations, cultural gap between those involved, especially where the parties are from very different cultural environments

cultural divergence differences among cultures, especially those that persist despite globalization processes

culture shared way of life of a group of people which distinguishes it from other groups and is passed from one generation to the next

current account in connection with an economy's balance of payments, account based on trade in goods, services, and profits and interest earned from overseas assets

customs union regional grouping in which member states remove all trade barriers among themselves and adopt a common set of external barriers

D

debt financing raising capital by borrowing

deflation general decline in prices in an economy, associated with recession and falling demand

deforestation the felling of forests for fuel or to use the land for other purposes

democracy system of elected government based on free and fair elections and universal suffrage

demographic change changes in whole populations brought about by rises and falls in the birth rate and death rate, as well as migration of people

depression situation in which an economy deteriorates significantly, diminishing by one-tenth in size

derivative financial instrument whose value is dependent on another asset class such as stock

developed countries countries whose economies have become industrialized and have reached high income levels

developing countries countries in the process of industrialization and building technological capacity

directors people appointed by the company to bear ultimate responsibility for the company's activities

Dispute Settlement Understanding (DSU) WTO framework for the settlement of trade disputes between member states

dumping sale of goods abroad at below the price charged for comparable goods in the producing country

E

East African Community (EAC) common market of East African countries

eclectic paradigm theory of FDI by Dunning based on three sets of advantages: ownership (O), location (L) and internalization (I); also known as the 'OLI paradigm'

ecology study of the relationship between organisms and their environment, including changes in their distribution and numbers

Economic and Monetary Union (EMU) EU programme centred on the single currency and an independent central bank which sets monetary policy for eurozone member states

Economic Community of West African States (ECOWAS) organization for co-operation among West African states

economic development can refer to any change in a country's overall balance of economic activities, but usually refers to industrialization and associated technological changes leading to economic growth and changes in society marked by a shift from rural to urban environments

economic growth a country's increase in national income over time; negative growth occurs when the economy is contracting

economic indicators statistical measures used to analyse a national economy; notable indicators are economic growth and GDP per capita

economic union regional grouping in which member states unify all their economic policies, including monetary, fiscal and welfare policies

emerging economies/markets fast-growing developing countries, typically becoming increasingly globalized

empowerment approach to management which focuses on individual responsibility

entrepreneur a person who starts up a business and imbues it with the energy and drive necessary to compete in markets

environmental degradation environmental change caused mainly by human activity which has detrimental effects on ecological systems

environmental management assessing environmental impacts and devising suitable strategies across a company's total operations

environmental, social and governance reporting (ESG) reporting framework for companies that covers a range of CSR issues, including human rights and responses to environmental pollution

equity in corporate finance, the share capital of a company

equity financing raising capital by issuing shares

ethical relativism approach to ethics which holds that principles are not absolute but dependent on values that differ from culture to culture

ethics the study of basic concepts of good and bad, right and wrong which relate to all people as human beings

ethnocentrism unquestioning belief that one's own culture and ways of doing things are the best

euro the single currency of the EU

eurobond a bond denominated in a currency other than the one of the country in which it is issued

European Convention on Human Rights (ECHR) human rights convention from the Council of Europe, dating from 1953; contains mainly the rights contained in the ICCPR

European Court of Human Rights court established by the Council of Europe which hears cases of alleged breaches of the European Convention on Human Rights brought by individuals in member states

European Court of Justice (ECJ) highest court for interpreting EU law

European Economic Area (EEA) grouping of the European Free Trade Area (EFTA) and the EU

European Free Trade Area (EFTA) grouping formed in 1960 by countries not signed up to the Treaty of Rome (which created what is now the EU)

European Patent Office (EPO) patent office of the EU, aiming to facilitate patent applications across all EU member states

European Union (EU) regional grouping of European countries which evolved from trade agreements to deeper economic integration

eurozone member states of the EU which have satisfied the Maastricht criteria and joined the EMU

executive with reference to governments, the function of government that administers laws and policies

executive directors directors who actively manage the company

export selling products in a country other than the one in which they were made

export processing zones (EPZ) associated with export-oriented industrialization, geographic areas where goods can be imported and exported duty-free

F

Fairtrade Foundation a charity that promotes a fair deal for poor agricultural producers in developing countries, licensing producer organizations to use the Fairtrade logo

FDI inflows aggregate value of investments which flow into a country

FDI inward stock the total value of foreign investments that a country has attracted

FDI outflows aggregate value of investments from a country's organizations to overseas destinations

FDI outward stock the total value of foreign investments made by a country's nationals

federal system system of government in which authority is divided between the centre and regional units

fiduciary duty duty of trust to act honestly and in the best interests of another; applies to the duty of directors owed to their company

finance and accounting business function which concerns control over the revenues and outgoings of the business, aiming to balance the books and to generate sufficient profits for the future health of the firm

first-mover advantage precept that countries or firms which are first to produce a new product gain an advantage in markets which makes it virtually impossible for others to catch up

fiscal policy budgetary policies for balancing public spending with taxation and other income in a national economy

Fordism approach to an industrial organization based on large factories producing standardized products for mass consumption; named after the automobile magnate, Henry Ford

foreign direct investment (FDI) a mode of internationalization whereby a company invests in productive assets in a foreign country, using its ownership stake to exert control over operations

for-profit organizations enterprises that aim to make money, allowing the gains to be used as owners desire

franchise business agreement whereby a business uses the brand, products and business format of another firm under licence

free trade agreement (FTA) treaty agreement between countries which aims to liberalize trade between them; can be bilateral or multilateral

free trade area regional grouping in which member states agree to remove trade barriers among themselves, but keep their separate national barriers against trade with non-member states

futures contract contract to carry out a particular transaction on a designated date in the future

G

G7 (Group of Seven) grouping of 7 advanced economies (US, Canada, UK, France, Germany, Italy and Japan); with the addition of Russia, it is known as the G8

G20 grouping of 20 developed, developing and emerging economies, brought together by the IMF in 1999, which meets regularly, focusing mainly on financial stability

General Agreement on Tariffs and Trade (GATT) succession of multilateral agreements on reducing trade barriers

genetically-modified organisms (GMOs) plants and animals that have been altered genetically in ways that do not occur in nature

Gini index tool used by economists to measure income inequality

globalization processes by which products, people, companies, money and information are able to move quickly around the world

globalization of markets MNEs' ability to serve consumers across the world with their products, taking account of different products for different national markets

globalized production MNEs' ability to locate different stages of production in the most advantageous location; associated with supply chains

Global Reporting Initiative (GRI) recognized set of guidelines for sustainability reporting by companies

global warming global rise in temperatures impacting on all forms of life, caused by the build-up of heat-trapping gases, or 'greenhouse gases' (GHG), in the earth's atmosphere

gold standard the setting of exchange rates based on the value of gold (operated from the 1870s to 1914)

governance a broader concept than 'government' involving interactions among a range of governmental and quasi-governmental bodies as well as civil society organizations

government structures and processes of the state by which laws are made and administered; also refers to the particular office holders at any given time

greenfield investment FDI which focuses on a new project, such as a factory, in a foreign location

greenhouse gases (GHG) mixture of heat-trapping gases, mainly carbon dioxide (CO_2), held to cause global warming

Gross Domestic Product (GDP) the value of the total economic activity produced within a country in a single year, including both domestic and foreign producers

Gross National Income (GNI) the total income from all the final products and services produced by a national economy within a single year

guanxi personal relations which establish the trust and mutual obligations necessary for business in China

H

hedge a financial tool or arrangement which insures a firm against adverse currency movements in its international financial activities

hedge fund investment fund managed by an individual or firm which is active in securities markets

high-context culture culture in which communication relies heavily on the behavioural dimension, such as 'body language'

Hinduism polytheistic religion whose adherents are predominantly concentrated in the Indian subcontinent

holding company company, often referred to as the 'parent' company, which owns a number of subsidiaries

horizontal integration merger or acquisition between two or more companies in the same industry

Human Development Index (HDI) UN ranking of countries based on economic, health and education criteria

human resource management (HRM) all aspects of the management of people in the organization, including recruitment, training, and rewarding the workforce

human rights basic, universal rights enjoyed by all individuals which transcend social and cultural differences

hybrid system a system of government in which the president is directly elected, and the prime minister, who heads the cabinet, is chosen by the legislative assembly

I

ideology all-encompassing system of beliefs and values, or 'world-view'

import the purchase of goods or services from a supplier in another country

import quota a barrier to trade which consists of limiting the quantity of an imported product that can legally enter a country

import substitution approach to economic development which favours producing goods for domestic consumption that otherwise would have been imported

inclusive growth economic growth that takes in improved living standards and greater economic security for all in a society

independent trade union organization of workers unconnected to owners of the business or government

industrialization transformation of an economy from mainly agricultural production for domestic consumption to one based on factory production, with potential for export

inequality economic indicator referring to the difference in wealth or income between the richest and poorest in society

inflation the continuing general rise in prices in an economy

initial public offering (IPO) first offering by a company of its shares to the public on a stock exchange; also known as 'flotation'

innovation wide range of activities which seek new and improved products and services, or new ways of carrying out an organization's activities

innovation system the structures and institutions by which a country's innovation activities are encouraged and facilitated, both directly and indirectly

intangible assets rights over products, such as trademarks and patents, which can be exploited commercially; they can be contrasted with tangible assets

intellectual property (IP) property in intangible assets, such as patents, copyrights and trademarks, which can be legally protected from use by others unless permission is obtained from the owner

interconnectedness improved communications across national borders, facilitated mainly by advances in technology, computing and the internet

interdependence links based on complementarities and co-operation between two or more countries or organizations

inter-generational justice concept which underlies the principle of sustainability, implying that moral obligations are owed to future generations

Intergovernmental Panel on Climate Change (IPCC) UN body of scientists that brings together evidence of climate change and issues reports

intermediate goods components and parts which cross national borders before being made into final products

international business business activities that straddle two or more countries

International Centre for Settlement of Investment Disputes (ICSID) tribunal system set up by the World Bank which is tasked with handling investor-state disputes arising under treaties

International Covenant on Civil and Political Rights (ICCPR) UN human rights treaty setting out rights to life and individual freedoms, such as freedom of speech and expression

International Covenant on Economic, Social and Cultural Rights (ICESCR) UN human rights treaty setting out rights to well-being, education, health and cultural participation

International Court of Justice (ICJ) UN-sponsored international court which hears legal cases relating to disputes between member states

International Criminal Court (ICC) court established under the auspices of the UN and the International Court of Justice which hears cases involving crimes against humanity and war crimes

International Labour Organization (ILO) UN organization that sets international labour standards

international law body of rules recognized by the international community as governing relations between sovereign states

International Monetary Fund (IMF) agency of the UN which oversees the international monetary and financial systems

International Organization for Standardization (ISO) body which oversees quality and environmental standards recognized across industries

invention product or process which can be described as 'new' in that it makes a significant qualitative leap forward from the state of existing knowledge

investor-state dispute settlement (ISDS) provision in a treaty that allows companies from one of the ratifying countries who invest in another ratifying country to bring cases in a tribunal when they feel their businesses have been prejudiced in the host country

Islam monotheistic religion based on the teachings of the prophet Muhammad as revealed in the Koran; followers are referred to as Muslims

J

joint venture an agreement between companies to form a new entity to carry out a business purpose, often an FDI project

judicial with reference to governments, the function of government that interprets the law and provides checks on the other two branches, the executive and legislative

judicial system system of courts, usually divided between civil courts and criminal courts

just-in-time (JIT) manufacturing system of manufacturing which relies on a continuous flow of materials

K

keiretsu grouping of Japanese companies characterized by inter-firm ties and cross-shareholdings

L

law rule or body of rules perceived as binding because it emanates from state authorities with powers of enforcement

lean production approach to mass production that aims to reduce waste and maintain continuous flow; associated with Japanese car company, Toyota

least-developed countries the world's poorest developing countries, mainly in sub-Saharan Africa

legal risk uncertainties surrounding legal liabilities, their implementation in differing legal systems, and the observance of fairness and impartiality in judicial proceedings in differing locations

legislation laws enacted by lawmaking processes set out in national constitutions; also known as statute law

legislative the lawmaking function within government; often referred to as the legislative 'branch'

legislative assembly body of elected representatives within a state, which has lawmaking responsibilities

leverage extent to which a company relies on debt financing

leveraged buy-out (LBO) acquisition of a company's equity by a firm or group of individuals, financed by borrowing

liberal market economy capitalist economic system in which supply and demand, as well as prices, are determined by free markets

limited liability principle that the shareholder is liable up to the amount invested for liabilities incurred by the company

litigation the use of judicial procedures and the court system to bring claims for damages and other remedies in legal cases

lobbying political activities of businesses and other groups that seek to influence policies, laws and the decisions made by public officeholders

local content requirements trade policy that requires foreign investors to use local component suppliers in, for example, manufacturing

location advantages inherent advantages of a country or region, such as access to transport, access to raw materials and low labour costs

low-context culture culture in which communication is clear and direct rather than relying on patterns of behaviour

M

macroeconomics the study of national economies

management process of planning, organizing, leading and controlling the work of organization members

market a location or framework facilitating exchange transactions, either with formal standing or informally; countries can be referred to as 'national markets'

marketing satisfying the needs and expectations of customers; includes a range of related activities, such as product offering, branding, advertising, pricing and distribution of goods

Mercosur South American common market

merger coming together of two or more companies to form a new company

microeconomics the study of economic activity at the level of individuals and firms

migration movement of people from one place to another, which can be within a country or between countries, with a view to making a new life in the new location

Millennium Development Goals (MDGs) goals designated by the UN Millennium Summit of 2000, which set targets for improving human well-being in developing regions

mixed economy economic system which combines market elements with state controls

modes of internationalization methods by which companies expand internationally, including FDI

monetary policy economic policies for determining the amount of money in supply, rates of interest, and exchange rates

monopoly domination by one firm over the market for particular goods or services, enabling the firm to determine price and supply

morality standards of behaviour considered right and wrong

most-favoured-nation (MFN) principle GATT principle by which the most favourable tariff treatment negotiated with one country is extended to similar goods from all countries

multilateral treaty international agreement binding many countries

multinational enterprise (MNE) an organization which acquires ownership or other contractual ties in other organizations (including companies and unincorporated businesses) outside its home country

multi-party system system in which many political parties participate, representing a wide spectrum of views; in elections, no single party is likely to obtain a majority, and a coalition government is often the outcome

N

national budget balance the extent to which public spending is balanced by receipts from taxes and other sources; budget deficits are common

national culture distinctive values, behavioural norms and shared history which distinguish one nation from other

national debt the total debt accumulated by a central government's borrowings over the years

national economy the aggregate of economic activities of governments, businesses and individuals within the national framework of a nation-state

nation-state social, administrative and territorial unit into which the world's peoples are divided

negligence breach of a duty to take reasonable care which causes injury or other harm to another; actionable in civil courts

non-executive directors part-time directors who are independent of a company's management and owners

non-governmental organization (NGOs) voluntary organization formed by private individuals for a particular shared purpose

non-tariff barriers in trade, legal requirements in a country, such as health and safety standards, that act to prevent the imports from other countries that are not in conformity

North American Free Trade Agreement (NAFTA) free trade area comprising the US, Canada and Mexico

not-for-profit organizations organizations such as charities which exist for the purpose of promoting good causes rather than to make a profit

O

offshoring contracting out of a business activity or function, usually to a low-cost location, often carrying negative connotations

oligopoly domination of an industry by a few very large firms

operations the entire process of producing and delivering a product to a consumer; covers tangible goods and services, and often a combination of both

option contractual device used to allow a person or company the right to purchase something of value at a future date; often used in hedging against currency risk

organizational culture an organization's values, behavioural norms and management style; also known as 'corporate culture'

Organization for Economic Co-operation and Development (OECD) organization of the world's main developed economies which supports market economies and democratic institutions

outsourced production agreement between a company, usually a brand owner, and another company, usually in a low-cost location, to make the products designed by the first of the companies

outsourcing the process by which an owner contracts out to another firm a business process, such as product manufacturing or a business service, usually under a licence agreement

ownership advantages resources specific to a firm, such as patents, which can be exploited for competitive advantage

P

parliamentary system system of government in which voters directly elect members of parliament from whom a prime minister is chosen

patent type of intellectual property which gives its owner an exclusive right for a limited period to exploit the invention, to license others to use it, and to stop all unauthorized exploitation of the invention

patentable invention a new product or process which can be applied industrially

'pegged' exchange rate exchange rate which links the value of a currency to that of another, usually stronger, currency

PEST analysis of a national environment which stands for political, economic, social and technological dimensions

philanthropy voluntary giving of money or other resources to good causes, often charities

planned economy economic system based on total state ownership of the means of production in which the state controls prices and output

pluralism existence in society of a multiplicity of groups and interests independent of the state, characterized by freedom of association; includes political parties and independent trade unions

plurilateral trade agreement trade agreement among a number of countries in different regions that come together deliberately for the purpose of liberalizing trade and investment among them; separate from the WTO's multilateral system

political party organization of people with similar political beliefs, which aims to put forward candidates for office and influence government policies

political risk uncertainties associated with the exercise of governmental power within a country, and from external forces

political union regional grouping in which member states transfer sovereignty to regional political and lawmaking institutions, creating a new 'superstate'

politics processes by which a social group allocates the exercise of power and authority for the group as a whole

polycentrism openness to other cultures and ways of doing things

portfolio investment buying shares or other securities of a company with a view to making financial gain on the investment

presidential system system of government in which the head of the executive branch, the president, is elected by the voters, either directly or through an electoral college (as in the US)

primary production agriculture, mining and fishing

primary stakeholders stakeholders directly involved in a firm's business

private equity fund investment fund managed on behalf of wealthy investors which is active in equity markets; noted for a focus on short-term gains

private international law the body of law for determining questions concerning which national law prevails in cases between individuals and companies in different countries

private limited company company whose shares are not publicly traded on a stock exchange

privatization process of transforming a state-owned enterprise into a public company and selling off a proportion of shares to the public, usually while retaining a stake and a controlling interest by the government

production under licence production of a product by a contractor under an agreement whereby it obtains permission from the company owning the brand, designs, patent or other IP rights

product liability liability of a producer of a defective product to consumers harmed by the product; can extend to suppliers

product life cycle theory theory of the evolution of a product in stages, from innovation in its home market to dissemination and production in overseas markets

product recall withdrawal of a product from the marketplace due to defects which might cause harm to consumers

proportional representation principle underlying systems of electoral representation in which seats are allocated in proportion to the votes obtained by each candidate or party

protectionism government trade policy of favouring home producers and discouraging imports

public law body of law covering relations between citizens and the state

public limited company (PLC) company which lists on a stock exchange and offers shares to the public

'pull' factors factors in a country which attract foreign investors

Purchasing Power Parity (PPP) means of estimating the number of units of the foreign currency which would be needed to buy goods or services equivalent to those which the US dollar would buy in the US

'push' factors factors in a company's home country which persuade it to pursue growth potential overseas

Q

quantitative easing (QE) monetary policy of creating money to purchase assets, mainly government bonds, with the aim of stimulating the economy

R

reasonable care test used in law to determine whether a person has acted negligently

recession two consecutive quarters of negative economic growth in an economy

referendum a type of direct democracy in which electors cast a vote on a particular issue

regionalization growing economic links and co-operation within a geographic region, both on the part of businesses and governments

regional trade agreement (RTA) free trade agreement among a number of countries in the same broad geographic region

regulation rules relating to a particular type of activity or sector; covers both formal legal requirements and less formal guidance such as codes of practice

relational contracting business dealings in which personal relations between the parties are more important than formal written agreements

religion set of beliefs and moral precepts which guide people in their lives, often contained in sacred scriptures and propounded by spiritual leaders

remittances money sent by migrant workers back to their families in their home location

research and development (R&D) seeking new knowledge and applications which can lead to new and improved products or processes

rule of law principle of supremacy of the law over both governments and citizens, entailing equality before the law and an independent judiciary

S

scientific management theory of management in which each worker's task is strictly defined and is part of a production process that is controlled in minute detail; devised by Frederick Taylor

secondary production industrial production, concentrated in factories

secondary stakeholders stakeholders indirectly involved in a firm's business

Securities and Exchange Commission (SEC) US stock market regulator

separation of powers in systems of government, the division between legislative, executive and judicial functions, or branches, with checks and balances to prevent one branch becoming dominant

share in a company, represents ownership of the company to the extent of the amount invested

shareholders legal owners of a company, known as 'members', who enjoy rights such as receiving dividends from company profits

Shari'a the authoritative source of Islamic law

small-to-medium-sized enterprise (SME) business ranging from a micro-enterprise of just one person to a firm with up to 249 employees

social enterprise an enterprise which lies somewhere between the for-profit and not-for-profit organization, aiming to make money but using it mainly for social causes

social market economy capitalist market economy with a strong social justice dimension, including substantial welfare state provisions

social responsibility the role of the organization in society with implied duties to communities and the environment

sole trader a person who is in business on his or her own account, also referred to as a self-employed person; the business of the sole trader has no separate existence from its owner

sovereignty supreme legal authority in the state; also mutual recognition of states in international relations

sovereign wealth fund entity controlled by a government which invests state funds and pursues an investment strategy; often active in global financial markets

spillover effects benefits to local firms in host countries from FDI, including technological capabilities and local supply contracts

stakeholder broad category including individuals, groups and even society generally that exerts influence on the company or that the company is in a position to influence

stakeholder theory management theory which focuses on the many different groups and interests that affect the company

stock exchanges regulated markets in which shares in public companies and other securities are traded

subculture minority culture in a society, often associated with immigrant communities

subsidiary company a company owned wholly or substantially by another company which is in a position to exert control

subsidies payments from public funds to support domestic industries; there are also export subsidies to home producers to bolster a country's exports

superpower in international politics, a state that is able to impose its power over other countries

supranational legal institutions above those of domestic law; characterizes EU law

sustainability the principle of taking into account the needs of today's inhabitants of the planet in ways which do not constitute a detriment to the ability of future generations to do the same

sustainable consumption principle that consumer lifestyle and purchasing decisions should take account of the environmental needs of future generations

sustainable development view of economic development involving continuing investment for future generations, taking into account the long-term viability of industries, both in terms of human values and environmental protection

Sustainable Development Goals (SDGs) UN development goals, superseding the Millennium Development Goals (MDGs), covering environmental, institutional and governance issues

T

tangible assets physical property such as machinery and goods

tariff tax imposed by governments on imported goods and services

technological diffusion processes by which advances in technology spread from one country to another, usually from developed to developing countries

technology methodical application of scientific knowledge for practical purposes

technology transfer process of acquiring technology from another country, especially in manufacturing, whereby skilled workers in the host country are able to learn from the technology of the foreign investor

terrorism action by an individual or group intended to inflict dramatic and deadly injury on civilians and create an atmosphere of fear, generally for a political or ideological purpose

tertiary sector the third type of economic activity (following primary and secondary) which consists of services, such as financial services

third-party verification the use of outside specialist services or certification to monitor CSR and environmental performance

tort in common law countries, branch of law which concerns obligations not to cause harm to others in society

trade the exchange of something of value, usually goods or services, for a price, usually money

Trade-Related Aspects of Intellectual Property Rights (TRIPS) multilateral international agreement on the protection of intellectual property which aims to bring national legal regimes into harmony

Transatlantic Trade and Investment Partnership (TTIP) proposed trade and investment agreement between the EU and the US

transboundary pollution the transmission of pollutants through the water, soil and air from one national jurisdiction to another

transition economies economies such as those of Eastern Europe and the CIS (Commonwealth of Independent States, including Russia) which are making the transition from planned economies to market-based economies

Trans-Pacific Partnership (TPP) trade and investment agreement among 12 countries bordering the Pacific, including the US and Japan

treaties instruments of international law

triad countries advanced economies of North America, the EU and Japan; Australia and New Zealand are also in this category

triple-bottom-line reporting corporate reporting focusing on social and environmental aspects of the company, in addition to traditional financial information

two-party system political system in which there are two major political parties, alternating between government and opposition depending on the outcome of elections

U

unemployment the percentage of people in a country's labour force who are willing to work but are without jobs

unitary system system of authority within a state in which all authority radiates out from the centre

United Nations (UN) the world's largest and most authoritative inter-governmental organization

United Nations Educational, Scientific and Cultural Organization (UNESCO) UN agency that promotes peace and security through collaboration in these areas, notably in respect of upholding human rights

Universal Declaration of Human Rights (UDHR) first comprehensive statement of human rights; passed by the UN General Assembly in 1948

urbanization process of large-scale shift of population from rural areas to cities

utilitarianism philosophical thinking based on the individualist view of human nature that each person has wants and needs which are pursued in a self-interested way

V

value chain concept which identifies the value created at each stage in a production process

vertical integration acquisition of firms involved in successive stages of a production process

voluntary export restraint (VER) tool of government trade policy by which trading partners wishing to export into a country are encouraged to limit their exports, or else incur the imposition of tariffs or import quotas

W

Washington consensus market-oriented outlook adopted by the World Bank and IMF

World Bank organization established in the aftermath of the Second World War to fund development projects and broader development programmes

World Trade Organization (WTO) successor organization to the GATT, set up to regulate world trade and settle trade disputes among member countries

Z

zero-hours contract employment arrangement whereby the worker is available for work but paid only for the hours worked, and the employer has no commitment to provide work

INDEX OF ORGANIZATIONS

x

x

INDEX OF PEOPLE

SUBJECT INDEX